Programming Home Projects with Microsoft® Small Basic

Kidware Software
PO Box 701
Maple Valley, WA 98038

http://www.computerscienceforkids.com
http://www.kidwaresoftware.com

Kidware Software LLC
PO Box 701
Maple Valley, Washington 98038
1.425.413.1185
www.kidwaresoftware.com
www.computerscienceforkids.com
www.biblebytebooks.com

Printed in the United States of America

ISBN-13: 978-1-937161-39-2

Previous edition published as "Home Projects with Microsoft Small Basic"

Cover Design by Stephanie Conrod
Copy Edit by Jessica Conrod
Book Cover Illustration by Kevin Brockschmidt

This guide was developed for the course, "Programming Home Projects with Microsoft Small Basic," produced by Kidware Software, Maple Valley, Washington. It is not intended to be a complete reference to the Small Basic language. Please consult the Microsoft website for detailed reference information.

About The Authors

Philip Conrod has authored, co-authored and edited numerous computer programming books for kids, teens and adults. Philip holds a BS in Computer Information Systems and a Master's certificate in the Essentials of Business Development from Regis University. Philip started programming computers in 1977 at 13 years of age. Philip has also held various Information Technology leadership roles in companies like Sundstrand Aerospace, Safeco Insurance Companies, FamilyLife, Kenworth Truck Company, PACCAR and Darigold. Philip serves as the President & Publisher of Kidware Software, LLC. He is the proud father of three "techie" daughters. Philip and his family live in Maple Valley, Washington.

Lou Tylee holds BS and MS degrees in Mechanical Engineering and a PhD in Electrical Engineering. Lou has been programming computers since 1969 when he took his first Fortran course in college. He has written software to control suspensions for high speed ground vehicles, monitor nuclear power plants, lower noise levels in commercial jetliners, compute takeoff speeds for jetliners, locate and identify air and ground traffic and to let kids count bunnies, learn how to spell and do math problems. He has written several on-line texts teaching Visual Basic, Visual C# and Java to thousands of people. He taught a beginning Visual Basic course for over 15 years at a major university. Currently, Lou works as an engineer at a major Seattle aerospace firm. He is the proud father of five children and proud husband of his special wife. Lou and his family live in Seattle, Washington.

Acknowledgements

I want to thank my three wonderful daughters - Stephanie, Jessica and Chloe, who helped with various aspects of the book publishing process including software testing, book editing, creative design and many other more tedious tasks like finding errors and typos. I could not have accomplished this without all your hard work, love and support.

I also want to thank my multi-talented co-author, Lou Tylee, for doing all the real hard work necessary to develop, test, debug, and keep current all the 'kid-friendly' applications, games and base tutorial text found in this book. Lou has tirelessly poured his heart and soul into so many previous versions of this tutorial and there are so many beginners who have benefited from his work over the years. Lou is by far one of the best application developers and tutorial writers I have ever worked with. Thank you Lou for collaborating with me on this book project.

Last, but definitely not least, I want to thank my best friend Jesus, who has always been there by my side giving me wisdom and guidance. Without you, this book would have never been printed and published.

1. Writing Programs Using Small Basic

2. Overview of Small Basic Programming

3. Debugging a Small Basic Project

4. Dual-Mode Stopwatch Project

5. Consumer Loan Assistant Project

6. Flash Card Math Quiz Project

7. Multiple Choice Exam Project

8. Blackjack Card Game Project

9. Weight Monitor Project

10. Home Inventory Manager Project

11. Snowball Toss Game Project

Appendix I. Small Basic Colors

Appendix II. Sharing a Small Basic Program

Description

PROGRAMMING HOME PROJECTS WITH SMALL BASIC explains (in simple, easy-to-follow terms) how to build useful Small Basic Windows program for use around the home. Students learn about program design, Small Basic objects, many elements of the Small Basic language, and how to debug and distribute finished programs. The programs built include:

- **Dual-Mode Stopwatch** - Allows you to time tasks you may be doing.
- **Consumer Loan Assistant** - Helps you see just how much those credit cards are costing you.
- **Flash Card Math Quiz** - Lets you practice basic addition, subtraction, multiplication and division skills.
- **Multiple Choice Exam** - Quizzes a user on matching pairs of items, like countries/capitals, words/meanings, books/authors.
- **Blackjack Card Game** - Play the classic card game against the computer.
- **Weight Monitor** - Track your weight each day and monitor your progress toward established goals.
- **Home Inventory Manager** - Helps you keep track of all your belongings.
- **Snowball Toss Game** - Lets you throw snowballs at another player or against the computer - has varying difficulties.

The product includes over 600 pages of self-study notes, all Small Basic source code and all needed graphics and sound files.

Course Prerequisites

To grasp the concepts presented in **PROGRAMMING HOME PROJECTS WITH SMALL BASIC**, you should possess a working knowledge of the Windows operating system. You should know how to use Windows Explorer to locate, copy, move and delete files. You should be familiar with the simple tasks of using menus, toolbars, resizing windows, and moving windows around.

You should have had some exposure to Small Basic programming (or some other programming language). We offer two beginning programming tutorials (**SMALL BASIC FOR KIDS** and **BEGINNING SMALL BASIC**) that would help you gain this needed exposure.

Software Requirements

Regarding software requirements, to use Small Basic, you (and your potential users) must be using Windows 7, 2000, or Windows XP. These notes and all programs are developed using Windows Vista. And, of course, you need to have the Small Basic product installed on your computer (Version 1.0 or higher). It is available for free download from Microsoft. Follow this link for complete instructions for downloading and installing Small Basic on your computer:

http://www.kidwaresoftware.com/sbasic.htm

System Requirements

You will need the following hardware and software to complete the exercises in this book:

- Microsoft Windows XP with Service Pack 3
- Microsoft Small Basic v1.0
- 766 MHz Pentium or compatible processor (1.5 Ghz Pentium Recommended)
- 256 MB RAM (512MB or more recommended)
- Video Monitor (1024 x768) with High Color 16 bit)
- CD-ROM or DVD-ROM Drive
- Microsoft Mouse or compatible pointing device

Using Programming Home Projects With Small Basic

If you purchased this book through a 3rd Party Book Store, the source code solutions and multimedia files for this tutorial are included in a downloadable compressed ZIP file that is available for download directly from our webpage at:

http://www.computerscienceforkids.com/PHPSB-Registration.aspx

Please complete the online registration web form at the webpage above with your name, shipping address, email address, date of purchase, online or physical store name, and your order confirmation number from that store. After we receive all this information from you we will email you a download link for the Program Solution and Multimedia Files associated with this book.

WARNING: If you purchased this book **"used"** or **"second hand"** you are NOT licensed or entitled to download the Program Solution Files. However, you can purchase the Download Only version of this book as an E-Book at a discounted price which allows you access to the program solutions and multimedia files required for completing this tutorial.

The course code for **PROGRAMMING HOME PROJECTS WITH SMALL BASIC** are included in one or more ZIP file(s). Use your favorite 'unzipping' application to write all files to your computer. The course is included in the folder entitled **HomeSB**. This folder contains two other folders: **HomeSB Notes** and **HomeSB Projects**. There's a chance when you copy the files to your computer, they will be written as '**Read-Only**.' To correct this (in **Windows Explorer** or **My Computer**), right-click the **HomeSB** folder and remove the check next to **Read only**. Make sure to choose the option to apply this change to all sub-folders and files.

1. Writing Programs Using Small Basic

Preview

In this first chapter, we will do an overview of how to write a program using Small Basic. You'll get a brief history of Small Basic and look into use of the Small Basic development environment.

Introducing Programming Home Projects With Small Basic

In these notes, we will use Small Basic to build many fun projects you can use around your home. The projects you will build are:

- **Dual-Mode Stopwatch** – Measures total and elapsed time.
- **Consumer Loan Assistant** – Helps you determine just how much those loans cost you.
- **Flash Card Math Quiz** – Practice basic math skills with timed drills.
- **Multiple Choice Exam** – Set up exams matching like terms.
- **Blackjack Card Game** – The classic casino game.
- **Weight Tracker** - Track your weight each day.
- **Home Inventory Manager** – Keep track of all the stuff you own for insurance purposes.
- **Snowball Toss Game** – A little game using sounds and animation.

Each project will be addressed in a single chapter. Complete step-by-step instructions covering every project detail will be provided. Before beginning the projects, however, we will review the Small Basic development environment in the remainder of this chapter. Then, we provide an overview of the Small Basic programming language (Chapter 2) and instructions on using the Small Basic debugger tools (Chapter 3). The projects will begin with Chapter 4.

Requirements for Programming Home Projects With Small Basic

Before starting, let's examine what you need to successfully build the programs included with **Programming Home Projects With Small Basic**. As far as computer skills, you should be comfortable working within the Windows environment. You should know how to run programs, find and create folders, and move and resize windows.

As far as programming skills, we assume you have had some exposure to computer programming using some language. If that language is **Small Basic**, great!! We offer two tutorials **Small Basic for Kids** and **Beginning Small Basic**, that could help you gain that exposure (see our website for details). But, if you've ever programmed in any language (Visual Basic, C, C++, C#, Java, J#, Ada, even FORTRAN), you should be able to follow what's going on. Even if you are a veteran programmer, we suggest you go through the first three chapters before attacking the programs. This review will give you some idea of the terminology we use in referring to different parts of a Small Basic program.

Regarding software requirements, to use Small Basic, you must be using Windows 7, 2000, Windows XP, Windows NT or Windows Vista. These notes and all programs are developed using Windows Vista and Version 1.0 of Small Basic. And, of course, you need to have the Small Basic product installed on your computer. It is available for free download from Microsoft. Follow this link for complete instructions for downloading and installing Small Basic on your computer:

http://www.smallbasic.com

Introducing Small Basic

In the late 1970's and early 1980's, it seems there were computers everywhere with names like Commodore 64, Texas Instruments 99/4A, Atari 400, Coleco Adam, Timex Sinclair and the IBM PC-Jr. Stores like Sears, JC Penneys and even K Mart sold computers.

One thing these machines had in common was that they were all programmed in some version of Microsoft's BASIC. Each computer had its own fans and own magazines. Users would wait each month for the next issue of a magazine with BASIC programs you could type into your computer and try at home.

This was a fun and exciting time for the beginning programmer, but the fun times ended with the introduction of the IBM-PC in the early 1980's. Bigger and faster computers brought forth bigger languages and bigger development environments. These new languages were expensive to acquire and difficult for the beginning programmer to grasp.

Which brings us to **Small Basic**, which I would call a relative of the early, original BASIC language. The development of Small Basic is an attempt to rekindle the exciting days when just about anyone could sit down at a computer and write a simple program using the BASIC language.

Those of you who wrote programs on those old "toy" computers will recognize the simplicity of the Small Basic language and the ease of its use. And, you will also notice Small Basic is a great environment for writing and testing code, something missing in the early 1980's. For those of you new to programming, I hope you can feel the excitement we old timers once had. For the old timers, I hope you rekindle your programming skills with this new product.

Small Basic possesses many features of more powerful (and more expensive) programming languages:

- Easy-to-use, Integrated Development Environment (IDE)
- Response to mouse and keyboard actions
- Full array of mathematical, string handling, and graphics functions
- Can easily work with arrays
- Sequential file support

Starting Small Basic

We assume you have Small Basic installed and operational on your computer. Once installed, to start Small Basic:

- Click on the **Start** button on the Windows task bar
- Select **Programs**, then **Small Basic**
- Click on **Microsoft Small Basic**

(Some of the headings given here may differ slightly on your computer, but you should have no trouble finding the correct ones.) The Small Basic program should start.

After installation and trying to start, you may see an error message that announces Small Basic cannot be started. If this occurs, try downloading and installing the latest version of the Microsoft .NET framework at:

http://msdn.microsoft.com/en-us/netframework/aa569263.aspx

This contains some files that Small Basic needs to operate and such files may not be on your computer.

Upon starting, my screen shows:

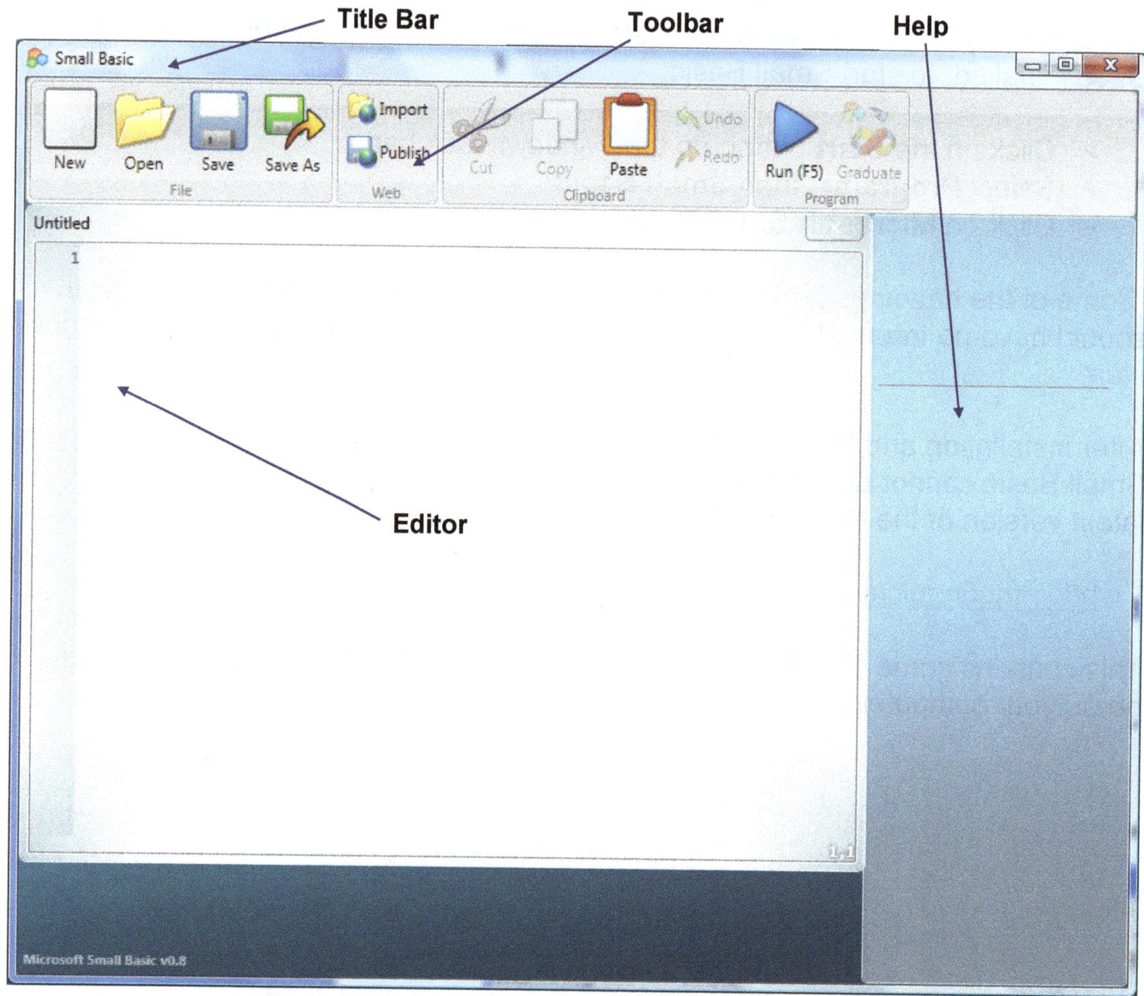

This window displays the **Small Basic Development Environment**. There are many areas of interest on the screen. At the top of the window is the **Title Bar**. The title bar gives us information about what program we're using and what Small Basic program we are working with.

Below the title bar is a **Toolbar**. Here, little buttons with pictures allow us to control Small Basic.

In the middle of the screen is the **Editor**. This is where we will write our Small Basic programs. To the right is a **Help** area. Small Basic has great help features when writing programs. This area will display hints and tips while we write code.

Running a Small Basic Program

Let's write our first Small Basic program. When you start, a new editor window appears. You can also get a new editor window by clicking the **New** toolbar button. Type these two lines in the editor window:

```
TextWindow.Title = "Hello Program"
TextWindow.WriteLine("This is the first line of the program.")
```

The editor window should look like this:

```
Untitled *
TextWindow.Title = "Hello Program"
TextWindow.WriteLine("This is the first line of the program.")
```

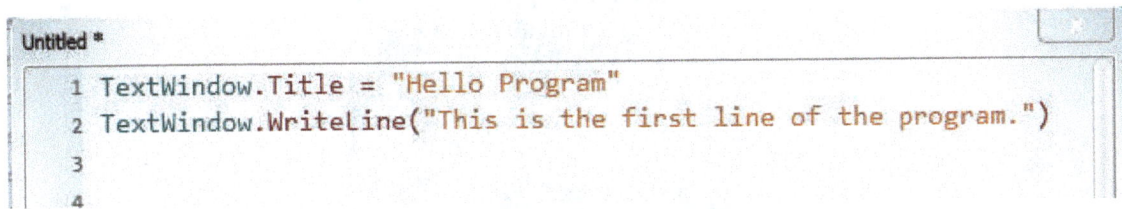

Notice as you started typing the first line, this popped-up:

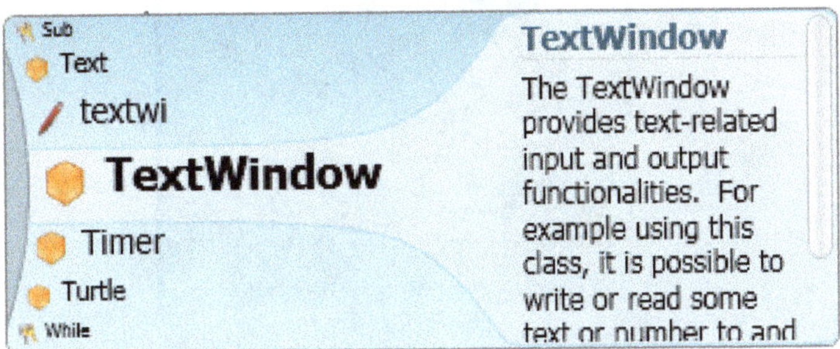

Small Basic has "intellisense" and uses this to make typing suggestions. You can just keep typing or accept its suggestion by scrolling through the pop-up list and pressing the **Enter** key.

Also, notice this appeared in the help area:

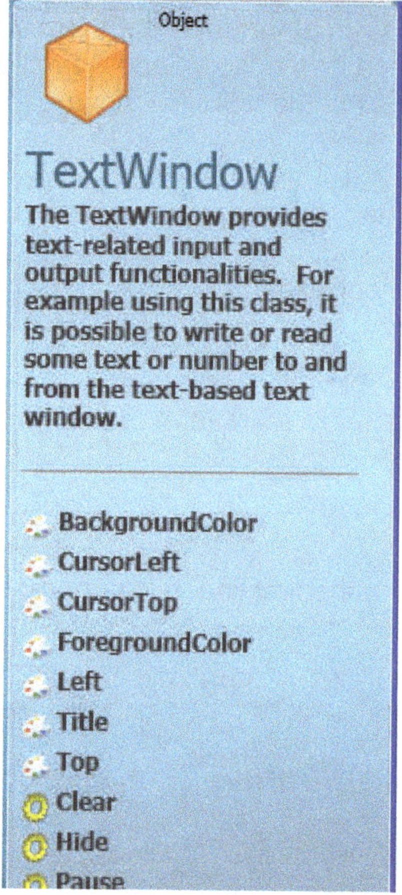

Once you typed **TextWindow**, the help feature displayed all it knows about the **TextWindow** to help you in your programming.

The **TextWindow** is a Small Basic **object**. It displays text output. The object has **properties**, **methods** and **events**. There are many objects in Small Basic. They will be reviewed in Chapter 2.

Let's run the program. Simply click the **Run** button on the toolbar to see:

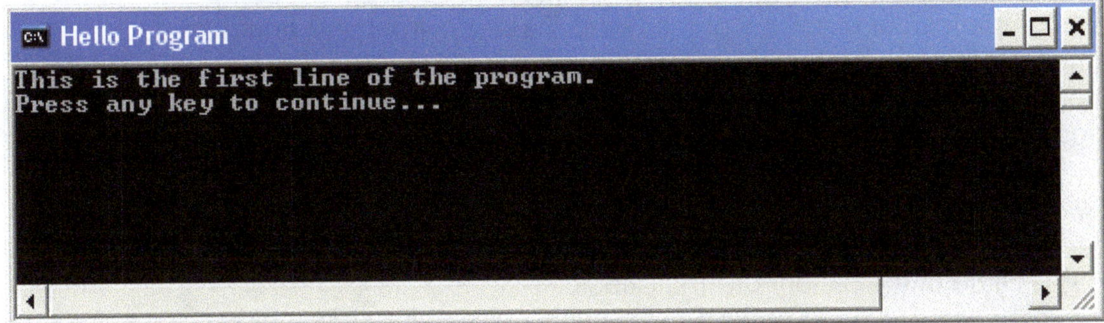

This is the text window displaying the program output. I have resized the window a bit. To stop the program, click the **X** in the upper right corner of the window.

That's all there is to writing a Small Basic program. Type the code in the editor window. Click the **Run** button to run the code. We will learn a lot of Small Basic code as we build the games in this course. Chapter 3 reviews most elements of the Small Basic language.

Other useful toolbar buttons are:

Open – Open a previously saved Small Basic program
Save – Save a Small Basic program
Save As – Save a Small Basic program with a different name

We suggest saving each Small Basic program in its own folder.

There are also the **Cut**, **Copy**, **Paste**, **Undo**, and **Redo** buttons for common editing tasks. Learn to use these – they will save you lots of time typing code.

Chapter Review

This completes our overview of the Small Basic environment and a brief demonstration of how to write a Small Basic program. If you've used Small Basic before, this material should be familiar. If you've programmed with other languages, you should have a fairly clear understanding of what's going on.

After completing this chapter, you should understand:

- A little of the history of Small Basic.
- The various parts of the Small Basic integrated development environment.
- The utility of "intellisense" and the Small Basic help panel.
- How to write code using the code editor.
- How to run a Small Basic program.

Before starting the home projects in Chapter 4, we need to review the language of Small Basic (Chapter 2) and learn how to debug projects (Chapter 3).

2. Overview of Small Basic Programming

Review and Preview

In this chapter, we provide an overview of Small Basic programming. We first look at the objects used to build projects. We then provide an overview of many of the elements of the language used in Small Basic. This will give us the foundation needed to begin building home projects.

This chapter is essentially a self-contained guide to the Small Basic language. While building the projects, you can refer back to this chapter when needed.

Objects, Properties, Methods and Events

Objects are used by the Small Basic language to help build programs. An object can have **properties**, **methods** and/or **events**.

A **property** describes something about the object. In Chapter 1, we had this simple line of code:

```
TextWindow.Title = "Hello Program"
```

Here **TextWindow** is the object, **Title** is the property (the information that appears in the window title bar) and "**Hello Program**" is the value of the property. So, in general, to set the **Property** of an **Object**, you use this "dot-notation":

Object.Property = Value

A **method** does something to an object. Again, in Chapter 1, we had this line:

```
TextWindow.WriteLine("This is the first line of the program.")
```

Here, **WriteLine** is the method (it writes information in the text window) and the item in the parentheses is called the method argument. The argument (or sometimes arguments) provides information needed by the method to do its job. To apply a **Method** to an **Object**, use:

Object.Method(Arguments)

Sometimes, the method may compute and return a value. In this case, that **Value** is found using:

Value = Object.Method(Arguments)

Lastly, an **event** is something that happens to an object. Example events are pressing a mouse button or pressing a key on the keyboard. To respond to an event, the event must be assigned a **subroutine** (a self-contained segment of program code) that is called if the event occurs. To assign the subroutine **EventSub** to the **Event** for **Object**, use:

```
Object.Event = EventSub
```

We now look at objects we will use in the course to build our projects. For each object, we review some of the properties, methods and events (if any).

TextWindow Object

The **TextWindow** is an object where we can receive text input and write text output. In the programs written in this course, we will use the text window to set options and provide feeback. We saw the text window in the little example in Chapter 1.

TextWindow **Properties:**

BackgroundColor	Gets or sets the background color of the text to be output in the text window.
CursorLeft	Gets or sets the cursor's column position in the text window.
CursorTop	Gets or sets the cursor's row position in the text window.
ForegroundColor	Gets or sets the foreground color of the text to be output in the text window.
Title	Gets or sets the title for the text window.

TextWindow **Methods**:

Clear()
Clears the text window.

Hide()
Hides the text window.

Pause()
Waits for user input before returning.

Read()
Reads a line of text from the text window. This method will not return until the user presses **Enter**. Returns entered text.

ReadNumber()
Reads a number from the text window. This method will not return until the user presses **Enter**. Returns entered number.

Show()
Shows the text window.

Write(data)

Writes text or number (**data**) to the text window. Unlike **WriteLine**, this will not append a new line character, which means, anything written to the text window after this call will be on the same line.

WriteLine(data)

Writes text or number (**data**) to the text window. A new line character will be appended to the output, so that the next time something is written to the text window, it will go in a new line.

TextWindow **Example**:

This code shows the text window, asks for an input and writes that input back to the text window:

```
TextWindow.Show()
TextWindow.Write("Enter a number ")
A = TextWindow.ReadNumber()
TextWindow.WriteLine(A)
```

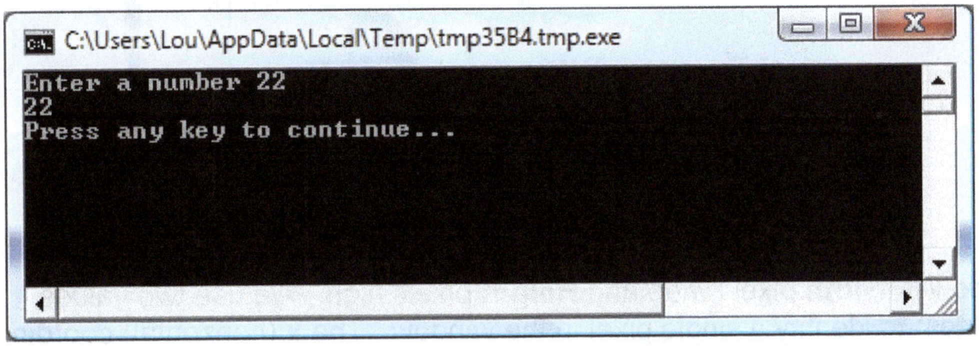

```
C:\Users\Lou\AppData\Local\Temp\tmp35B4.tmp.exe
Enter a number 22
22
Press any key to continue...
```

GraphicsWindow Object

The **GraphicsWindow** object is the cornerstone of our project building. In the graphics window, we can draw lines, shapes, and text in many colors. We can receive mouse and keyboard input from a user. The coordinate system used by the graphics window is:

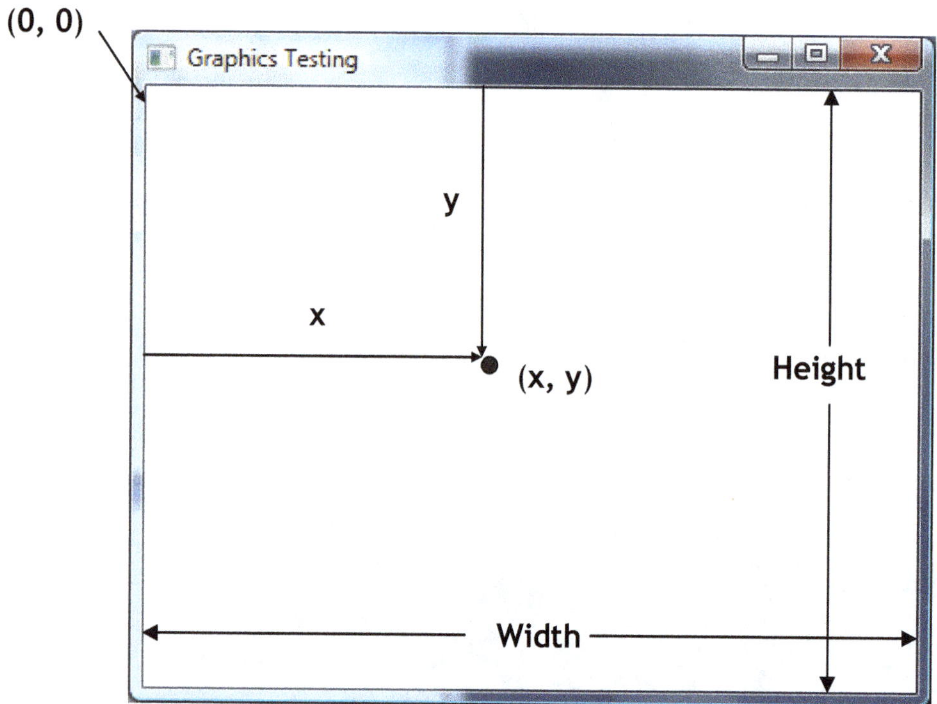

The window is **Width** pixels wide and **Height** pixels high. We use two values (coordinates) to identify a single pixel in the window. The **x** (horizontal) coordinate increases from left to right, starting at **0**. The **y** (vertical) coordinate increases from top to bottom, also starting at **0**. Points in the region are referred to by the two coordinates enclosed in parentheses, or **(x, y)**.

Each program will be developed within the graphics window. This window has many properties, methods and events. As you build the projects, you will become familiar with the use of most of these.

GraphicsWindow **Properties**:

BackgroundColor	Gets or sets the background color of the graphics window.
BrushColor	Gets or sets the brush color to be used to fill shapes drawn on the graphics window.
FontBold	Gets or sets whether or not the font to be used when drawing text on the graphics window, is bold.
FontSize	Gets or sets the font size to be used when drawing text on the graphics window.
Height	Gets or sets the height of the graphics window.
LastKey	Gets the last key that was pressed or released.
LastText	Gets the last text that was entered on the graphics window.
MouseX	Gets the x-position of the mouse relative to the graphics window.
MouseY	Gets the y-position of the mouse relative to the graphics window.
PenColor	Gets or sets the color of the pen used to draw shapes on the graphics window.
PenWidth	Gets or sets the width of the pen used to draw shapes on the graphics window.
Title	Gets or sets the title for the graphics window.
Width	Gets or sets the width of the graphics window.

GraphicsWindow **Methods**:

Clear()
Clears the window.

DrawEllipse(x, y, w, h)
Draws an ellipse (width **w**, height **h**) at (**x, y**) on the screen using the selected pen.

DrawImage(image, x, y)
Draws the specified **image** from memory on to the screen at (**x, y**).

DrawLine(x1, y1, x2, y2)
Draws a line from one point (**x1, y1**) to another (**x2, y2**).

DrawRectangle(x, y, w, h)
Draws a rectangle (width **w**, height **h**) on the screen at (**x, y**) using the selected pen.

DrawResizedImage(image, x, y, w, h)
Draws the specified **image** from memory on to the screen at (**x, y**), in the specified size (width **w**, height **h**).

DrawText(x, y, text)
Draws a line of **text** on the screen at the specified location (**x, y**).

DrawTriangle(x1, y1, x2, y2, x3, y3)
Draws a triangle connecting the three input points on the screen using the selected pen.

FillEllipse(x, y, w, h)
Fills an ellipse (width **w**, height **h**) on the screen at (**x, y**) using the selected brush.

FillRectangle(x, y, w, h)
Fills a rectangle (width **w**, height **h**) on the screen at (**x, y**) using the selected brush.

FillTriangle(x1, y1, x2, y2, x3, y3)
Fills a triangle connecting the three input points on the screen using the selected brush.

GetColorFromRGB(red, green, blue)
Constructs a color give the **red**, **green**, **blue** values (0-255). Returns the color.

GetRandomColor()
Gets a valid random color. Returns the color.

Hide()
Hides the graphics window.

Show()
Shows the graphics window to enable interactions with it.

ShowMessage(text, title)
Displays a message box (with message **text** and **title**) to the user.

GraphicsWindow **Events**:

KeyDown	Raises an event when a key is pressed down on the keyboard.
KeyUp	Raises an event when a key is released on the keyboard.
MouseDown	Raises an event when the mouse button is clicked down.
MouseMove	Raises an event when the mouse is moved around.
MouseUp	Raises an event when the mouse button is released.
TextInput	Raises an event when text is entered on the graphics window.

GraphicsWindow **Example**:

This code displays a graphics window 400 pixels wide by 150 pixels high with a yellow background. It draws "**Graphics Window**" in black near the center in a large font:

```
GraphicsWindow.Show()
GraphicsWindow.Width = 400
GraphicsWindow.Height = 150
GraphicsWindow.BackgroundColor = "Yellow"
GraphicsWindow.FontSize = 36
GraphicsWindow.BrushColor = "Black"
GraphicsWindow.DrawText(20, 40, "Graphics Window")
```

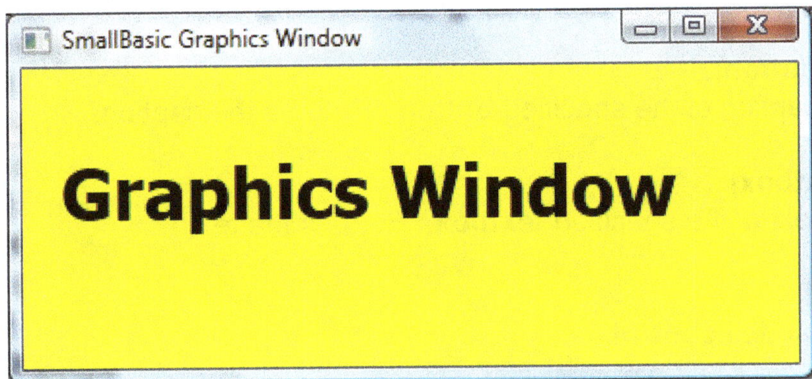

Many more examples of graphics methods are given later in this chapter.

Controls Object

The **Controls** object allows you to use three controls in your Small Basic programs – a **Button,** a **TextBox** and a **MultiLineTextBox**. The **Button** control is used to begin, interrupt, or end a particular process. The **TextBox** and **MultiLineTextBox** are used to both receive input from a user and to provide information to a user.

Controls **Properties**:

LastClickedButton	Gets the last button that was clicked on the graphics window.
LastTypedTextBox	Gets the last text box that text was typed into.

Controls **Methods**:

AddButton(caption, x, y)
Adds a button with **caption** to the graphics window at (**x, y**). Returns the added button.

AddMultiLineTextBox(x, y)
Adds a multi-line text box to the graphics window at (**x, y**). Returns the added text box.

AddTextBox(x, y)
Adds a single line text box to the graphics window at (**x, y**). Returns the added text box.

GetButtonCaption(button)
Gets the current caption of the specified **button**. Returns the caption.

GetTextBoxText(textbox)
Gets the current text of the specified **textbox**. Returns the text.

HideControl(control)
Hides an already added **control**.

Move(control, x, y)
Moves the **control** with the specified name to a new position (**x, y**).

Remove(control)
Removes a **control** from the graphics window.

SetButtonCaption(button, caption)
Sets the **caption** of the specified **button**.

SetTextBoxText(textbox, text)
Sets the **text** of the specified **textbox**.

SetSize(control, w, h)
Sets the size (width **w**, height **h**) of the **control**.

ShowControl(control)
Shows a previously hidden **control**.

Controls **Events**:

ButtonClicked	Raises an event when any button control is clicked.
TextTyped	Raises an event when text is typed into any textbox.

Some features of the **Button** control:

- The background is gray in color.
- The text color is the value of **GraphicsWindow.BrushColor** when the button is created.
- The text font assumes the values of **GraphicsWindow.FontSize** and **GraphicsWindow.FontBold** when the button is created.

Button Control **Example**:

This code creates a button (caption **This Button**, size 100 pixels by 40 pixels) in the graphics window:

```
GraphicsWindow.Show()
GraphicsWindow.Width = 400
GraphicsWindow.Height = 150
GraphicsWindow.BrushColor = "Black"
ThisButton = Controls.AddButton("This Button", 10, 10)
Controls.SetSize(ThisButton, 100, 40)
```

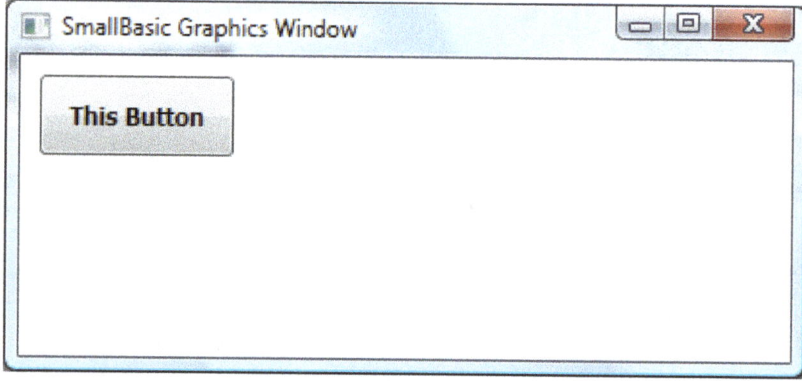

Some features of the **TextBox** and **MultiLineTextBox** controls:

- The background is white in color.
- The text color is the value of **GraphicsWindow.BrushColor** when the text box is created.
- The text font assumes the values of **GraphicsWindow.FontSize** and **GraphicsWindow.FontBold** when the text box is created.

TextBox Control **Example**:

This code creates a text box (size 200 pixels by 40 pixels) in the graphics window:

```
GraphicsWindow.Show()
GraphicsWindow.Width = 400
GraphicsWindow.Height = 150
GraphicsWindow.BrushColor = "Black"
GraphicsWindow.FontSize = 18
ThisTextBox = Controls.AddTextBox(10, 10)
Controls.SetSize(ThisTextBox, 200, 40)
Controls.SetTextBoxText(ThisTextBox, "This is my text box!")
```

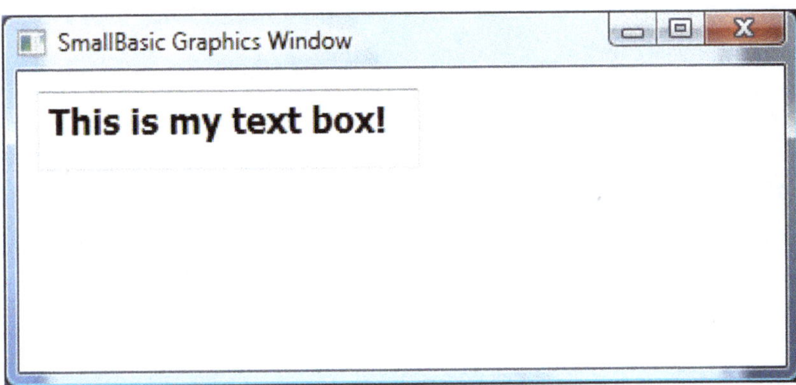

Program Object

The **Program** object (or more properly class) helps with program execution.

Program **Properties**:

Directory Gets the executing program's directory.

Program **Methods:**

Delay(milliseconds)
Delays program execution by the specified amount of **milliseconds**.

End()
Ends the program.

Text Object

The **Text** object provides helpful operations when working with strings of text.

Text **Methods:**

Append(text1, text2)

Appends two text inputs (**text1**, **text2**) and returns the result as another text. This operation is particularly useful when dealing with unknown text in variables which could accidentally be treated as numbers and get added, instead of getting appended.

ConvertToLowerCase(text)

Converts the given **text** to lower case. Returns the converted text.

ConvertToUpperCase(text)

Converts the given **text** to upper case. Returns the converted text.

GetLength(text)

Gets the length of the given **text**. Returns the length (number of characters).

GetSubText(text, start, length)

Gets a subtext from the given **text**. Returns the text starting at **start** and **length** characters long. Returns the subtext.

GetSubTextToEnd(text, start)

Gets a subtext from the given **text** from a specified position (**start**) to the end. Returns the subtext.

IsSubText(text, subtext)

Gets whether or not a given **subtext** is a subset of the larger **text**. Returns "**true**" if subtext is found in text.

Mouse Object

The **Mouse** object (or more properly class) helps decide if mouse is being used.

Mouse **Properties**:

IsLeftButtonDown	Gets whether or not the left button is pressed.
IsRightButtonDown	Gets whether or not the right button is pressed.

ImageList Object

The **ImageList** object (or more properly class) helps to load and store images in variables.

ImageList **Methods:**

ClipImage(image, x, y, w, h)
Clips a portion of a given **image** and returns a new image. The clipping rectangle is at (**x, y**) in the image and width **w**, height **h**. Returns the clipped image.

GetHeightOfImage(image)
Gets the height of the stored **image**. Returns the height.

GetWidthOfImage(image)
Gets the width of the stored **image**. Returns the width.

LoadImage(filename)
Loads an image from a file or the internet into memory (**filename** can be a local file or a URL). Returns the name of the image that was loaded.

Shapes Object

The **Shapes** object allows you to add, move and rotate shapes to the graphics window. Shapes are drawn and filled with the current pen and brush settings.

Shapes **Methods:**

AddEllipse(w, h)
Adds an ellipse shape with the specified width **w** and height **h**. Returns the ellipse.

AddImage(image)
Adds an **image** as a shape that can be moved, animated or rotated. Returns the image.

AddLine(x1, y1, x2, y2)
Adds a line between the specified points (**x1, y1**) and (**x2, y2**). Returns the line.

AddRectangle(w, h)
Adds a rectangle shape with the specified width **w** and height **h**. Returns the rectangle.

AddText(text)
Adds **text** as a shape that can be moved, animated or rotated. Returns the text shape.

AddTriangle(x1, y1, x2, y2, x3, y3)
Adds a triangle shape represented by the specified points. Returns the triangle.

Animate(shape, x, y, duration)
Animates a **shape** with the specified name to a new position (**x, y**). The animation lasts **duration** milliseconds.

GetLeft(shape)
Gets the left coordinate of the specified **shape**. Returns the left coordinate.

GetTop(shape)
Gets the top coordinate of the specified **shape**. Returns the top coordinate.

Move(shape, x, y)
Moves the shape with the specified name to a new position (**x, y**).

Remove(shape)
Removes a **shape** from the graphics window.

Rotate(shape, angle)
Rotates the **shape** with the specified name to the specified **angle** (in degrees).

SetText(shape, text)
Sets **text** of already added **shape**.

Shapes **Example**:

This code draws a red rectangle with a blue border and rotates it 30 degrees:

```
GraphicsWindow.Show()
GraphicsWindow.Width = 400
GraphicsWindow.Height = 150
GraphicsWindow.PenColor = "Blue"
GraphicsWindow.PenWidth = 5
GraphicsWindow.BrushColor = "Red"
MyShape = Shapes.AddRectangle(70, 100)
Shapes.Move(MyShape, 100, 20)
Shapes.Rotate(MyShape, 30)
```

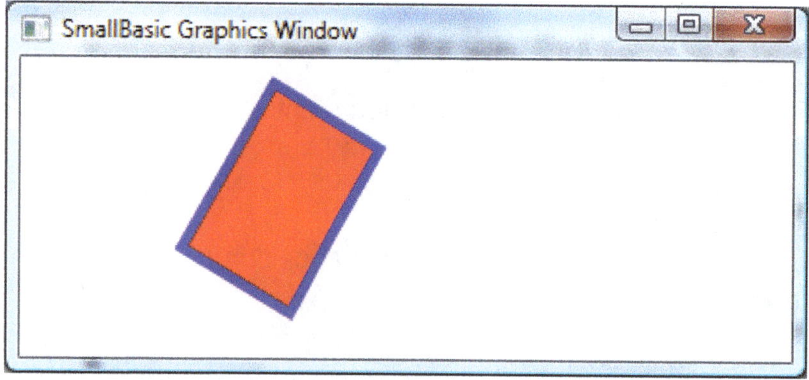

File Object

The **File** object provides methods to access, read and write information from and to a file on disk. You provide the complete filepath to the file.

File **Methods:**

AppendContents(file, contents)
Opens the specified **file** and appends the **contents** to the end of the file. Returns "**SUCCESS**" if successful, otherwise returns "**FAILED**".

GetFiles(path)
Gets all the files in the specified directory **path**. If the operation was successful, this will return the files as an array. Otherwise, it will return "**FAILED**".

InsertLine(file, line number, contents)
Opens the specified **file** and inserts the **contents** at the specified **line number**. This operation will not overwrite any existing content at the specified line. Returns "**SUCCESS**" if successful, otherwise returns "**FAILED**".

ReadContents(file)
Opens a **file** and reads the entire file's contents. Returns the contents of the file.

ReadLine(file, line number)
Opens the specified **file** and reads the contents at the specified **line number**. Returns the text at the specified line.

WriteContents(file, contents)
Opens a **file** and writes the specified **contents** into it, replacing the original contents with the new content. Returns "**SUCCESS**" if successful, otherwise returns "**FAILED**".

WriteLine(file, line number, contents)
Opens the specified **file** and write the **contents** at the specified **line number**. This operation will overwrite any existing content at the specified line. Returns "**SUCCESS**" if successful, otherwise returns "**FAILED**".

Timer Object

The **Timer** object provides an easy way for doing something repeatedly with a constant interval between.

Timer **Properties:**

Interval	Gets or sets the interval (in milliseconds) specifying how often the timer should raise the **Tick** event.

Timer **Methods:**

Pause()
Pauses the timer. Tick events will not be raised.

Resume()
Resumes the timer from a paused state. Tick events will now be raised.

Timer **Events:**

Tick	Raises an event when the timer ticks.

Sound Object

The **Sound** object provides operations that allow the playback of sounds. Some sample sounds are provided along with the library.

Sound **Methods:**

Pause(file)
Pauses playback of an audio **file**. If the file was not already playing, this operation will not do anything.

Play(file)
Plays an audio **file**. If the file was already paused, this operation will resume from the position where the playback was paused.

PlayAndWait(file)
Plays an audio **file** and waits until it is finished playing. If the file was already paused, this operation will resume from the position where the playback was paused.

PlayBellRing()
Plays the bell ring sound.

PlayBellRingAndWait()
Plays the bell ring sound and waits for it to finish.

PlayChime()
Plays the chime sound.

PlayChimeAndWait()
Plays the chime sound and waits for it to finish.

PlayChimes()
Plays the chimes sound.

PlayChimesAndWait()
Plays the chimes sound and waits for it to finish.

PlayClick()
Plays the click sound.

PlayClickAndWait()
Plays the click sound and waits for it to finish.

Stop(file)
Stops playback of an audio **file**. If the file was not already playing, this operation will not do anything.

The Small Basic Language

We have completed our review of Small Basic objects. Now, we are concerned with writing code for our programs. We will provide an overview of many of the elements of the language used in Small Basic. But first, a little history lesson.

The BASIC language was developed in the early 1960's at Dartmouth College as a device for teaching programming to "ordinary" people. There is a reason it's called BASIC:

B (eginner's)
A (All-Purpose)
S (Symbolic)
I (Instruction)
C (Code)

When timesharing systems were introduced in the 1960's, BASIC was the language of choice. Many of the first computer simulation games (Star Trek, for example) were written in timeshare BASIC.

In the mid-1970's, two college students decided that the new Altair microcomputer needed a BASIC language interpreter. They sold their product on cassette tape for a cost of $350. You may have heard of these entrepreneurs: Bill Gates and Paul Allen!

Every BASIC written since then has been based on that early version. Examples include: GW-Basic, QBasic, QuickBasic, Visual Basic. All the toy computers of the early 80's (anyone remember TI99/4A, Commodore 64, Timex, Atari 400?) used BASIC for programming.

Small Basic continues the tradition of BASIC programming. It uses the simple concepts of the early BASIC language with a modern development environment.

We provide an overview of the BASIC language used in the Small Basic environment. If you've ever used another programming language (or some version of BASIC), you will see equivalent structures in the language of Small Basic.

Variables

Variables are used by Small Basic to hold information needed by an application. Variables must be properly named. Rules used in naming variables:

- No more than 40 characters
- They may include letters, numbers, and underscore (_)
- The first character must be a letter
- You cannot use a reserved word (keywords used by Small Basic)

Use meaningful variable names that help you (or other programmers) understand the purpose of the information stored by the variable.

Examples of acceptable variable names:

```
StartingTime        Interest_Value        Letter05
JohnsAge            Number_of_Days        TimeOfDay
```

Small Basic Data Types

Each variable is used to store information of a particular **type**. Small Basic uses three types of data: **numeric**, **string** (or text) and **Boolean** variables. You must always know the type of information stored in a particular variable.

Numeric variables can store integer or decimal numbers. They can be positive or negative.

A **string** variable is just that – one that stores a string (list) of various characters. A string can be a name, a string of numbers, a sentence, a paragraph, any characters at all. And, many times, a string will contain no characters at all (an empty string). We will use lots of strings in Small Basic, so it's something you should become familiar with. Strings are always enclosed in quotes ("). Examples of strings:

"I am a Small Basic programmer"   "012345"   "Title   Author"

Boolean variables can have one of two different string values: "**true**" or "**false**". The quotes are need to indicate these are string values. Boolean variables are helpful in making decisions.

With all the different variable types, we need to be careful not to improperly mix types. We can only do mathematical operations on numbers (integer and decimal types). String types must only work with other string types. Boolean types are used for decisions.

Small Basic has no requirements (or capabilities) for declaring variables before they are used. They are essentially declared the first time they are used.

Arrays

Small Basic has facilities for handling arrays, which provide a way to store a large number of variables under the same name. Each variable, called an element, in an array must have the same data type, and they are distinguished from each other by an array index which is enclosed in brackets **[ ].**

Arrays are used in a manner identical to that of regular variables. For example, the ninth element of an array named **Item** is:

```
Item[9]
```

The index on an array variable begins at 0 and ends at the highest value used. Hence, the **Item** array in the above example actually has **ten** elements, ranging from Item[0] to Item[9]. This is different than other languages. You use array variables just like any other variable - just remember to include its name and its index. Many times, the 0 index is ignored and we just start with item 1. But sometimes the 0th element cannot be ignored. You will see examples of both 0-based and 1-based arrays in the course examples.

You can have multi-dimensional arrays. A two-dimensional array element is written as:

```
AnotherArray[2][7]
```

This refers to the element in the 2nd row and 7th column of the array **AnotherArray**.

Intellisense Feature

Working within the code editor window is easy. You will see that typing code is just like using any word processor. The usual navigation and editing features are all there.

feature that you will become comfortable with and amazed with is called **Intellisense**. As you type code, the Intellisense feature will, at times, provide assistance in completing lines of code. For example, once you type an object name and a dot (.), a drop-down list of possible properties and methods will appear. When we use methods and events, suggested values for arguments will be provided in the Small Basic help panel.

Intellisense is a very useful part of Small Basic. You should become acquainted with its use and how to select suggested values. We tell you about now so you won't be surprised when little boxes start popping up as you type code.

Small Basic Statements and Expressions

The simplest (and most common) statement in Small Basic is the **assignment** statement. It consists of a variable name, followed by the assignment operator (=), followed by some sort of **expression**. The expression on the right hand side is evaluated, then the variable (or property) on the left hand side of the assignment operator is **replaced** by that value of the expression.

Examples:

```
StartTime = Now
ExplorerName = "Captain Spaulding"
TextWindow.Title = "My Program"
BitCount = ByteCount * 8
Energy = Mass * LightSpeed * LightSpeed
NetWorth = Assets - Liabilities
```

The assignment statement stores information.

Comment statements begin with a single quote ('). For example:

```
' This is a comment
x = 2 * y ' another way to write a comment
```

You, as a programmer, should decide how much to comment your code. Consider such factors as reuse, your audience, and the legacy of your code. In our notes and examples, we try to insert comment statements when necessary to explain some detail.

Small Basic Arithmetic Operators

Operators modify values of variables. The simplest **operators** carry out **arithmetic** operations. There are four **arithmetic operators** in Small Basic.

Addition is done using the plus (+) sign and **subtraction** is done using the minus (-) sign. Simple examples are:

Operation	Example	Result
Addition	7 + 2	9
Addition	3.4 + 8.1	11.5
Subtraction	6 - 4	2
Subtraction	11.1 – 7.6	3.5

Multiplication is done using the asterisk (*) and **division** is done using the slash (/). Simple examples are:

Operation	Example	Result
Multiplication	8 * 4	32
Multiplication	2.3 * 12.2	28.06
Division	12 / 2	6
Division	45.26 / 6.2	7.3

The mathematical operators have the following **precedence** indicating the order they are evaluated without specific groupings:

1. Multiplication (*) and division (/)
2. Addition (+) and subtraction (-)

If multiplications and divisions or additions and subtractions are in the same expression, they are performed in left-to-right order. **Parentheses** around expressions are used to force some desired precedence.

Comparison and Logical Operators

There are six **comparison** operators in Small Basic used to compare the value of two expressions (the expressions must be of the same data type). These are the basis for making decisions:

Operator	Comparison
>	Greater than
<	Less than
>=	Greater than or equal to
<=	Less than or equal to
=	Equal to
<>	Not equal to

It should be obvious that the result of a comparison operation is a Boolean value (**"true"** or **"false"**). **Examples**:

A = 9.6, B = 8.1, A **>** B returns "true"
A = 14, B = 14, A **<** B returns "false"
A = 14, B = 14, A **>=** B returns "true"
A = 7, B = 11, A **<=** B returns "true"
A = "Small", B="Small", A **=** B returns "true"
A = "Basic", B = "Basic", A **<>** B returns "false"

Logical operators operate on Boolean data types, providing a Boolean result. They are also used in decision making. We will use two **logical** operators

Operator	Operation
And	Logical And
Or	Logical Or

The **And** operator checks to see if two different Boolean data types are both “true”. If both are “true”, the operator returns a “true”. Otherwise, it returns a “false” value. Examples:

A = “true”, B = “true”, then A **And** B = “true”
A = “true”, B = “false”, then A **And** B = “false”
A = “false”, B = “true”, then A **And** B = “false”
A = “false”, B = “false”, then A **And** B = “false”

The **Or** operator checks to see if either of two Boolean data types is “true”. If either is “true”, the operator returns a “true”. Otherwise, it returns a “false” value. Examples:

A = “true”, B = “true”, then A **Or** B = “true”
A = “true”, B = “false”, then A **Or** B = “true”
A = “false”, B = “true”, then A **Or** B = “true”
A = “false”, B = “false”, then A **Or** B = “false”

Logical operators follow arithmetic operators in precedence. Use of these operators will become obvious as we delve further into coding.

Concatenation Operator

To **concatentate** two string data types (tie them together), use the **+** symbol, the string concatenation operators:

```
CurrentTime = "The current time is" + Clock.Time
SampleText = "Hook this " + "to this"
```

Small Basic Methods

Small Basic offers a rich assortment of built-in **methods** that compute or provide various quantities. The general form of a method is:

```
ReturnedValue = ObjectName.MethodName(Arguments)
```

where **Arguments** represents a comma-delimited list of information needed by **MethodName** to perform its computation. Once the arguments are supplied to the method it returns a value (**ReturnedValue**) for use in an application.

Some methods do not return a value, but only perform a task. To use these methods, just type:

```
ObjectName.MethodName(Arguments)
```

String Methods

Small Basic offers a powerful set of methods to work with string type variables, which are very important in Small Basic. These methods are associated with the **Text** object.

To determine the number of characters in (or length of) a string variable, we use the **GetLength** method. Using **MyString** as example:

```
MyString = "Small Basic is fun!"
LenString = Text.GetLength(MyString)
```

LenString will have a value of **19**. Characters in the string variable start at index 1 and end at 19.

You can extract substrings of characters. The **GetSubText** method is used for this task. You specify the string, the starting position and the number of characters to extract. This example starts at character 2 and extracts 6 characters:

```
MyString = "Small Basic is fun!"
SubString = Text.GetSubText(MyString, 2, 6)
```

The **SubString** variable is equal to **"mall B"** Notice you can use this to extract from 1 to as many characters as you wish.

Perhaps, you just want a far left portion of a string. Use the **GetSubText** method with a starting position of 1. This example extracts the 3 left-most characters from a string:

```
MyString = "Small Basic is fun!"
LeftString = Text.GetSubText(MyString, 1, 3)
```

The **LeftString** variable is equal to **"Sma"**

To get the far right portion of a string, use the **GetSubTextToEnd** method. Specify the character to start with and the right portion of the string is returned. To get 6 characters at the end of our example, you would use:

```
MyString = "Small Basic is fun!"
RightString = Text.GetSubTextToEnd(MyString, 13)
```

The **RightString** variable is equal to **"s fun!"**

Many times, you want to convert letters to upper case or vice versa. Small Basic provides two methods for this purpose: **ConvertToUpperCase** and **ConvertToLowerCase**. The ConvertToUpperCase method will convert all letters in a string variable to upper case, while the ConvertToLowerCase method will convert all letters to lower case. Any non-alphabetic characters are ignored in the conversion. And, if a letter is already in the desired case, it is left unmodified. For our example (modified a bit):

```
MyString = "Read About Small Basic in 2010!”
A = Text.ConvertToUpperCase(MyString)
B = Text.ConvertToLowerCase(MyString)
```

The first conversion using **ConvertToUpperCase** will result in:

```
A = “READ ABOUT SMALL BASIC IN 2010!”
```

And the second conversion using **ConvertToLowerCase** will yield:

```
B = “read about small basic in 2010!”
```

Math Methods

Another set of methods we need are mathematical methods (yes, programming involves math!) Small Basic provides a set of methods that perform tasks such as square roots, trigonometric relationships, and exponential functions.

Each of the Small Basic math functions comes from the **Math** class. All this means is that each method name must be preceded by **Math.** (say Math-dot) to work properly. The methods and the returned values are:

Math Method	Value Returned
`Math.Abs`	Returns the absolute value of a specified number.
`Math.Ceiling`	Gets an integer that is greater than or equal to the specified decimal number. For example, 32.233 will return 33.
`Math.Cos`	Returns a value containing the cosine of the specified angle in radians.
`Math.Floor`	Gets an integer that is less than or equal to the specified decimal number. For example, 32.233 will return 32.
`Math.GetDegrees`	Converts a given angle in radians to degrees.
`Math.GetRadians`	Converts a given angle in degrees to radians.
`Math.Log`	Gets the logarithm (base 10) value of the given number.
`Math.Max`	Returns the larger of two numbers.
`Math.Min`	Returns the smaller of two numbers.
`Math.NaturalLog`	Gets the natural logarithm value of the given number.
`Math.Pi`	A constant that specifies the ratio of the circumference of a circle to its diameter (3.14159265359…).
`Math.Power`	Raises a number to a specified power.
`Math.Remainder`	Divides the first number by the second and returns the remainder.
`Math.Round`	Returns the number nearest the specified value.
`Math.Sin`	Returns a value containing the sine of the specified angle in radians.
`Math.SquareRoot`	Returns a value specifying the square root of a number.
`Math.Tan`	Returns a value containing the tangent of an angle in radians.

Examples:

`Math.Abs(-5.4)` returns the absolute value of –5.4 (returns 5.4)
`Math.Cos(2.3)` returns the cosine of an angle of 2.3 radians
`Math.Max(7, 10)` returns the larger of the two numbers (returns 10)
`Math.Power(2, 4)` returns 2 raised to the fourth power (16)
`Math.SquareRoot(4.5)` returns the square root of 4.5

Random Numbers

We single out one math method for its importance. In writing games and learning software, we use a random number generator to introduce unpredictability. The **Math.GetRandomNumber** method is used in Small Basic for random numbers.

Whenever you need a random whole number (integer) value, use this method:

```
Math.GetRandomNumber(Limit)
```

This statement generates a random value that is between 1 and **Limit**. For example, the method:

```
Math.GetRandomNumber(5)
```

will generate random numbers from 1 to 5. The possible values will be 1, 2, 3, 4 and 5.

A roll of a die can produce a number from 1 to 6. To use **GetRandomNumber** to roll a die, we would write:

```
DieNumber = Math.GetRandomNumber(6)
```

For a deck of cards, the random integers would range from 1 to 52 since there are 52 cards in a standard playing deck. Code to do this:

```
CardNumber = Math.GetRandomNumber(52)
```

If we want a number between -100 and 100, we would use:

```
YourNumber = 101 -Math.GetRandomNumber(201)
```

Check the examples above to make sure you see how the random number generator produces the desired range of integers.

Graphics Methods

All of our projects will be “hosted” by the Small Basic graphics window. To put anything in the graphics window, it must be “drawn” there using one of the many Small Basic graphics methods. Even text has to be drawn! Let’s take a look at these methods.

Recall the coordinate system used by the graphics window is:

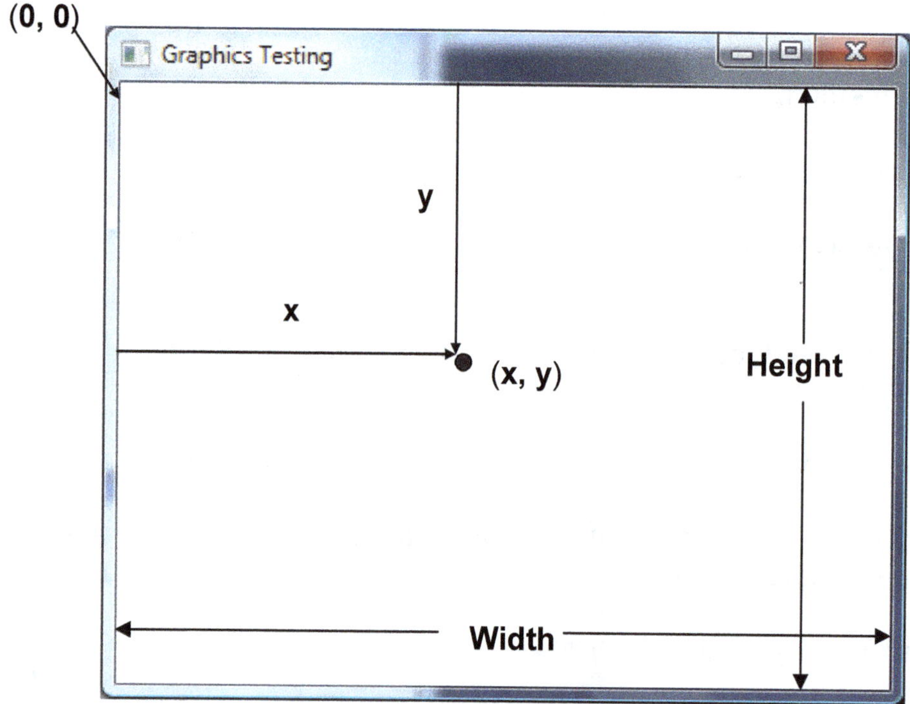

The window is **Width** pixels wide and **Height** pixels high. We use two values (coordinates) to identify a single pixel in the window. The **x** (horizontal) coordinate increases from left to right, starting at **0**. The **y** (vertical) coordinate increases from top to bottom, also starting at **0**. Points in the region are referred to by the two coordinates enclosed in parentheses, or **(x, y)**.

To draw lines and shapes, we use a **pen**. You can choose color and width. Lines of code that accomplish this task are:

```
GraphicsWindow.PenColor = Color
GraphicsWindow.PenWidth = Width
```

where **Color** is the color your pen will draw in and **Width** is the integer width (a value of 1 by default) of the line (in pixels) drawn. This pen will draw a solid line. To specify a color, you use a color name like “Red”, “White” or “Blue”. Appendix I lists the multitude of colors available with Small Basic.

The Small Basic **DrawLine** method is used to connect two points with a straight-line segment. If we wish to connect the point (**x1**, **y1**) with (**x2**, **y2**), the statement is:

```
GraphicsWindow.DrawLine(x1, y1, x2, y2)
```

The line will draw in the current pen **Color** and **Width**. Example that draws a blue line of width 1:

```
GraphicsWindow.PenColor = "Blue"
GraphicsWindow.PenWidth = 1
GraphicsWindowGraphicsWindow.DrawLine(20, 50, 380, 280)
```

The Small Basic **DrawRectangle** method is used to draw a rectangle. To draw a rectangle, we specify the upper left hand corner’s coordinate (**x**, **y**) and the **width** and **height** of the rectangle. To draw such a rectangle in the graphics window:

```
GraphicsWindow.DrawRectangle(x, y, width, height)
```

The rectangle will draw with the current pen. To draw a blue rectangle (pen width 2) with the upper left corner at (20, 50), width 150 and height 100, use this code:

```
GraphicsWindow.PenColor = "Blue"
GraphicsWindow.PenWidth = 2
GraphicsWindow.DrawRectangle(20, 50, 150, 100)
```

The Small Basic **DrawEllipse** method is used to draw an ellipse. To draw an ellipse, we specify the upper left hand corner's coordinate (**x**, **y**) and the **width** and **height** of the ellipse. To draw such an ellipse in the graphics window:

```
GraphicsWindow.DrawEllipse(x, y, width, height)
```

The ellipse will draw with the current pen. To draw a green ellipse (pen width 3) with the upper left corner at (20, 50), width 150 and height 100, use this code:

```
GraphicsWindow.PenColor = "Green"
GraphicsWindow.PenWidth = 3
GraphicsWindow.DrawEllipse(20, 50, 150, 100)
```

A **brush** is like a "wide" pen. It is used to fill areas with a color. It has a single property (**Color**). To set the brush color, use:

```
GraphicsWindow.BrushColor = Color
```

A brush is 'solid' – filling areas completely with the specified color

To fill rectangles and ellipses with the current brush color, use the **FillRectangle** and **FillEllipse** methods. They have the same arguments as **DrawRectangle** and **DrawEllipse**, respectively.

To add text information to the graphics window, we use the Small Basic **DrawText** method – yes, text is "drawn" to the window. The **DrawText** method is:

```
GraphicsWindow.DrawText(x, y, text)
```

In this statement, **text** represents the string to print in the window and the point (**x, y**) is where the string will be located. The string will draw in the graphics window using the current brush color using the default font. Note this method uses the brush color, not the pen color – text is truly drawn like other graphics objects.

Here's an example using **DrawText**:

```
GraphicsWindow.BrushColor = "Blue"
GraphicsWindow.DrawText(40, 100, "Isn't Small Basic fun?")
```

This puts the line "Isn't Small Basic fun?" at (40, 100) in the graphics window. The text will be blue in color. By setting the (x, y) point, you can left or right justify the text, or center it horizontally and/or vertically by knowing the window dimensions. The font size can be changed by setting the **FontSize** property and **FontBold** determines if the font is bold or not.

Shapes Objects

Related to graphics methods are **Shapes** objects. A **Shapes** object is a rectangular region we can add, move and remove within the graphics window. Such an object makes animation (moving objects) very simple. We can have shapes that are rectangles, ellipses and even images! Let's look at each.

To create a rectangular shape (**MyRectangle**) that is **W** pixels wide and **H** pixels high, use the **AddRectangle** method:

```
MyRectangle = Shapes.AddRectangle(W, H)
```

This will create a 'bordered' rectangle. The current pen color and pen width establishes the rectangle's border color, while the current brush color establishes the fill color. By default, it will be put in the upper left corner of the graphics window.

Analogously, to create an elliptical shape (**MyEllipse**) that is **W** pixels wide and **H** pixels high, use the **AddEllipse** method:

```
MyEllipse = Shapes.AddEllipse(W, H)
```

This will create a 'bordered' ellipse. The current pen color and pen width establishes the ellipse border color, while the current brush color establishes the fill color. By default, it will be put in the upper left corner of the graphics window.

To create a shape with an image, we need two steps. First, we must load the image, then create the shape. Assume you have **jpg** image file (a digital photo) named **MyImage.jpg**. (You can use other image files types too). The file with this image must be in the same folder as your Small Basic program. The image is loaded using the **LoadImage** method of the **ImageList** object:

```
MyImage = ImageList.LoadImage(Program.Directory +
"\MyImage.jpg")
```

Then the image shape (**MyImageShape**) is created using:

```
MyImageShape = Shapes.AddImage(MyImage)
```

The shape will be placed in the upper left corner of the graphics window.

Moving **Shapes** objects in a graphics window is easy to do. It is a simple two step process: use some rule to determine a new position, then redraw it in this new position using the **Shapes** object **Move** method. If you have a shape object named **MyShape** and you want to move it to (**NewX**, **NewY**), the code is:

```
Shapes.Move(MyShape, NewX, NewY)
```

This code will 'erase' **MyShape** at its current position, then 'redraw' it at the newly specified position. Successive transfers (or moves) gives the impression of motion, or animation.

Small Basic Decisions - If Statements

The concept of an **If** statement for making a decision is very simple. We check to see if a particular condition is "true". If so, we take a certain action. If not, we do something else. **If** statements are also called **branching** statements. **Branching** statements are used to cause certain actions within a program if a certain condition is met.

The simplest branching statement is:

```
If (Condition) Then
   [process this code]
EndIf
```

Here, if **Condition** is **"**true", the code bounded by the If/EndIf is executed. If Condition is "false", nothing happens and code execution continues after the EndIf statement.

Example:

```
If (Balance - Check < 0) Then
  Trouble = "true"
  GraphicsWindow.BackgroundColor = "Red"
EndIf
```

In this case, if Balance - Check is less than zero, two lines of information are processed: Trouble is set to "true" and the window turns red. Notice the indentation of the code between the **If** and **EndIf** lines. The Small Basic Intellisense feature will automatically do this indentation. It makes understanding (and debugging) your code much easier.

What if you want to do one thing if a condition is "true" and another if it is "false"? Use an **If/Then/Else/EndIf** block:

```
If (Condition) Then
   [process this code]
Else
   [process this code]
EndIf
```

In this block, if Condition is "true", the code between the If and Else lines is executed. If Condition is "false", the code between the Else and EndIf statements is processed.

Example:

```
If (Balance - Check < 0) Then
  Trouble = "true"
  GraphicsWindow.BackgroundColor = "Red"
Else
  Trouble = "false"
  GraphicsWindow.BackgroundColor = "Black"
EndIf
```

Here, the same two lines are executed if you are overdrawn (Balance - Check < 0), but if you are not overdrawn (**Else**), the Trouble flag is turned off and your window is black.

Finally, we can test multiple conditions by adding the **ElseIf** statement:

```
If (Condition1) Then
   [process this code]
ElseIf (Condition2) Then
   [process this code]
ElseIf (Condition3) Then
   [process this code]
Else
   [process this code]
EndIf
```

In this block, if Condition1 is "true", the code between the If and first ElseIf line is executed. If Condition1 is "false", Condition2 is checked. If Condition2 is "true", the indicated code is executed. If Condition2 is not true, Condition3 is checked. Each subsequent condition in the structure is checked until a "true" condition is found, a Else statement is reached or the EndIf is reached.

Example:

```
If (Balance - Check < 0) Then
  Trouble = "true"
  GraphicsWindow.BackgroundColor = "Red"
ElseIf (Balance - Check = 0) Then
  Trouble = "false"
  GraphicsWindow.BackgroundColor = "Yellow"
Else
  Trouble = "false"
  GraphicsWindow.BackgroundColor = "Black"
EndIf
```

Now, one more condition is added. If your Balance equals the Check amount (**ElseIf** Balance - Check = 0), you're still not in trouble and the screen is yellow.

In using branching statements, make sure you consider all viable possibilities in the If/Else/EndIf structure. Also, be aware that each If and ElseIf in a block is tested sequentially. The first time an If test is met, the code associated with that condition is executed and the If block is exited. If a later condition is also "true", it will never be considered.

Small Basic Looping

Many applications require repetition of certain code segments. For example, you may want to roll a die (simulated die of course) until it shows a six. Or, you might generate financial results until a certain sum of returns has been achieved. This idea of repeating code is called iteration or **looping**.

In Small Basic, one way of looping is with the **While** loop:

```
While (Condition)
  ' Small Basic code block to repeat while Condition is true
EndWhile
```

In this structure, all code between While and EndWhile is repeated **while** the given logical **Condition** is "**true**".

Note a **While** loop structure will not execute even once if Condition is "false" the first time through. If we do enter the loop (Condition is "true"), it is assumed at some point Condition will become false to allow exiting. Once this happens, code execution continues at the statement following the EndWhile statement. This brings up a very important point about loops – if you get in one, make sure you get out at some point. In the While loop, if Condition is always "true", you will loop forever – something called an infinite loop.

Here is an example:

```
Counter = 1
While (Counter <= 1000)
  Counter = Counter + 1
EndWhile
```

This loop repeats as long as (**While**) the variable Counter is less than or equal to 1000.

Another example:

```
Rolls = 0
Counter = 0
While (Counter < 10)
  ' Roll a simulated die
  Roll = Roll + 1
  If (Math.GetRandomNumber(6) = 6) Then
    Counter = Counter + 1
  EndIf
EndWhile
```

This loop repeats while the **Counter** variable remains less than 10. The counter variable is incremented (increased by one) each time a simulated die rolls a 6. The **Roll** variable tells you how many rolls of the die were needed to roll 10 sixes. Theoretically, it should take 60 rolls since there is a 1 in 6 chance of rolling a six.

As mentioned, if the logical condition used by a While loop is "false" the first time the loop is encountered, the code block in the While loop will not be executed. This may be acceptable behavior – it may not be.

We can build a loop that will always be executed at least once. To do this we need to introduce the Small Basic **Goto** statement. A Goto allows you to transfer code execution to anywhere in your code. A Goto requires a **label**. A label is like a bookmark – it can be named anything you want. A label name is always followed by a colon. An example is:

```
MyLabel:
```

Anytime we want to transfer program execution to this label statement, we use a Goto:

```
Goto MyLabel
```

You do not write the colon in the Goto statement.

Using these new concepts in a loop, we have what we'll call a **Goto loop**:

```
MyLabel:
  ' Small Basic code block to process
If (Condition) Then
  Goto MyLabel
EndIf
```

The code block repeats as long as **Condition** is "true". Unlike the While loop, this loop is always executed at least once. Somewhere in the loop, Condition should be changed to "false" to allow exiting.

Let's look at examples of the **Goto** loop. What if we want to keep adding three to a **Sum** until the value exceeds 50. This loop will do it:

```
Sum = 0
SumLoop:
  Sum = Sum + 3
If (Sum <= 50) Then
  Goto SumLoop
EndIf
```

Or, another dice example:

```
Sum = 0
Roll = 0
SumLoop:
  ' Roll a simulated die
  Die = Math.GetRandomNumber(6)
  Sum = Sum + Die
  Roll = Roll + 1
If (Sum <= 30) Then
  Goto SumLoop
EndIf
```

This loop rolls a simulated die (**Die**) while the **Sum** of the rolls does not exceed 30. It also keeps track of the number of rolls (**Roll**) needed to achieve this sum.

You need to decide which of the loop structures (While, Goto) fits your program. Recall the major difference is that a Goto loop is always executed at least once; a While loop may never be executed.

And, make sure you can always get out of a loop. In both looping structures, this means that, at some point, the checking logical condition must become "false" to allow exiting the loop. When you exit a While loop, processing continues at the next Small Basic statement after the EndWhile. In a Goto loop, processing continues at the Small Basic statement after the If structure checking whether the loop should repeat.

If, at some point in the code block of a loop, you decide you need to immediately leave the loop or move to another point in the code, a **Goto** statement can also do this. You just need a label statement at the appropriate place. When the **Goto** statement is encountered, processing is immediately transferred to the labeled statement.

Small Basic Counting

With While loop structures, we usually didn't know, ahead of time, how many times we execute a loop or iterate. If you know how many times you need to iterate on some code, you want to use Small Basic **counting**. Counting is useful for adding items to a list or perhaps summing a known number of values to find an average.

Small Basic counting is accomplished using the **For** loop:

```
For Variable = Start To End Step Increment
  ' Small Basic code to execute goes here]
EndFor
```

In this loop, **Variable** is the counter (doesn't necessarily need to be a whole number). The first time through the loop, Variable is initialized at **Start**. Each time the corresponding **EndFor** statement is reached, Variable is incremented by an amount **Increment**. If the **Step** value is omitted, a default increment value of one is used. Negative increments are also possible. The counting repeats until Variable equals or exceeds the final value **End**.

Example:

```
For Degrees = 0 To 360 Step 10
  'convert to radians
  R = Degrees * Math.PI / 180
  A = Math.Sin(R)
  B = Math.Cos(R)
  C = Math.Tan(R)
EndFor
```

In this example, we compute trigonometric functions for angles from 0 to 360 degrees in increments (steps) of 10 degrees.

Another Example:

```
For Countdown = 10 To 0 Step -1
  TextWindow.WriteLine(Countdown + " Seconds")
EndFor
```

NASA called and asked us to countdown from 10 to 0. The loop above accomplishes the task.

And, Another Example:

```
Sum = 0
For I = 1 to 100
  Sum = Sum + MyValues[I]
EndFor
Average = Sum / 100
```

This code finds the average value of 100 numbers stored in the array MyValues. It first sums each of the values in a **For** loop. That sum is then divided by the number of terms (100) to yield the average.

You may exit a For loop early using an **Goto** statement. This will transfer program control to the corresponding labeled statement, usually the line after the EndFor.

Small Basic Subroutines

In the looping discussion, we saw how code in one particular block could be repeated until some desired condition was met. Many times in Small Basic programs, we might have a need to repeat a certain block of code at several different points in the program. Why would you want to do this?

Say we had a game that requires us to roll 5 dice and add up their individual values to yield a sum. What if we needed to do this at 10 different places in our program? We could write the code, then copy and paste it to the 10 different places. I think you can see problems already. What if you need to change the code? You would need to change it in 10 different places. What if you needed to put the code in another place in your program? You would need to do another 'copy and paste' operation. There's a better way. And that way is to use a Small Basic **subroutine**.

A subroutine allows you to write the code to perform certain tasks just once. Then, whenever you need to access the code in your program, you can "call it.," providing any information it might need to do its tasks. Subroutines are the building blocks of a Small Basic program. Using subroutines in your Small Basic programs can help divide a complex application into more manageable units of code. Just think of a subroutine as a code block you can access from anywhere in a Small Basic program. When you call the subroutine, program control goes to that subroutine, performs the assigned tasks and returns to the calling program. It's that easy.

Subroutines are also an important part of object events. When an event occurs, program control transfers to the subroutine assigned to that event.

Let's see how to create and call a subroutine. Subroutines go at the end of your '**main'** program code. A subroutine named **MySubroutine** would have the form (starts with a **Sub** keyword and ends with **EndSub**):

```
Sub MySubroutine
  ' Code to be executed in the subroutine
EndSub
```

You execute, or call, this subroutine using:

```
MySubroutine()
```

The parentheses are needed to tell the computer you are executing a subroutine. When the subroutine is called, the corresponding code is executed until the **EndSub** line is reached. At this point, program execution returns to the 'main' code after the line calling the subroutine.

A subroutine can access and use any variable you use in your program. Likewise, your program can use any variables defined in your subroutines. In computer talk, we say the variables in a Small Basic program have **global scope**.

Let's try to make this clearer by looking at a subroutine example. We'll do the dice example of rolling five dice and computing their sum. The subroutine that accomplishes this task is:

```
Sub RollDice
  Die1 = Math.GetRandomNumber(6)
  Die2 = Math.GetRandomNumber(6)
  Die3 = Math.GetRandomNumber(6)
  Die4 = Math.GetRandomNumber(6)
  Die5 = Math.GetRandomNumber(6)
  SumDice = Die1 + Die2 + Die3 + Die4 + Die5
EndSub
```

This subroutine is named **RollDice** and the variable **SumDice** has the resulting sum.

Using this subroutine, any time you need the sum of five dice in your program, you would use:

```
RollDice()
A = SumDice
```

After this code is executed, the variable **A** will have sum of five dice.

As you progress in your Small Basic programming education, you will become more comfortable with using subroutines and see how useful they are. In the remainder of this course, we will use subroutines for all of the code. Study each example to help learn how to build and use subroutines.

Chapter Review

After completing this chapter, you should understand:

- Use of the **TextWindow.**
- Use of the **GraphicsWindow.**
- Use of other objects.
- How to play sounds using the **Sound** object.
- How to properly use variables.
- Small Basic statements.
- The assignment operator, mathematics operators, comparison and logic operators and concatenation operators.
- The wide variety of built-in Small Basic methods, especially string methods and mathematics methods.
- How to use graphics methods to draw in the graphics window.
- The **If/Then/ElseIf/Else/EndIf** structure used for branching and decisions.
- How the **While** loop and **Goto** loop work.
- How the **For** loop is used for counting.
- The importance of subroutines in Small Basic programs.

We now have the foundation needed to write code for our programs. We will begin our first project in Chapter 4, once we have a brief discussion of debugging programs (Chapter 3).

This page intentionally not left blank.

3. Debugging a Small Basic Program

Review and Preview

As you begin building projects using **Programming Home Projects With Small Basic**, you will undoubtedly encounter errors in your code. In this chapter, we look at handling errors in projects. After this, we begin building projects (at last).

Debugging a Small Basic Program

No matter how well you plan your program and no matter how careful you are in implementing your ideas in Small Basic code, you will make mistakes. Errors, or what computer programmers call **bugs**, do creep into your program. You may have already encountered a few in the programs we've built so far. Perhaps you spelled a keyword wrong, forgot a punctuation mark or misspelled a variable name. These are all examples of program bugs. You, as a programmer, need to have a strategy for finding and eliminating those bugs. The process of eliminating bugs in a program is called **debugging**. Unfortunately, there are not a lot of hard, fast rules for finding bugs in a program. Each programmer has his or her own way of attacking bugs. You will develop your ways. We can come up with some general strategies, though, and that's what we'll give you here.

Program errors, or bugs, can be divided into three types:

- **Syntax** errors
- **Run-time** errors
- **Logic** errors

Syntax errors occur when you make an error typing a line of Small Basic code. Something is misspelled or something is left out that needs to be there. Your program won't run if there are any syntax errors. **Run-time errors** occur when you try to run your program. It will stop abruptly because something has happened beyond its control. **Logic errors** are the toughest to find. Your program will run okay, but the results it gives are not what you expected. Let's examine each error type and address possible debugging methods.

Syntax Errors

Syntax errors are the easiest to identify and eliminate. The Small Basic development environment is a big help in finding syntax errors. Syntax errors will occur as you're writing Small Basic code.

Start Small Basic. We'll type in a few snippets of code to see how different bugs are identified. Let's look at some typical errors. In the editor, type these two lines of code:

```
MyNumber = 7
TextWindow.WriteLine(MyNmber)
```

We've misspelled the assigned variable name (**MyNumber**) in the **WriteLine** statement.

Try running this and below the editor you will see the message:

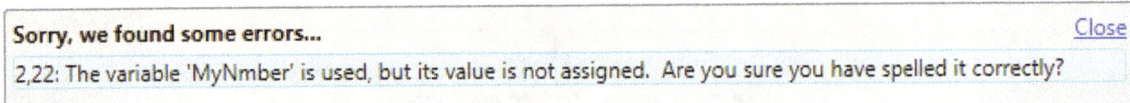

Sorry, we found some errors... Close

2,22: The variable 'MyNmber' is used, but its value is not assigned. Are you sure you have spelled it correctly?

The 2,22 implies there is an error in Line 2, Column 22. It tells you it does not recognize the variable **MyNmber** and asks if you misspelled it. We did. Small Basic is pretty smart!

Correct that error, but misspell **WriteLine** as **WriteLne**:

```
MyNumber = 7
TextWindow.WriteLne(MyNumber)
```

Try running and Small Basic will tell you the problem:

```
Sorry, we found some errors...
2,12: Cannot find operation 'WriteLne' in 'TextWindow'.
```

Correct your error. But, change the first line as shown (leave out the assignment operator):

```
MyNumber  7
TextWindow.WriteLine(MyNumber)
```

Try running and you'll get this error message:

```
Sorry, we found some errors...
1,11: Unrecognized statement encountered.
```

You are being told this (line 1 again) is not a recognized statement and the problem is somewhere around Column 11. You should immediately see the problem and be able to fix it. Fix the error.

Let's try one other example. Change the second line by adding an additional parenthesis at the end of the **WriteLine** method:

```
MyNumber = 7
TextWindow.WriteLine(MyNumber))
```

Try running and you receive this message:

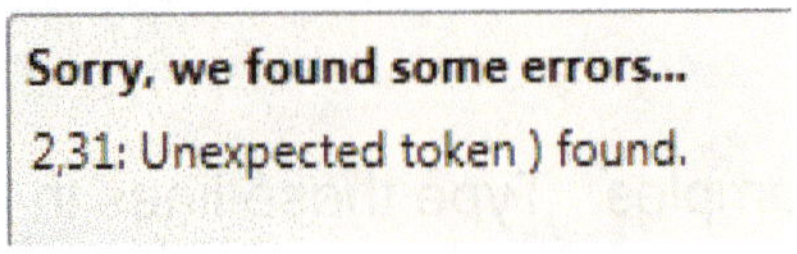

Sorry, we found some errors...
2,31: Unexpected token) found.

The problem is clear – you have one too many right parentheses.

So when you try to run with syntax errors, the Small Basic environment will kindly point out your errors to you so you can fix them. Note that syntax errors usually result because of incorrect typing, either misspellings, additions or omissions - another great reason to improve your typing skills, if they need it.

Run-Time Errors

Once you have written your code and eliminated all identified syntax errors, obtaining a successful compilation, you try to run your program. If the program runs, great! But, many times, your program may stop and tell you it found an error - this is a run-time error. You need to figure out why it stopped and fix the problem. At this writing, the Small Basic environment does not give you much useful information when a run-time error occurs. Many times, the program will just stop.

Let's look at a couple of examples. Type these lines in the editor:

```
MyNumber = 7
MyOtherNumber = 0
TextWindow.WriteLine(MyNumber / MyOtherNumber)
```

Yes, I know we'll get a divide by zero (a classic run-time error), but that's the point here – to illustrate potential errors. The program should not run, giving you some indication you are dividing by zero. If you run the program, it runs without error, printing a zero as the division result:

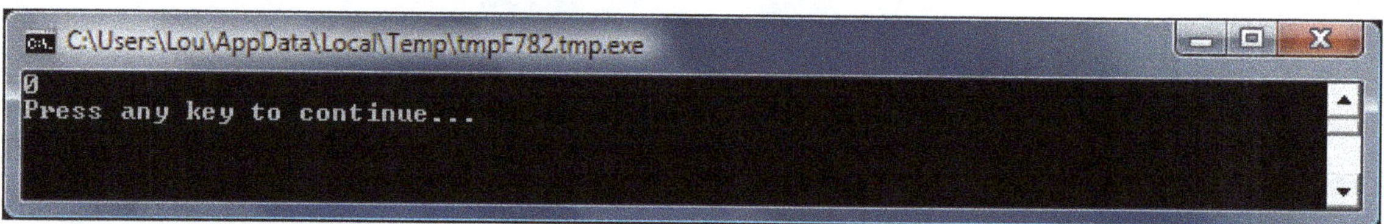

This needs to be corrected in future Small Basic versions.

Another common run-time error occurs when using one of Small Basic's built-in functions. Errors result if you use the wrong type or value as one of the arguments. Try these two lines of code:

```
MyNumber = -7
TextWindow.WriteLine(Math.SquareRoot(MyNumber))
```

We attempt to take the square root of a negative number (not allowed). When we run the program, we get some indication that something is wrong, but it is not very explicit:

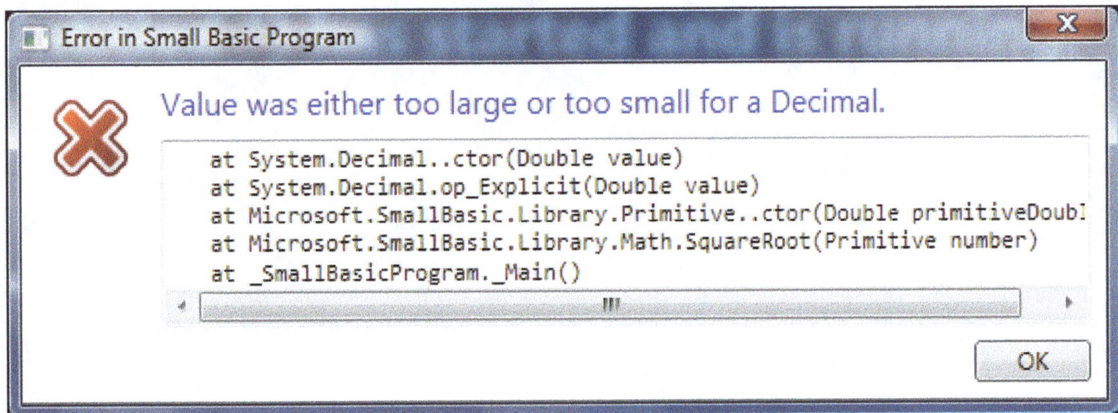

Click **OK** and the program just stops:

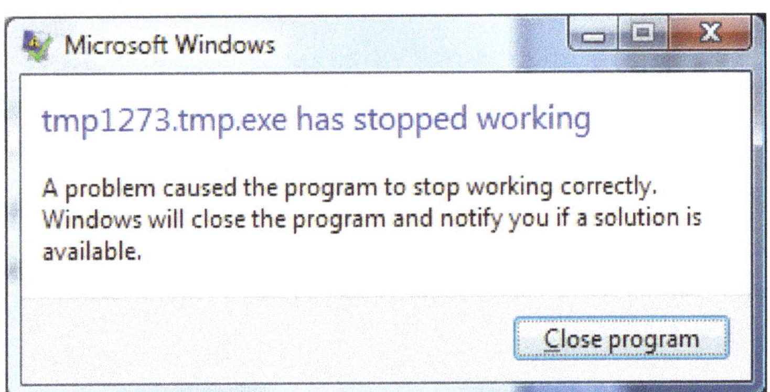

We've seen just a couple of possible run-time errors. There are others and you'll see them as you start building programs. And, unfortunately, the current Small Basic program is not very helpful in pointing out where errors are. Hopefully, this situation will change with future versions. One last thing about run-time errors. Small Basic will not find all errors at once. It will stop at the first run-time error it encounters. After you fix that error, there may be more. You have to fix run-time errors one at a time.

Logic Errors

Logic errors are the most difficult to find and eliminate. These are errors that don't keep your program from running, but cause incorrect or unexpected results. The only thing you can do at this point, if you suspect logic errors exist, is to dive into your program and make sure everything is coded exactly as you want it. Finding logic errors is a time-consuming art, not a science. There are no general rules for finding logic errors. Each programmer has his or her own particular way of searching for logic errors.

With the example we have been using, a logic error would be setting a variable to an incorrect value. Or, perhaps you add two numbers together when you should have subtracted. Logic errors are mistakes you have inadvertently introduced into your Small Basic code. And, unfortunately, these errors are not pointed out to you. Hence, eliminating logic errors is not always easy.

Advanced programming languages use something called a **debugger** that helps in the identification of logic errors. Using a debugger lets you examine variable values, stop your code wherever and whenever you want, and run your program line-by-line. Small Basic does not offer a debugger. So, for now, you need to learn to eliminate logic errors by paying close attention to your code. And, the best approach is to be so careful that you don't have any logic errors to worry about.

Chapter Review

After completing this chapter, you should understand:

- The different types of errors.
- Ways to track errors.

We can now start building some projects.

4. Dual-Mode Stopwatch Project

Review and Preview

We've completed our review of the Small Basic development environment, the objects and language needed to program using Small Basic and techniques for debugging projects. We can finally start building some home projects.

For each project built, we provide step-by-step instructions in designing and building the window's graphic interface and detailed explanations of the code behind the projects.

The first project we build is a **Dual-Mode Stopwatch** that allows you to time tasks you may be doing.

Project Design Considerations

Before building this first project, let's look at some of the things that should be considered to make a useful project. A first consideration should be to determine what processes and functions you want your application to perform. What are the inputs and outputs? Develop a framework or flow chart of all your application's processes.

Decide what controls you need. Use buttons and text boxes as needed.

Design your user interface. What do you want your window to look like? Consider appearance and ease of use. Make the interface consistent with other Windows applications. Familiarity is good in program design.

Write your code. Make your code readable and traceable - future code modifiers (including yourself) will thank you. Consider developing reusable code - subroutines with utility outside your current development. This will save you time in future developments.

Make your code 'user-friendly.' Make operation of your application obvious to the user. Step the user through its use. Try to anticipate all possible ways a user can mess up in using your application. It's fairly easy to write an application that works properly when the user does everything correctly. It's difficult to write an application that can handle all the possible wrong things a user can do and still not bomb out.

Debug your code completely before giving it to others. There's nothing worse than having a user call you to point out flaws in your application. A good way to find all the bugs is to let several people try the code - a mini beta-testing program.

Dual-Mode Stopwatch Project Preview

In this chapter, we will build a **dual-mode stopwatch**. The stopwatch can be started and stopped when desired. Two times are tracked: the time that elapses while the stopwatch is active (the running time) and the total time elapsed between first starting and finally stopping the stopwatch.

The finished project is saved as **Stopwatch** in the **HomeSB\HomeSB Projects\Stopwatch** folder. Start Small Basic and open the finished program. **Run** the program (click the **Run** toolbar button or press <**F5**>). The stopwatch will appear in its 'initial' state, with the displayed times set at zero and the **Start** and **Exit** buttons visible:

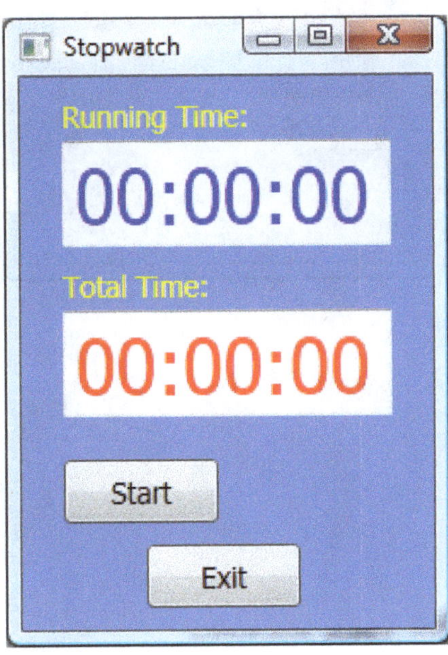

Click the **Start** button to start the stopwatch. Its caption will change (now reading **Stop**) and the **Exit** button will disappear - the two displayed times will be the same (updating every second). We call this the ‘running’ state:

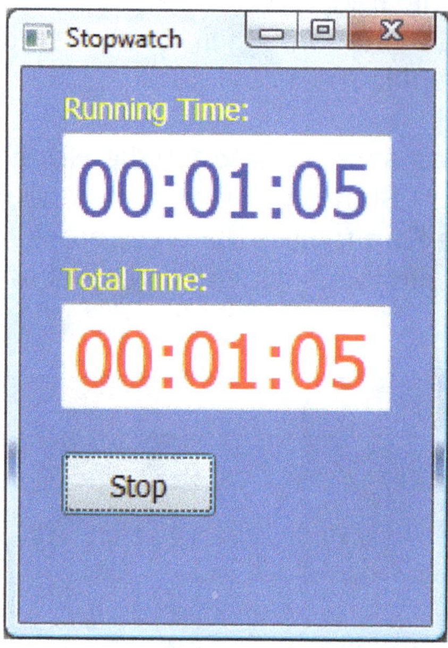

At some point, click **Stop**. When I did, the window appears as:

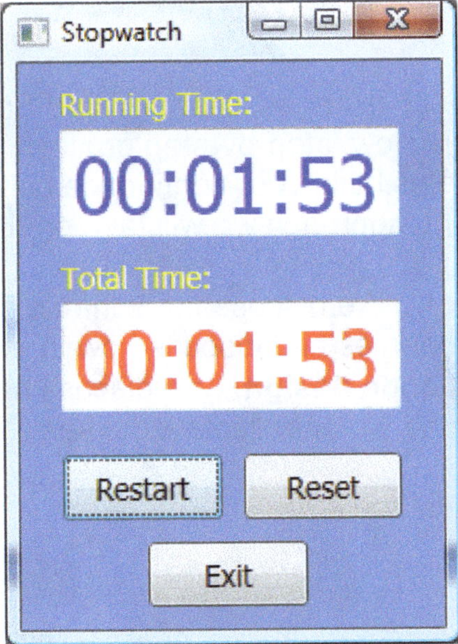

At this point ('stopped' state), all buttons are visible and you have three options. You can click **Exit** to stop the project. You can click **Reset** to set both times back to zero and return the project to its initial state. Or, you can click the button now labeled **Restart** to restart the timer. When I do this, after a short wait, I get:

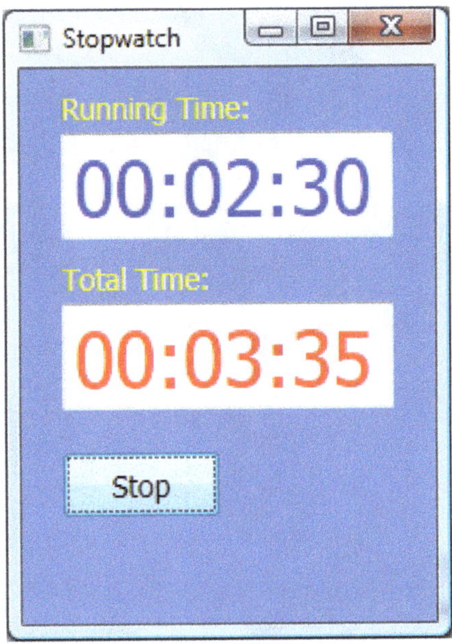

The stopwatch is running again, but the two displayed times are different. The **Total Time** is the amount of time elapsed since we first started the stopwatch. The **Running Time** is the total time less time when the stopwatch is in stopped mode. Based on these values, this stopwatch has spent 1:05 waiting around.

Continue starting, stopping, restarting and resetting the stopwatch to understand its operation. Click **Exit** when you're done to stop the project. Look over the code, if you like.

You will now build this project in stages. As you build Small Basic projects, we always recommend taking a slow, step-by-step process. It minimizes programming errors and helps build your confidence as things come together in a complete project. This is the approach we will take on all projects in these notes.

We address **window design**. We discuss the controls needed to build the window, establish initial properties and discuss how to change the state of the controls. And, we address **code design**. We discuss how to do the necessary mathematics to determine the various displayed times.

Project Window Design

Since this is our first project, let's look briefly at the idea of game **window design**. This is a first step in building a Small Basic program where you decide what you want to display to the user in the graphics window. In this **window design** phase, you need to know what inputs you need from the user and how you want to show them outputs.

Make initial sketches of where you want certain game elements to appear. Always have an area to provide messages to the user – messages like how to start/stop the game and messages on how they are progressing in the game. Use button controls to perform specific tasks (start, stop, change options) in your program. Use text box controls to display information or get user input.

In your design, since you are using the graphics window, make sure you incorporate graphics elements of colors and shapes. Make the window pleasant to look at and easy to understand. Finalize your sketch on graph paper to help with positioning parts of the final layout. Make notes for dimensions and locations of different components.

Translate your sketch to actual Small Basic code to draw the window elements. With Small Basic, you can make quick changes and see the results of these changes immediately. The window design process is iterative – meaning you will always be tweaking certain items until you are satisfied with your window design. For the programs in these notes, we present our ideas for windows. Feel free to modify them in any way you choose.

Stopwatch Window Design

Here is the sketch for the window layout of the **Stopwatch** program:

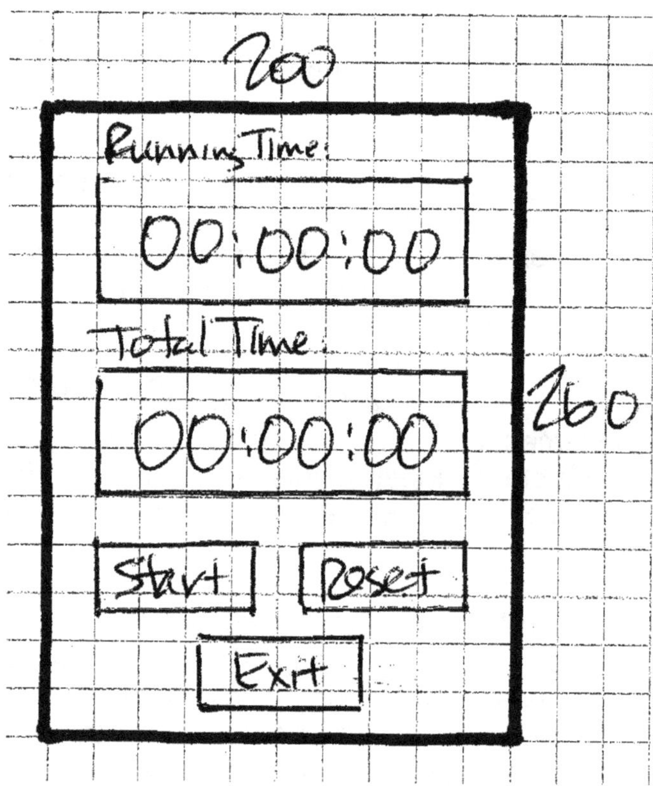

Two **Shapes** objects will be used for time displays. Button controls start, stop and reset the stopwatch and stop the application.

We will begin writing code for the **Stopwatch** program. We will write the code in several steps. As a first step, we write the code that sets up the display in the window. Then, we will write the code that takes the stopwatch from 'initial' state to its 'running' state, following clicking of the **Start** button. During the code development process, recognize you may modify a particular procedure several times before arriving at the finished product.

Before starting, make sure you have established a folder on your computer for building Small Basic programs. Always save your programs in this folder. Do not save them in the folder used in these notes (**HomeSB\HomeSB Projects**). Leave this folder intact so you can always reference the finished programs, if needed.

Start a new program in Small Basic. Once started, we suggest you immediately save the program with a name you choose. This sets up the folder and file structure needed for your program.

Window Design – Time Displays

The first step is to establish the two time displays in the **Stopwatch** window. Type this code in the code editor:

```
' Stopwatch
InitializeProgram()

Sub InitializeProgram
  'graphics window
  GraphicsWindow.Width = 200
  GraphicsWindow.Height = 260
  GraphicsWindow.Title = "Stopwatch"
  GraphicsWindow.BackgroundColor = "CornflowerBlue"
  'add labels and text shapes
  GraphicsWindow.BrushColor = "Yellow"
  GraphicsWindow.FontBold = "false"
  GraphicsWindow.FontSize = 14
  GraphicsWindow.DrawText(20, 10, "Running Time:")
  GraphicsWindow.DrawText(20, 90, "Total Time:")
  GraphicsWindow.BrushColor = "White"
  GraphicsWindow.FillRectangle(20, 30, 160, 50)
  GraphicsWindow.FillRectangle(20, 110, 160, 50)
  GraphicsWindow.BrushColor = "Blue"
  GraphicsWindow.FontSize = 36
  RunningDisplay = Shapes.AddText("00:00:00")
  Shapes.Move(RunningDisplay, 25, 30)
  GraphicsWindow.BrushColor = "Red"
  TotalDisplay = Shapes.AddText("00:00:00")
  Shapes.Move(TotalDisplay, 25, 110)
EndSub
```

This code translates the top part of our window sketch into code. The first line of code calls a subroutine **InitializeProgram** where we will put all code needed to set up the program for use. All remaining code here goes in that subroutine. We set up the window size and color. Then the **Shapes** objects (**RunningDisplay** and **TotalDisplay**) with appropriate labels are added to the window (the shapes are placed on top of white rectangles drawn in the graphics window). Note how we change **FontSize** and **BrushColor** set before creating the shapes. These new values are used by the text shapes. With many projects in this course, you will find such text shapes are useful for information that needs to be changed periodically.

Save and **Run** the project (click the **Run** button in the toolbar). You should see the initialized times:

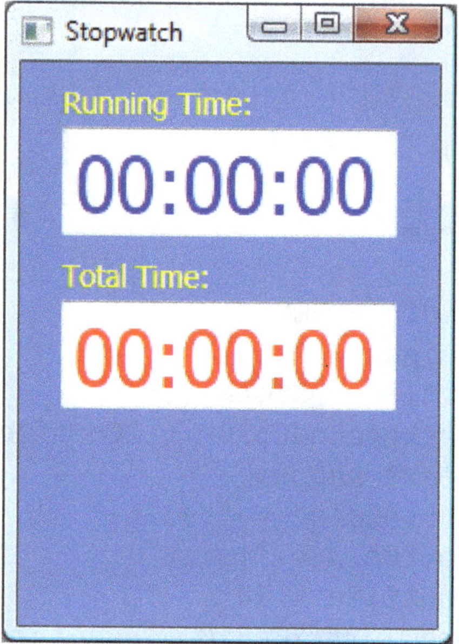

Window Design – Add Buttons

The **Stopwatch** uses three buttons: one to start/stop/pause (**StartStopButton**), one to reset (**ResetButton**) and one to exit (**ExitButton**). Add this code at the end of the **InitializeProgram** subroutine:

```
'add buttons
GraphicsWindow.BrushColor = "Black"
GraphicsWindow.FontSize = 14
StartStopButton = Controls.AddButton("Start", 20, 180)
Controls.SetSize(StartStopButton, 75, 30)
ResetButton = Controls.AddButton("Reset", 105, 180)
Controls.SetSize(ResetButton, 75, 30)
Controls.HideControl(ResetButton)
ExitButton = Controls.AddButton("Exit", 60, 220)
Controls.SetSize(ExitButton, 75, 30)
```

We initially hide **ResetButton** since we can't click it initially.

Save and **Run** the program to see the added buttons:

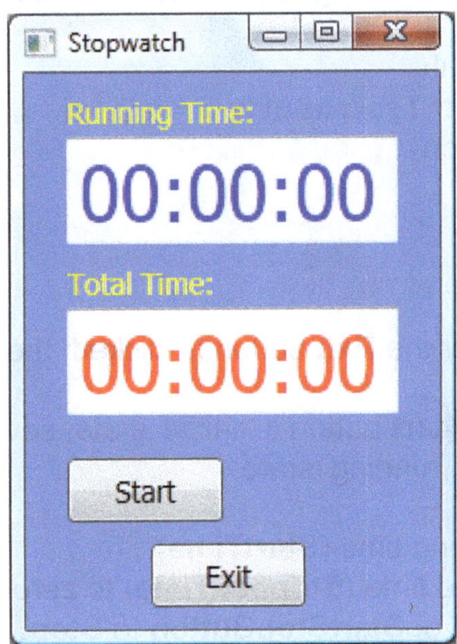

Code Design – Initial to Running State

At this point in our development, we have two choices – either click **StartStopButton** (the button with **Start**) or click **ExitButton** (the button with **Exit**). (Recall the **Reset** button is initially hidden – you can't click this button until the stopwatch has been running.) We write code for both options.

First, add this line at the end of **InitializeProgram** to recognize button clicks:

```
Controls.ButtonClicked = ButtonClickedSub
```

Then, add the **ButtonClickedSub** subroutine which is called when a button is clicked:

```
Sub ButtonClickedSub
  B = Controls.LastClickedButton
EndSub
```

The variable **B** holds the name of the clicked button.

Now, add the shaded code to recognize and react to clicking on **ExitButton**:

```
Sub ButtonClickedSub
  B = Controls.LastClickedButton
  If (B = ExitButton) Then
    Program.End()
  EndIf
EndSub
```

This simply says whenever the **Exit** button is clicked, the program ends.

When the user clicks the **Start** button in 'initial' state, several things must happen to switch the stopwatch to 'running' state:

- Determine the starting time (**StartTime**).
- Initialize the stopped time (**StoppedTime**) to zero.
- Change the caption of **StartStopButton** to **Stop**.
- Hide **ExitButton**.

Add the shaded code to the **ButtonClickedSub** subroutine to recognize clicking **StartStopButton**:

```
Sub ButtonClickedSub
  B = Controls.LastClickedButton
  If (B = ExitButton) Then
    Program.End()
  ElseIf (B = StartStopButton) Then
    StartStopButtonClicked()
  EndIf
EndSub
```

The code for the **StartStopButtonClicked** subroutine that implements the listed steps is then:

```
Sub StartStopButtonClicked
  'initial to running state
  StartTime = Clock.ElapsedMilliseconds
  StoppedTime = 0
  Controls.SetButtonCaption(StartStopButton, "Stop")
  Controls.HideControl(ExitButton)
EndSub
```

Note use of the **ElapsedMilliseconds** property of the **Clock** object to obtain the starting time (in milliseconds – there are 1000 milliseconds in one second).

Code Design – Update Display

Save and **Run** the project. Click the **Start** button and you should see:

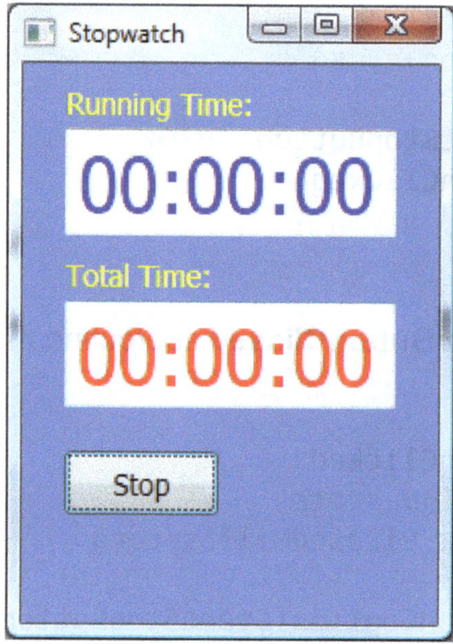

The project is now in 'running' state. However, nothing is changing in the displays.

We will use a Small Basic **Timer** object to update the displayed times. This object generates a **Tick** event every **Interval** (a **Timer** property) milliseconds. We write code for the**Tick** event's subroutine to update the displayed times.

We set the **Timer** object's **Interval** property to 1000 milliseconds, or 1 second. Hence, every second, the timer control's **Tick** event is invoked. Add this code to **InitializeProgram** (at end) to initialize the timer:

```
Timer.Interval = 1000
Timer.Tick = TimerTickSub
Timer.Pause()
```

With each call to the **TimerTickSub** subroutine, we need to:

- Determine the current time (**CurrentTime**).
- Subtract the current time from the start time to obtain the total time (**TotalTime**).
- Subtract the stopped time from the total time to get the running time (**RunningTime**).
- Display the running and total times in the appropriate shape objects.

We find all times using the **ElapsedMilliseconds** method and all time differences are converted from milliseconds to seconds. Once we have a time difference in seconds, how do we display such a time in the desired format of **hours:minutes:seconds**? We need to do this twice in each call to **TimerTickSub**, once for the running time and once for the total time. Add this subroutine to your program to do the conversion:

```
Sub HMS
  'Break time down into hours, minutes, and seconds
  HH = Math.Floor(TimeValue / 3600)
  MM = Math.Floor((TimeValue - HH * 3600) / 60 )
  SS = Math.Floor(TimeValue) - HH * 3600 - MM * 60
  HMSDisplay = HH + ":"
  If (HH < 10) Then
    HMSDisplay = "0" + HMSDisplay
  EndIf
  If (MM < 10) Then
    HMSDisplay = HMSDisplay + "0" + MM + ":"
  Else
    HMSDisplay = HMSDisplay + MM + ":"
  EndIf
  If (SS < 10) Then
    HMSDisplay = HMSDisplay + "0" + SS
  Else
    HMSDisplay = HMSDisplay + SS
  EndIf
EndSub
```

In this subroutine, the total seconds (**TimeValue**) is the value to display. The hours (**HH**) are extracted using the integer part of a division. Once the seconds attributed to any **HH** value are subtracted from **TimeValue**, the minutes (**MM**) are extracted. Any remaining value in **TimeValue**, once the seconds associated with the hours and minutes are removed, are the displayed seconds (**SS**) value. The returned value (**HMSDisplay**) is a string in the desired **HH:MM:SS** format for display. Work through this subroutine with an example to convince yourself it works.

The **HMS** subroutine is used in the **TimerTickSub** subroutine, which has the steps outlined earlier. That code is:

```
Sub TimerTickSub
  'Determine total and running times in seconds
  CurrentTime = Clock.ElapsedMilliseconds
  TotalTime = (CurrentTime - StartTime) / 1000
  RunningTime = TotalTime - StoppedTime
  'Display times
  TimeValue = TotalTime
  HMS()
  Shapes.SetText(TotalDisplay, HMSDisplay)
  TimeValue = RunningTime
  HMS()
  Shapes.SetText(RunningDisplay, HMSDisplay)
EndSub
```

You should be able to see how this procedure computes the needed times and displays them using the **HMS** subroutine.

And, lastly, add the shaded line to the **StartStopButtonClicked** subroutine to start the timer when the **Start** button is clicked:

```
Sub StartStopButtonClicked
  'initial to running state
  StartTime = Clock.ElapsedMilliseconds
  StoppedTime = 0
  Controls.SetButtonCaption(StartStopButton, "Stop")
  Controls.HideControl(ExitButton)
  Timer.Resume()
EndSub
```

Code Design – Running to Stopped State

Save and **Run** the project. Click the **Start** button. The times should now be updating every second:

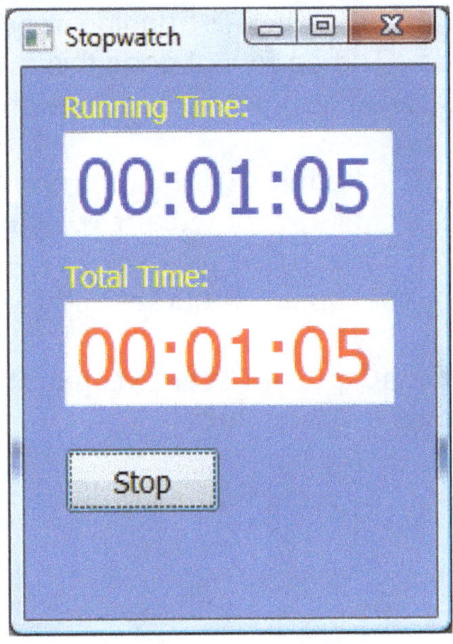

The project is now in the 'running' state. Only one option exists at this point – click **Stop** to put the stopwatch in 'stopped' state.

When a user clicks **Stop** (**StartStopButton**), the following things need to happen:

- Determine the stop time (**StopTime**, not to be confused with the stopped time).
- Stop the timer to stop updating the displays.
- Change the caption of **StartStopButton** to **Restart**
- Show **ResetButton**.
- Show **ExitButton**.

The button now marked **Stop** is button named **StartStopButton**. We have already added some code to the **StartStopButtonClicked** subroutine (when the button is used to start the stopwatch). It is common practice to have one button control have multiple purposes - we just need to have some way to distinguish which "mode" the button is in when it is clicked. In this project, we use the caption of the button. If the caption is **Start**, we switch to 'running' mode. If the caption is **Stop**, we switch to 'stopped' mode. The code that does this is (modifications to the current **StartStopButtonClicked** subroutine code are shaded):

```
Sub StartStopButtonClicked
  If (Controls.GetButtonCaption(StartStopButton)= "Start") Then
    'initial to running state
    StartTime = Clock.ElapsedMilliseconds
    StoppedTime = 0
    Controls.SetButtonCaption(StartStopButton, "Stop")
    Controls.HideControl(ExitButton)
    Timer.Resume()
  ElseIf (Controls.GetButtonCaption(StartStopButton) = "Stop")
Then
    'running to stopped state
    StopTime = Clock.ElapsedMilliseconds
    Timer.Pause()
    Controls.SetButtonCaption(StartStopButton, "Restart")
    Controls.ShowControl(ResetButton)
    Controls.ShowControl(ExitButton)
  EndIf
EndSub
```

Make the noted modifications to the code. Notice the **ElseIf** line is displayed on two lines in these notes due to margin restrictions. Make sure this is typed on one line in the code editor. Look for similar occurrences throughout the notes for this course.

Code Design – Stopped State

Save and **Run** the project. Click the **Start** button. Let the stopwatch run for a while, then click **Stop**. The stopwatch will go to 'stopped' state:

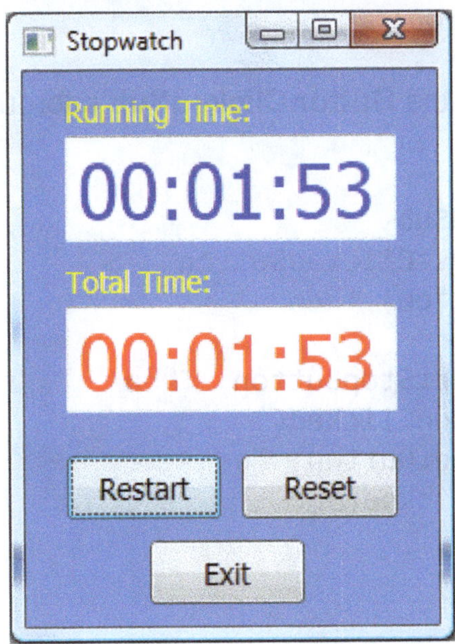

In this state, there are three possible options – clicking **Restart** (**StartStopButton**), clicking **Reset** (**ResetButton**) or clicking **Exit** (**ExitButton**). We'll address each possibility in reverse order.

If **Exit** is clicked, the project ends. We have already written the code for this possibility.

If **Reset** is clicked, we want to return the stopwatch to its 'initial' state. The steps to do this are:

- Reset the displayed times to **00:00:00**
- Change the caption of **StartStopButton** to **Start**
- Hide **ResetButton**.

Add the shaded code to the **ButtonClickedSub** subroutine to recognize clicking **Reset**:

```
Sub ButtonClickedSub
  B = Controls.LastClickedButton
  If (B = ExitButton) Then
    Program.End()
  ElseIf (B = StartStopButton) Then
    StartStopButtonClicked()
  ElseIf (B = ResetButton) Then
    ResetButtonClicked()
  EndIf
EndSub
```

Then the **ResetButtonClicked** subroutine is:

```
Sub ResetButtonClicked
  'return to initial state
  Shapes.SetText(RunningDisplay, "00:00:00")
  Shapes.SetText(TotalDisplay, "00:00:00")
  Controls.SetButtonCaption(StartStopButton, "Start")
  Controls.HideControl(ResetButton)
EndSub
```

If **Restart** is clicked while in 'stopped' state, the **StartStopButtonClicked** subroutine is called. This is another use for **StartStopButton**. We need to modify the code already in that procedure to handle such an event

When a user clicks **Restart** (**StartStopButton**), the following things need to happen:

- Update (increment) the stopped time – add in the difference between the current time and the **StopTime**, the time when the **Stop** button was clicked.
- Change the caption of **StartStopButton** to **Stop**
- Hide **ResetButton**.
- Hide **ExitButton**.
- Start the timer.

The modified **StartStopButtonClicked** subroutine that implements these new steps (changes are shaded) is:

```
Sub StartStopButtonClicked
  If (Controls.GetButtonCaption(StartStopButton)= "Start") Then
    'initial to running state
    StartTime = Clock.ElapsedMilliseconds
    StoppedTime = 0
    Controls.SetButtonCaption(StartStopButton, "Stop")
    Controls.HideControl(ExitButton)
    Timer.Resume()
  ElseIf (Controls.GetButtonCaption(StartStopButton) = "Stop")
Then
    'running to stopped state
    StopTime = Clock.ElapsedMilliseconds
    Timer.Pause()
    Controls.SetButtonCaption(StartStopButton, "Restart")
    Controls.ShowControl(ResetButton)
    Controls.ShowControl(ExitButton)
  ElseIf (Controls.GetButtonCaption(StartStopButton) =
"Restart") Then
    'stopped to running state
    StoppedTime = StoppedTime + (Clock.ElapsedMilliseconds -
StopTime) / 1000
    Controls.SetButtonCaption(StartStopButton, "Stop")
    Controls.HideControl(ResetButton)
    Controls.HideControl(ExitButton)
    Timer.Resume()
  EndIf
EndSub
```

Notice how **StoppedTime** is updated. Implement the noted changes.

Save and **Run** the project. At some point, click **Stop**. When I did, the window appears as:

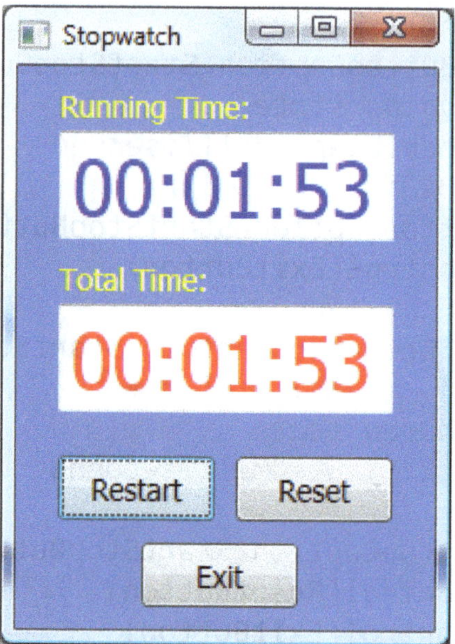

After a wait, click **Restart**. When I do this, I get:

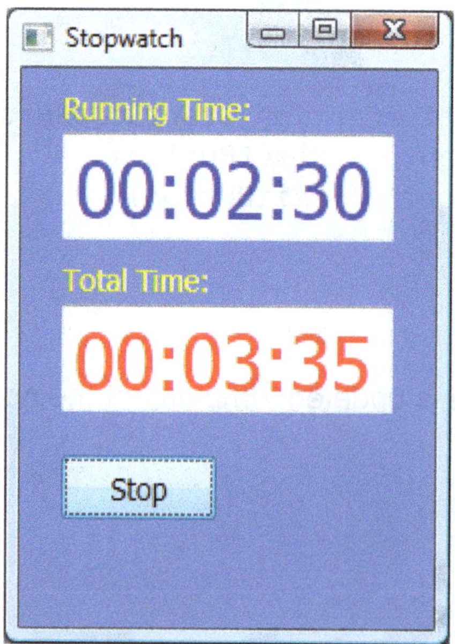

The stopwatch is running again, but the two displayed times are different. The **Total Time** is the amount of time elapsed since we first started the stopwatch. The **Running Time** is the total time less time when the stopwatch is in stopped mode. Based on these values, this stopwatch has spent 1:05 waiting around. Click **Stop** – make sure the **Reset** option works. The program is finished.

Dual-Mode Stopwatch Project Code Listing

Here is the complete listing of the **Stopwatch** Small Basic program:

```
' Stopwatch
InitializeProgram()

Sub InitializeProgram
  'graphics window
  GraphicsWindow.Width = 200
  GraphicsWindow.Height = 260
  GraphicsWindow.Title = "Stopwatch"
  GraphicsWindow.BackgroundColor = "CornflowerBlue"
  'add labels and text shapes
  GraphicsWindow.BrushColor = "Yellow"
  GraphicsWindow.FontBold = "false"
  GraphicsWindow.FontSize = 14
  GraphicsWindow.DrawText(20, 10, "Running Time:")
  GraphicsWindow.DrawText(20, 90, "Total Time:")
  GraphicsWindow.BrushColor = "White"
  GraphicsWindow.FillRectangle(20, 30, 160, 50)
  GraphicsWindow.FillRectangle(20, 110, 160, 50)
  GraphicsWindow.BrushColor = "Blue"
  GraphicsWindow.FontSize = 36
  RunningDisplay = Shapes.AddText("00:00:00")
  Shapes.Move(RunningDisplay, 25, 30)
  GraphicsWindow.BrushColor = "Red"
  TotalDisplay = Shapes.AddText("00:00:00")
  Shapes.Move(TotalDisplay, 25, 110)
  'add buttons
  GraphicsWindow.BrushColor = "Black"
  GraphicsWindow.FontSize = 14
  StartStopButton = Controls.AddButton("Start", 20, 180)
  Controls.SetSize(StartStopButton, 75, 30)
  ResetButton = Controls.AddButton("Reset", 105, 180)
  Controls.SetSize(ResetButton, 75, 30)
  Controls.HideControl(ResetButton)
  ExitButton = Controls.AddButton("Exit", 60, 220)
  Controls.SetSize(ExitButton, 75, 30)
  Controls.ButtonClicked = ButtonClickedSub
  Timer.Interval = 1000
  Timer.Tick = TimerTickSub
  Timer.Pause()
EndSub

Sub ButtonClickedSub
```

```
  B = Controls.LastClickedButton
  If (B = ExitButton) Then
    Program.End()
  ElseIf (B = StartStopButton) Then
    StartStopButtonClicked()
  ElseIf (B = ResetButton) Then
    ResetButtonClicked()
  EndIf
EndSub

Sub StartStopButtonClicked
  If (Controls.GetButtonCaption(StartStopButton)= "Start") Then
    'initial to running state
    StartTime = Clock.ElapsedMilliseconds
    StoppedTime = 0
    Controls.SetButtonCaption(StartStopButton, "Stop")
    Controls.HideControl(ExitButton)
    Timer.Resume()
  ElseIf (Controls.GetButtonCaption(StartStopButton) = "Stop")
Then
    'running to stopped state
    StopTime = Clock.ElapsedMilliseconds
    Timer.Pause()
    Controls.SetButtonCaption(StartStopButton, "Restart")
    Controls.ShowControl(ResetButton)
    Controls.ShowControl(ExitButton)
  ElseIf (Controls.GetButtonCaption(StartStopButton) = "Restart")
Then
    'stopped to running state
    StoppedTime = StoppedTime + (Clock.ElapsedMilliseconds -
StopTime) / 1000
    Controls.SetButtonCaption(StartStopButton, "Stop")
    Controls.HideControl(ResetButton)
    Controls.HideControl(ExitButton)
    Timer.Resume()
  EndIf
EndSub

Sub HMS
  'Break time down into hours, minutes, and seconds
  HH = Math.Floor(TimeValue / 3600)
  MM = Math.Floor((TimeValue - HH * 3600) / 60 )
  SS = Math.Floor(TimeValue) - HH * 3600 - MM * 60
  HMSDisplay = HH + ":"
  If (HH < 10) Then
    HMSDisplay = "0" + HMSDisplay
```

```
  EndIf
  If (MM < 10) Then
    HMSDisplay = HMSDisplay + "0" + MM + ":"
  Else
    HMSDisplay = HMSDisplay + MM + ":"
  EndIf
  If (SS < 10) Then
    HMSDisplay = HMSDisplay + "0" + SS
  Else
    HMSDisplay = HMSDisplay + SS
  EndIf
EndSub

Sub TimerTickSub
  'Determine total and running times in seconds
  CurrentTime = Clock.ElapsedMilliseconds
  TotalTime = (CurrentTime - StartTime) / 1000
  RunningTime = TotalTime - StoppedTime
  'Display times
  TimeValue = TotalTime
  HMS()
  Shapes.SetText(TotalDisplay, HMSDisplay)
  TimeValue = RunningTime
  HMS()
  Shapes.SetText(RunningDisplay, HMSDisplay)
EndSub

Sub ResetButtonClicked
  'return to initial state
  Shapes.SetText(RunningDisplay, "00:00:00")
  Shapes.SetText(TotalDisplay, "00:00:00")
  Controls.SetButtonCaption(StartStopButton, "Start")
  Controls.HideControl(ResetButton)
EndSub
```

Dual-Mode Stopwatch Project Review

The **Dual-Mode Stopwatch** project is now complete. **Save** and **Run** the project and make sure it works as promised. Check that you can move from state to state correctly. Use it to time tasks as you work on your computer.

If there are errors in your implementation, go back over the steps of window and code design. Go over the developed code – make sure you understand how different parts of the project were coded. As mentioned in the beginning of this chapter, the completed project is saved as **Stopwatch** in the **HomeSB\HomeSB Projects\Stopwatch** folder.

While completing this project, new concepts and skills you should have gained include:

- Proper steps in project design.
- Capabilities and use of the different objects and controls.
- How to find and display differences between two times.

Dual-Mode Stopwatch Project Enhancements

There are always things you can do to improve a project. At the end of each chapter, we will give you some ideas for the current project. For the dual-mode stopwatch, some possibilities are:

- Whenever you stop the stopwatch, save that time. Then, when you ultimately stop the watch, provide a review mode. In review, you can see how much time was spent running the stopwatch and how much time was spent stopped.
- Provide an immediate feedback on each segment of elapsed time – a lap timing feature.

This page intentionally not left blank.

5. Consumer Loan Assistant Project

Review and Preview

Ever wonder just how much those credit card accounts are costing you? This project will help you get a handle on consumer debt. The **Consumer Loan Assistant Project** we build computes payments and loan terms given balance and interest information. We look at input validation and use of the message box for user information.

Consumer Loan Assistant Project Preview

In this chapter, we will build a **consumer loan assistant**. You input a loan balance and yearly interest rate. You then have two options: (1) enter the desired number of payments and the loan assistant computes the monthly payment, or (2) enter the desired monthly payment and the loan assistant determines the number of payments you will make. An analysis of your loan, including total of payments and interest paid is also provided.

The finished project is saved as **LoanAssistant** in the **HomeSB\HomeSB Projects\LoanAssistant** folder. Start Small Basic and open the finished program. **Run** the program (click the **Run** toolbar button or press <**F5**>). The loan assistant will appear as:

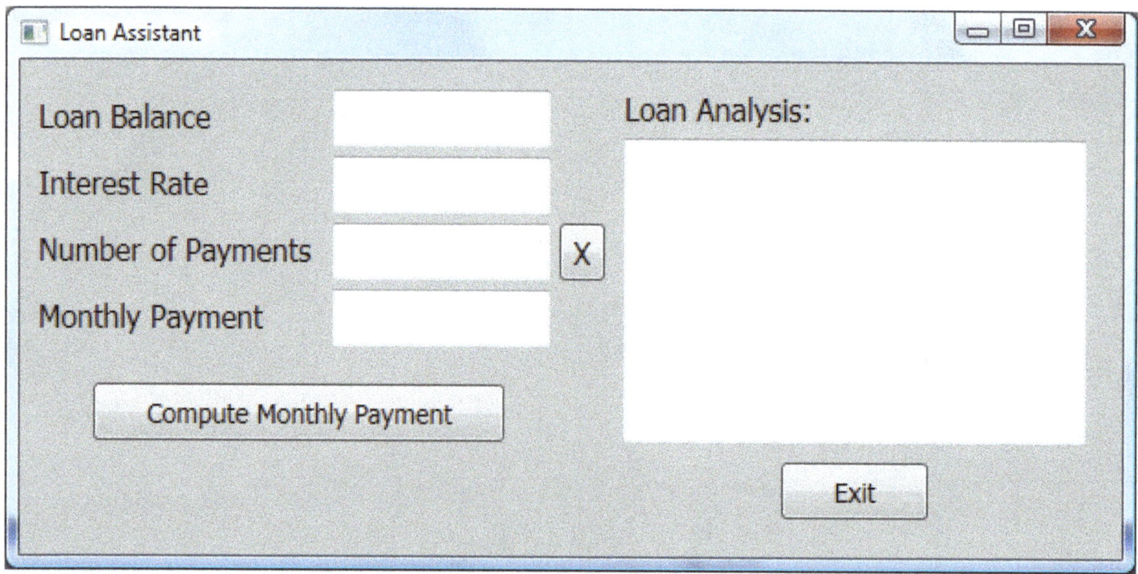

In this initial configuration, you enter a **Loan Balance**, an **Interest Rate** (annual rate as a percentage) and a **Number of Payments** value. Click **Compute Monthly Payment**. The payment will appear in the **Monthly Payment** text box and a complete loan analysis will appear in the large text box.

Here are some numbers I tried:

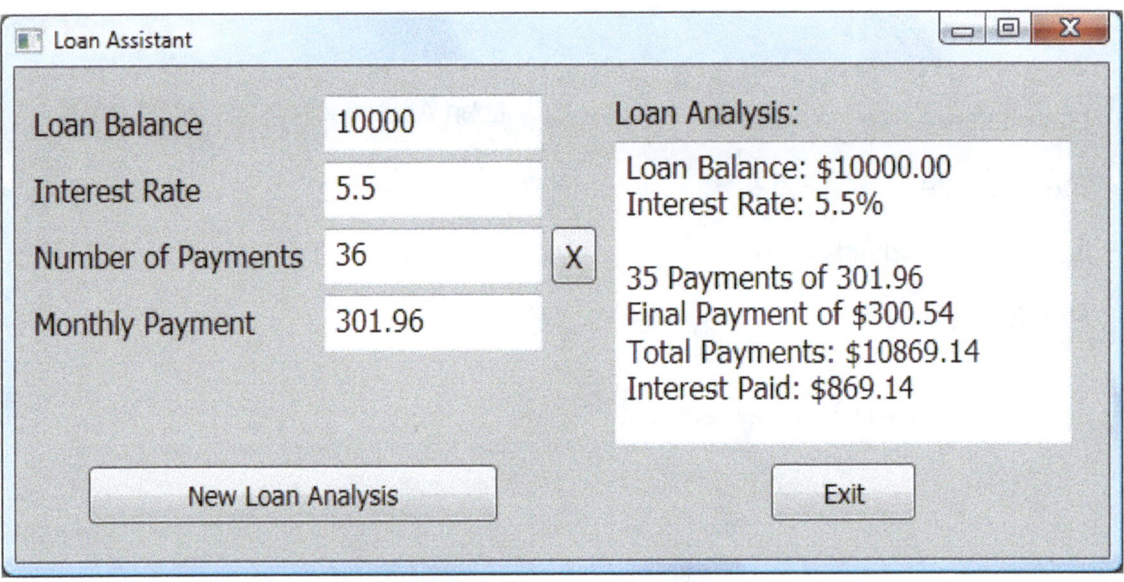

So, if I borrow $10,000 at 5.5% interest, I will pay $301.96 for three years (36 months). More specific details on exact payment amounts, including total interest paid, is shown under **Loan Analysis**.

At this point, you can click **New Loan Analysis** to try some new values:

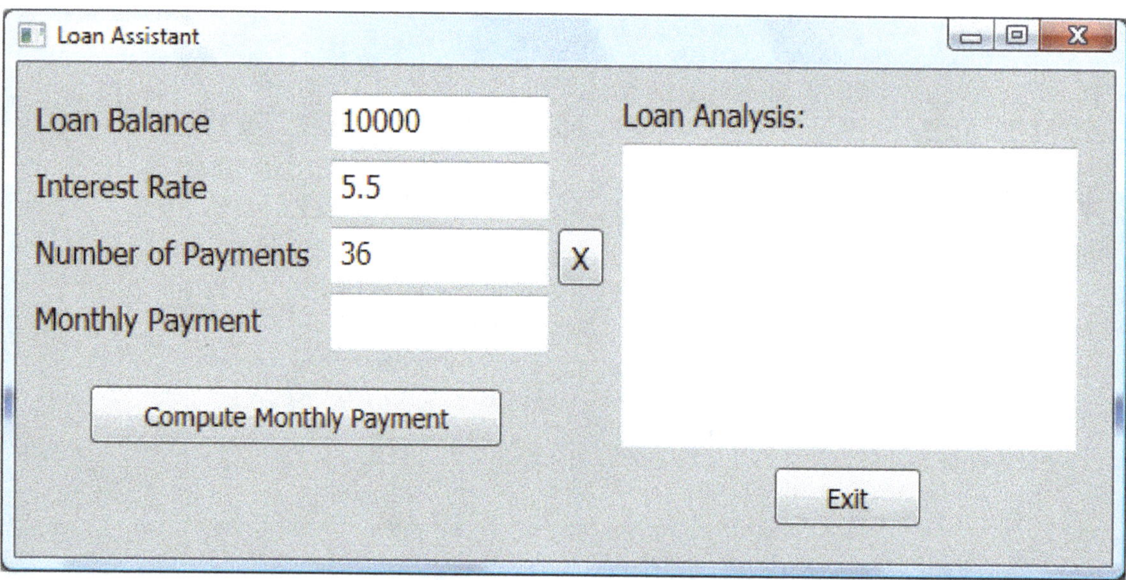

Note the **Loan Balance**, **Interest Rate**, and **Number of Payments** entries remain. Only the **Monthly Payment** and the **Loan Analysis** have been cleared. This lets you try different values with minimal typing of new entries. Change any entry you like to see different results – or even change them all. Try as many combinations as you like.

At some point, clear the text boxes and click the button with an **X** next to the **Number of Payments** text box. You will see:

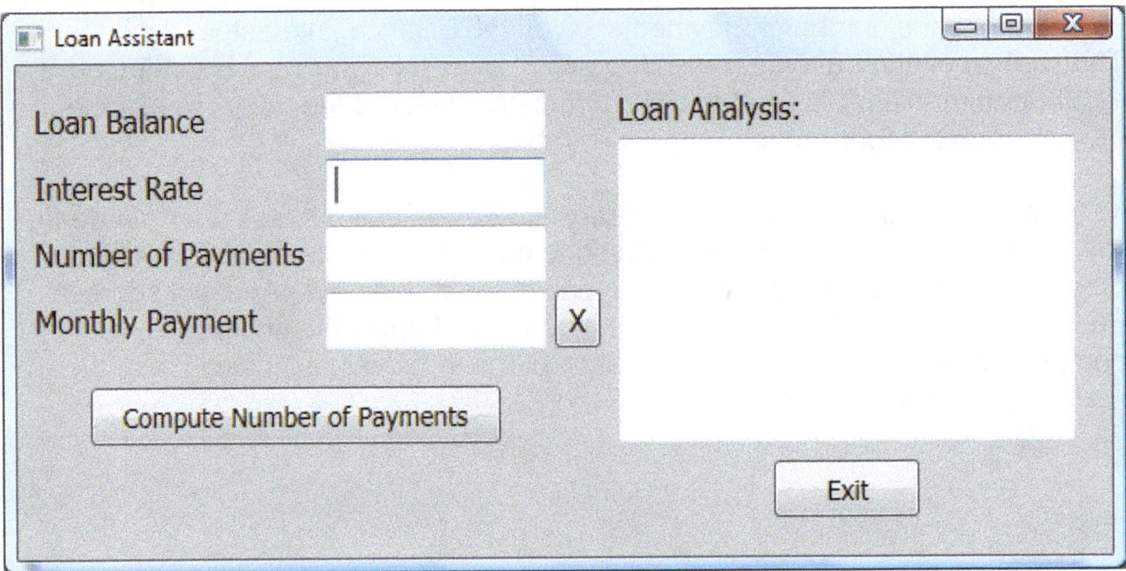

Notice the button control now says **Compute Number of Payments**. The button with an **X** has moved to the **Monthly Payment** text box. In this configuration, you enter a **Loan Balance**, an **Interest Rate** and a **Monthly Payment**. The loan assistant will determine how many payments you need to pay off the loan. Here are some numbers I tried:

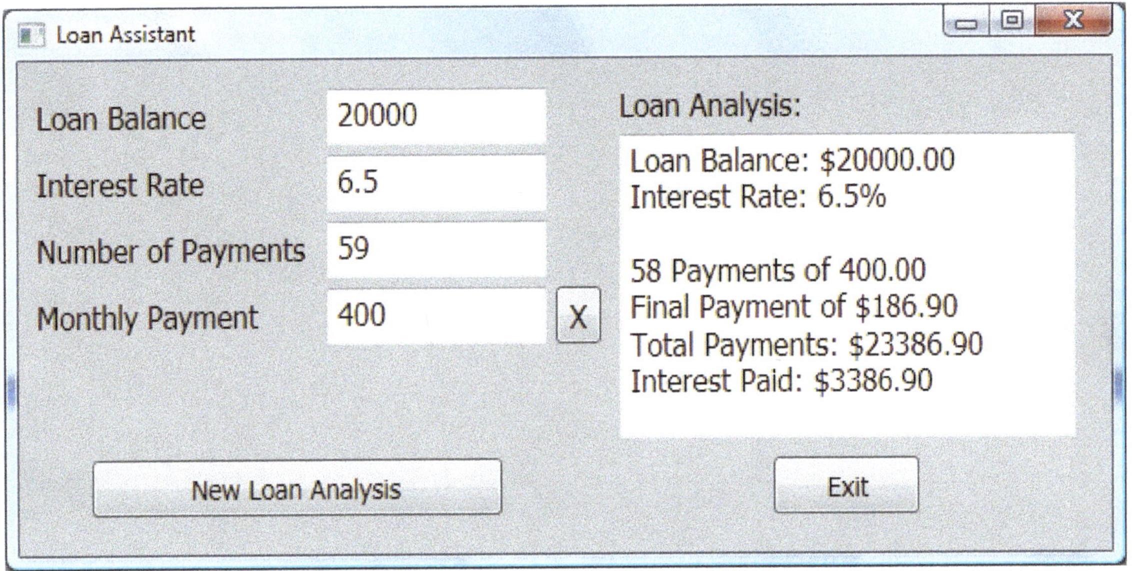

It will take 59 payments (the last one is smaller) to pay off this particular loan. Again, you can click **New Loan Analysis** to try other values and see the results.

That's all you do with the loan assistant project – there's a lot going on behind the scenes though. The loan assistant has two modes of operation. It can compute the monthly payment, given the balance, interest and number of payments. Or, it can compute the number of payments, given the balance, interest, and payment. The caption on the button beneath the entry boxes tells you what is computed. The button marked **X** is used to switch from one mode to the next. To exit the project, click the **Exit** button.

You will now build this project in several stages. We first address **window design**. We discuss the controls and object used to build the window, establish initial properties, and discuss switching from one mode to the next. And, we address **code design** in detail. We cover the mathematics behind the financial computations. We also discuss validation of the input values, making sure the user only types valid entries.

Loan Assistant Window Design

Here is the sketch for the window layout of the **Loan Assistant** program:

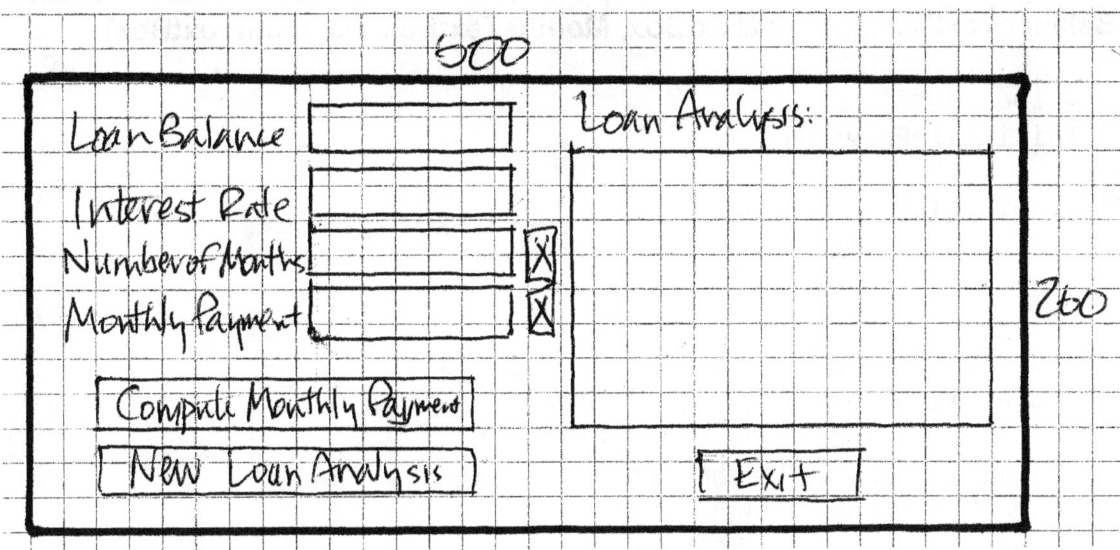

Label information is drawn to the window. Two button controls are used to compute results and to start a new analysis. Two small button controls (marked with X) control whether you compute the number of payments or the payment amount. One button exits the project. Four text box controls are used for inputs and a multi-line text box is used to present the loan analysis results.

We will begin writing code for the application. We will write the code in several steps. As a first step, we write code that places the controls and labeling information on the window. Then, we write the code that switches the application between its two possible modes of operation: (1) compute monthly payment, or (2) compute number of payments.

Start a new program in Small Basic. Once started, we suggest you immediately save the program with a name you choose. This sets up the folder and file structure needed for your program.

Window Design – Input Text Boxes

The first step is to establish the four text boxes used for input and the associated labeling information. This code sets up the initial window and the labels/text boxes (**BalanceTextBox**, **InterestTextBox**, **MonthsTextBox**, **PaymentTextBox**):

```
' Loan Assistant
InitializeProgram()

Sub InitializeProgram
  'graphics window
  GraphicsWindow.Width = 600
  GraphicsWindow.Height = 260
  GraphicsWindow.Title = "Loan Assistant"
  GraphicsWindow.BackgroundColor = "LightGray"
  'add labels text boxes
  GraphicsWindow.BrushColor = "Black"
  GraphicsWindow.FontBold = "false"
  GraphicsWindow.FontSize = 16
  GraphicsWindow.DrawText(10, 20, "Loan Balance")
  GraphicsWindow.DrawText(10, 55, "Interest Rate")
  GraphicsWindow.DrawText(10, 90, "Number of Payments")
  GraphicsWindow.DrawText(10, 125, "Monthly Payment")
  BalanceTextBox = Controls.AddTextBox(170, 15)
  Controls.SetSize(BalanceTextBox, 120, 30)
  InterestTextBox = Controls.AddTextBox(170, 50)
  Controls.SetSize(InterestTextBox, 120, 30)
  MonthsTextBox = Controls.AddTextBox(170, 85)
  Controls.SetSize(MonthsTextBox, 120, 30)
  PaymentTextBox = Controls.AddTextBox(170, 120)
  Controls.SetSize(PaymentTextBox, 120, 30)
EndSub
```

The first line of code calls a subroutine **InitializeProgram** where we will put all code needed to set up the program for use. All remaining code here goes in that subroutine. Locations of each element are taken from the sketch. All use a black brush with size 16 font.

Save and **Run** the program. The text boxes are displayed:

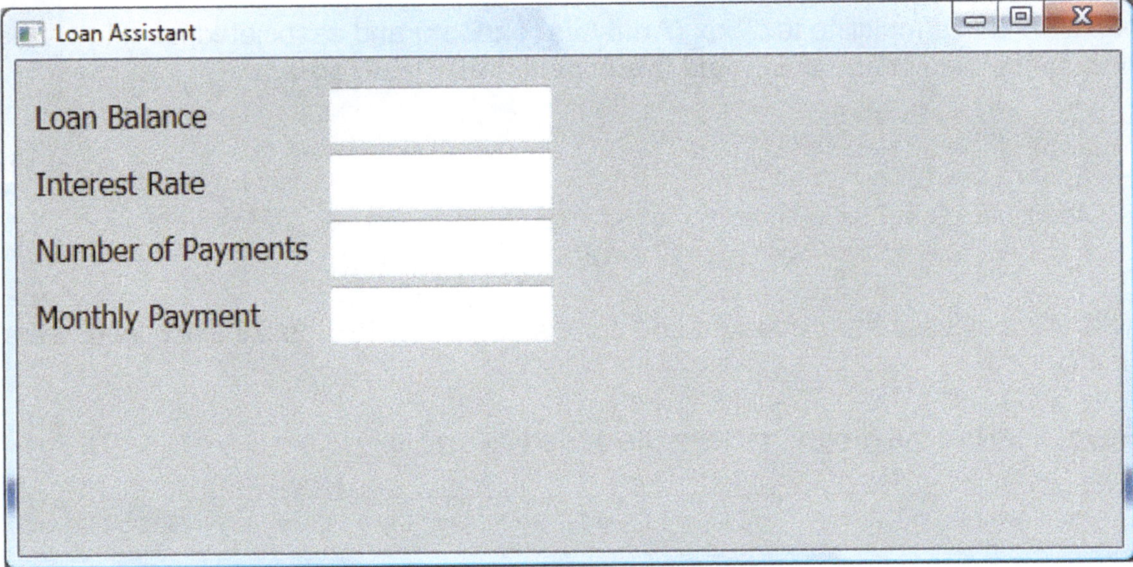

Window Design – Loan Analysis

Next, we add a multiline text box (**AnalysisTextBox**) and associated label to display the loan information. Add this code to **InitializeProgram**:

```
'add analysis text box
GraphicsWindow.DrawText(330, 15, "Loan Analysis:")
AnalysisTextBox = Controls.AddMultiLineTextBox(330, 40)
Controls.SetSize(AnalysisTextBox, 250, 160)
```

This text box uses the same font and color as the other text boxes since values are unchanged.

Save and **Run** the program to see the added elements:

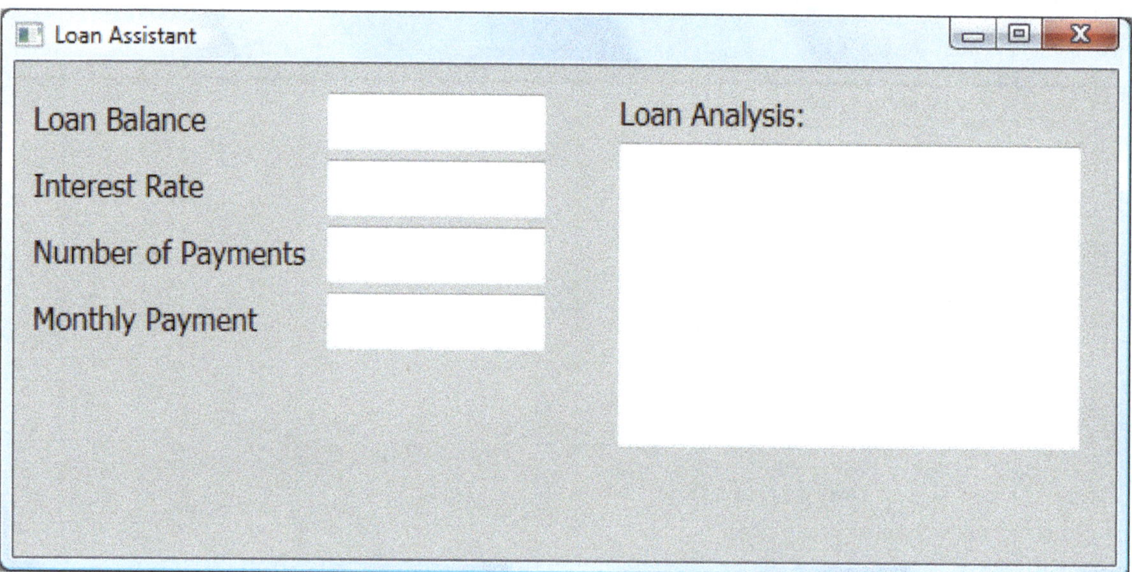

Window Design – Add Buttons

We complete the window design by adding button controls to the window. Five buttons are needed. One (**ComputeButton**) is used to compute the loan payment or number of months. A button (**NewLoanButton**) is used to start a new analysis. And, one (**ExitButton**) is used to exit the program. We also need two small buttons with an '**X**' that are used to switch program modes (**MonthsButton** and **PaymentButton**). Here's the code that adds these buttons. Add this to **InitializeProgram**:

```
'add buttons
GraphicsWindow.FontSize = 14
ComputeButton = Controls.AddButton("Compute Monthly Payment",
40, 170)
Controls.SetSize(ComputeButton, 225, 30)
NewLoanButton = Controls.AddButton("New Loan Analysis", 40,
210)
Controls.SetSize(NewLoanButton, 225, 30)
ExitButton = Controls.AddButton("Exit", 415, 210)
Controls.SetSize(ExitButton, 80, 30)
GraphicsWindow.FontSize = 16
MonthsButton = Controls.AddButton("X", 295, 85)
Controls.SetSize(MonthsButton, 25, 30)
PaymentButton = Controls.AddButton("X", 295, 120)
Controls.SetSize(PaymentButton, 25, 30)
```

Save and **Run** the program. The finished window is seen:

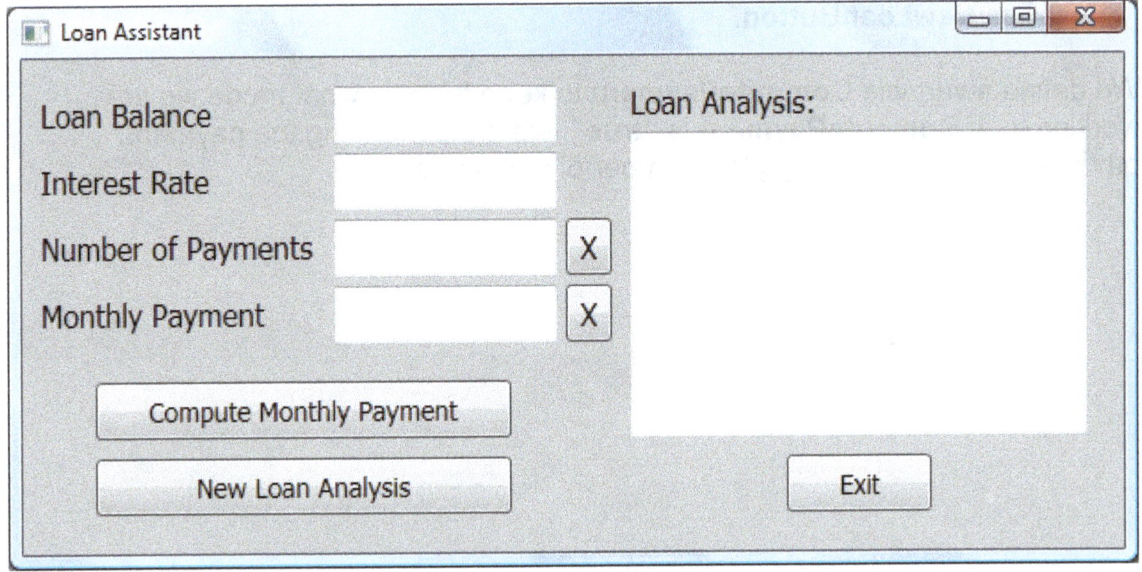

Code Design – Switching Modes

There are two modes the loan assistant can operate in. In the first mode, you enter a loan balance, an interest rate and a number of payments. The assistant then computes the monthly payment. In the second mode, you enter a loan balance, an interest rate and a monthly payment. The assistant computes the number of payments. The buttons with **X** control which mode the assistant operates in. Click the **X** (**PaymentButton**) next to the payment text box and you switch to the first mode (compute monthly payment). Click the **X** (**MonthsButton**) next to the number of payments text box and you switch to the second mode (compute number of payments). Let's look at the steps for each operation.

When the user clicks the **X** next to the monthly payment text box (**PaymentButton**), the steps are taken:

- Hide **PaymentButton**.
- Show **MonthsButton**.
- Blank out **PaymentTextBox**.
- Set caption of **ComputeButton** to **Compute Monthly Payment**.
- Hide **NewLoanButton**.

When you click the **X** next to the number of payments text box (**MonthsButton**), we essentially 'reverse' the steps just listed:

- Show **PaymentButton**.
- Hide **MonthsButton**.
- Blank out **MonthsTextBox**.
- Set caption of **ComputeButton** to **Compute Number of Payments**.
- Hide **NewLoanButton**.

We define a variable **ComputePayment** to keep track of what mode we are working in. If **ComputePayment** is **"true"**, we are computing the payment, otherwise we are computing the number of payments.

Add this line at the end of the **InitializeProgram** subroutine to allow recognition of button clicks:

```
Controls.ButtonClicked = ButtonClickedSub
```

And, add the **ButtonClickedSub** subroutine to see which button was clicked.:

```
Sub ButtonClickedSub
  B = Controls.LastClickedButton
  If (B = PaymentButton) Then
    PaymentButtonClicked()
  ElseIf (B = MonthsButton) Then
    MonthsButtonClicked()
  EndIf
EndSub
```

We have added code to see if either **PaymentButton** or **MonthsButton** is clicked. If so, the appropriate subroutine (**PaymentButtonClicked** or **MonthsButtonClicked**) is called.

The code for the **PaymentButtonClicked** subroutine that implements the listed steps is then:

```
Sub PaymentButtonClicked
  ' will compute payment
  ComputePayment = "true"
  Controls.HideControl(PaymentButton)
  Controls.ShowControl(MonthsButton)
  Controls.SetTextBoxText(PaymentTextBox, "")
  Controls.SetButtonCaption(ComputeButton, "Compute Monthly
Payment")
  Controls.HideControl(NewLoanButton)
EndSubEndSub
```

The code for the **MonthsButtonClicked** subroutine is:

```
Sub MonthsButtonClicked
  ' will compute months
  ComputePayment = "false"
  Controls.ShowControl(PaymentButton)
  Controls.HideControl(MonthsButton)
  Controls.SetTextBoxText(MonthsTextBox, "")
  Controls.SetButtonCaption(ComputeButton, "Compute Number of
Payments")
  Controls.HideControl(NewLoanButton)
EndSubEndSub
```

We would like the application to begin in the mode where the monthly payment is computed. One way we could do this is repeat the code in the **PaymentButtonClicked** subroutine at the beginning of the program. But an easier approach is to have the application 'simulate' clicking on the **PaymentButton** when the application begins. This can be done at the end of **InitializeProgram** with the single line:

```
PaymentButtonClicked()
```

Save and **Run** the project. If the code is entered correctly, the window should appear in the 'compute payment' mode:

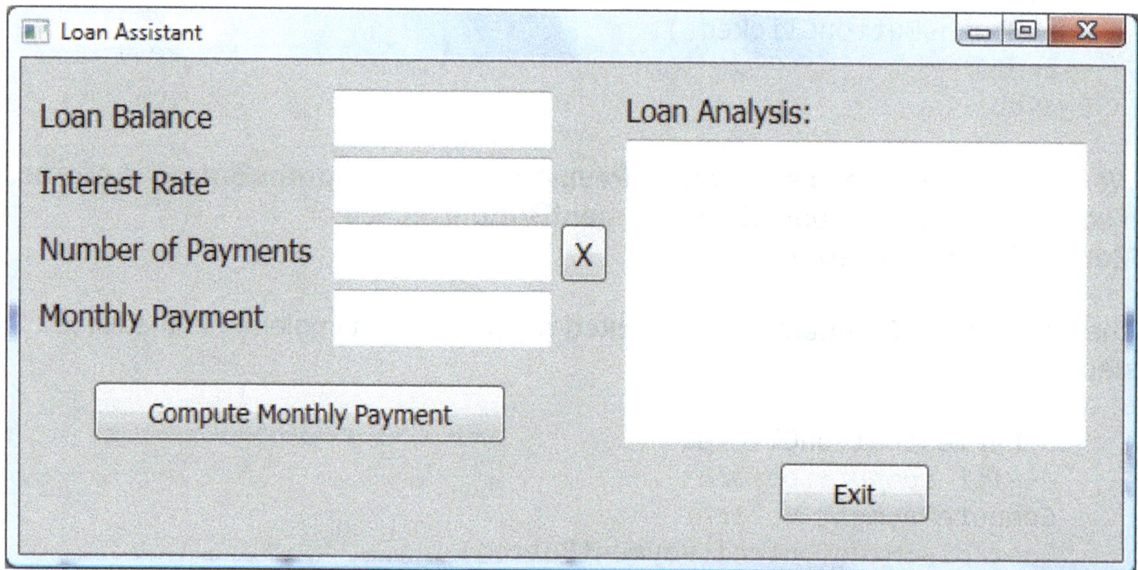

The **ComputeButton** caption is **Compute Monthly Payment**. The **NewLoanButton** is hidden.

Click the **X** next to **Number of Payments** and you switch to the 'compute number of payments' mode:

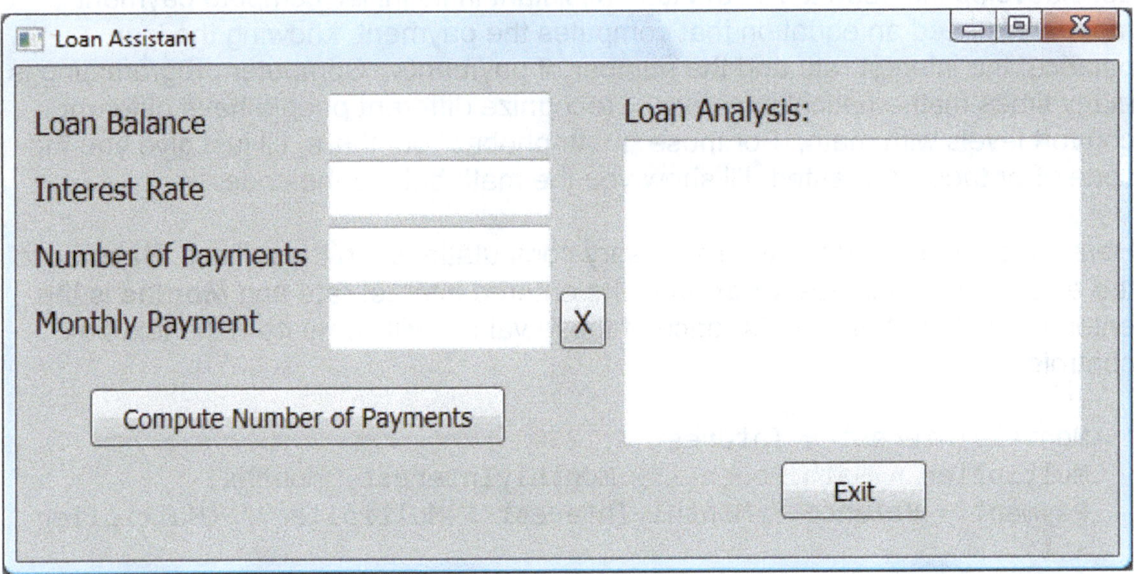

The **X** button now appears next to **Monthly Payment**. And, the **ComputeButton** caption is **Compute Number of Payments**.

The mode switching should be working correctly. Now, let's write the code behind the needed computations.

Code Design – Computing Monthly Payment

Let's develop the code to run the loan assistant in its initial 'compute payment' mode. We need an equation that computes the payment, knowing the loan balance, the interest rate and the number of payments. Computer programming is many times mathematical in nature. I recognize different people have different comfort levels with math. For those "math-phobes" out there, I'll just give you the code. For those interested, I'll show you the math behind the code.

Here's the code that does the necessary computations. In these lines, **Balance** is the entered loan balance, **Interest** is the entered interest rate and **Months** is the entered number of payments (each of these values will come from the text box controls):

```
MonthlyInterest = Interest / 1200
Multiplier = Math.Power(1 + MonthlyInterest, Months)
Payment = Balance * MonthlyInterest * Multiplier / (Multiplier
- 1)
```

In this code, the input interest (a yearly percentage) is converted to a monthly interest (**MonthlyInterest**). This conversion is done by dividing by 12 (the number of months in a year) times 100 (to convert percentage to a decimal number). A **Multiplier** term is formed using the **Power** method (we raise **1 + MonthlyInterest** to the **Months** power). These values are then used to compute **Payment**.

If you don't want to see mathematics, **stop now**!! Skip ahead to the code steps for the **ComputeButtonClicked** subroutine. If you're still with me, I'll go over the steps that derive the code above. Let B represent the initial loan balance, i the monthly interest and P the monthly payment (we'll be solving an equation for this value). With this notation, the product of B times i (Bi) represents one month's interest on the existing balance. We add this interest to the balance then subtract the payment to obtain the balance after one payment, B_1:

$$B_1 = B + Bi - P = B(1 + i) - P$$

Using the same approach, the balance after two payments (B_2) would be:

$$B_2 = B_1 + B_1i - P = B_1(1 + i) - P$$

Substituting the previous equation for B_1 into this equation gets things in terms of the original balance:

$$B_2 = [B(1 + i) – P](1 + i) – P = B(1 + i)^2 – P(1 + i) - P$$

Doing the same for B_3, we can show:

$$B_3 = B(1 + i)^3 – P(1 + i)^2 – P(1 + i) - P$$

Noting the trend in this relation, we can obtain an expression for B_N (the balance after N payments, when the loan is finally paid off):

$$B_N = B(1 + i)^N – P \sum_{k=0}^{N-1} (1 + i)^k$$

The Greek sigma in the above equation simply indicates that you add up all the corresponding elements next to the sigma.

After N payments, we want the balance of the loan to be zero. If we set B_N to zero in the above equation, we obtain a value for P, the payment:

$$P = B(1 + i)^N / \sum_{k=0}^{N-1} (1 + i)^k$$

This is the desired result and we could easily code it using a For loop to evaluate the summation in the denominator. We can avoid this step by consulting a handbook on “finite series.” The denominator term actually has a “closed-form” (one not requiring the summation). It is (trust me on this):

$$\sum_{k=0}^{N-1} (1 + i)^k = [(1 + i)^N – 1]/i$$

Try a few values of i and N to convince yourself this works (if you need convincing). Substituting this into the equation for P and flipping a few terms around gives us the final equation for computing P:

$$P = Bi(1 + i)^N / [(1 + i)^N – 1]$$

Compare this equation to the code we gave you. You should see the code matches this equation (**B** is **Balance**, **i** is **MonthlyInterest**, **N** is **Months** and **P** is **Payment**).

When the user clicks **Compute Monthly Payment** (**ComputeButton**), the following steps are taken:

- Obtain the **Balance** value from user input.
- Obtain the **Interest** value from user input.
- Obtain the **Months** value from user input.
- Compute **Payment** using given code.
- Display **Payment** in **PaymentTextBox**.

Add the shaded code to **ButtonClickedSub** to detect clicks on **ComputeButton**:

```
Sub ButtonClickedSub
  B = Controls.LastClickedButton
  If (B = PaymentButton) Then
    PaymentButtonClicked()
  ElseIf (B = MonthsButton) Then
    MonthsButtonClicked()
  ElseIf (B = ComputeButton) Then
    ComputeButtonClicked()
  EndIf
EndSub
```

The subroutine **ComputeButtonClicked** is called when this button is clicked.

Now, the **ComputeButtonClicked** subroutine that implements the above steps are:

```
Sub ComputeButtonClicked
  Balance = Controls.GetTextBoxText(BalanceTextBox)
  Interest = Controls.GetTextBoxText(InterestTextBox)
  MonthlyInterest = Interest / 1200
  'Compute loan payment
  Months = Controls.GetTextBoxText(MonthsTextBox)
  Multiplier = Math.Power(1 + MonthlyInterest, Months)
  Payment = Balance * MonthlyInterest * Multiplier /
(Multiplier - 1)
  Controls.SetTextBoxText(PaymentTextBox, Payment)
EndSub
```

Save and Run the project. Enter some numbers for balance, interest and number of payments, then click **Compute Monthly Payment**. Here's my run:

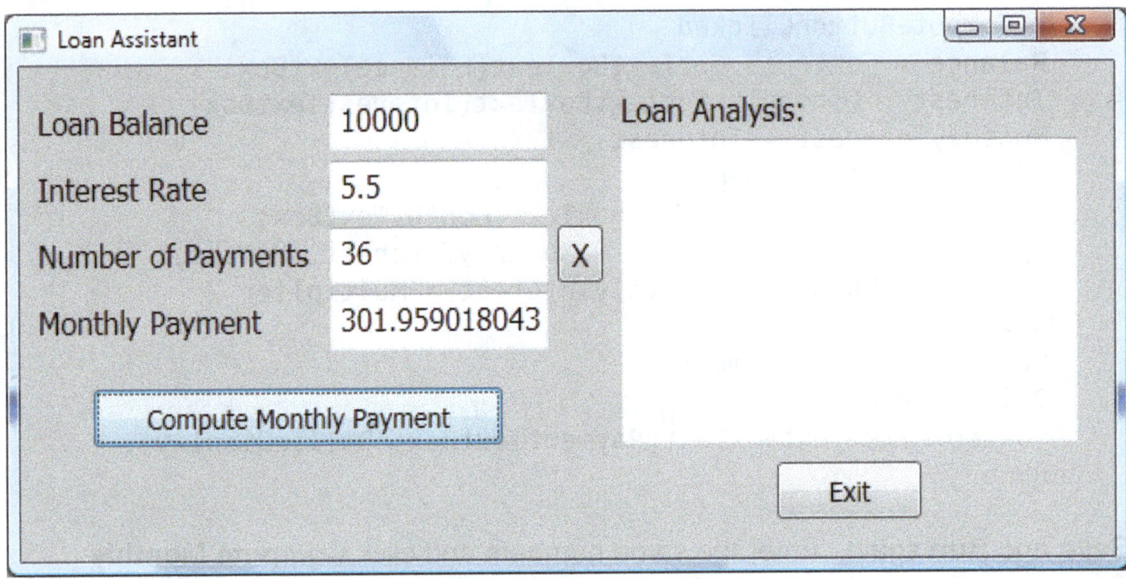

A $10,000 loan at 5.5% yearly interest has a monthly payment of $301.959018043. Just a few too many decimal places.

When we compute **Payment**, as seen, it will most likely have more than the usual two decimal places used to display dollar amounts. Here is a subroutine (**DollarFormat**) that takes an amount (**DollarAmount**) and creates a display value (**DollarDisplay**) with exactly two decimal places:

```
Sub DollarFormat
  'provide DollarAmount - return DollarDisplay (0.00 format)
  'get dollars
  Dollars = Math.Floor(DollarAmount)
  'get cents
  Cents = Math.Round((DollarAmount - Dollars) * 100)
  DollarDisplay = Text.Append(Dollars, ".")
  If (Cents < 10) Then
    DollarDisplay = Text.Append(Text.Append(DollarDisplay,
"0"), Cents)
  Else
    DollarDisplay = Text.Append(DollarDisplay, Cents)
  EndIf
EndSub
```

This code gets the decimal part of **DollarAmount** and rounds it to a **Cents** value between 0 and 100. It then develops **DollarDisplay**.

Add the **DollarFormat** subroutine to your program and make the shaded changes to **ComputeButtonClicked**:

```
Sub ComputeButtonClicked
  Balance = Controls.GetTextBoxText(BalanceTextBox)
  Interest = Controls.GetTextBoxText(InterestTextBox)
  MonthlyInterest = Interest / 1200
  'Compute loan payment
  Months = Controls.GetTextBoxText(MonthsTextBox)
  Multiplier = Math.Power(1 + MonthlyInterest, Months)
  Payment = Balance * MonthlyInterest * Multiplier /
(Multiplier - 1)
  DollarAmount = Payment
  DollarFormat()
  Controls.SetTextBoxText(PaymentTextBox, DollarDisplay)
EndSub
```

Save and **Run** again. Enter the same numbers and click **Compute Monthly Payment**. The result now only has two decimal places:

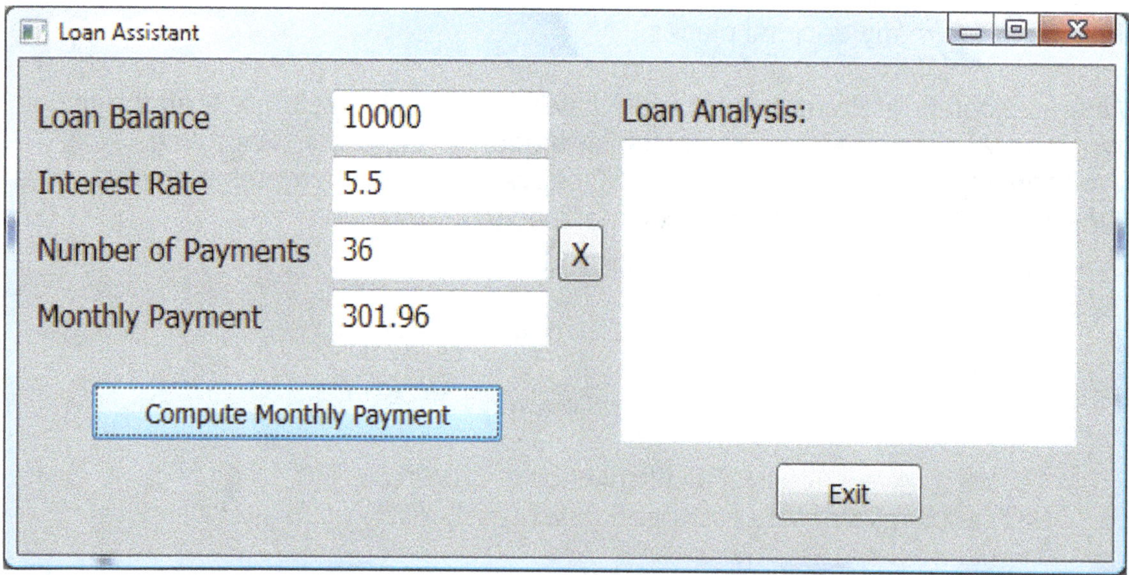

Click **Exit**. Nothing should happen. We haven't written any code behind this button yet. Let's correct that before moving on.

Add the shaded code to the **ButtonClickedSub** subroutine:

```
Sub ButtonClickedSub
  B = Controls.LastClickedButton
  If (B = PaymentButton) Then
    PaymentButtonClicked()
  ElseIf (B = MonthsButton) Then
    MonthsButtonClicked()
  ElseIf (B = ComputeButton) Then
    ComputeButtonClicked()
  ElseIf (B = ExitButton) Then
    Program.End()
  EndIf
EndSub
```

We simply end the program when **Exit** is clicked. Resave and rerun the program to make sure **Exit** works now.

Code Design – Computing Number of Payments

The second mode of operation for the loan assistant is 'compute number of payments' mode. We need an equation the computes the number of payments, knowing the loan balance, the interest rate and the monthly payment. Again, a bit of math is involved. And, again, for those interested, I'll show you the math behind the code.

Here's the code that does the necessary computations. In these lines, **Balance** is the entered loan balance, **Interest** is the entered interest rate and **Payment** is the entered monthly payment (each of these values will come from the text box controls):

```
MonthlyInterest = Interest / 1200
Months = Math.Floor((Math.Log(Payment) - Math.Log(Payment -
Balance * MonthlyInterest)) / Math.Log(1 + MonthlyInterest))
```

In this code, we again use the **MonthlyInterest** value. The number of payments (**Months,** an integer) is computed using the **Math.Log** function. This is a mathematical logarithm.

All "math-phobes," skip ahead to the code to modify the **ComputeButtonClicked** subroutine. For those interested, let's see where that logarithm comes from. The equation we derived for the **Payment** (**P**) was:

$$P = Bi(1 + i)^N / [(1 + i)^N - 1]$$

where **B** is **Balance**, **i** is **MonthlyInterest**, and **N** is **Months**. In the current mode, we want to solve for N, given B, i, and P. Multiply both sides of the equation by the denominator on the right side to get:

$$[(1 + i)^N - 1]P = Bi(1 + i)^N$$

Multiply out the left side:

$$(1 + i)^N P - P = Bi(1 + i)^N$$

Then collect terms:

$$(P - Bi)(1 + i)^N = P$$

or

$(1 + i)^N = P / (P - Bi)$

Now, take the logarithm (hopefully you remember how these work) of both sides to yield:

$N\log(1 + i) = \log(P) - \log(P - Bi)$

Or, solving for N, our desired result:

$N = [\log(P) - \log(P - Bi)] / \log(1 + i)$

Look back at the code and you should see this equation. In the code, we use the **Math.Floor** function to insure N is an integer value (we can't make a fractional payment).

So when the user clicks **Compute Number of Payments** (**ComputeButton** when **ComputePayment** is **"false"**), the following steps are taken:

- Obtain the **Balance** value from user input.
- Obtain the **Interest** value from user input.
- Obtain the **Payment** value from user input.
- Compute **Months** using given code.
- Display **Months** in **MonthsTextBox**.

The modifed **ComputeButtonClicked** subroutine that implements these steps are (new code is shaded, notice we now look **ComputePayment** to see what 'mode' we are in):

```
Sub ComputeButtonClicked
  Balance = Controls.GetTextBoxText(BalanceTextBox)
  Interest = Controls.GetTextBoxText(InterestTextBox)
  MonthlyInterest = Interest / 1200
  If (ComputePayment) Then
    'Compute loan payment
    Months = Controls.GetTextBoxText(MonthsTextBox)
    Multiplier = Math.Power(1 + MonthlyInterest, Months)
    Payment = Balance * MonthlyInterest * Multiplier /
(Multiplier - 1)
    DollarAmount = Payment
    DollarFormat()
    Controls.SetTextBoxText(PaymentTextBox, DollarDisplay)
  Else
    'Compute number of payments
    Payment = Controls.GetTextBoxText(PaymentTextBox)
    Months = Math.Floor((Math.Log(Payment) - Math.Log(Payment -
Balance * MonthlyInterest)) / Math.Log(1 + MonthlyInterest))
    Controls.SetTextBoxText(MonthsTextBox, Months)
  EndIf
EndSub
```

Save and **Run** the application. Make sure it still works in the initial mode for computing the monthly payment. When you're sure this is working okay, click the **X** next to the number of payment text box to switch to 'compute number of payments' mode.

Type in some values for balance, interest and payment. Click **Compute Number of Payments**. Here's a run I made:

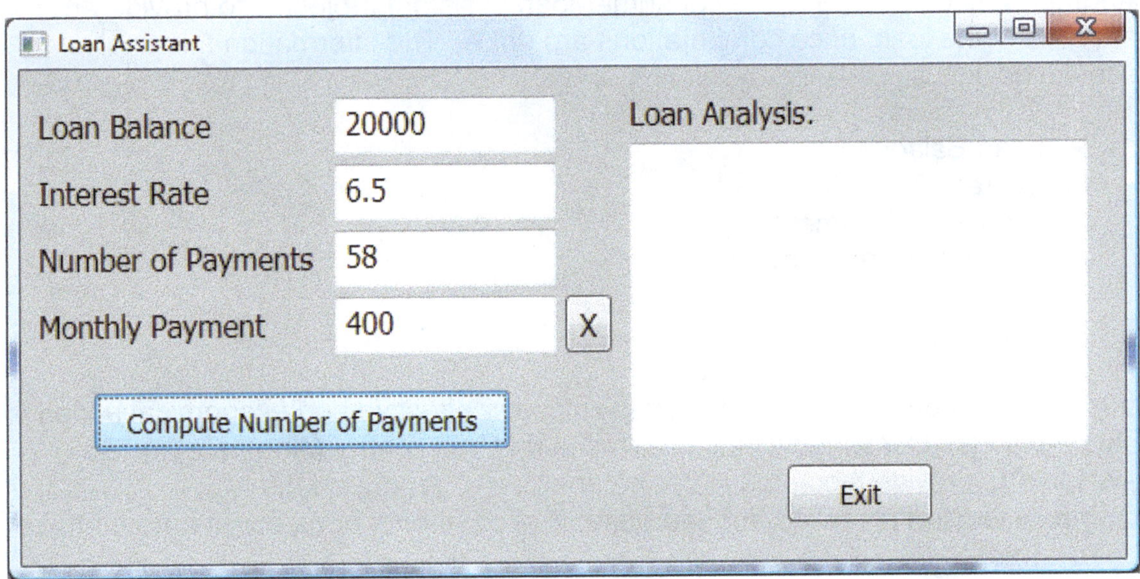

This tells me if I borrow $20, 000 at 6.5% interest, I would need to make 58 monthly payments of $400 to pay the loan back. If you have a good memory (or look back earlier in this chapter), you'll remember we tried this when demonstrating the loan assistant project. In that earlier run, we obtained a value of 59 monthly payments. Is this a mistake? No – you'll see why next.

Code Design – Loan Analysis

Another desired feature of the consumer loan assistant project is to provide an analysis of the loan, once computations are done. The information this analysis should include is:

- Loan Balance
- Interest Rate
- Number of Payments
- Amount of Each Payment
- Total of Payments Made
- Total Interest Paid

Such information is very useful in analyzing how effective and economical a loan payoff plan is. Our window has a multi-line text box control (**AnalysisTextBox**) available to provide these results. The analysis is generated after **ComputeButton** is clicked and the number of payments or payment amount have been computed.

At first, generating a loan analysis seems like a simple task. The balance (**Balance**) and interest rate (**Interest**) are input numbers. The number of payments (**Months**) and monthly payment (**Payment**) are either input or computed. So, it seems the total of payments would be given by:

```
TotalPayments = Months * Payment
```

while the interest paid would be:

```
InterestPaid = TotalPayments - Balance
```

The second equation is correct (assuming **TotalPayments** is correct). But, the first equation (for **TotalPayments**) doesn't quite apply. It's not that simple.

The code used for computing the payment amount (**ComputePayment** is **"true"**) and the number of payments (**ComputePayment** is **"false"**) is not exact. Truncation errors (making sure payments only have two decimal places) can affect the final payment amount. And, forcing the number of payments to be an integer value can result in significant errors in the final payment, perhaps even necessitating a final payment (remember the example we just ran?). We need to develop an analysis that recognizes the possibility of such errors and make necessary adjustments.

Here's the approach we will take. If the loan has N payments of P dollars, we will process all but the last payment and see what the remaining balance is at that point. If that balance is less than P, that will become the final payment. If that balance is greater than P, a payment of P will be applied and an additional payment of the final balance will be created. The displayed loan analysis will then show the final payment and the associated total of payments and interest paid.

For those of you who have avoided all the mathematical derivations up to this point, you need to know how to process a single payment to reduce the loan balance. If B is the current loan balance, i the monthly interest rate and P the payment. The balance (B_{after}) after the payment is:

$$B_{after} = B + Bi - P$$

This equation simply says the new balance is the old balance incremented by interest owed (Bi), then decreased by the payment amount (P). We use this equation to compute the final payment in the loan analysis.

The steps behind generating the loan analysis are:

- Display **Balance**.
- Display **Interest**.
- Compute **FinalPayment** (adding a payment, if necessary).
- Compute and display total of payments.
- Compute and display interest paid.
- Hide **ComputeButton**.
- Hide **MonthsButton**.
- Hide **PaymentButton**.
- Show **NewLoanButton**.

Each of these steps is performed in the **ComputeButtonClicked** subroutine. The modified procedure is (changes are shaded):

```
Sub ComputeButtonClicked
  Balance = Controls.GetTextBoxText(BalanceTextBox)
  Interest = Controls.GetTextBoxText(InterestTextBox)
  MonthlyInterest = Interest / 1200
  If (ComputePayment) Then
    'Compute loan payment
    Months = Controls.GetTextBoxText(MonthsTextBox)
    Multiplier = Math.Power(1 + MonthlyInterest, Months)
    Payment = Balance * MonthlyInterest * Multiplier /
(Multiplier - 1)
    DollarAmount = Payment
    DollarFormat()
    Controls.SetTextBoxText(PaymentTextBox, DollarDisplay)
  Else
    'Compute number of payments
    Payment = Controls.GetTextBoxText(PaymentTextBox)
    Months = Math.Floor((Math.Log(Payment) - Math.Log(Payment -
Balance * MonthlyInterest)) / Math.Log(1 + MonthlyInterest))
    Controls.SetTextBoxText(MonthsTextBox, Months)
  EndIf
  CRLF = Text.GetCharacter(13)
  'reset payment prior to analysis to fix at two decimals
  Payment = Controls.GetTextBoxText(PaymentTextBox)
  'show analysis
  DollarAmount = Balance
  DollarFormat()
  DisplayText = "Loan Balance: $" + DollarDisplay
  DisplayText = DisplayText + CRLF + "Interest Rate: " +
Interest + "%"
  'process all but last payment
  LoanBalance = Balance
  For PaymentNumber = 1 To Months - 1
    LoanBalance = LoanBalance + LoanBalance * MonthlyInterest -
Payment
  EndFor
  'find final payment
  FinalPayment = LoanBalance
  If FinalPayment > Payment Then
    'apply one more payment
    LoanBalance = LoanBalance + LoanBalance * MonthlyInterest -
Payment
    FinalPayment = LoanBalance
    Months = Months + 1
```

```
    Controls.SetTextBoxText(MonthsTextBox, Months)
  EndIf
  DollarAmount = Payment
  DollarFormat()
  DisplayText = DisplayText + CRLF + CRLF + (Months - 1) + "
Payments of " + DollarDisplay
  DollarAmount = FinalPayment
  DollarFormat()
  DisplayText = DisplayText + CRLF + "Final Payment of $" +
DollarDisplay
  DollarAmount = (Months - 1) * Payment + FinalPayment
  DollarFormat()
  DisplayText = DisplayText + CRLF + "Total Payments: $" +
DollarDisplay
  DollarAmount = (Months - 1) * Payment + FinalPayment -
Balance
  DollarFormat()
  DisplayText = DisplayText + CRLF + "Interest Paid: $" +
DollarDisplay
  Controls.SetTextBoxText(AnalysisTextBox, DisplayText)
  Controls.HideControl(ComputeButton)
  Controls.HideControl(MonthsButton)
  Controls.HideControl(PaymentButton)
  Controls.ShowControl(NewLoanButton)
EndSub
```

You should be able to identify all the steps of the loan analysis, especially the final payment adjustment.

A couple of comments. In the top of the analysis code, we reassign the **Payment** value to the displayed value in the **PaymentTextBox**. The displayed value is formatted to two decimal places. Through this reassignment, we make sure **Payment** is just two decimal places. Second, note the analysis in the text box is essentially just one long string. To start a new line, we use a variable **CRLF**, which stands for a carriage return, line feed (a throwback to typewriter days). In "ASCII" code, character 13 represents this function:

```
CRLF = Text.GetCharacter(13)
```

Save and **Run** the project. Enter values for balance, interest and number of payments. Click **Compute Monthly Payment** . Here are the results for the example I've been using:

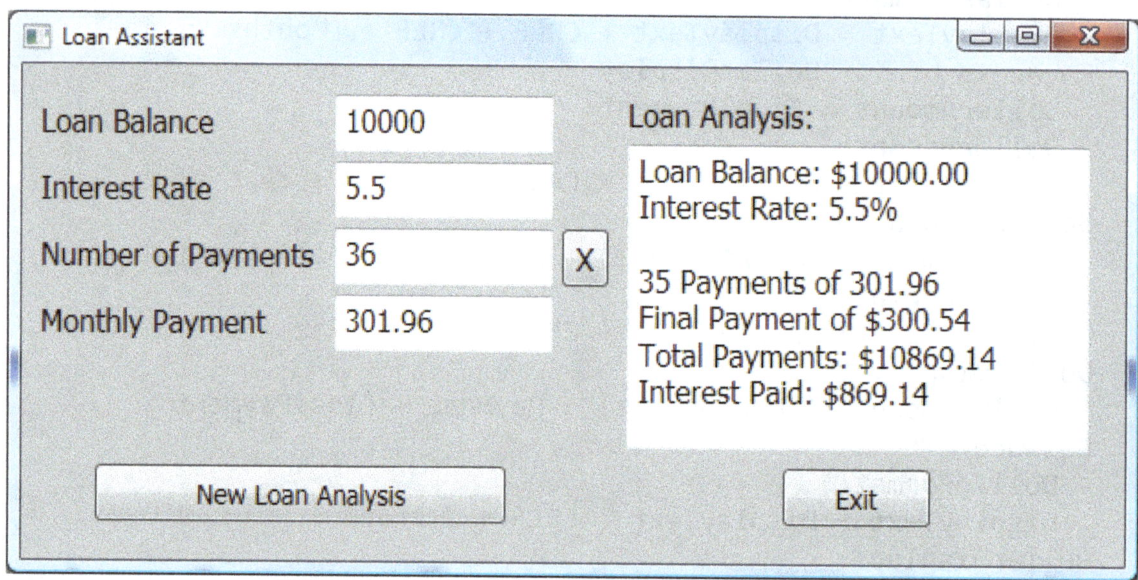

Note the slight adjustment to the final payment amount. Note the **New Loan Analysis** button. You can't do another analysis at this point since **ComputeButton** is hidden – we'll fix that in the next section. Click **Exit**.

Run the project again, this time clicking the **X** next to the **Number of Payments** text box. Enter values for balance, interest and payment, then click **Compute Number of Payments**. Continuing with the example I've been using (remember we got 58 payments before?) shows:

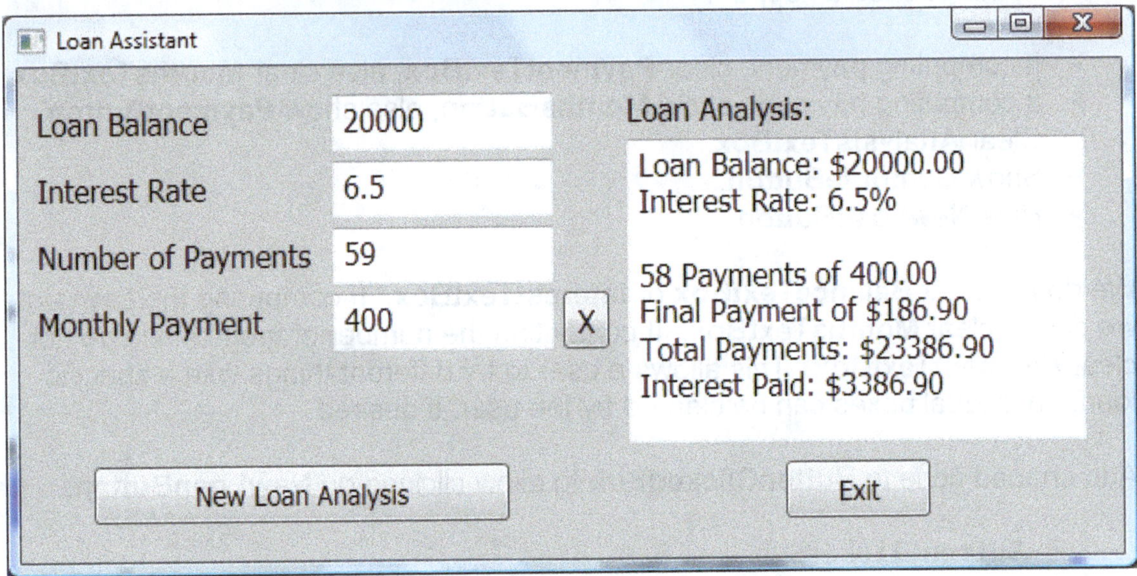

We now get 59 rather than 58 payments, the same result we saw earlier in the chapter. It was determined that once 58 payments of $400.00 per month were applied, there was still a balance, necessitating a 59th payment of $186.90. Click **Exit**, since you can't do anything else at this point.

Code Design – New Loan Analysis

Following an analysis, we would like the capability of performing a new analysis. When a user clicks the **New Loan Analysis** button (**NewLoanButton**), the following things should happen:

- If computing payment, clear **PaymentTextBox**, else clear **MonthsTextBox**.
- If computing payment, show **MonthsButton**, else show **PaymentButton**.
- Clear **AnalysisTextBox**.
- Show **ComputeButton**.
- Hide **NewLoanButton**.

We do not clear **BalanceTextBox** or **InterestTextBox**. If computing the payment, we do not clear **MonthsTextBox**. If computing the number of months, we do not clear **PaymentTextBox**. This allows a user to try different things with a specific loan. Individual boxes can be cleared by the user, if desired.

Add shaded code to **ButtonClickedSub** to allow clicking on **NewLoanButton**:

```
Sub ButtonClickedSub
  B = Controls.LastClickedButton
  If (B = PaymentButton) Then
    PaymentButtonClicked()
  ElseIf (B = MonthsButton) Then
    MonthsButtonClicked()
  ElseIf (B = ComputeButton) Then
    ComputeButtonClicked()
  ElseIf (B = ExitButton) Then
    Program.End()
  ElseIf (B = NewLoanButton) Then
    NewLoanButtonClicked()
  EndIf
EndSub
```

And, the **NewLoanButtonClicked** subroutine is:

```
Sub NewLoanButtonClicked
  'clear computed value and analysis
  If ComputePayment Then
    Controls.SetTextBoxText(PaymentTextBox, "")
    Controls.ShowControl(MonthsButton)
  Else
    Controls.SetTextBoxText(MonthsTextBox, "")
    Controls.ShowControl(PaymentButton)
  EndIf
  Controls.SetTextBoxText(AnalysisTextBox, "")
  Controls.ShowControl(ComputeButton)
  Controls.HideControl(NewLoanButton)
EndSub
```

Enter this code into your program.

Save and **Run** the project. The project should now have total ability to compute monthly payments or number of payments, providing complete loan analysis results. Play with the project as much as you'd like.

Improving a Small Basic Project

The consumer loan assistant project works fine in its current configuration, but there are some hidden problems. You may have uncovered some of them already. This is something you, as a programmer, will do a lot. You will build a project and, while running it and testing it, will uncover weaknesses that need to be eliminated. These weaknesses could be actual errors in the application or just things that, if eliminated, make your application easier to use. Some weaknesses are easy to find, some more subtle.

You will find, as you progress as a programmer, that you will spend much of your time improving your projects. You will always find ways to add features to a project and to make it more appealing to your user base. You should never be satisfied with your first solution to a problem. There will always be room for improvement. And Small Basic provides a perfect platform for adding improvements to an application. You can easily add features and test them to see if the desired performance enhancements are attained.

If you run the loan assistant project a few more times, you can identify some weaknesses:

- For example, what happens if you input a zero interest? The program will give incorrect results because the formulas implemented in code will not work properly with zero interest.
- What happens if you forget to input a value (leaving a text box empty)? You could get unpredictable results.
- Notice you can type any characters you want in the text boxes when you should just be limited to numbers and a single decimal point – any other characters will cause the program to work incorrectly.
- A subtle problem arises when using the 'compute number of months' mode. In this configuration, the minimum desired payment must exceed the loan balance times the monthly interest. If it doesn't, you will never get the loan paid off – your balance will just keep growing (!), something called negative amortization.

We can (and will) address each of these points as we improve the loan assistant project.

Code Design – Zero Interest

If you are lucky enough to find a bank or someone to give you a loan at zero percent interest, congratulations!! However, you can't use the current code to compute payment information. Try it if you like – you'll receive incorrect results.

The formulas used in the code assume a non-zero interest rate. If **Interest** is zero, we can use much simpler formulas. For the 'compute payment' mode, the code is simply:

```
Payment = Balance / Months
```

While for the 'compute number of payments' mode, the code is:

```
Months = Math.Floor(Balance / Payment)
```

The modified **ComputeButtonClicked** subroutine (changes are shaded, some unmodified code is not shown for brevity):

```
Sub ComputeButtonClicked
    .
    .
  If (ComputePayment) Then
    'Compute loan payment
    Months = Controls.GetTextBoxText(MonthsTextBox)
    If (Interest = 0) Then
      Payment = Balance / Months
    Else
      Multiplier = Math.Power(1 + MonthlyInterest, Months)
      Payment = Balance * MonthlyInterest * Multiplier /
(Multiplier - 1)
    EndIf
    DollarAmount = Payment
    DollarFormat()
    Controls.SetTextBoxText(PaymentTextBox, DollarDisplay)
  Else
    'Compute number of payments
    Payment = Controls.GetTextBoxText(PaymentTextBox)
    If (Interest = 0) Then
      Months = Math.Floor(Balance / Payment)
    Else
      Months = Math.Floor((Math.Log(Payment) - Math.Log(Payment
- Balance * MonthlyInterest)) / Math.Log(1 + MonthlyInterest))
    EndIf
    Controls.SetTextBoxText(MonthsTextBox, Months)
  EndIf
    .
    .
EndSub
```

Save and **Run** the application, making sure zero interest works under each mode. Notice adjustments to the final payment are only made when the balance is not an exact multiple of the payment. Make sure the non-zero interest options still work, too. Always make sure when you make changes to your code that you haven't disturbed portions that are working satisfactorily.

ShowMessage Method

If one of the text box controls (that should have an entry) is empty or not numeric, we need to inform the user of such an error and give him/her a chance to correct it. Similarly, when using the 'compute number of months' mode, if the user enters a payment that is too low, we need to tell the user a minimum payment will be used. We can do both of these tasks using the **GraphicsWindow ShowMessage** method. This method lets you display a small message box to your user. It can be used to display error messages, describe potential problems or just to show the result of some computation. The user responds by clicking an **OK** button in the message box

To use the **ShowMessage** method, you decide what the **Text** of the message should be and what **Title** you desire for the box. Then, to display the message box in code, you use:

```
GraphicsWindow.ShowMessage(Text, Title)
```

ShowMessage **Example**:

If you use this code:

```
GraphicsWindow.Show()
GraphicsWindow.ShowMessage("Quick Message for You", "Hey
You!!")
```

The resulting message box:

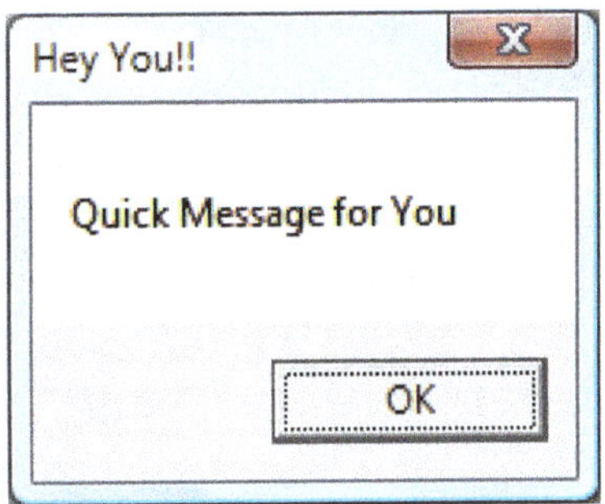

You will find a lot of uses for this message boxas you progress in Small Basic.

Code Design – Input Validation

The code to check each text box entry (**Number**) for validity is similar. The steps are:

- Check to see if **Number** is blank.
- If **Number** is blank, display message box telling user so.
- If **Number** is not blank, check to make sure all characters in text box are numeric (numerals or a single decimal point). If not numeric, inform the user.

This subroutine (**ValidateNumber**) checks for entry validity. You supply a **NumberToCheck**. If the number is valid (not blank, only numbers and at most one decimal), the variable **NumberIsValid** will have a value of "**true**", otherwise it will be "**false**.". Add the subroutine to your program:

```
Sub ValidateNumber
  'sees if NumberToCheck has only digits and a single decimal
and is not blank
  NumberIsValid = "true"
  If (NumberToCheck = "") Then
    NumberIsValid = "false"
    Goto ExitValidateNumber
  EndIf
  DecimalCount = 0
  For I = 1 To Text.GetLength(NumberToCheck)
    CC = Text.GetCharacterCode(Text.GetSubText(NumberToCheck,
I, 1))
    If (CC = Text.GetCharacterCode(".")) Then
      DecimalCount = DecimalCount + 1
      If (DecimalCount > 1) Then
        NumberIsValid = "false"
        Goto ExitValidateNumber
      EndIf
    ElseIf (CC < Text.GetCharacterCode("0") Or CC >
Text.GetCharacterCode("9")) Then
      NumberIsValid = "false"
      Goto ExitValidateNumber
    EndIf
  EndFor
ExitValidateNumber:
EndSub
```

All modifications for checking for valid text box entries go in the **ComputeButtonClicked** subroutine. The modified subroutine (changes are shaded, with some unmodified code not shown) that implements each of the above steps for each text box control is:

```
Sub ComputeButtonClicked
  Balance = Controls.GetTextBoxText(BalanceTextBox)
  NumberToCheck = Balance
  ValidateNumber()
  If (NumberIsValid = "false") Then
    GraphicsWindow.ShowMessage("Loan Balance is blank or
contains non-numeric characters.", "Invalid Input")
    Goto ExitComputeButtonClicked
  EndIf
  Interest = Controls.GetTextBoxText(InterestTextBox)
  NumberToCheck = Interest
  ValidateNumber()
  If (NumberIsValid = "false") Then
    GraphicsWindow.ShowMessage("Interest Rate is blank or
contains non-numeric characters.", "Invalid Input")
    Goto ExitComputeButtonClicked
  EndIf
  MonthlyInterest = Interest / 1200
  If (ComputePayment) Then
    'Compute loan payment
    Months = Controls.GetTextBoxText(MonthsTextBox)
    NumberToCheck = Months
    ValidateNumber()
    If (NumberIsValid = "false") Then
      GraphicsWindow.ShowMessage("Number of Months is blank or
contains non-numeric characters.", "Invalid Input")
      Goto ExitComputeButtonClicked
    EndIf
    If (Interest = 0) Then
      Payment = Balance / Months
    Else
      Multiplier = Math.Power(1 + MonthlyInterest, Months)
      Payment = Balance * MonthlyInterest * Multiplier /
(Multiplier - 1)
    EndIf
    DollarAmount = Payment
    DollarFormat()
    Controls.SetTextBoxText(PaymentTextBox, DollarDisplay)
  Else
    'Compute number of payments
    Payment = Controls.GetTextBoxText(PaymentTextBox)
```

```
    NumberToCheck = Payment
    ValidateNumber()
    If (NumberIsValid = "false") Then
      GraphicsWindow.ShowMessage("Monthly Payment is blank or
contains non-numeric characters.", "Invalid Input")
      Goto ExitComputeButtonClicked
    EndIf
    If (Interest = 0) Then
      Months = Math.Floor(Balance / Payment)
    Else
      Months = Math.Floor((Math.Log(Payment) - Math.Log(Payment
- Balance * MonthlyInterest)) / Math.Log(1 + MonthlyInterest))
    EndIf
    Controls.SetTextBoxText(MonthsTextBox, Months)
  EndIf
   .
   .
ExitComputeButtonClicked:
EndSub
```

After making these modifications, **Save** and **Run** the project. Make sure each input validation works correctly. Make sure it works in both computation modes. And, make sure your changes have not affected previously correct calculations. Here's what appears when I leave **BalanceTextBox** blank and click **Compute Payment**:

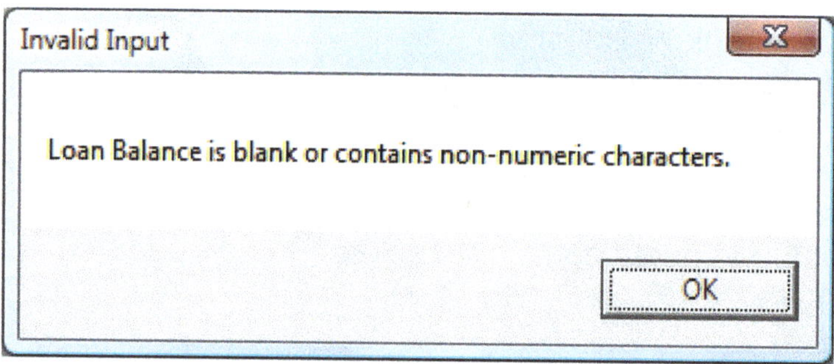
Invalid Input
Loan Balance is blank or contains non-numeric characters.
OK

The user clicks **OK** for another chance at inputting a non-blank value.

We have one last input validation to implement and then the consumer loan assistant project is complete (unless you can think of other improvements). Recall, when computing the number of months, we must enter a minimum payment or the balance will continue to grow. The minimum payment is the loan balance times the monthly interest:

```
MinimumPayment = Balance * MonthlyInterest
```

If this payment is made each month, it is called an "interest only" loan. This means, we just pay the interest owed each month, never decreasing the balance. Since our goal is to decrease the balance, we will suggest to the user a minimum payment at least $1 greater than the interest only option, or we will use:

```
MinimumPayment = Balance * MonthlyInterest + 1
```

The steps for minimum payment validation are (only needed when **ComputePayment** is **"false"**):

- If entered **Payment** is less than minimum value, display message box informing user of minimum needed and display minimum payment in **PaymentTextBox**. Continue computations using minimum payment.
- If entered **Payment** is above minimum value, continue as usual.

These modifications go in the **ComputeButtonClicked** subroutine. The modifications are shaded (again, unmodified code is not shown for brevity):

```
Sub ComputeButtonClicked
  .
  .
  'Compute number of payments
  Payment = Controls.GetTextBoxText(PaymentTextBox)
  NumberToCheck = Payment
  ValidateNumber()
  If (NumberIsValid = "false") Then
    GraphicsWindow.ShowMessage("Monthly Payment is blank or
contains non-numeric characters.", "Invalid Input")
    Goto ExitComputeButtonClicked
  EndIf
  If (Payment <= Balance * MonthlyInterest + 1.0) Then
    DollarAmount = Math.Floor(Balance * MonthlyInterest +
1.0)
    DollarFormat()
    Controls.SetTextBoxText(PaymentTextBox, DollarDisplay)
    GraphicsWindow.ShowMessage("Minimum payment must be $" +
DollarDisplay + ". Payment has been set to that value.", "Input
Error")
    Payment = DollarAmount
  EndIf
  .
  .
EndSub
```

Make the indicated changes.

While implementing improvements to the loan assistant project, we have made many modifications to the **ComputeButtonClicked** subroutine. For reference, consult the **Loan Assistant Project Code Listing** for the final version of the subroutine.

Save and **Run** the loan assistant project. Switch to 'compute number of payments' mode. Enter a **Loan Balance** and an **Interest Rate**. Enter a "too low" **Monthly Payment** amount. Here's some numbers I used:

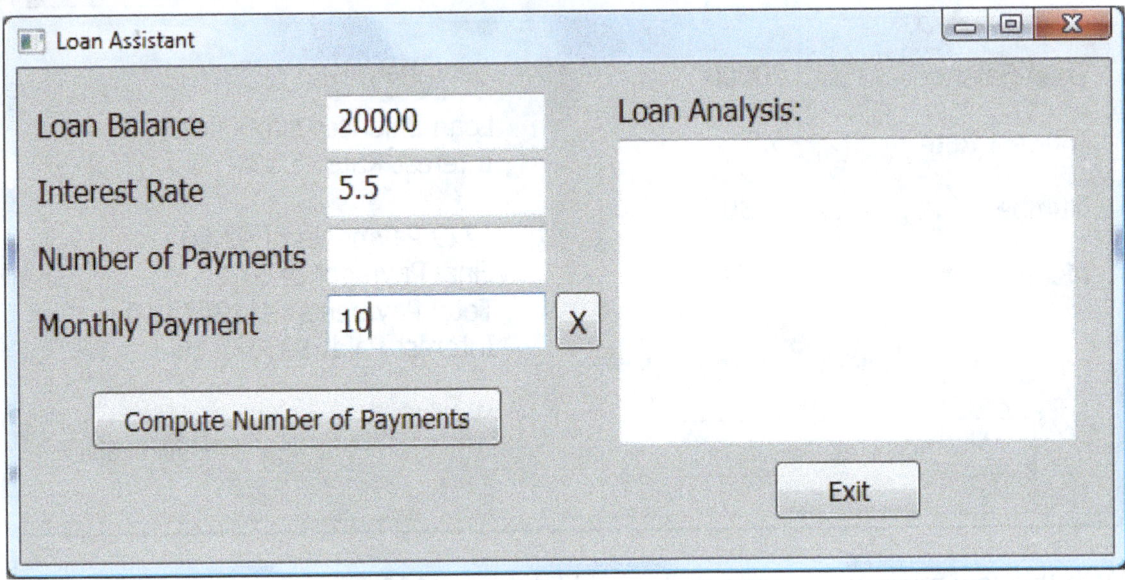

Now, click **Compute Number of Payments**. A message box like this should appear:

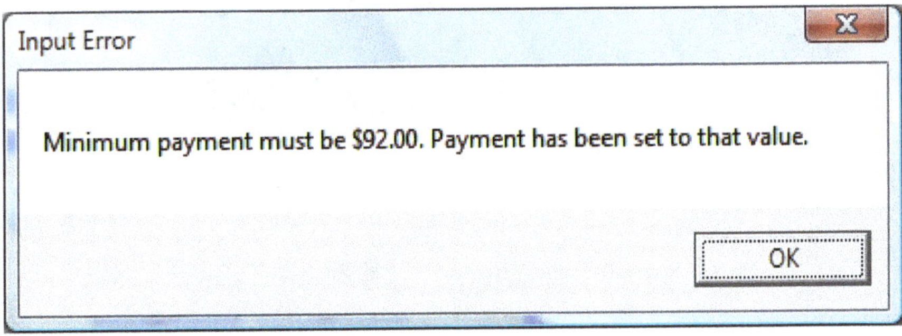

Click **OK** and analysis will proceed using the suggested minimum payment ($92.00 in my example):

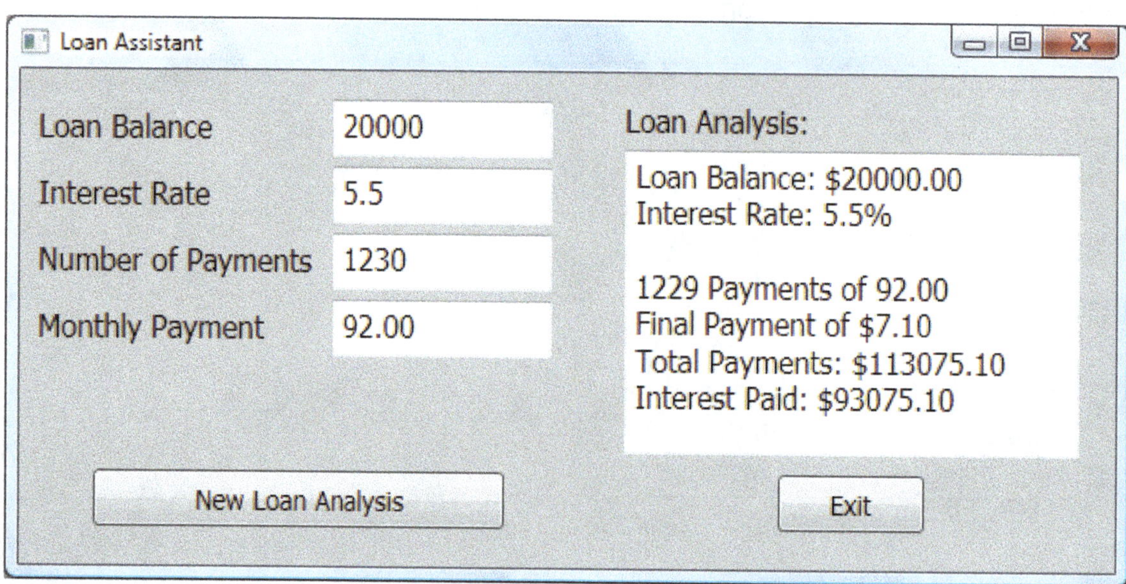

With this low minimum payment, it would take over 100 years to pay off the loan!! And, unfortunately, many credit card companies don't let you know how many years it takes to pay off a balance if you just make the minimum payment each month. This new project arms you with the tool you need to make such computations.

Consumer Loan Assistant Project Code Listing

Here is the complete listing of the **Consumer Loan Assistant** Small Basic program:

```
' Loan Assistant
InitializeProgram()

Sub InitializeProgram
  'graphics window
  GraphicsWindow.Width = 600
  GraphicsWindow.Height = 260
  GraphicsWindow.Title = "Loan Assistant"
  GraphicsWindow.BackgroundColor = "LightGray"
  'add labels text boxes
  GraphicsWindow.BrushColor = "Black"
  GraphicsWindow.FontBold = "false"
  GraphicsWindow.FontSize = 16
  GraphicsWindow.DrawText(10, 20, "Loan Balance")
  GraphicsWindow.DrawText(10, 55, "Interest Rate")
  GraphicsWindow.DrawText(10, 90, "Number of Payments")
  GraphicsWindow.DrawText(10, 125, "Monthly Payment")
  BalanceTextBox = Controls.AddTextBox(170, 15)
  Controls.SetSize(BalanceTextBox, 120, 30)
  InterestTextBox = Controls.AddTextBox(170, 50)
  Controls.SetSize(InterestTextBox, 120, 30)
  MonthsTextBox = Controls.AddTextBox(170, 85)
  Controls.SetSize(MonthsTextBox, 120, 30)
  PaymentTextBox = Controls.AddTextBox(170, 120)
  Controls.SetSize(PaymentTextBox, 120, 30)
  'add analysis text box
  GraphicsWindow.DrawText(330, 15, "Loan Analysis:")
  AnalysisTextBox = Controls.AddMultiLineTextBox(330, 40)
  Controls.SetSize(AnalysisTextBox, 250, 160)
  'add buttons
  GraphicsWindow.FontSize = 14
  ComputeButton = Controls.AddButton("Compute Monthly Payment",
40, 170)
  Controls.SetSize(ComputeButton, 225, 30)
  NewLoanButton = Controls.AddButton("New Loan Analysis", 40, 210)
  Controls.SetSize(NewLoanButton, 225, 30)
  ExitButton = Controls.AddButton("Exit", 415, 210)
  Controls.SetSize(ExitButton, 80, 30)
  GraphicsWindow.FontSize = 16
  MonthsButton = Controls.AddButton("X", 295, 85)
  Controls.SetSize(MonthsButton, 25, 30)
```

```
  PaymentButton = Controls.AddButton("X", 295, 120)
  Controls.SetSize(PaymentButton, 25, 30)
  Controls.ButtonClicked = ButtonClickedSub
  PaymentButtonClicked()
EndSub

Sub ButtonClickedSub
  B = Controls.LastClickedButton
  If (B = PaymentButton) Then
    PaymentButtonClicked()
  ElseIf (B = MonthsButton) Then
    MonthsButtonClicked()
  ElseIf (B = ComputeButton) Then
    ComputeButtonClicked()
  ElseIf (B = ExitButton) Then
    Program.End()
  ElseIf (B = NewLoanButton) Then
    NewLoanButtonClicked()
  EndIf
EndSub

Sub PaymentButtonClicked
  ' will compute payment
  ComputePayment = "true"
  Controls.HideControl(PaymentButton)
  Controls.ShowControl(MonthsButton)
  Controls.SetTextBoxText(PaymentTextBox, "")
  Controls.SetButtonCaption(ComputeButton, "Compute Monthly
Payment")
  Controls.HideControl(NewLoanButton)
EndSub

Sub MonthsButtonClicked
  ' will compute months
  ComputePayment = "false"
  Controls.ShowControl(PaymentButton)
  Controls.HideControl(MonthsButton)
  Controls.SetTextBoxText(MonthsTextBox, "")
  Controls.SetButtonCaption(ComputeButton, "Compute Number of
Payments")
  Controls.HideControl(NewLoanButton)
EndSub

Sub ComputeButtonClicked
  Balance = Controls.GetTextBoxText(BalanceTextBox)
  NumberToCheck = Balance
```

```
  ValidateNumber()
  If (NumberIsValid = "false") Then
    GraphicsWindow.ShowMessage("Loan Balance is blank or contains
non-numeric characters.", "Invalid Input")
    Goto ExitComputeButtonClicked
  EndIf
  Interest = Controls.GetTextBoxText(InterestTextBox)
  NumberToCheck = Interest
  ValidateNumber()
  If (NumberIsValid = "false") Then
    GraphicsWindow.ShowMessage("Interest Rate is blank or contains
non-numeric characters.", "Invalid Input")
    Goto ExitComputeButtonClicked
  EndIf
  MonthlyInterest = Interest / 1200
  If (ComputePayment) Then
    'Compute loan payment
    Months = Controls.GetTextBoxText(MonthsTextBox)
    NumberToCheck = Months
    ValidateNumber()
    If (NumberIsValid = "false") Then
      GraphicsWindow.ShowMessage("Number of Months is blank or
contains non-numeric characters.", "Invalid Input")
      Goto ExitComputeButtonClicked
    EndIf
    If (Interest = 0) Then
      Payment = Balance / Months
    Else
      Multiplier = Math.Power(1 + MonthlyInterest, Months)
      Payment = Balance * MonthlyInterest * Multiplier /
(Multiplier - 1)
    EndIf
    DollarAmount = Payment
    DollarFormat()
    Controls.SetTextBoxText(PaymentTextBox, DollarDisplay)
  Else
    'Compute number of payments
    Payment = Controls.GetTextBoxText(PaymentTextBox)
    NumberToCheck = Payment
    ValidateNumber()
    If (NumberIsValid = "false") Then
      GraphicsWindow.ShowMessage("Monthly Payment is blank or
contains non-numeric characters.", "Invalid Input")
      Goto ExitComputeButtonClicked
    EndIf
    If (Payment <= Balance * MonthlyInterest + 1.0) Then
```

```
      DollarAmount = Math.Floor(Balance * MonthlyInterest + 1.0)
      DollarFormat()
      Controls.SetTextBoxText(PaymentTextBox, DollarDisplay)
      GraphicsWindow.ShowMessage("Minimum payment must be $" +
DollarDisplay + ". Payment has been set to that value.", "Input
Error")
      Payment = DollarAmount
    EndIf
    If (Interest = 0) Then
      Months = Math.Floor(Balance / Payment)
    Else
      Months = Math.Floor((Math.Log(Payment) - Math.Log(Payment -
Balance * MonthlyInterest)) / Math.Log(1 + MonthlyInterest))
    EndIf
    Controls.SetTextBoxText(MonthsTextBox, Months)
  EndIf
  CRLF = Text.GetCharacter(13)
  'reset payment prior to analysis to fix at two decimals
  Payment = Controls.GetTextBoxText(PaymentTextBox)
  'show analysis
  DollarAmount = Balance
  DollarFormat()
  DisplayText = "Loan Balance: $" + DollarDisplay
  DisplayText = DisplayText + CRLF + "Interest Rate: " + Interest
+ "%"
  'process all but last payment
  LoanBalance = Balance
  For PaymentNumber = 1 To Months - 1
    LoanBalance = LoanBalance + LoanBalance * MonthlyInterest -
Payment
  EndFor
  'find final payment
  FinalPayment = LoanBalance
  If FinalPayment > Payment Then
    'apply one more payment
    LoanBalance = LoanBalance + LoanBalance * MonthlyInterest -
Payment
    FinalPayment = LoanBalance
    Months = Months + 1
    Controls.SetTextBoxText(MonthsTextBox, Months)
  EndIf
  DollarAmount = Payment
  DollarFormat()
  DisplayText = DisplayText + CRLF + CRLF + (Months - 1) + "
Payments of " + DollarDisplay
  DollarAmount = FinalPayment
```

```
  DollarFormat()
  DisplayText = DisplayText + CRLF + "Final Payment of $" +
DollarDisplay
  DollarAmount = (Months - 1) * Payment + FinalPayment
  DollarFormat()
  DisplayText = DisplayText + CRLF + "Total Payments: $" +
DollarDisplay
  DollarAmount = (Months - 1) * Payment + FinalPayment - Balance
  DollarFormat()
  DisplayText = DisplayText + CRLF + "Interest Paid: $" +
DollarDisplay
  Controls.SetTextBoxText(AnalysisTextBox, DisplayText)
  Controls.HideControl(ComputeButton)
  Controls.HideControl(MonthsButton)
  Controls.HideControl(PaymentButton)
  Controls.ShowControl(NewLoanButton)
ExitComputeButtonClicked:
EndSub

Sub DollarFormat
  'provide DollarAmount - return DollarDisplay (0.00 format)
  'get dollars
  Dollars = Math.Floor(DollarAmount)
  'get cents
  Cents = Math.Round((DollarAmount - Dollars) * 100)
  DollarDisplay = Text.Append(Dollars, ".")
  If (Cents < 10) Then
    DollarDisplay = Text.Append(Text.Append(DollarDisplay, "0"),
Cents)
  Else
    DollarDisplay = Text.Append(DollarDisplay, Cents)
  EndIf
EndSub

Sub NewLoanButtonClicked
  'clear computed value and analysis
  If ComputePayment Then
    Controls.SetTextBoxText(PaymentTextBox, "")
    Controls.ShowControl(MonthsButton)
  Else
    Controls.SetTextBoxText(MonthsTextBox, "")
    Controls.ShowControl(PaymentButton)
  EndIf
  Controls.SetTextBoxText(AnalysisTextBox, "")
  Controls.ShowControl(ComputeButton)
  Controls.HideControl(NewLoanButton)
```

```
EndSub

Sub ValidateNumber
  'sees if NumberToCheck has only digits and a single decimal and
is not blank
  NumberIsValid = "true"
  If (NumberToCheck = "") Then
    NumberIsValid = "false"
    Goto ExitValidateNumber
  EndIf
  DecimalCount = 0
  For I = 1 To Text.GetLength(NumberToCheck)
    CC = Text.GetCharacterCode(Text.GetSubText(NumberToCheck, I,
1))
    If (CC = Text.GetCharacterCode(".")) Then
      DecimalCount = DecimalCount + 1
      If (DecimalCount > 1) Then
        NumberIsValid = "false"
        Goto ExitValidateNumber
      EndIf
    ElseIf (CC < Text.GetCharacterCode("0") Or CC >
Text.GetCharacterCode("9")) Then
      NumberIsValid = "false"
      Goto ExitValidateNumber
    EndIf
  EndFor
ExitValidateNumber:
EndSub
```

Consumer Loan Assistant Project Review

The **Consumer Loan Assistant** project is now complete. **Save** and **Run** the project and make sure it works as designed. Check that you can move back and forth between computation modes. Use the project to make informed payment decisions regarding any loans or credit cards you may have.

If there are errors in your implementation, go back over the steps of window and code design. Use the debugger when needed. Go over the developed code – make sure you understand how different parts of the project were coded. As mentioned in the beginning of this chapter, the completed project is saved as **LoanAssistant** in the **HomeSB\HomeSB Projects\LoanAssistant** folder.

While completing this project, new concepts and skills you should have gained include:

- Proper use of the text box control.
- Different ways to improve a Small Basic project.
- How to do input validation.
- How to use message boxes in conjunction with input validation.

This project also showed that once you have built a working project, there is often still a lot of work to do. Much of the code in the loan assistant project was added to improve the application – making it more user friendly and less susceptible to erroneous entries. As mentioned previously in these notes, it is relatively easy to write a project that works properly when the user does everything correctly. It's difficult and takes time to write a project that can handle all the possible wrong things a user can do and still not bomb out. Added improvements separate the good projects from the adequate projects.

Consumer Loan Assistant Project Enhancements

Possible enhancements to the consumer loan assistant project include:

- Many times, you know how much you can afford monthly and want to know how much you can borrow. Add a capability to compute balance, given interest, months and payment. Follow similar steps for computing the other parameters.
- Add single payment processing capability so you can see how much the balance decreases each month and how much interest you are paying. Show results in the current text box or add other controls.
- Add the capability to stop after a certain number of payments have been processed.
- Add an output to the loan analysis that tells you what date your loan will be paid off based on the number of monthly payments.

6. Flash Card Math Quiz Project

Review and Preview

In this chapter, we build a project that lets kids (or adults) practice their basic addition, subtraction, multiplication and division skills. The **Flash Card Math Quiz Project** allows you to select problem type, what numbers you want to use and has three timing options. We also look at using random numbers and accepting keyboard input.

Flash Card Math Quiz Project Preview

In this chapter, we will build a **flash card math** program. Random math problems (selectable from addition, subtraction, multiplication, and/or division) using the numbers from 0 to 9 are presented. Timing options are available to help build both accuracy and speed.

The finished project is saved as **FlashCard** in the **HomeSB\HomeSB Projects\FlashCard** folder. Start Small Basic and open the finished project. **Run** the project (click **Run** in the toolbar or press <**F5**>). The flash card math program will appear as:

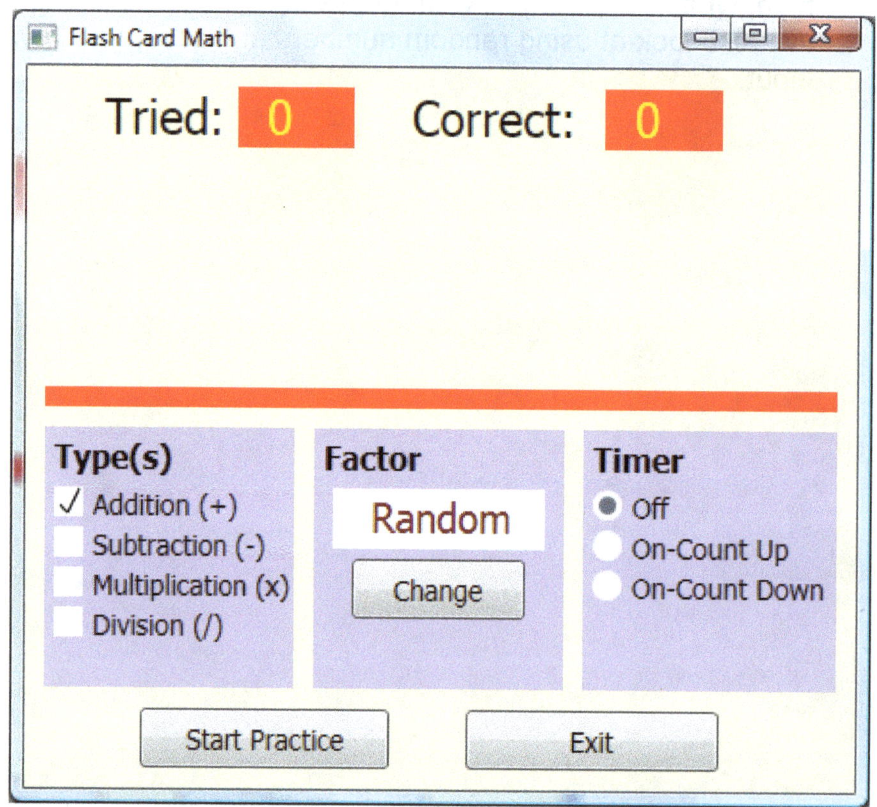

Many options are available. First, choose problem type from the **Type** box. Choose from **Addition**, **Subtraction**, **Multiplication**, and/or **Division** problems (click on your choice; you may choose more than one problem type). Choose your **Factor** (use the **Change** button), any number from 0 to 9, or choose **Random** for random factors. These options may be changed at any time. To practice math facts, click on the **Start Practice** button.

When I click **Start Practice** (using the default choices), I see:

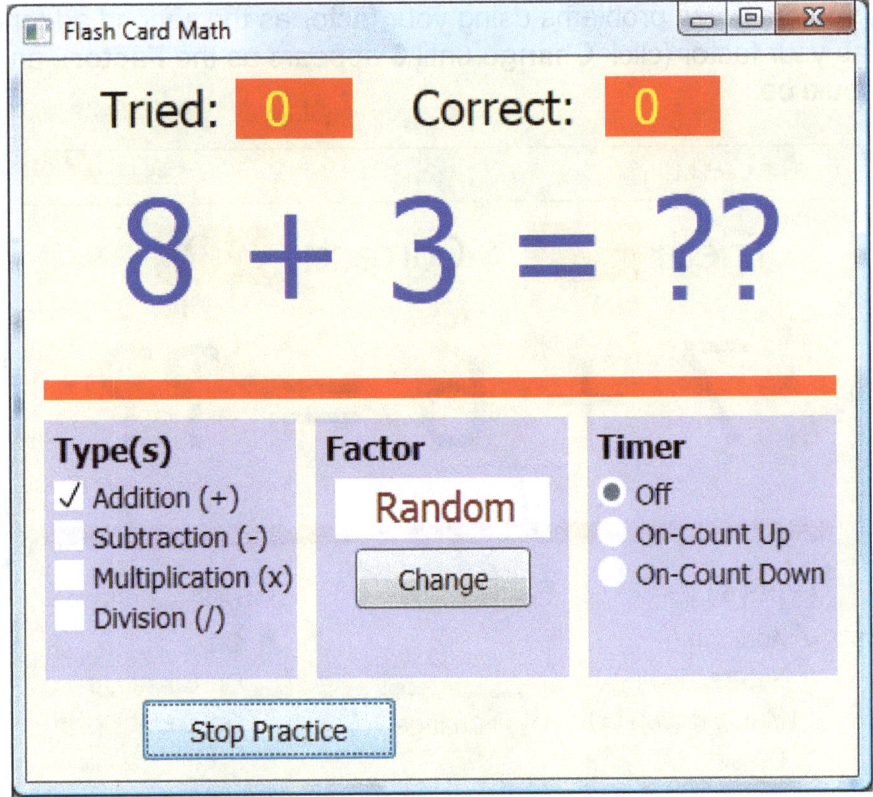

You can now see there is a large display in the middle where the problem (8 + 3 =) is displayed. The program is waiting for an answer to this problem. Type your answer. If it is correct, the number next to **Correct:** is incremented. Whether correct or not, another problem is presented.

A few notes on entering your answer. The primary goal of the program is to build speed in solving simple problems. As such, you have one chance to enter an answer - there is no erasing. If the answer has more than two digits (the number of digits in the answer is shown using question marks), type your answer from left to right. For example, if the answer is 10, type a 1 then a 0. Try several addition problems to see how answers are entered. You can stop practicing math problems, at any time, by clicking the **Stop Practice** button.

Other problem types can be selected and a new factor chosen at any time. Each problem is generated randomly, based on problem type and factor value. For **Addition**, you are given problems using your factor as the second addend. If you choose **6** as your factor (click **Change** until **6** appears as the **Factor**), an example problem would be:

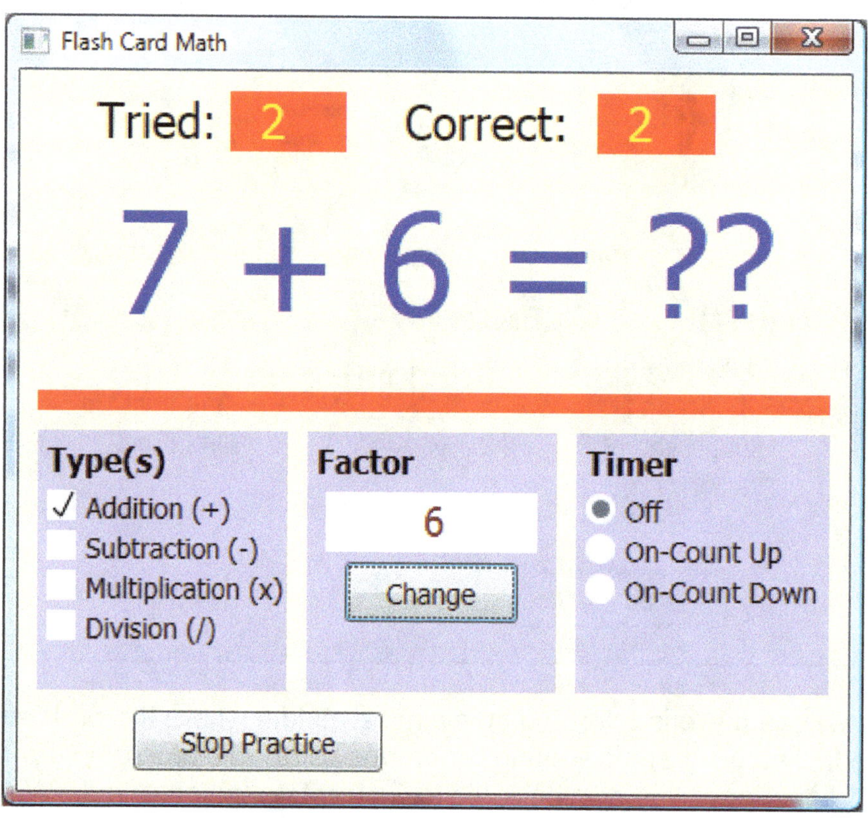

For **Subtraction** (click **Subtraction** under **Type** – note the added check mark) you are given problems using your factor as the subtrahend (the number being subtracted). Selecting a factor of **5**, an example subtraction problem is:

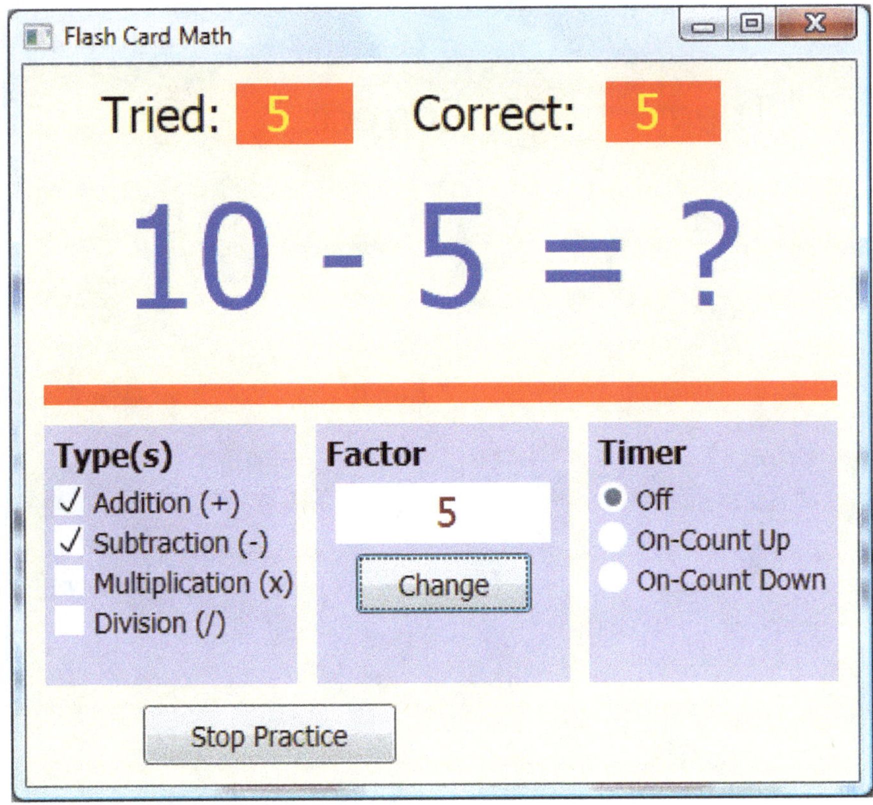

For **Multiplication**, you are given problems using your factor as the multiplier (the number you're multiplying by). If a factor of **9** is selected, an example multiplication problem is:

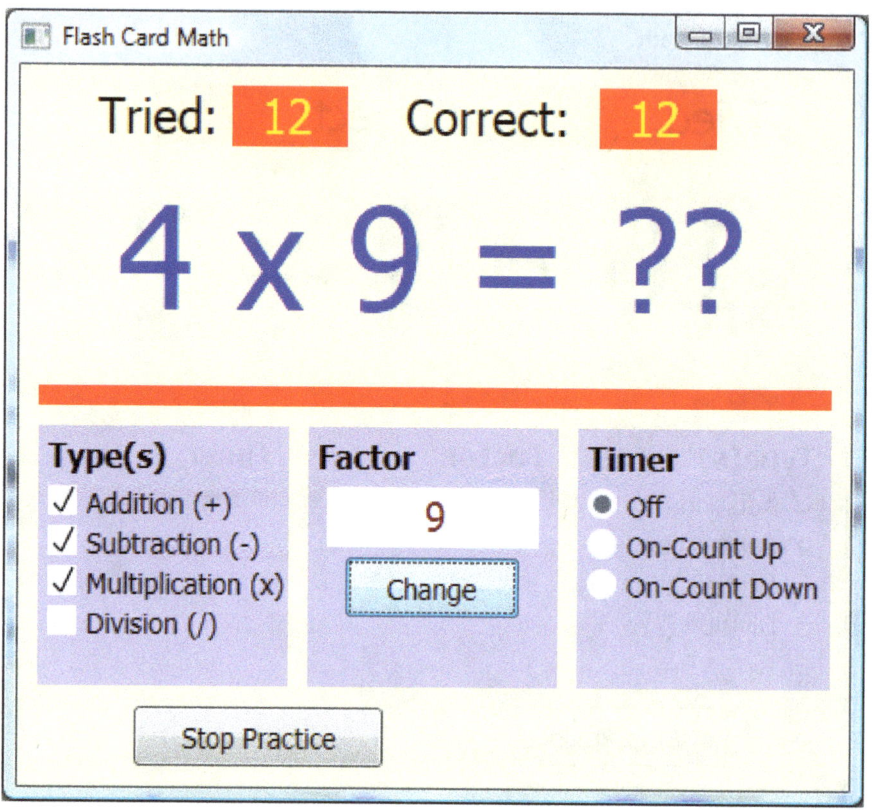

Lastly, for **Division**, you are given problems using your factor as the divisor (the number you are dividing by). If the selected factor is 4, a typical division problem would be:

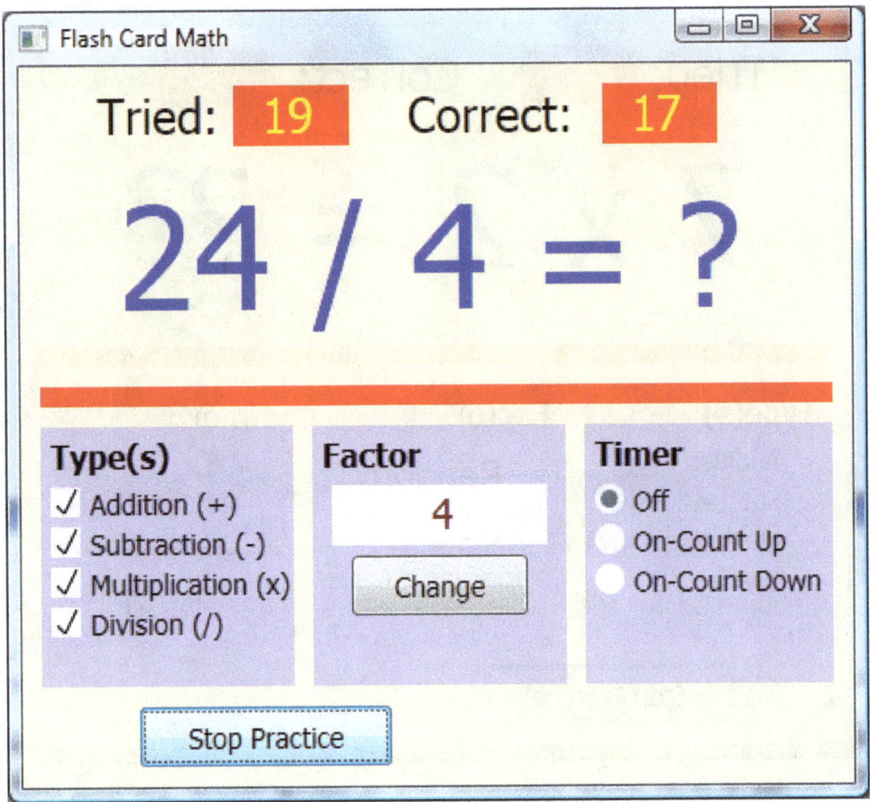

As mentioned, you do not have to choose a specific factor – **Random** factors can be chosen. Try all kinds of factors with all kinds of problem types.

There is another option to consider when using the flash card math project – the corresponding option choices are in the **Timer** box. These options can only be selected when not solving problems. There are three choices here. If you select **Off**, you solve problems until you click **Stop Practice**. If you select **On-Count Up**, a timer will appear and the computer will keep track of how long you were solving problems (a maximum of 30 minutes is allowed). If you select **On-Count Down**, a timer will appear, along with +/- buttons. The buttons are used to set how long you want to solve problems (a maximum of 30 minutes is allowed). The timer will then count down, allowing you to solve problems until the allotted time expires.

Try the timer options if you'd like. Here's the beginning of a run I made using the **On-Count Down** option (starting at 1 minute):

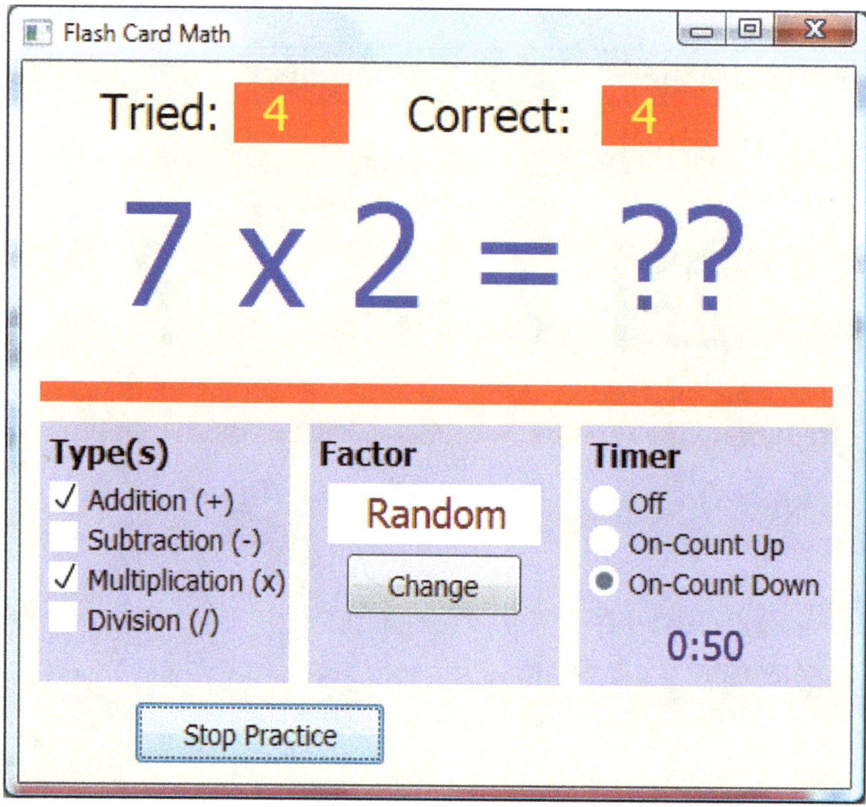

Once you are done practicing math problems (either you clicked **Stop Practice** or time ran out with the **On-Count Down** option), a message box appears giving you the results of your little quiz. This box tells you how many problems you solved and how many you got correct (including a percentage score). If the timer was on, you are also told how long you were solving problems and how much time (on average) you spent on each problem. Here's the message box I saw when I finished the quiz I started above:

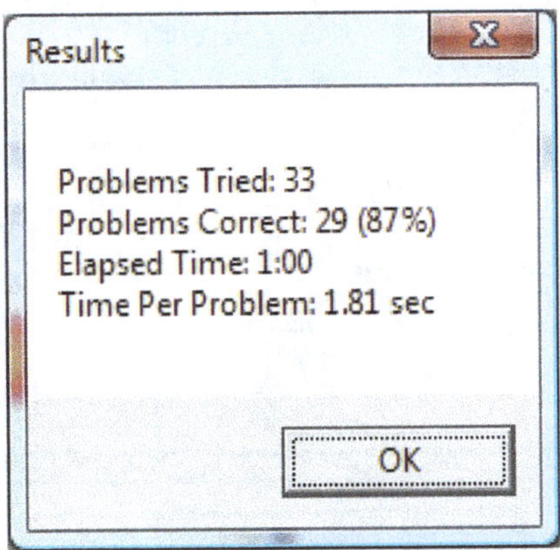

Click **OK** and you can try again. Click the **Exit** button in **Flash Card Math** when you are done solving problems.

You will now build this project in several stages. We first address **window design**. We discuss the controls used to build the window and establish initial properties. And, we address **code design** in detail. We cover random generation of problems, selection of the various program options, and how to use timing.

Flash Card Math Window Design

Here is the sketch for the window layout of the **Flash Card Math** program:

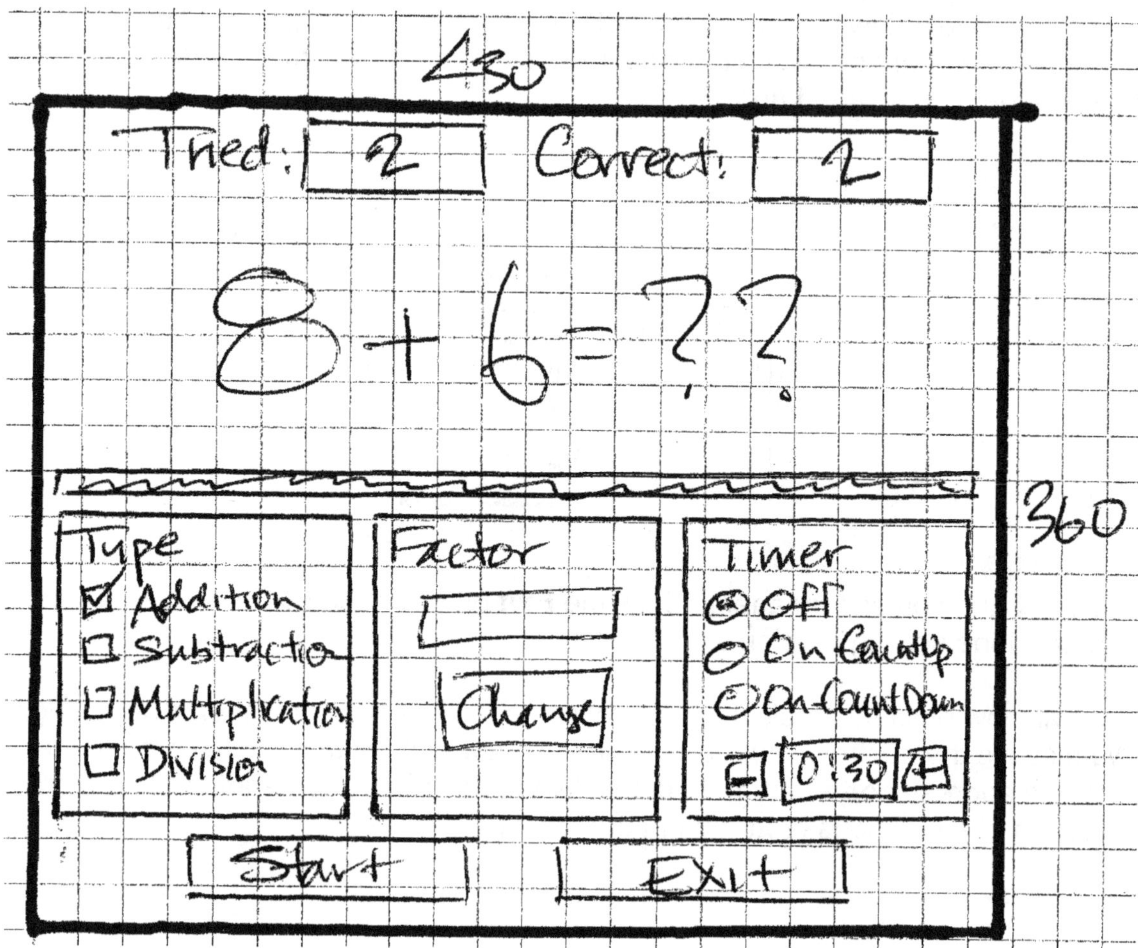

There's a lot here. Two labeled text shapes are used for scoring. There's a large text shape in the middle of the window used to display the math problem. A dividing rectangle separates the problem display from option choices and buttons. Two button controls (at the bottom of the window) are used to start and stop the problems and to exit the project. There are three rectangles used to group option choices. The first holds four "check boxes" used to select problem type. The second holds a button and display used to select numbers used in the problems. The third box holds three little circles used to select the timing option. Two small button controls (marked with – and +) are used to adjust the amount of time used in the flash card drills.

We will begin writing code for the application. We will write the code in several steps. We start with the code needed to add all the above elements to the program window. The program will be built in its default configuration: **Addition** problems, **Random** factor and timer **Off**. Later, we add code to change these default values.

Start a new program in Small Basic. Once started, we suggest you immediately save the program with a name you choose. This sets up the folder and file structure needed for your program.

Window Design – Scoring and Problem Display

We begin by setting up the graphics window and adding the text shapes that display the number of problems tried (**TriedDisplay**) and the number answered correctly (**CorrectDisplay**). We also add an empty text shape (**ProblemDisplay**, with a very large font) to display the problem to answer and draw a red, dividing rectangle. Add this code to your program:

```
' Flash Card Math
InitializeProgram()

Sub InitializeProgram
  'graphics window
  GraphicsWindow.Width = 430
  GraphicsWindow.Height = 360
  GraphicsWindow.Title = "Flash Card Math"
  GraphicsWindow.BackgroundColor = "LightYellow"
  'labels/scores
  GraphicsWindow.BrushColor = "Black"
  GraphicsWindow.FontBold = "false"
  GraphicsWindow.FontSize = 24
  GraphicsWindow.DrawText(40, 10, "Tried:")
  GraphicsWindow.DrawText(200, 10, "Correct:")
  GraphicsWindow.BrushColor = "Red"
  GraphicsWindow.FillRectangle(110, 10, 60, 30)
  GraphicsWindow.FillRectangle(300, 10, 60, 30)
  GraphicsWindow.BrushColor = "Yellow"
  TriedDisplay = Shapes.AddText("0")
  Shapes.Move(TriedDisplay, 125, 10)
  CorrectDisplay = Shapes.AddText("0")
  Shapes.Move(CorrectDisplay, 315, 10)
  'problem display
  GraphicsWindow.BrushColor = "Blue"
  GraphicsWindow.FontSize = 72
  ProblemDisplay = Shapes.AddText("")
  Shapes.Move(ProblemDisplay, 50, 50)
  'divider
  GraphicsWindow.BrushColor = "Red"
  GraphicsWindow.FillRectangle(10, 160, 410, 10)
EndSub
```

The first line of code calls a subroutine **InitializeProgram** where we will put all code needed to set up the program for use. All remaining code here goes in that subroutine.

As written, you won't see a problem since **ProblemDisplay** is blank. To get an idea of what a problem will look like, temporarily change the line setting the text to:

```
ProblemDisplay = Shapes.AddText("8 + 7 = 15")
```

Now, **Save** and **Run** the program. You should see:

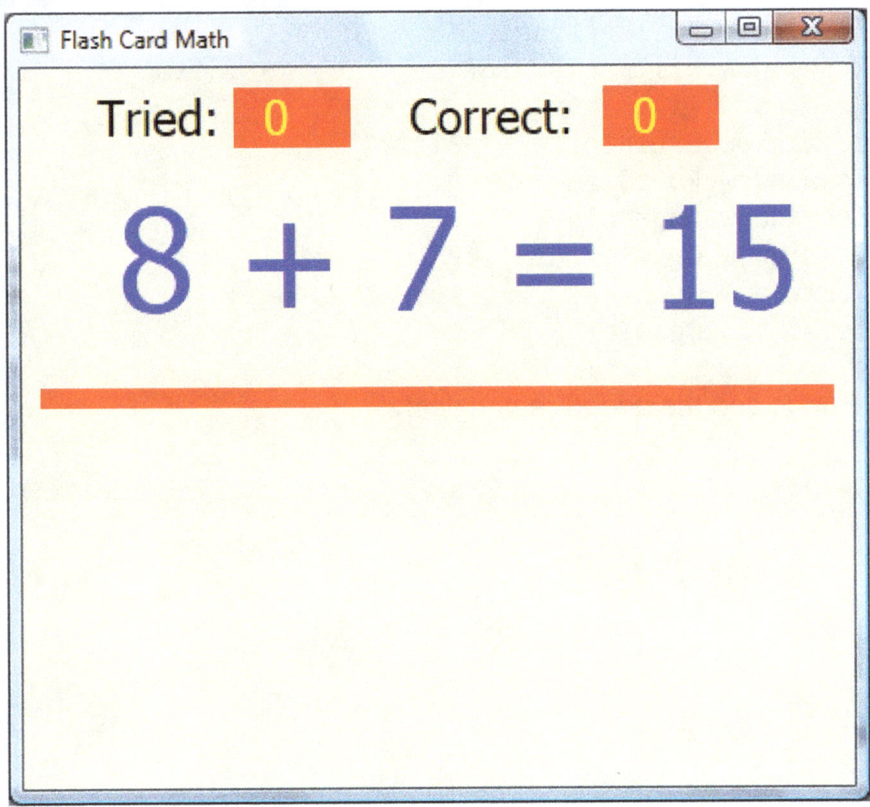

Notice how we put the text shapes (**TriedDisplay** and **CorrectDisplay**) on red rectangles to give them some background. You may wonder how we knew to use **FontSize** of **72** in the problem display. There was no magic - we just tried different values until we got a nice display.

Remember to change the line setting the problem display back to:

```
ProblemDisplay = Shapes.AddText("")
```

Next, we start writing the code to choose the program options. Before doing this, add this code (in **InitializeProgram**) to draw and label the three blue rectangles to hold each option choice:

```
'problem types/factor/timer
GraphicsWindow.BrushColor = GraphicsWindow.GetColorFromRGB(192,
192, 255)
GraphicsWindow.FillRectangle(10, 180, 130, 130)
GraphicsWindow.FillRectangle(150, 180, 130, 130)
GraphicsWindow.FillRectangle(290, 180, 130, 130)
GraphicsWindow.BrushColor = "Black"
GraphicsWindow.FontSize = 16
GraphicsWindow.FontBold = "true"
GraphicsWindow.DrawText(15, 185, "Type(s)")
GraphicsWindow.DrawText(155, 185, "Factor")
GraphicsWindow.DrawText(295, 185, "Timer")
```

Save and **Run** to see the added rectangles:

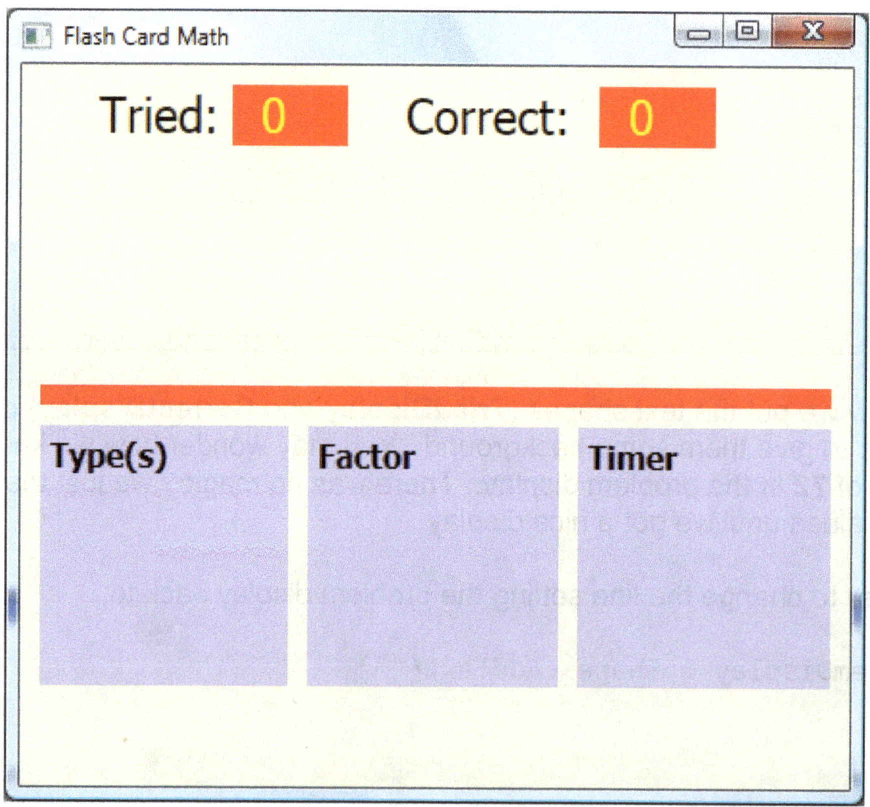

Window Design – Choosing Problem Types

In the **Flash Card Math** program, you can practice any of the four basic arithmetic operations: addition, subtraction, multiplication and/or division. We want to provide the user with a convenient way to choose among the problem types. Here's a display of the method chosen:

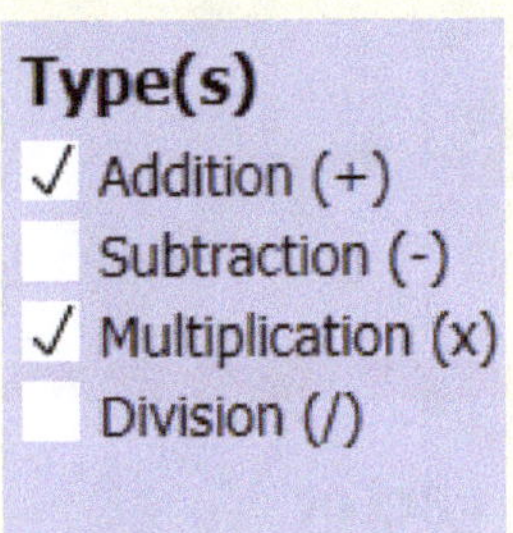

White squares are drawn next to the choices. When a user clicks a square, if there is no check mark there, one appears (selecting that problem type). If a check mark is already there, it disappears (deselecting that problem type).

The code to implement the selection process is a bit complicated and will be discussed later. For now, we draw the display assuming only **Addition** problems (default choice) are available. Add this code to **InitializeProgram**:

```
'problem types
GraphicsWindow.BrushColor = "Black"
GraphicsWindow.FontSize = 14
GraphicsWindow.FontBold = "false"
GraphicsWindow.DrawText(35, 210, "Addition (+)")
GraphicsWindow.DrawText(35, 230, "Subtraction (-)")
GraphicsWindow.DrawText(35, 250, "Multiplication (x)")
GraphicsWindow.DrawText(35, 270, "Division (/)")
GraphicsWindow.BrushColor = "White"
GraphicsWindow.FillRectangle(15, 210, 15, 15)
GraphicsWindow.FillRectangle(15, 230, 15, 15)
GraphicsWindow.FillRectangle(15, 250, 15, 15)
GraphicsWindow.FillRectangle(15, 270, 15, 15)
ProblemSelected[1] = "true"
ProblemSelected[2] = "false"
ProblemSelected[3] = "false"
ProblemSelected[4] = "false"
```

This code draws four white squares with the appropriate labels. An array **ProblemSelected** is used to specify which problem types are selected. For now, only element 1 (**Addition** problems) is "**true**".

Save and **Run** the program. The selection squares appear:

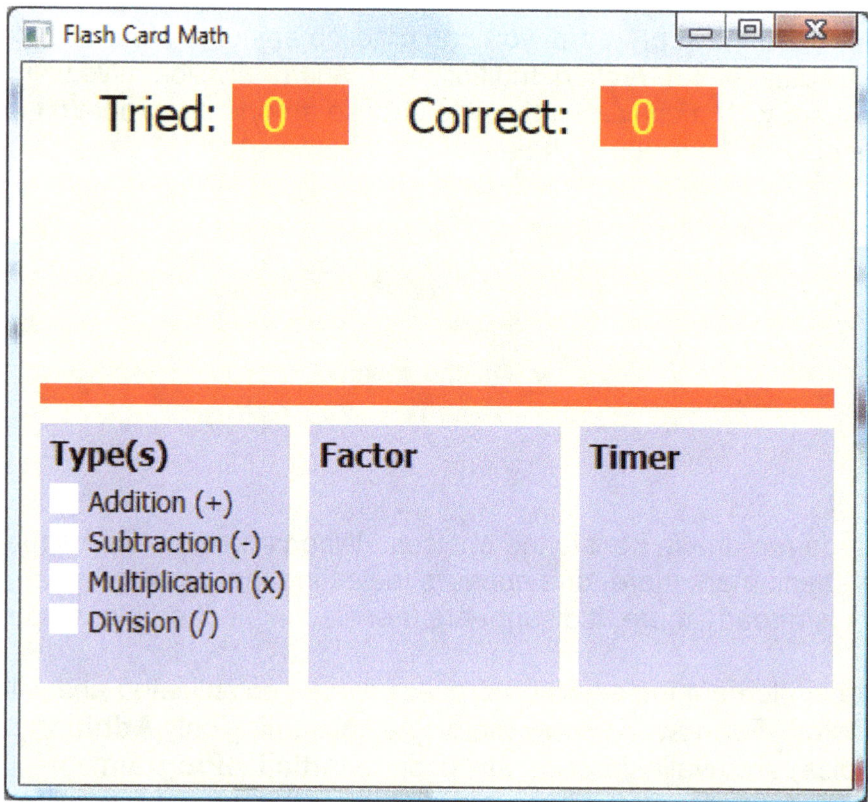

No check mark appears in the square indicating that **Addition** problems are selected. We will correct that when we write code for the selection process.

Window Design - Factor Selection

A user can choose a particular number (factor) from 0 to 9 to practice math problems or can choose a random factor. This choice is made in the **Factor** selection box. Like we did for the problem type selection, we simply set up the window for the default choice (**Random** factor), then later address the code for changing the factor.

Add this code to **InitializeProgram**:

```
'factor
GraphicsWindow.BrushColor = "White"
GraphicsWindow.FillRectangle(160, 210, 110, 30)
GraphicsWindow.BrushColor = "DarkRed"
GraphicsWindow.FontSize = 20
FactorDisplay = Shapes.AddText("Random")
Shapes.Move(FactorDisplay, 180, 212)
FactorChoice = -1
GraphicsWindow.BrushColor = "Black"
GraphicsWindow.FontSize = 14
FactorButton = Controls.AddButton("Change", 170, 245)
Controls.SetSize(FactorButton, 90, 30)
```

This places a text shape (**FactorDisplay**) on top of a white rectangle to show which factor is selected (shows **Random** for now). A button control (**FactorButton**) will be used to change this display. The variable **FactorChoice** keeps track of the selected factor. If it is positive, its value is the selected factor (0 to 9). When its value is -1 (the default value here), a random factor is used.

Save and **Run** the program to see the factor selection box:

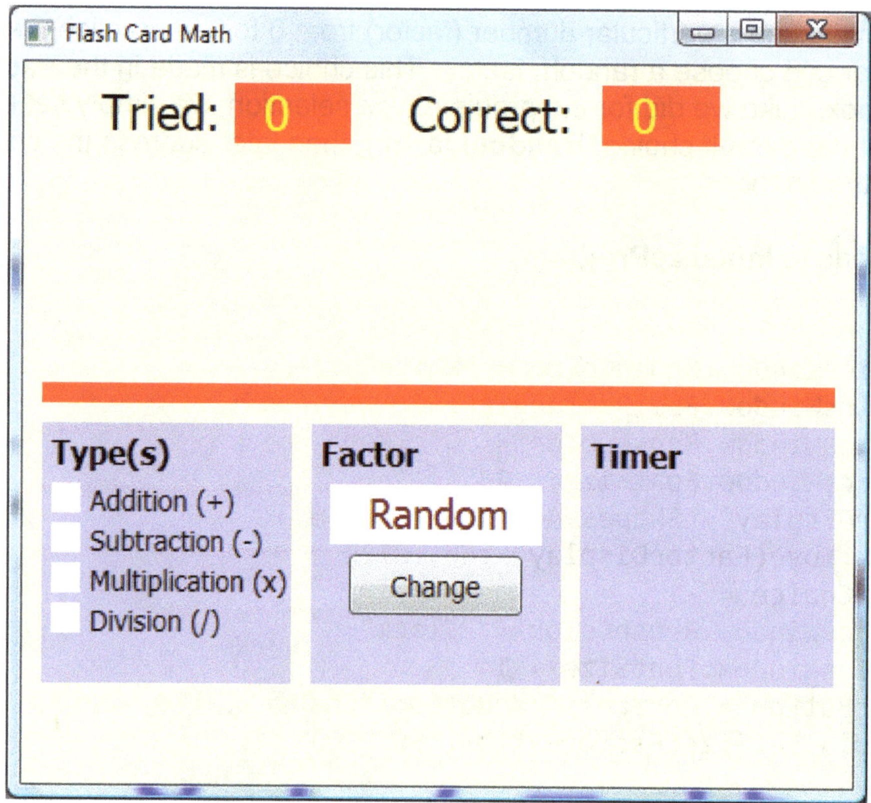

Later, we write code to change the displayed factor when the **Change** button is clicked.

Window Design - Timer Options

In the **Flash Card Math** program, you can time your practice if you choose. There are three choices: timer **Off**, timer **On – Count Up**, timer **On – Count Down**. Like the problem type selection, we want to provide the user with a convenient way to choose the timer option. The difference between this selection and that of problem type is that only one choice can be made. Here's a display of the method chosen:

White circles are drawn next to the choices. When a user clicks a circle, that circle is marked (selecting that timer option). All other choices become 'unmarked'. When one of the timer **On** options is selected, timing information and buttons to change times will be displayed under the circles.

Also, like the problem type selection, the code behind selecting timing options is involved and will be discussed later. Here, we write code to build the display and use the default option of timer **Off**. Add this code to **InitializeProgram**:

```
'timer choices
GraphicsWindow.BrushColor = "Black"
GraphicsWindow.FontSize = 14
GraphicsWindow.FontBold = "false"
GraphicsWindow.DrawText(315, 210, "Off")
GraphicsWindow.DrawText(315, 230, "On-Count Up")
GraphicsWindow.DrawText(315, 250, "On-Count Down")
GraphicsWindow.BrushColor = "White"
GraphicsWindow.FillEllipse(295, 210, 15, 15)
GraphicsWindow.FillEllipse(295, 230, 15, 15)
GraphicsWindow.FillEllipse(295, 250, 15, 15)
TimerChoice = 0 ' 0-off, 1 -on/up, 2- on/down
GraphicsWindow.BrushColor = "DarkBlue"
GraphicsWindow.FontSize = 20
TimeDisplay = Shapes.AddText("0:30")
Shapes.Move(TimeDisplay, 335, 277)
GraphicsWindow.BrushColor = "Black"
GraphicsWindow.FontSize = 14
TimerPlusButton = Controls.AddButton("+", 390, 275)
```

```
Controls.SetSize(TimerPlusButton, 20, 30)
TimerMinusButton = Controls.AddButton("-", 300, 275)
Controls.SetSize(TimerMinusButton, 20, 30)
```

This code draws the circles (ellipses) next to the labeled choices. A variable **TimerChoice** stores which option is selected (0-off, 1-on, count up, 2-on, count down). It is set to zero initially (timer is off). A text shape (**TimeDisplay**) is used to display time when the timer is used and two buttons (**TimerPlusButton**, **TimerMinusButton**) are used to adjust the timer in the count down situation.

Save and **Run** the program to see the new additions:

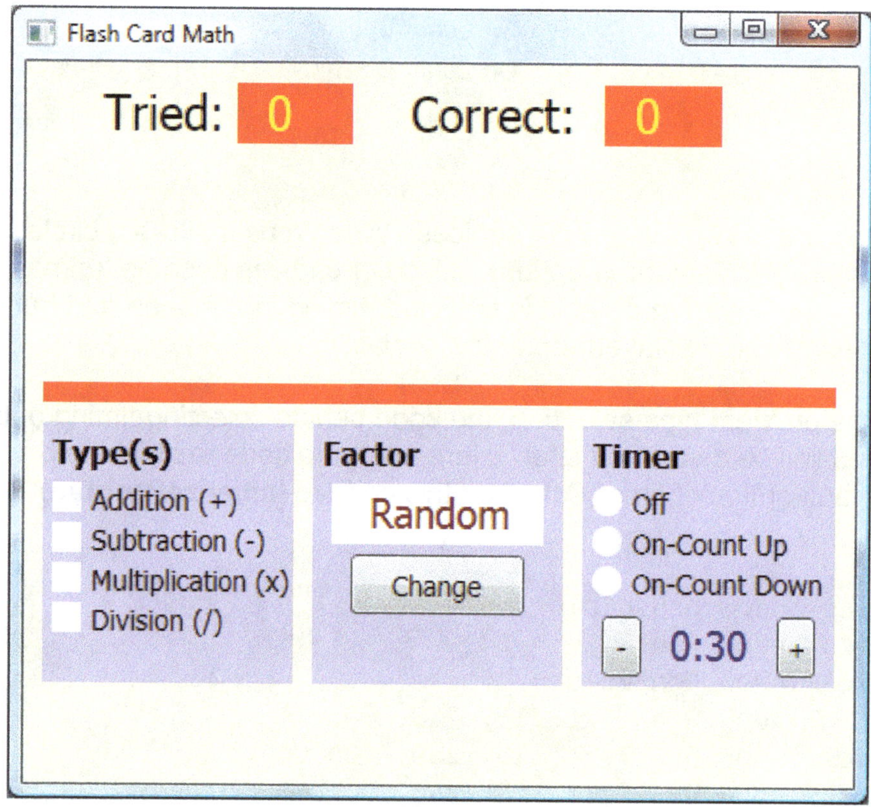

No selection mark appears in the circle indicating the **Timer** is **Off**. We will correct that when we write code for the selection process. **TimeDisplay** and the two adjustment buttons should not appear in the default configuration (timer **Off**), so add these three lines in **InitializeProgram** (after the code just added to create them) to hide these controls:

```
Shapes.HideShape(TimeDisplay)
Controls.HideControl(TimerMinusButton)
Controls.HideControl(TimerPlusButton)
```

Rerun the program to make sure the controls are hidden.

Window Design - Add Buttons

The final element needed in the window are the two buttons to control the program operation. One button (**StartStopButton**) is used to start and stop practice of math problems. One button (**ExitButton**) is used to stop the program. Add this code to **InitializeProgram**:

```
'buttons
GraphicsWindow.BrushColor = "Black"
GraphicsWindow.FontSize = 14
StartStopButton = Controls.AddButton("Start Practice", 60, 320)
Controls.SetSize(StartStopButton, 130, 30)
ExitButton = Controls.AddButton("Exit", 230, 320)
Controls.SetSize(ExitButton, 130, 30)
```

Save and **Run** the program to see the final window design:

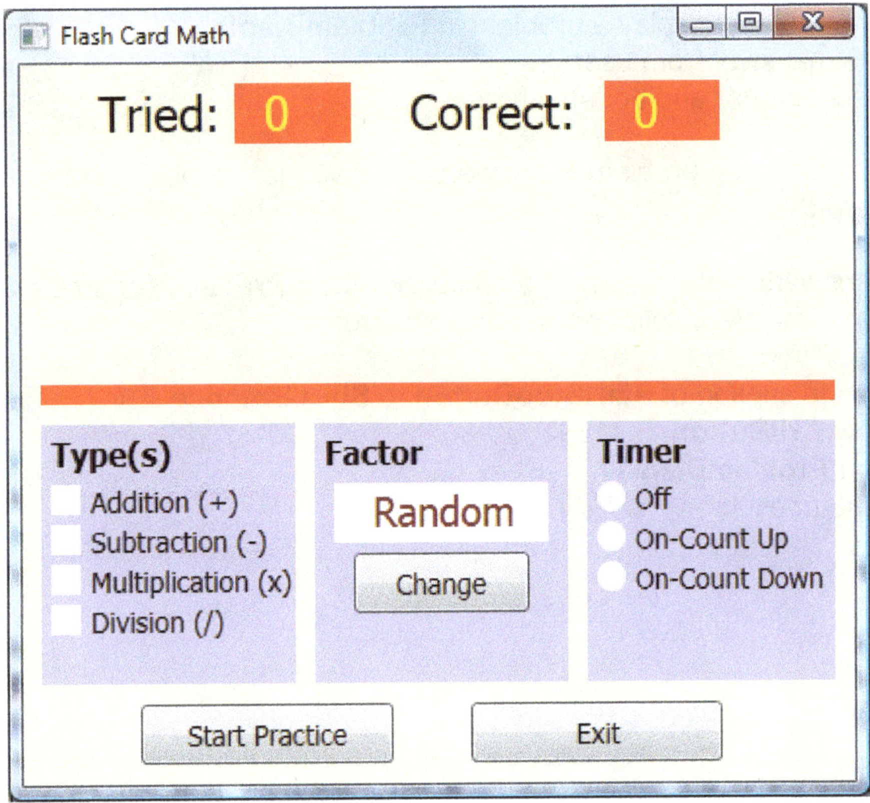

We now start writing the code behind choosing all the options and generating and solving problems. As a first step, we write the code that generates a random problem and gets the answer from the user, updating the score.

Code Design – Start Practice

The idea of the flash card math project is to display a problem, receive an answer from the user and check for correctness. Problems can be of four different types with different factor choices and different timer options. For now, we work with **Addition** problems with **Random** factors. And, we will ignore the timer options. Once this initial code is working satisfactorily, other problem types and factors and timing will be considered. Again, this step-by-step approach to building a project is far simpler than trying to build everything at once.

Things begin by clicking the **Start Practice** button (**StartStopButton**). When this happens, the following steps are taken:

- Change caption of **StartStopButton** to **Stop Practice**.
- Hide **ExitButton**.
- Set number of problems tried (**NumberTried**) and number correct (**NumberCorrect**) to zero.
- Generate and display a problem in **ProblemDisplay**.
- Obtain answer from user.
- Check answer and update score.

Once each generated problem is answered, subsequent problems are generated and answered.

The user answers problems until he/she clicks **Stop Practice** (or time elapses in timed drills). The steps followed at this point are:

- Change caption of **StartStopButton** to **Start Practice**
- Show **ExitButton**.
- Clear **ProblemDisplay**.
- Present results.

The code behind the listed steps is fairly straightforward. First, add this line at the end of **InitializeProgram** to allow detection of button clicks:

```
Controls.ButtonClicked = ButtonClickedSub
```

And the corresponding subroutine (**ButtonClickedSub**) called when a button is clicked:

```
Sub ButtonClickedSub
  B = Controls.LastClickedButton
  If (B = StartStopButton) Then
    StartStopButtonClicked()
  ElseIf (B = ExitButton) Then
    Program.End()
  EndIf
EndSub
```

We have added possibilities for clicking on either **StartStopButton** or **ExitButton**. As seen, if a user clicks the **ExitButton**, the program simply ends.

Now, use this code in the **StartStopButtonClicked** subroutine (implements the steps above, except for presenting results):

```
Sub StartStopButtonClicked
  If (Controls.GetButtonCaption(StartStopButton) = "Start
Practice") Then
    Controls.SetButtonCaption(StartStopButton, "Stop Practice")
    Controls.HideControl(ExitButton)
    NumberTried = 0
    NumberCorrect = 0
    Shapes.SetText(TriedDisplay, "0")
    Shapes.SetText(CorrectDisplay, "0")
    GetProblem()
  Else
    Controls.SetButtonCaption(StartStopButton, "Start
Practice")
    Controls.ShowControl(ExitButton)
    Shapes.SetText(ProblemDisplay, "")
  EndIf
EndSub
```

This code uses a subroutine **GetProblem** to generate the random problem and display it in **ProblemDisplay**. Add this nearly empty procedure (we'll fill it in soon).

```
Sub GetProblem
  Shapes.SetText(ProblemDisplay, "Problem!!")
EndSub
```

Save and **Run** the project. Click **Start Practice** to make sure buttons change as planned. You will also see the generated "problem":

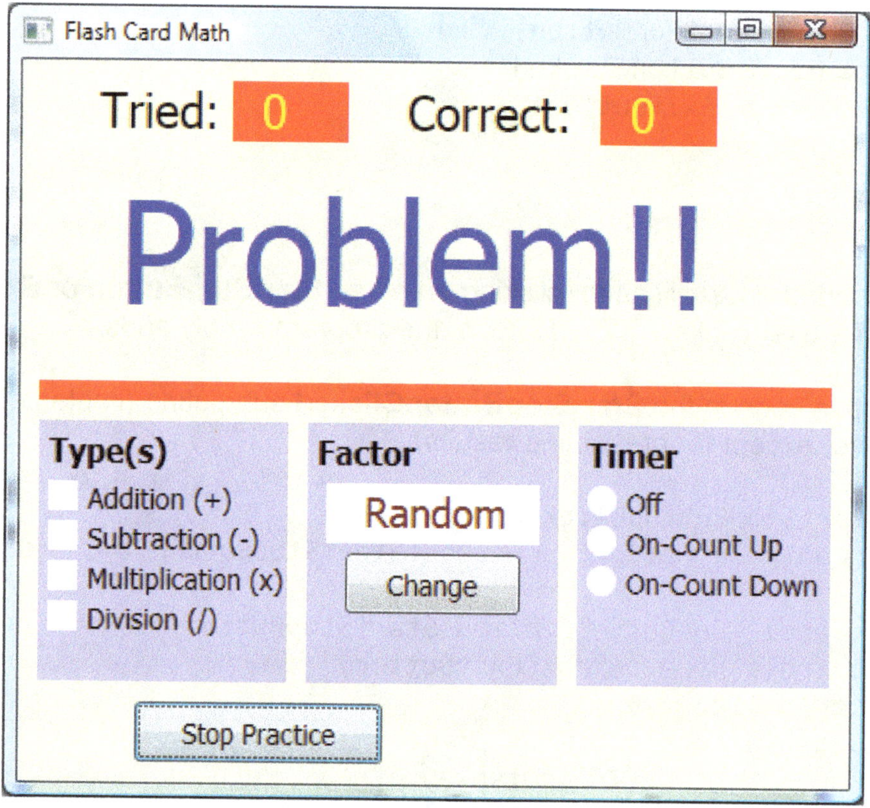

Now, click **Stop Practice**. Make sure **Exit** works.

This framework seems acceptable. We continue code design by discussing **problem generation** and **obtaining an answer** (including **scoring**) from the user. Then, later we discuss **timing** and **presenting the results**.

Code Design – Problem Generation

To generate a problem, we examine the current options selected by the user and produce a random problem based on these selections. All code will be in the **GetProblem** subroutine currently in the framework code. And, even though we are only using **Addition** problems with **Random** factors in this initial design, we will write code for all possibilities.

The steps involved in generating a random flash card problem are:

- Select problem type (random selection based on checked choices in **Type** box)
- Generate factor (based on selection in **Factor** box)
- Formulate problem and determine correct answer.
- Display problem in **ProblemDisplay** text shape, replacing correct answer with question marks (?) in place of digits. An example of the desired form of the returned value is:

  8 + 6 = ??

  where question marks tell the user how many digits are in the correct answer.
- Initialize **YourAnswer** to blank and **DigitNumber** (used to check if you have typed in all the digits to the answer).

Let's look at each step of the problem generation process. The first step is to choose a random problem type from the maximum of four possibilities. We will use a simple approach, first generating a random number from 1 to 4 (1 representing addition, 2 representing subtraction, 3 representing multiplication and 4 representing division). If the corresponding element of the **ProblemSelected** array is "**true**" (meaning that check box is checked), that will be the problem type. It that element of **ProblemSelected** is "**false**", we choose another random number. We continue this process until a problem type is selected. Notice this approach assumes at least one check box is always selected. We will make sure this is the case when developing code for the problem type option. There are more efficient ways to choose problem type which don't involve loops, but, for this simple problem, this works quite well.

A snippet of code that performs the choice of problem type (**ProblemType**) is:

```
ProblemType = 0
While (ProblemType = 0)
  P = Math.GetRandomNumber(4)
  If (P = 1 And ProblemSelected[1]) Then
    'Addition
    ProblemType = P
  ElseIf (P = 2 And ProblemSelected[2]) Then
    'Subtraction
    ProblemType = P
  ElseIf (P = 3 And ProblemSelected[3]) Then
    'Multiplication
    ProblemType = P
  ElseIf (P = 4 And ProblemSelected[4]) Then
    'Division
    ProblemType = P
  EndIf
EndWhile
```

Once a problem type is selected, we determine the factor used to generate a problem. It can be a selected value from 0 to 9, or a random value from 0 to 9, based on the value selected in the **Factor** box. For now, we assume that value is provided by a subroutine **GetFactor** that determines a **Factor** value, based on problem type **ProblemType**.

Each problem has four variables associated with it: **Factor**, representing the value returned by **GetFactor**, **Number**, the other number used in the math problem, **CorrectAnswer**, the problem answer, and **Problem**, a string representation of the unsolved problem. Once a problem type and factor have been determined, we find values for each of these variables. Each problem type has unique considerations for problem generation. Let's look at each type.

For **Addition** problems (**ProblemType = 1**), the selected factor is the second **addend** in the problem. The string form of addition problems (**Problem**) will be:

Number + Factor =

where **Number** is a random value from 0 to 9, while recall **Factor** is the selected factor. A snippet of code to generate an addition problem and determine the **CorrectAnswer** is:

```
Number = Math.GetRandomNumber(10) - 1
GetFactor()
CorrectAnswer = Number + Factor
Problem = Number + " + " + Factor + " = "
```

For **Subtraction** problems (**ProblemType = 2**), the factor is the **subtrahend** (the number being subtracted). The string form of subtraction problems (**Problem**) will be:

Number - Factor =

We want all the possible answers to be positive numbers between 0 and 9. Because of this, we formulate the problem in a backwards sense, generating a random answer (**CorrectAnswer**), then computing **Number** based on that answer and the known factor (**Factor**). The code that does this is:

```
GetFactor()
CorrectAnswer = Math.GetRandomNumber(10) - 1
Number = CorrectAnswer + Factor
Problem = Number + " - " + Factor + " = "
```

For **Multiplication** problems (**ProblemType = 3**), the selected factor is the **multiplier** (the number you're multiplying by) in the problem. The string form of multiplication problems (**Problem**) will be:

Number x Factor =

where **Number** is a random value from 0 to 9, and **Factor** is the factor. A snippet of code to generate a multiplication problem and the **CorrectAnswer** is:

```
Number = Math.GetRandomNumber(10) - 1
GetFactor()
CorrectAnswer = Number * Factor
Problem = Number + " x " + Factor + " = "
```

For **Division** problems (**ProblemType = 4**), the factor is the **divisor** (the number doing the dividing). The string form of division problems (**Problem**) will be:

Number / Factor =

Like in subtraction, we want all the possible answers to be positive numbers between 0 and 9. So, we again formulate the problem in a backwards sense, generating a random answer (**CorrectAnswer**), then computing **Number** based on that answer and the known factor (**Factor**). The code that does this is:

```
GetFactor()
CorrectAnswer = Math.GetRandomNumber(10) - 1
Number = CorrectAnswer * Factor
Problem = Number + " / " + Factor + " = "
```

Note with division, we must make sure the factor is never zero (can't divide by zero).

The **GetFactor** routine provides the factor based on the selected value (**FactorChoice**) in the **Factor** box and problem type **ProblemType**. For random factors, it will make sure a zero is not returned if a division problem is being generated. The **GetFactor** subroutine is thus:

```
Sub GetFactor
  If (FactorChoice = -1) Then
    If (ProblemType = 4) Then
      Factor = Math.GetRandomNumber(9)
    Else
      Factor = Math.GetRandomNumber(10) - 1
    EndIf
  Else
    Factor = FactorChoice
  EndIf
EndSub
```

If the Random (**FactorChoice = -1**) option is selected, 0 to 9 is returned for addition, subtraction and multiplication problems; 1 to 9 is returned for division problems (**ProblemType = 4**). In other cases, the selected factor is returned (we will have to make sure zero is not a choice when doing division).

The **GetProblem** subroutine is nearly complete. We want to return the **Problem** variable with appended question marks that represent the number of digits (**NumberDigits**) in the correct answer and we need to initialize **YourAnswer** and **DigitNumber**. The code snippet that does this is:

```
If (CorrectAnswer < 10) Then
  NumberDigits = 1
  Shapes.SetText(ProblemDisplay, Problem + "?")
Else
  NumberDigits = 2
  Shapes.SetText(ProblemDisplay, Problem + "??")
EndIf
YourAnswer = ""
DigitNumber = 1
```

We can now assemble all the little code snippets into a final form for the **GetProblem** subroutine. To build the **GetProblem** subroutine, first eliminate the single line of code that displays "**Problem!!**". Then, start with the snippet that selects problem type. Add each problem generation segment (one for each of the four mathematical operations) in its corresponding location. Finally, add the question mark appending code. The finished function is:

```
Sub GetProblem
  ProblemType = 0
  While (ProblemType = 0)
    P = Math.GetRandomNumber(4)
    If (P = 1 And ProblemSelected[1]) Then
      'Addition
      ProblemType = P
      Number = Math.GetRandomNumber(10) - 1
      GetFactor()
      CorrectAnswer = Number + Factor
      Problem = Number + " + " + Factor + " = "
    ElseIf (P = 2 And ProblemSelected[2]) Then
      'Subtraction
      ProblemType = P
      GetFactor()
      CorrectAnswer = Math.GetRandomNumber(10) - 1
      Number = CorrectAnswer + Factor
      Problem = Number + " - " + Factor + " = "
    ElseIf (P = 3 And ProblemSelected[3]) Then
      'Multiplication
      ProblemType = P
      Number = Math.GetRandomNumber(10) - 1
      GetFactor()
      CorrectAnswer = Number * Factor
      Problem = Number + " x " + Factor + " = "
    ElseIf (P = 4 And ProblemSelected[4]) Then
      'Division
      ProblemType = P
      GetFactor()
      CorrectAnswer = Math.GetRandomNumber(10) - 1
      Number = CorrectAnswer * Factor
      Problem = Number + " / " + Factor + " = "
    EndIf
  EndWhile
  If (CorrectAnswer < 10) Then
    NumberDigits = 1
    Shapes.SetText(ProblemDisplay, Problem + "?")
  Else
    NumberDigits = 2
```

```
    Shapes.SetText(ProblemDisplay, Problem + "??")
  EndIf
EndSub
```

Add this to the project along with the code for **GetFactor**.

Save and **Run** the project. Click **Start Practice** and you should see a random addition problem:

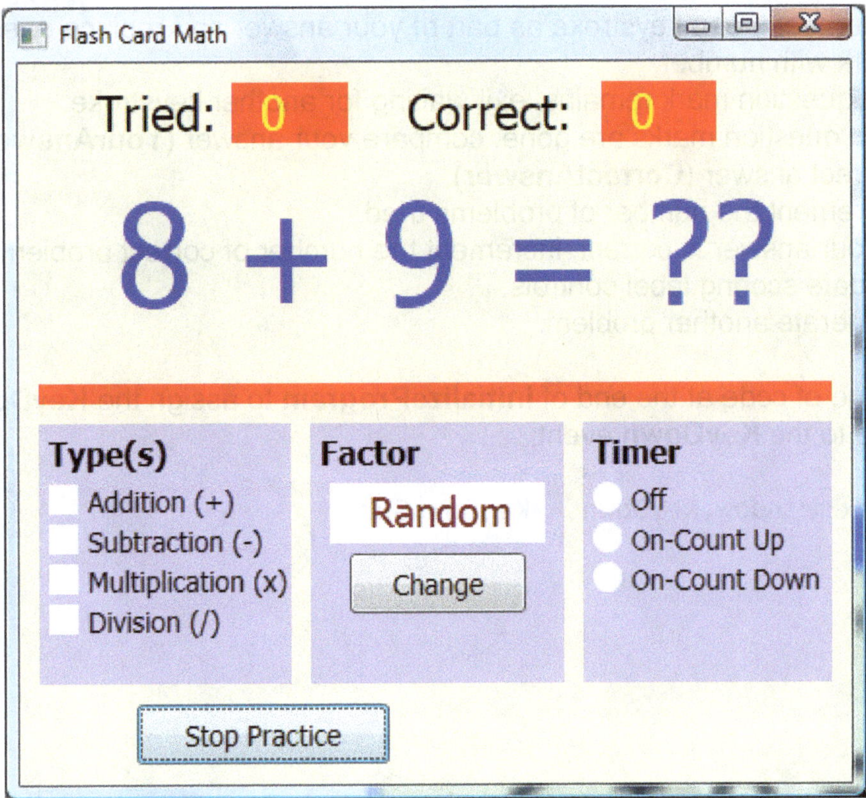

The two question marks tell us there are two digits in the correct answer. We'll see how to get that answer next. At this point, all you can do is click **Stop Practice**. You can then click **Start Practice** to see another addition problem if you'd like. View as many random addition problems as you want.

Code Design – Obtaining Answer

Once a problem is displayed, the user can enter the digits in the answer. These digits will be entered using the keyboard. The keystrokes will be handled by the graphics window **KeyDown** event.

The steps for obtaining and checking an answer are:

- Make sure keystroke is a number (0 to 9).
- If number, keep keystroke as part of your answer and replace question mark with number.
- If a question mark remains, exit waiting for another keystroke.
- If all question marks are gone, compare your answer (**YourAnswer**) with correct answer (**CorrectAnswer**).
- Increment the number of problems tried.
- If your answer is correct, increment the number of correct problems.
- Update scoring label controls.
- Generate another problem.

Add this line of code at the end of **InitializeProgram** to assign the **KeyDownSub** subroutine to the **KeyDown** event:

```
GraphicsWindow.KeyDown = KeyDownSub
```

The **KeyDownSub** subroutine that incorporates the steps listed above is then:

```
Sub KeyDownSub
  If (Controls.GetButtonCaption(StartStopButton) = "Stop
Practice") Then
    'can only check keystrokes when practicing-only allow
number keys
    'number is last character in keypressed
    KeyPressed = Text.GetSubTextToEnd(GraphicsWindow.LastKey,
Text.GetLength(GraphicsWindow.LastKey))
    If (Text.GetCharacterCode(KeyPressed) >=
Text.GetCharacterCode("0") And
Text.GetCharacterCode(KeyPressed) <=
Text.GetCharacterCode("9")) Then
      YourAnswer = Text.Append(YourAnswer, KeyPressed)
      If DigitNumber <> NumberDigits Then
        DigitNumber = DigitNumber + 1
        Shapes.SetText(ProblemDisplay, Problem + YourAnswer +
"?")
      Else
        NumberTried = NumberTried + 1
        'check answer
        If (YourAnswer = CorrectAnswer) Then
          NumberCorrect = NumberCorrect + 1
        EndIf
        Shapes.SetText(TriedDisplay, NumberTried)
        Shapes.SetText(CorrectDisplay, NumberCorrect)
        GetProblem()
      EndIf
    EndIf
  EndIf
EndSub
```

In the first few lines of code, we make sure we are solving problems before allowing any keystrokes. Notice how all digits in your answer (represented by the typed character in **KeyPressed**) are saved and concatenated into **YourAnswer**. Also, notice how the displayed problem is updated, overwriting a question mark, with each keystroke. As mentioned earlier, the program only gives you one chance to enter an answer - there is no erasing.

Save and **Run** the project. You should now be able to answer as many random addition problems as you'd like. Try it. Make sure the score is updating properly. Here's my window after trying a few problems:

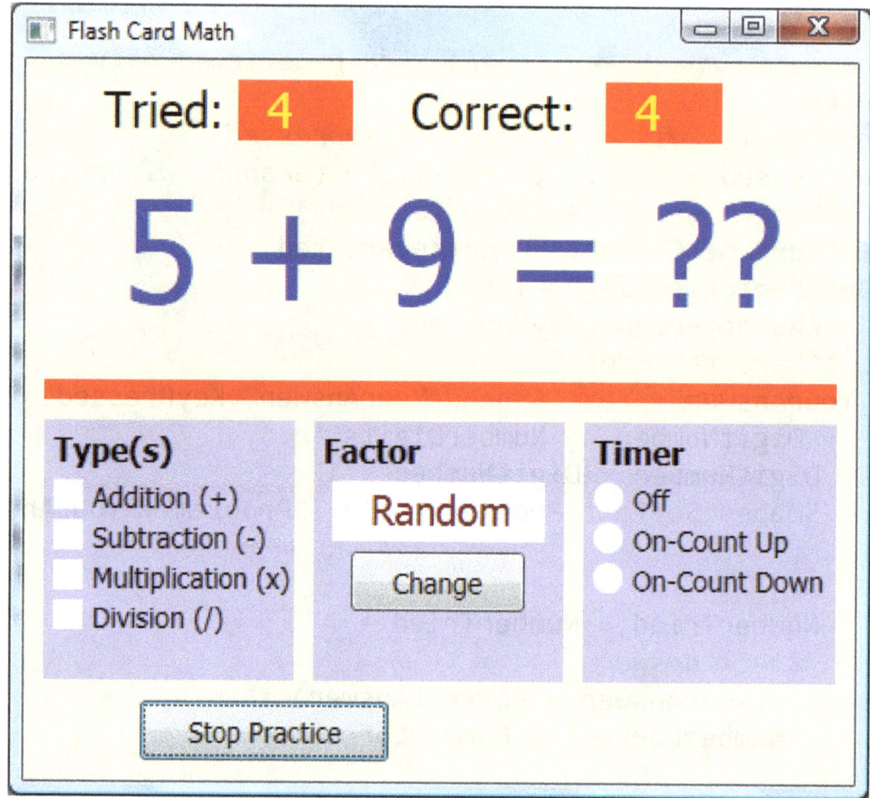

You can stop practicing problems, at any time, by clicking the **Stop Practice** button. Random addition problems will get boring after a while. Let's add the logic for other problem types and other factors.

Code Design – Choosing Problem Type

The selection of problem type seems simple. Choose the check box or check boxes you want and the correct problem will be generated. But there are a couple of problems we've alluded to. We need to keep a user from "unchecking" all the boxes, leaving no problem type to select. We must make sure at least one box is always selected. And, if **Division** problems are selected, we cannot allow zero (0) to be used as a factor.

Here, we write code to mark and unmark check boxes and to address the first problem (always having one problem selected). The problem of a zero factor in division problems is addressed when we discuss factors in the next section. Let's review the location of each check box (all squares with 15 pixel sides). This will define the 'clickable' areas.

Addition – Check box is at (15, 210)
Subtraction – Check box is at (15, 230)
Multiplication – Check box is at (15, 250)
Division – Check box is at (15, 270)

To allow detection of mouse clicks, add this single line of code at the end of **InitializeProgram**:

```
GraphicsWindow.MouseDown = MouseDownSub
```

Now, in the **MouseDownSub** subroutine, we do the following:

- Determine which check box was clicked (**ProblemTypeClicked**).
- If clicked box is checked (**ProblemSelected** is "**true**"), uncheck the box unless the number of boxes checked (**Selections**) is one. Decrement **Selections** if possible.
- If selected box is unchecked (**ProblemSelected** is "**false**"), check the box and increment **Selections**.

The initial selection is **Addition** problems. Add this initialization code to **InitializeProgram** after the code setting the initial values of the **ProblemSelected** array.

```
Selections = 1
ProblemTypeClicked = 1
MarkProblemType()
```

Note the initialization code calls a subroutine (**MarkProblemType**) to place an initial check mark next to **Addition**. That routine is:

```
Sub MarkProblemType
  If (ProblemTypeClicked < 0) Then
    ProblemTypeClicked = Math.Abs(ProblemTypeClicked)
    GraphicsWindow.BrushColor = "White"
    GraphicsWindow.FillRectangle(15, 190 + ProblemTypeClicked *
20, 15, 15)
  Else
    GraphicsWindow.PenColor = "Black"
    GraphicsWindow.PenWidth = 1
    GraphicsWindow.DrawLine(18, 199 + ProblemTypeClicked * 20,
22, 203 + ProblemTypeClicked * 20)
    GraphicsWindow.DrawLine(22, 203 + ProblemTypeClicked * 20,
28, 191 + ProblemTypeClicked * 20)
  EndIf
EndSub
```

This subroutine will place a check mark (drawn using two **DrawLine** methods within the selected check box) when **ProblemTypeClicked** is positive. When **ProblemTypeClicked** is negative, the check mark is removed (the box is cleared).

With this information, the **MouseDownSub** procedure that implements the needed steps is:

```
Sub MouseDownSub
  X = GraphicsWindow.MouseX
  Y = GraphicsWindow.MouseY
  'problem selections - must always have at least one selected
  If (X > 15 And X < 30 And Y > 210 And Y < 285) Then
    If (Y > 210 And Y < 225) Then
      'clicked addition
      ProblemTypeClicked = 1
    ElseIf (Y > 230 And Y < 245) Then
      'clicked subtraction
      ProblemTypeClicked = 2
    ElseIf (Y > 250 And Y < 265) Then
      'clicked multiplication
      ProblemTypeClicked = 3
    ElseIf (Y > 270 And Y < 285) Then
      'clicked division
      ProblemTypeClicked = 4
    EndIf
    If (ProblemSelected[ProblemTypeClicked] And Selections <>
1) Then
      'clear choice if not last one selected
      Selections = Selections - 1
      ProblemSelected[ProblemTypeClicked] = "false"
      ProblemTypeClicked = -ProblemTypeClicked
      MarkProblemType()
    ElseIf (ProblemSelected[ProblemTypeClicked] = "false") Then
      'mark choice
      Selections = Selections + 1
      ProblemSelected[ProblemTypeClicked] = "true"
      MarkProblemType()
    EndIf
  EndIf
EndSub
```

You should be able to see how the various steps are implemented. In particular, note when a box is to be cleared, the **ProblemTypeClicked** is converted to a negative number before calling **MarkProblemType**. Enter this code into your project.

Save and **Run** the project. Make sure all the newly installed code is doing its job. Try to "uncheck" all the problem type boxes – one box will always remain. You can now solve any problem type. If you change options while solving problems, the changes will be seen once you finish solving the current problem. Try solving problems, changing problem type. Here's my window while solving a division problem (note the check marks):

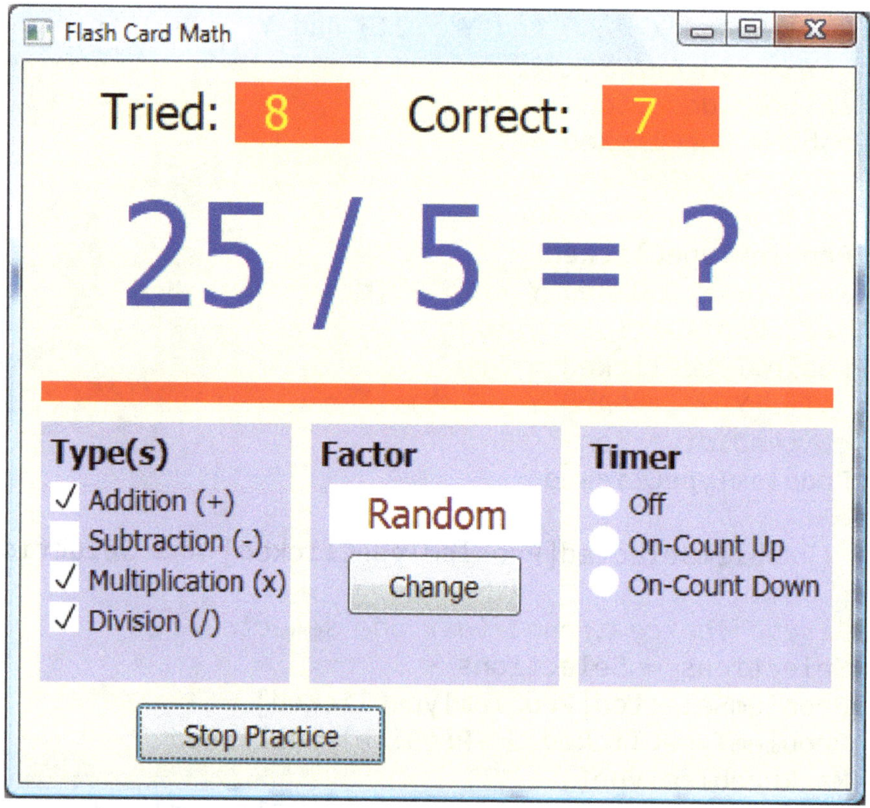

Next, we remove the random factor restriction.

Code Design – Changing Factor

Thus far, we have only used a random factor in problems. To add the capability of other factors, we need code for clicking the **FactorButton**. With each click of that button, we cycle through values of **FactorChoice** (0 through 9, -1 for random factors) and display that choice in the text shape (**FactorDisplay**).

Add the shaded code to **ButtonClickSub** to detect clicks of **FactorButton**:

```
Sub ButtonClickedSub
  B = Controls.LastClickedButton
  If (B = StartStopButton) Then
    StartStopButtonClicked()
  ElseIf (B = ExitButton) Then
    Program.End()
  ElseIf (B = FactorButton) Then
    FactorButtonClicked()
  EndIf
EndSub
```

Add the **FactorButtonClicked** subroutine to cycle through and display factor values:

```
Sub FactorButtonClicked
  'change factor choice
  FactorChoice = FactorChoice + 1
  If (FactorChoice > 9) Then
    FactorChoice = -1
    Shapes.SetText(FactorDisplay, "Random")
  Else
    Shapes.SetText(FactorDisplay, Text.Append("     ",
FactorChoice))
  EndIf
EndSub
```

Save and **Run** the program. Click **Start Practice**. Click **Change** and watch the values change. Here is my window showing an **Addition** problem with a selected **Factor** of 6:

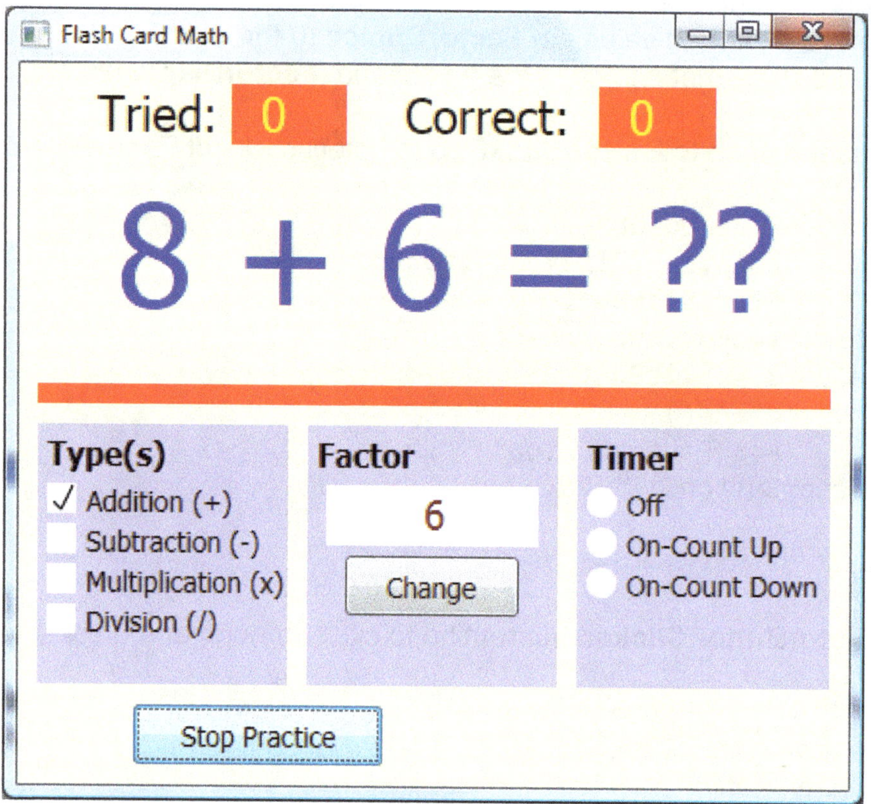

We need two changes related to not allowing a zero factor for **Division** problems. First, make the shaded change to the **FactorButtonClicked** subroutine:

```
Sub FactorButtonClicked
  'change factor choice
  FactorChoice = FactorChoice + 1
  If (FactorChoice > 9) Then
    FactorChoice = -1
    Shapes.SetText(FactorDisplay, "Random")
  Else
    If (ProblemSelected[4] And FactorChoice = 0) Then
      'no zero if doing division
      FactorChoice = 1
    EndIf
    Shapes.SetText(FactorDisplay, Text.Append("      ",
FactorChoice))
  EndIf
EndSub
```

Here, if **Division** is a selected problem type and a zero factor is selected, the zero factor will be skipped over.

Second, make the shaded change to the **MouseDownSub** subroutine:

```
Sub MouseDownSub
  X = GraphicsWindow.MouseX
  Y = GraphicsWindow.MouseY
  'problem selections - must always have at least one selected
  If (X > 15 And X < 30 And Y > 210 And Y < 285) Then
    If (Y > 210 And Y < 225) Then
     'clicked addition
     ProblemTypeClicked = 1
    ElseIf (Y > 230 And Y < 245) Then
      'clicked subtraction
      ProblemTypeClicked = 2
    ElseIf (Y > 250 And Y < 265) Then
      'clicked multiplication
     ProblemTypeClicked = 3
    ElseIf (Y > 270 And Y < 285) Then
     'clicked division
      ProblemTypeClicked = 4
    EndIf
    If (ProblemSelected[ProblemTypeClicked] And Selections <>
1) Then
      'clear choice if not last one selected
      Selections = Selections - 1
```

```
        ProblemSelected[ProblemTypeClicked] = "false"
        ProblemTypeClicked = -ProblemTypeClicked
        MarkProblemType()
      ElseIf (ProblemSelected[ProblemTypeClicked] = "false") Then
        'mark choice
        Selections = Selections + 1
        ProblemSelected[ProblemTypeClicked] = "true"
        MarkProblemType()
        'make sure zero not selected factor if division selected
        If (ProblemTypeClicked = 4 And FactorChoice = 0) Then
          FactorButtonClicked()
        EndIf
      EndIf
    EndIf
  EndSub
```

In this added code, if a user selects **Division** and zero is the factor, we simulate a click on **FactorButton** to increment the factor to one.

Save and **Run** the program again. Check **Division** problems. Click on the **Change** button and notice the zero factor never appears. Uncheck **Division** problems. Choose 0 as a factor using the **Change** button. Now, check **Division** again. Notice the factor is changed to 1 and the 0 option does not appear with subsequent clicks on **Change**. You can now solve any problem type with any factor.

Code Design – Timing Options

Having coded problem generation and answer checking, we can now address the use of timing in the flash card math project. Up to now, we've assumed the timer is off (**TimerChoice = 0**). We have two possibilities for a timer: (1) one where the timer counts up, keeping track how long you are solving problems (**TimerChoice = 1**), and (2) one where the timer counts down from some preset value (**TimerChoice = 2**). In both cases, a text shape (**TimeDisplay**) displays the time in **minutes:seconds** form. In the second case, two button controls (**TimerMinusButton** and **TimerPlusButton**) are used to set the value. The timing will be controlled with a **Timer** object with an interval of 1 second (1000 milliseconds).

We allow changing problem type and factors while solving problems. It wouldn't make sense to be able to change timer options while solving problems – the times would not be correct. We will only allow selection of timer options prior to clicking **Start Practice**. First, we write code to mark the circles next to the three timing options (only one option can be selected). Here are the locations of the circles (all 15 pixel diameters). This will define the 'clickable' areas.

Off – Circle is at (295, 210)
On, Count Up – Circle is at (295, 230)
On, Count Down – Circle is at (295, 250)

Add the shaded code to **ButtonDownSub** to detect the appropriate mouse clicks:

```
Sub MouseDownSub
  X = GraphicsWindow.MouseX
  Y = GraphicsWindow.MouseY
  'problem selections - must always have at least one selected
   .
   .
  If (Controls.GetButtonCaption(StartStopButton) = "Start
Practice") Then
    'timer selections - only one can be selected
    If (X > 295 And X < 310 And Y > 210 And Y < 265) Then
      'problem selections - must always have at least one
selected
      If (Y > 210 And Y < 225) Then
        'clicked timer off
        TimerChoice = 0
        MarkTimerChoice()
      ElseIf (Y > 230 And Y < 245) Then
        'clicked timer on - count up
        TimerChoice = 1
        MarkTimerChoice()
      ElseIf (Y > 250 And Y < 265) Then
        'clicked timer on - count down
        TimerChoice = 2
        MarkTimerChoice()
      EndIf
    EndIf
  EndIf
EndSub
```

Note changes can only be made when **StartStopButton** displays a **Start Practice** caption.

This code uses a subroutine (**MarkTimerChoice**) to mark the selected option and unmark the others. That routine is:

```
Sub MarkTimerChoice
  GraphicsWindow.BrushColor = "White"
  GraphicsWindow.FillEllipse(295, 210, 15, 15)
  GraphicsWindow.FillEllipse(295, 230, 15, 15)
  GraphicsWindow.FillEllipse(295, 250, 15, 15)
  GraphicsWindow.BrushColor = "SlateGray"
  GraphicsWindow.FillEllipse(298, 213 + TimerChoice * 20, 9, 9)
EndSub
```

The initial selection is **Off**. Add this line after the line setting the initial value of **TimerChoice** in **InitializeProgram**:

```
MarkTimerChoice()
```

Save and **Run** the program. Notice the initial selection of the **Off** option:

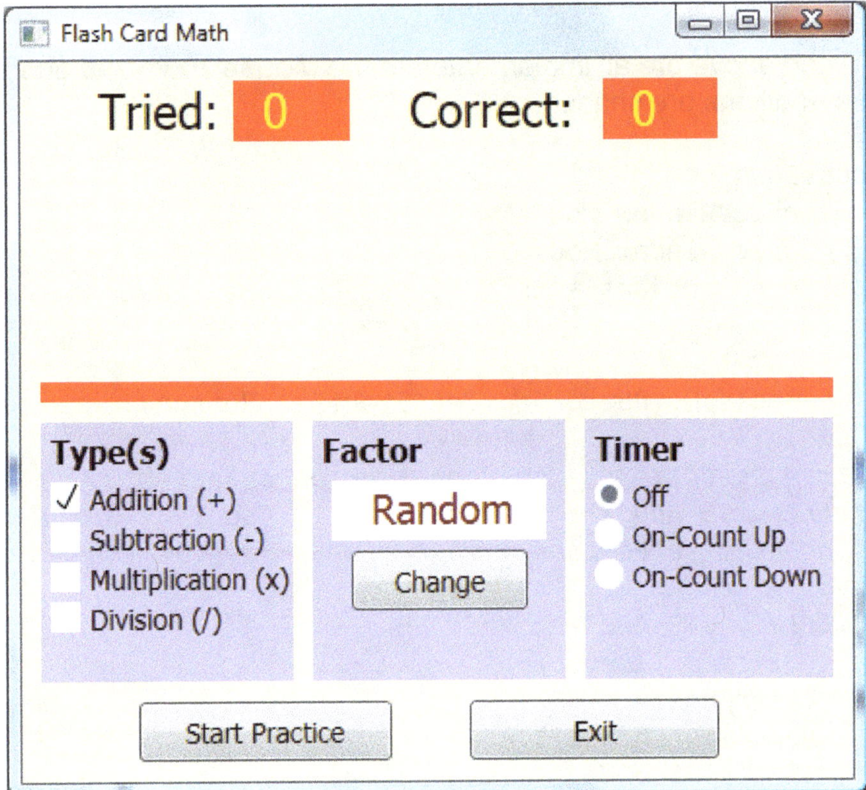

Choose other **Timer** options to make sure proper marking is done.

Other steps must be followed when we switch from one timing option to the next. We will use a variable (**ProblemTime**) to store the time value (whether counting up or down) in seconds. When counting down, **ProblemTime** will start at 30 times **TimerIndex** (a value set by the two timer control buttons). Those steps followed when changing options are:

- If Off (**TimerChoice = 0**) is selected: hide **TimerDisplay, TimerMinusButton, TimerPlusButton**.
- If On-Count Up (**TimerChoice = 1**) is selected, show **TimerDisplay** and hide **TimerMinusButton** and **TimerPlusButton**. Initialize **ProblemTime** to 0. Display **ProblemTime**.
- If On-Count Down (**TimerChoice = 2**) is selected, show **TimerDisplay**, **TimerMinusButton, TimerPlusButton.** Initialize **ProblemTime** to 30 times **TimerIndex**. Display **ProblemTime**.

Before attacking this code, add a line to **InitializeProgram** (after the call to **MarkTimerChoice**) setting an initial value for **TimerIndex**:

```
TimerIndex = 1
```

The steps listed above are all implemented in the **MouseDownSub** subroutine. The needed additions are shaded:

```
Sub MouseDownSub
  X = GraphicsWindow.MouseX
  Y = GraphicsWindow.MouseY
  'problem selections - must always have at least one selected
  .
  .
  If (Controls.GetButtonCaption(StartStopButton) = "Start
Practice") Then
    'timer selections - only one can be selected
    If (X > 295 And X < 310 And Y > 210 And Y < 265) Then
      'problem selections - must always have at least one
selected
      If (Y > 210 And Y < 225) Then
        'clicked timer off
        TimerChoice = 0
        MarkTimerChoice()
        Shapes.HideShape(TimeDisplay)
        Controls.HideControl(TimerMinusButton)
        Controls.HideControl(TimerPlusButton)
      ElseIf (Y > 230 And Y < 245) Then
        'clicked timer on - count up
        TimerChoice = 1
        MarkTimerChoice()
```

```
          Shapes.ShowShape(TimeDisplay)
          Controls.HideControl(TimerMinusButton)
          Controls.HideControl(TimerPlusButton)
          ProblemTime = 0
          FormatTime()
          Shapes.SetText(TimeDisplay, FormattedTime)
        ElseIf (Y > 250 And Y < 265) Then
          'clicked timer on - count down
          TimerChoice = 2
          MarkTimerChoice()
          Shapes.ShowShape(TimeDisplay)
          Controls.ShowControl(TimerMinusButton)
          Controls.ShowControl(TimerPlusButton)
          ProblemTime = 30 * TimerIndex
          FormatTime()
          Shapes.SetText(TimeDisplay, FormattedTime)
        EndIf
      EndIf
    EndIf
  EndSub
```

This subroutine uses another subroutine **FormatTime** that converts **ProblemTime** (seconds) as a **FormattedTime** in 00:00 format:

```
Sub FormatTime
  Minutes = Math.Floor(ProblemTime / 60)
  Seconds = ProblemTime - Minutes * 60
  If (Seconds < 10) Then
    FormattedTime = Minutes + ":0" + Seconds
  Else
    FormattedTime = Minutes + ":" + Seconds
  EndIf
EndSub
```

This subroutine takes the time (**ProblemTime**) in seconds and breaks it into minutes and seconds. Add this new code to your project.

Let's check both timer options to make sure the window changes as desired. **Save** and **Run** the program. Click **On-Count Up**. You should see:

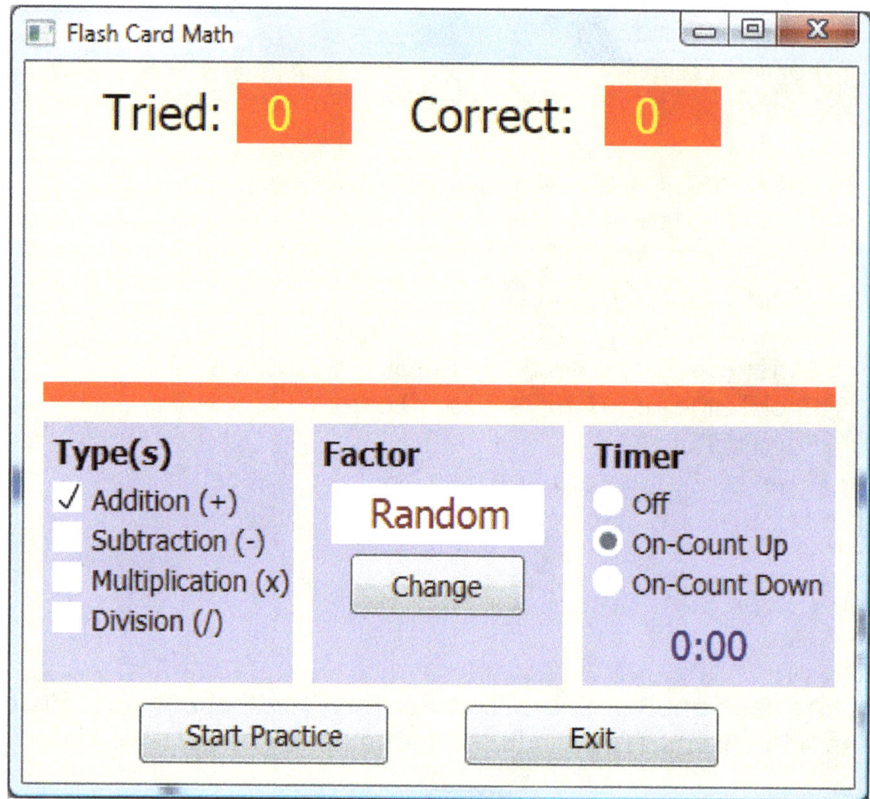

The 'count-up' time is displayed.

Now, choose **On-Count Down** to see:

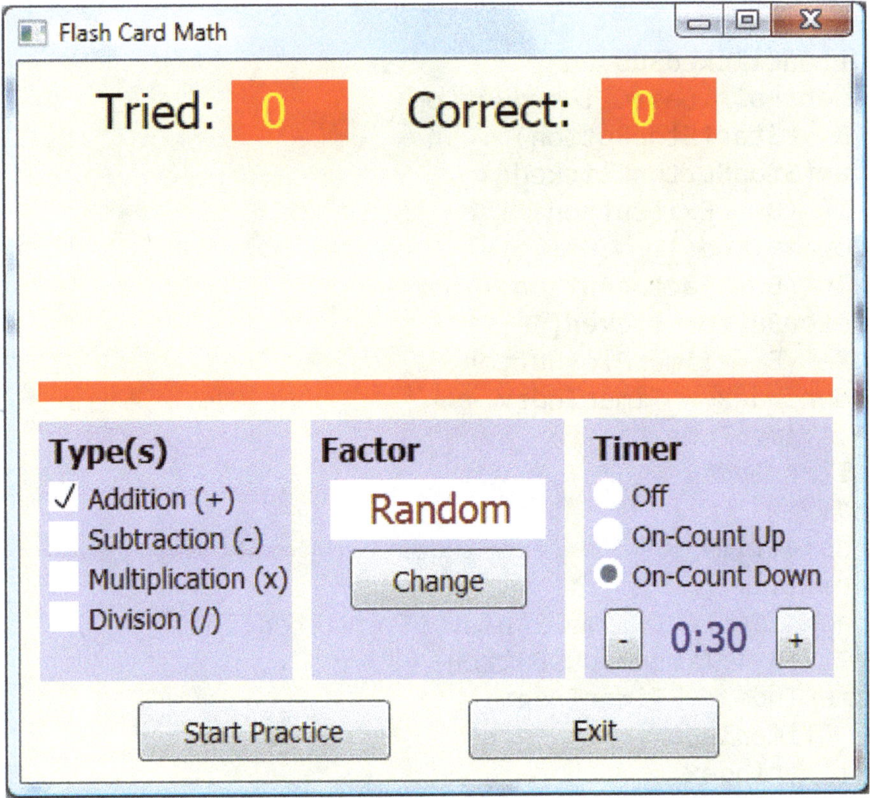

The 'count-down' time is displayed along with adjustment button controls. In this mode, **TimerIndex** is used to initialize the **ProblemTime** variable. This value is changed by clicking on the +/- control buttons (**TimerPlusButton** and **TimerMinusButton**). We will keep **TimerIndex** between 1 and 60. This allows a maximum of 30 minutes (1800 seconds) for a timed flash card math session.

Add the shaded code to **ButtonClickedSub** to detect clicking on these buttons and adjustment of the **TimerIndex** value (along with the **TimeDisplay**):

```
Sub ButtonClickedSub
  B = Controls.LastClickedButton
  If (B = StartStopButton) Then
    StartStopButtonClicked()
  ElseIf (B = ExitButton) Then
    Program.End()
  ElseIf (B = FactorButton) Then
    FactorButtonClicked()
  ElseIf (B = TimerPlusButton) Then
    TimerIndex = TimerIndex + 1
    If (TimerIndex > 60) Then
      TimerIndex = 60
    EndIf
    ProblemTime = 30 * TimerIndex
    FormatTime()
    Shapes.SetText(TimeDisplay, FormattedTime)
  ElseIf (B = TimerMinusButton) Then
    TimerIndex = TimerIndex - 1
    If (TimerIndex < 1) Then
      TimerIndex = 1
    EndIf
    ProblemTime = 30 * TimerIndex
    FormatTime()
    Shapes.SetText(TimeDisplay, FormattedTime)
  EndIf
EndSub
```

A **Timer** object will be used to control the time display. Add these at the end of **InitializeProgram** to set the **Interval** and establish the **Tick** event subroutine (**TimerTickSub**):

```
Timer.Interval = 1000
Timer.Tick = TimerTickSub
Timer.Pause()
```

Clicking **Start Practice** will start the timing process; the steps are:

- If **Off** (**TimerChoice = 0**) is selected, do nothing else.
- If **On-Count Up** (**TimerChoice = 1**) is selected:
  - Initialize **ProblemTime** to zero; display **ProblemTime**.
  - Start timer.
- If **On-Count Down** (**TimerChoice = 2**) is selected:
  - Initialize **ProblemTime** to 30 times **TimerIndex**; display **ProblemTime**.
  - Hide **TimerPlusButton** and **TimerMinusButton**.
  - Start timer.

Clicking **Stop Practice** will stop the timing process. The corresponding steps:

- Stop timer.
- Show **TimerPlusButton** and **TimerMinusButton** if **TimerChoice = 2**.

Each of these steps is handled in the **StartStopButton** subroutine. The modified procedure (changes are shaded) is:

```
Sub StartStopButtonClicked
  If (Controls.GetButtonCaption(StartStopButton) = "Start
Practice") Then
    Controls.SetButtonCaption(StartStopButton, "Stop Practice")
    Controls.HideControl(ExitButton)
    NumberTried = 0
    NumberCorrect = 0
    Shapes.SetText(TriedDisplay, "0")
    Shapes.SetText(CorrectDisplay, "0")
    GetProblem()
    If (TimerChoice <> 0) Then
      If (TimerChoice = 1) Then
        ProblemTime = 0
      Else
        ProblemTime = 30 * TimerIndex
        Controls.HideControl(TimerMinusButton)
        Controls.HideControl(TimerPlusButton)
      EndIf
      FormatTime()
```

```
      Shapes.SetText(TimeDisplay, FormattedTime)
      Timer.Resume()
    EndIf
  Else
    Controls.SetButtonCaption(StartStopButton, "Start
Practice")
    Controls.ShowControl(ExitButton)
    Shapes.SetText(ProblemDisplay, "")
    Timer.Pause()
    If (TimerChoice = 2) Then
      Controls.ShowControl(TimerMinusButton)
      Controls.ShowControl(TimerPlusButton)
    EndIf
  EndIf
EndSub
```

Make the indicated changes. We're almost ready to try the timing – just one more procedure to code.

When the timer is running, the time display (**TimeDisplay**) is updated every second (we use an **Interval** property of 1000). The displayed time is incremented if counting up, decremented if counting down. The steps involved for counting up are:

- Increment **ProblemTime** by 1.
- Display **ProblemTime**.
- If **ProblemTime** is 1800 (30 minutes), stop solving problems.

Note we limit the total solving time to 30 minutes.

The steps for counting down are:

- Decrement **ProblemTime** by 1.
- Display **ProblemTime**.
- If **ProblemTime** is 0, stop solving problems.

The code to update the displayed time is placed in the **TimerTickSub** subroutine. The code that implements the above steps are:

```
Sub TimerTickSub
  If (TimerChoice = 1) Then
    ProblemTime = ProblemTime + 1
    FormatTime()
    Shapes.SetText(TimeDisplay, FormattedTime)
    If ProblemTime >= 1800 Then
      StartStopButtonClicked()
    EndIf
  Else
    ProblemTime = ProblemTime - 1
    FormatTime()
    Shapes.SetText(TimeDisplay, FormattedTime)
    If (ProblemTime = 0) Then
      StartStopButtonClicked()
    EndIf
  EndIf
EndSub
```

Notice to stop solving problems, we simulate a click on **Stop Practice** (the **StartStopButton** button). Add this procedure to the project.

We're done implementing the modifications to add timing in the flash card math project. **Save** and **Run** the project. You want to make sure all the timer options work correctly. First, check to see that the project still works correctly with no timer.

Once you are convinced the no timer option still works, stop solving problems and choose the **On-Count Up** option. **Run** the project. Make sure the timer increments properly. Here's a run I just started:

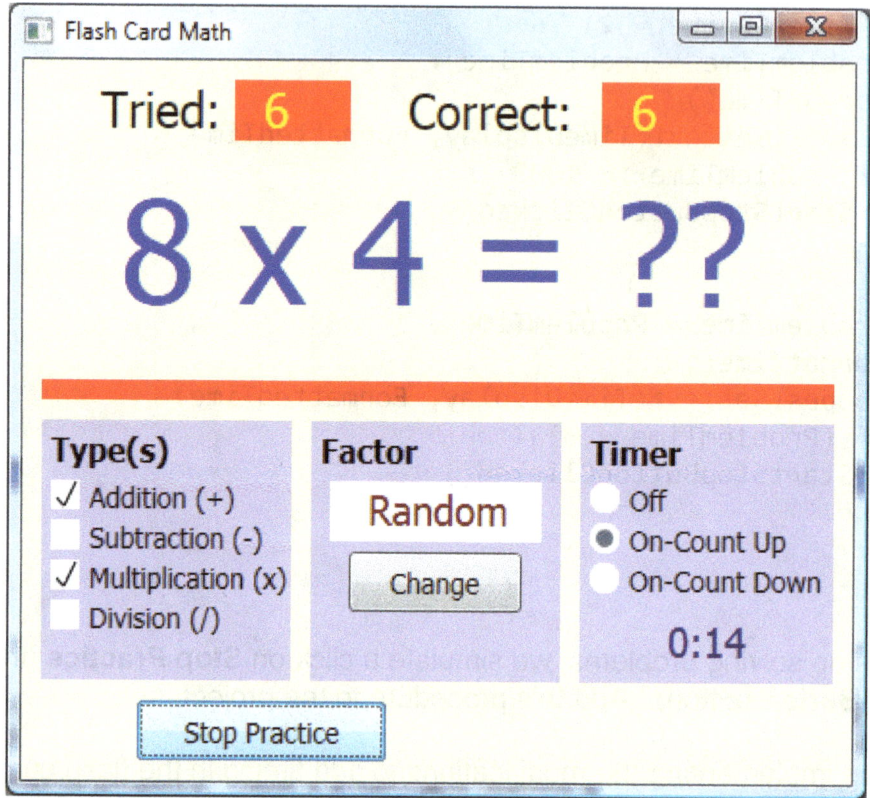

Click **Stop Practice** at some point. You should also make sure the program automatically stops after 30 minutes (go have lunch while the program runs).

Choose the **On-Count Down** option. Change the amount of allowed time using the vertical scroll bar. Make sure it reaches a maximum of 30:00 (it has a minimum of 0:30). **Run** the project. Make sure the time decrements correctly. Here's a run I made using a starting time of 1:00:

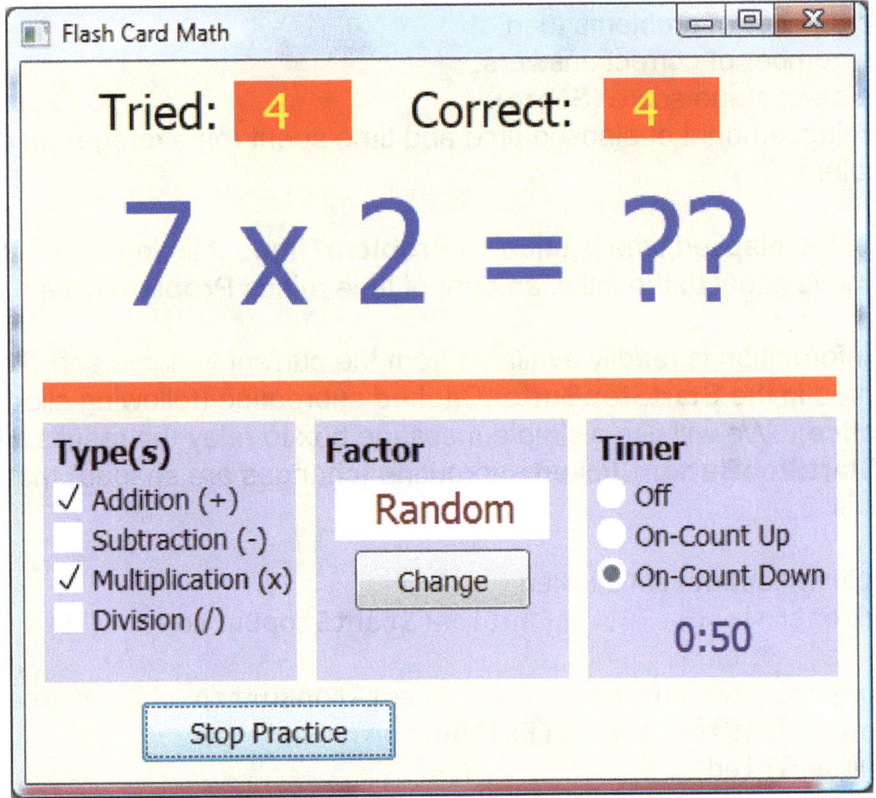

Make sure the program stops once the time elapses.

Code Design – Presenting Results

Once a user stops solving problems, we want to let he/she know how well they did in answering problems. The information of use would be:

- The number of problems tried.
- The number of correct answers.
- The percentage score (**Score**).
- If timing, amount of elapsed time and time spent (on average) on each problem.

If timing up, the elapsed time is equal to **ProblemTime**. If timing down, the elapsed time is equal to the initial amount of time minus **ProblemTime**.

All of this information is readily available from the current variable set. The results are presented in the **StartStopButtonClicked** subroutine (following clicking of **Stop Practice**). We will use a simple message box to relay the results. The modified **StartStopButtonClicked** subroutine (changes are shaded) that displays the results is:

```
Sub StartStopButtonClicked
  If (Controls.GetButtonCaption(StartStopButton) = "Start
Practice") Then
    Controls.SetButtonCaption(StartStopButton, "Stop Practice")
    Controls.HideControl(ExitButton)
    NumberTried = 0
    NumberCorrect = 0
    Shapes.SetText(TriedDisplay, "0")
    Shapes.SetText(CorrectDisplay, "0")
    GetProblem()
    If (TimerChoice <> 0) Then
      If (TimerChoice = 1) Then
        ProblemTime = 0
      Else
        ProblemTime = 30 * TimerIndex
        Controls.HideControl(TimerMinusButton)
        Controls.HideControl(TimerPlusButton)
      EndIf
      FormatTime()
      Shapes.SetText(TimeDisplay, FormattedTime)
      Timer.Resume()
    EndIf
  Else
    Controls.SetButtonCaption(StartStopButton, "Start
Practice")
    Controls.ShowControl(ExitButton)
```

```
    Shapes.SetText(ProblemDisplay, "")
    Timer.Pause()
    If (TimerChoice = 2) Then
      Controls.ShowControl(TimerMinusButton)
      Controls.ShowControl(TimerPlusButton)
    EndIf
    If (NumberTried > 0) Then
      CRLF = Text.GetCharacter(13)
      Score = Math.Floor(100 * (NumberCorrect / NumberTried))
      Message = "Problems Tried: " + NumberTried + CRLF
      Message = Message + "Problems Correct: " + NumberCorrect
+ " (" + Score + "%)" + CRLF
      If (TimerChoice = 0) Then
        Message = Message + "Timer Off"
      Else
        If (TimerChoice = 2) Then
          ProblemTime = 30 * TimerIndex - ProblemTime
        EndIf
        FormatTime()
        Message = Message + "Elapsed Time: " + FormattedTime +
CRLF
        Message = Message + "Time Per Problem: " +
Math.Floor(100 * (ProblemTime / NumberTried)) / 100 + " sec"
      EndIf
      GraphicsWindow.ShowMessage(Message, "Results")
    EndIf
  EndIf
EndSub
```

Add the noted changes.

One last time – **Save** and **Run** the project. Solve some problems and see the results. Make sure the results display correctly whether timing or not. Here is a set of results I received while using the timing down option:

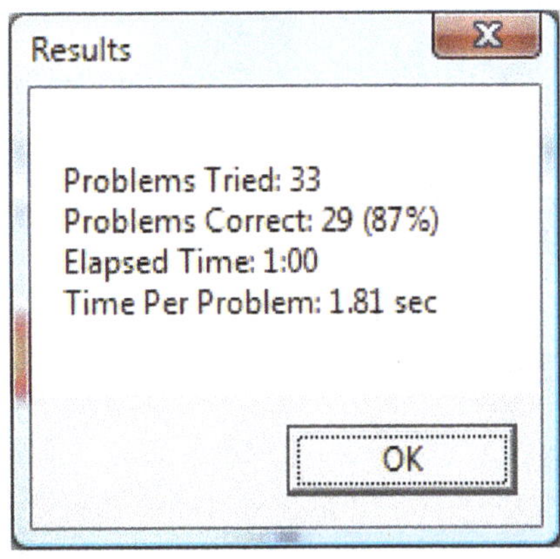

Flash Card Math Quiz Project Code Listing

Here is the complete listing of the **Flash Card Math Quiz** Small Basic program:

```
' Flash Card Math
InitializeProgram()

Sub InitializeProgram
  'graphics window
  GraphicsWindow.Width = 430
  GraphicsWindow.Height = 360
  GraphicsWindow.Title = "Flash Card Math"
  GraphicsWindow.BackgroundColor = "LightYellow"
  'labels/scores
  GraphicsWindow.BrushColor = "Black"
  GraphicsWindow.FontBold = "false"
  GraphicsWindow.FontSize = 24
  GraphicsWindow.DrawText(40, 10, "Tried:")
  GraphicsWindow.DrawText(200, 10, "Correct:")
  GraphicsWindow.BrushColor = "Red"
  GraphicsWindow.FillRectangle(110, 10, 60, 30)
  GraphicsWindow.FillRectangle(300, 10, 60, 30)
  GraphicsWindow.BrushColor = "Yellow"
  TriedDisplay = Shapes.AddText("0")
  Shapes.Move(TriedDisplay, 125, 10)
  CorrectDisplay = Shapes.AddText("0")
  Shapes.Move(CorrectDisplay, 315, 10)
  'problem display
  GraphicsWindow.BrushColor = "Blue"
  GraphicsWindow.FontSize = 72
  ProblemDisplay = Shapes.AddText("")
  Shapes.Move(ProblemDisplay, 50, 50)
  'divider
  GraphicsWindow.BrushColor = "Red"
  GraphicsWindow.FillRectangle(10, 160, 410, 10)
  'problem types/factor/timer
  GraphicsWindow.BrushColor = GraphicsWindow.GetColorFromRGB(192,
192, 255)
  GraphicsWindow.FillRectangle(10, 180, 130, 130)
  GraphicsWindow.FillRectangle(150, 180, 130, 130)
  GraphicsWindow.FillRectangle(290, 180, 130, 130)
  GraphicsWindow.BrushColor = "Black"
  GraphicsWindow.FontSize = 16
  GraphicsWindow.FontBold = "true"
  GraphicsWindow.DrawText(15, 185, "Type(s)")
  GraphicsWindow.DrawText(155, 185, "Factor")
```

```
GraphicsWindow.DrawText(295, 185, "Timer")
'problem types
GraphicsWindow.BrushColor = "Black"
GraphicsWindow.FontSize = 14
GraphicsWindow.FontBold = "false"
GraphicsWindow.DrawText(35, 210, "Addition (+)")
GraphicsWindow.DrawText(35, 230, "Subtraction (-)")
GraphicsWindow.DrawText(35, 250, "Multiplication (x)")
GraphicsWindow.DrawText(35, 270, "Division (/)")
GraphicsWindow.BrushColor = "White"
GraphicsWindow.FillRectangle(15, 210, 15, 15)
GraphicsWindow.FillRectangle(15, 230, 15, 15)
GraphicsWindow.FillRectangle(15, 250, 15, 15)
GraphicsWindow.FillRectangle(15, 270, 15, 15)
ProblemSelected[1] = "true"
ProblemSelected[2] = "false"
ProblemSelected[3] = "false"
ProblemSelected[4] = "false"
Selections = 1
ProblemTypeClicked = 1
MarkProblemType()
'factor
GraphicsWindow.BrushColor = "White"
GraphicsWindow.FillRectangle(160, 210, 110, 30)
GraphicsWindow.BrushColor = "DarkRed"
GraphicsWindow.FontSize = 20
FactorDisplay = Shapes.AddText("Random")
Shapes.Move(FactorDisplay, 180, 212)
FactorChoice = -1
GraphicsWindow.BrushColor = "Black"
GraphicsWindow.FontSize = 14
FactorButton = Controls.AddButton("Change", 170, 245)
Controls.SetSize(FactorButton, 90, 30)
'timer choices
GraphicsWindow.BrushColor = "Black"
GraphicsWindow.FontSize = 14
GraphicsWindow.FontBold = "false"
GraphicsWindow.DrawText(315, 210, "Off")
GraphicsWindow.DrawText(315, 230, "On-Count Up")
GraphicsWindow.DrawText(315, 250, "On-Count Down")
GraphicsWindow.BrushColor = "White"
GraphicsWindow.FillEllipse(295, 210, 15, 15)
GraphicsWindow.FillEllipse(295, 230, 15, 15)
GraphicsWindow.FillEllipse(295, 250, 15, 15)
TimerChoice = 0 ' 0-off, 1 -on/up, 2- on/down
MarkTimerChoice()
```

```
  TimerIndex = 1
  GraphicsWindow.BrushColor = "DarkBlue"
  GraphicsWindow.FontSize = 20
  TimeDisplay = Shapes.AddText("0:30")
  Shapes.Move(TimeDisplay, 335, 277)
  GraphicsWindow.BrushColor = "Black"
  GraphicsWindow.FontSize = 14
  TimerPlusButton = Controls.AddButton("+", 390, 275)
  Controls.SetSize(TimerPlusButton, 20, 30)
  TimerMinusButton = Controls.AddButton("-", 300, 275)
  Controls.SetSize(TimerMinusButton, 20, 30)
  Shapes.HideShape(TimeDisplay)
  Controls.HideControl(TimerMinusButton)
  Controls.HideControl(TimerPlusButton)
  'buttons
  GraphicsWindow.BrushColor = "Black"
  GraphicsWindow.FontSize = 14
  StartStopButton = Controls.AddButton("Start Practice", 60, 320)
  Controls.SetSize(StartStopButton, 130, 30)
  ExitButton = Controls.AddButton("Exit", 230, 320)
  Controls.SetSize(ExitButton, 130, 30)
  Controls.ButtonClicked = ButtonClickedSub
  GraphicsWindow.KeyDown = KeyDownSub
  GraphicsWindow.MouseDown = MouseDownSub
  Timer.Interval = 1000
  Timer.Tick = TimerTickSub
  Timer.Pause()
EndSub

Sub ButtonClickedSub
  B = Controls.LastClickedButton
  If (B = StartStopButton) Then
    StartStopButtonClicked()
  ElseIf (B = ExitButton) Then
    Program.End()
  ElseIf (B = FactorButton) Then
    FactorButtonClicked()
  ElseIf (B = TimerPlusButton) Then
    TimerIndex = TimerIndex + 1
    If (TimerIndex > 60) Then
      TimerIndex = 60
    EndIf
    ProblemTime = 30 * TimerIndex
    FormatTime()
    Shapes.SetText(TimeDisplay, FormattedTime)
  ElseIf (B = TimerMinusButton) Then
```

```
    TimerIndex = TimerIndex - 1
    If (TimerIndex < 1) Then
      TimerIndex = 1
    EndIf
    ProblemTime = 30 * TimerIndex
    FormatTime()
    Shapes.SetText(TimeDisplay, FormattedTime)
  EndIf
EndSub

Sub StartStopButtonClicked
  If (Controls.GetButtonCaption(StartStopButton) = "Start
Practice") Then
    Controls.SetButtonCaption(StartStopButton, "Stop Practice")
    Controls.HideControl(ExitButton)
    NumberTried = 0
    NumberCorrect = 0
    Shapes.SetText(TriedDisplay, "0")
    Shapes.SetText(CorrectDisplay, "0")
    GetProblem()
    If (TimerChoice <> 0) Then
      If (TimerChoice = 1) Then
        ProblemTime = 0
      Else
        ProblemTime = 30 * TimerIndex
        Controls.HideControl(TimerMinusButton)
        Controls.HideControl(TimerPlusButton)
      EndIf
      FormatTime()
      Shapes.SetText(TimeDisplay, FormattedTime)
      Timer.Resume()
    EndIf
  Else
    Controls.SetButtonCaption(StartStopButton, "Start Practice")
    Controls.ShowControl(ExitButton)
    Shapes.SetText(ProblemDisplay, "")
    Timer.Pause()
    If (TimerChoice = 2) Then
      Controls.ShowControl(TimerMinusButton)
      Controls.ShowControl(TimerPlusButton)
    EndIf
    If (NumberTried > 0) Then
      CRLF = Text.GetCharacter(13)
      Score = Math.Floor(100 * (NumberCorrect / NumberTried))
      Message = "Problems Tried: " + NumberTried + CRLF
```

```
      Message = Message + "Problems Correct: " + NumberCorrect + "
(" + Score + "%)" + CRLF
      If (TimerChoice = 0) Then
        Message = Message + "Timer Off"
      Else
        If (TimerChoice = 2) Then
          ProblemTime = 30 * TimerIndex - ProblemTime
        EndIf
        FormatTime()
        Message = Message + "Elapsed Time: " + FormattedTime +
CRLF
        Message = Message + "Time Per Problem: " + Math.Floor(100
* (ProblemTime / NumberTried)) / 100 + " sec"
      EndIf
      GraphicsWindow.ShowMessage(Message, "Results")
    EndIf
  EndIf
EndSub

Sub GetProblem
  ProblemType = 0
  While (ProblemType = 0)
    P = Math.GetRandomNumber(4)
    If (P = 1 And ProblemSelected[1]) Then
      'Addition
      ProblemType = P
      Number = Math.GetRandomNumber(10) - 1
      GetFactor()
      CorrectAnswer = Number + Factor
      Problem = Number + " + " + Factor + " = "
    ElseIf (P = 2 And ProblemSelected[2]) Then
      'Subtraction
      ProblemType = P
      GetFactor()
      CorrectAnswer = Math.GetRandomNumber(10) - 1
      Number = CorrectAnswer + Factor
      Problem = Number + " - " + Factor + " = "
    ElseIf (P = 3 And ProblemSelected[3]) Then
      'Multiplication
      ProblemType = P
      Number = Math.GetRandomNumber(10) - 1
      GetFactor()
      CorrectAnswer = Number * Factor
      Problem = Number + " x " + Factor + " = "
    ElseIf (P = 4 And ProblemSelected[4]) Then
      'Division
```

```
      ProblemType = P
      GetFactor()
      CorrectAnswer = Math.GetRandomNumber(10) - 1
      Number = CorrectAnswer * Factor
      Problem = Number + " / " + Factor + " = "
    EndIf
  EndWhile
  YourAnswer = ""
  DigitNumber = 1
  If (CorrectAnswer < 10) Then
    NumberDigits = 1
    Shapes.SetText(ProblemDisplay, Problem + "?")
  Else
    NumberDigits = 2
    Shapes.SetText(ProblemDisplay, Problem + "??")
  EndIf
EndSub

Sub GetFactor
  If (FactorChoice = -1) Then
    If (ProblemType = 4) Then
      Factor = Math.GetRandomNumber(9)
    Else
      Factor = Math.GetRandomNumber(10) - 1
    EndIf
  Else
    Factor = FactorChoice
  EndIf
EndSub

Sub KeyDownSub
  If (Controls.GetButtonCaption(StartStopButton) = "Stop
Practice") Then
    'can only check keystrokes when practicing-only allow number
keys
    'number is last character in keypressed
    KeyPressed = Text.GetSubTextToEnd(GraphicsWindow.LastKey,
Text.GetLength(GraphicsWindow.LastKey))
    If (Text.GetCharacterCode(KeyPressed) >=
Text.GetCharacterCode("0") And Text.GetCharacterCode(KeyPressed)
<= Text.GetCharacterCode("9")) Then
      YourAnswer = Text.Append(YourAnswer, KeyPressed)
      If DigitNumber <> NumberDigits Then
        DigitNumber = DigitNumber + 1
        Shapes.SetText(ProblemDisplay, Problem + YourAnswer + "?")
      Else
```

```
        NumberTried = NumberTried + 1
        'check answer
        If (YourAnswer = CorrectAnswer) Then
          NumberCorrect = NumberCorrect + 1
        EndIf
        Shapes.SetText(TriedDisplay, NumberTried)
        Shapes.SetText(CorrectDisplay, NumberCorrect)
        GetProblem()
      EndIf
    EndIf
  EndIf
EndSub

Sub MouseDownSub
  X = GraphicsWindow.MouseX
  Y = GraphicsWindow.MouseY
  'problem selections - must always have at least one selected
  If (X > 15 And X < 30 And Y > 210 And Y < 285) Then
    If (Y > 210 And Y < 225) Then
     'clicked addition
     ProblemTypeClicked = 1
    ElseIf (Y > 230 And Y < 245) Then
      'clicked subtraction
      ProblemTypeClicked = 2
    ElseIf (Y > 250 And Y < 265) Then
      'clicked multiplication
     ProblemTypeClicked = 3
    ElseIf (Y > 270 And Y < 285) Then
     'clicked division
      ProblemTypeClicked = 4
    EndIf
    If (ProblemSelected[ProblemTypeClicked] And Selections <> 1)
Then
      'clear choice if not last one selected
      Selections = Selections - 1
      ProblemSelected[ProblemTypeClicked] = "false"
      ProblemTypeClicked = -ProblemTypeClicked
      MarkProblemType()
    ElseIf (ProblemSelected[ProblemTypeClicked] = "false") Then
      'mark choice
      Selections = Selections + 1
      ProblemSelected[ProblemTypeClicked] = "true"
      MarkProblemType()
      'make sure zero not selected factor if division selected
      If (ProblemTypeClicked = 4 And FactorChoice = 0) Then
        FactorButtonClicked()
```

```
      EndIf
    EndIf
  EndIf
  If (Controls.GetButtonCaption(StartStopButton) = "Start
Practice") Then
    'timer selections - only one can be selected
    If (X > 295 And X < 310 And Y > 210 And Y < 265) Then
      'problem selections - must always have at least one selected
      If (Y > 210 And Y < 225) Then
        'clicked timer off
        TimerChoice = 0
        MarkTimerChoice()
        Shapes.HideShape(TimeDisplay)
        Controls.HideControl(TimerMinusButton)
        Controls.HideControl(TimerPlusButton)
      ElseIf (Y > 230 And Y < 245) Then
        'clicked timer on - count up
        TimerChoice = 1
        MarkTimerChoice()
        Shapes.ShowShape(TimeDisplay)
        Controls.HideControl(TimerMinusButton)
        Controls.HideControl(TimerPlusButton)
        ProblemTime = 0
        FormatTime()
        Shapes.SetText(TimeDisplay, FormattedTime)
      ElseIf (Y > 250 And Y < 265) Then
        'clicked timer on - count down
        TimerChoice = 2
        MarkTimerChoice()
        Shapes.ShowShape(TimeDisplay)
        Controls.ShowControl(TimerMinusButton)
        Controls.ShowControl(TimerPlusButton)
        ProblemTime = 30 * TimerIndex
        FormatTime()
        Shapes.SetText(TimeDisplay, FormattedTime)
      EndIf
    EndIf
  EndIf
EndSub

Sub MarkProblemType
  If (ProblemTypeClicked < 0) Then
    ProblemTypeClicked = Math.Abs(ProblemTypeClicked)
    GraphicsWindow.BrushColor = "White"
    GraphicsWindow.FillRectangle(15, 190 + ProblemTypeClicked *
20, 15, 15)
```

```
  Else
    GraphicsWindow.PenColor = "Black"
    GraphicsWindow.PenWidth = 1
    GraphicsWindow.DrawLine(18, 199 + ProblemTypeClicked * 20, 22,
203 + ProblemTypeClicked * 20)
    GraphicsWindow.DrawLine(22, 203 + ProblemTypeClicked * 20, 28,
191 + ProblemTypeClicked * 20)
  EndIf
EndSub

Sub FactorButtonClicked
  'change factor choice
  FactorChoice = FactorChoice + 1
  If (FactorChoice > 9) Then
    FactorChoice = -1
    Shapes.SetText(FactorDisplay, "Random")
  Else
    If (ProblemSelected[4] And FactorChoice = 0) Then
      'no zero if doing division
      FactorChoice = 1
    EndIf
    Shapes.SetText(FactorDisplay, Text.Append("      ",
FactorChoice))
  EndIf
EndSub

Sub MarkTimerChoice
  GraphicsWindow.BrushColor = "White"
  GraphicsWindow.FillEllipse(295, 210, 15, 15)
  GraphicsWindow.FillEllipse(295, 230, 15, 15)
  GraphicsWindow.FillEllipse(295, 250, 15, 15)
  GraphicsWindow.BrushColor = "SlateGray"
  GraphicsWindow.FillEllipse(298, 213 + TimerChoice * 20, 9, 9)
EndSub

Sub FormatTime
  Minutes = Math.Floor(ProblemTime / 60)
  Seconds = ProblemTime - Minutes * 60
  If (Seconds < 10) Then
    FormattedTime = Minutes + ":0" + Seconds
  Else
    FormattedTime = Minutes + ":" + Seconds
  EndIf
EndSub

Sub TimerTickSub
```

```
  If (TimerChoice = 1) Then
    ProblemTime = ProblemTime + 1
    FormatTime()
    Shapes.SetText(TimeDisplay, FormattedTime)
    If ProblemTime >= 1800 Then
      StartStopButtonClicked()
    EndIf
  Else
    ProblemTime = ProblemTime - 1
    FormatTime()
    Shapes.SetText(TimeDisplay, FormattedTime)
    If (ProblemTime = 0) Then
      StartStopButtonClicked()
    EndIf
  EndIf
EndSub
```

Flash Card Math Quiz Project Review

The **Flash Card Math Quiz** project is now complete. **Save** and **Run** the project and make sure it works as designed. Recheck that all options work and interact properly. Let your kids (or anyone else) have fun tuning up their basic math skills.

If there are errors in your implementation, go back over the steps of window and code design. Use the debugger when needed. Go over the developed code – make sure you understand how different parts of the project were coded. As mentioned in the beginning of this chapter, the completed project is saved as **FlashCard** in the **HomeSB\HomeSB Projects\FlashCard** folder.

While completing this project, new concepts and skills you should have gained include:

- How to make selections among options.
- Use of the KeyDown event for input.
- Using a message box to report results.

Flash Card Math Quiz Project Enhancements

Possible enhancements to the flash card math project include:

- As implemented, the only feedback a user gets about entered answers is an update of the score. Some kind of audible feedback would be a big improvement (a positive sound for correct answer, a negative sound for a wrong answer). We discuss adding sounds to a project in the final chapter – you might like to look ahead.
- When a user stops answering problems, it would be nice to have a review mode where the problems missed are presented. You would need some way to save each problem that was answered incorrectly.
- Kids like rewards. As you gain more programming skills, a nice visual display of some sort for good work would be a fun addition.
- Currently, once a problem is answered, the next problem is immediately displayed. Some kind of delay (perhaps make it optional and adjustable) might be desired.

This page intentionally not left blank.

7. Multiple Choice Exam Project

Review and Preview

In this chapter, we build a project that quizzes a user on matching pairs of items – for example, states (or countries) and capital cities, words and meanings, books and authors, inventions and inventors.

The **Multiple Choice Exam Project** allows you to select which item is given and which should be provided as the answer and whether the answers should be multiple choice or typed in. The project introduces reading information from files.

Multiple Choice Exam Project Preview

In this chapter, we will build a **multiple choice exam** program. Random items from a provided list are displayed to the user. The user picks the item that matches (or goes with the displayed item). For example, if a country is listed, the user may be asked for the capital city. Answers can be multiple choice or typed in.

The finished project is saved as **MultipleChoice** in the **HomeSB\HomeSB Projects\MultipleChoice** folder. Start Small Basic and open the finished project. **Run** the project (click **Run** in the toolbar or press <**F5**>). The multiple choice exam program will appear as:

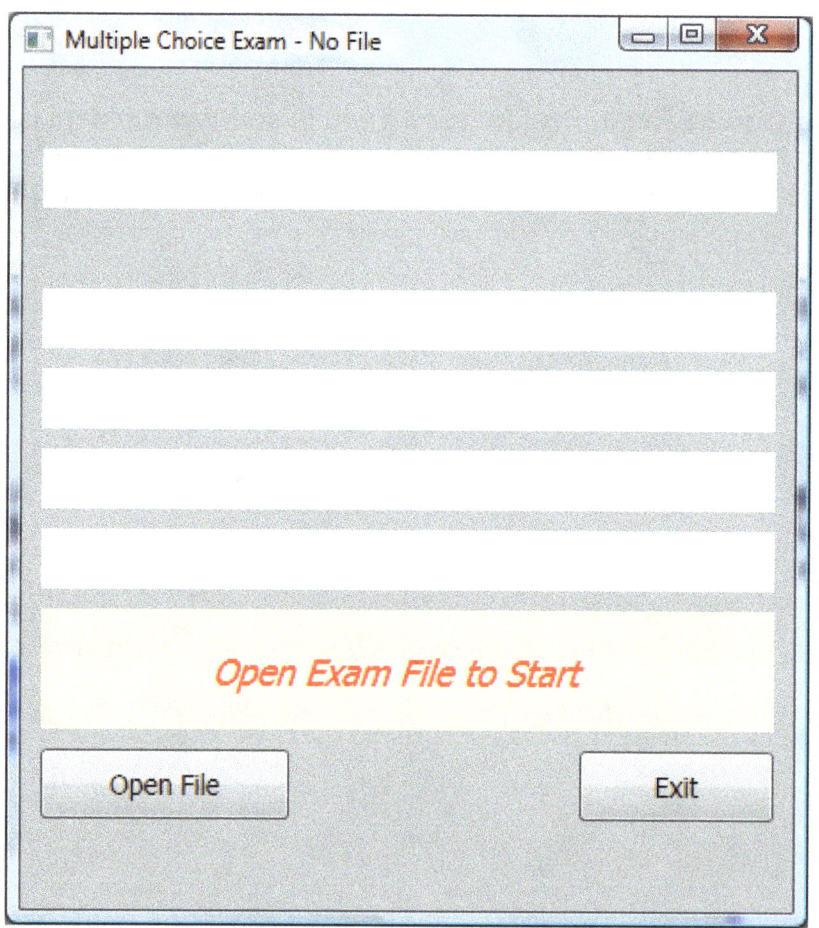

In the message area you see "***Open Exam File to Start***". The information used for a multiple choice exam is stored in files you build (we will discuss how to do this). So, the first step is to open and load such a file. Click **Open File**. A text window will appear:

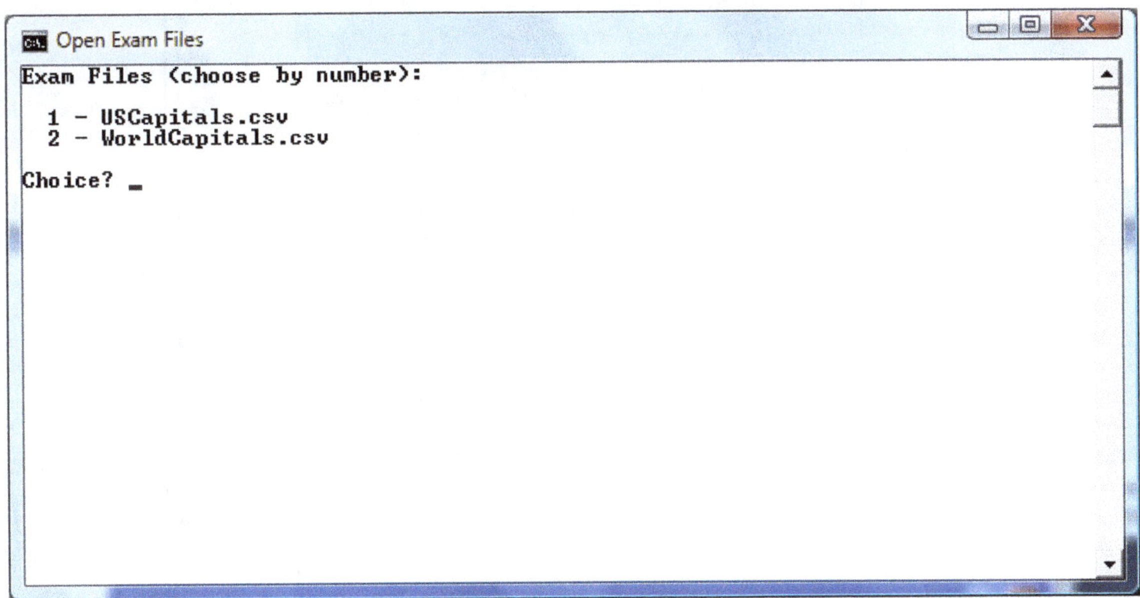

This window displays two example data files included with the program - **USCapitals.csv** (listing states and capitals) and **WorldCapitals.csv** (listing countries and capitals). Choose **WorldCapitals.csv** by pressing 2 and then pressing **Enter**.

The file will open and the project window should now appear as:

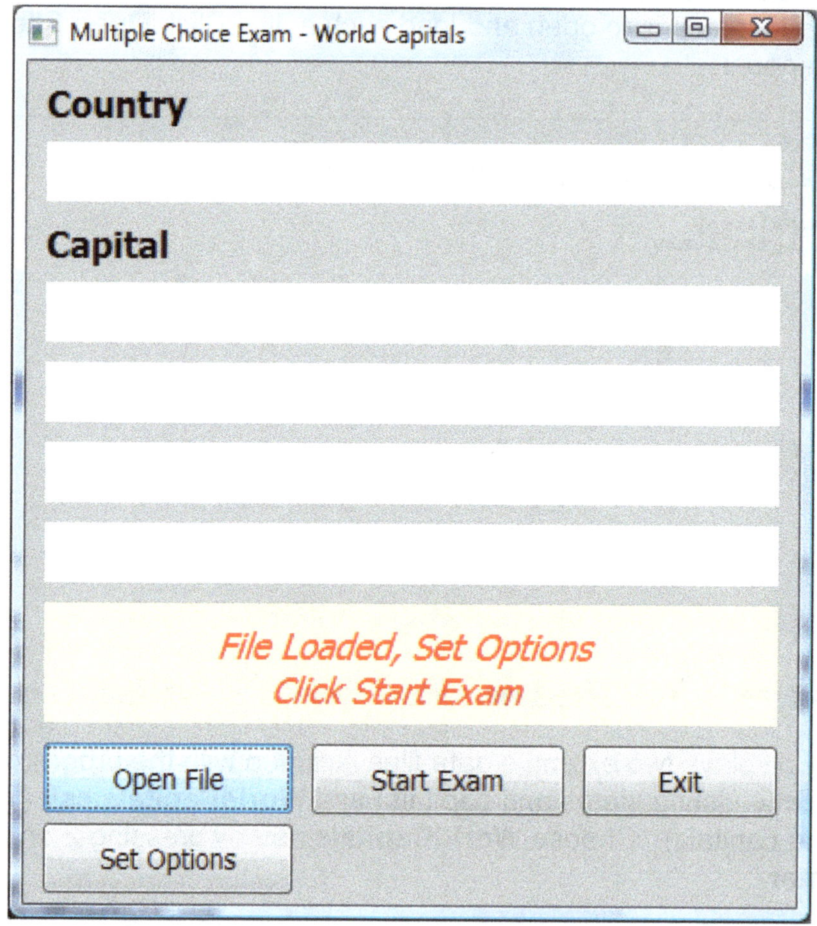

Notice headers (**Country** and **Capital**) are now listed on the window. The window has a caption (**Multiple Choice Exam – World Capitals**) with the exam title. The program is now asking you to set options before starting the exam.

Click the **Set Options** button. A text window will appear asking you to decide which options you want. Two choices are made. In this example, you are asked whether you want to name the **Capital**, given the **Country**, or vice versa:

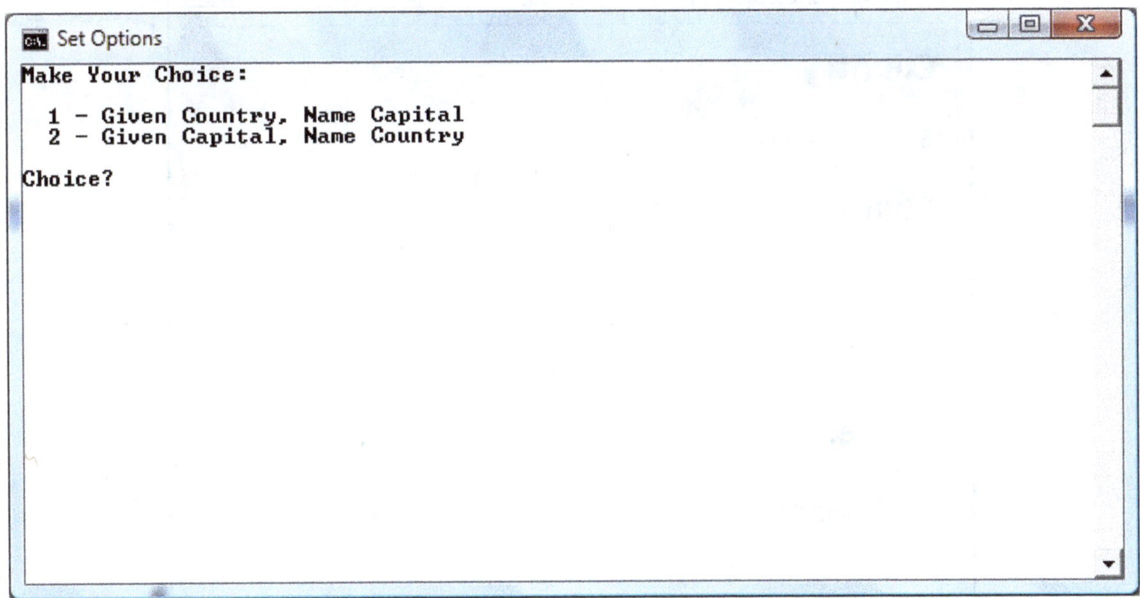

Let's choose **Given Country, Name Capital** (Option 1). The other choice is whether you want to be provided with a list of multiple choice answers or you want to type in your answer:

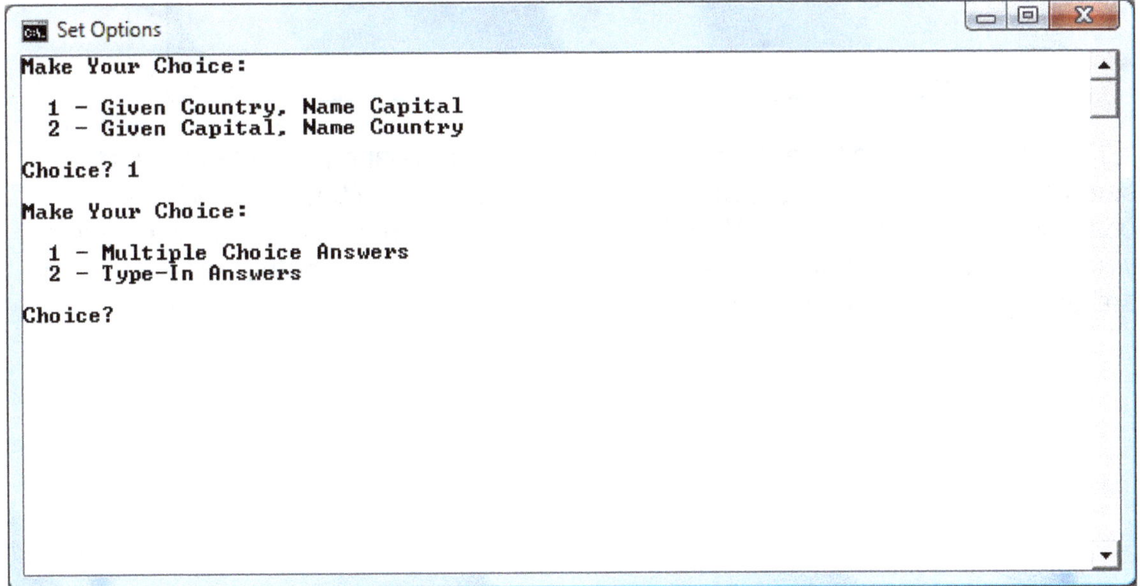

Choose **Multiple Choice Answers** (Option 1).

We're ready to start the exam. Click the button marked **Start Exam** and you will see:

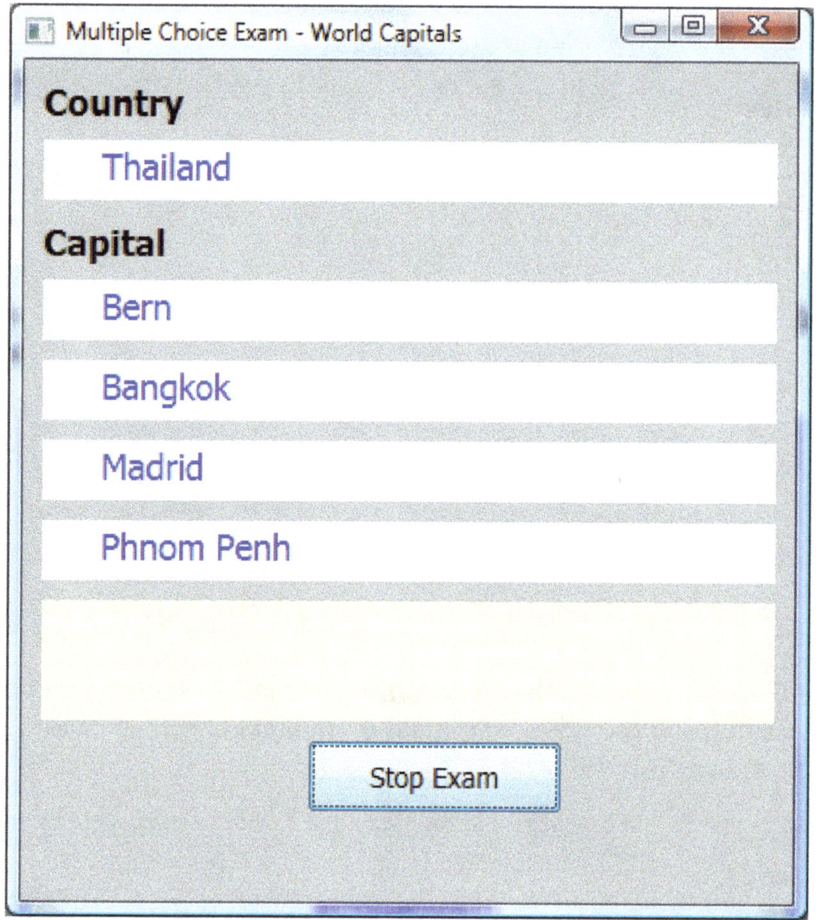

Your entries will be different since the exam questions and possible answers are selected randomly. This question asks for the capital of **Thailand** and four possible answers are listed. You click on your choice of capital. You will be told if you are correct or not and given the opportunity to answer another question. You are only given one chance to get the correct answer.

I know the capital of **Thailand** is **Bangkok**. When I click that selection, I see:

At this point, you have two choices – click **Next Question** to continue or click **Stop Exam** to stop. Try a few more questions.

At some point, when you answer incorrectly, you will see a screen similar to this:

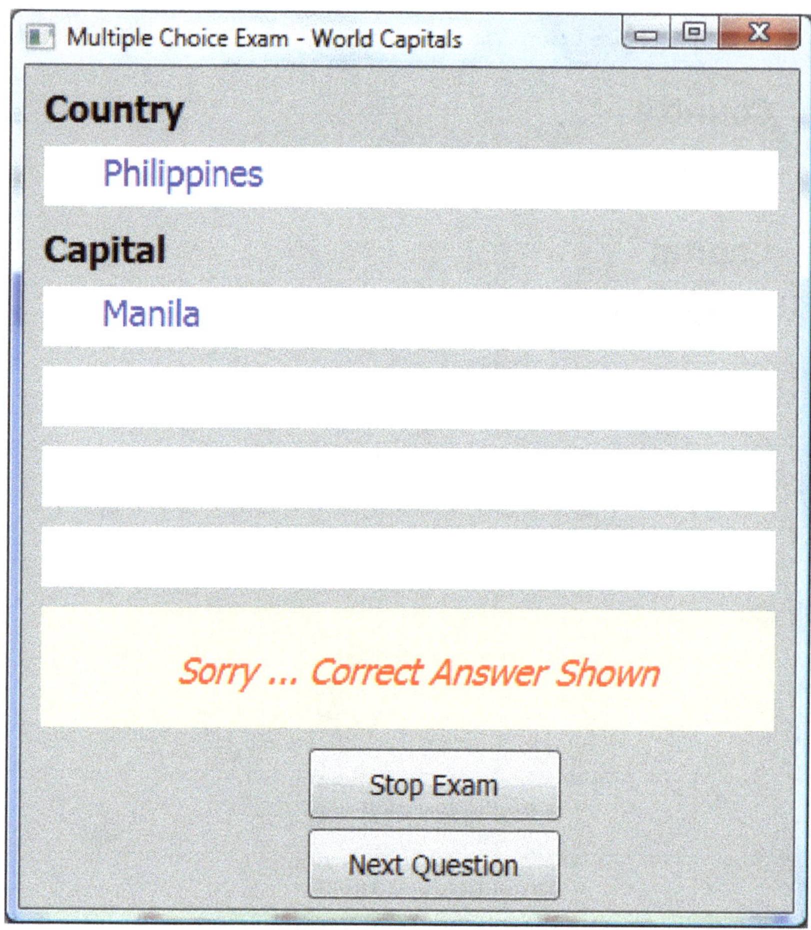

So, with an incorrect answer, you are told so and given the correct answer. Keep answering questions as long as you'd like. When you finally click **Stop Exam**, you will be shown a message box with the exam results. Mine for a short exam is:

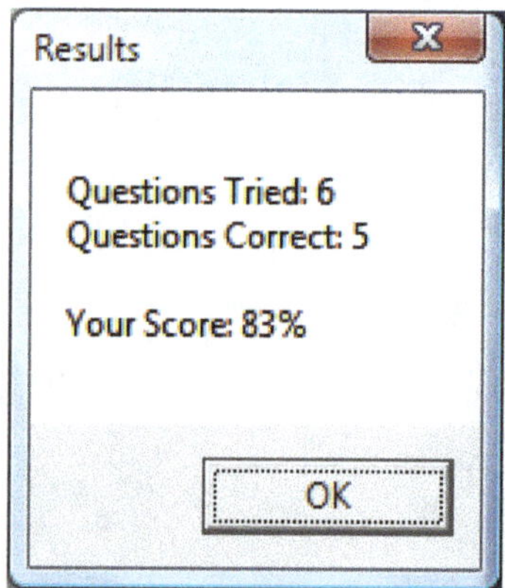

Click **OK** in the message box and your form returns to its initial configuration:

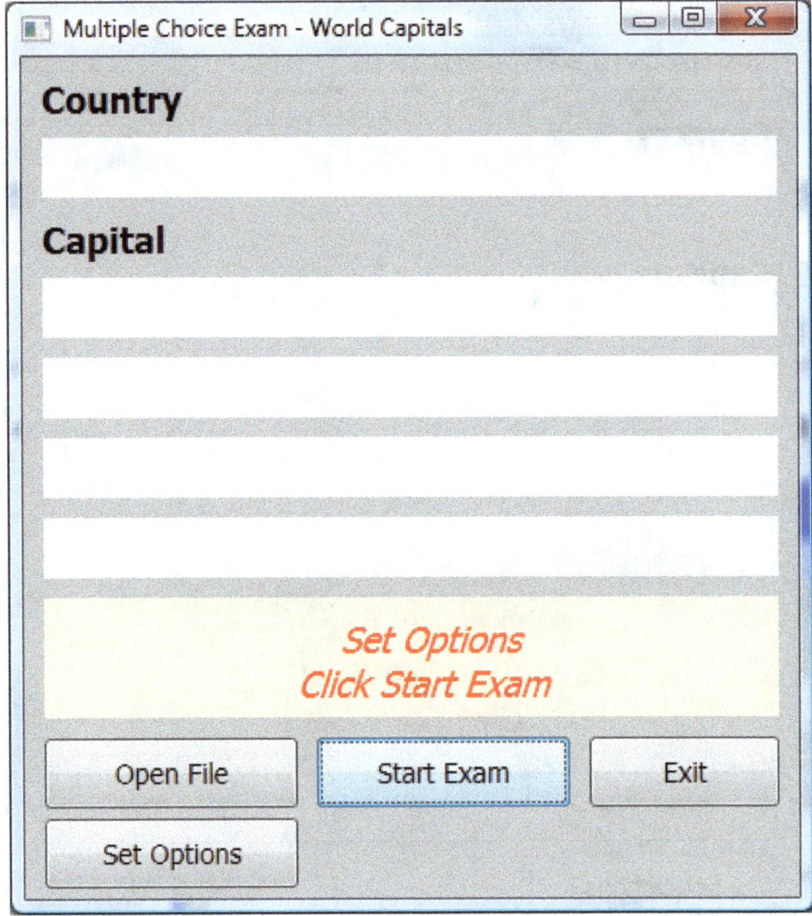

At this point, you can change any option and start a new exam, start a new exam with the same options or load a new exam file. Or, you can click **Exit** to stop the program.

Click the **Set Options** button, choose **Given Country, Name Capital** and choose **Type In Answer**. You will see:

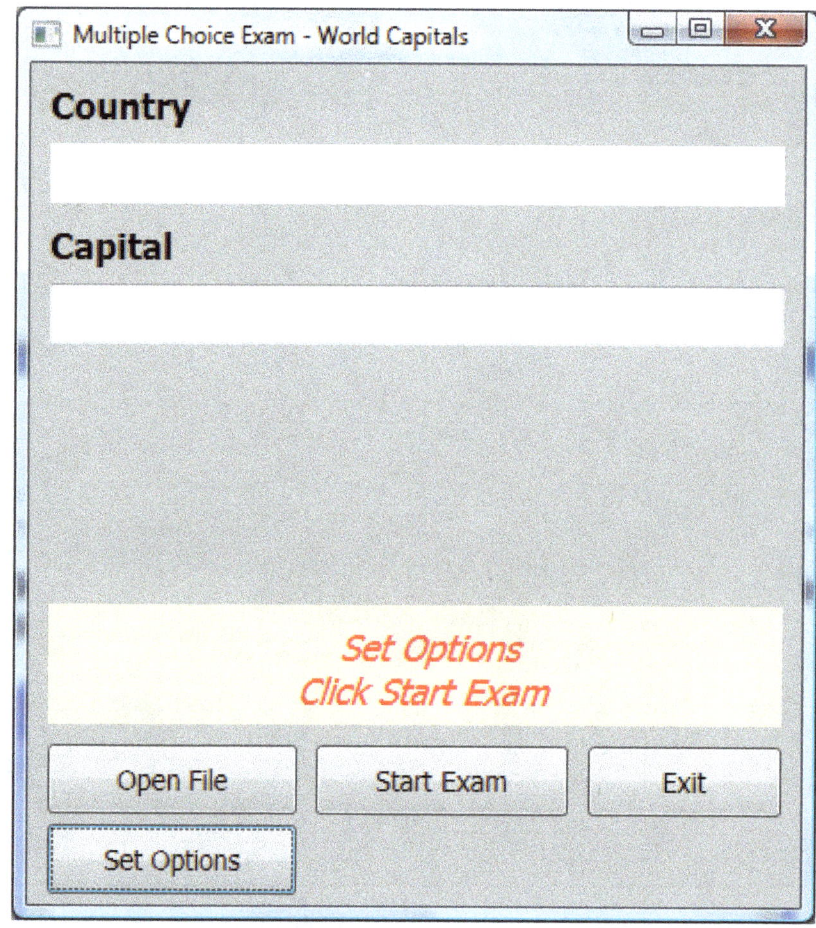

The window has reconfigured – the four multiple choice answer areas (shapes) have been replaced by a single text box control where your answer is typed. Click **Start Exam**.

The first question is displayed (again, yours will be different):

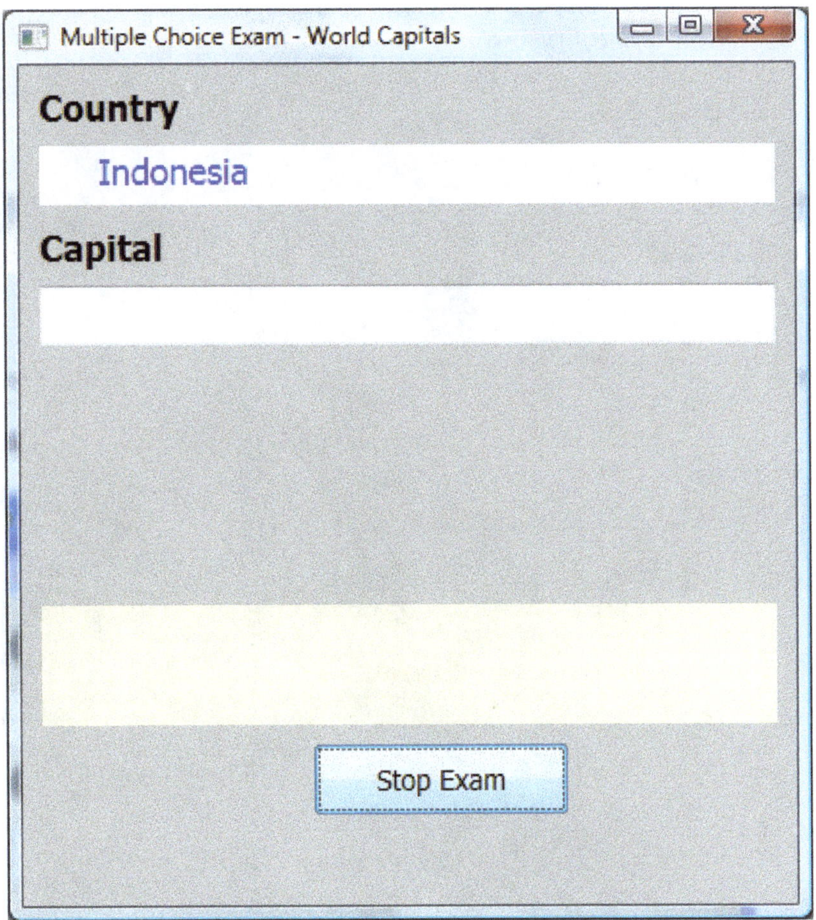

The capital of **Indonesia** is **Jakarta**. If you type **Jakarta** in the text box and press <**Enter**> you will be told this is a correct answer. The program allows your answers to be case-insensitive (we'll show you how to do this in the code design), so even if you type **jakarta**, you are credited with a correct answer.

When I type **jakarta** in the text box and press <**Enter**>, I see:

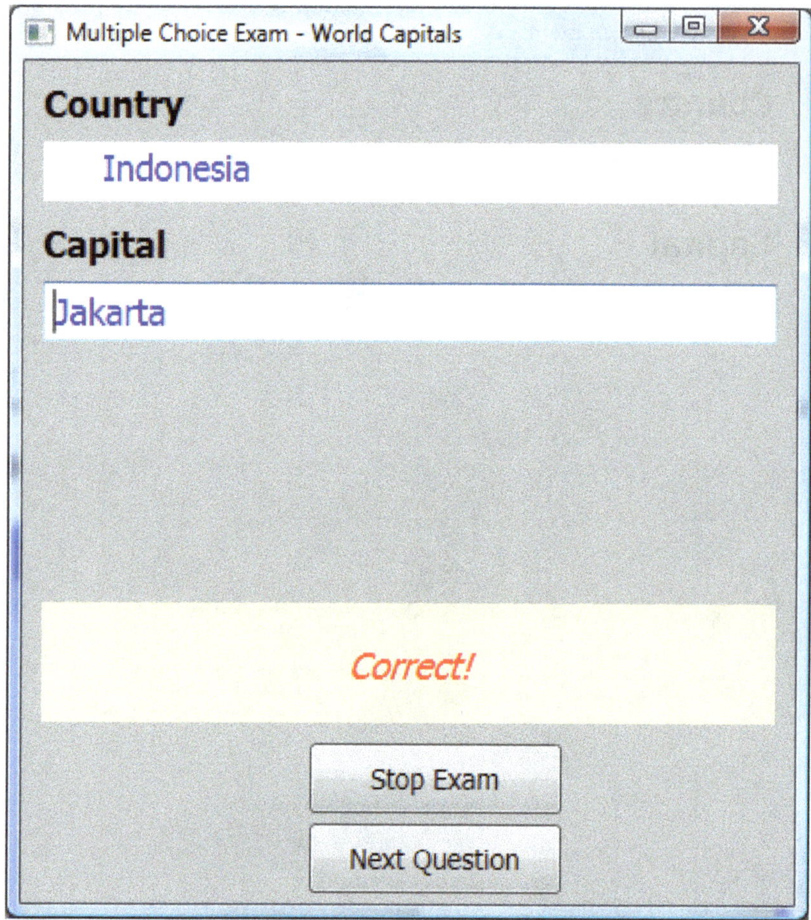

As mentioned, the answer is accepted and the 'capitalization' is corrected.

Now, let's look at a really neat feature of the program. Many times, when typing answers, you might know the answer but not the correct spelling. This happens a lot with kids – could you spell **Jakarta** when you were young? Rather than telling a user the answer is wrong, it would be nice to credit a user with the correct answer if the spelling is close. How do you do such magic, you ask? We'll see in the code design section. For now, let's just try it.

After getting credit for my **Indonesia** question, the next question presented was (again, your question will be different, but try misspelling an answer):

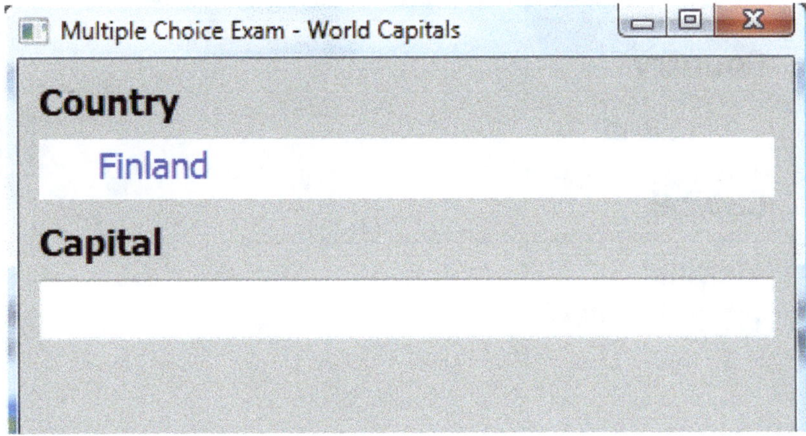

I know the capital of **Finland** is **Helskinki**, but what if I mistakenly spell it as **hellsinky**:

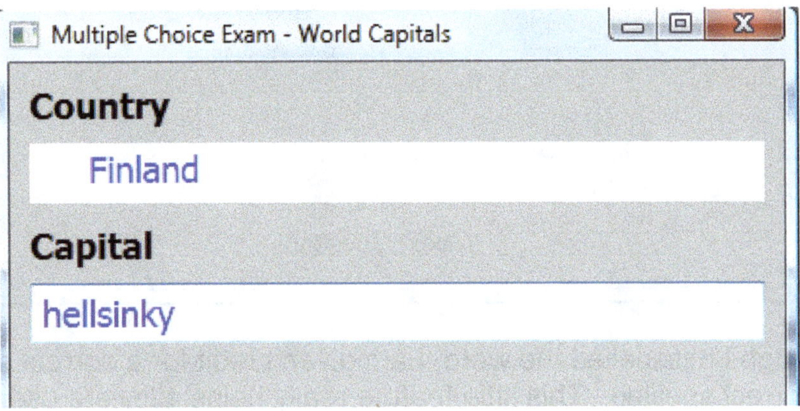

When I press <**Enter**>, I see:

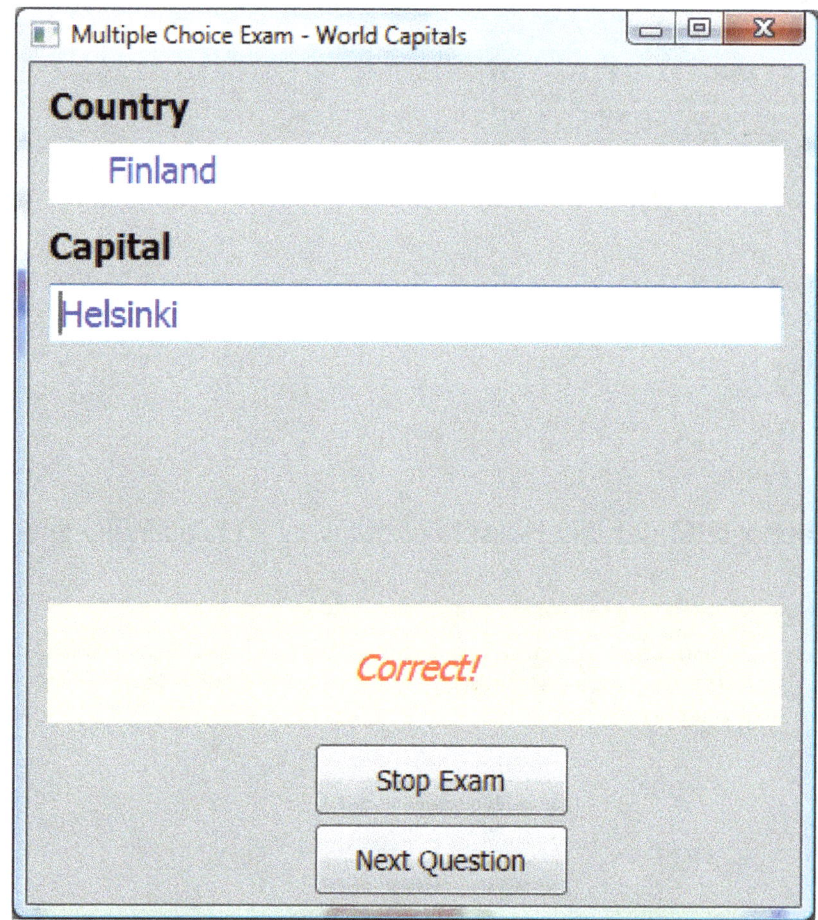

So, even though I misspelled the word, I am given credit for a correct answer and shown the correct spelling. This little feature really helps alleviate user's frustration at not quite knowing how to spell an answer – this is especially useful with kids.

I think you see the idea of the program. Try as many questions, with as many different options, as you like. Maybe load in the **USCapitals.csv** file. When you are finally, finished click **Exit** to stop.

You will now build this project in several stages. We address **window design**. We discuss the controls used to build the form and establish initial properties. And, we address **code design** in detail. We cover opening and loading exam files, establishing and switching configurations for different options, validation of both multiple choice and typed in answers and presenting results. And, we show how we did the trick to check for "close spelling"?

Multiple Choice Exam Window Design

Here is the sketch for the window layout of the **Multiple Choice Exam** program:

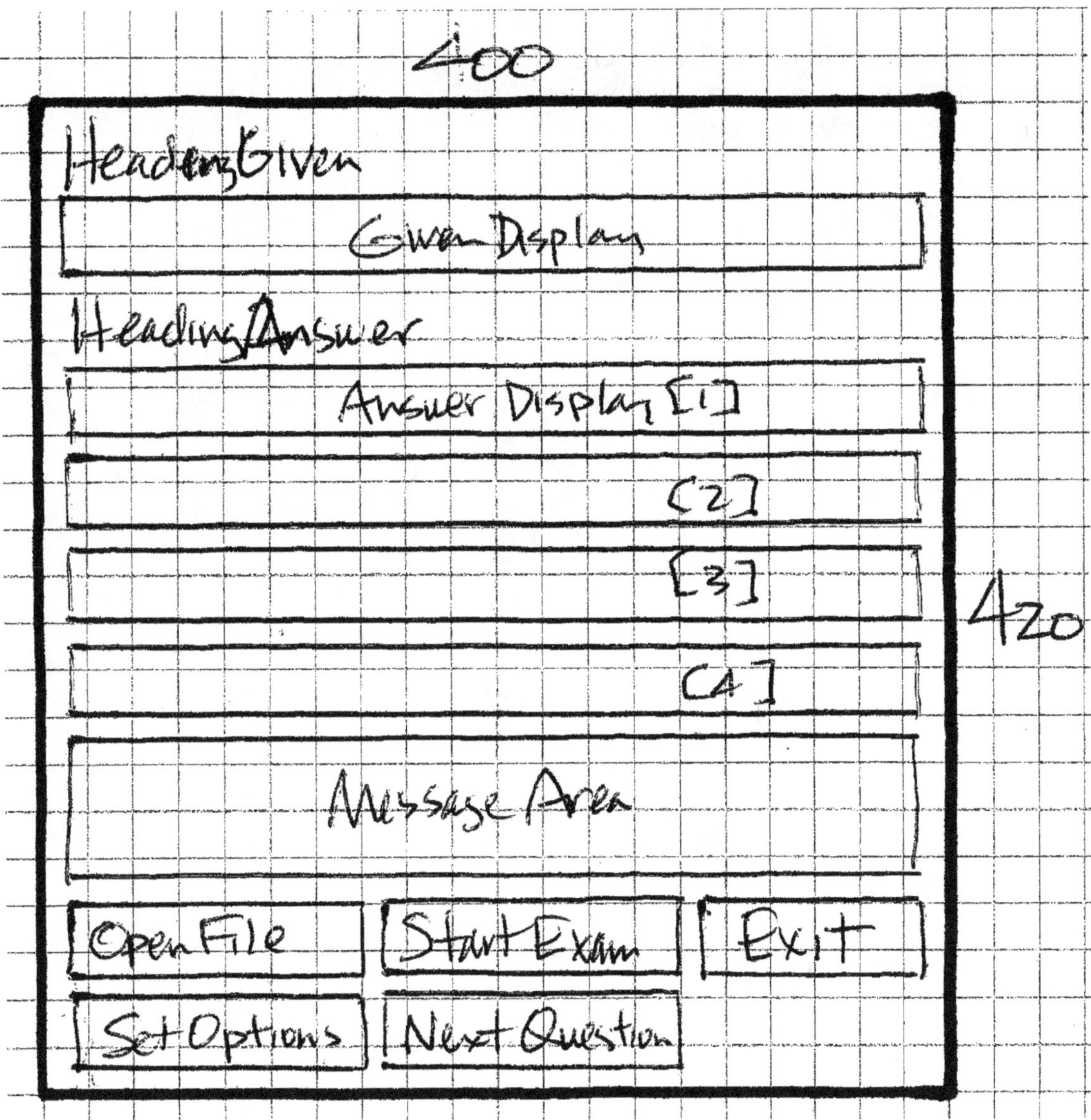

Two text shapes are used for heading information. Four text shapes on white backgrounds are used for multiple choice answers and a text shape on a yellow background is used to provide comments to the user. For typed-in answers, we will use a text box control in place of multiple choice answers. Two button controls are used to move from question to question and to start and stop the exam. A button is used to open exam files and use them in the project. Buttons are also used to set options and exit the program.

We will begin writing code for the application. We will write the code in several steps. We start with the code needed to add all the above elements to the program window. The program will be built in its default configuration of providing multiple choice answers. Later, we add code to change this default value.

Start a new program in Small Basic. Once started, we suggest you immediately save the program with a name you choose. This sets up the folder and file structure needed for your program.

Window Design – Adding Shapes

The headings, given information and multiple choice answers will all be displayed in **Shapes** objects with text information. Add this code to initialize the graphics window and display these shapes:

```
'Multiple Choice Exam
InitializeProgram()

Sub InitializeProgram
  'graphics window
..GraphicsWindow.Show()
..GraphicsWindow.Width = 400
..GraphicsWindow.Height = 420
..GraphicsWindow.BackgroundColor = "LightGray"
..GraphicsWindow.Title = "Multiple Choice Exam - No File"
..'headings
..GraphicsWindow.BrushColor = "Black"
..GraphicsWindow.FontSize = 18
..GraphicsWindow.FontBold = "true"
..HeadingGiven = Shapes.AddText("")
..Shapes.Move(HeadingGiven, 10, 10)
..HeadingAnswer = Shapes.AddText("")
..Shapes.Move(HeadingAnswer, 10, 80)
..GraphicsWindow.BrushColor = "White"
..GraphicsWindow.FillRectangle(10, 40, 380, 30)
..GraphicsWindow.FillRectangle(10, 110, 380, 30)
..GraphicsWindow.FillRectangle(10, 150, 380, 30)
..GraphicsWindow.FillRectangle(10, 190, 380, 30)
..GraphicsWindow.FillRectangle(10, 230, 380, 30)
..'shapes for given and mc answers
..GraphicsWindow.FontBold = "false"
..GraphicsWindow.BrushColor = "Blue"
..GivenDisplay = Shapes.AddText("")
..Shapes.Move(GivenDisplay, 40, 42)
..AnswerDisplay[1] = Shapes.AddText("")
..Shapes.Move(AnswerDisplay[1], 40, 112)
..AnswerDisplay[2] = Shapes.AddText("")
..Shapes.Move(AnswerDisplay[2], 40, 152)
..AnswerDisplay[3] = Shapes.AddText("")
..Shapes.Move(AnswerDisplay[3], 40, 192)
..AnswerDisplay[4] = Shapes.AddText("")
..Shapes.Move(AnswerDisplay[4], 40, 232)
..Header1Given = "true"
..MCAnswers = "true"
EndSub
```

The first line of code calls a subroutine **InitializeProgram** where we will put all code needed to set up the program for use. All remaining code here goes in that subroutine. We have a heading for given information (**HeadingGiven**) along with the shape for displaying this information (**GivenDisplay**). There is also a heading for the answers (**HeadingAnswer**) and the four possible multiple choice answer shapes (**AnswerDisplay[1], AnswerDisplay[2], AnswerDisplay[3], AnswerDisplay[4]**). All of the shapes (except headings) are placed on white rectangular backgrounds. We also initialize variables used to keep track of selected options (**Header1Given** and **MCAnswers**).

Save and **Run** the program. You should see the blank headings and shapes:

We need to anticipate a later need for a text box if using typed-in answers. We will put this control in the same location as the first multiple choice answer (and make it the same size) and hide it for now. Add this code to **InitializeProgram**:

```
'text box for type in answers
AnswerTextBox = Controls.AddTextBox(10, 110)
Controls.SetSize(AnswerTextBox, 380, 30)
Controls.HideControl(AnswerTextBox)
```

Lastly, we add the message area. It is a shape (**MessageArea**) on a yellow rectangle. Add this code to **InitializeProgram**:

```
'message display
GraphicsWindow.BrushColor = "LightYellow"
GraphicsWindow.FillRectangle(10, 270, 380, 60)
GraphicsWindow.BrushColor = "Red"
GraphicsWindow.FontSize = 18
GraphicsWindow.FontBold = "false"
GraphicsWindow.FontItalic = "true"
MessageArea = Shapes.AddText("Open Exam File to Start")
Shapes.Move(MessageArea, 100, 290)
```

Run and **Save** the program. You should now see the added message:

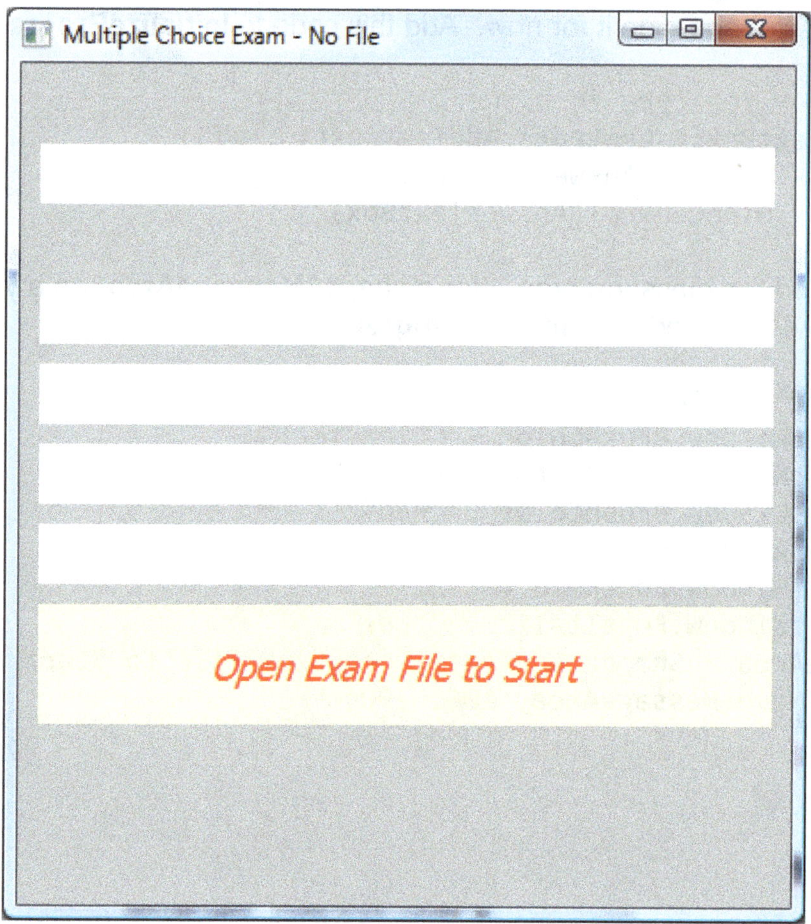

Window Design – Adding Buttons

Five buttons are used in the program. **OpenButton** is used to open and load exam file, **OptionsButton** is used to set options, **StartStopButton** is used to start and stop exams, **NextButton** is used (during exams) to move to another question, and **ExitButton** is used to stop the program. In the initial configuration, only **OpenButton** and **ExitButton** are shown.

Add this code to **InitializeProgram** to create the needed buttons (and hide three of them):

```
'buttons
GraphicsWindow.BrushColor = "Black"
GraphicsWindow.FontSize = 14
GraphicsWindow.FontItalic = "false"
GraphicsWindow.FontBold = "false"
OpenButton = Controls.AddButton("Open File", 10, 340)
Controls.SetSize(OpenButton, 130, 35)
OptionsButton = Controls.AddButton("Set Options", 10, 380)
Controls.SetSize(OptionsButton, 130, 35)
StartStopButton = Controls.AddButton("Start Exam", 150, 340)
Controls.SetSize(StartStopButton, 130, 35)
NextButton = Controls.AddButton("Next Question", 150, 380)
Controls.SetSize(NextButton, 130, 35)
ExitButton = Controls.AddButton("Exit", 290, 340)
Controls.SetSize(ExitButton, 100, 35)
Controls.HideControl(OptionsButton)
Controls.HideControl(StartStopButton)
Controls.HideControl(NextButton)
```

Save and **Run** the program. The **Open File** button and **Exit** button are visible:

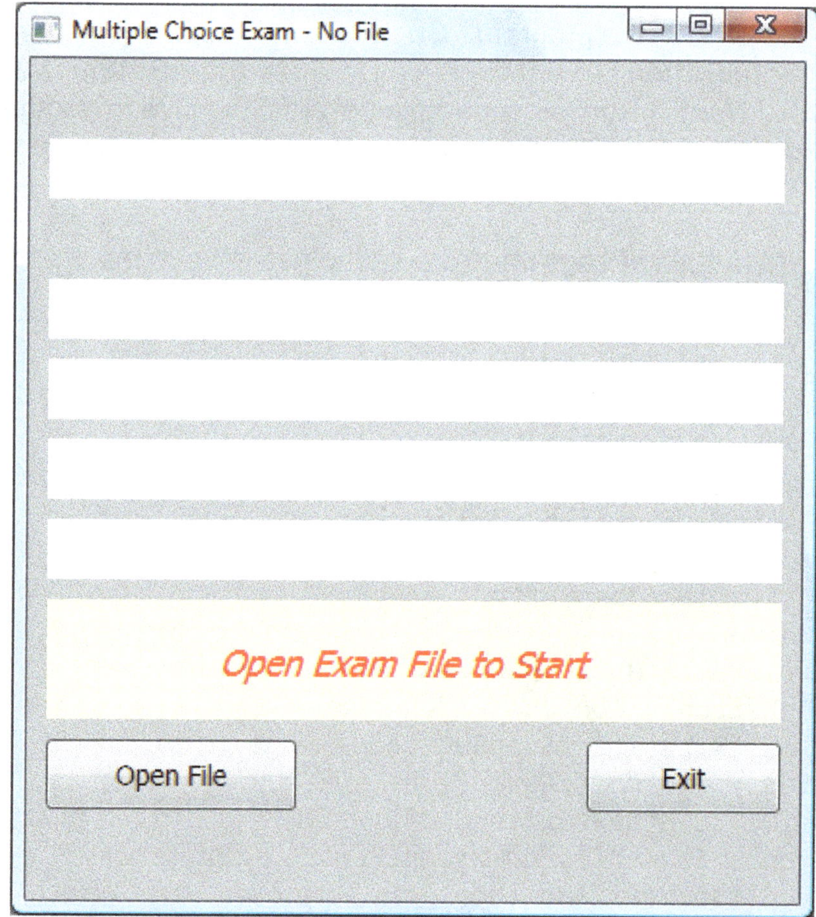

Notice at this point, the only thing a user can do is click **Open File** or click **Exit**. The code behind the **Exit** button is simple (we will add it when we code the **Open File** button). The code for the **Open File** button is far more involved. We'll spend a lot of time talking about it, building it in stages. We discuss file format, ways to generate exam files, how to open exam files, and how to read information from the exam files.

Code Design – Exam File Format

The files used to store information for multiple choice exams have a specific format – you need to insure any files you generate conform to this standard. The files used are called **sequential files**, indicating they are just line after line of information.

To generate a file, you need to have two lists of matching terms (in our sample files, the lists are states and capitals and countries and capitals). Each term should have an identifying header. And each file (exam) should have a title. Once you have this information, the first line of the file is the exam title, followed by a comma (,). The second line is the two headers describing the listed terms, separated by a comma. Subsequent lines are the pairs of terms, each pair separated by a comma – the program will allow up to 100 matching pairs.

Using Windows Notepad, open the **USCapitals.csv** file in the **HomeSB\HomeSB Projects\MultipleChoice** folder. When Notepad opens, choose **Open** under the **File** menu. Then, choose **All Files** under **Files of Type** in the **Open** dialog box (by default, only files with **txt** extensions are shown). Choose the file and click **Open**. Note the format:

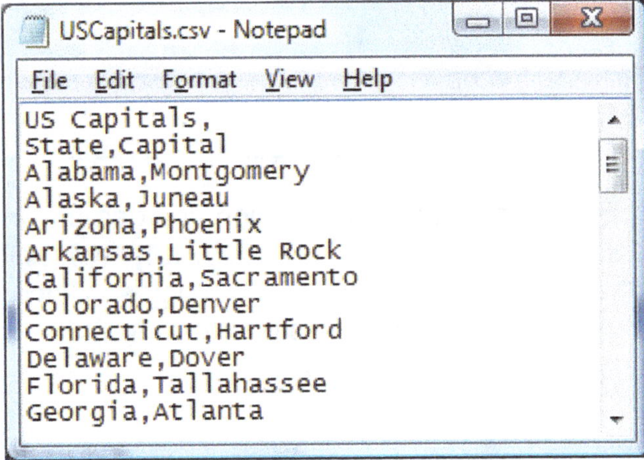
USCapitals.csv - Notepad

File Edit Format View Help

```
US Capitals,
State,Capital
Alabama,Montgomery
Alaska,Juneau
Arizona,Phoenix
Arkansas,Little Rock
California,Sacramento
Colorado,Denver
Connecticut,Hartford
Delaware,Dover
Florida,Tallahassee
Georgia,Atlanta
```

The first line shows the title (**US Capitals**) with an ending comma (don't forget this comma when generating a file). The second line are the headers (**State** and **Capital**), separated by a comma. Following the headers are the 50 pairs of states and capitals, separated by commas. All files must be in this form. Let's see how you can generate such files.

Code Design – Generating Exam Files

You will eventually want to use exam files other than the two examples included. Hence, you need to know how to generate such files. First, you need to have your list of terms (the list must have at least five pairs of items). Choose a title and the two headers. Once you have this information, you need to save it in the proper file format with a **csv** extension. The extension **csv** stands for **comma separated values** – that's why we saw all the commas in the **USCapitals.csv** file.

One way to generate an exam file is use a simple word processor such as the Windows **Notepad**. Start a new file and simply type in the information in the proper format like this:

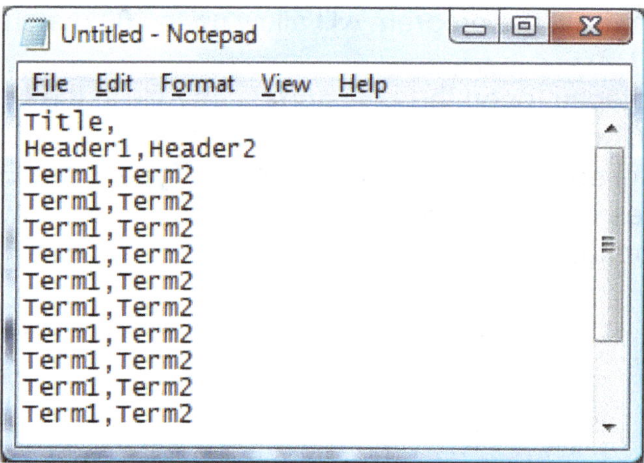

There are very few restrictions on the information you can use in an exam file. Entries can be letters, numbers, spaces and nearly any "typeable" character. A major restriction is that the entries can have <u>no commas</u>. Since we use a comma as a **delimiter** (the character that separates one term from the other), any other comma in a line would result in an error.

When the file is complete, save it with a **csv** extension in the same folder as your program. Notepad, by default, will want to save your file with a **txt** extension. To bypass this, when the **Save** dialog opens, choose **All Files** in the **Save as type** drop-down as shown:

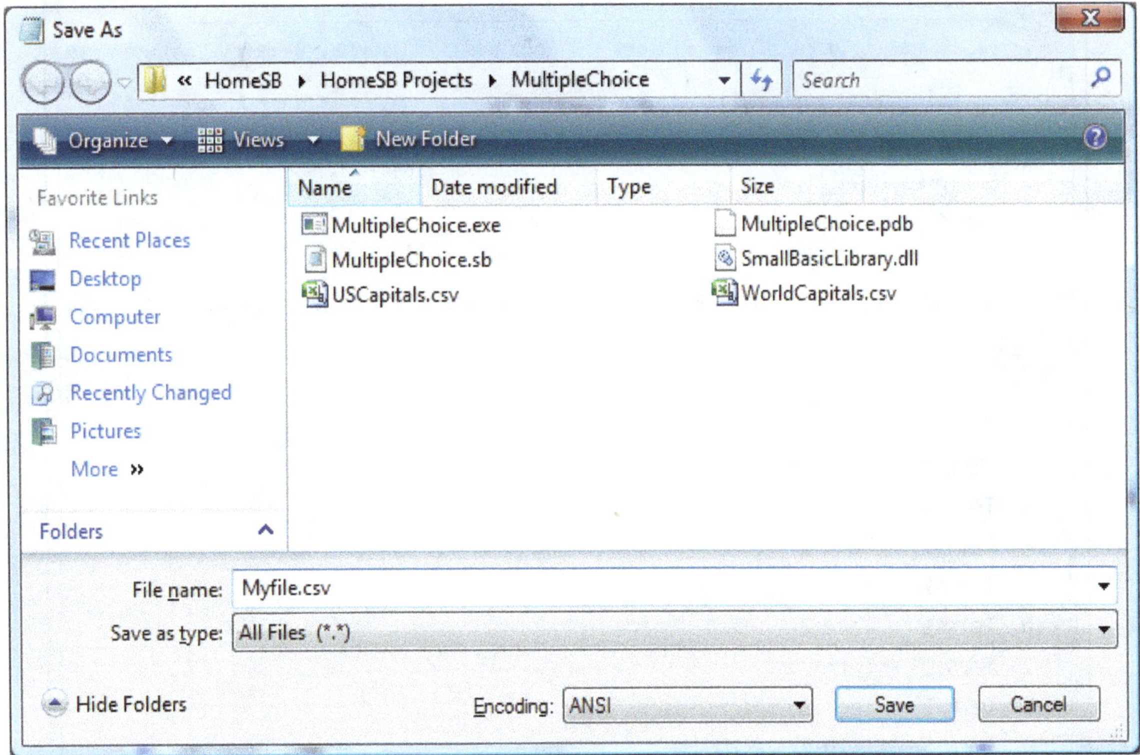

Type your file name with the **csv** extension and click **Save**. Make sure you have saved your file in the same folder as your **Multiple Choice Exam** program.

A spreadsheet program such as Microsoft's **Excel** can also be used to generate an exam file. To do this, start Excel. A blank worksheet should appear. Type the information in the spreadsheet cells something like this:

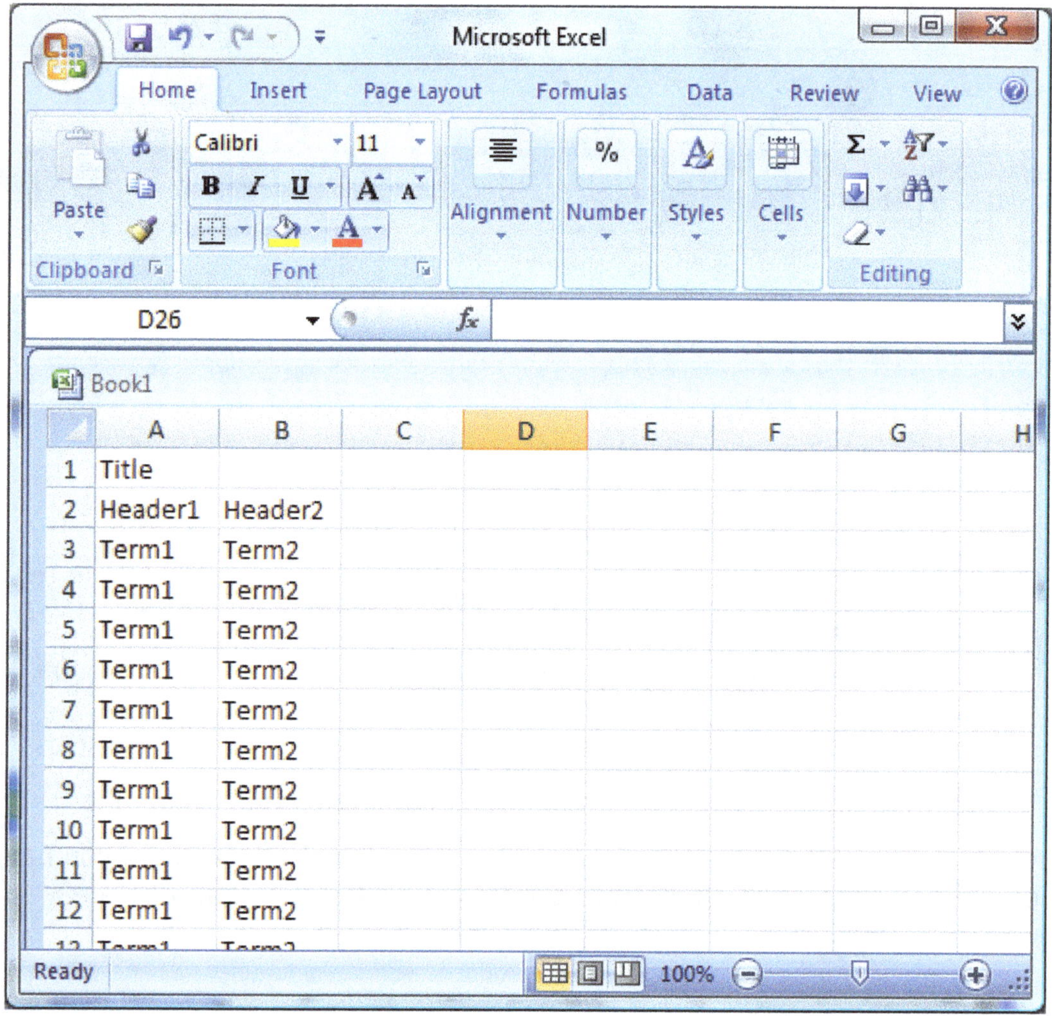

Once you've entered all your terms, choose **File**, then click **Save As**. When the **Save As** window appears, choose **CSV** under **Save as type** as shown below:

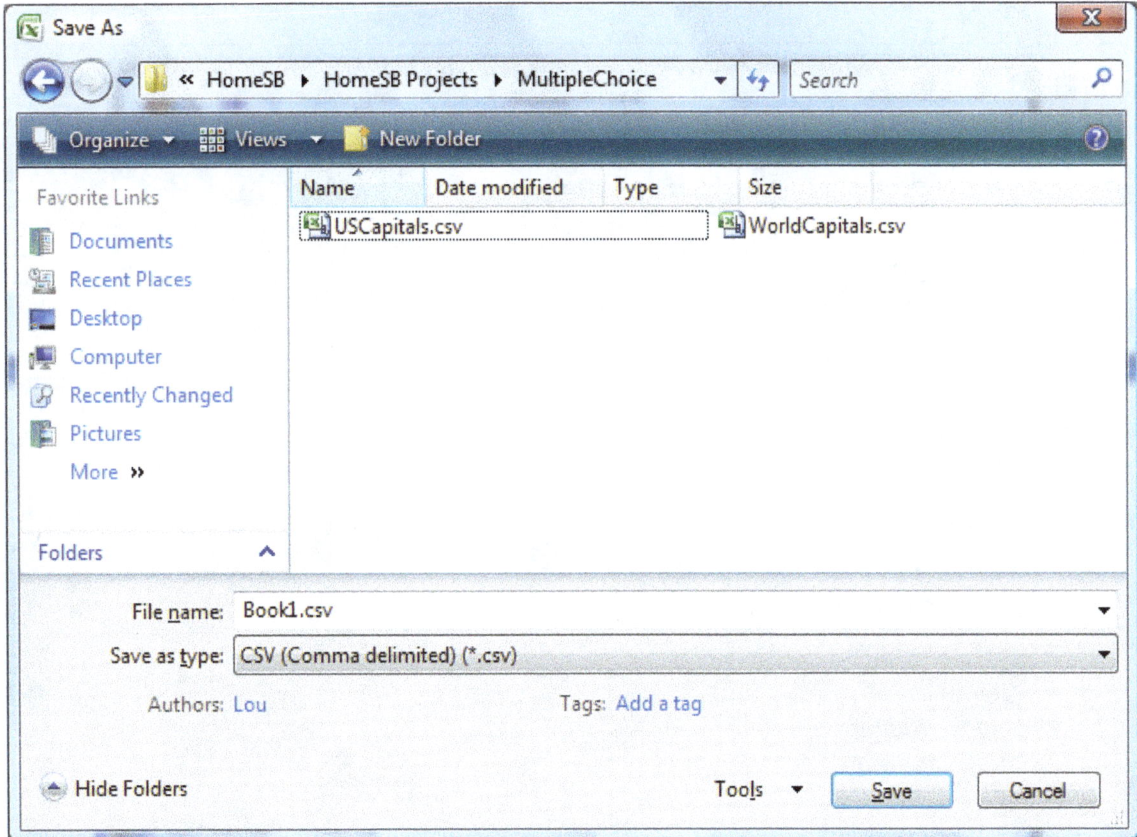

The information in the spreadsheet will be saved as a comma-separated file in the format used by the multiple choice exam project. Again, make sure you save the file in the same folder as your exam program.

You can also open the example exam files in Excel. Choose **Open** under the **File** menu, then choose one of the samples – you have to set **Files of type** to **All Files** when selecting the file. Here's the **WorldCapitals.csv** file in Excel:

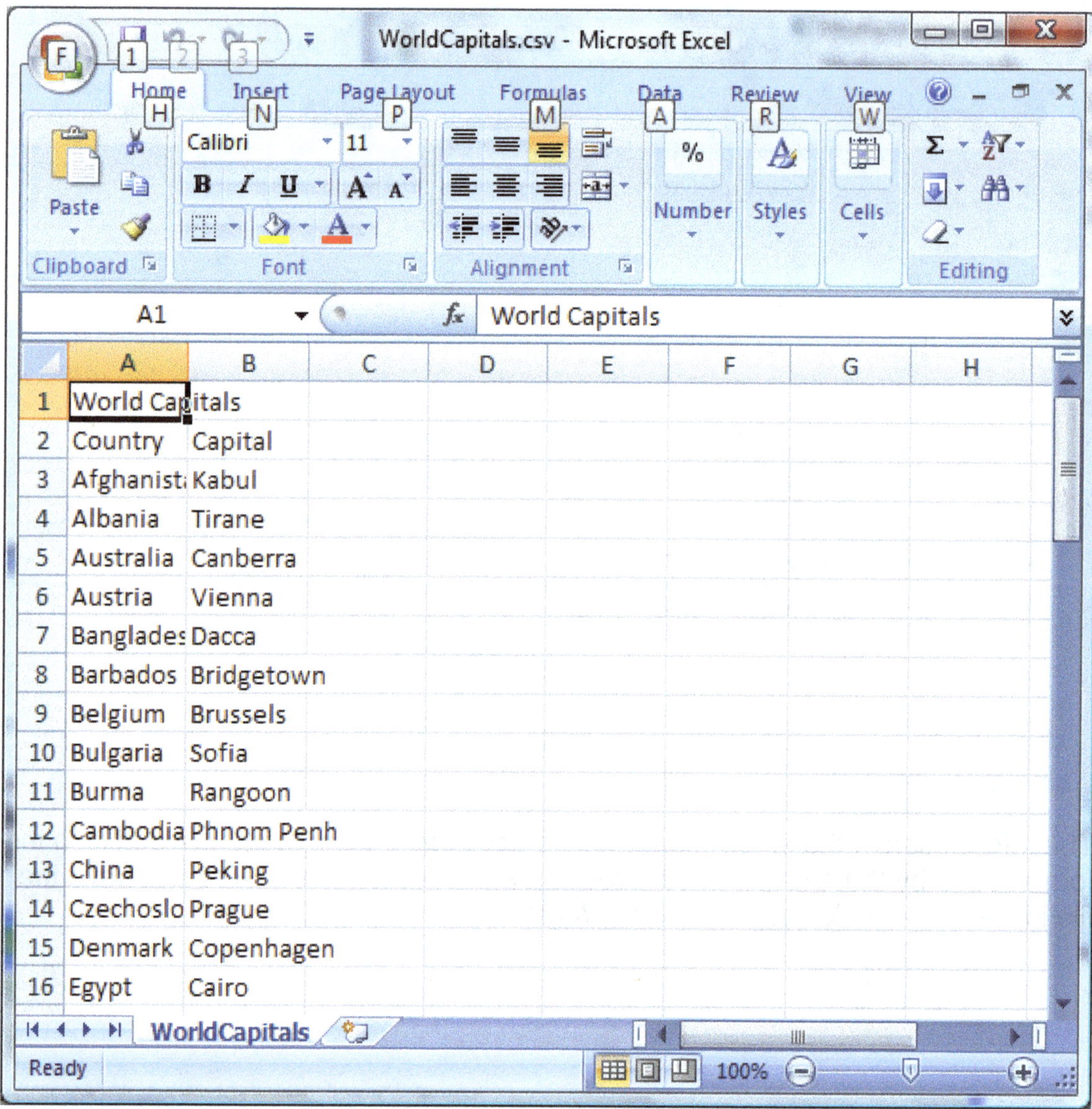

Now, let's see how to open exam files in our project.

Code Design – Opening an Exam File

When a user clicks the **Open File** button, the project should display all the exam files in the program folder and ask the user to select one. Upon that selection, the program will open the file, read in the information and place that information in the proper program variables. Once this is done, the user can begin to take a quiz. All of this will happen in the **OpenButtonClicked** subroutine. We will begin building that procedure. As a first step, let's look at the step of finding exam files.

The **GetFiles** method of the Small Basic **File** object will return all the files found in a particular folder. If the path to the folder is **FilePath**, the statement to do this is:

```
Files = File.GetFiles(FilePath)
```

Files is now an array containing the names (and associated paths) of all files found in **FilePath**. To find exam files, we would look at each item in this array and save the ones with a **csv** extension. Let's code up this first step.

Add this line at the end of **InitializeProgram** to detect button clicks:

```
Controls.ButtonClicked = ButtonClickedSub
```

Then, add the **ButtonClickedSub** subroutine:

```
Sub ButtonClickedSub
  B = Controls.LastClickedButton
  If (B = ExitButton) Then
    Program.End()
  ElseIf (B = OpenButton) Then
    OpenButtonClicked()
  EndIf
EndSub
```

Here, we have added code for **ExitButton** and **OpenButton**. If **OpenButton** is clicked, we call the **OpenButtonClicked** subroutine.

Add the **OpenButtonClicked** subroutine with the code needed to find exam files (files with **csv** extensions):

```
Sub OpenButtonClicked
  GraphicsWindow.Hide()
  TextWindow.Show()
  TextWindow.BackgroundColor = "White"
  TextWindow.ForegroundColor = "Black"
  TextWindow.Clear()
  TextWindow.Title = "Open Exam Files"
  'find csv files in program directory
  AllFiles = File.GetFiles(Program.Directory)
  NumberFiles = Array.GetItemCount(AllFiles)
  NumberCSVFiles = 0
  For I = 1 To NumberFiles
    'check for csv extension
    If (Text.IsSubText(AllFiles[I], ".csv")) Then
      NumberCSVFiles = NumberCSVFiles + 1
      CSVFiles[NumberCSVFiles] = AllFiles[I]
    EndIf
  EndFor
  If (NumberCSVFiles = 0) Then
    TextWindow.WriteLine("No exam files found.")
    TextWindow.Pause()
  Else
    TextWindow.WriteLine("Exam Files (choose by number):")
    TextWindow.WriteLine("")
    For I = 1 To NumberCSVFiles
      TextWindow.CursorLeft = 2
      TextWindow.Write(I + " - ")
      'strip off directory for display of name
      TextWindow.WriteLine(text.GetSubTextToEnd(CSVFiles[I],
Text.GetLength(Program.Directory) + 2))
    EndFor
    TextWindow.WriteLine("")
    GetFileNumber:
    TextWindow.Write("Choice? ")
    J = TextWindow.ReadNumber()
    If (J < 1 Or J > NumberCSVFiles) Then
      Goto GetFileNumber
    EndIf
  EndIf
  TextWindow.Hide()
  GraphicsWindow.Show()
EndSub
```

Let's explain what goes on here. A text window is used to display the exam files. **AllFiles** contains all files in the **Program.Directory** folder. There are **NumberFiles** such files. We loop through these files looking for a **csv** extension. All these files (there are **NumberCSVFiles** such files) are stored in the array **CSVFiles**. These files are listed (without the **Program.Directory**) for the user to choose from.

Copy the sample exam files (**USCapitals.csv** and **WorldCapitals.csv**) and any other exam files you may have created to your program folder. **Save** and **Run** the program. Click **Open File**. You should see this text window displaying the exam files it found:

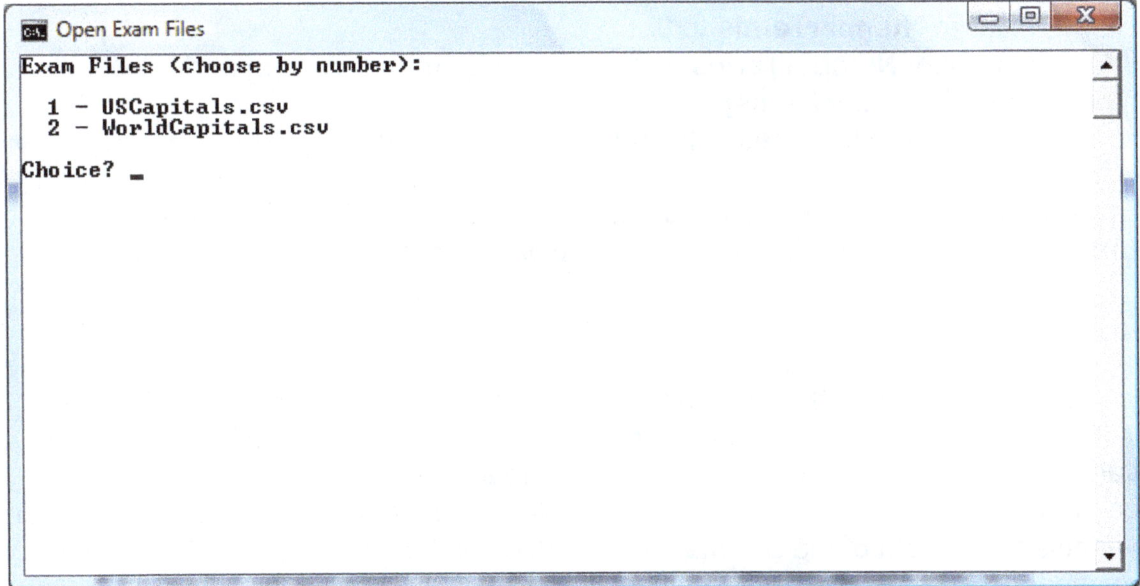

You can select a file, but nothing will happen. We need code to open the file and read information from it. We will discuss how to do that next.

Code Design – Reading an Exam File

Once an exam file is selected, we can read in the information from the file, line-by-line, and obtain needed program variables. Let's first discuss those variables. The file will provide us with the exam title (**ExamTitle**), two headers (**Header1**, **Header2**) and lists of exam terms in two arrays (**Term1**, **Term2**). We have arbitrarily set the limit on array length to be 100.

The steps to follow after selecting an exam file are:

- Read in first line, obtain **ExamTitle**.
- Read in second line, obtain **Header1** and **Header2**
- Initialize **NumberTerms** to 0.
- Increment **NumberTerms**, read in **Term1[NumberTerms]** and **Term2[NumberTerms]**
- Continue reading lines until end of file is reached.

Let's see how to read the lines and get the needed variables. To read line **LineNumber** from file **FileName**, use the **ReadLine** method of the **File** object:

```
FileLine = File.ReadLine(FileName, LineNumber)
```

where **FileLine** will be the line. In the exam file, this line (except for the first line) will have one variable, a comma, then another variable. To obtain the individual variables, we need to 'parse' the line. This means we will identify where the comma is in the line then extract one variable to the left of the comma and another variable to the right of the comma. This parsing is done with various **Text** object methods.

To determine the location of the comma in **FileLine**, we use the **GetIndexOf** method. In the expression:

```
CL = Text.GetIndexOf(FileLine, ",")
```

The variable **CL** will tell us which character in **FileLine** is a comma. The characters of **FileLine** are numbered from **1** to **Text.GetLength(FileLine),** the number of characters, or length, of **FileLine**. As an example, say **FileLine** is given by:

```
First,Second
```

Note **Text.GetLength(FileLine)** is **12**. If we apply the above **GetIndexOf** method to this line, we will find **CL** is **6**, or the comma is the 6th character in **FileLine**.

For multiple choice exam files, to extract the characters to the left of the comma (located at **CL**) in **FileLine**, we start at character **1** and extract **CL – 1** characters using the **GetSubTextOf** method:

```
LeftSide = Text.GetSubText(FileLine, 1, CL - 1)
```

The string to the right of the comma starts at character **CL + 1** and is extracted using the **GetSubTextToEnd** method:

```
RightSide = Text.GetSubTextToEnd(FileLine, CL + 1)
```

To convince you that this works, let's return to the example with:

```
First,Second
```

where recall **CL** is **6** and **Text.GetLength(FileLine)** is **12**. Using the **LeftSide** relation, we see:

```
LeftSide = Text.GetSubText(FileLine, 1, 6 - 1)
         = Text.GetSubText(FileLine, 1, 5)
```

Starting at the first character and extracting five characters, we get:

```
LeftSide = First
```

Success. Now, using the **RightString** relation, we see:

```
RightSide = Text.GetSubTextToEnd(FileLine, 6 + 1)
          = Text.GetSubTextToEnd(FileLine, 7)
```

Starting at the 7th character and extracting the remaining characters (including the 7th character), we get:

```
RightSide = Second
```

It works!!

All we need to know now is how to determine when we've reached the end of the exam file, so we know we have all the terms. After each line is read, we check for a blank line. When such a line is found, the end-of-file is reached.

We can now write the code to implement the steps to read and establish the variable values. The modified **OpenButtonClicked** subroutine (changes are shaded) is:

```
Sub OpenButtonClicked
    .
    .
    GetFileNumber:
    TextWindow.Write("Choice? ")
    J = TextWindow.ReadNumber()
    If (J < 1 Or J > NumberCSVFiles) Then
      Goto GetFileNumber
    EndIf
    'read info from file
    FileLine = File.ReadLine(CSVFiles[J], 1)
    ExamTitle = Text.GetSubText(FileLine, 1,
Text.GetLength(FileLine) - 1)
    FileLine = File.ReadLine(CSVFiles[J], 2)
    CL = Text.GetIndexOf(FileLine, ",")
    Header1 = Text.GetSubText(FileLine, 1, CL - 1)
    Header2 = Text.GetSubTextToEnd(FileLine, CL + 1)
    NumberTerms = 0
    NextLine:
    FileLine = File.ReadLine(CSVFiles[J], NumberTerms + 3)
    If (FileLine <> "") Then
      NumberTerms = NumberTerms + 1
      CL = Text.GetIndexOf(FileLine, ",")
      Term1[NumberTerms] = Text.GetSubText(FileLine, 1, CL - 1)
      Term2[NumberTerms] = Text.GetSubTextToEnd(FileLine, CL +
1)
      If (NumberTerms < 100) Then
        Goto NextLine
      EndIf
    EndIf
  EndIf
  TextWindow.Hide()
  GraphicsWindow.Show()
EndSub
```

You should be able to see all the steps in the code – we read the title, read the headers, then read in each set of variables. **Save** and **Run** the project. Click **Open File**. Select and process an exam file. Nothing exciting will happen. The code will just run and the interface won't change.

Let's add the code that changes the window so it is ready to start an exam. The steps are (assuming an exam file has been read correctly):

- Establish **Title** property for window.
- Set **text** for **HeadingGiven** and **HeadingAnswer** (based on **Header1Given** variable).
- Show **StartStopButton**.
- Show **OptionsButton**.
- Set **text** for **MessageArea** to indicate the file is loaded.

The code for each of these steps also goes in the **OpenButtonClicked** subroutine. The changes are shaded:

```
Sub OpenButtonClicked
    .
    .
    GetFileNumber:
    TextWindow.Write("Choice? ")
    J = TextWindow.ReadNumber()
    If (J < 1 Or J > NumberCSVFiles) Then
      Goto GetFileNumber
    EndIf
    'read info from file
    FileLine = File.ReadLine(CSVFiles[J], 1)
    ExamTitle = Text.GetSubText(FileLine, 1,
Text.GetLength(FileLine) - 1)
    FileLine = File.ReadLine(CSVFiles[J], 2)
    CL = Text.GetIndexOf(FileLine, ",")
    Header1 = Text.GetSubText(FileLine, 1, CL - 1)
    Header2 = Text.GetSubTextToEnd(FileLine, CL + 1)
    NumberTerms = 0
    NextLine:
    FileLine = File.ReadLine(CSVFiles[J], NumberTerms + 3)
    If (FileLine <> "") Then
      NumberTerms = NumberTerms + 1
      CL = Text.GetIndexOf(FileLine, ",")
      Term1[NumberTerms] = Text.GetSubText(FileLine, 1, CL - 1)
      Term2[NumberTerms] = Text.GetSubTextToEnd(FileLine, CL +
1)
      If (NumberTerms < 100) Then
        Goto NextLine
```

```
      EndIf
    EndIf
    'establish window title
    GraphicsWindow.Title = "Multiple Choice Exam - " +
ExamTitle
    'set up headers items
    If (Header1Given) Then
      Shapes.SetText(HeadingGiven, Header1)
      Shapes.SetText(HeadingAnswer, Header2)
    Else
      Shapes.SetText(HeadingGiven, Header1)
      Shapes.SetText(HeadingAnswer, Header2)
    EndIf
    Controls.ShowControl(StartStopButton)
    Controls.ShowControl(OptionsButton)
    Shapes.SetText(MessageArea, "File Loaded, Set Options" +
CRLF + "      Click Start Exam")
    Shapes.Move(MessageArea, 100, 280)
  EndIf
  TextWindow.Hide()
  GraphicsWindow.Show()
EndSub
```

This subroutine uses a variable **CRLF** to define a new line in the message. Add this single line in **InitializeProgram** to define **CRLF**:

```
CRLF = Text.GetCharacter(13)
```

Save and **Run** the project. Load in an exam file. When I loaded **USCapitals.csv**, the window looks like this:

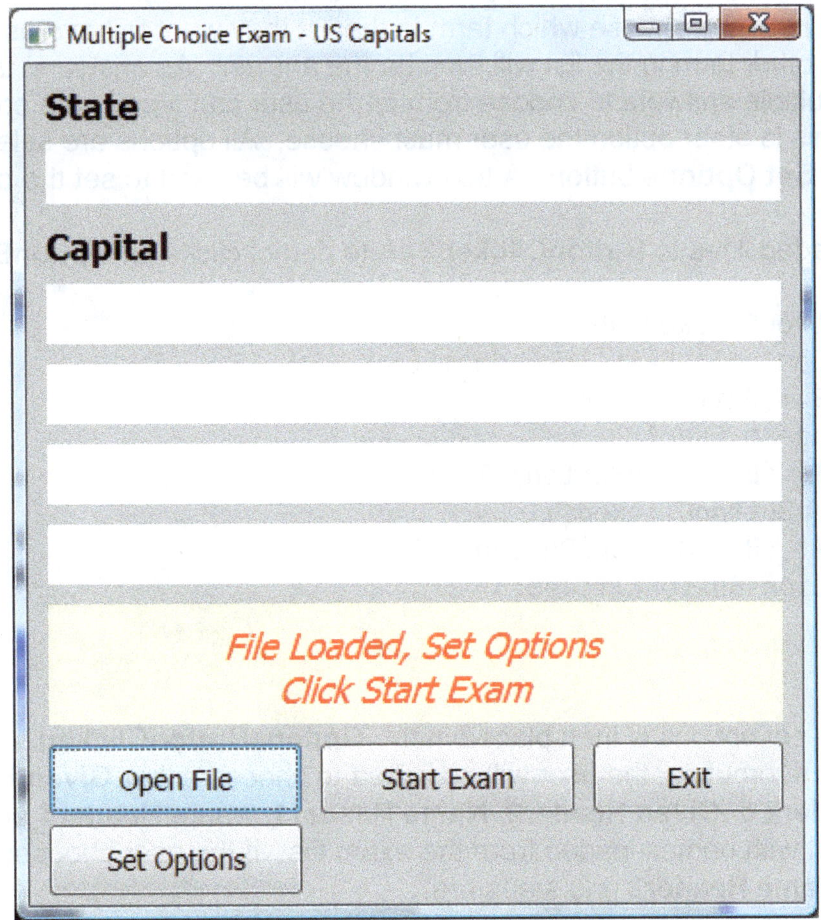

The window is ready for a multiple choice exam, where you name the **Capital**, given the **State** (default options). At this point, the user can change options if desired, then click **Start Exam** to start an exam. We'll look at the code to do that next.

Window Design – Selecting Options

Once an exam file is opened, the user needs to make two decisions before taking an exam. First, they choose which term in the list they want to have as the 'given' value. The other term in the list will then be the answer. As answers, the user can be given multiple answers to choose from or the user can type in the correct answer. This is other option the user must choose. All options are selected after clicking the **Set Options** button. A text window will be used to set the options.

Add the shaded lines to **ButtonClickedSub** to detect clicks on **OptionButton**:

```
Sub ButtonClickedSub
  B = Controls.LastClickedButton
  If (B = ExitButton) Then
    Program.End()
  ElseIf (B = OpenButton) Then
    OpenButtonClicked()
  ElseIf (B = OptionsButton) Then
    OptionsButtonClicked()
  EndIf
EndSub
```

The code to set options is then placed in the **OptionsButtonClicked** subroutine. First, in that subroutine, the user will be asked to choose either **Given Header1, Name Header2** or **Given Header2, Name Header1**, where **Header1** and **Header2** are replaced with names loaded from the exam file. If the user chooses **Given Header1, Name Header2**, the steps are:

- Set **Header1Given** to "**true**"
- Set **text** of **HeadingGiven** to **Header1**
- Set **text** of **HeadingAnswer** to **Header2**

Conversely, if the user chooses **Given Header2, Name Header1**, the steps are:

- Set **Header1Given** to "**false**"
- Set **text** of **HeadingGiven** to **Header2**
- Set **text** of **HeadingAnswer** to **Header1**

Next, the user is asked if they prefer **Multiple Choice Answers** or **Type-In Answers**. This results of this choice requires reconfiguration of the window. The multiple choice option requires four shapes to present the possible answers, while the type in option requires a single text box for entry of the answer. The steps involved in choosing the **Multiple Choice Answers** option are:

- Set **MCAnswers** to "**true**"
- Show four shape controls (**AnswerDisplay** array).
- Hide text box control (**AnswerTextBox**).

And, conversely, if the **Type In Answer** option is chosen, the steps are:

- Set **MCAnswers** to "**false**"
- Hide the four shape controls (**AnswerDisplay** array).
- Hide text box control (**AnswerTextBox**).

The **OptionsButtonClicked** subroutine that implements these steps is:

```
Sub OptionsButtonClicked
  GraphicsWindow.Hide()
  TextWindow.Show()
  TextWindow.BackgroundColor = "White"
  TextWindow.ForegroundColor = "Black"
  TextWindow.Clear()
  TextWindow.Title = "Set Options"
  TextWindow.WriteLine("Make Your Choice:")
  TextWindow.WriteLine("")
  TextWindow.CursorLeft = 2
  TextWindow.WriteLine("1 - Given " + Header1 + ", Name " +
Header2)
  TextWindow.CursorLeft = 2
  TextWindow.WriteLine("2 - Given " + Header2 + ", Name " +
Header1)
  TextWindow.WriteLine("")
  GetGiven:
  TextWindow.Write("Choice? ")
  A = TextWindow.ReadNumber()
  If (A = 1) Then
    Header1Given = "true"
    Shapes.SetText(HeadingGiven, Header1)
    Shapes.SetText(HeadingAnswer, Header2)
  ElseIf (A = 2) Then
    Header1Given = "false"
    Shapes.SetText(HeadingGiven, Header2)
    Shapes.SetText(HeadingAnswer, Header1)
  Else
```

```
    Goto GetGiven
   EndIf
   TextWindow.CursorTop = 7
   TextWindow.WriteLine("Make Your Choice:")
   TextWindow.WriteLine("")
   TextWindow.CursorLeft = 2
   TextWindow.WriteLine("1 - Multiple Choice Answers")
   TextWindow.CursorLeft = 2
   TextWindow.WriteLine("2 - Type-In Answers")
   TextWindow.WriteLine("")
   GetAnswer:
   TextWindow.Write("Choice? ")
   A = TextWindow.ReadNumber()
   If (A = 1) Then
     MCAnswers = "true"
     Shapes.SetText(GivenDisplay, "")
     GraphicsWindow.BrushColor = "White"
     GraphicsWindow.FillRectangle(10, 110, 380, 30)
     GraphicsWindow.FillRectangle(10, 150, 380, 30)
     GraphicsWindow.FillRectangle(10, 190, 380, 30)
     GraphicsWindow.FillRectangle(10, 230, 380, 30)
     For I = 1 To 4
       Shapes.SetText(AnswerDisplay[I], "")
       Shapes.ShowShape(AnswerDisplay[I])
     EndFor
     Controls.HideControl(AnswerTextBox)
   ElseIf (A = 2) Then
     MCAnswers = "false"
     Shapes.SetText(GivenDisplay, "")
     GraphicsWindow.BrushColor = GraphicsWindow.BackgroundColor
     GraphicsWindow.FillRectangle(10, 110, 380, 30)
     GraphicsWindow.FillRectangle(10, 150, 380, 30)
     GraphicsWindow.FillRectangle(10, 190, 380, 30)
     GraphicsWindow.FillRectangle(10, 230, 380, 30)
     For I = 1 To 4
       Shapes.HideShape(AnswerDisplay[I])
     EndFor
     Controls.ShowControl(AnswerTextBox)
   Else
     Goto GetAnswer
   EndIf
   TextWindow.Hide()
   GraphicsWindow.Show()
 EndSub
```

Save and **Run** the project. Open an example exam file (I used **USCapitals.csv**). Click **Set Options** and this text window appears:

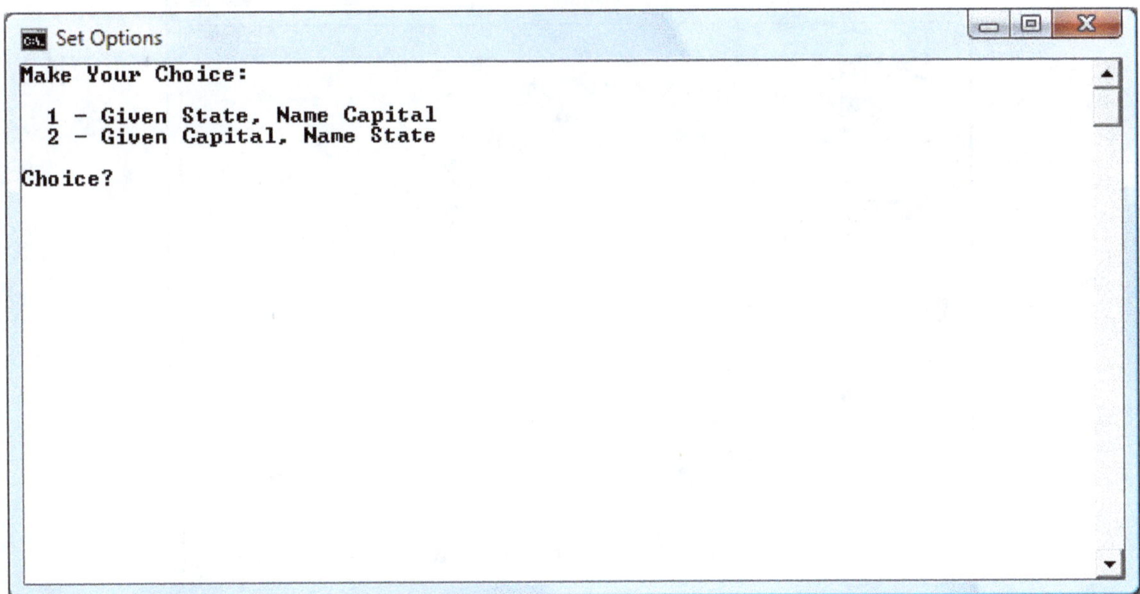
Set Options
Make Your Choice:
1 - Given State, Name Capital
2 - Given Capital, Name State
Choice?

Choose **Given Capital, Name State** (Option 2). Then, you see:

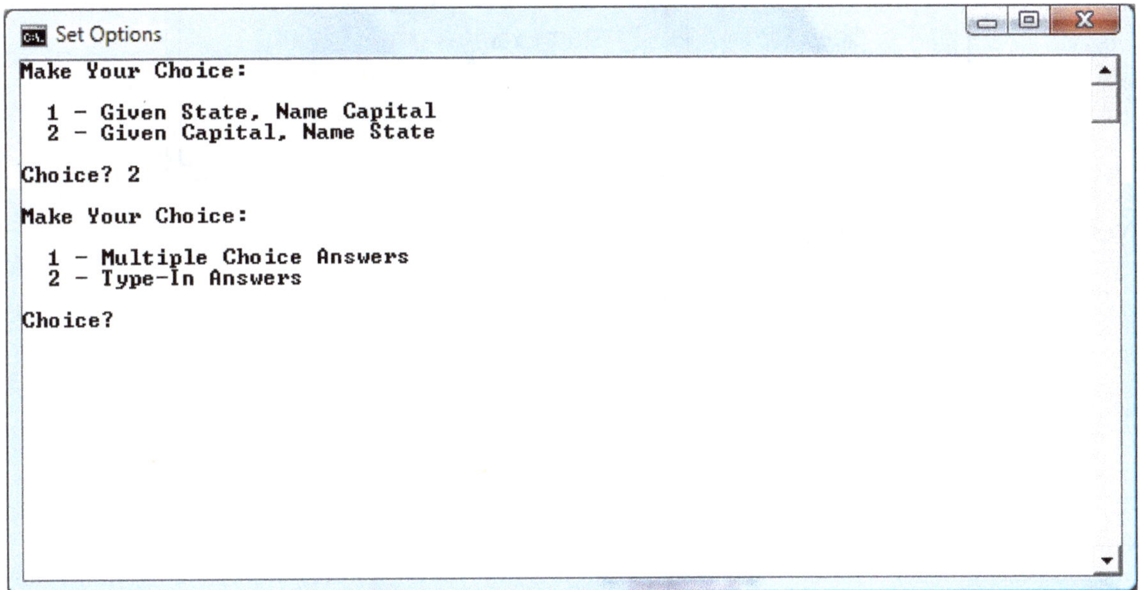
Set Options
Make Your Choice:
1 - Given State, Name Capital
2 - Given Capital, Name State
Choice? 2
Make Your Choice:
1 - Multiple Choice Answers
2 - Type-In Answers
Choice?

Choose **Multiple Choice Answers** (Option 1).

You should see:

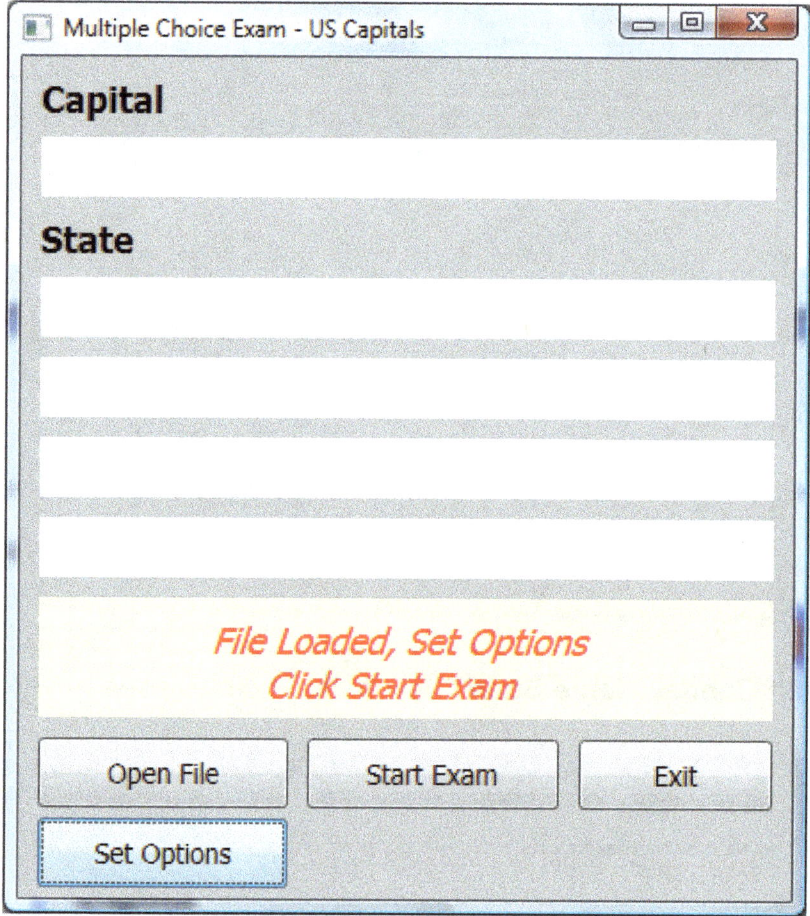

Note the proper headers.

By default, the multiple choice answer option is shown. Click Set Options again, this time **Type In Answers**. This changes the window to:

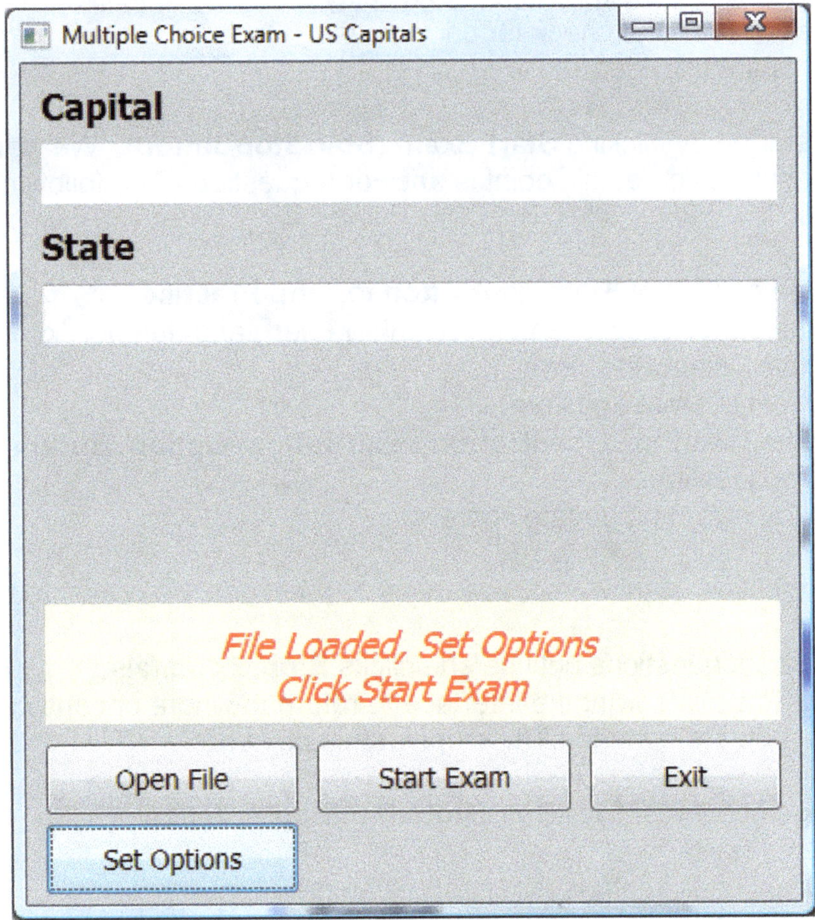

Make sure you can change back to the **Multiple Choice Answers** option.

We've completed the code for opening exam files and configuring the interface (by choosing options). It is now time to address the code to present an exam to the user.

Code Design – Start Exam

The idea of a multiple choice exam is to display a random question, obtain an answer from the user and check for correctness. Once an exam is complete, scoring results are provided.

An exam is started by clicking **Start Exam** (**StartStopButton**). We want to make sure all the user can do at this point is answer a question. The following steps should occur:

- Change caption of **StartStopButton** to **Stop Practice**
- Set number of questions tried (**NumberTried**) and number correct (**NumberCorrect**) to zero.
- Clear text of **MessageArea**.
- Hide **Next Button**, **OpenButton**, **ExitButton**, **OptionsButton**.
- Present question.
- Check answer and update score.

Once each question is answered, subsequent questions are presented.

The user answers questions until he/she clicks **Stop Exam** (also **StartStopButton**). We want the interface to return to where options can be selected or a new file opened. The steps at this point are:

- Change caption of **StartStopButton** to **Stop Practice**
- Present results.
- Clear text of all controls (shapes/text boxes).
- Set text of **MessageArea** to indicate a new exam can be started.
- Hide **NextButton**.
- Show **OpenButton**, **ExitButton**, **OptionsButton**.

Let's build a framework for the code that implements most of these steps (we'll look at presenting results later). Add the shaded lines to **ButtonClickedSub** to detect clicks on **StartStopButton**:

```
Sub ButtonClickedSub
  B = Controls.LastClickedButton
  If (B = ExitButton) Then
    Program.End()
  ElseIf (B = OpenButton) Then
    OpenButtonClicked()
  ElseIf (B = OptionsButton) Then
    OptionsButtonClicked()
  ElseIf (B = StartStopButton) Then
    StartStopButtonClicked()
  EndIf
EndSub
```

The **StartStopButtonClicked** subroutine that implements the listed steps (again, except for results) is:

```
Sub StartStopButtonClicked
  If (Controls.GetButtonCaption(StartStopButton) = "Start
Exam") Then
    Controls.SetButtonCaption(StartStopButton, "Stop Exam")
    ' Reset the score
    NumberTried = 0
    NumberCorrect = 0
    Shapes.SetText(MessageArea, "")
    Controls.HideControl(NextButton)
    Controls.HideControl(OpenButton)
    Controls.HideControl(ExitButton)
    Controls.HideControl(OptionsButton)
    NextQuestion()
  Else
    Controls.SetButtonCaption(StartStopButton, "Start Exam")
    Shapes.SetText(GivenDisplay, "")
    If (MCAnswers) Then
      Shapes.SetText(AnswerDisplay[1], "")
      Shapes.SetText(AnswerDisplay[2], "")
      Shapes.SetText(AnswerDisplay[3], "")
      Shapes.SetText(AnswerDisplay[4], "")
    Else
      Controls.SetTextBoxText(AnswerTextBox, "")
    EndIf
    Shapes.SetText(MessageArea, "    Set Options" + CRLF +
"Click Start Exam")
```

```
      Shapes.Move(MessageArea, 140, 280)
      Controls.HideControl(NextButton)
      Controls.ShowControl(OpenButton)
      Controls.ShowControl(ExitButton)
      Controls.ShowControl(OptionsButton)
    EndIf
  EndSub
```

Add this code to the project.

This code uses a subroutine **NextQuestion** to generate a random question. Add this empty procedure to the project:

```
  Sub NextQuestion
  EndSub
```

We'll write code for this procedure next, once we make sure the changes just made work.

Save and **Run** the project. Open an exam file. Make sure the **Start Exam** and **Stop Exam** buttons function properly, changing the interface as desired.

Code Design - Question Generation

To generate a question, we examine the options selected by the user and produce a random question based on these selections. The code to generate such a question will be in the **NextQuestion** general procedure.

The steps involved in generating a random question are:

- Clear **text** of **MessageArea**.
- Select random item from term list as the "correct answer" (**CorrectAnswer**).
- Set text of **DisplayGiven** to 'given' term.
- If **Multiple Choice Answers** is selected:
  - Generate four possible answers (one of which is the correct answer)
  - Display answers in shapes.
- If **Type In Answers** is selected:
  - Clear **AnswerTextBox**.

The code to select a question, set **DisplayGiven** and to set up for **type in answers** is straightforward.

The code for the **NextQuestion** procedure for these steps is:

```
Sub NextQuestion
  Shapes.SetText(MessageArea, "")
  ' Generate the next question based on selected options
  CorrectAnswer = Math.GetRandomNumber(NumberTerms)
  GraphicsWindow.BrushColor = "Blue"
  GraphicsWindow.FontSize = 18
  GraphicsWindow.FontBold = "false"
  GraphicsWindow.BrushColor = "Blue"
  If (Header1Given) Then
    Shapes.SetText(GivenDisplay, Term1[CorrectAnswer])
  Else
    Shapes.SetText(GivenDisplay, Term2[CorrectAnswer])
  EndIf
  If (MCAnswers) Then
    ' Multiple choice answers
  Else
    ' Type-in answers
    Controls.SetTextBoxText(AnswerTextBox, "")
  EndIf
EndSub
```

Add this code to the project. **Save** and **Run** the project if you'd like to see if you can type in answers (make sure you select this option).

The code for **multiple choice answers** is more detailed and we need to spend some time looking at it. The tricky part of this code is to select the four multiple choices, one of which is the correct answer. The approach we follow is to first select four terms at random from the **NumberTerms** possibilities, making sure we don't select the correct answer (index is **CorrectAnswer**). Once we have these four possibilities, we replace one at random with the correct answer. Let's look at the steps.

First, we need some way to know if we have already selected a previously chosen answer possibility. We will use an array **TermUsed** to tell us if a term has been used. Each element in this array is initialized to **"false"**, indicating all are available. The code snippet that accomplishes this task is:

```
For I = 1 To NumberTerms
  TermUsed[I] = "false"
EndFor
```

A loop is used to pick the four random answer possibilities. An array **Index** stores the four selected indices. The code snippet is:

```
' Pick four random possiblities
For I = 1 To 4
  GetJ:
  J = Math.GetRandomNumber(NumberTerms)
  If (TermUsed[J] Or J = CorrectAnswer) Then
    Goto GetJ
  EndIf
  TermUsed[J] = "true"
  Index[I] = J
EndFor
```

See how this works? For each of the four answers (selected with the **For** loop), a random index **J** is selected making sure the corresponding term has not been selected before and is not the **CorrectAnswer**.

Once the array **Index** is established, one item in the array is replaced with **CorrectAnswer**. The line of code that accomplishes this replacement is:

```
' Replace one with correct answer
Index[Math.GetRandomNumber(4)] = CorrectAnswer
```

Now, depending on which is term is given and which is the answer, the **Index** array establishes the contents of the text shapes used for multiple choice answers.

The modified **NextQuestion** subroutine that incorporates the code for multiple choice answers (changes are shaded) is:

```
Sub NextQuestion
  Shapes.SetText(MessageArea, "")
  ' Generate the next question based on selected options
  CorrectAnswer = Math.GetRandomNumber(NumberTerms)
  GraphicsWindow.BrushColor = "Blue"
  GraphicsWindow.FontSize = 18
  GraphicsWindow.FontBold = "false"
  GraphicsWindow.BrushColor = "Blue"
  If (Header1Given) Then
    Shapes.SetText(GivenDisplay, Term1[CorrectAnswer])
  Else
    Shapes.SetText(GivenDisplay, Term2[CorrectAnswer])
  EndIf
  If (MCAnswers) Then
    ' Multiple choice answers
    For I = 1 To NumberTerms
```

```
      TermUsed[I] = "false"
    EndFor
    ' Pick four random possiblities
    For I = 1 To 4
      GetJ:
      J = Math.GetRandomNumber(NumberTerms)
      If (TermUsed[J] Or J = CorrectAnswer) Then
        Goto GetJ
      EndIf
      TermUsed[J] = "true"
      Index[I] = J
    EndFor
    ' Replace one with correct answer
    Index[Math.GetRandomNumber(4)] = CorrectAnswer
    ' Display multiple choice answers
    If (Header1Given) Then
      Shapes.SetText(AnswerDisplay[1], Term2[Index[1]])
      Shapes.SetText(AnswerDisplay[2], Term2[Index[2]])
      Shapes.SetText(AnswerDisplay[3], Term2[Index[3]])
      Shapes.SetText(AnswerDisplay[4], Term2[Index[4]])
    Else
      Shapes.SetText(AnswerDisplay[1], Term1[Index[1]])
      Shapes.SetText(AnswerDisplay[2], Term1[Index[2]])
      Shapes.SetText(AnswerDisplay[3], Term1[Index[3]])
      Shapes.SetText(AnswerDisplay[4], Term1[Index[4]])
    EndIf
  Else
    ' Type-in answers
    Controls.SetTextBoxText(AnswerTextBox, "")
  EndIf
EndSub
```

Make the noted modifications.

Save and **Run** the project. Open an example exam file. Using default options and the **USCapitals.csv** file, clicking **Start Exam**, I see (you will see different results because of the Random object):

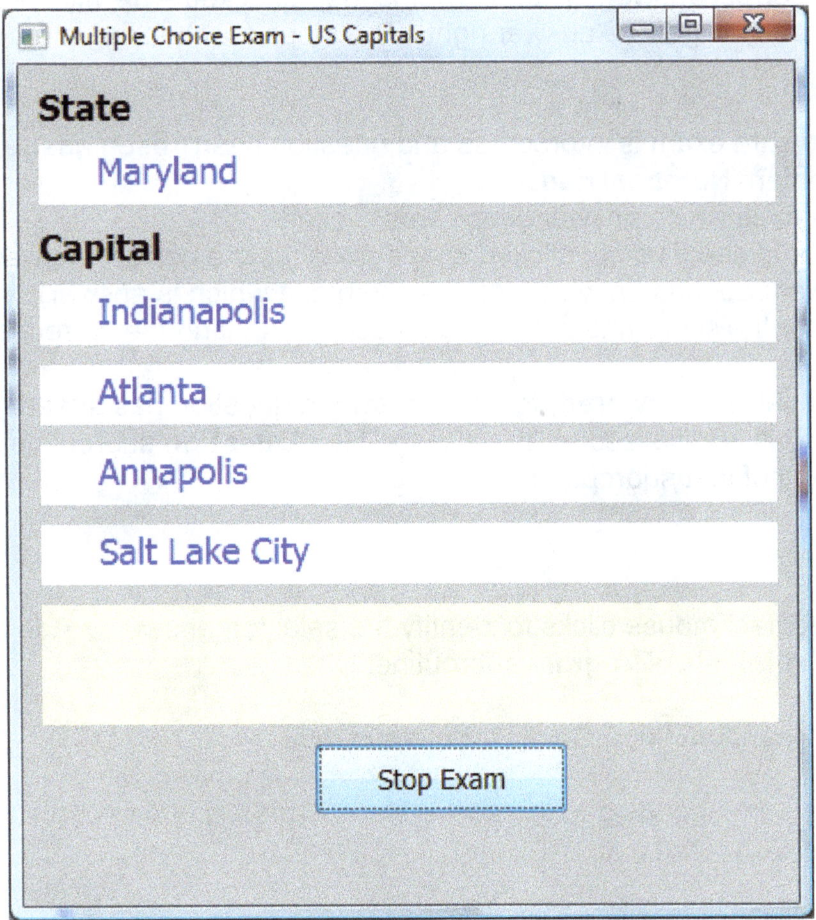

The given **State** is **Maryland**. Note the four possible **State** answers (three random and one the correct answer, **Annapolis**). The multiple choice logic seems to be working. All you can do at this point is click **Stop Exam**. You can then click **Start Exam** to see another question (changing options if you wish). View as many questions, with different options, as you wish. Next, we'll see how to get answers to these questions – we consider both multiple choice and type in answers.

Code Design – Checking Multiple Choice Answers

Once a question is presented using multiple choice answers, the user is asked to click on the correct answer. That answer is then checked - we will only give the user one chance to get the answer right. The steps for checking a multiple choice answer:

- Make sure exam is in progress and question hasn't been answered already.
- Increment **NumberTried**.
- Determine which answer shape was clicked.
- Check to see if text of clicked shape matches the correct answer (correct answer depends on which term is given and which is answer).
- Update the score and provide feedback, presenting the correct answer.

We use a variable (**Answered**) to let us know if a question has already been answered. This is initialized to "false" in the **NextQuestion** subroutine. Add this line at the end of that subroutine:

```
Answered = "false"
```

We want to detect mouse clicks to identify the selected answers. Add this line at the end of the **InitializeProgram** subroutine:

```
GraphicsWindow.MouseDown = MouseDownSub
```

So, the code corresponding to the above steps is placed in a subroutine named **MouseDownSub**. That code is:

```
Sub MouseDownSub
  ' If exam not in progress or already answered, exit
  If (Controls.GetButtonCaption(StartStopButton) = "Start Exam"
Or Answered) Then
    Goto ExitMouseDownSub
  EndIf
  ' find out which answer was clicked
  X = GraphicsWindow.MouseX
  Y = GraphicsWindow.MouseY
  If (X > 10 And X < 390 And Y > 110 And Y < 260) Then
    NumberTried = NumberTried + 1
    If (Y > 110 And Y < 140) Then
      AnswerClicked = 1
    ElseIf (Y > 150 And Y < 180) Then
      AnswerClicked = 2
    ElseIf (Y > 190 And Y < 220) Then
      AnswerClicked = 3
    ElseIf (Y > 230 And Y < 260) Then
```

```
      AnswerClicked = 4
    EndIf
    Correct = "false"
    If (Header1Given) Then
      If Term2[Index[AnswerClicked]] = Term2[CorrectAnswer]
Then
        Correct = "true"
      EndIf
    Else
      If Term1[Index[AnswerClicked]] = Term1[CorrectAnswer]
Then
        Correct = "true"
      EndIf
    EndIf
    Answered = "true"
    UpdateScore()
  EndIf
  ExitMouseDownSub:
EndSub
```

This code uses a subroutine **UpdateScore** to update the scoring and prepare the user interface for the next question. The procedure uses the value of **Correct**. If **Correct** is **"true"** if the answer was answered correct, **"false"** is incorrect. The steps involved:

- If answer is correct: increment **NumberCorrect** and set text of **MessageArea** to "**Correct!**"
- If answer is incorrect: set text of **MessageArea** to "**Sorry ... Correct Answer Shown**"
- If multiple choice answers are used: put correct answer in **AnswerDisplay[1]**, clear all other label controls.
- If type in answers are used: put correct answer in **AnswerTextBox**.
- Show **StartStopButton**.
- Show **NextButton**.

The code for **UpdateScore** is:

```
Sub UpdateScore
  ' Check if answer is correct
  If (Correct) Then
    NumberCorrect = NumberCorrect + 1
    Shapes.SetText(MessageArea, "Correct!")
    Shapes.Move(MessageArea, 170, 290)
  Else
    Shapes.SetText(MessageArea, "Sorry ... Correct Answer
Shown")
    Shapes.Move(MessageArea, 80, 290)
  EndIf
  ' Display correct answer
  If (MCAnswers) Then
    If (Header1Given) Then
      Shapes.SetText(AnswerDisplay[1], Term2[CorrectAnswer])
    Else
      Shapes.SetText(AnswerDisplay[1], Term1[CorrectAnswer])
    EndIf
    Shapes.SetText(AnswerDisplay[2], "")
    Shapes.SetText(AnswerDisplay[3], "")
    Shapes.SetText(AnswerDisplay[4], "")
  Else
    If (Header1Given) Then
      Controls.SetTextBoxText(AnswerTextBox,
Term2[CorrectAnswer])
    Else
      Controls.SetTextBoxText(AnswerTextBox,
Term1[CorrectAnswer])
    EndIf
  EndIf
  Controls.ShowControl(StartStopButton)
  Controls.ShowControl(NextButton)
EndSub
```

Add the **MouseDownSub** and **UpdateScore** (this routine will also be used when checking typed in answers) code to the project.

Notice after displaying the correct answer, the button marked **Next Question** appears. Clicking this button will present another question to the user. The code simply involves hiding the button, once clicked, then invoking the existing **NextQuestion** subroutine. Add the shaded lines to **ButtonClickedSub** to implement these steps:

```
Sub ButtonClickedSub
  B = Controls.LastClickedButton
  If (B = ExitButton) Then
    Program.End()
  ElseIf (B = OpenButton) Then
    OpenButtonClicked()
  ElseIf (B = OptionsButton) Then
    OptionsButtonClicked()
  ElseIf (B = StartStopButton) Then
    StartStopButtonClicked()
  ElseIf (B = NextButton) Then
    Controls.HideControl(NextButton)
    NextQuestion()
  EndIf
EndSub
```

We are now ready to take exams with multiple choice answers

Save and **Run** the project. Open an exam file. Select options (obviously choose multiple choice answers). For the example here, I use the **WorldCapitals.csv** file, providing capitals, given the country. The first question I see is:

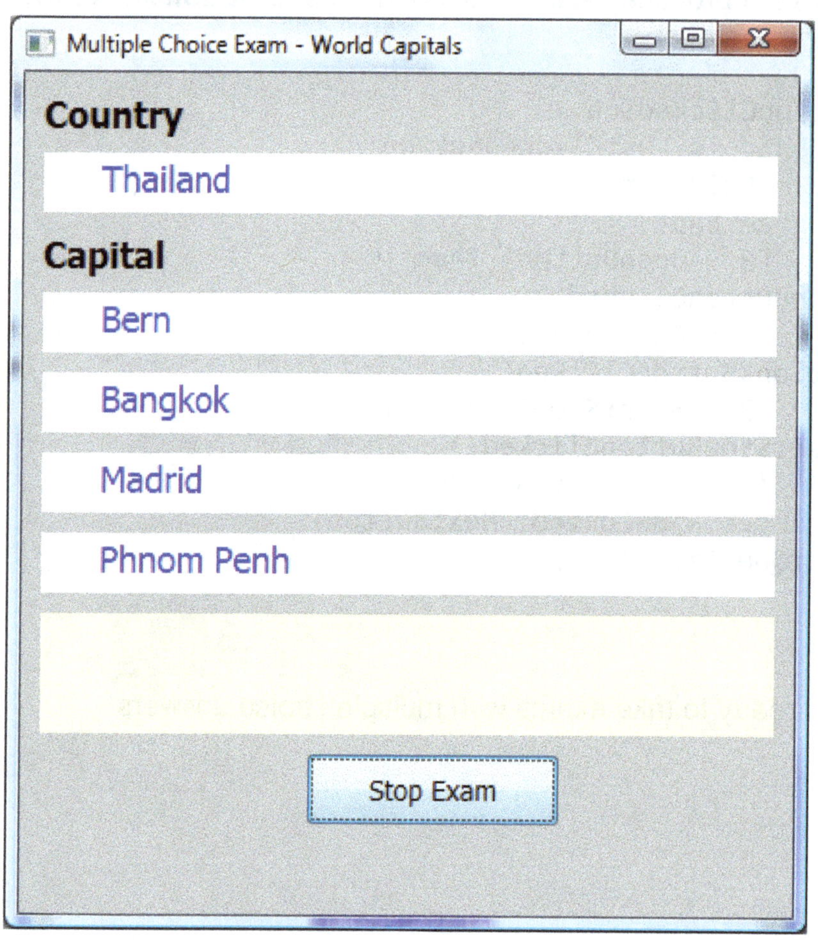

When I click **Bangkok**, I see:

At this point, I can click **Next Question** for another question, or click **Stop Exam** to stop this test. Answer as many questions as you like.

At some point, answer incorrectly. When I do, I see:

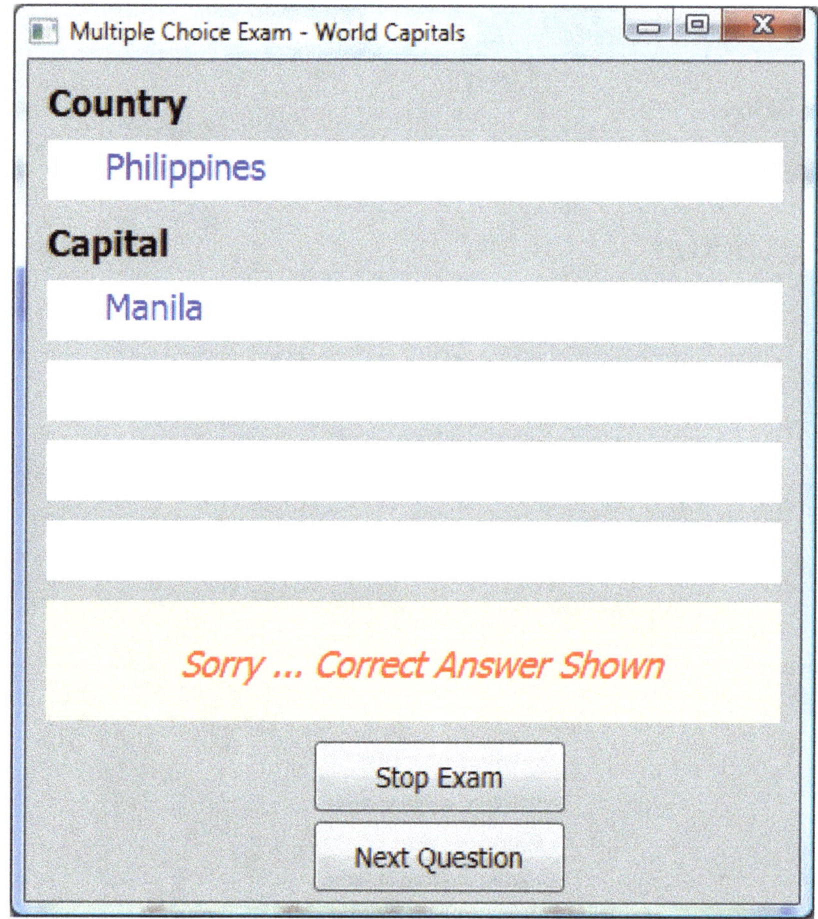

So, with an incorrect answer, you are told so and given the correct answer. The only difference between the results of a correct and incorrect answer is the message displayed to the user (and the score, of course).

Code Design – Checking Type In Answers

Problems can arise when using text box controls. When a user types an answer, a first consideration that must be made is whether any typed keys are unacceptable. Recall in the loan assistant, we only allowed numeric inputs. In this project, we will allow all keystrokes. A second question is how do we know when a user is done entering an answer? You could have a button to click that says **Check Answer** or have the user press a certain key. In this exam project, we will check the answer once a user presses the <**Enter**> key.

We need to consider case sensitivity when entering alphabetic entries. For example, in the **USCapitals.csv** file, the capital of the state of **Washington** (our home state) is saved as **Olympia**. If a user types **olympia** (all lower case), do we really want to tell the user the answer is incorrect? Or, what if they type **Olimpia**, a very close spelling? What do we do in this situation? We will solve both of these problems, addressing case-sensitivity first.

Once a user types an answer and presses <**Enter**>, we take these steps:

- Make sure question hasn't been answered already.
- Increment **NumberTried**.
- Convert text in **AnswerTextBox** (user answer) to all upper case.
- Convert correct answer to all upper case.
- Compare upper case strings to see if they are equal.
- Update the score and provide feedback, presenting the correct answer.

The method **Text.ConvertToUpperCase** converts a string value to all upper case. The method ignores any non-letter characters.

To detect the <**Enter**> key, we use the **KeyDown** event of the graphics window. Add this single line to **InitializeProgram**:

```
GraphicsWindow.KeyDown = KeyDownSub
```

We place the code to check a typed answer in the **KeyDownSub** subroutine (processing the code when the <**Enter**> key is pressed). The procedure is:

```
Sub KeyDownSub
  ' If exam not in progress or already answered, exit
  If (Controls.GetButtonCaption(StartStopButton) = "Start Exam"
Or Answered) Then
    Goto ExitTextTypedSub
  EndIf
  'wait for <Enter>
  If (GraphicsWindow.LastKey = "Return") Then
    NumberTried = NumberTried + 1
    UCTypedAnswer =
Text.ConvertToUpperCase(Controls.GetTextBoxText(AnswerTextBox))
    If (Header1Given) Then
      UCAnswer = Text.ConvertToUpperCase(Term2[CorrectAnswer])
    Else
      UCAnswer = Text.ConvertToUpperCase(Term2[CorrectAnswer])
    EndIf
    Correct = "false"
    UpdateScore()
  EndIf
  ExitTextTypedSub:
EndSub
```

Note the use of the **LastKey** method to see when <**Enter**> is pressed. Also note the use of the **ConvertToUpperCase** method. This code also uses the **UpdateScore** subroutine to update the score and display after answering. Add this procedure to the project.

Save and **Run** the project. Select an exam file (I used **WorldCapitals.csv**). Choose the **Type In Answers** option. Click **Start Exam**. My first question appears as:

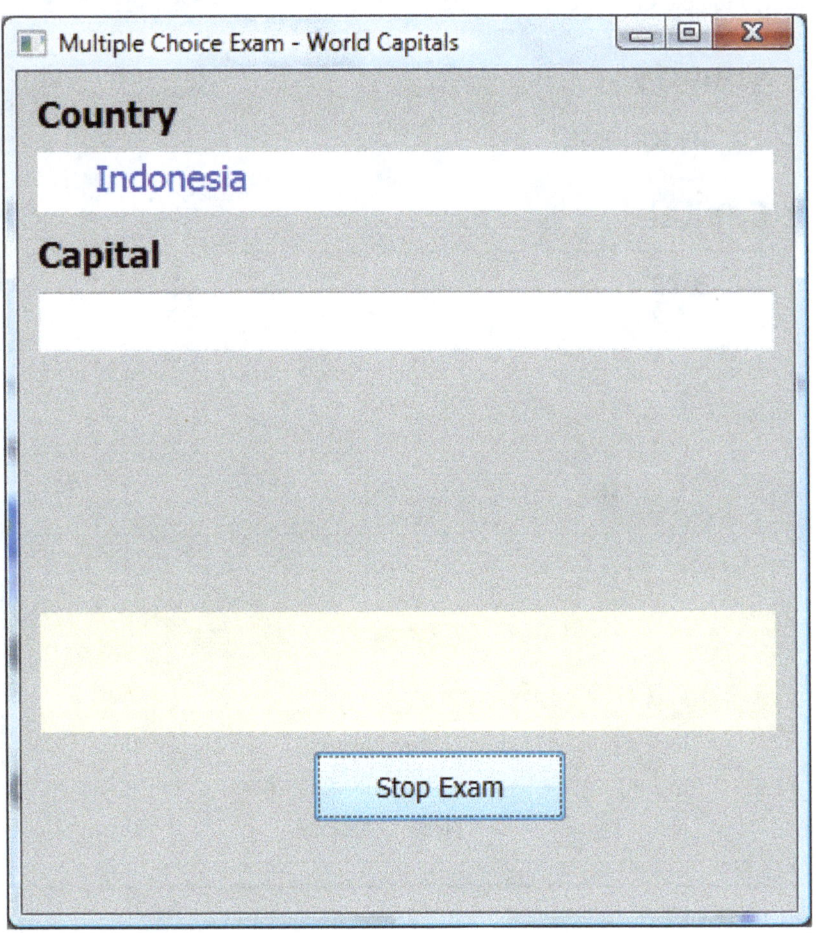

Click the text box to type your answer. If I type **Jakarta**, the correct answer with correct letter case, then press <**Enter**>, I am told the answer is correct:

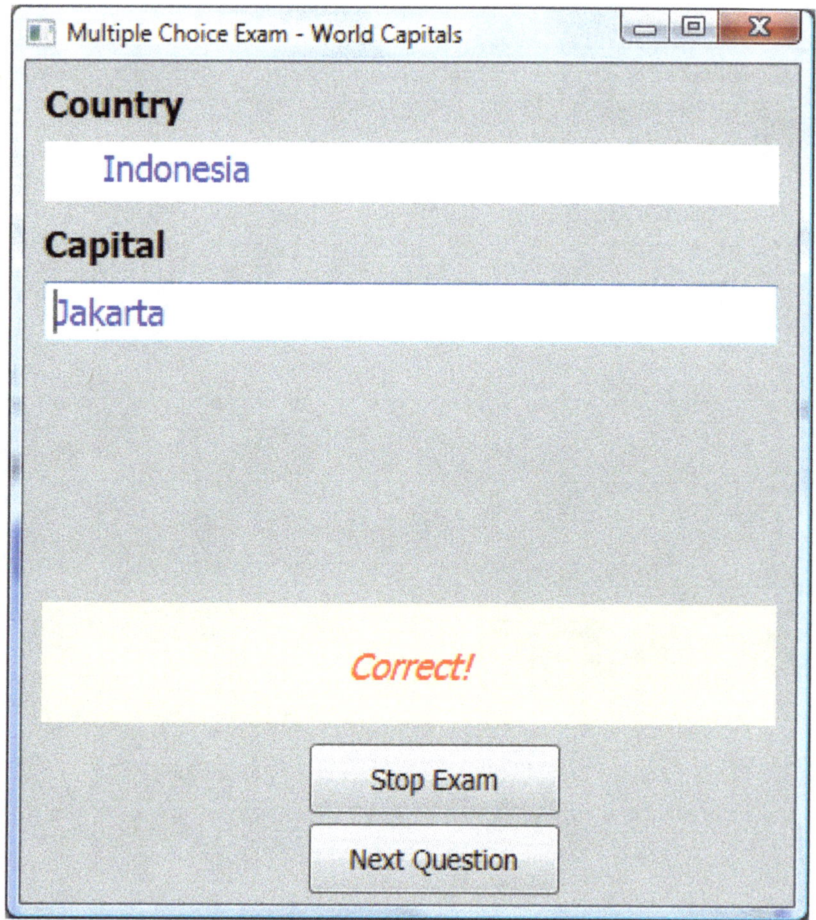

Click **Next Question**.

The next question is:

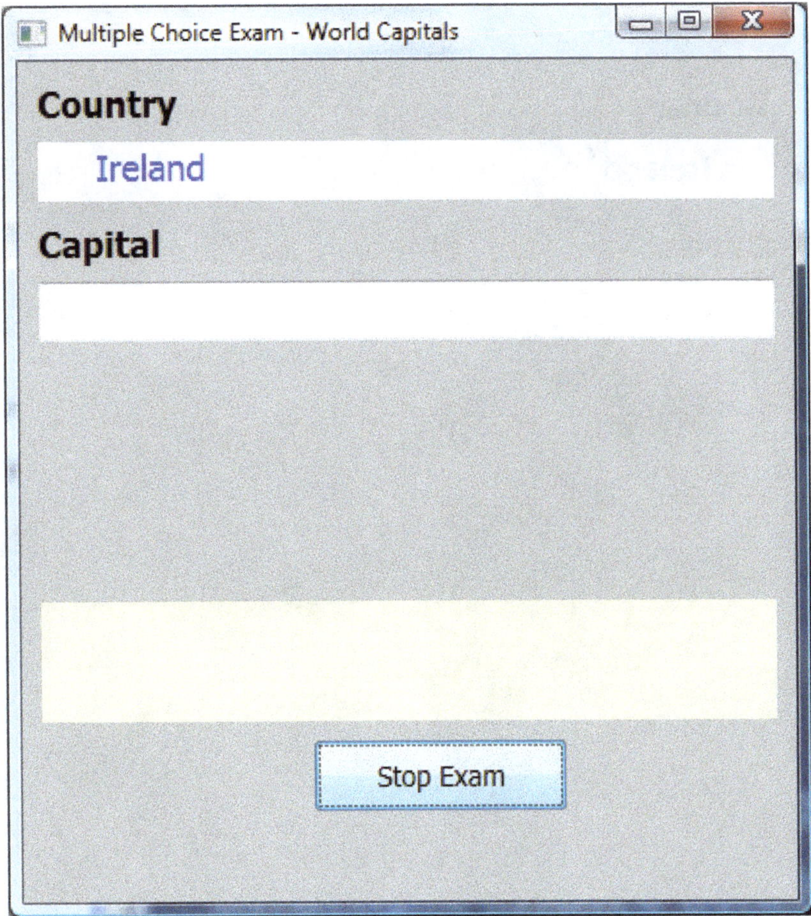

The capital of **Ireland** is **Dublin**. If you type **Dublin** in the text box area and press <**Enter**> you will be told this is a correct answer. Let's make sure the answers are not case-sensitive.

When I type **dublin** in the text box and click <**Enter**>, I see:

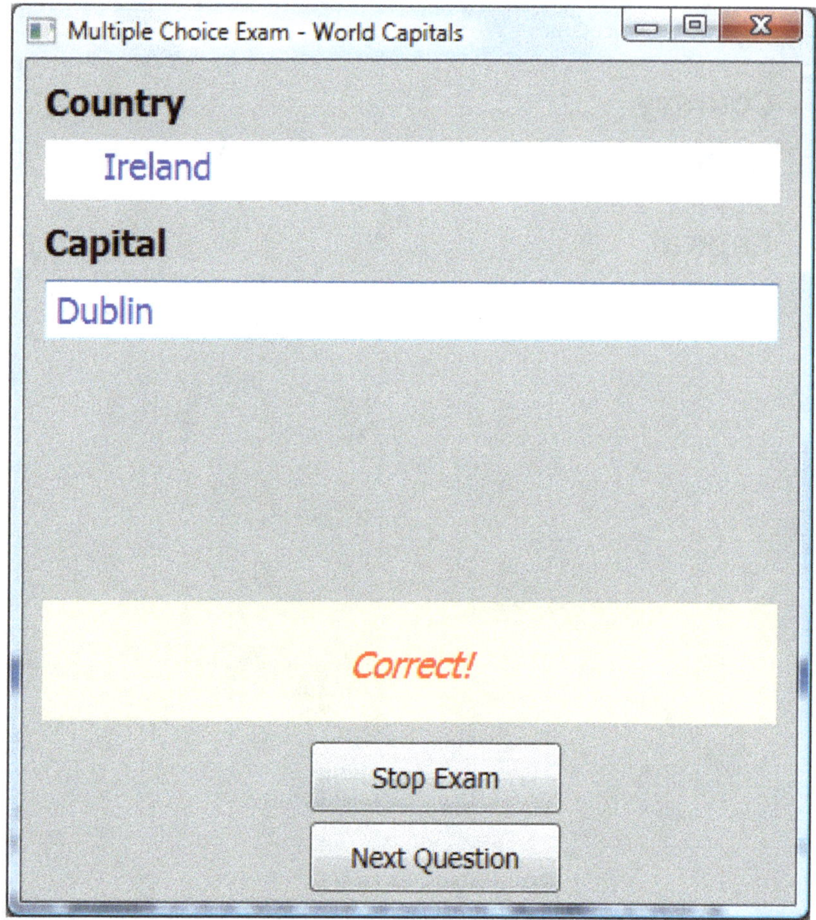

The answer is accepted and the 'capitalization' is corrected.

Continue trying correct and incorrect answers, checking to make sure case-insensitivity is properly incorporated into the project. Try typing an answer with spelling 'close to' the correct spelling. You will be told you are incorrect. This can be frustrating to the 'spelling challenged' and especially frustrating for children learning how to spell. If your spelling is 'close' you should be rewarded and gently corrected, not told you are wrong. Stop the exam and the project and we'll fix this problem.

Code Design – Checking Spelling

The techniques behind checking for 'close spelling' are called **Soundex** checks. Words, or terms, are assigned something called a **Soundex code**. Any two terms with the same Soundex code will have similar spellings. This is how spell checker programs work. When you misspell a word, you are presented with a list of words with similar Soundex codes from which to choose possible corrections. In our multiple choice exam project, if the Soundex code for a user typed response is equal to the Soundex code for the actual answer, we will credit the user with a correct answer.

The technique we use to determine Soundex codes is based on an article in an issue of **Byte** magazine from the early 1980's. As a historical footnote, early programmers were always eager to get the latest issue of **Byte**. It would contain programs you could type into your computer and try. These programs were usually written in the BASIC language. The code here is based on one of these programs. It's fun to go to a local library and look at old issues of **Byte** magazine. You'll find ads for computers with 8K (yes, I said 8K) of memory for just $500. And, you'll see 1/12th page ads for a little Bellevue, Washington, company just getting started in the computer business – yes, Microsoft.

To determine the **Soundex** code **SXCode** for a word **SXWord** (whose first character must be a letter), these steps are followed:

- Convert **SXWord** to all upper case (call the result **UCW**)
- Set the first character of **SXCode** to the first character of **UCW**.
- Cycle through all remaining characters in **UCW**, one at a time.
- Assign letter characters in **UCW** a corresponding numerical value from **0** to **9**, according to provided table. Numerical values are not given to any non-letter characters.
- If numerical value is non-zero and not equal to the previous character's numerical value, append that number to the end of the Soundex code **SXCode**.

The numerical codes associated with the 26 letters of the English alphabet are:

A = 0	B = 1	C = 2	D = 3	E = 0	F = 1	G = 2
H = 0	I = 0	J = 2	K = 2	L = 4	M = 5	N = 5
O = 0	P = 1	Q = 2	R = 6	S = 2	T = 3	U = 0
V = 1	W =0	X = 2	Y = 0	Z = 2		

Notice the vowels (A, E, I, O, U) and soft consonants (H, W, Y) have zero values. These values are stored in an array **SXValue**.

You should see that a **Soundex** code will be a string starting with a letter, followed by a sequence of numbers (none of which are zero) with no identical consecutive numbers. Let's try it with an example to see how it works, then we'll write the code. We'll use the word 'beautiful'. We'll misspell it as 'buetifull'. First, convert both words to upper case. Initialize the Soundex codes for both to the first letter of the word (both will be **B**). So, obviously a condition for two Soundex codes to match is that the first letter of the two words being compared must be the same. Now, go through all subsequent letters in each capitalized word and assign the corresponding numerical value to the letters. The results are:

```
BEAUTIFUL     Code: B00030104
BUETIFULL     Code: B00301044
```

Remove the zeroes and repeated values to get the final codes:

```
BEAUTIFUL     Code: B314
BUETIFULL     Code: B314
```

The two codes match, hence have similar spellings. Can you find other words with the same code. Some I came up with are: bad ball (the space is ignored by Soundex), bedful, and bait pail. So, Soundex doesn't always work – call some one 'bait pail' instead of 'beautiful' and you'll see what I mean!

The code to compute a Soundex code will be in a subroutine **Soundex**. You provide the subroutine with the word the code is being computed for (**SXWord**). The routine computes the **Soundex code** for **SXWord** and puts it in **SXCode**:

```
Sub Soundex
  'SoundEx values
  SXValue["A"] = 0
  SXValue["B"] = 1
  SXValue["C"] = 2
  SXValue["D"] = 3
  SXValue["E"] = 0
  SXValue["F"] = 1
  SXValue["G"] = 2
  SXValue["H"] = 0
  SXValue["I"] = 0
  SXValue["J"] = 2
  SXValue["K"] = 2
  SXValue["L"] = 4
  SXValue["M"] = 5
  SXValue["N"] = 5
  SXValue["O"] = 0
  SXValue["P"] = 1
  SXValue["Q"] = 2
```

```
    SXValue["R"] = 6
    SXValue["S"] = 2
    SXValue["T"] = 3
    SXValue["U"] = 0
    SXValue["V"] = 1
    SXValue["W"] =0
    SXValue["X"] = 2
    SXValue["Y"] = 0
    SXValue["Z"] = 2
    'Generates Soundex code (SXCode) for SXWord
    UCW = Text.ConvertToUpperCase(SXWord)
    L = Text.GetLength(UCW)
    SXCode = ""
    If (L <> 0) Then
      'Set first character
      SXCode = Text.GetSubText(UCW, 1, 1)
      If (L > 1) Then
        For I = 2 To L
          'Get next character
          NC = Text.GetSubText(UCW, I, 1)
          'Get numerical value
          NV = SXValue[NC]
          'Append NV if not zero and not previous character
          If (NV <> "0" And NV <> Text.GetSubText(SXCode,
  Text.GetLength(SXCode), 1)) Then
            SXCode = SXCode + NV
          EndIf
        EndFor
      EndIf
    EndIf
  EndSub
```

Add this routine to the project.

To use the **Soundex** subroutine, we must modify code in the **KeyDownSub** subroutine to not only check for exact spelling, but for equal **Soundex** codes. The modified code is shaded (most unmodified code is not shown):

```
Sub KeyDownSub
  ' If exam not in progress or already answered, exit
  If (Controls.GetButtonCaption(StartStopButton) = "Start Exam"
Or Answered) Then
    Goto ExitTextTypedSub
  EndIf
  'wait for <Enter>
  If (GraphicsWindow.LastKey = "Return") Then
    NumberTried = NumberTried + 1
    UCTypedAnswer =
Text.ConvertToUpperCase(Controls.GetTextBoxText(AnswerTextBox))
    If (Header1Given) Then
      UCAnswer = Text.ConvertToUpperCase(Term2[CorrectAnswer])
    Else
      UCAnswer = Text.ConvertToUpperCase(Term1[CorrectAnswer])
    EndIf
    Correct = "false"
    'get SoundEx codes for typed and actual answers
    SXWord = UCTypedAnswer
    Soundex()
    TypedSXCode = SXCode
    SXWord = UCAnswer
    Soundex()
    AnswerSXCode = SXCode
    If (UCTypedAnswer = UCAnswer Or TypedSXCode = AnswerSXCode)
Then
      Correct = "true"
    EndIf
    UpdateScore()
  EndIf
  ExitTextTypedSub:
EndSub
```

Make these changes. Now, let's give the Soundex code a try!

Save and run the project. Select an exam file (I again used **WorldCapitals.csv**). Choose the **Type In Answers** option. Click **Start Exam**. My first question appears as:

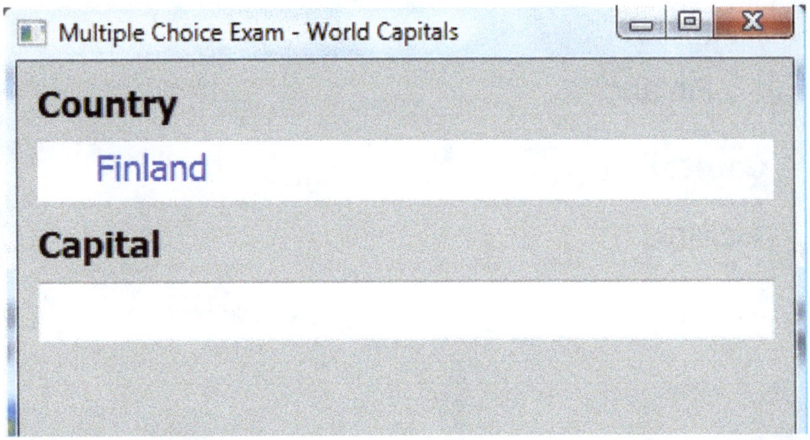

The capital of **Finland** is **Helsinki** (Soundex code is **H4252**), but what if I mistakenly spell it as **hellsinky**:

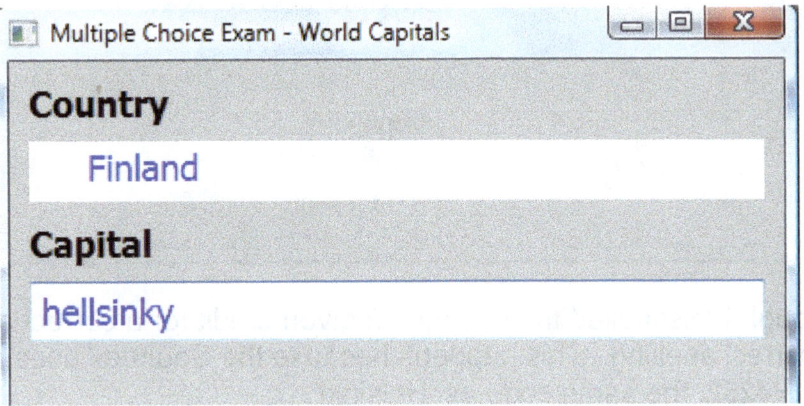

When I press <**Enter**>, I see:

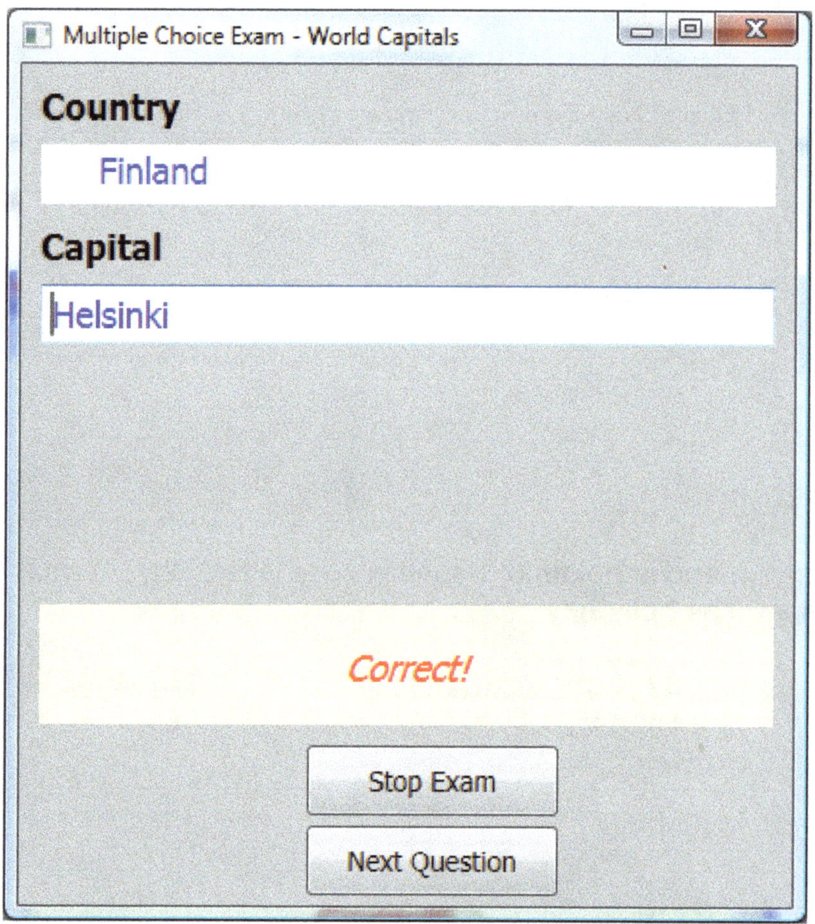

So, even though I misspelled the word, I am given credit for a correct answer and shown the correct spelling. This happens because the Soundex code for ‘hellsinky’ is **H4252**, the same code as ‘Helsinki’.

The program is nearly complete. Keep trying exams with different options to make sure everything works correctly. Play with the type in answers to see how well the Soundex codes work. How close does the spelling really need to be? Click **Exit** to stop the program when you want.

Code Design – Presenting Results

Once a user stops a particular exam, we want to let them know how well they did in answering questions. The information of use would be:

- The number of questions tried (**NumberTried**).
- The number of correct answers (**NumberCorrect**).
- The percentage score.

All of this information is available from the defined variables.

The exam results are presented in the **StartStopButtonClicked** subroutine (following clicking of **Stop Exam**). A message box is used to display the results. The modified procedure (changes are shaded) is:

```
Sub StartStopButtonClicked
  If (Controls.GetButtonCaption(StartStopButton) = "Start
Exam") Then
    Controls.SetButtonCaption(StartStopButton, "Stop Exam")
    ' Reset the score
    NumberTried = 0
    NumberCorrect = 0
    Shapes.SetText(MessageArea, "")
    Controls.HideControl(NextButton)
    Controls.HideControl(OpenButton)
    Controls.HideControl(ExitButton)
    Controls.HideControl(OptionsButton)
    NextQuestion()
  Else
    Controls.SetButtonCaption(StartStopButton, "Start Exam")
    Shapes.SetText(GivenDisplay, "")
    If (NumberTried > 0) Then
      Message = "Questions Tried: " + NumberTried + CRLF
      Message = Message + "Questions Correct: " + NumberCorrect
+ CRLF + CRLF
      Message = Message + "Your Score: " + Math.Floor(100 *
(NumberCorrect / NumberTried)) + "%"
      GraphicsWindow.ShowMessage(Message, "Results")
    EndIf
    If (MCAnswers) Then
      Shapes.SetText(AnswerDisplay[1], "")
      Shapes.SetText(AnswerDisplay[2], "")
      Shapes.SetText(AnswerDisplay[3], "")
      Shapes.SetText(AnswerDisplay[4], "")
    Else
      Controls.SetTextBoxText(AnswerTextBox, "")
    EndIf
    Shapes.SetText(MessageArea, "    Set Options" + CRLF +
"Click Start Exam")
    Shapes.Move(MessageArea, 140, 280)
    Controls.HideControl(NextButton)
    Controls.ShowControl(OpenButton)
    Controls.ShowControl(ExitButton)
    Controls.ShowControl(OptionsButton)
  EndIf
EndSub
```

And, one last time, save and run the project. Load in an exam file. Take some kind of exam. Answer some questions – miss a few to make sure the scoring works. At some point, click **Stop Exam** and some results should appear. Here's a message box I received after taking an exam:

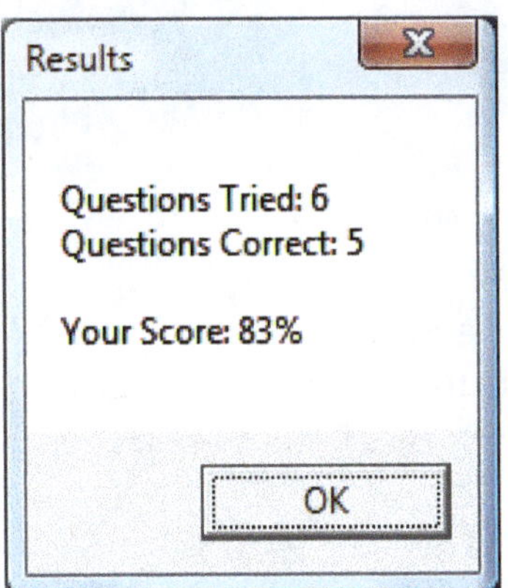

Multiple Choice Exam Project Code Listing

Here is the complete listing of the **Multiple Choice Exam** Small Basic program:

```
'Multiple Choice Exam
InitializeProgram()

Sub InitializeProgram
  'graphics window
  GraphicsWindow.Width = 400
  GraphicsWindow.Height = 420
  GraphicsWindow.BackgroundColor = "LightGray"
  GraphicsWindow.Title = "Multiple Choice Exam - No File"
  'headings
  GraphicsWindow.BrushColor = "Black"
  GraphicsWindow.FontSize = 18
  GraphicsWindow.FontBold = "true"
  HeadingGiven = Shapes.AddText("")
  Shapes.Move(HeadingGiven, 10, 10)
  HeadingAnswer = Shapes.AddText("")
  Shapes.Move(HeadingAnswer, 10, 80)
  GraphicsWindow.BrushColor = "White"
  GraphicsWindow.FillRectangle(10, 40, 380, 30)
  GraphicsWindow.FillRectangle(10, 110, 380, 30)
  GraphicsWindow.FillRectangle(10, 150, 380, 30)
  GraphicsWindow.FillRectangle(10, 190, 380, 30)
  GraphicsWindow.FillRectangle(10, 230, 380, 30)
  'shapes for given and mc answers
  GraphicsWindow.FontBold = "false"
  GraphicsWindow.BrushColor = "Blue"
  GivenDisplay = Shapes.AddText("")
  Shapes.Move(GivenDisplay, 40, 42)
  AnswerDisplay[1] = Shapes.AddText("")
  Shapes.Move(AnswerDisplay[1], 40, 112)
  AnswerDisplay[2] = Shapes.AddText("")
  Shapes.Move(AnswerDisplay[2], 40, 152)
  AnswerDisplay[3] = Shapes.AddText("")
  Shapes.Move(AnswerDisplay[3], 40, 192)
  AnswerDisplay[4] = Shapes.AddText("")
  Shapes.Move(AnswerDisplay[4], 40, 232)
  Header1Given = "true"
  MCAnswers = "true"
  'text box for type in answers
  AnswerTextBox = Controls.AddTextBox(10, 110)
  Controls.SetSize(AnswerTextBox, 380, 30)
  Controls.HideControl(AnswerTextBox)
```

```
  'message display
  GraphicsWindow.BrushColor = "LightYellow"
  GraphicsWindow.FillRectangle(10, 270, 380, 60)
  GraphicsWindow.BrushColor = "Red"
  GraphicsWindow.FontSize = 18
  GraphicsWindow.FontBold = "false"
  GraphicsWindow.FontItalic = "true"
  MessageArea = Shapes.AddText("Open Exam File to Start")
  Shapes.Move(MessageArea, 100, 290)
  'buttons
  GraphicsWindow.BrushColor = "Black"
  GraphicsWindow.FontSize = 14
  GraphicsWindow.FontItalic = "false"
  GraphicsWindow.FontBold = "false"
  OpenButton = Controls.AddButton("Open File", 10, 340)
  Controls.SetSize(OpenButton, 130, 35)
  OptionsButton = Controls.AddButton("Set Options", 10, 380)
  Controls.SetSize(OptionsButton, 130, 35)
  StartStopButton = Controls.AddButton("Start Exam", 150, 340)
  Controls.SetSize(StartStopButton, 130, 35)
  NextButton = Controls.AddButton("Next Question", 150, 380)
  Controls.SetSize(NextButton, 130, 35)
  ExitButton = Controls.AddButton("Exit", 290, 340)
  Controls.SetSize(ExitButton, 100, 35)
  Controls.HideControl(OptionsButton)
  Controls.HideControl(NextButton)
  Controls.HideControl(StartStopButton)
  Controls.ButtonClicked = ButtonClickedSub
  GraphicsWindow.MouseDown = MouseDownSub
  GraphicsWindow.KeyDown = KeyDownSub
  CRLF = Text.GetCharacter(13)
EndSub

Sub ButtonClickedSub
  B = Controls.LastClickedButton
  If (B = ExitButton) Then
    Program.End()
  ElseIf (B = OpenButton) Then
    OpenButtonClicked()
  ElseIf (B = OptionsButton) Then
    OptionsButtonClicked()
  ElseIf (B = StartStopButton) Then
    StartStopButtonClicked()
  ElseIf (B = NextButton) Then
    Controls.HideControl(NextButton)
    NextQuestion()
```

```
  EndIf
EndSub

Sub OpenButtonClicked
  GraphicsWindow.Hide()
  TextWindow.Show()
  TextWindow.BackgroundColor = "White"
  TextWindow.ForegroundColor = "Black"
  TextWindow.Clear()
  TextWindow.Title = "Open Exam Files"
  'find csv files in program directory
  AllFiles = File.GetFiles(Program.Directory)
  NumberFiles = Array.GetItemCount(AllFiles)
  NumberCSVFiles = 0
  For I = 1 To NumberFiles
    'check for csv extension
    If (Text.IsSubText(AllFiles[I], ".csv")) Then
      NumberCSVFiles = NumberCSVFiles + 1
      CSVFiles[NumberCSVFiles] = AllFiles[I]
    EndIf
  EndFor
  If (NumberCSVFiles = 0) Then
    TextWindow.WriteLine("No exam files found.")
    TextWindow.Pause()
  Else
    TextWindow.WriteLine("Exam Files (choose by number):")
    TextWindow.WriteLine("")
    For I = 1 To NumberCSVFiles
      TextWindow.CursorLeft = 2
      TextWindow.Write(I + " - ")
      'strip off directory for display of name
      TextWindow.WriteLine(text.GetSubTextToEnd(CSVFiles[I],
Text.GetLength(Program.Directory) + 2))
    EndFor
    TextWindow.WriteLine("")
    GetFileNumber:
    TextWindow.Write("Choice? ")
    J = TextWindow.ReadNumber()
    If (J < 1 Or J > NumberCSVFiles) Then
      Goto GetFileNumber
    EndIf
    'read info from file
    FileLine = File.ReadLine(CSVFiles[J], 1)
    ExamTitle = Text.GetSubText(FileLine, 1,
Text.GetLength(FileLine) - 1)
    FileLine = File.ReadLine(CSVFiles[J], 2)
```

```
    CL = Text.GetIndexOf(FileLine, ",")
    Header1 = Text.GetSubText(FileLine, 1, CL - 1)
    Header2 = Text.GetSubTextToEnd(FileLine, CL + 1)
    NumberTerms = 0
    NextLine:
    FileLine = File.ReadLine(CSVFiles[J], NumberTerms + 3)
    If (FileLine <> "") Then
      NumberTerms = NumberTerms + 1
      CL = Text.GetIndexOf(FileLine, ",")
      Term1[NumberTerms] = Text.GetSubText(FileLine, 1, CL - 1)
      Term2[NumberTerms] = Text.GetSubTextToEnd(FileLine, CL + 1)
      If (NumberTerms < 100) Then
        Goto NextLine
      EndIf
    EndIf
    'establish window title
    GraphicsWindow.Title = "Multiple Choice Exam - " + ExamTitle
    'set up headers items
    If (Header1Given) Then
      Shapes.SetText(HeadingGiven, Header1)
      Shapes.SetText(HeadingAnswer, Header2)
    Else
      Shapes.SetText(HeadingGiven, Header1)
      Shapes.SetText(HeadingAnswer, Header2)
    EndIf
    Controls.ShowControl(StartStopButton)
    Controls.ShowControl(OptionsButton)
    Shapes.SetText(MessageArea, "File Loaded, Set Options" + CRLF
+ "      Click Start Exam")
    Shapes.Move(MessageArea, 100, 280)
  EndIf
  TextWindow.Hide()
  GraphicsWindow.Show()
EndSub

Sub OptionsButtonClicked
  GraphicsWindow.Hide()
  TextWindow.Show()
  TextWindow.BackgroundColor = "White"
  TextWindow.ForegroundColor = "Black"
  TextWindow.Clear()
  TextWindow.Title = "Set Options"
  TextWindow.WriteLine("Make Your Choice:")
  TextWindow.WriteLine("")
  TextWindow.CursorLeft = 2
```

```
  TextWindow.WriteLine("1 - Given " + Header1 + ", Name " +
Header2)
  TextWindow.CursorLeft = 2
  TextWindow.WriteLine("2 - Given " + Header2 + ", Name " +
Header1)
  TextWindow.WriteLine("")
  GetGiven:
  TextWindow.Write("Choice? ")
  A = TextWindow.ReadNumber()
  If (A = 1) Then
    Header1Given = "true"
    Shapes.SetText(HeadingGiven, Header1)
    Shapes.SetText(HeadingAnswer, Header2)
  ElseIf (A = 2) Then
    Header1Given = "false"
    Shapes.SetText(HeadingGiven, Header2)
    Shapes.SetText(HeadingAnswer, Header1)
  Else
    Goto GetGiven
  EndIf
  TextWindow.CursorTop = 7
  TextWindow.WriteLine("Make Your Choice:")
  TextWindow.WriteLine("")
  TextWindow.CursorLeft = 2
  TextWindow.WriteLine("1 - Multiple Choice Answers")
  TextWindow.CursorLeft = 2
  TextWindow.WriteLine("2 - Type-In Answers")
  TextWindow.WriteLine("")
  GetAnswer:
  TextWindow.Write("Choice? ")
  A = TextWindow.ReadNumber()
  If (A = 1) Then
    MCAnswers = "true"
    Shapes.SetText(GivenDisplay, "")
    GraphicsWindow.BrushColor = "White"
    GraphicsWindow.FillRectangle(10, 110, 380, 30)
    GraphicsWindow.FillRectangle(10, 150, 380, 30)
    GraphicsWindow.FillRectangle(10, 190, 380, 30)
    GraphicsWindow.FillRectangle(10, 230, 380, 30)
    For I = 1 To 4
      Shapes.SetText(AnswerDisplay[I], "")
      Shapes.ShowShape(AnswerDisplay[I])
    EndFor
    Controls.HideControl(AnswerTextBox)
  ElseIf (A = 2) Then
    MCAnswers = "false"
```

```
    Shapes.SetText(GivenDisplay, "")
    GraphicsWindow.BrushColor = GraphicsWindow.BackgroundColor
    GraphicsWindow.FillRectangle(10, 110, 380, 30)
    GraphicsWindow.FillRectangle(10, 150, 380, 30)
    GraphicsWindow.FillRectangle(10, 190, 380, 30)
    GraphicsWindow.FillRectangle(10, 230, 380, 30)
    For I = 1 To 4
      Shapes.HideShape(AnswerDisplay[I])
    EndFor
    Controls.ShowControl(AnswerTextBox)
  Else
    Goto GetAnswer
  EndIf
  TextWindow.Hide()
  GraphicsWindow.Show()
EndSub

Sub StartStopButtonClicked
  If (Controls.GetButtonCaption(StartStopButton) = "Start Exam")
Then
    Controls.SetButtonCaption(StartStopButton, "Stop Exam")
    ' Reset the score
    NumberTried = 0
    NumberCorrect = 0
    Shapes.SetText(MessageArea, "")
    Controls.HideControl(NextButton)
    Controls.HideControl(OpenButton)
    Controls.HideControl(ExitButton)
    Controls.HideControl(OptionsButton)
    NextQuestion()
  Else
    Controls.SetButtonCaption(StartStopButton, "Start Exam")
    Shapes.SetText(GivenDisplay, "")
    If (NumberTried > 0) Then
      Message = "Questions Tried: " + NumberTried + CRLF
      Message = Message + "Questions Correct: " + NumberCorrect +
CRLF + CRLF
      Message = Message + "Your Score: " + Math.Floor(100 *
(NumberCorrect / NumberTried)) + "%"
      GraphicsWindow.ShowMessage(Message, "Results")
    EndIf
    If (MCAnswers) Then
      Shapes.SetText(AnswerDisplay[1], "")
      Shapes.SetText(AnswerDisplay[2], "")
      Shapes.SetText(AnswerDisplay[3], "")
      Shapes.SetText(AnswerDisplay[4], "")
```

```
    Else
      Controls.SetTextBoxText(AnswerTextBox, "")
    EndIf
    Shapes.SetText(MessageArea, "    Set Options" + CRLF + "Click
Start Exam")
    Shapes.Move(MessageArea, 140, 280)
    Controls.HideControl(NextButton)
    Controls.ShowControl(OpenButton)
    Controls.ShowControl(ExitButton)
    Controls.ShowControl(OptionsButton)
  EndIf
EndSub

Sub NextQuestion
  Shapes.SetText(MessageArea, "")
  ' Generate the next question based on selected options
  CorrectAnswer = Math.GetRandomNumber(NumberTerms)
  GraphicsWindow.BrushColor = "Blue"
  GraphicsWindow.FontSize = 18
  GraphicsWindow.FontBold = "false"
  GraphicsWindow.BrushColor = "Blue"
  If (Header1Given) Then
    Shapes.SetText(GivenDisplay, Term1[CorrectAnswer])
  Else
    Shapes.SetText(GivenDisplay, Term2[CorrectAnswer])
  EndIf
  If (MCAnswers) Then
    ' Multiple choice answers
    For I = 1 To NumberTerms
      TermUsed[I] = "false"
    EndFor
    ' Pick four random possiblities
    For I = 1 To 4
      GetJ:
      J = Math.GetRandomNumber(NumberTerms)
      If (TermUsed[J] Or J = CorrectAnswer) Then
        Goto GetJ
      EndIf
      TermUsed[J] = "true"
      Index[I] = J
    EndFor
    ' Replace one with correct answer
    Index[Math.GetRandomNumber(4)] = CorrectAnswer
    ' Display multiple choice answers
    If (Header1Given) Then
      Shapes.SetText(AnswerDisplay[1], Term2[Index[1]])
```

```
      Shapes.SetText(AnswerDisplay[2], Term2[Index[2]])
      Shapes.SetText(AnswerDisplay[3], Term2[Index[3]])
      Shapes.SetText(AnswerDisplay[4], Term2[Index[4]])
    Else
      Shapes.SetText(AnswerDisplay[1], Term1[Index[1]])
      Shapes.SetText(AnswerDisplay[2], Term1[Index[2]])
      Shapes.SetText(AnswerDisplay[3], Term1[Index[3]])
      Shapes.SetText(AnswerDisplay[4], Term1[Index[4]])
    EndIf
  Else
    ' Type-in answers
    Controls.SetTextBoxText(AnswerTextBox, "")
  EndIf
  Answered = "false"
EndSub

Sub MouseDownSub
  ' If exam not in progress or already answered, exit
  If (Controls.GetButtonCaption(StartStopButton) = "Start Exam" Or
Answered) Then
    Goto ExitMouseDownSub
  EndIf
  ' find out which answer was clicked
  X = GraphicsWindow.MouseX
  Y = GraphicsWindow.MouseY
  If (X > 10 And X < 390 And Y > 110 And Y < 260) Then
    NumberTried = NumberTried + 1
    If (Y > 110 And Y < 140) Then
      AnswerClicked = 1
    ElseIf (Y > 150 And Y < 180) Then
      AnswerClicked = 2
    ElseIf (Y > 190 And Y < 220) Then
      AnswerClicked = 3
    ElseIf (Y > 230 And Y < 260) Then
      AnswerClicked = 4
    EndIf
    Correct = "false"
    If (Header1Given) Then
      If Term2[Index[AnswerClicked]] = Term2[CorrectAnswer] Then
        Correct = "true"
      EndIf
    Else
      If Term1[Index[AnswerClicked]] = Term1[CorrectAnswer] Then
        Correct = "true"
      EndIf
    EndIf
```

```
    Answered = "true"
    UpdateScore()
  EndIf
  ExitMouseDownSub:
EndSub

Sub UpdateScore
  ' Check if answer is correct
  If (Correct) Then
    NumberCorrect = NumberCorrect + 1
    Shapes.SetText(MessageArea, "Correct!")
    Shapes.Move(MessageArea, 170, 290)
  Else
    Shapes.SetText(MessageArea, "Sorry ... Correct Answer Shown")
    Shapes.Move(MessageArea, 80, 290)
  EndIf
  ' Display correct answer
  If (MCAnswers) Then
    If (Header1Given) Then
      Shapes.SetText(AnswerDisplay[1], Term2[CorrectAnswer])
    Else
      Shapes.SetText(AnswerDisplay[1], Term1[CorrectAnswer])
    EndIf
    Shapes.SetText(AnswerDisplay[2], "")
    Shapes.SetText(AnswerDisplay[3], "")
    Shapes.SetText(AnswerDisplay[4], "")
  Else
    If (Header1Given) Then
      Controls.SetTextBoxText(AnswerTextBox, Term2[CorrectAnswer])
    Else
      Controls.SetTextBoxText(AnswerTextBox, Term1[CorrectAnswer])
    EndIf
  EndIf
  Controls.ShowControl(StartStopButton)
  Controls.ShowControl(NextButton)
EndSub

Sub KeyDownSub
  ' If exam not in progress or already answered, exit
  If (Controls.GetButtonCaption(StartStopButton) = "Start Exam" Or
Answered) Then
    Goto ExitTextTypedSub
  EndIf
  'wait for <Enter>
  If (GraphicsWindow.LastKey = "Return") Then
    NumberTried = NumberTried + 1
```

```
    UCTypedAnswer =
Text.ConvertToUpperCase(Controls.GetTextBoxText(AnswerTextBox))
    If (Header1Given) Then
      UCAnswer = Text.ConvertToUpperCase(Term2[CorrectAnswer])
    Else
      UCAnswer = Text.ConvertToUpperCase(Term1[CorrectAnswer])
    EndIf
    Correct = "false"
    'get SoundEx codes for typed and actual answers
    SXWord = UCTypedAnswer
    Soundex()
    TypedSXCode = SXCode
    SXWord = UCAnswer
    Soundex()
    AnswerSXCode = SXCode
    If (UCTypedAnswer = UCAnswer Or TypedSXCode = AnswerSXCode)
Then
      Correct = "true"
    EndIf
    UpdateScore()
  EndIf
  ExitTextTypedSub:
EndSub

Sub Soundex
  'SoundEx values
  SXValue["A"] = 0
  SXValue["B"] = 1
  SXValue["C"] = 2
  SXValue["D"] = 3
  SXValue["E"] = 0
  SXValue["F"] = 1
  SXValue["G"] = 2
  SXValue["H"] = 0
  SXValue["I"] = 0
  SXValue["J"] = 2
  SXValue["K"] = 2
  SXValue["L"] = 4
  SXValue["M"] = 5
  SXValue["N"] = 5
  SXValue["O"] = 0
  SXValue["P"] = 1
  SXValue["Q"] = 2
  SXValue["R"] = 6
  SXValue["S"] = 2
  SXValue["T"] = 3
```

```
  SXValue["U"] = 0
  SXValue["V"] = 1
  SXValue["W"] =0
  SXValue["X"] = 2
  SXValue["Y"] = 0
  SXValue["Z"] = 2
  'Generates Soundex code (SXCode) for SXWord
  UCW = Text.ConvertToUpperCase(SXWord)
  L = Text.GetLength(UCW)
  SXCode = ""
  If (L <> 0) Then
    'Set first character
    SXCode = Text.GetSubText(UCW, 1, 1)
    If (L > 1) Then
      For I = 2 To L
        'Get next character
        NC = Text.GetSubText(UCW, I, 1)
        'Get numerical value
        NV = SXValue[NC]
        'Append NV if not zero and not previous character
        If (NV <> "0" And NV <> Text.GetSubText(SXCode,
Text.GetLength(SXCode), 1)) Then
          SXCode = SXCode + NV
        EndIf
      EndFor
    EndIf
  EndIf
EndSub
```

Multiple Choice Exam Project Review

The **Multiple Choice Exam** project is now complete. **Save** and **Run** the project and make sure it works as designed. Recheck that all options work and interact properly. Create some exam files (or use the two examples) and have fun learning.

If there are errors in your implementation, go back over the steps of window and code design. Use the debugger when needed. Go over the developed code – make sure you understand how different parts of the project were coded. As mentioned in the beginning of this chapter, the completed project is saved as **MultipleChoice** in the **HomeSB\HomeSB Projects\MultipleChoice** folder.

While completing this project, new concepts and skills you should have gained include:

- How to locate files.
- Creating and saving an exam file.
- Opening a sequential file, inputting and parsing data lines.
- Checking spelling using Soundex codes.

Multiple Choice Exam Project Enhancements

Possible enhancements to the multiple choice exam project include:

- The only feedback a user gets about entered answers is a displayed message. Some kind of audible feedback would be nice (a positive sound for correct answer, a negative sound for a wrong answer). We discuss adding sounds to a project in the final chapter – you might like to look ahead.
- Modify the program and scoring system to allow multiple tries at the answer. Award higher scores for fewer missed guesses. If using type in answers, you would need some kind of 'I Give Up' button or just give a specified number of guesses.
- The user only learns the results (score) after an exam. Add some features that always display the current results.
- Add an option that allows a user to review the entries in an exam file.
- Build an 'Exam Builder' tool that lets a user enter the needed information and save the exam file. You need to know how to save sequential files, a topic discussed in Chapter 9.

8. Blackjack Card Game Project

Review and Preview

The first popular computer games appeared in the early 1970's with the introduction of timeshare computing. There was a classic set of DEC (Digital Equipment Corporation) programs written in BASIC for timeshare users. The set included gambling games, simulations and the ever-popular Star Trek game. A favorite DEC BASIC program was the casino card game Blackjack.

In this chapter, we build a version of that game. The **Blackjack Card Game Project** allows a single player to compete against the computer dealer. The project discusses the math and logic involved in shuffling and displaying a deck of cards. The project also reveals how dangerous gambling can be. You will indeed see that the odds are stacked against you so keep you real money in your wallet!

Blackjack Card Game Project Preview

In this chapter, we will build a **Blackjack card game** program. This program allows a single player to compete against the computer dealer. The idea of Blackjack is to score higher than the dealer's hand without exceeding twenty-one points. Cards count their value, except face cards (Jacks, Queens, Kings) count for ten, and Aces count for either one or eleven (you pick). If you beat the dealer, you get 10 points. If you get Blackjack (21 with just two cards) and beat the dealer, you get 15 points. If the dealer beats you, you lose 10 points. Before trying the program, let's review the rules used in this version of Blackjack and see how the program works.

Blackjack starts by giving two cards (from a standard 52 card deck – reshuffles are done when only a few cards remain) to the dealer (one face down) and two cards to the player (you). The player decides whether to **Hit** (receive another card) or **Stay** (stop receiving cards). The player can choose as many extra cards as desired. If the player's score exceeds 21 before staying, it is a loss (-10 points) and we say the player **busted**. If the player does not exceed 21, it becomes the dealer's turn. The dealer must add cards to his score until 16 is exceeded. When this occurs, if the dealer also exceeds 21 (**busts**) or if his score is less than the player's, he loses (+10 points for you). If the dealer's score is greater than the player's score (and under 21), the dealer wins (-10 points for you). If the dealer and the player have the same score, it is called a **push** (no points added or subtracted). The dealer must always take an Ace to be 11 points, unless it causes him to bust.

If either the player or dealer get 'Blackjack' which is defined as 21 points with just two cards (an Ace and a card worth 10 points), they automatically win. If the dealer gets Blackjack, the player loses 10 points. If the player gets Blackjack, he wins 15 points. If both the dealer and the player get Blackjack, it's a push.

A special rule for this version of Blackjack (not used in casinos) involves the number of cards received. Theoretically, you can have eleven cards given to you and still not bust! We don't want to display that many cards since it would be a rare occurrence. You can see in the interface, we limit the display to six cards. So, a special rule in this implementation is that, if the player gets six cards and has 21 or fewer points, the player is declared a winner. Similarly, if the player has fewer than six cards and the dealer is able to draw six cards without exceeding 16 points (since the dealer must stop adding cards after 16 points), the dealer wins, regardless of score.

There are lots of rules here. Let's see these rules in action. The finished project is saved as **Blackjack** in the **HomeSB\HomeSB Projects\Blackjack** folder. Start Small Basic and open the finished project. **Run** the project (click **Run** in the toolbar or press <**F5**>). The Blackjack program will appear as (you will see different cards – the results are random):

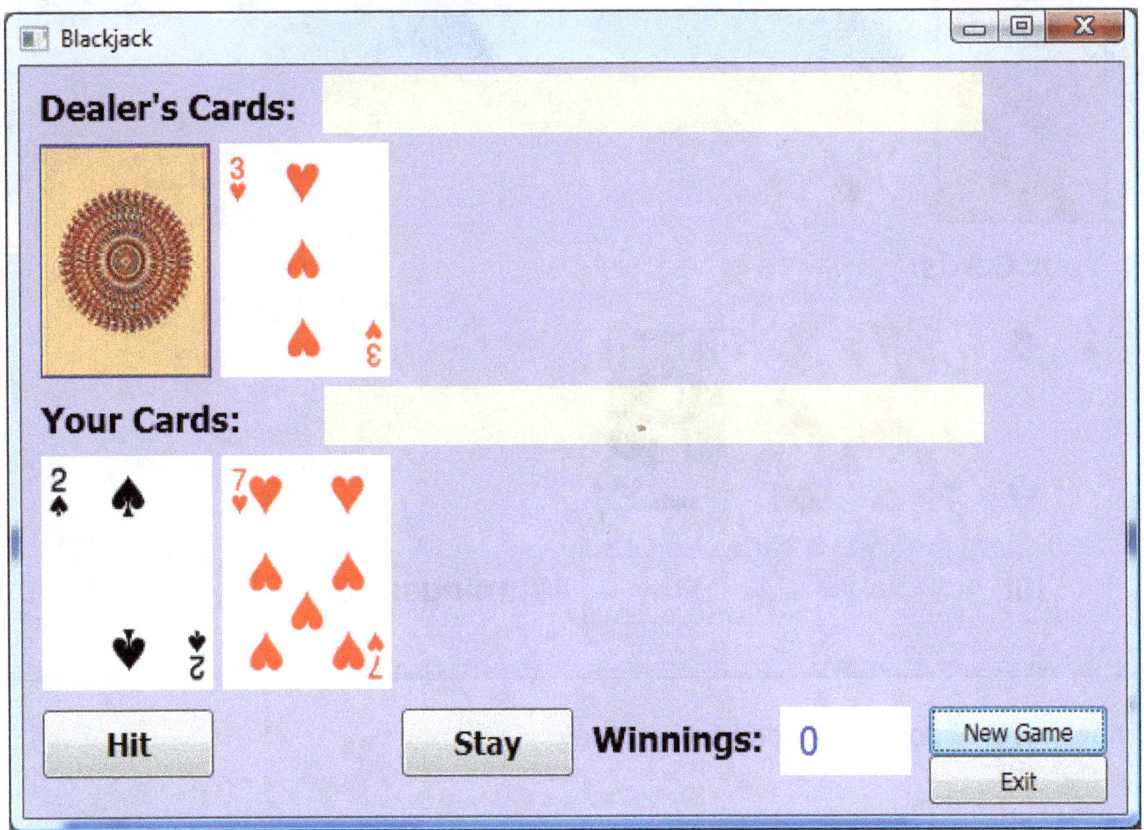

Notice the displayed card images. In card lingo, the displayed cards are referred to **hands**. The dealer plays one hand, while the player plays the other hand. One of the dealer's cards is face down – the other is a 3. I have a 2 and a 7 showing (9 points). I can either get another card (**Hit**) or stop (**Stay**). I think you'd agree that **Hit** is the correct choice since I'm far from 21.

When I click **Hit**, I receive a Jack, worth 10 points.

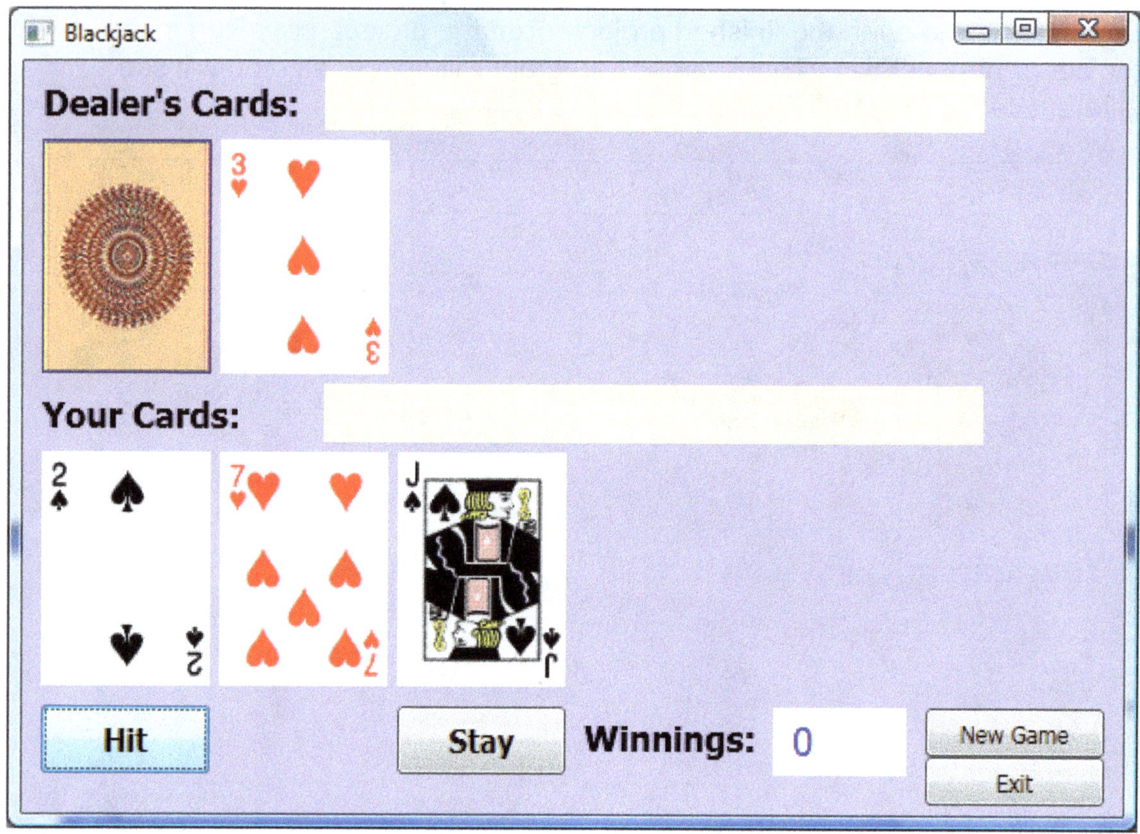

I now have 19 points – a good time to **Stay**.

After clicking **Stay**, the dealer plays out his cards according to the prescribed rules:

The first card is 'flipped' over revealing a 6, giving the dealer 9 points. Since the score is under 16, another card must be taken. That card is a Queen, giving the dealer 19 points – we tie (or in card talk **push**). Notice the messages telling me the results and displaying my winnings. Click **Deal** to play another hand.

The next hand I see is:

I have 20 points, so I'll choose **Stay**.

I click **Stay** and the dealer plays out:

The face-down card is revealed to be a 2. The dealer has 12 points and must take another card – a 7 – giving him 19 points. The dealer is restricted by the rules to stop at this point (even though it's a loss). The dealer loses since his score is less than mine. My 20 beats his 19 – I win!

After playing a few more hands, I got these cards.:

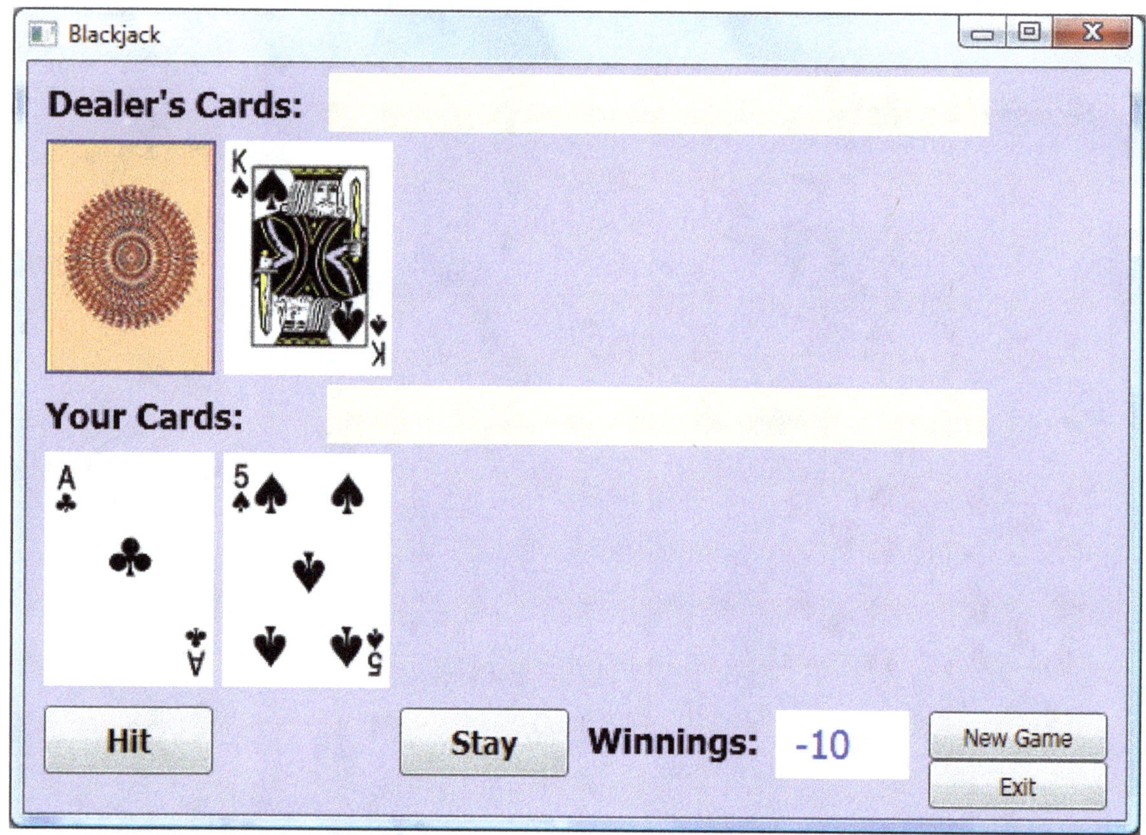

Recall, an Ace can be either 1 or 11 points. Choosing 1 in this case gives me 6 points (1 + 5). I choose to **Hit**.

After a **Hit**, I see:

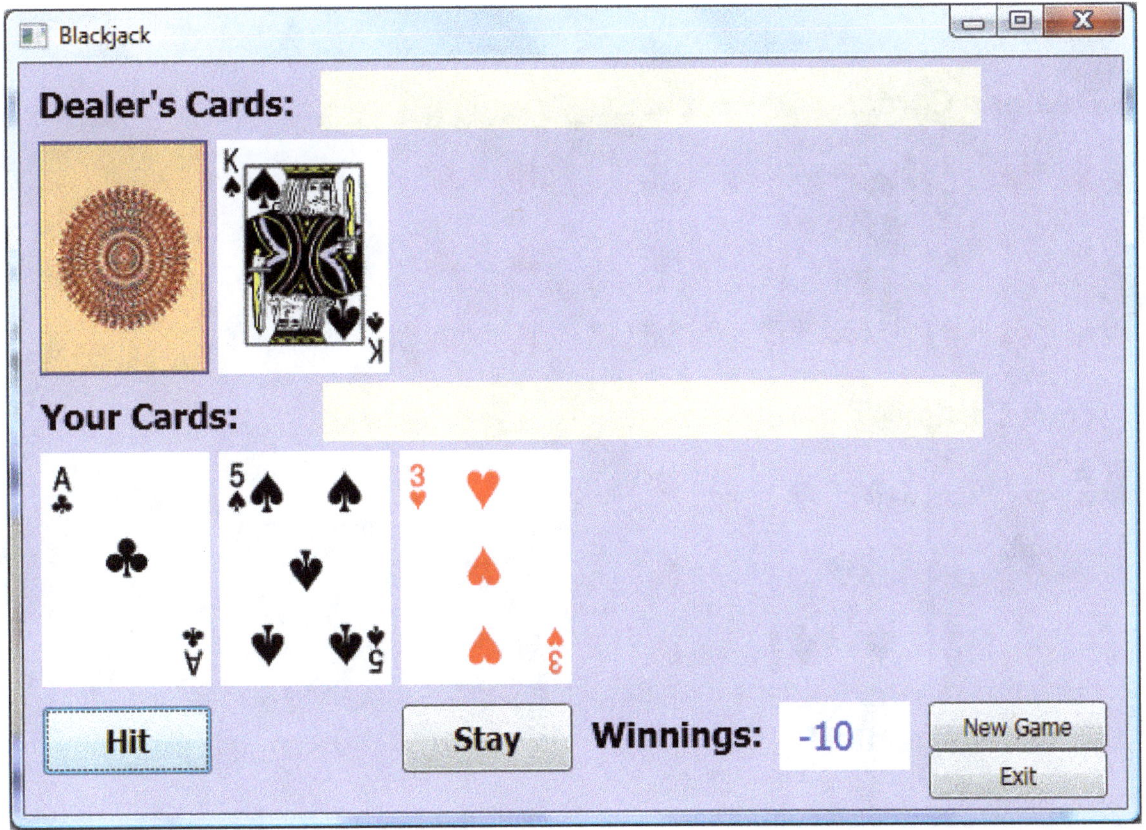

If I now take the Ace to be 11 points, I have 19 (11 + 5 + 3). I choose to **Stay**.

After clicking **Stay**, the dealer plays his cards according to the rules:

The dealer reveals his first card (2), giving him 12 points (2 + 10). The dealer takes another card (3), to give him 15 points. He must take another – a 7 which puts him over 21 – or we say the dealer **busts**. I win again.

As I play more hands, winning a few, losing a few, in one game I got Blackjack (21 points with two cards):

I won 15 points with this hand (obviously I have lost a few hands after my initial success, since my total winnings are just 15).

Continue playing hands until you understand how the rules of the game, especially those that the dealer uses, are applied. Try to figure out some good strategy for playing Blackjack. At any point, a new game can be started (resetting the winnings) by clicking the **New Game** button. Clicking **Exit** will stop the **Blackjack** program.

You will now build this project in several stages. We address **window design**. We discuss the controls used to build the form and establish initial properties. And, we address **code design** in detail. We will discuss how to shuffle a deck of cards and how to display the card images. We also cover the logic behind the complicated rules of play and how to determine who wins (or if it is a push).

Blackjack Window Design

Here is the sketch for the window layout of the **Blackjack** program:

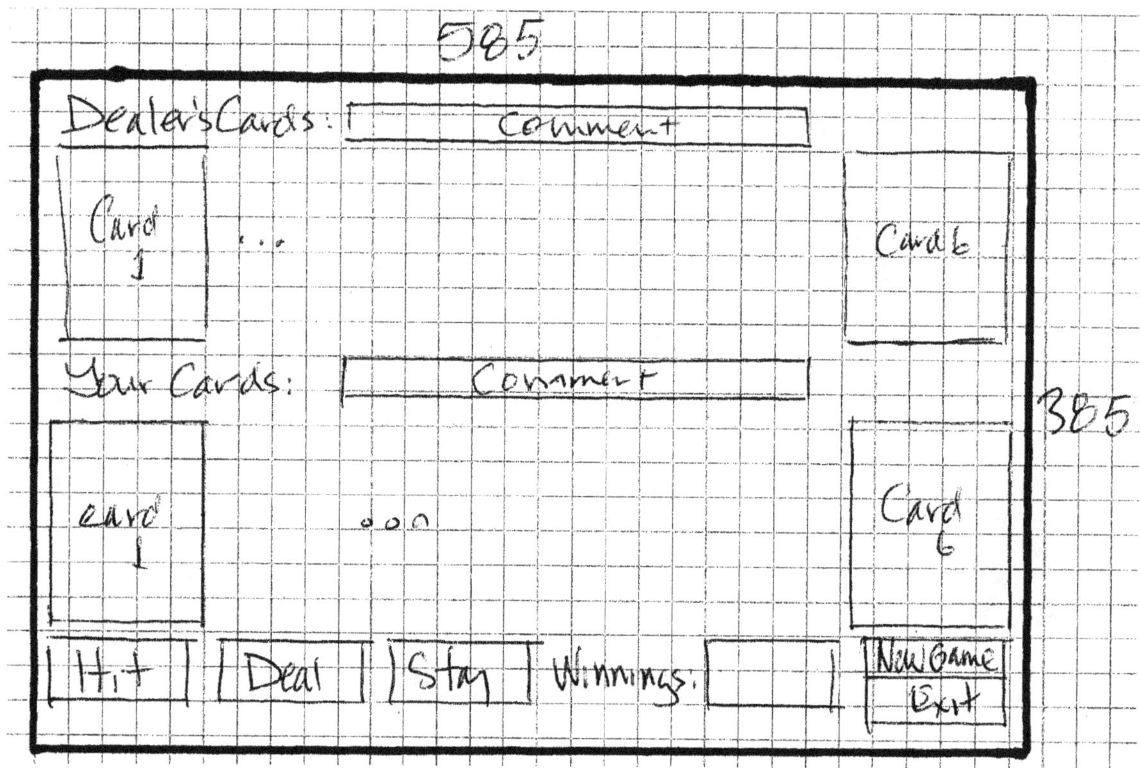

Text shapes are used for header information and to provide feedback and winnings information to the player. Three button controls (**Hit**, **Deal**, **Stay**) are used by the player to 'talk to' the dealer. An additional two buttons are used to start a new game and exit the program. Cards will be displayed under the **Dealer's Cards** and **Your Cards** headers. The will be drawn as images 90 pixels wide by 120 pixels high.

Defining the interface for this project is straightforward - the code behind the interface is not trivial. As we saw when playing the game, there are lots of rules involved with playing Blackjack and we need to determine some way to display the cards. We will build the code slowly. First, let's define the window elements.

Start a new program in Small Basic. Once started, we suggest you immediately save the program with a name you choose. This sets up the folder and file structure needed for your program.

Window Design – Headings and Comments

The headings (**Dealer's Cards**, **Your Cards**) are drawn to the window and the corresponding comments (**DealerComment**, **PlayerComment**) are displayed in **Shapes** objects with text information. Add this code to initialize the graphics window and display these elements:

```
'Blackjack
InitializeProgram()

Sub InitializeProgram
  'graphics window
  GraphicsWindow.Show()
  GraphicsWindow.Width = 585
  GraphicsWindow.Height = 385
  GraphicsWindow.BackgroundColor =
GraphicsWindow.GetColorFromRGB(192, 192, 255)
  GraphicsWindow.Title = "Blackjack"
  'headings/comment areas
  GraphicsWindow.BrushColor = "Black"
  GraphicsWindow.FontSize = 18
  GraphicsWindow.FontBold = "true"
  GraphicsWindow.DrawText(10, 10, "Dealer's Cards:")
  GraphicsWindow.DrawText(10, 170, "Your Cards:")
  GraphicsWindow.BrushColor = "LightYellow"
  GraphicsWindow.FillRectangle(160, 5, 350, 30)
  GraphicsWindow.FillRectangle(160, 165, 350, 30)
  GraphicsWindow.BrushColor = "Blue"
  GraphicsWindow.FontBold = "false"
  DealerComment = Shapes.AddText("")
  Shapes.Move(DealerComment, 170, 10)
  PlayerComment = Shapes.AddText("")
  Shapes.Move(PlayerComment, 170, 170)
EndSub
```

The first line of code calls a subroutine **InitializeProgram** where we will put all code needed to set up the program for use. All remaining code here goes in that subroutine.

Save and **Run** the program. Blank comments are seen:

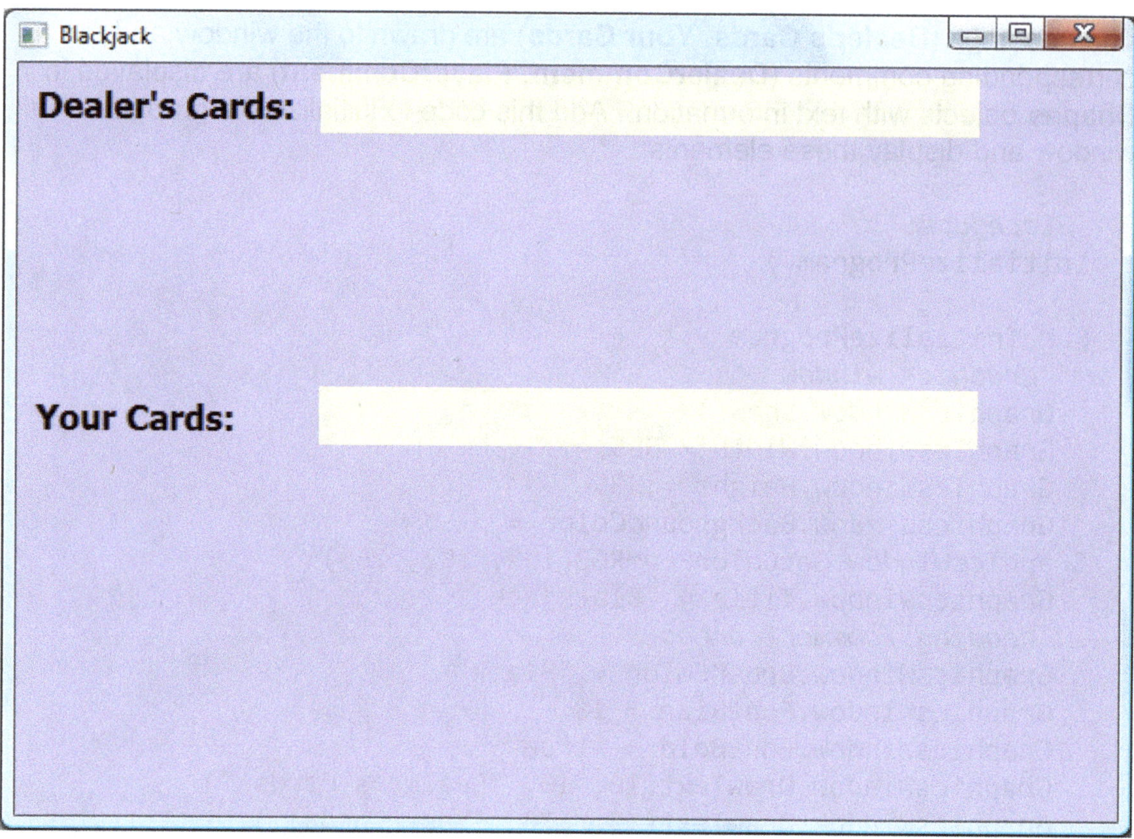

Window Design – Winnings

Similar code is used to display your winnings while playing Blackjack. Add this code to **InitializeProgram**:

```
'winnings display
GraphicsWindow.BrushColor = "Black"
GraphicsWindow.FontBold = "true"
GraphicsWindow.DrawText(300, 335, "Winnings:")
GraphicsWindow.BrushColor = "White"
GraphicsWindow.FillRectangle(400, 330, 70, 35)
GraphicsWindow.BrushColor = "Blue"
GraphicsWindow.FontSize = 20
GraphicsWindow.FontBold = "false"
WinningsDisplay = Shapes.AddText("0")
Shapes.Move(WinningsDisplay, 410, 335)
```

The text shape **WinningsDisplay** is used to show the winnings.

Save and **Run** the program. The initialized winnings (zero) are displayed.

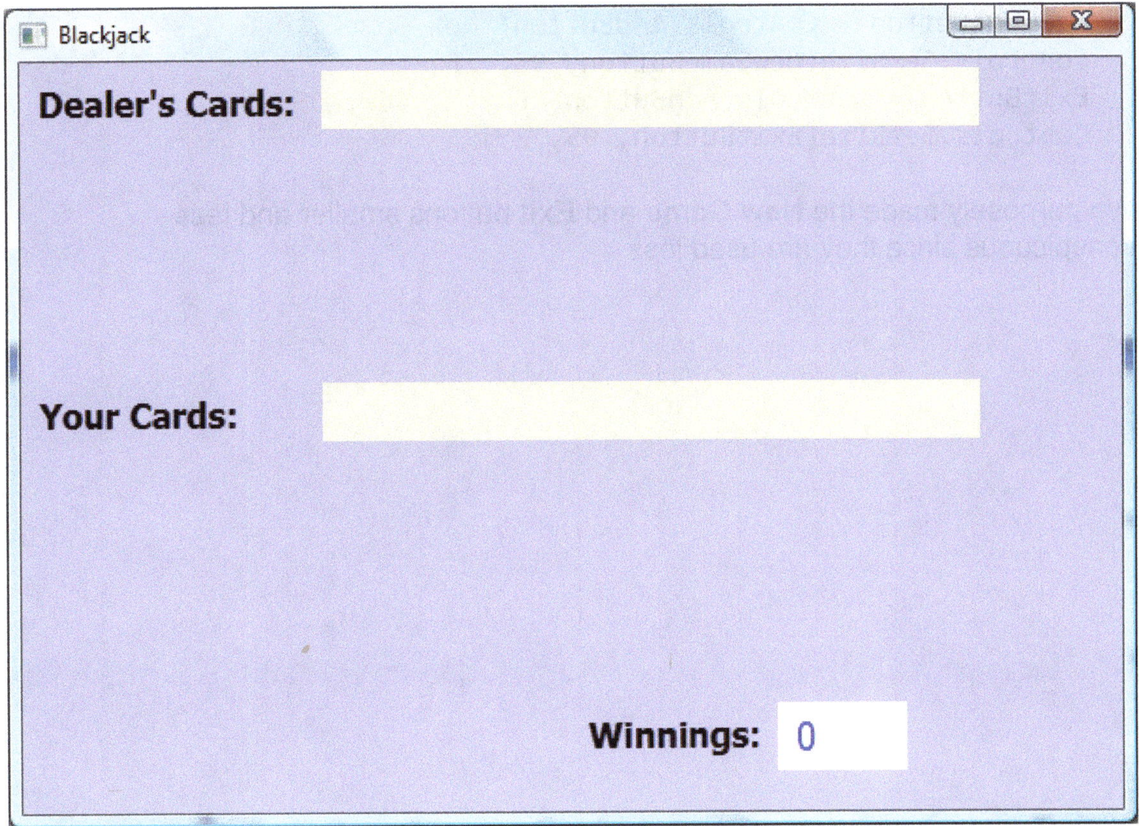

Window Design – Adding Buttons

Five buttons are used in the program. **HitButton** is used to tell the dealer you want an additional card. **StayButton** is used to tell the dealer you want no more cards. **DealButton** tells the dealer you want to start a new hand. Lastly, **NewGameButton** restarts the program and **ExitButton** stops the program.

Add this code (in **InitializeProgram**) to create and place the five buttons:

```
'buttons
GraphicsWindow.BrushColor = "Black"
GraphicsWindow.FontSize = 16
GraphicsWindow.FontBold = "true"
HitButton = Controls.AddButton("Hit", 10, 330)
Controls.SetSize(HitButton, 90, 35)
DealButton = Controls.AddButton("Deal", 105, 330)
Controls.SetSize(DealButton, 90, 35)
StayButton = Controls.AddButton("Stay", 200, 330)
Controls.SetSize(StayButton, 90, 35)
GraphicsWindow.FontSize = 12
GraphicsWindow.FontBold = "false"
NewGameButton = Controls.AddButton("New Game", 480, 330)
Controls.SetSize(NewGameButton, 95, 25)
ExitButton = Controls.AddButton("Exit", 480, 355)
Controls.SetSize(ExitButton, 95, 25)
```

We purposely made the **New Game** and **Exit** buttons smaller and less conspicuous since they are used less.

Save and **Run** the program. The buttons will appear:

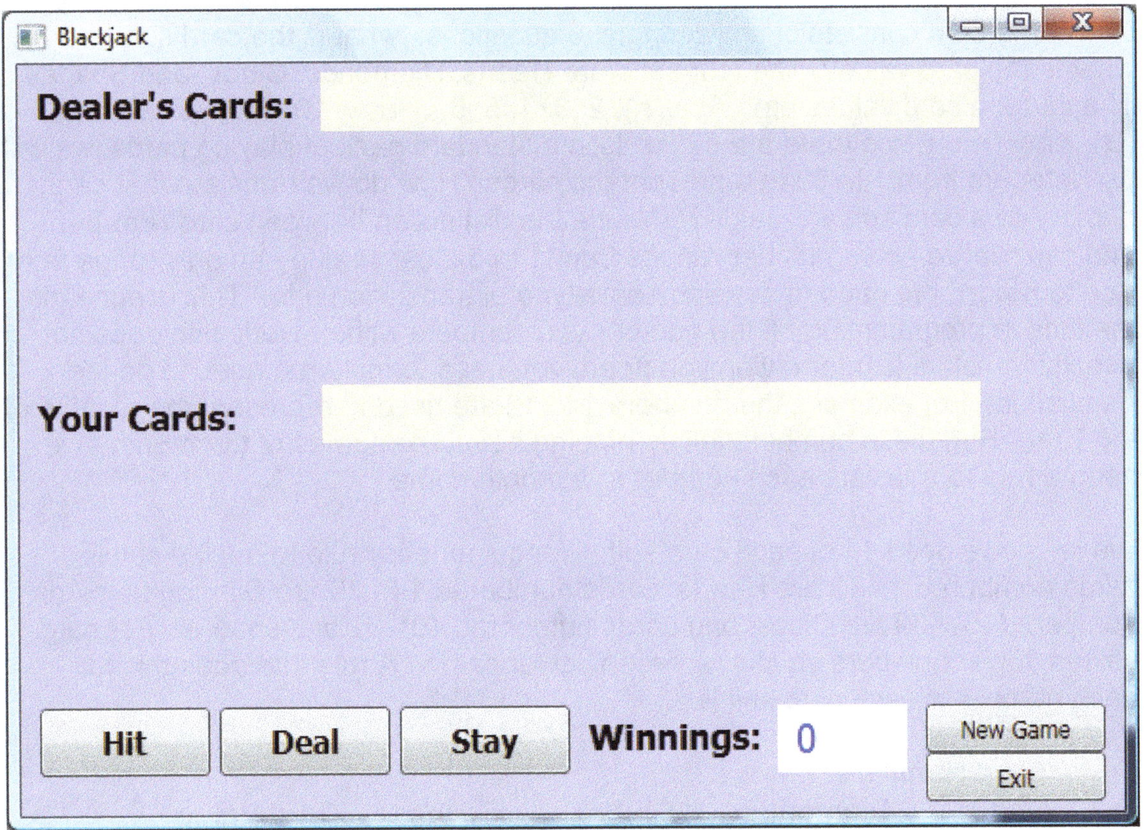

The game window is complete. Now, let's code game play. Many tasks are repeated in the Blackjack card game. We need to shuffle a deck of cards, deal a new hand, display cards for the dealer and player as play continues, and end a hand when a winner is declared. The approach we take is to build the code in modules that perform these repeated tasks. As we build the modules (subroutines), we use them to write code for the button click procedures. One drawback to this modular approach is that we will have to write lots of code before anything can be tested. As a first step, we write the code that defines a deck of cards.

Code Design – Card Definition and Display

Defining a card consists of answering two questions: what is the card suit and what is the card value? The four suits are Hearts, Diamonds, Clubs, and Spades. The thirteen card values are: Ace (A), 2, 3, 4, 5, 6, 7, 8, 9, 10, Jack (J), Queen (Q), King (K). Since there are 52 cards in a standard deck of playing cards, we will use integers from 1 to 52 to represent the cards. How do we translate that card number to a card suit and value? (Notice the distinction between card **number** and card **value** - card number ranges from 1 to 52, card value can only range from Ace to King.) We need to develop some type of translation rule. This is done all the time in programming. If the number you compute with or work with does not directly translate to information you need, you need to make up rules to do the translation. For example, the numbers 1 to 12 are used to represent the months of the year. But, these numbers tell us nothing about the names of the month - we need a rule to translate each number to a month name.

We know we need 13 of each card suit. Hence, an easy rule to decide suit is: cards numbered 1 - 13 are Hearts, cards numbered 14 - 26 are Diamonds, cards numbered 27 - 39 are Clubs, and cards numbered 40 - 52 are Spades. For card values, lower numbers should represent lower cards. A rule that does this for each number in each card suit is:

Card Numbers				
Hearts	**Diamonds**	**Clubs**	**Spades**	**Card Value**
1	14	27	40	A
2	15	28	41	2
3	16	29	42	3
4	17	30	43	4
5	18	31	44	5
6	19	32	45	6
7	20	33	46	7
8	21	34	47	8
9	22	35	48	9
10	23	36	49	10
11	24	37	50	J
12	25	38	51	Q
13	26	39	52	K

As examples, notice card number 12 is a Queen of Hearts. Card number 31 is a 5 of Clubs. These card numbers will be used to establish the image file associated with the card.

As an aside, if you have used KIDware's **Beginning Small Basic**, you will notice the rules for displaying cards here are slightly different than those used in the Card Wars project. In Card Wars, Ace was a high card, where here it is considered a low card.

We will use 52 different image files to display cards in the **Blackjack** program. As mentioned, a card number is used to establish the image file that represents the corresponding card. In the **HomeSB\HomeSB Projects\CardGraphics** folder are 52 graphics files (**gif** files) that represent the 52 playing cards (these images were found on the Internet). The files are named **card01.gif** to **card52.gif**. And, yes, the file numbers (the last two digits in the name) correspond to the card numbers we've assigned. So **card12.gif** is a Queen of Hearts and **card31.gif** is a 5 of Clubs. Open the files in a graphics program if you like. So, once we know a card number, we know which file is used to display that card.

Two approaches can be taken to display cards in the Blackjack program. The first is that whenever a card must be displayed, we could load the appropriate file into an image using the **ImageList.LoadImage** method. Then, it could be displayed in the graphics window. In this approach, every time a card is needed, the program would have to find the file and load it from disk. This approach would require multiple accesses to disk files, slowing down the program. The second approach (and the one we use) is to preload all image files (still using **ImageList.LoadImage** method) into an array of images. Then, when a card must be displayed, we can draw the image using the appropriate array element. This is a much faster approach and only requires opening the image files one time. The preloading of images is done when we initialize the program window.

Before coding this initialization, we address where the image files should be located in the project file structure. The accepted standard for using files (graphics files, sound files, data files, configuration files) associated with a project is to store those files in the same folder as the program. Copy the 52 card graphics (plus the file **cardback.gif**, which holds the image to represent the back of a card) into your project's folder. If you want, open and view the folder in the **HomeSB\HomeSB Projects\Blackjack** project to see these files in the included project.

We will define 53 images for card display – one for the card back (**CardBack**) and an array of 52 images (**CardImage**) for the individual cards. Now, the code that establishes these images is:

```
'Load card images
CardBack = ImageList.LoadImage(Program.Directory +
"\cardback.gif")
For CardNumber = 1 To 52
  ImageFile = Program.Directory + "\card"
  If (CardNumber < 10) Then
    ImageFile = ImageFile + Text.Append("0", CardNumber)
+".gif"
  Else
    ImageFile = ImageFile + CardNumber +".gif"
  EndIf
  CardImage[CardNumber] = ImageList.LoadImage(ImageFile)
EndFor
```

In this code, we first set **CardBack**. Then, for all 52 cards, we form the appropriate file name and load the 52 **CardImage** values from file. Note use of the **Program.Directory** parameter (it "points" to your program's folder) and the need for an additional backslash (\) in the path name.

Add the initialization code to **InitializeProgram** (after code for buttons), then **Save** and **Run** the project. If the program runs without errors, things are probably okay. If there are errors, you need to correct them. One thing to check is to make sure the image files are in your program's folder. As a test, add this line after the code loading the images:

```
GraphicsWindow.DrawImage(CardImage[12], 10, 40)
```

This draws the first dealer card at (10, 40). Now, **Run** the program again. If everything works, you should see the Queen of Hearts (card number 12):

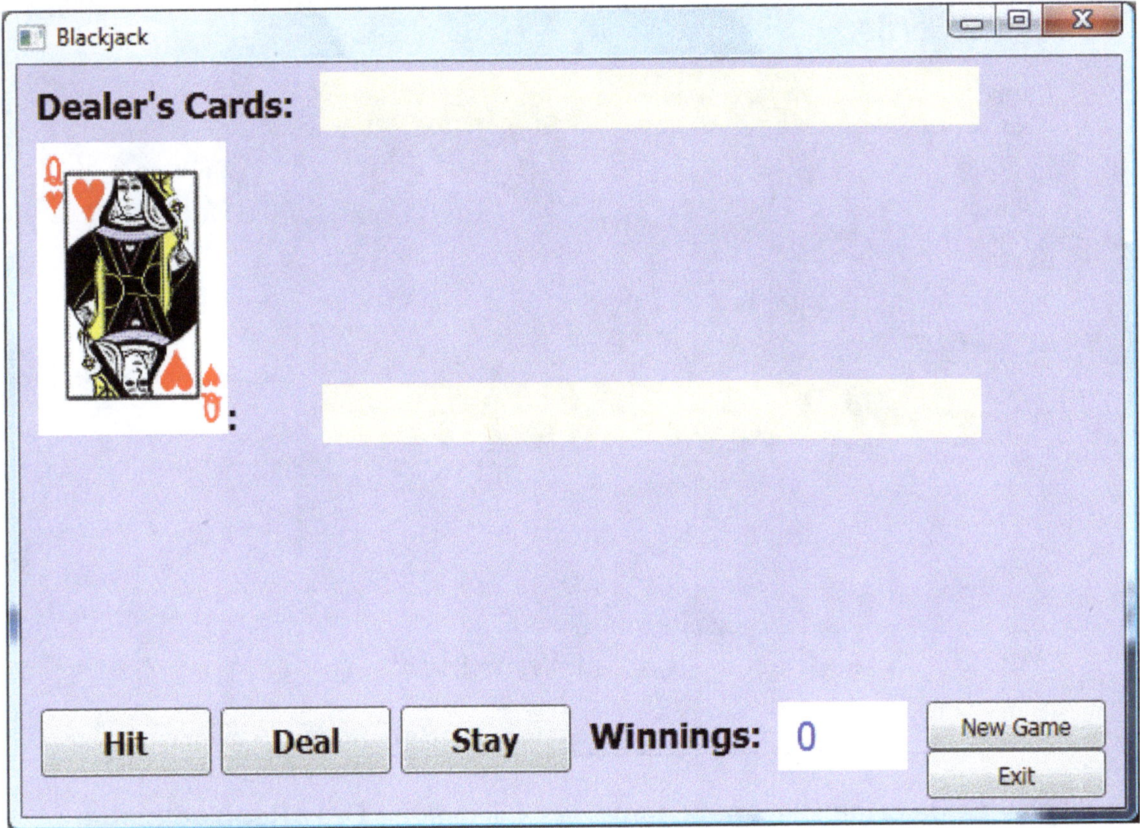

The **DrawImage** method draws an image in full-size. As seen, the card's a little bigger than we want (it wipes out one of the headings), but we can fix that.

In the **Blackjack** program, card images will be 90 pixels wide by 120 pixels high. To display the images in this size, we use the **DrawResizedImage** method which has two additional arguments defining width and height. To draw the Queen of Hearts in the proper size, change the test line of code to:

```
GraphicsWindow.DrawResizedImage(CardImage[12], 10, 40, 90, 120)
```

Save and **Run** and the queen appears properly sized:

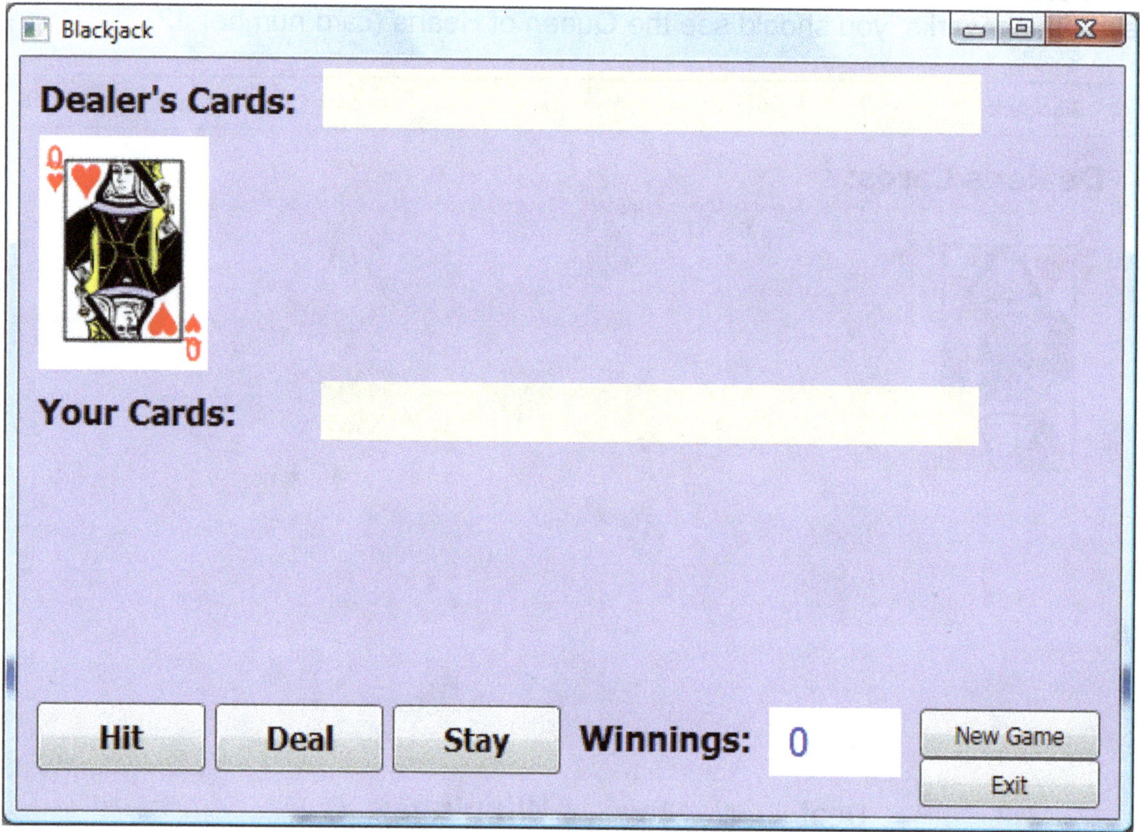

To display cards in the **Blackjack** game, we will use the **DrawResizedImage** method (using a width of 90 and height of 120). The cards will be evenly spaced (six cards maximum) under the proper heading (**Dealer's Cards** or **Your Cards**). Remove the test line of code.

At this point, we have an array (**CardImage**) of the graphics used to represent each of the 52 cards. In Blackjack, each card also has a point value. An Ace (initially, at least) is worth 1 point, the cards 2 through 10 have points value equal to their card value. And, the face cards (Jack, Queen, King) are each worth 10 points. An array (**CardPoints**) is used to hold the point value for each card. Modify the code just entered to establish the elements of this array (changes are shaded):

```
'Load card images
CardBack = ImageList.LoadImage(Program.Directory +
"\cardback.gif")
For CardNumber = 1 To 52
  ImageFile = Program.Directory + "\card"
  If (CardNumber < 10) Then
    ImageFile = ImageFile + Text.Append("0", CardNumber)
+".gif"
  Else
    ImageFile = ImageFile + CardNumber +".gif"
  EndIf
  CardImage[CardNumber] = ImageList.LoadImage(ImageFile)
  J = Math.Remainder(CardNumber - 1, 13) + 1 ' a number from 1
(A) to 13 (K)
  If (J < 11) Then
    ' A through 10
    CardPoints[CardNumber] = J
  Else
    'Jack, Queen, King
    CardPoints[CardNumber] = 10
  EndIf
EndFor
```

This new code uses the **Remainder** method (returns the remainder when the first number in the parentheses is divided by the second number) to assign a point value to a card (**CardNumber**) from 1 to 52. The expression using the **Remainder** method converts any card number to a number from 1 to 13, regardless of suit. The result is then used to assign the point value. Try a few values to convince yourself this works. Make the noted modifications. **Save** and **Run** the project, if you'd like.

We now have all the information we need to define a card and we know how to display the corresponding image. The array **CardImage** has images for specific cards, while the array **CardPoints** has the corresponding point values. The index on the array, **CardNumber**, ranges from 1 to 52 (Ace of Hearts to King of Spades). Let's learn how to "shuffle" these cards.

Code Design – Card Shuffle

With 52 cards, we need to randomly sort the integers from 1 to 52 to "simulate" the shuffling process. How do we do this?

Usually when we need a computer version of something we can do without a computer, it is fairly easy to write down the steps taken and duplicate them in code. When we shuffle a deck of cards, we separate the deck in two parts, then interleaf the cards as we fan each part, making that familiar shuffling noise. I don't know how you could write code to do this. We'll take another approach which is hard or tedious to do off the computer, but is easy to do on a computer.

We perform what is called a "one card shuffle." In a one card shuffle, you pull a single card (at random) out of the deck and lay it aside on a pile. Repeat this 52 times and the cards are shuffled. Try it! I think you see this idea is simple, but doing a one card shuffle with a real deck of cards would be awfully time-consuming. We'll use the idea of a one card shuffle here, with a slight twist. Rather than lay the selected card on a pile, we will swap it with the bottom card in the stack of cards remaining to be shuffled. This takes the selected card out of the deck and replaces it with the remaining bottom card. The result is the same as if we lay it aside.

Here's how the shuffle works with N numbers:

- Start with a list of N consecutive integers.
- Randomly pick one item from the list. Swap that item with the last item. You now have one fewer items in the list to be sorted (called the remaining list), or N is now N - 1.
- Randomly pick one item from the remaining list. Swap it with the item on the bottom of the remaining list. Again, your remaining list now has one fewer items.
- Repeatedly remove one item from the remaining list and swap it with the item on the bottom of the remaining list until you have run out of items. When done, the list will have been replaced with the original list in random order.

The code to do a one card shuffle, or sort **NIntegers** integers, is placed in a subroutine named **SortIntegers**. The code computes an array (**SortedArray**) containing the randomly sorted integers. The code is:

```
Sub SortIntegers
  'Randomly sorts NIntegers integers and puts results in
SortedArray
  'Order all elements initially
  For II = 1 To NIntegers
    SortedArray[II] = II
  EndFor
  'JJ is the number of integers remaining
  For JJ = NIntegers To 2 Step -1
    II = Math.GetRandomNumber(JJ)
    TT = SortedArray[JJ]
    SortedArray[JJ] = SortedArray[II]
    SortedArray[II] = TT
  EndFor
EndSub
```

You should be able to see each step of the shuffle procedure. This subroutine is general (sorting **NIntegers** integers) and can be used in other projects requiring random lists of integers.

Add the **SortIntegers** subroutine to your Blackjack project. It will be used every time we need to shuffle the 52 cards. In the project, we will use an array **Card** (with 52 elements) to hold the randomly sorted integers (the shuffled cards). A variable **CurrentCard** will be used to indicate the current index of the **Card** array being used. The snippet of code that does a shuffle is:

```
NIntegers = 52
SortIntegers()
Card = SortedArray
CurrentCard = 1
```

In this code, we obtain the shuffled cards in **Card** and set **CurrentCard** to one so we are 'pointing' to the first card in the deck.

We can now use the shuffling process and card descriptions to begin building modules to play the Blackjack game.

Code Design – Start New Game

To start a new **Blackjack** game, a user clicks the **New Game** button. The steps in this procedure are:

- Set winnings (**Winnings**) to zero and reset winnings display.
- Shuffle cards.
- Start a new hand.

Add this line of code at the end of **InitializeProgram** to detect button clicks:

```
Controls.ButtonClicked = ButtonClickedSub
```

And, add the subroutine **ButtonClickedSub** which calls **NewGameButtonClicked** when **NewGameButton** is clicked:

```
Sub ButtonClickedSub
  B = Controls.LastClickedButton
  If (B = NewGameButton) Then
    NewGameButtonClicked()
  EndIf
EndSub
```

The code for the **NewGameButtonClicked** subroutine is:

```
Sub NewGameButtonClicked
  'start new game - clear winnings and start over
  Winnings = 0
  Shapes.SetText(WinningsDisplay, "0")
  NIntegers = 52
  SortIntegers()
  Card = SortedArray
  CurrentCard = 1
  NewHand()
EndSub
```

The steps are obvious. This procedure uses a subroutine **NewHand** to start a new hand of Blackjack. We will code that next, but let's take care of a couple of other tasks first.

Add the shaded code to **ButtonClickedSub** to handle clicking **ExitButton**:

```
Sub ButtonClickedSub
  B = Controls.LastClickedButton
  If (B = NewGameButton) Then
    NewGameButtonClicked()
  ElseIf (B = ExitButton) Then
    Program.End()
  EndIf
EndSub
```

When the Blackjack program first begins, we also want to start a new game. Add this line at the end of **InitializeProgram**. This line will cause the **NewGameButtonClicked** subroutine to be executed when the program begins:

```
NewGameButtonClicked()
```

Save the program. If you try to run it, you will be told the subroutine **NewHand** is not defined. Let's define it.

Code Design – Start New Hand

Each "round" of Blackjack begins with a new hand. In a new hand, two dealer cards (one face down) and two player cards are displayed and the interface is set so the player can begin playing his hand. Many steps are required to start a new hand:

- Clear all cards.
- Clear dealer and player comments.
- Show **Hit** button.
- Show **Stay** button.
- Hide **Deal** button.
- Reshuffle if necessary (if more than 35 cards have been used).
- Add two cards to dealer hand.
- Add two cards to player hand.
- Check if either hand is a Blackjack. If so, end the hand.

Several variables are used to know the status of the dealer and player hands. **NumberCardsDealer** tells us how many cards are currently in the dealer's hand, **AcesDealer** tells us how many of those cards are Aces, and **ScoreDealer** tells us the dealer point total. We track Aces separately since their score can be either a 1 or 11. **NumberCardsPlayer** tells us how many cards are currently in the player's hand, **AcesPlayer** tells us how many of those cards are Aces, and **ScorePlayer** tells us the player point total. In the **NewHand** procedure, all of these will be initialized at zero, prior to adding cards to the hands.

The **NewHand** subroutine that implements the listed steps is:

```
Sub NewHand
  'Deal a new hand
  'Clear table of cards
  GraphicsWindow.BrushColor = GraphicsWindow.BackgroundColor
  GraphicsWindow.FillRectangle(10, 40, 565, 120)
  GraphicsWindow.FillRectangle(10, 200, 565, 120)
  Shapes.SetText(DealerComment, "")
  Shapes.SetText(PlayerComment, "")
  Controls.ShowControl(HitButton)
  Controls.ShowControl(StayButton)
  Controls.HideControl(DealButton)
  'reshuffle occasionally
  If (CurrentCard > 35) Then
    NIntegers = 52
    SortIntegers()
    Card = SortedArray
    CurrentCard = 1
  EndIf
  'Get two dealer cards
  ScoreDealer = 0
  AcesDealer = 0
  NumberCardsDealer = 0
  AddDealerCard()
  AddDealerCard()
  'Get two player cards
  ScorePlayer = 0
  AcesPlayer = 0
  NumberCardsPlayer = 0
  AddPlayerCard()
  AddPlayerCard()
  'Check for blackjacks
  If (ScoreDealer = 11 And AcesDealer = 1) Then
    ScoreDealer = 21
  EndIf
  If (ScorePlayer = 11 And AcesPlayer = 1) Then
    ScorePlayer = 21
  EndIf
  If (ScoreDealer = 21 And ScorePlayer = 21) Then
    Shapes.SetText(DealerComment,"Dealer has Blackjack!")
    Shapes.SetText(PlayerComment, "And, you have Blackjack .. a
push!")
    Change = 0
    EndHand()
  ElseIf (ScoreDealer = 21) Then
```

```
    Shapes.SetText(DealerComment,"Dealer has Blackjack!")
    Shapes.SetText(PlayerComment, "You lose ...")
    Change = -10
    EndHand()
  ElseIf (ScorePlayer = 21) Then
    Shapes.SetText(DealerComment,"Dealer loses ...")
    Shapes.SetText(PlayerComment, "You have Blackjack!")
    Change = 15
    EndHand()
  EndIf
EndSub
```

Let's look at the **NewHand** procedure in a little detail. The cards are cleared by drawing filled rectangles in the card display areas. A reshuffle is done when **CurrentCard** is greater than **35**. The dealer hand status variables are set to zero and two cards are added to the dealer hand using a subroutine **AddDealerCard**. Similarly for the player's hand, two cards are added using **AddPlayerCard**. We will write these procedures soon (they update the three status variables for the dealer and player).

The last part of the procedure checks each hand for Blackjack (having an Ace and a card worth 10 points, a 10, a Jack, a Queen, or a King). If either has a Blackjack, comments are displayed, the change in winnings (**Change**) is determined and the subroutine **EndHand** is called. In this procedure, the player's winnings are updated and the player is allowed to play again.

Add the **NewHand** subroutine to your project. **Save** your work. We still can't test the project. We still need three more subroutines which we'll code next – **EndHand**, **AddDealerCard**, **AddPlayerCard**.

Code Design – End Hand

When a hand has ended, we want to tell the player whether he/she won and update their winnings. A new hand can then be dealt. The steps involved in ending a hand are:

- Display the dealer's face down card (just to make sure it is showing)
- Update **Winnings** and display new value.
- Hide **Hit** button.
- Hide **Stay** button.
- Show **Deal** button.

Since the first dealer card is shown face down (unless there is a Blackjack or until the player stays or busts), we need a variable to hold that card's image (**DealerFaceDown**). This variable will be established in the **AddDealerCard** procedure.

The **EndHand** subroutine that accomplishes the above tasks is:

```
Sub EndHand
  'make sure dealer cards are seen
  GraphicsWindow.DrawResizedImage(DealerFaceDown, 10, 40, 90,
120)
  'Hand has ended - update winnings
  Winnings = Winnings + Change
  Shapes.SetText(WinningsDisplay, Winnings)
  Controls.HideControl(HitButton)
  Controls.HideControl(StayButton)
  Controls.ShowControl(DealButton)
EndSub
```

Add **EndHand** to your project and **Save**. Just two more subroutines and we can see if all this works! We need to add cards to the dealer and player hands.

Code Design – Display Dealer Card

Here, we build a subroutine to add a card to the dealer's hand and display that card. The **CurrentCard** variable, used with the **Card** array, identifies the card added to the dealer's hand. Recall three variables (**NumberCardsDealer**, **AcesDealer**, **ScoreDealer**) are used to provide specifics about the dealer's hand. Also, recall **DealerFaceDown** saves the dealer's face down card.

Knowing **CurrentCard**, the steps involved in adding a card to the dealer's hand are:

- Determine **CardNumber** from the **Card** array.
- Increment **NumberCardsDealer**.
- If displaying first card:
  - Set **DealerFaceDown** to **CardImage[CardNumber]**.
  - Display dealer's first card as **CardBack**.
- If display second through sixth card:
  - Display **CardImage[CardNumber]** at corresponding location.
- Increment dealer's score by **CardPoints[CardNumber]**
- Increment **AcesDealer**, if card is an Ace.
- Increment **CurrentCard**.

In these steps, if we are adding the first card, we save the image and display the card back. For other cards, the appropriate image is displayed. We then update the score, noting if an Ace has been added. As a last step, the current card index is incremented by one. At all times, we know the status of the dealer's hand (number of cards, number of aces and score).

The steps of the process to add a card to the dealer's hand are coded in a subroutine named **AddDealerCard**:

```
Sub AddDealerCard
  CardNumber = Card[CurrentCard]
  'Adds a card to dealer hand
  NumberCardsDealer = NumberCardsDealer + 1
  If (NumberCardsDealer = 1) Then
    DealerFaceDown = CardImage[CardNumber]
    GraphicsWindow.DrawResizedImage(CardBack, 10, 40, 90, 120)
  Else
    GraphicsWindow.DrawResizedImage(CardImage[CardNumber], 10 +
(NumberCardsDealer - 1) * 95, 40, 90, 120)
  EndIf
  ScoreDealer = ScoreDealer + CardPoints[CardNumber]
  If (CardPoints[CardNumber] = 1) Then
    AcesDealer = AcesDealer + 1
  EndIf
  CurrentCard = CurrentCard + 1
EndSub
```

Add this subroutine to your project. Notice how **NumberCardsDealer** is used to space the cards across the window. Also notice the score (**ScoreDealer**) always considers Aces as a single point. This may change when final hands are considered.

Code Design – Display Player Card

The procedure to add a card to the player's hand is similar to the code just developed. The only difference is that there is never a 'face-down' card in the player's hand. The **CurrentCard** variable, used with the **Card** array, identifies the card added to the player's hand. Three variables (**NumberCardsPlayer**, **AcesPlayer**, **ScorePlayer**) are used to provide specifics about the player's hand.

Knowing **CurrentCard**, the steps involved in adding a card to the player's hand are:

- Determine **CardNumber** from the **Card** array.
- Increment **NumberCardsPlayer**.
- Display **CardImage[CardNumber]** at appropriate location.
- Increment player's score by **CardPoints[CardNumber]**
- Increment **AcesPlayer**, if card is an Ace.
- Increment **CurrentCard**.

In these steps, the appropriate image is displayed. We then update the score, noting if an Ace has been added. As a last step, the current card index is incremented by one. At all times, we know the status of the player's hand (number of cards, number of aces and score).

The steps of the process to add a card to the player's hand are coded in a subroutine named **AddPlayerCard**:

```
Sub AddPlayerCard
  CardNumber = Card[CurrentCard]
  'Adds a card to player hand
  NumberCardsPlayer = NumberCardsPlayer + 1
  GraphicsWindow.DrawResizedImage(CardImage[CardNumber], 10 +
(NumberCardsPlayer - 1) * 95, 200, 90, 120)
  ScorePlayer = ScorePlayer + CardPoints[CardNumber]
  If (CardPoints[CardNumber] = 1) Then
    AcesPlayer = AcesPlayer + 1
  EndIf
  CurrentCard = CurrentCard + 1
EndSub
```

Add this subroutine to your project. Again, notice how **NumberCardsPlayer** is used to position the cards and the score (**ScorePlayer**) always considers Aces as a single point. This may change when final hands are considered.

After all the code we have added, we are finally at a point to try running the project. **Save** and **Run** the project to make sure there are no errors in the code. If there are no errors, the window with the first hand should appear. Here's what I see:

You should see something similar, unless there is a Blackjack. If one of the first hands is a Blackjack, you will see messages to say so and the window will be set so a new hand can be dealt (the **Deal** button will be enabled).

If you encounter errors in trying to run the project, you need to go back over all the code and see what went wrong. Hopefully, by taking things slow and step-by-step, fixing problems should be straightforward. In the current mode, the user can click **Hit** or **Stay**. If there is a Blackjack, the user can click **Deal**. The last remaining programming tasks are to code the **Click** events for these three buttons. The subroutines we have written will help in this additional coding. The **Deal** button has the simplest coding, so we'll do it first.

Code Design – Deal New Hand

When a hand has ended, the user can either start a new game, exit the program or deal a new hand. We have already written code for starting a new game and exiting the program. Here we write code for dealing a new hand, once the user clicks the **Deal** button.

The code for clicking on **DealButton** is made simple because of all the code we have already developed. It is a single line of code that calls the existing **NewHand** procedure. Add the shaded code to the ButtonClickedSub subroutine:

```
Sub ButtonClickedSub
  B = Controls.LastClickedButton
  If (B = NewGameButton) Then
    NewGameButtonClicked()
  ElseIf (B = ExitButton) Then
    Program.End()
  ElseIf (B = DealButton) Then
    NewHand()
  EndIf
EndSub
```

Code Design – Player 'Hit'

When a player chooses the **Hit** button, a new card is added to his/her hand and the results evaluated. The steps are:

- Add a player card.
- If player's score exceeds 21, end hand announcing player has busted.
- If player has 6 cards, end hand announcing player has won.

As mentioned earlier in this chapter, this last step is a special rule used in our version of Blackjack.

The code is placed in **ButtonClickedSub** subroutine (changes are shaded):

```
Sub ButtonClickedSub
  B = Controls.LastClickedButton
  If (B = NewGameButton) Then
    NewGameButtonClicked()
  ElseIf (B = ExitButton) Then
    Program.End()
  ElseIf (B = DealButton) Then
    NewHand()
  ElseIf (B = HitButton) Then
    'Add a card if player requests
    AddPlayerCard()
    If (ScorePlayer > 21) Then
      Shapes.SetText(DealerComment, "Dealer wins")
      Shapes.SetText(PlayerComment, "You busted!")
      Change = -10
      EndHand()
    ElseIf (NumberCardsPlayer = 6) Then
      Shapes.SetText(DealerComment, "No dealer play")
      Shapes.SetText(PlayerComment, "You win - 6 cards and not
over 21!")
      Change = 10
      EndHand()
    EndIf
  EndIf
EndSub
```

Make the noted additions.

Save and **Run** the project. Try the **Hit** button. Keep adding cards until you bust (exceed 21) or get 6 cards. You can't choose to **Stay** – we need to write some code behind that procedure. Once you bust or get 6 cards, you can click **Deal** to try again. You won't be able to test the **Hit** button if there is an initial Blackjack. In this case, click the **Deal** button until hands without a Blackjack appear. Then try the **Hit** button.

Code Design – Player 'Stay'

We save the most detailed event– clicking the **Stay** button - for last. Lots of things need to happen in this code. We need to determine player's final score, then allow the dealer to play out his hand according to the fixed set of rules. There are lots of decisions to be made. The procedure steps are:

- Hide **Hit** button.
- Hide **Stay** button.
- Determine player's highest possible score without exceeding 21 (accounting for any aces).
- Display the dealer's face down card.
- Play dealer's hand (repeat all steps until hand is ended):
  - Determine dealer's highest possible score without exceeding 21 (accounting for any aces).
  - If dealer's score is above 16, determine winner and end hand.
  - If dealer has six cards and still under 16, end hand and declare dealer the winner.
  - Add card to dealer's hand.
  - If above 21, end hand and declare player the winner.

As you can see most of the logic is in playing the dealer's hand. Also, notice the special "six card" rule we use.

Determining either the player's or dealer's score (considering the possibility of Aces) is a little tricky. Let's look at a snippet of code that does the task for the player:

```
If (AcesPlayer <> 0 And ScorePlayer <= 11) Then
  ScorePlayer = ScorePlayer + 10
  AcesPlayer = AcesPlayer - 1
EndIf
```

Recall the running score (**ScorePlayer**) always considers Aces as one point. If the player has no Aces, there is no score adjustment. Otherwise 10 points is added to the score, if that adjusted score would not exceed 21. If a player has multiple Aces, only one can count for 11 points (would exceed 21, otherwise). Similar code is used for the dealer score.

Add the shaded lines to **ButtonClickedSub** to detect clicks on **StayButton**:

```
Sub ButtonClickedSub
  B = Controls.LastClickedButton
  If (B = NewGameButton) Then
    NewGameButtonClicked()
  ElseIf (B = ExitButton) Then
    Program.End()
  ElseIf (B = DealButton) Then
    NewHand()
  ElseIf (B = HitButton) Then
    'Add a card if player requests
    AddPlayerCard()
    If (ScorePlayer > 21) Then
      Shapes.SetText(DealerComment, "Dealer wins")
      Shapes.SetText(PlayerComment, "You busted!")
      Change = -10
      EndHand()
    ElseIf (NumberCardsPlayer = 6) Then
      Shapes.SetText(DealerComment, "No dealer play")
      Shapes.SetText(PlayerComment, "You win - 6 cards and not
over 21!")
      Change = 10
      EndHand()
    EndIf
  ElseIf (B = StayButton) Then
    StayButtonClicked()
  EndIf
EndSub
```

The **StayButtonClicked** subroutine is:

```
Sub StayButtonClicked
  Controls.HideControl(HitButton)
  Controls.HideControl(StayButton)
  'Check for aces in player hand and adjust score
  'to highest possible
  If (AcesPlayer <> 0 And ScorePlayer <= 11) Then
    ScorePlayer = ScorePlayer + 10
    AcesPlayer = AcesPlayer - 1
  EndIf
  'Uncover dealer face down card and play dealer hand
  GraphicsWindow.DrawResizedImage(DealerFaceDown, 10, 40, 90,
120)
  CheckLoop:
    ScoreTemp = ScoreDealer
    AcesTemp = AcesDealer
    'Check for aces and adjust score
    If (AcesDealer <> 0 And ScoreDealer <= 11) Then
      ScoreDealer = ScoreDealer + 10
      AcesDealer = AcesDealer - 1
    EndIf
    'add card unless score above 16 or dealer has 6 cards
    If (ScoreTemp > 16) Then
      If (ScoreTemp > ScorePlayer) Then
        Shapes.SetText(DealerComment, "Dealer wins with " +
ScoreTemp)
        Shapes.SetText(PlayerComment, "You lose with " +
ScorePlayer)
        Change = -10
        EndHand()
      ElseIf (ScoreTemp = ScorePlayer) Then
        Shapes.SetText(DealerComment, "Dealer has " +
ScoreTemp)
        Shapes.SetText(PlayerComment, "So do you ... a push!")
        Change = 0
        EndHand()
      Else
        Shapes.SetText(DealerComment, "Dealer loses with " +
ScoreTemp)
        Shapes.SetText(PlayerComment, "You win with " +
ScorePlayer)
        Change = 10
        EndHand()
      EndIf
      Goto ExitStayButtonClicked
```

```
    ElseIf (NumberCardsDealer = 6) Then
      Shapes.SetText(DealerComment, "Dealer wins ... 6 cards
and not over 16!")
      Shapes.SetText(PlayerComment, "You lose ...")
      Change = -10
      EndHand()
      Goto ExitStayButtonClicked
    Else
      AddDealerCard()
      'dealer loses if busted
      If (ScoreDealer > 21) Then
        Shapes.SetText(DealerComment, "Dealer busts!")
        Shapes.SetText(PlayerComment, "You win!!")
        Change = 10
        EndHand()
        Goto ExitStayButtonClicked
      EndIf
    EndIf
    Goto CheckLoop
  ExitStayButtonClicked:
  EndSub
```

Notice the code to determine player and dealer scores. For the dealer, we use temporary variables (**ScoreTemp** and **AcesTemp**) to represent the dealer score. We don't want to destroy the values of **ScoreDealer** and **AcesDealer** in case more cards may be added. A loop structure is implemented to allow the dealer to continue to add cards to his hand until the hand ends. Notice whenever a call to **EndHand** is encountered, it is followed by a subsequent **Goto ExitStayButtonClicked** statement to leave the subroutine so the dealer no longer adds cards. Add this final subroutine to the project.

Save and **Run** the project. You should now have a complete, running version of the Blackjack game. Have fun playing it! See if you can come up with some kind of winning strategy. Here's the first game I played. It was a push after taking a hit:

In the next game, I won after taking a single hit:

In a later game, I won after taking one hit. Notice the Ace in my hand counts as 11:

And, in one game, I got Blackjack!!

Blackjack Card Game Project Code Listing

Here is the complete listing of the **Blackjack Card Game** Small Basic program:

```
'Blackjack
InitializeProgram()

Sub InitializeProgram
  'graphics window
  GraphicsWindow.Width = 585
  GraphicsWindow.Height = 385
  GraphicsWindow.BackgroundColor =
GraphicsWindow.GetColorFromRGB(192, 192, 255)
  GraphicsWindow.Title = "Blackjack"
  'headings/comment areas
  GraphicsWindow.BrushColor = "Black"
  GraphicsWindow.FontSize = 18
  GraphicsWindow.FontBold = "true"
  GraphicsWindow.DrawText(10, 10, "Dealer's Cards:")
  GraphicsWindow.DrawText(10, 170, "Your Cards:")
  GraphicsWindow.BrushColor = "LightYellow"
  GraphicsWindow.FillRectangle(160, 5, 350, 30)
  GraphicsWindow.FillRectangle(160, 165, 350, 30)
  GraphicsWindow.BrushColor = "Blue"
  GraphicsWindow.FontBold = "false"
  DealerComment = Shapes.AddText("")
  Shapes.Move(DealerComment, 170, 10)
  PlayerComment = Shapes.AddText("")
  Shapes.Move(PlayerComment, 170, 170)
  'winnings display
  GraphicsWindow.BrushColor = "Black"
  GraphicsWindow.FontBold = "true"
  GraphicsWindow.DrawText(300, 335, "Winnings:")
  GraphicsWindow.BrushColor = "White"
  GraphicsWindow.FillRectangle(400, 330, 70, 35)
  GraphicsWindow.BrushColor = "Blue"
  GraphicsWindow.FontSize = 20
  GraphicsWindow.FontBold = "false"
  WinningsDisplay = Shapes.AddText("0")
  Shapes.Move(WinningsDisplay, 410, 335)
  'buttons
  GraphicsWindow.BrushColor = "Black"
  GraphicsWindow.FontSize = 16
  GraphicsWindow.FontBold = "true"
  HitButton = Controls.AddButton("Hit", 10, 330)
  Controls.SetSize(HitButton, 90, 35)
```

```
  DealButton = Controls.AddButton("Deal", 105, 330)
  Controls.SetSize(DealButton, 90, 35)
  StayButton = Controls.AddButton("Stay", 200, 330)
  Controls.SetSize(StayButton, 90, 35)
  GraphicsWindow.FontSize = 12
  GraphicsWindow.FontBold = "false"
  NewGameButton = Controls.AddButton("New Game", 480, 330)
  Controls.SetSize(NewGameButton, 95, 25)
  ExitButton = Controls.AddButton("Exit", 480, 355)
  Controls.SetSize(ExitButton, 95, 25)
  'Load card images
  CardBack = ImageList.LoadImage(Program.Directory +
"\cardback.gif")
  For CardNumber = 1 To 52
    ImageFile = Program.Directory + "\card"
    If (CardNumber < 10) Then
      ImageFile = ImageFile + Text.Append("0", CardNumber) +".gif"
    Else
      ImageFile = ImageFile + CardNumber +".gif"
    EndIf
    CardImage[CardNumber] = ImageList.LoadImage(ImageFile)
    J = Math.Remainder(CardNumber - 1, 13) + 1 ' a number from 1
(A) to 13 (K)
    If (J < 11) Then
      ' A through 10
      CardPoints[CardNumber] = J
    Else
      'Jack, Queen, King
      CardPoints[CardNumber] = 10
    EndIf
  EndFor
  Controls.ButtonClicked = ButtonClickedSub
  NewGameButtonClicked()
EndSub

Sub SortIntegers
  'Randomly sorts NIntegers integers and puts results in
SortedArray
  'Order all elements initially
  For II = 1 To NIntegers
    SortedArray[II] = II
  EndFor
  'JJ is the number of integers remaining
  For JJ = NIntegers To 2 Step -1
    II = Math.GetRandomNumber(JJ)
    TT = SortedArray[JJ]
```

```
    SortedArray[JJ] = SortedArray[II]
    SortedArray[II] = TT
  EndFor
EndSub

Sub ButtonClickedSub
  B = Controls.LastClickedButton
  If (B = NewGameButton) Then
    NewGameButtonClicked()
  ElseIf (B = ExitButton) Then
    Program.End()
  ElseIf (B = DealButton) Then
    NewHand()
  ElseIf (B = HitButton) Then
    'Add a card if player requests
    AddPlayerCard()
    If (ScorePlayer > 21) Then
      Shapes.SetText(DealerComment, "Dealer wins")
      Shapes.SetText(PlayerComment, "You busted!")
      Change = -10
      EndHand()
    ElseIf (NumberCardsPlayer = 6) Then
      Shapes.SetText(DealerComment, "No dealer play")
      Shapes.SetText(PlayerComment, "You win - 6 cards and not
over 21!")
      Change = 10
      EndHand()
    EndIf
  ElseIf (B = StayButton) Then
    StayButtonClicked()
  EndIf
EndSub

Sub NewGameButtonClicked
  'start new game - clear winnings and start over
  Winnings = 0
  Shapes.SetText(WinningsDisplay, "0")
  NIntegers = 52
  SortIntegers()
  Card = SortedArray
  CurrentCard = 1
  NewHand()
EndSub

Sub NewHand
  'Deal a new hand
```

```
  'Clear table of cards
  GraphicsWindow.BrushColor = GraphicsWindow.BackgroundColor
  GraphicsWindow.FillRectangle(10, 40, 565, 120)
  GraphicsWindow.FillRectangle(10, 200, 565, 120)
  Shapes.SetText(DealerComment, "")
  Shapes.SetText(PlayerComment, "")
  Controls.ShowControl(HitButton)
  Controls.ShowControl(StayButton)
  Controls.HideControl(DealButton)
  'reshuffle occasionally
  If (CurrentCard > 35) Then
    NIntegers = 52
    SortIntegers()
    Card = SortedArray
    CurrentCard = 1
  EndIf
  'Get two dealer cards
  ScoreDealer = 0
  AcesDealer = 0
  NumberCardsDealer = 0
  AddDealerCard()
  AddDealerCard()
  'Get two player cards
  ScorePlayer = 0
  AcesPlayer = 0
  NumberCardsPlayer = 0
  AddPlayerCard()
  AddPlayerCard()
  'Check for blackjacks
  If (ScoreDealer = 11 And AcesDealer = 1) Then
    ScoreDealer = 21
  EndIf
  If (ScorePlayer = 11 And AcesPlayer = 1) Then
    ScorePlayer = 21
  EndIf
  If (ScoreDealer = 21 And ScorePlayer = 21) Then
    Shapes.SetText(DealerComment,"Dealer has Blackjack!")
    Shapes.SetText(PlayerComment, "And, you have Blackjack .. a
push!")
    Change = 0
    EndHand()
  ElseIf (ScoreDealer = 21) Then
    Shapes.SetText(DealerComment,"Dealer has Blackjack!")
    Shapes.SetText(PlayerComment, "You lose ...")
    Change = -10
    EndHand()
```

```
  ElseIf (ScorePlayer = 21) Then
    Shapes.SetText(DealerComment,"Dealer loses ...")
    Shapes.SetText(PlayerComment, "You have Blackjack!")
    Change = 15
    EndHand()
  EndIf
EndSub

Sub EndHand
  'make sure dealer cards are seen
  GraphicsWindow.DrawResizedImage(DealerFaceDown, 10, 40, 90, 120)
  'Hand has ended - update winnings
  Winnings = Winnings + Change
  Shapes.SetText(WinningsDisplay, Winnings)
  Controls.HideControl(HitButton)
  Controls.HideControl(StayButton)
  Controls.ShowControl(DealButton)
EndSub

Sub AddDealerCard
  CardNumber = Card[CurrentCard]
  'Adds a card to dealer hand
  NumberCardsDealer = NumberCardsDealer + 1
  If (NumberCardsDealer = 1) Then
    DealerFaceDown = CardImage[CardNumber]
    GraphicsWindow.DrawResizedImage(CardBack, 10, 40, 90, 120)
  Else
    GraphicsWindow.DrawResizedImage(CardImage[CardNumber], 10 +
(NumberCardsDealer - 1) * 95, 40, 90, 120)
  EndIf
  ScoreDealer = ScoreDealer + CardPoints[CardNumber]
  If (CardPoints[CardNumber] = 1) Then
    AcesDealer = AcesDealer + 1
  EndIf
  CurrentCard = CurrentCard + 1
EndSub

Sub AddPlayerCard
  CardNumber = Card[CurrentCard]
  'Adds a card to player hand
  NumberCardsPlayer = NumberCardsPlayer + 1
  GraphicsWindow.DrawResizedImage(CardImage[CardNumber], 10 +
(NumberCardsPlayer - 1) * 95, 200, 90, 120)
  ScorePlayer = ScorePlayer + CardPoints[CardNumber]
  If (CardPoints[CardNumber] = 1) Then
    AcesPlayer = AcesPlayer + 1
```

```
  EndIf
  CurrentCard = CurrentCard + 1
EndSub

Sub StayButtonClicked
  Controls.HideControl(HitButton)
  Controls.HideControl(StayButton)
  'Check for aces in player hand and adjust score
  'to highest possible
  If (AcesPlayer <> 0 And ScorePlayer <= 11) Then
    ScorePlayer = ScorePlayer + 10
    AcesPlayer = AcesPlayer - 1
  EndIf
  'Uncover dealer face down card and play dealer hand
  GraphicsWindow.DrawResizedImage(DealerFaceDown, 10, 40, 90, 120)
  CheckLoop:
    ScoreTemp = ScoreDealer
    AcesTemp = AcesDealer
    'Check for aces and adjust score
    If (AcesDealer <> 0 And ScoreDealer <= 11) Then
      ScoreDealer = ScoreDealer + 10
      AcesDealer = AcesDealer - 1
    EndIf
    'add card unless score above 16 or dealer has 6 cards
    If (ScoreTemp > 16) Then
      If (ScoreTemp > ScorePlayer) Then
        Shapes.SetText(DealerComment, "Dealer wins with " +
ScoreTemp)
        Shapes.SetText(PlayerComment, "You lose with " +
ScorePlayer)
        Change = -10
        EndHand()
      ElseIf (ScoreTemp = ScorePlayer) Then
        Shapes.SetText(DealerComment, "Dealer has " + ScoreTemp)
        Shapes.SetText(PlayerComment, "So do you ... a push!")
        Change = 0
        EndHand()
      Else
        Shapes.SetText(DealerComment, "Dealer loses with " +
ScoreTemp)
        Shapes.SetText(PlayerComment, "You win with " +
ScorePlayer)
        Change = 10
        EndHand()
      EndIf
      Goto ExitStayButtonClicked
```

```
    ElseIf (NumberCardsDealer = 6) Then
      Shapes.SetText(DealerComment, "Dealer wins ... 6 cards and
not over 16!")
      Shapes.SetText(PlayerComment, "You lose ...")
      Change = -10
      EndHand()
      Goto ExitStayButtonClicked
    Else
      AddDealerCard()
      'dealer loses if busted
      If (ScoreDealer > 21) Then
        Shapes.SetText(DealerComment, "Dealer busts!")
        Shapes.SetText(PlayerComment, "You win!!")
        Change = 10
        EndHand()
        Goto ExitStayButtonClicked
      EndIf
    EndIf
    Goto CheckLoop
ExitStayButtonClicked:
EndSub
```

Blackjack Card Game Project Review

The **Blackjack Card Game Project** is now complete. **Save** and **Run** the project and make sure it works as designed. Play lots of games to make sure winners are always declared correctly and that the dealer logic is implemented correctly. You may have to play lots of hands before both the dealer and player have Blackjack. And, you may have to play many, many hands to see if the special "six card" rule works correctly.

If there are errors in your implementation, go back over the steps of window and code design. Use the debugger when needed. Go over the developed code – make sure you understand how different parts of the project were coded. As mentioned in the beginning of this chapter, the completed project is saved as **Blackjack** in the **HomeSB\HomeSB Projects\Blackjack** folder.

While completing this project, new concepts and skills you should have gained include:

- Displaying graphics using **DrawResizedImage**.
- How to define a deck of cards using card number indices.
- How to store a graphics file in an image array.
- How to "shuffle" a deck of cards using the **SortIntegers** subroutine.

Blackjack Card Game Project Enhancements

Possible enhancements to the Blackjack card game project include:

- As you probably know, Blackjack is a dangerous gambling game. The idea is for you (the player) to win as much money as possible from the dealer. Our version of Blackjack is a simplification of the casino version. The casino version allows betting – our version doesn't (you either win or lose 10 points with each hand; well, you win 15 if you get a Blackjack. Casinos tend to make a lot of profit from uneducated players. Our purpose here is to educate you on how the odds are stacked against you. We recommend you enjoy this game at home and keep your hard earned money in your wallet!

- Casinos also allow you, in certain cases, to double your bet after a hand has been dealt. And, if your two initial cards are the same, you can split them and play two hands. Not being a gambler, I don't know all the specifics behind "double-down" and "splitting." If you want, you can try and implement these modifications to the program.

- Some casinos have different rules for dealer play. In our version, an Ace must always take on its highest value (without exceeding 21 of course). In other versions, the dealer has discretion. Perhaps, you would like to give the dealer in your program this discretion.

- To make play more difficult, some casinos play Blackjack with more than one deck of cards. Maybe have the number of card decks being used be an option in your program. In such a case, or even in the current configuration, it might be nice to announce to the player when a reshuffle of the cards is done.

- Now that you know the high risks involved with gambling, let's move on to a more practical application.

9. Weight Monitor Project

Review and Preview

Everyone these days seems to be watching their weight. In the **Weight Monitor Project**, we build a program that tracks your weight each day and helps you follow progress toward goals. Plots of your daily weight are provided along with a computation of the trend in your weight. Sequential file input and output is introduced.

Weight Monitor Project Preview

In this chapter, we will build a **weight monitor** program. This program allows you to enter your weight each day, then examine a plot to observe trends. All values are saved in a file you specify when you create the program.

The finished project is saved as **Weight** in the **HomeSB\HomeSB Projects\Weight** folder. Start Small Basic and open the finished project. **Run** the project (click **Run** in the toolbar or press <**F5**>). When the program begins, it will automatically open your weight file and display the results.:

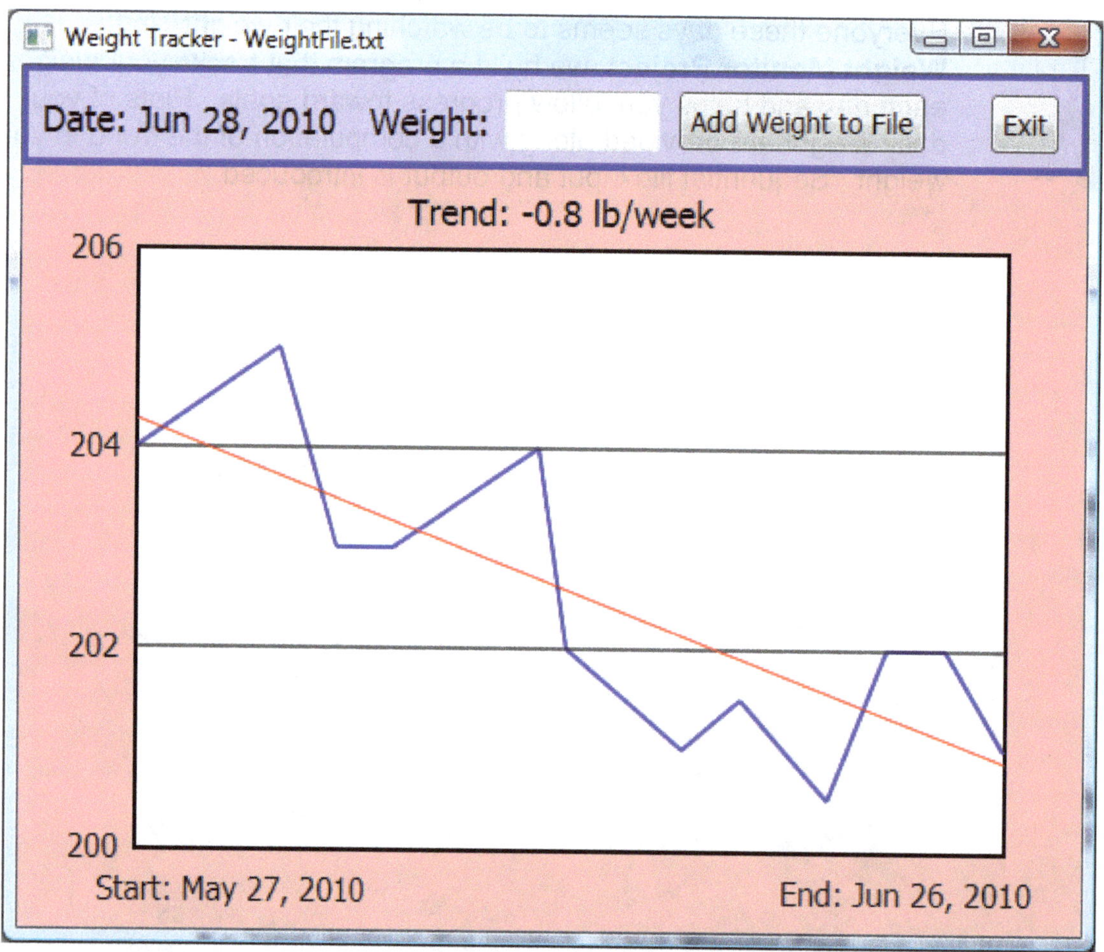

The program indicates we are working with a file named **WeightFile.txt** (see the title area). This is a file you specify. Today's date is displayed at the top of the window. At this point, you enter a weight in the text box control and press <**Enter**> or click **Add Weight to File**. Give it a try.

When I enter my weight (201.5), I see:

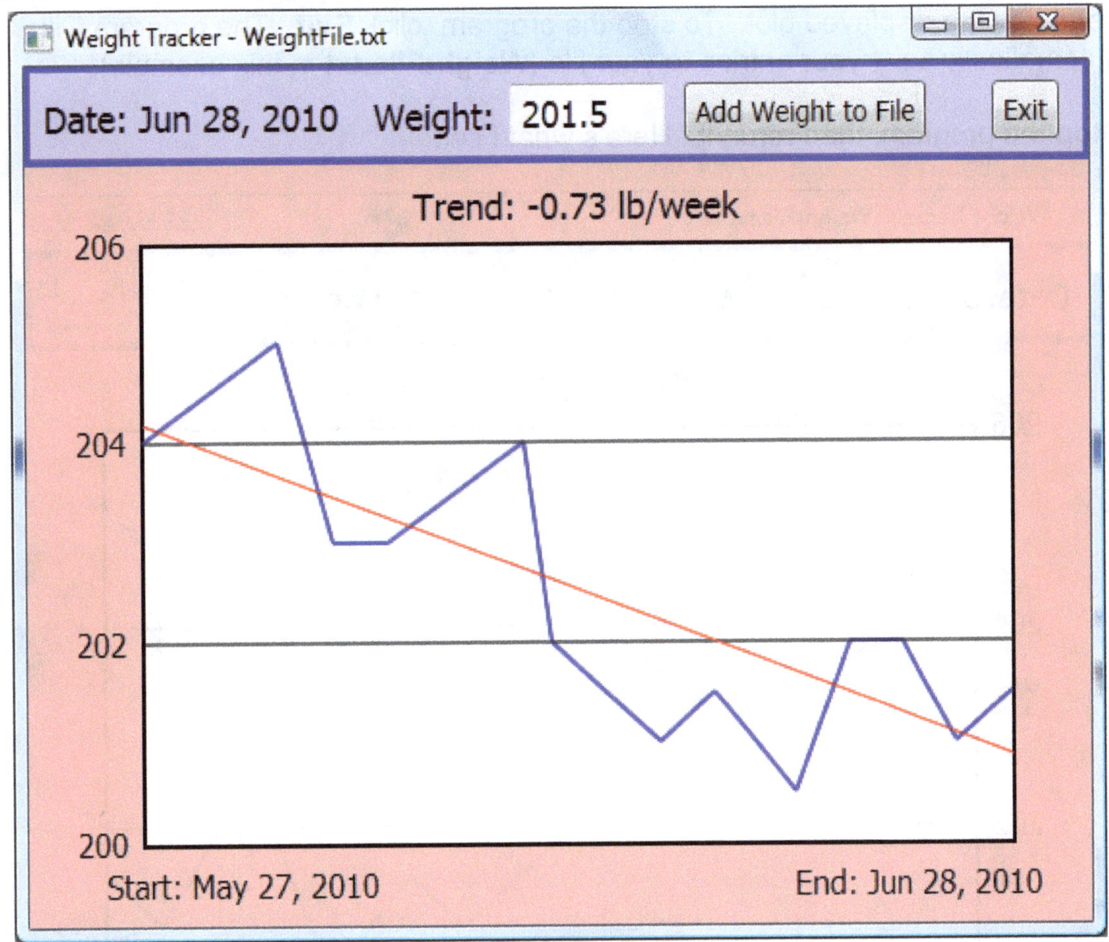

The date and weight have been added to the file. The plot is updated, showing the recorded weights over the specified time period. At the top of the plot, I am shown an indication of the trend in my weight (going down at 0.73 pounds each week – a good trend).

That's all you do with the weight monitor project. Periodically run the program (every day if you like) and enter your weight for the current day. View your weight trends on the displayed plot. To stop the program, click **Exit**. The program will automatically save your entries to your file (**WeightFile.txt** in this example).

Stop the program, then rerun it. Here's what I see:

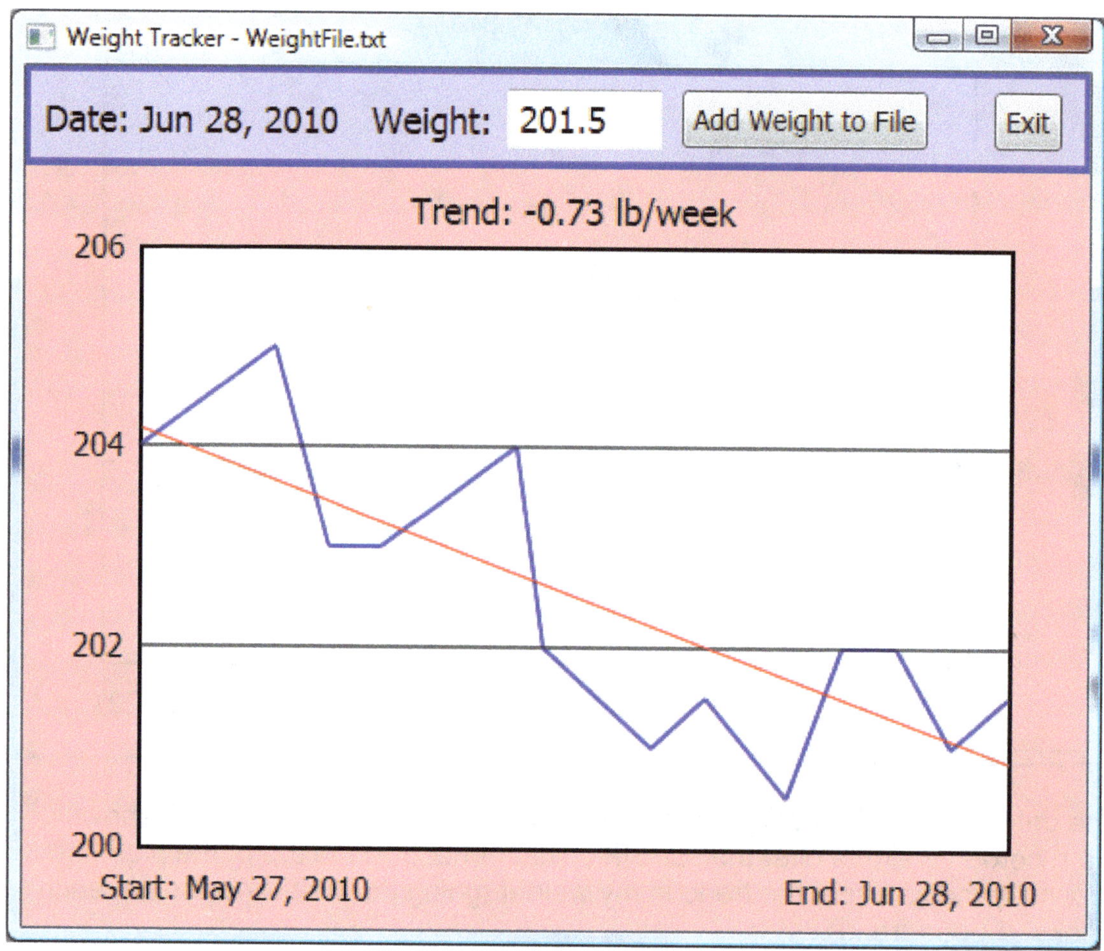

We see today's date, along with the weight entered for today, and also see the updated plot. All we can do at this point is modify today's entry.

If I change it to 202, I see:

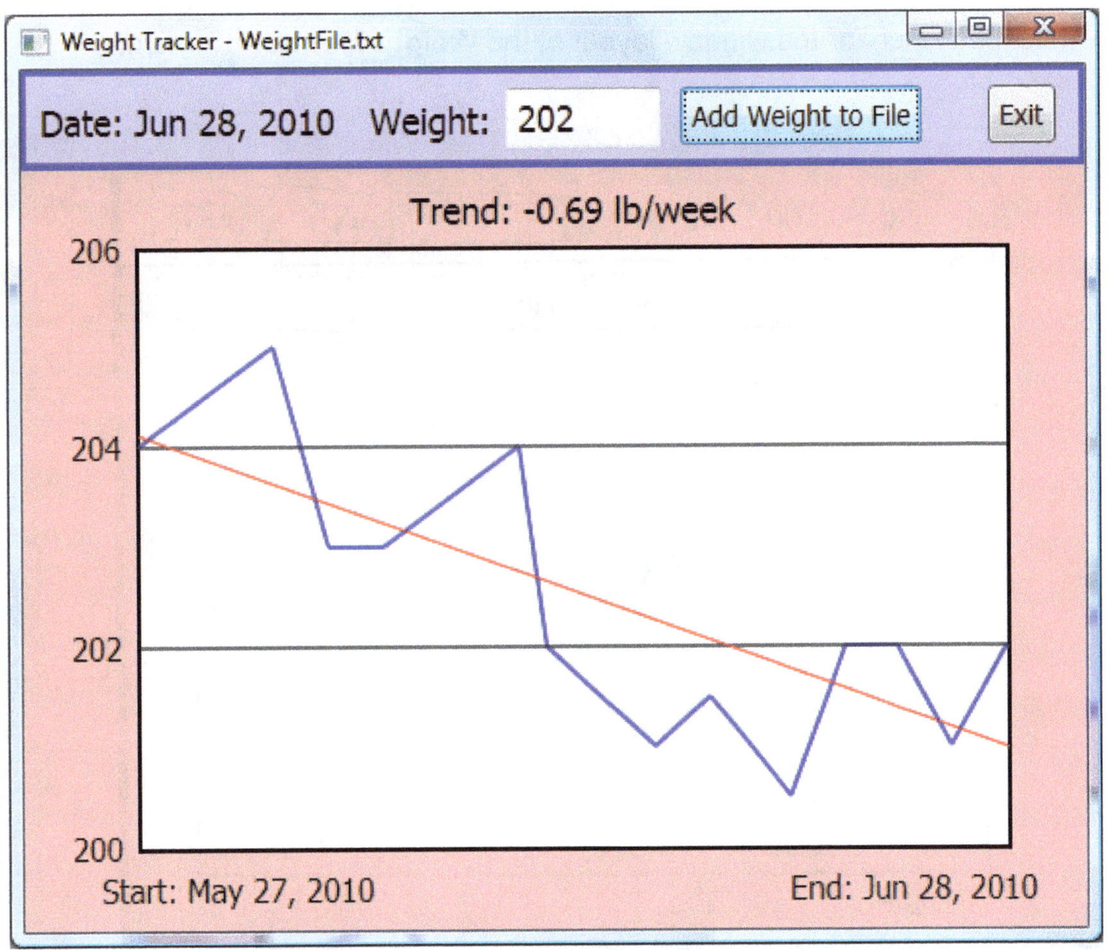

Note the plot and trend value change slightly.

You will now build this project in several stages. We first address **window design**. We discuss the controls used to build the window and establish initial properties. And, we address **code design** in detail. We discuss how to open and save the weight files. We discuss the graphics methods behind generating a line plot like the one used to display the weight trend.

Weight Monitor Window Design

Here is the sketch for the window layout of the **Weight Monitor** program:

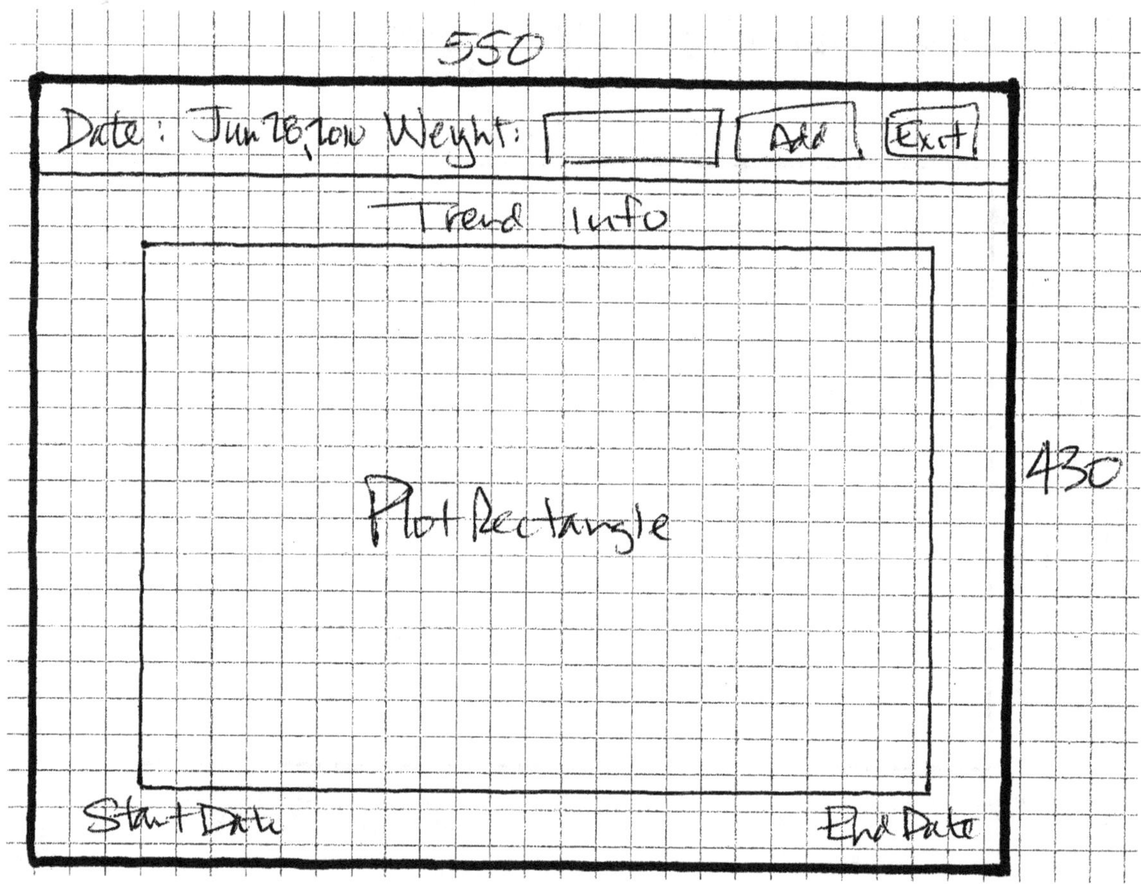

The date will be displayed at the top of the window. A text box is used to accept a weight value. Button controls are used to add to the weight file and exit the program. The weight values will be plotted in the lower part of the window. Appropriate labeling will be provided.

We will begin writing code. As always, the code will be written in steps. We'll begin by writing code draws the top part of the window: date display, weight text box and button controls.

Start a new program in Small Basic. Once started, we suggest you immediately save the program with a name you choose. This sets up the folder and file structure needed for your program.

Window Design – Date Display

The idea of the **Weight Monitor** is to enter your weight on the current day and have it saved. Hence, a needed feature is a display of the current date. The Small Basic **Clock** object provides the needed information:

`Clock.Month`	Specifies current month (1-12)
`Clock.Day`	Specifies current day (1-12)
`Clock.Year`	Specifies current year

Rather than use a number to indicate month, we will use a three letter abbreviation (e.g. **Jan** instead of **1**).

We will write the date in the window using the **DrawText** method. Add this code to your code editor to initialize the graphics window and display today's date:

```
' Weight Tracker
InitializeProgram()

Sub InitializeProgram
  'graphics window
  GraphicsWindow.Width = 550
  GraphicsWindow.Height = 430
  GraphicsWindow.Title = "Weight Tracker"
  GraphicsWindow.BackgroundColor =
GraphicsWindow.GetColorFromRGB(192, 192, 255)
  GraphicsWindow.PenColor = "Blue"
  GraphicsWindow.PenWidth = 5
  GraphicsWindow.DrawRectangle(0, 0, GraphicsWindow.Width, 49)
  'month arrays
  MonthName[1] = "Jan"
  MonthName[2] = "Feb"
  MonthName[3] = "Mar"
  MonthName[4] = "Apr"
  MonthName[5] = "May"
  MonthName[6] = "Jun"
  MonthName[7] = "Jul"
  MonthName[8] = "Aug"
  MonthName[9] = "Sep"
  MonthName[10] = "Oct"
  MonthName[11] = "Nov"
  MonthName[12] = "Dec"
  'date
  GraphicsWindow.BrushColor = "Black"
  GraphicsWindow.FontBold = "false"
  GraphicsWindow.FontSize = 18
```

```
  GraphicsWindow.DrawText(10, 15, "Date: " +
MonthName[Clock.Month] + " " + Clock.Day + ", " + Clock.year)
EndSub
```

The first line of code calls a subroutine **InitializeProgram** where we will put all code needed to set up the program for use. All remaining code here goes in that subroutine. Note how the month number is converted to a three letter abbreviation using the **MonthName** array.

Save and **Run** the program. Today's date (will be different for you) will be displayed in a rectangle at the top of the blue window:

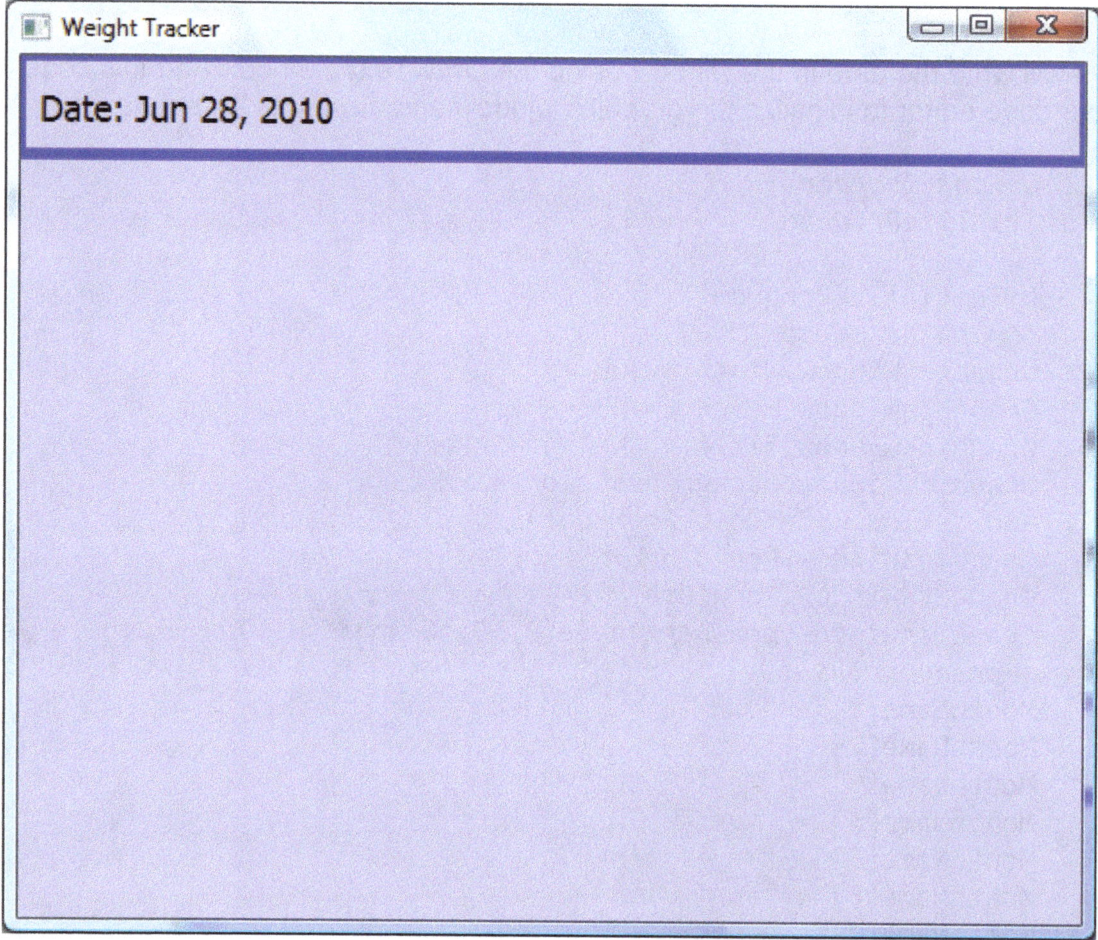

Window Design – Weight Entry

A text box (**WeightTextBox**) will be used to accept a user's entry of their current weight. Add these lines (to **InitializeProgram**) to add the weight text box and corresponding label:

```
'weight
GraphicsWindow.DrawText(180, 15, "Weight: ")
WeightTextBox = Controls.AddTextBox(250, 10)
Controls.SetSize(WeightTextBox, 80, 30)
```

Save and **Run** the program to see the added elements:

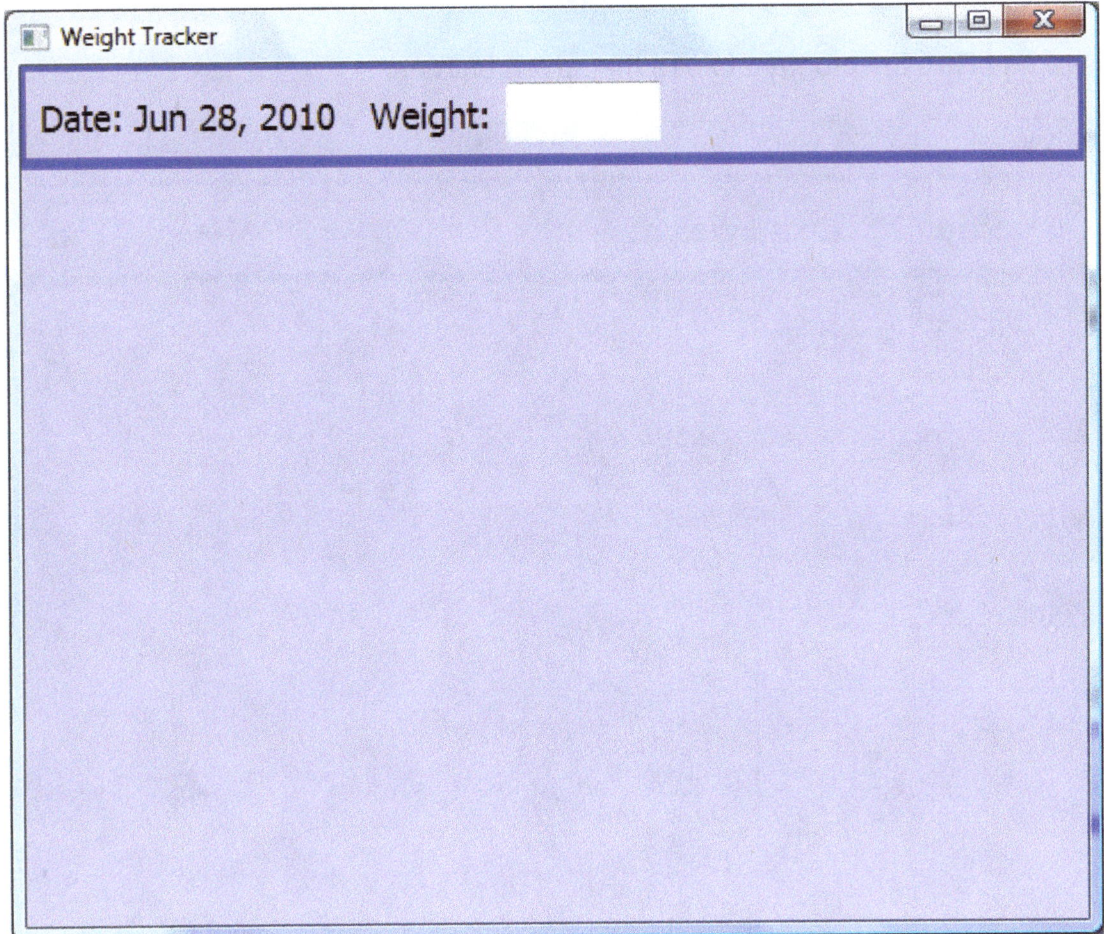

Window Design – Add Buttons

Two button controls are used in the program. **AddWeightButton** is used to add an entered weight to the weight file. **ExitButton** is used to stop the program. Add the code to create these buttons to **InitializeProgram**:

```
'buttons
GraphicsWindow.BrushColor = "Black"
GraphicsWindow.FontSize = 14
GraphicsWindow.FontBold = "false"
AddWeightButton = Controls.AddButton("Add Weight to File", 340,
10)
ExitButton = Controls.AddButton("Exit", 500, 10)
```

Save and **Run** the program to see the added buttons:

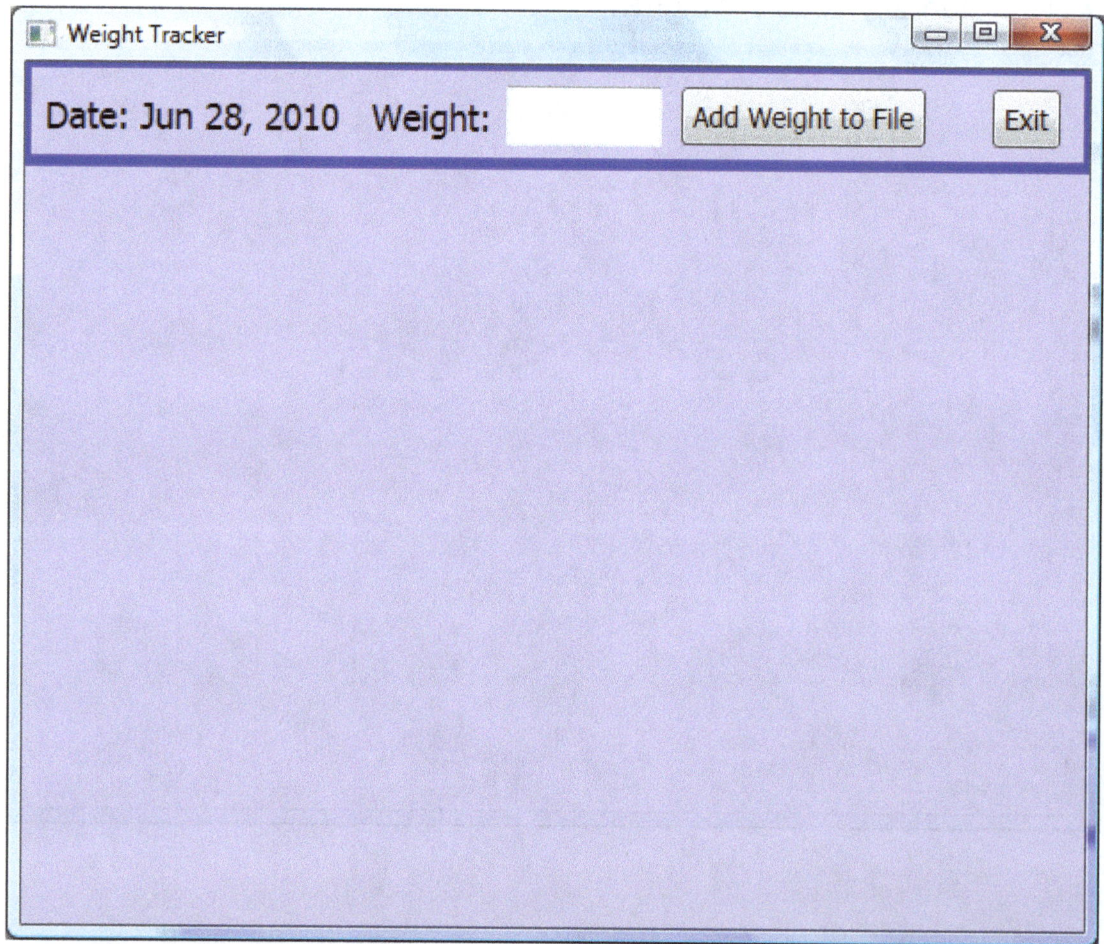

The interface is done at this point. We now need to write the code that opens a weight file, plots the weight values, allows you to enter today's weight, then saves the file when the program is stopped.

Code Design – Specifying a Weight File

All entered weights (and accompanying dates) are saved in a file you specify (using the variable **WeightFile**). The file must be in your program folder. For now, we will use a sample file included with these notes. The sample file is named **WeightFile.txt** and is saved in the **HomeSB\HomeSB Projects\Weight** folder. Copy this file to your program's folder. Later, after the program is built and running, you can use your own weight file.

Add this code to **InitializeProgram** to identify your weight file and show the file name in the window title area:

```
'specify weight file
WeightFile = "WeightFile.txt"
GraphicsWindow.Title = GraphicsWindow.Title + " - " +
WeightFile
```

Save and **Run** the program to see that the file name is displayed:

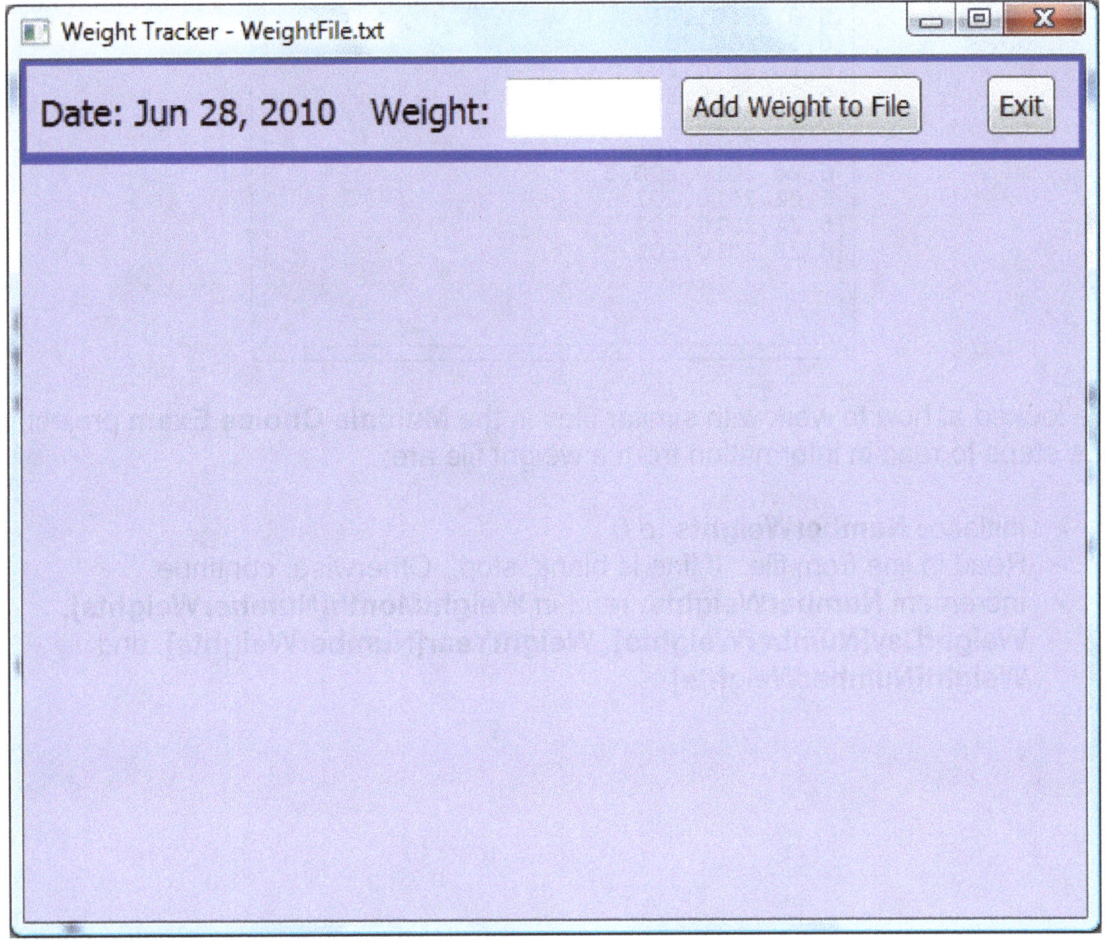

Code Design – Opening Weight File

When the program starts, we want to open the specified weight file (**WeightFile**) and read in date and weight information from the file. The weight file is saved in a specific format. Each line in the file has date and weight information as follows:

Month,Day,Year,Weight

Where **Month** is the month number, **Day** the day number, **Year** the year number, and **Weight** the weight for the corresponding date. In the program, each item is stored in its own array. Those arrays are, respectively, **WeightMonth**, **WeightDay**, **WeightYear** and **Weight**.

Open the sample file (**WeightFile.txt**) to see the specified format:

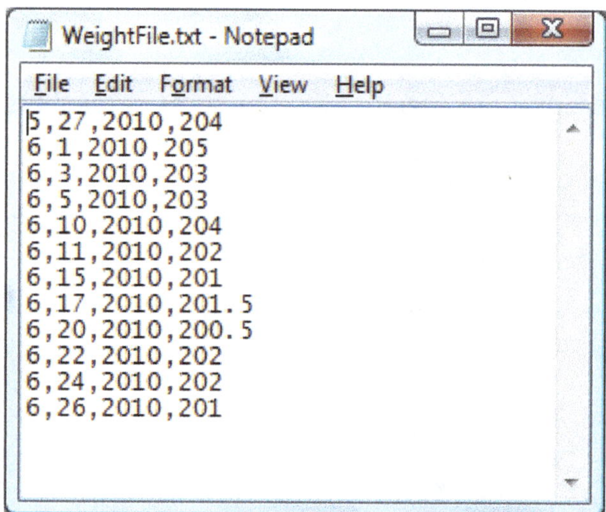

We looked at how to work with similar files in the **Multiple Choice Exam** project. The steps to read in information from a weight file are:

- Initialize **NumberWeights** to 0.
- Read in line from file. If line is blank, stop. Otherwise, continue.
- Increment **NumberWeights**, read in **WeightMonth[NumberWeights], WeightDay[NumberWeights], WeightYear[NumberWeights]**, and **Weight[NumberWeights]**.

Let's review how to read the lines and get the needed variables. To read line **LineNumber** from file **FileName**, use the **ReadLine** method of the **File** object:

```
FileLine = File.ReadLine(FileName, LineNumber)
```

where **FileLine** will be the line. In the weight file, this line will have four values, each separated by a comma. To obtain the individual variables, we 'parse' the line. We identify where a comma is in the line then extract one variable to the left of the comma, saving the part of the line to the right of the comma. We locate a comma in the saved part and extract one variable to the left of that comma. We repeat this process until all four variables are extracted. Recall we use **Text** object methods to do these steps.

To determine the location of the comma in **FileLine**, we use the **GetIndexOf** method. In the expression:

```
CL = Text.GetIndexOf(FileLine, ",")
```

The left portion of the line is extracted using:

```
LeftSide = Text.GetSubText(FileLine, 1, CL - 1)
```

And the right portion is given by:

```
RightSide = Text.GetSubTextToEnd(FileLine, CL + 1)
```

Let's see how this works with the weight file. We will put the code needed to open the weight file and extract the variables in a subroutine called **OpenWeightFile**. Hence, add this single line in **InitializeProgram** (following the lines establishing a value for **WeightFile**):

```
OpenWeightFile()
```

Now, add the **OpenWeightFile** subroutine:

```
Sub OpenWeightFile
  NumberWeights = 0
  ReadWeight:
  FileLine = File.ReadLine(Program.Directory + "\" +
WeightFile, NumberWeights + 1)
  If (FileLine <> "") Then
    NumberWeights = NumberWeights + 1
    'find month/shorten FileLine
    CL = Text.GetIndexOf(FileLine, ",")
    WeightMonth[NumberWeights] = Text.GetSubText(FileLine, 1,
CL - 1)
    FileLine = Text.GetSubTextToEnd(FileLine, CL + 1)
    'find day/shorten FileLine
    CL = Text.GetIndexOf(FileLine, ",")
    WeightDay[NumberWeights] = Text.GetSubText(FileLine, 1, CL
- 1)
    FileLine = Text.GetSubTextToEnd(FileLine, CL + 1)
    'find year/shorten FileLine
    CL = Text.GetIndexOf(FileLine, ",")
    WeightYear[NumberWeights] = Text.GetSubText(FileLine, 1, CL
- 1)
    'find weight (what's left)
    Weight[NumberWeights] = Text.GetSubTextToEnd(FileLine, CL +
1)
    Goto ReadWeight
  EndIf
EndSub
```

This code implements the steps listed. In each line, it searches for commas, parsing out the four needed variables. When done, we have the four arrays (**WeightMonth**, **WeightDay**, **WeightYear**, **Weight**), each with **NumberWeights** elements.

To check that this all works, add this temporary line before the **Goto ReadWeight** line. This will print out the values (separated by colons) read in into a text window:

```
TextWindow.WriteLine(WeightMonth[NumberWeights] + ":" +
WeightDay[NumberWeights] + ":" + WeightYear[NumberWeights] +
":" + Weight[NumberWeights])
```

Save and **Run** the program. Find the text window that opens and you should see the file contents:

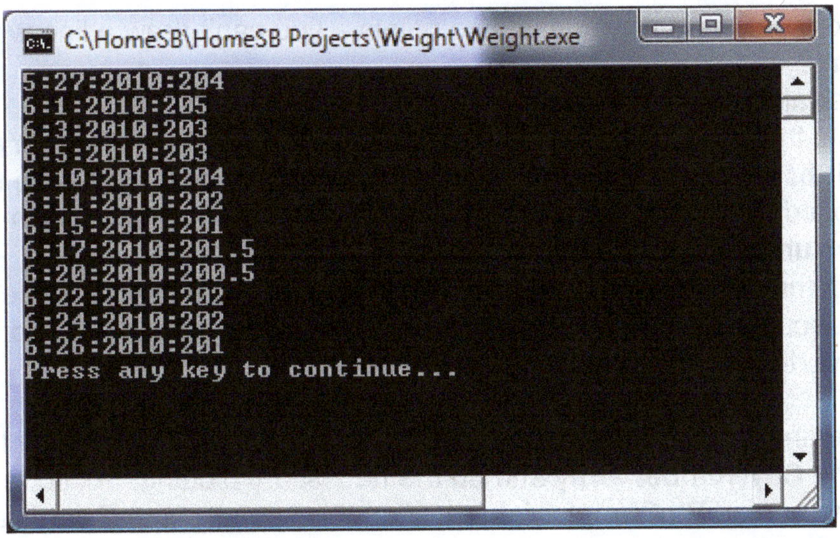

C:\HomeSB\HomeSB Projects\Weight\Weight.exe

```
5:27:2010:204
6:1:2010:205
6:3:2010:203
6:5:2010:203
6:10:2010:204
6:11:2010:202
6:15:2010:201
6:17:2010:201.5
6:20:2010:200.5
6:22:2010:202
6:24:2010:202
6:26:2010:201
Press any key to continue...
```

Remove the temporary line that generated this window and lets start the code for plotting the weights.

The weight plot will be drawn in the lower part of the graphics window. There are two primary tasks in drawing the weight plot. The first is to “connect the points” specified by the date and weight arrays with line segments. The second is to put useful labeling information around the plot. Let’s look at the plot drawing task first.

Code Design – Weight Plot

When a weight file is opened (or new weight value entered), we want to display a plot of the weights. To draw a plot, we use the Small Basic graphics methods. We generate what is known as a **line plot**, which connects Cartesian pairs of points (x and y values). The horizontal axis will be the number of days that have elapsed since the first weight entry. The vertical axis will be the corresponding weight value. Such a plot will give us some idea of any trends noted over time. The steps to generate such a plot are fairly simple:

- Make sure there are at least two points – you can't draw a line with fewer points!
- Clear any previous plot.
- Cycle through all values in **WeightMonth**, **WeightDay**, **WeightYear** and **Weight** arrays, extracting the date and weight values. Store the number of elapsed days (difference between 'current' date and first date) in an array **DayNumber**.
- Loop through all **DayNumber** and **Weight** array elements, connecting consecutive points (with **DayNumber** as the horizontal point and **Weight** as the vertical point) using the **DrawLine** method.

Let's do the first step here (clearing the plot). We will then explain how to generate the **DayNumber** array and do the necessary plotting. All code will be in a subroutine named **PlotWeightValues**. Add this line after the **OpenWeightFile** line in **InitializeProgram**.

```
PlotWeightValues()
```

We draw the plot area in the lower part of the window. The plot will be drawn in a white rectangular area (located at **PlotLeft**, **PlotTop**, with width **PlotWidth** and height **PlotHeight**) embedded in a larger red area. Add this code in **PlotWeightValues** to draw the blank plot area:

```
Sub PlotWeightValues
  If (NumberWeights < 2) Then
    Goto ExitPlotWeightValues
  EndIf
  'clear weight panel  'clear weight panel
  GraphicsWindow.BrushColor =
GraphicsWindow.GetColorFromRGB(255, 192, 192)
  GraphicsWindow.FillRectangle(0, 50, 550, 380)
  GraphicsWindow.BrushColor = "White"
  PlotLeft = 60
  PlotTop = 90
  PlotWidth = 450
  PlotHeight = 300
  GraphicsWindow.FillRectangle(PlotLeft, PlotTop, PlotWidth,
PlotHeight)
  GraphicsWindow.PenColor = "Black"
  GraphicsWindow.PenWidth = 2
  GraphicsWindow.DrawRectangle(PlotLeft, PlotTop, PlotWidth,
PlotHeight)
ExitPlotWeightValues:
EndSub
```

Notice if there are fewer than two weight values, we simply exit the subroutine.

Save and **Run** the program. The plot area will appear:

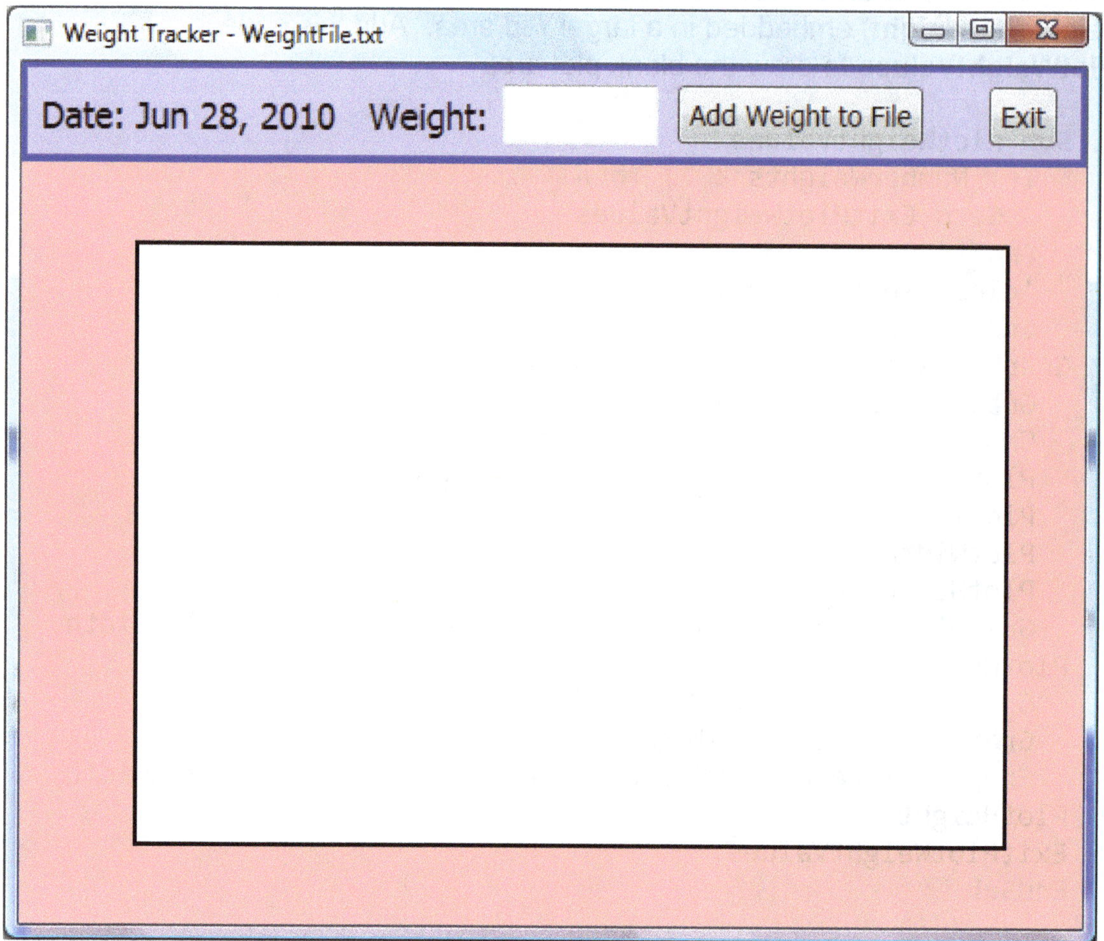

Code Design – Date Arithmetic

The horizontal axis on our plot will be the number of days (in array **DayNumber**) that have elapsed since the plot began (the first date in the weight file). We will use the **ComputeElapsedDays** subroutine (modified slightly) developed in the **Biorhythm Tracker** project to form this array.

Here are the steps:

- Define a reference date that represents '**day one**'. In this program, we use January 1, 2010 (this is the modification to **ComputeElapsedDays**, defining a new **BaseYear**.)
- For the first date in the weight file, determine how many days have elapsed since day one. Define that to be **FirstDayValue**. Set **DayNumber[1]** to **0** (since zero days have elapsed since the first day in the file).
- For each subsequent date (date **J**) in the weight file, determine how many days have elapsed since day one. Subtract **FirstDayValue** from that number and assign the result to **DayNumber[J]**.

The modified subroutine (new **BaseYear** value), **ComputeElapsedDays**, is:

```
Sub ComputeElapsedDays
  'number of days in each month
  MonthDays[1] = 31
  MonthDays[2] = 28
  MonthDays[3] = 31
  MonthDays[4] = 30
  MonthDays[5] = 31
  MonthDays[6] = 30
  MonthDays[7] = 31
  MonthDays[8] = 31
  MonthDays[9] = 30
  MonthDays[10] = 31
  MonthDays[11] = 30
  MonthDays[12] = 31
  'January 1, 2010 is Day 1
  BaseYear = 2010
  ElapsedDaysElapsedDays == 0  ElapsedDays = 0
  'Difference in years
  DeltaY = YY - BaseYear
  If (DeltaY > 0) Then
    'move to January 1 of current year
    For J = BaseYear To YY - 1
      'Leap year?
      If (Math.Remainder(J, 4) = 0) Then
        ElapsedDays = ElapsedDays + 366
```

```
      Else
        ElapsedDays = ElapsedDays + 365
      EndIf
    EndFor
  EndIf
  'Difference in months
  DeltaM = MM - 1
  If (DeltaM > 0) Then
    'move to current month
    For J = 1 To MM - 1
      'if february, leap year?
      If (J = 2) Then
        If (Math.Remainder(YY, 4) = 0) Then
          ElapsedDays = ElapsedDays + 29
        Else
          ElapsedDays = ElapsedDays + 28
        EndIf
      Else
        ElapsedDays = ElapsedDays + MonthDays[J]
      EndIf
    EndFor
  EndIf
  'difference in days
  ElapsedDays = ElapsedDays + DD - 1
EndSub
```

Add this subroutine to your program.

Now we use the **ComputeElapsedDays** subroutine to set up the **DayNumber** array for the weight file. We will do this in the **OpenWeightFile** subroutine. This insures all arrays are set up before plotting. Add the shaded code:

```
Sub OpenWeightFile
  NumberWeights = 0
  ReadWeight:
  FileLine = File.ReadLine(Program.Directory + "\" +
WeightFile, NumberWeights + 1)
  If (FileLine <> "") Then
    NumberWeights = NumberWeights + 1
    'find month/shorten FileLine
    CL = Text.GetIndexOf(FileLine, ",")
    WeightMonth[NumberWeights] = Text.GetSubText(FileLine, 1,
CL - 1)
    FileLine = Text.GetSubTextToEnd(FileLine, CL + 1)
    'find day/shorten FileLine
    CL = Text.GetIndexOf(FileLine, ",")
    WeightDay[NumberWeights] = Text.GetSubText(FileLine, 1, CL
- 1)
    FileLine = Text.GetSubTextToEnd(FileLine, CL + 1)
    'find year/shorten FileLine
    CL = Text.GetIndexOf(FileLine, ",")
    WeightYear[NumberWeights] = Text.GetSubText(FileLine, 1, CL
- 1)
    'find weight (what's left)
    Weight[NumberWeights] = Text.GetSubTextToEnd(FileLine, CL +
1)
    'establish day number
    MM = WeightMonth[NumberWeights]
    DD = WeightDay[NumberWeights]
    YY = WeightYear[NumberWeights]
    ComputeElapsedDays()
    If (NumberWeights = 1) Then
      FirstDayValue = DN
      DayNumber[1] = 0
    Else
      DayNumber[NumberWeights] = DN - FirstDayValue
    EndIf
    Goto ReadWeight
  EndIf
EndSub
```

We now have the values we need to draw the weight plot.

Code Design – Drawing the Plot

The plot will be drawn in the white rectangle in the middle of the plot area. The coordinate system for this rectangle is:

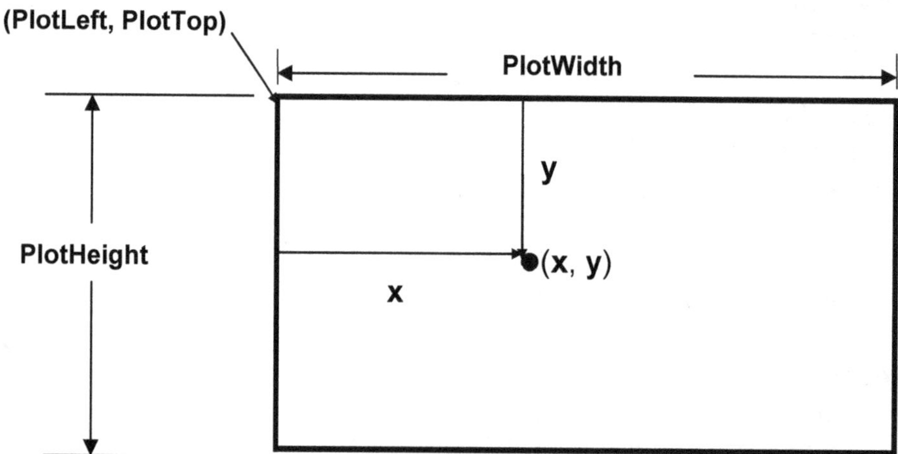

In this region, the horizontal (**x**) coordinate increases from left to right, starting at **0** and extending to **PlotWidth - 1**. The vertical (**y**) coordinate increases from top to bottom, starting at **0** and ending at **PlotHeight - 1**. All measurements are in units of **pixels**.

In the weight plot, the horizontal value (**D**, a date difference) will range from **0** (the first **DayNumber** in the weight file) to **DayNumber[NumberWeights]** (we'll call this $\mathbf{D}_{max}$, the difference between the last date in the file and the first date). This value increases from left to right. The vertical value (**W,** the weight) will range from the minimum weight value ($\mathbf{W}_{min}$) to the maximum weight value ($\mathbf{W}_{max}$) - we will need to find these extremes. This value increases from bottom to top. Hence, to plot our data, we need to compute where each (**D**, **W**) pair in our weight plot fits within the dimensions of the white plot rectangle. This is a straightforward coordinate conversion computation.

Let's look at the horizontal axis first. As seen in the previous diagram, the horizontal (**X** axis) in the rectangle is **PlotWidth** pixels wide. The far left pixel is at **X = PlotLeft** and the far right is at **X = PlotLeft + PlotWidth – 1**. **X** increases from left to right:

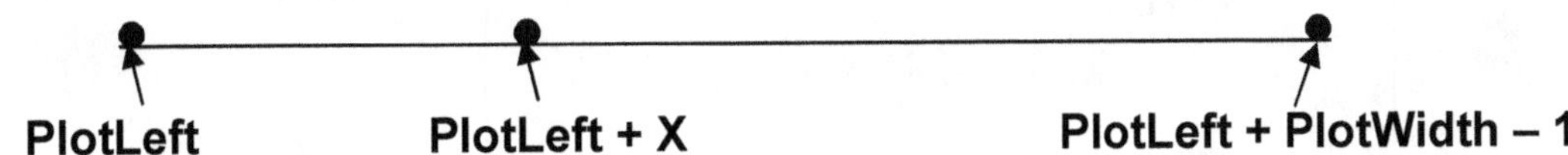

The horizontal plot value (**D**) runs from a minimum, **0**, at the left to a maximum, $\mathbf{D_{max}}$, at the right. Thus, the first pixel on the horizontal axis of our plot will be **0** and the last will be $\mathbf{D_{max}}$:

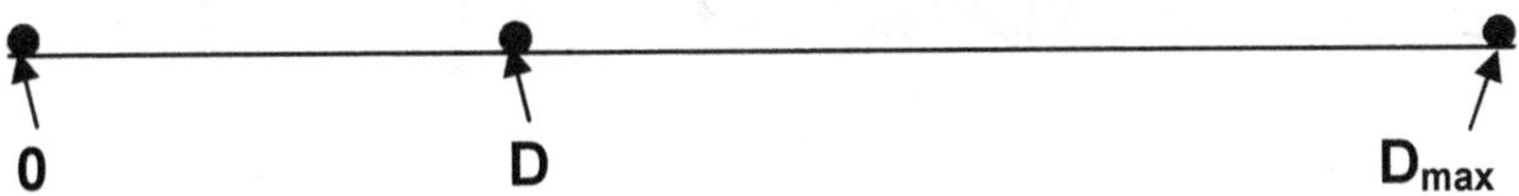

With these two depictions, we can compute the **X** value corresponding to a given **D** value using simple **proportions,** taking the distance from some point on each axis to the minimum and dividing by the total distance. The process is also called **linear interpolation**. These proportions show:

$$\frac{D - 0}{D_{max} - 1} = \frac{PlotLeft + X - 0}{PlotWidth - 1 - 0}$$

Solving this for **X** yields the desired conversion from a days value on the horizontal axis (**D**) to a graphics object value for plotting:

$$X = PlotLeft + D(PlotWidth - 1)/D_{max}$$

You can see this is correct at each extreme value. When **D = 0**, **X = PlotLeft**. When $\mathbf{D = D_{max}}$, **X = PlotLeft + PlotWidth – 1**.

Now, we find the corresponding conversion for the vertical axis. We'll place the two axes side-by-side for easy comparison (plot rectangle on left, weight axis on right):

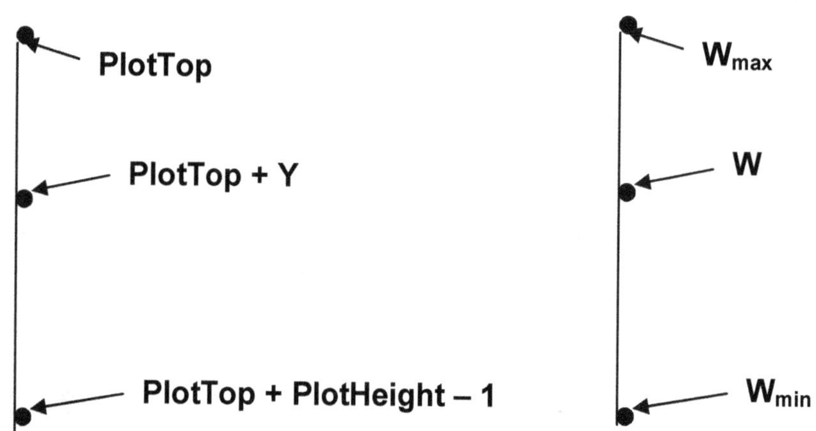

The vertical (**Y** axis) in the rectangle is **PlotHeight** pixels high. The topmost pixel is at **Y** = **PlotTop** and the bottom is at **Y** = **PlotTop + PlotHeight – 1. Y** increases from top to bottom. The vertical data (weight axis, **W**) in our weight plot, runs from a minimum, $\mathbf{W_{min}}$, at the bottom, to a maximum, $\mathbf{W_{max}}$, at the top. Thus, the top pixel on the vertical axis will be $\mathbf{W_{max}}$ and the bottom will be $\mathbf{W_{min}}$ (note the weight axis increases up, rather than down).

With these two depictions, we can compute the **Y** value corresponding to a given **W** value using linear interpolation. The computations show:

$$\frac{W - W_{min}}{W_{max} - W_{min}} = \frac{Y - (PlotHeight - 1)}{PlotTop - (PlotHeight - 1)}$$

Solving this for **Y** yields the desired conversion from a weight value on the vertical axis (**W**) to a graphics object value for plotting (this requires a bit algebra, but it's straightforward):

$$Y = PlotTop + (W_{max} - W)(PlotHeight - 1)/(W_{max} - W_{min})$$

Again, check the extremes. When $\mathbf{W = W_{min}}$, **Y** = **PlotTop + PlotHeight – 1**. When $\mathbf{W = W_{max}}$, **Y** = **PlotTop**. It looks good.

In summary, we will use these two equations whenever we need to do any coordinate conversions:

$$X = PlotLeft + D(PlotWidth - 1)/D_{max}$$

$$Y = PlotTop + (W_{max} - W)(PlotHeight - 1)/(W_{max} - W_{min})$$

Recall **D** is the **DayNumber** and **W** the correcpsonding **Weight** array element. D_{max} will be **DayNumber[NumberWeights]**. W_{max} and W_{min} are determined from the **Weight** array.

With the ability to transform coordinates, we can now rewrite the steps to generate a weight plot:

- Cycle through all values in the **Weight** array and determine the minimum and maximum weight values (W_{min} and W_{max}).
- Loop through all array elements. For each point, convert the **DayNumber** and **Weight** values to plot rectangle coordinates (**X, Y**), then connect the current point with the previous point using the **DrawLine** function.

The shaded code added to **PlotWeightValues** accomplishes these steps:

```
Sub PlotWeightValues
  If (NumberWeights < 2) Then
    Goto ExitPlotWeightValues
  EndIf
  'clear weight panel  'clear weight panel
  GraphicsWindow.BrushColor =
GraphicsWindow.GetColorFromRGB(255, 192, 192)
  GraphicsWindow.FillRectangle(0, 50, 550, 380)
  GraphicsWindow.BrushColor = "White"
  PlotLeft = 60
  PlotTop = 90
  PlotWidth = 450
  PlotHeight = 300
  GraphicsWindow.FillRectangle(PlotLeft, PlotTop, PlotWidth,
PlotHeight)
  GraphicsWindow.PenColor = "Black"
  GraphicsWindow.PenWidth = 2
  GraphicsWindow.DrawRectangle(PlotLeft, PlotTop, PlotWidth,
PlotHeight)
  Wmin = 1000.0
  Wmax = 0.0
  For I = 1 To NumberWeights
    Wmin = Math.Min(Weight[I], Wmin)
    Wmax = Math.Max(Weight[I], Wmax)
```

```
  EndFor
  GraphicsWindow.PenColor = "Blue"
  GraphicsWindow.PenWidth = 2
  XPrevious = PlotLeft
  YPrevious = PlotTop + (Wmax - Weight[1]) * (PlotHeight - 1) /
(Wmax - Wmin)
  For I = 2 To NumberWeights
    'connect current point to previous point
    XCurrent = PlotLeft + DayNumber[I] * (PlotWidth - 1) /
DayNumber[NumberWeights)
    YCurrent = PlotTop + (Wmax - Weight[I]) * (PlotHeight - 1)
/ (Wmax - Wmin)
    GraphicsWindow.DrawLine(XPrevious, YPrevious, XCurrent,
YCurrent)
    XPrevious = XCurrent
    YPrevious = YCurrent
  EndFor
ExitPlotWeightValues:
EndSub
```

Notice how the coordinate conversion equations are used and how the current and previous values are swapped.

Save and **Run** the project. The weight file will be opened and the values plotted in a line graph:

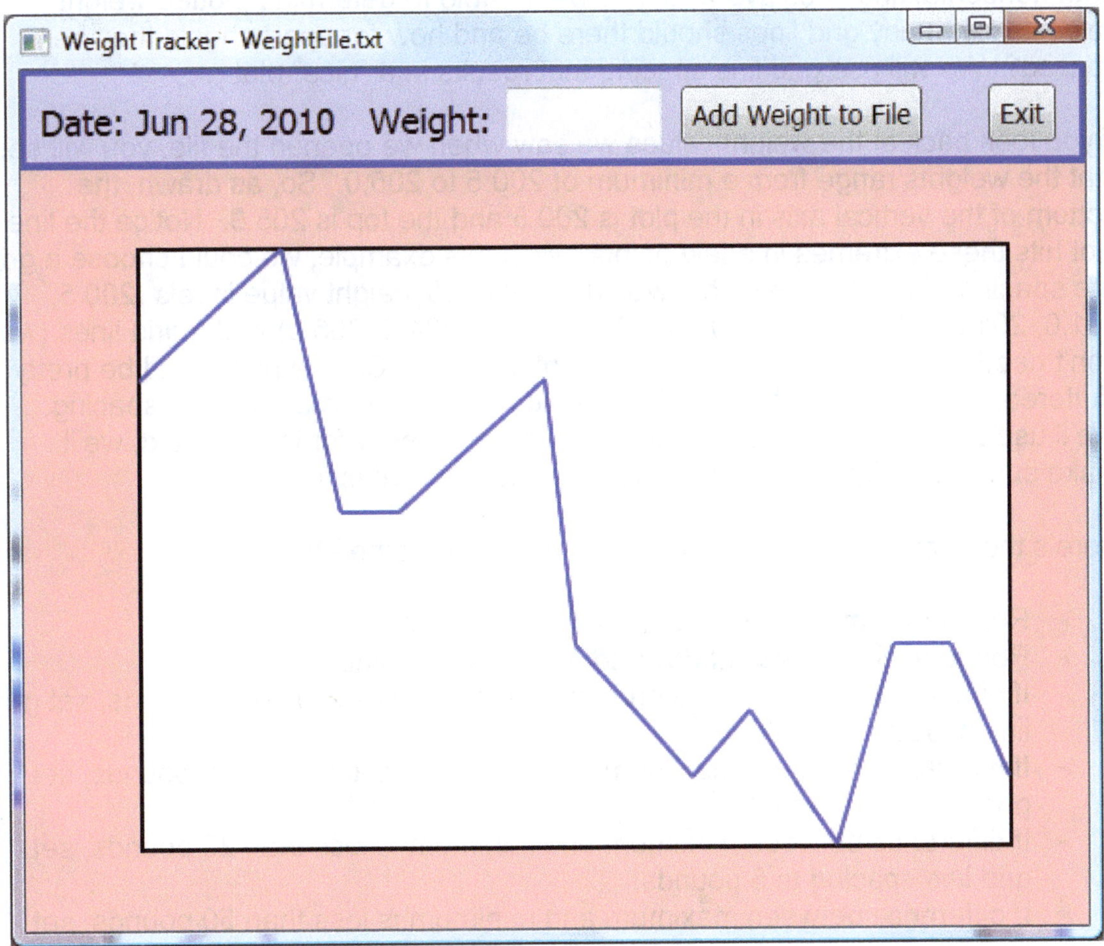

Success!

As drawn, the weight plot (though informative) is pretty boring. It lacks grid lines indicating weight values. And, it lacks labeling information to tell us what we're looking at. We need labels on the vertical axis telling us the weight range. We need labels on the horizontal axis telling us the represented date range. First, let's address grid lines.

Code Design – Grid Lines

With horizontal grid lines, we would be better able to determine plotted weight values. How many grid lines should there be and how far apart should they be spaced? We will use grid line spacing that results in a "nice" plot.

If you look back at the weight values we saw when we opened the file, you will see that the weights range from a minimum of 200.5 to 205.0. So, as drawn, the bottom of the vertical axis in the plot is 200.5 and the top is 205.0. Notice the line plot hits these extremes in a few points. With this example, we could choose a grid line spacing of 0.5 pounds. That would result in 10 weight value labels (200.5, 201.0, 201.5, 202.0, 202.5, 203.0, 203.5, 204.0, 204.5, 205.0) and 8 grid lines (we don't need grid lines at the bottom or top of the plot). Such a plot would be pretty cluttered, not a "nice" plot. Let's develop some rules for nicer grid line spacing. We'll use whole numbers for spacing and whole number for labels. And, we'll make sure the weight plot never touches either vertical extreme.

Here's the rules I use (you may come up with some others):

- Round maximum weight up to next integer value.
- Round minimum weight down to next integer value.
- If difference between maximum and minimum is less than 5 pounds, set grid line spacing to 1 pound.
- If difference between maximum and minimum is less than 10 pounds, set grid line spacing to 2 pounds.
- If difference between maximum and minimum is less than 25 pounds, set grid line spacing to 5 pounds.
- If difference between maximum and minimum is less than 50 pounds, set grid line spacing to 10 pounds.
- For larger differences, use a grid line spacing of 20 pounds.
- Adjust maximum value to next highest integer multiple of the grid line spacing (if necessary).
- Adjust minimum value to next lowest integer multiple of the grid line spacing (if necessary).

Once the grid line spacing is determined, the grid lines can be drawn using the **DrawLine** method. As stated, grid lines are drawn at each vertical position, except the bottom and top.

The modified **PlotWeightValues** subroutine that computes grid line spacing and draws the grid lines is (changes are shaded):

```
Sub PlotWeightValues
  If (NumberWeights < 2) Then
    Goto ExitPlotWeightValues
  EndIf
  'clear weight panel  'clear weight panel
  GraphicsWindow.BrushColor =
GraphicsWindow.GetColorFromRGB(255, 192, 192)
  GraphicsWindow.FillRectangle(0, 50, 550, 380)
  GraphicsWindow.BrushColor = "White"
  PlotLeft = 60
  PlotTop = 90
  PlotWidth = 450
  PlotHeight = 300
  GraphicsWindow.FillRectangle(PlotLeft, PlotTop, PlotWidth,
PlotHeight)
  GraphicsWindow.PenColor = "Black"
  GraphicsWindow.PenWidth = 2
  GraphicsWindow.DrawRectangle(PlotLeft, PlotTop, PlotWidth,
PlotHeight)
  Wmin = 1000.0
  Wmax = 0.0
  For I = 1 To NumberWeights
    Wmin = Math.Min(Weight[I], Wmin)
    Wmax = Math.Max(Weight[I], Wmax)
  EndFor
  'adjust Wmin/Wmax for 'nice' intervals
  If (Wmin = Wmax) Then
    Wmin = Wmax - 1
  EndIf
  Wmax = Math.Ceiling(Wmax + 0.5) 'round up
  Wmin = Math.Floor(Wmin - 0.5) 'round down
  If (Wmax - Wmin) <= 5.0 Then
    GridSpacing = 1.0
  ElseIf (Wmax - Wmin <= 10.0) Then
    GridSpacing = 2.0
  ElseIf (Wmax - Wmin <= 25.0) Then
    GridSpacing = 5.0
  ElseIf (Wmax - Wmin <= 50.0) Then
    GridSpacing = 10.0
  Else
    GridSpacing = 20.0
  EndIf
  If (Math.Remainder(Wmax, GridSpacing) <> 0) Then
```

```
    Wmax = GridSpacing * Math.Floor(Wmax / GridSpacing) +
GridSpacing
  EndIf
  If (Math.Remainder(Wmin, GridSpacing) <> 0) Then
    Wmin = GridSpacing * Math.Floor(Wmin / GridSpacing)
  EndIf
  Intervals = Math.Floor((Wmax - Wmin) / GridSpacing)
  GraphicsWindow.PenColor = "Blue"
  GraphicsWindow.PenWidth = 2
  XPrevious = PlotLeft
  YPrevious = PlotTop + (Wmax - Weight[1]) * (PlotHeight - 1) /
(Wmax - Wmin)
  For I = 2 To NumberWeights
    'connect current point to previous point
    XCurrent = PlotLeft + DayNumber[I] * (PlotWidth - 1) /
DayNumber[NumberWeights]
    YCurrent = PlotTop + (Wmax - Weight[I]) * (PlotHeight - 1)
/ (Wmax - Wmin)
    GraphicsWindow.DrawLine(XPrevious, YPrevious, XCurrent,
YCurrent)
    XPrevious = XCurrent
    YPrevious = YCurrent
  EndFor
  GraphicsWindow.PenColor = "Black"
  GraphicsWindow.PenWidth = 1
  WLegend = Wmin
  For I = 0 To Intervals
    YLegend = PlotTop + Math.Floor((Wmax - WLegend) *
(PlotHeight - 1) / (Wmax - Wmin))
    'draw grid line (except at top and bottom)
    If (I > 0 And I < Intervals) Then
      GraphicsWindow.DrawLine(PlotLeft, YLegend, PlotLeft +
PlotWidth, YLegend)
    EndIf
    WLegend = WLegend + GridSpacing
  EndFor
ExitPlotWeightValues:
EndSub
```

In this code, **GridSpacing** is the spacing between grid lines and **Intervals** is the number of grid intervals between **Wmin** and **Wmax**. **WLegend** is the weight value at the current grid line (it starts at **Wmin** and increases by **GridSpacing** after drawing a grid line). The grid lines are drawn with a black pen with 1 pixel width. You should see all the grid spacing calculation steps. Make the indicated changes in your project.

Save and **Run** the project. Here's the modified plot:

Notice the grid lines (they're spaced apart by 2 pounds, by the way). Notice the weight plot no longer touches the top or bottom of the plot area. This is a nicer plot. It's still not "nice enough." There's no indication of what the grid line spacing is. We don't know what the weight range is. We don't know what the date range is. All that information is provided with plot labeling.

Code Design – Plot Labels

We will add text information for labeling the weight axis first. When drawing the grid lines, we wrote code that specified the weight values (**WLegend**) for the labels. We just need to add code that places these values in the appropriate location in the plot area. For each **WLegend** value:

- Convert **WLegend** to a whole number (no decimals)
- Position string in proper vertical location.

The Y axis conversion equation helps position the string label vertically.

Each label will be "drawn" outside the plot rectangle. Here's a sketch that shows you how one label (for a weight value **W**) is positioned:

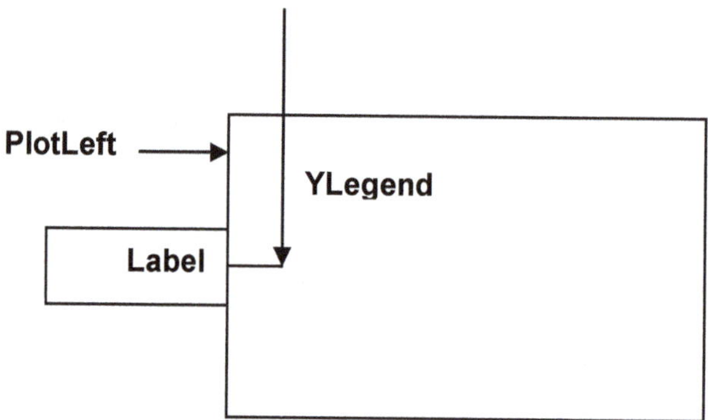

To horizontally position **Label**, I use:

```
x = PlotLeft - 35
```

To vertically position **Label**, use:

```
y = YLegend - 10
```

The pair (**x, y**) are used to position the label using **DrawText**. The numbers used to position this label were found by trial and error.

The code to draw the weight axis labels is processed at the end of the **PlotWeightValues** subroutine (modifications are shaded; much unmodified code is not shown):

```
Sub PlotWeightValues
  If (NumberWeights < 2) Then
    Goto ExitPlotWeightValues
  EndIf
  'clear weight panel
   .
   .
  GraphicsWindow.PenColor = "Black"
  GraphicsWindow.PenWidth = 1
  WLegend = Wmin
  GraphicsWindow.BrushColor = "Black"
  GraphicsWindow.FontSize = 16
  GraphicsWindow.FontBold = "false"
  For I = 0 To Intervals
    YLegend = PlotTop + Math.Floor((Wmax - WLegend) *
(PlotHeight - 1) / (Wmax - Wmin))
    'add label
    GraphicsWindow.DrawText(PlotLeft - 35, YLegend - 10,
WLegend)
    'draw grid line (except at top and bottom)
    If (I > 0 And I < Intervals) Then
      GraphicsWindow.DrawLine(PlotLeft, YLegend, PlotLeft +
PlotWidth, YLegend)
    EndIf
    WLegend = WLegend + GridSpacing
  EndFor
ExitPlotWeightValues:
EndSub
```

We use a black brush (plain, size 16 font) to draw the label. Make the noted changes to the subroutine.

Save and **Run** the project. Our plot now has very nice labels.

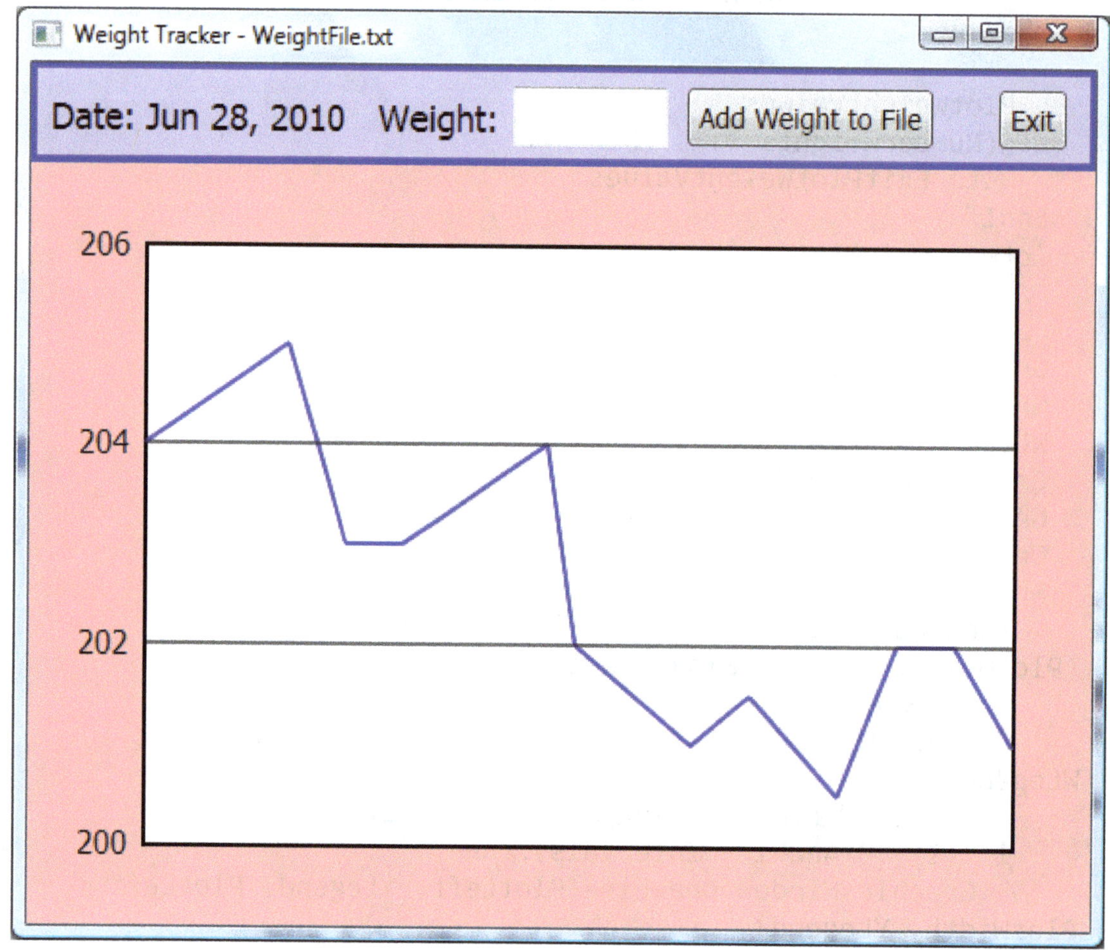

Now, we add labels to the horizontal weight plot axis. Recall this axis tells us how many days have elapsed since we started the weight file. We could label the axis with such day values, choosing an appropriate horizontal spacing. Instead of doing this, we will simply label the axis with the starting date and the ending date. We feel this is more meaningful information. The form of the labeling will be:

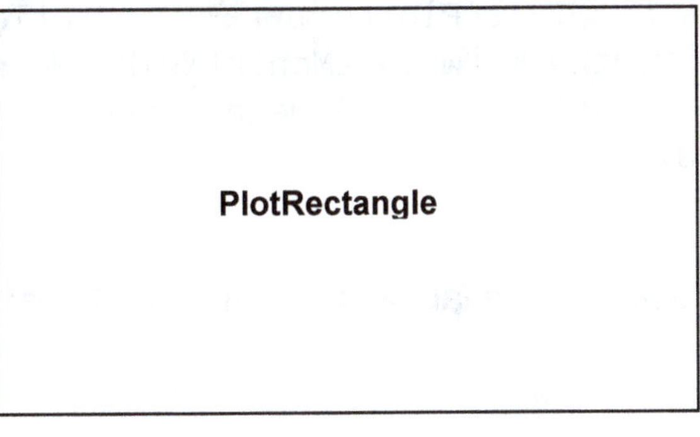

Start Date **End Date**

The code to generate these labels also goes in the **PlotWeightValues** subroutine. The new procedure is (once again, changes are shaded with much unmodified code not shown):

```
Sub PlotWeightValues
  If (NumberWeights < 2) Then
    Goto ExitPlotWeightValues
  EndIf
  'clear weight panel
   .
   .
  GraphicsWindow.PenColor = "Black"
  GraphicsWindow.PenWidth = 1
  WLegend = Wmin
  GraphicsWindow.BrushColor = "Black"
  GraphicsWindow.FontSize = 16
  GraphicsWindow.FontBold = "false"
  For I = 0 To Intervals
    YLegend = PlotTop + Math.Floor((Wmax - WLegend) *
(PlotHeight - 1) / (Wmax - Wmin))
    'add label
    GraphicsWindow.DrawText(PlotLeft - 35, YLegend - 10,
WLegend)
    'draw grid line (except at top and bottom)
    If (I > 0 And I < Intervals) Then
      GraphicsWindow.DrawLine(PlotLeft, YLegend, PlotLeft +
PlotWidth, YLegend)
```

```
    EndIf
    WLegend = WLegend + GridSpacing
  EndFor
  'add x Legends
  GraphicsWindow.DrawText(PlotLeft - 20, PlotTop + PlotHeight
+10, "Start: " + MonthName[WeightMonth[1]] + " " + WeightDay[1]
+ ", "+ WeightYear[1])
  GraphicsWindow.DrawText(PlotLeft + 335, PlotTop + PlotHeight
+ 10, "End: " + MonthName[WeightMonth[NumberWeights]] + " " +
WeightDay[NumberWeights] + ", "+ WeightYear[NumberWeights])
ExitPlotWeightValues:
EndSub
```

You should be able to see how the labels are formed and positioned. Make the noted changes.

Save and **Run** the project and you should see:

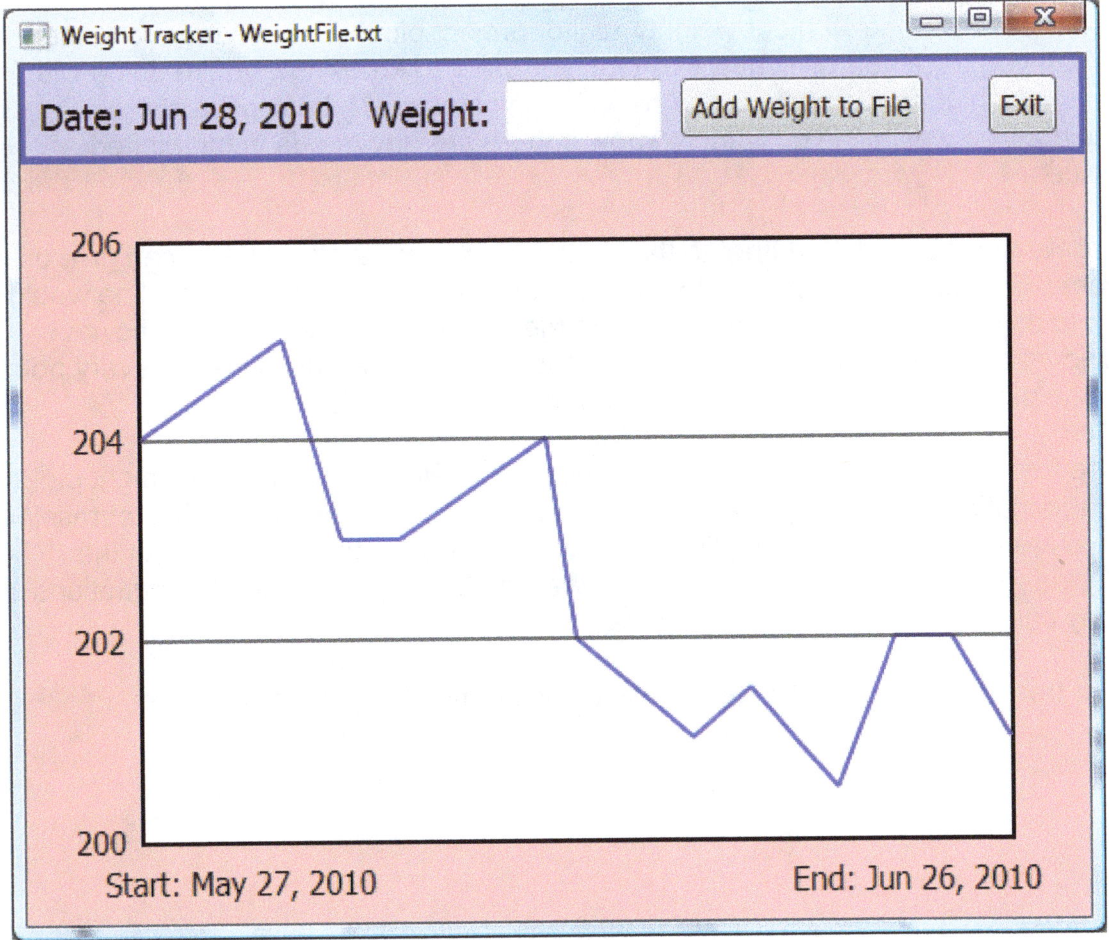

Don't you agree the plot looks much nicer with labels?

Code Design – Weight Plot Trend

We're almost done with our weight monitor project plot. Just one more change. When you track your weight with a plot, you want to know how you're doing with your weight management plan. Are you gaining weight? Losing weight? Maintaining weight? You want to know if there are any trends in the plotted values.

We want to add a '**trend line'** to the weight plot. Such a straight line can give us some idea of what direction our weight is going in. A very simple trend line would be to connect the first point in the plot to the last point. This approach, however, ignores all other points in the plot. The approach we take will consider every point in the plot, but, be forewarned, some mathematics is needed.

The trend line we use will represent a "best fit" to all the points in the weight plot. Mathematically speaking, we do a **linear regression** on the data. This regression involves calculus and solving linear equations, so we won't bore you with the details (unless you want to see them). We'll just give you the needed equations so they can be added to the project code.

Our trend line 'models' the weight values using the straight line equation:

$$\mathbf{W_m = TD + W_0}$$

where:

$\mathbf{W_m}$ – modeled weight
D – horizontal axis value (number of days since first weight entry)
T – trend value (pounds/day), called the slope of the line
$\mathbf{W_0}$ – modeled weight when **D = 0**

With the above model, the trend line connects two Cartesian end points: (**0**, $\mathbf{W_0}$) and ($\mathbf{D_{max}}$, $\mathbf{TD_{max}} + \mathbf{W_0}$). So, to draw the trend line, we need to know values for **T** and $\mathbf{W_0}$ (we know $\mathbf{D_{max}}$). Values for these two terms are found using the **DayNumber** and **Weight** arrays currently used to create the weight plots. To simplify all the math written out below, we will refer to **DayNumber** by **D** and **Weight** by **W**. The equations for **T** and $\mathbf{W_0}$, using these arrays are (these equations come from the linear regression we mentioned):

$$T = \frac{N\sum_{k=1}^{N} D(k)W(k) - \sum_{k=1}^{N} D(k) \sum_{k=1}^{N} W(k)}{N\sum_{k=1}^{N} D^2(k) - [\sum_{k=1}^{N} D(k)]^2}$$

$$W_0 = \frac{\sum_{k=1}^{N} D^2(k) \sum_{k=1}^{N} W(k) - \sum_{k=1}^{N} D(k) \sum_{k=1}^{N} D(k)W(k)}{N\sum_{k=1}^{N} D^2(k) - [\sum_{k=1}^{N} D(k)]^2}$$

where recall the Greek sigma in the above equations indicates you add up all the corresponding elements next to the sigma. Also, **N** is the number of elements in each array (**NumberWeights**).

I know the above equations are messy, but they yield a very nice trend line and are straightforward to program. You simply declare a variable for each of the summation terms and form the sums as you cycle through the two arrays **D** and **W**. Then a little math gives you values for **T** and $\mathbf{W_0}$.

For those interested in the mathematics involved in deriving these relations, I'll outline them for you. For those not interested, leave this paragraph now. The idea behind linear regression is to minimize the squared error between the modeled weight points and the actual weight points. That error (**E**) is given by:

$$\mathbf{E} = \sum_{k=1}^{N} \{W(k) - [TD(k) + W_0]\}^2$$

We want E to as small as possible, seeking the so-called least square error solution. For E to be minimum the partial derivative of E with respect to T and the partial derivative with respect to W_0 must be zero. Those derivatives are (here's where the calculus shows up):

$$2\sum_{k=1}^{N} \{W(k) - [TD(k) + W_0]\}D(k) = 0 \text{ (partial derivative with respect to T)}$$

$$2\sum_{k=1}^{N} \{W(k) - [TD(k) + W_0]\} = 0 \text{ (partial derivative with respect to } W_0\text{)}$$

If we rearrange these equations a bit, we get:

$$T\sum_{k=1}^{N} D^2(k) + W_0\sum_{k=1}^{N} D(k) = \sum_{k=1}^{N} D(k)W(k)$$

$$T\sum_{k=1}^{N} D(k) + W_0N = \sum_{k=1}^{N} W(k)$$

We have two linear equations with two unknowns (**T** and $\mathbf{W_0}$). We can use Cramer's rule to solve these equations to yield the previously seen relations for **T** and $\mathbf{W_0}$.

The code to compute and draw the trend line goes in **PlotWeightValues**. In addition to drawing the trend line, we add a label at the top of the plot to indicate a "weekly" trend value (**7 * T**), showing how much weight you are losing or gaining each week. The modified procedure is (changes are shaded):

```
Sub PlotWeightValues
  If (NumberWeights < 2) Then
    Goto ExitPlotWeightValues
  EndIf
  'clear weight panel  'clear weight panel
  GraphicsWindow.BrushColor =
GraphicsWindow.GetColorFromRGB(255, 192, 192)
  GraphicsWindow.FillRectangle(0, 50, 550, 380)
  GraphicsWindow.BrushColor = "White"
  PlotLeft = 60
  PlotTop = 90
  PlotWidth = 450
  PlotHeight = 300
  GraphicsWindow.FillRectangle(PlotLeft, PlotTop, PlotWidth,
PlotHeight)
  GraphicsWindow.PenColor = "Black"
  GraphicsWindow.PenWidth = 2
  GraphicsWindow.DrawRectangle(PlotLeft, PlotTop, PlotWidth,
PlotHeight)
  Wmin = 1000.0
  Wmax = 0.0
  SumD = 0.0
  SumD2 = 0.0
  SumW = 0.0
  SumDW = 0.0
  For I = 1 To NumberWeights
    Wmin = Math.Min(Weight[I], Wmin)
    Wmax = Math.Max(Weight[I], Wmax)
    'values for trend line
    SumD = SumD + DayNumber[I]
    SumD2 = SumD2 + DayNumber[I] * DayNumber[I]
    SumW = SumW + Weight[I]
    SumDW = SumDW + DayNumber[I] * Weight[I]
  EndFor
  'adjust Wmin/Wmax for 'nice' intervals
  If (Wmin = Wmax) Then
    Wmin = Wmax - 1
  EndIf
  Wmax = Math.Ceiling(Wmax + 0.5) 'round up
  Wmin = Math.Floor(Wmin - 0.5) 'round down
  If (Wmax - Wmin) <= 5.0 Then
```

```
      GridSpacing = 1.0
    ElseIf (Wmax - Wmin <= 10.0) Then
      GridSpacing = 2.0
    ElseIf (Wmax - Wmin <= 25.0) Then
      GridSpacing = 5.0
    ElseIf (Wmax - Wmin <= 50.0) Then
      GridSpacing = 10.0
    Else
      GridSpacing = 20.0
    EndIf
    If (Math.Remainder(Wmax, GridSpacing) <> 0) Then
      Wmax = GridSpacing * Math.Floor(Wmax / GridSpacing) +
  GridSpacing
    EndIf
    If (Math.Remainder(Wmin, GridSpacing) <> 0) Then
      Wmin = GridSpacing * Math.Floor(Wmin / GridSpacing)
    EndIf
    Intervals = Math.Floor((Wmax - Wmin) / GridSpacing)
    GraphicsWindow.PenColor = "Blue"
    GraphicsWindow.PenWidth = 2
    XPrevious = PlotLeft
    YPrevious = PlotTop + (Wmax - Weight[1]) * (PlotHeight - 1) /
  (Wmax - Wmin)
    For I = 2 To NumberWeights
      'connect current point to previous point
      XCurrent = PlotLeft + DayNumber[I] * (PlotWidth - 1) /
  DayNumber[NumberWeights]
      YCurrent = PlotTop + (Wmax - Weight[I]) * (PlotHeight - 1)
  / (Wmax - Wmin)
      GraphicsWindow.DrawLine(XPrevious, YPrevious, XCurrent,
  YCurrent)
      XPrevious = XCurrent
      YPrevious = YCurrent
    EndFor
    GraphicsWindow.PenColor = "Black"
    GraphicsWindow.PenWidth = 1
    WLegend = Wmin
    GraphicsWindow.BrushColor = "Black"
    GraphicsWindow.FontSize = 16
    GraphicsWindow.FontBold = "false"
    For I = 0 To Intervals
      YLegend = PlotTop + Math.Floor((Wmax - WLegend) *
  (PlotHeight - 1) / (Wmax - Wmin))
      'add label
      GraphicsWindow.DrawText(PlotLeft - 35, YLegend - 10,
  WLegend)
```

```
    'draw grid line (except at top and bottom)
    If (I > 0 And I < Intervals) Then
      GraphicsWindow.DrawLine(PlotLeft, YLegend, PlotLeft +
PlotWidth, YLegend)
    EndIf
    WLegend = WLegend + GridSpacing
  EndFor
  'add x legends
  GraphicsWindow.DrawText(PlotLeft - 20, PlotTop + PlotHeight
+10, "Start: " + MonthName[WeightMonth[1]] + " " + WeightDay[1]
+ ", "+ WeightYear[1])
  GraphicsWindow.DrawText(PlotLeft + 335, PlotTop + PlotHeight
+ 10, "End: " + MonthName[WeightMonth[NumberWeights]] + " " +
WeightDay[NumberWeights] + ", "+ WeightYear[NumberWeights])
  'trend computations
  T = (NumberWeights * SumDW - SumD * SumW) / (NumberWeights *
SumD2 - SumD * SumD)
  W0 = (SumD2 * SumW - SumD * SumDW) / (NumberWeights * SumD2 -
SumD * SumD)
  'draw line
  Y1 = PlotTop + Math.Floor((Wmax - W0) * (PlotHeight - 1) /
(Wmax - Wmin))
  Y2 = PlotTop + Math.Floor((Wmax - (T *
DayNumber[NumberWeights] + W0)) * (PlotHeight - 1) / (Wmax -
Wmin))
  GraphicsWindow.PenColor = "Red"
  GraphicsWindow.PenWidth = 1
  GraphicsWindow.DrawLine(PlotLeft, Y1, PlotLeft + PlotWidth ,
Y2)
  'draw trend title
  GraphicsWindow.BrushColor = "Black"
  GraphicsWindow.FontSize = 18
  S = "Trend: "
  If (T > 0) Then
    S = S + "+"
  EndIf
  S = S + Math.Floor(7 * 100 * T) / 100 + " lb/week"
  GraphicsWindow.DrawText(200, 60, S)
ExitPlotWeightValues:
EndSub
```

This is the final version of the **PlotWeightValues** subroutine. Make the noted changes. You should see how the trend line is computed and drawn. Also notice how the trend value is printed at the top of the plot.

Save and **Run** the project. You will see a nice red trend line and corresponding label indicating I'm losing nearly a pound a week:

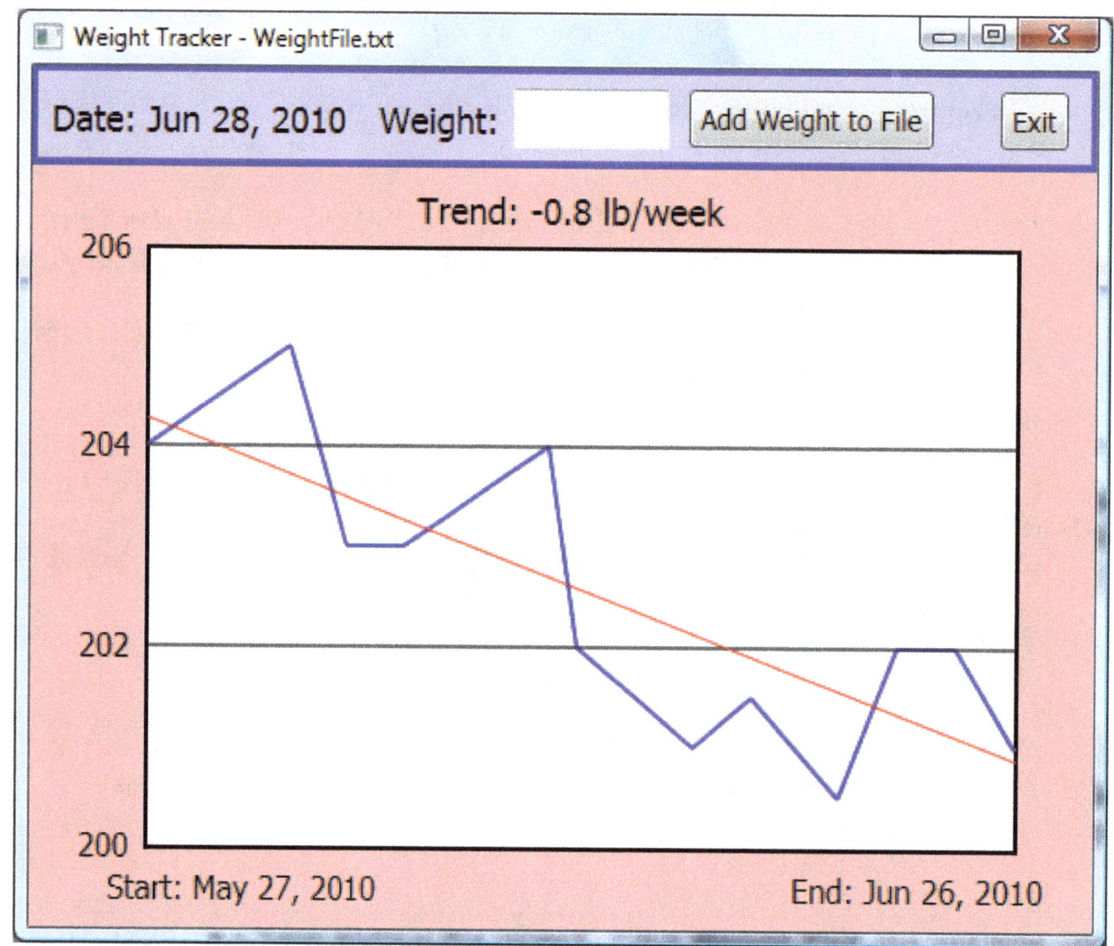

Code Design – Entering Weights

At this point, all we can do is open the existing weight file and plot the values. We need to add the ability to let a user add a weight value (in **WeightTextBox**) for the displayed date (the current day). Once entered, the user clicks **Add Weight to File** to have that entry (and the date information) put in the **DayNumber** and **Weight** arrays. Here, we write the code that accomplishes this task.

Once a user enters a weight, we need to process the following steps to add the entry to the arrays:

- See if entry already exists for current date; if so, overwrite the weight value.
- Add new date and new weight to arrays.
- Replot the weight values.

The code to implement these steps will be in the subroutine associated with clicking **AddWeightButton.**

Add this line of code at the end of **InitializeProgram** to recognize button clicks:

```
Controls.ButtonClicked = ButtonClickedSub
```

Add this code after opening the weight file:

```
'get today's day number
MM = Clock.Month
DD = Clock.Day
YY = Clock.Year
ComputeElapsedDays()
TodayDayNumber = ElapsedDays - FirstDayValue
```

This computes the day number (**TodayDayNumber**) for the current day. This has to be after the call to **OpenWeightFile** so we have a value for **FirstDayValue**.

Next add the **ButtonClickedSub** subroutine.

```
Sub ButtonClickedSub
  B = Controls.LastClickedButton
  If (B = AddWeightButton) Then
    AddWeightButtonClicked()
  EndIf
EndSub
```

Note clicking on **AddWeightButton** calls the **AddWeightButtonClicked** subroutine where we place the code to add a weight value to the arrays.

The **AddWeightButtonClicked** subroutine that implements the previously outlined steps:

```
Sub AddWeightButtonClicked
  'are adding or replacing today's weight?
  If (DayNumber[NumberWeights] <> TodayDayNumber) Then
    'adding value
    NumberWeights = NumberWeights + 1
    WeightMonth[NumberWeights] = Clock.Month
    WeightDay[NumberWeights] = Clock.Day
    WeightYear[NumberWeights] = Clock.Year
    DayNumber[NumberWeights] = TodayDayNumber
  EndIf
  Weight[NumberWeights] =
Controls.GetTextBoxText(WeightTextBox)
  PlotWeightValues()
EndSub
```

Notice how we increment **NumberWeights** only if this is a new entry.

Save and **Run** the project. Type a weight in the text box control and click the **Add Weight to File**. When I type my weight in for today (201.5), I see:

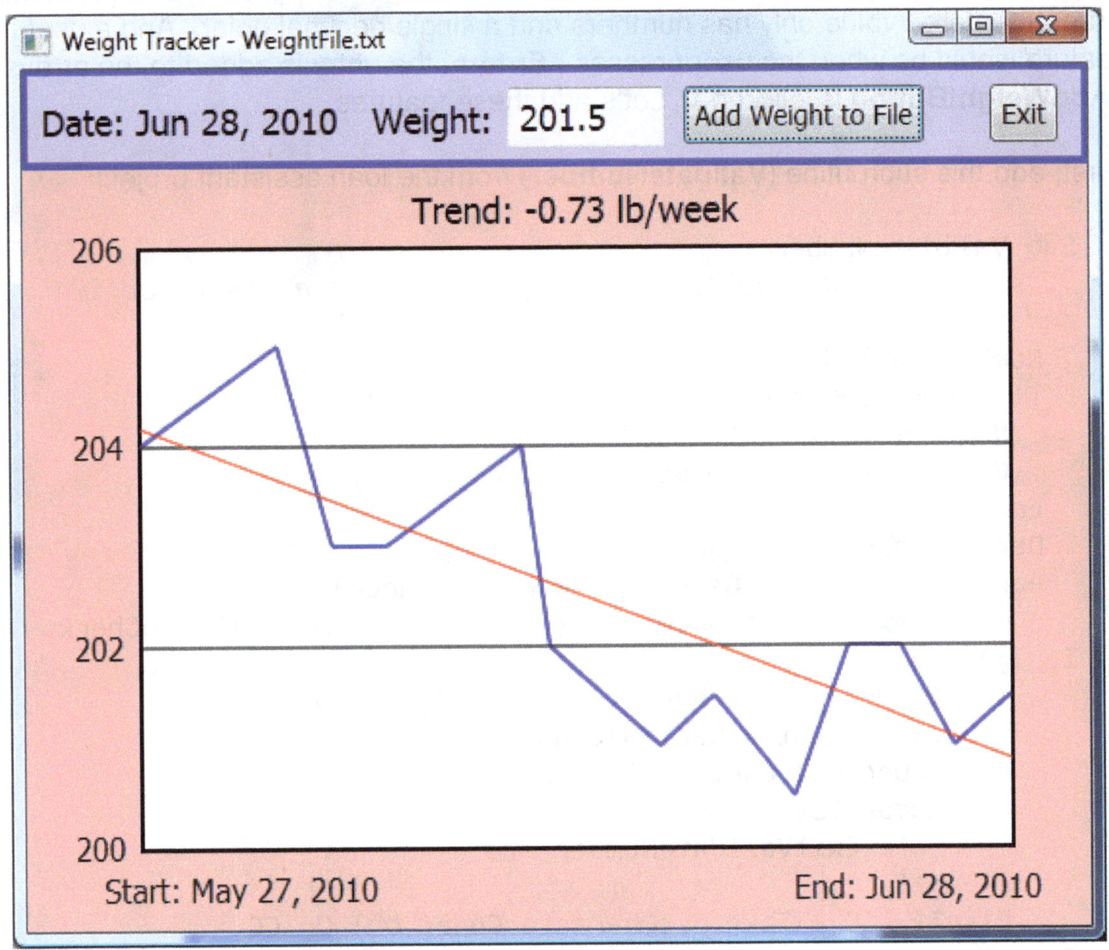

Note the new plot and adjusted trend values.

You may or may not have noted that when entering a weight in the text box, there are no restrictions on what you can type – it could even be blank!. We will borrow code we wrote way back in the loan assistant project to correct this. We will make sure an entered value only has numbers and a single decimal point. And a useful feature would be when the user presses <**Enter**>, the entry is added to the arrays (**AddWeightButton** is 'clicked'). Let's add these features.

First, add this subroutine (**ValidateNumber**) from the loan assistant project:

```
Sub ValidateNumber
  'sees if NumberToCheck has only digits and a single decimal
and is not blank
  NumberIsValid = "true"
  If (NumberToCheck = "") Then
    NumberIsValid = "false"
    Goto ExitValidateNumber
  EndIf
  DecimalCount = 0
  For I = 1 To Text.GetLength(NumberToCheck)
    CC = Text.GetCharacterCode(Text.GetSubText(NumberToCheck,
I, 1))
    If (CC = Text.GetCharacterCode(".")) Then
      DecimalCount = DecimalCount + 1
      If (DecimalCount > 1) Then
        NumberIsValid = "false"
        Goto ExitValidateNumber
      EndIf
    ElseIf (CC < Text.GetCharacterCode("0") Or CC >
Text.GetCharacterCode("9")) Then
      NumberIsValid = "false"
      Goto ExitValidateNumber
    EndIf
  EndFor
ExitValidateNumber:
EndSub
```

You provide a value – **NumberToCheck**. If it is a valid entry, the subroutine returns **NumberIsValid** as "true".

Add the shaded code to **AddWeightButtonClicked**:

```
Sub AddWeightButtonClicked
  'is weight valid?
  NumberToCheck = Controls.GetTextBoxText(WeightTextBox)
  ValidateNumber()
  If (NumberIsValid) Then
    'are adding or replacing today's weight?
    If (DayNumber[NumberWeights] <> TodayDayNumber) Then
      'adding value
      NumberWeights = NumberWeights + 1
      WeightMonth[NumberWeights] = Clock.Month
      WeightDay[NumberWeights] = Clock.Day
      WeightYear[NumberWeights] = Clock.Year
      DayNumber[NumberWeights] = TodayDayNumber
    EndIf
    Weight[NumberWeights] =
Controls.GetTextBoxText(WeightTextBox)
    PlotWeightValues()
  Else
    GraphicsWindow.ShowMessage("Entered weight is invalid
format or blank.  Please correct.", "Invalid Entry")
  EndIf
EndSub
```

If the entered weight is not valid, we display a message to that effect. This insures we don't get funny looking plots – invalid entries would yield a zero weight!

Save and **Run** the project. Click **Add Weight to File** without entering a value. You will see:

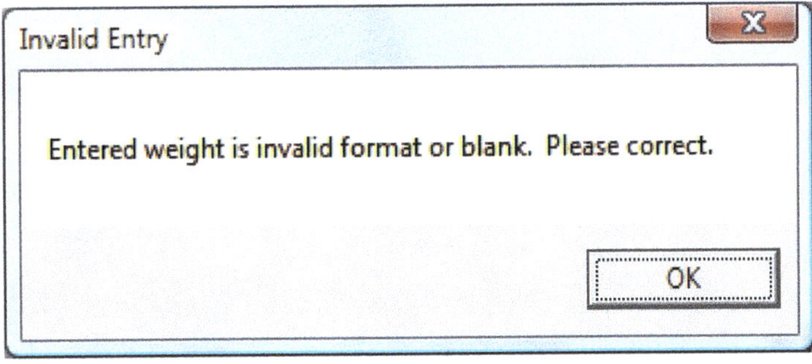

Type in a correct value to make sure the code accepts it.

The other feature we want is that when a user clicks <**Enter**> after entering a weight, the weight will processed (the same as if we click **AddWeightButton**). Add this line at the end of **InitializeProgram** to recognize pressing the <**Enter**> key:

```
GraphicsWindow.KeyDown = KeyDownSub
```

Then, add the **KeyDownSub** subroutine:

```
Sub KeyDownSub
  If (GraphicsWindow.LastKey = "Return") Then
    AddWeightButtonClicked()
  EndIf
EndSub
```

Save and **Run** the program again. Enter a weight for the displayed date and press <**Enter**>. Make sure it is entered just as if the **Add Weight to File** button is pressed. Keep changing today's weight to watch the plot change.

Code Design – Saving Weight Files

When a user exits the program (clicks **Exit**), we want to save date and weight information back to **WeightFile**. This insures any weight added for the current date is saved. This is a straightforward task. We simply write all **NumberWeights** elements of the **WeightMonth**, **WeightDay**, **WeightYear** and **Weight** arrays back to the file in the proper comma-separated format. This allows **WeightFile** to be opened and read the next time the program is run.

Add the shaded code to the **ButtonClickedSub** subroutine:

```
Sub ButtonClickedSub
  B = Controls.LastClickedButton
  If (B = AddWeightButton) Then
    AddWeightButtonClicked()
  ElseIf (B = ExitButton) Then
    'write out file and stop program
    For I = 1 To NumberWeights
      FileLine = WeightMonth[I] + "," + WeightDay[I] + "," +
WeightYear[I] + "," + Weight[I]
      File.WriteLine(Program.Directory + "\" + WeightFile, I,
FileLine)
    EndFor
    Program.End()
  EndIf
EndSub
```

When a user clicks **ExitButton**, the array elements are written back to **WeightFile** one line at a time. Then the program ends.

Save and **Run** the program. Enter a value for today's weight – I used 201.5 again:

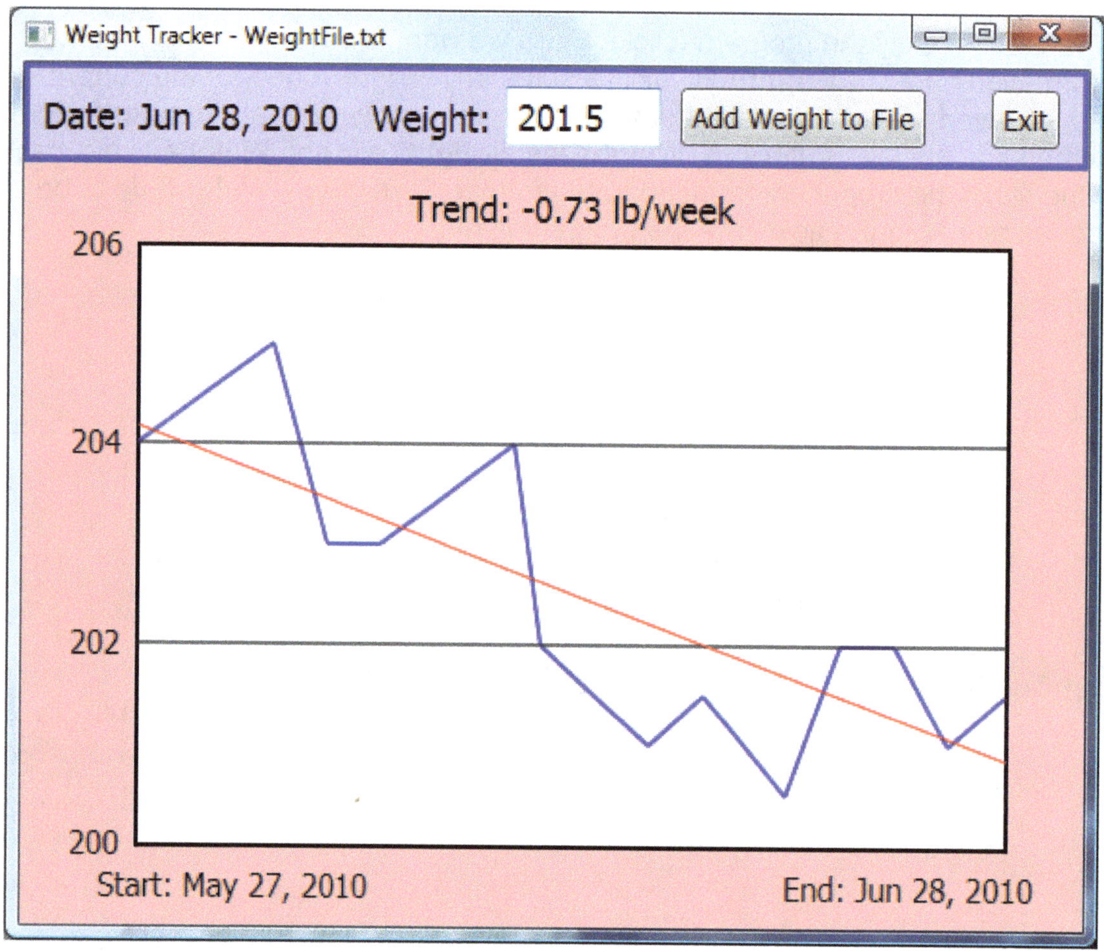

Click **Exit**. Go to your program folder and open **WeightFile.txt**. The new entry is there:

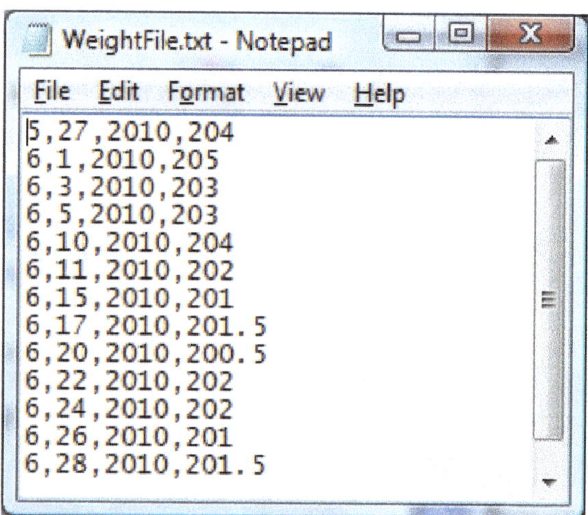

Now, **Run** again. You will see the same plot since the last value was saved:

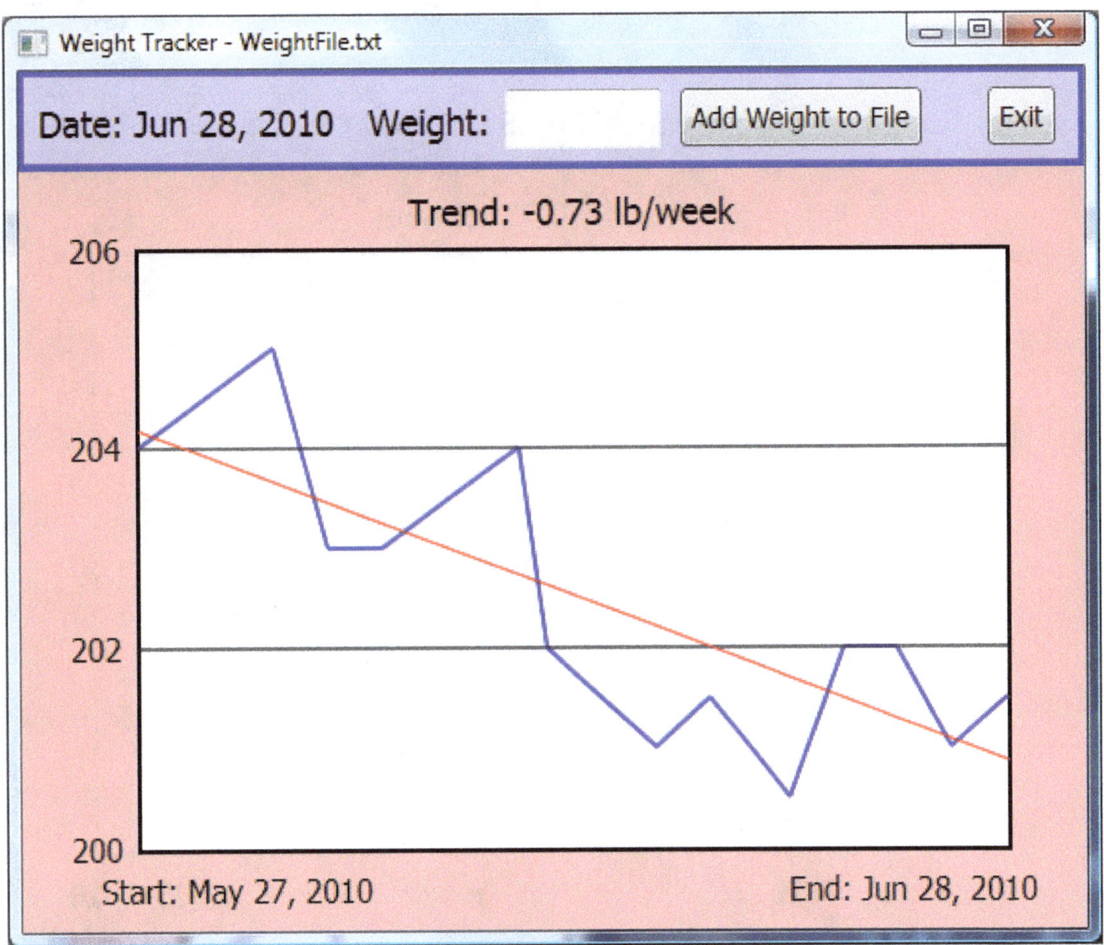

In the plot above, notice, even though there is a weight value for the current date (June 28), that value is not displayed in the text box. We should display the value so it can be edited if desired. To do that, add these lines of code in **InitializeProgram** after the lines establishing **TodayDayNumber**:

```
'if last value is today show it in text box
If (DayNumber[NumberWeights] = TodayDayNumber) Then
  Controls.SetTextBoxText(WeightTextBox, Weight[NumberWeights])
EndIf
PlotWeightValuesPlotWeightValues(()
```

Save and **Run** again. The current value (201.5) appears in the text box:

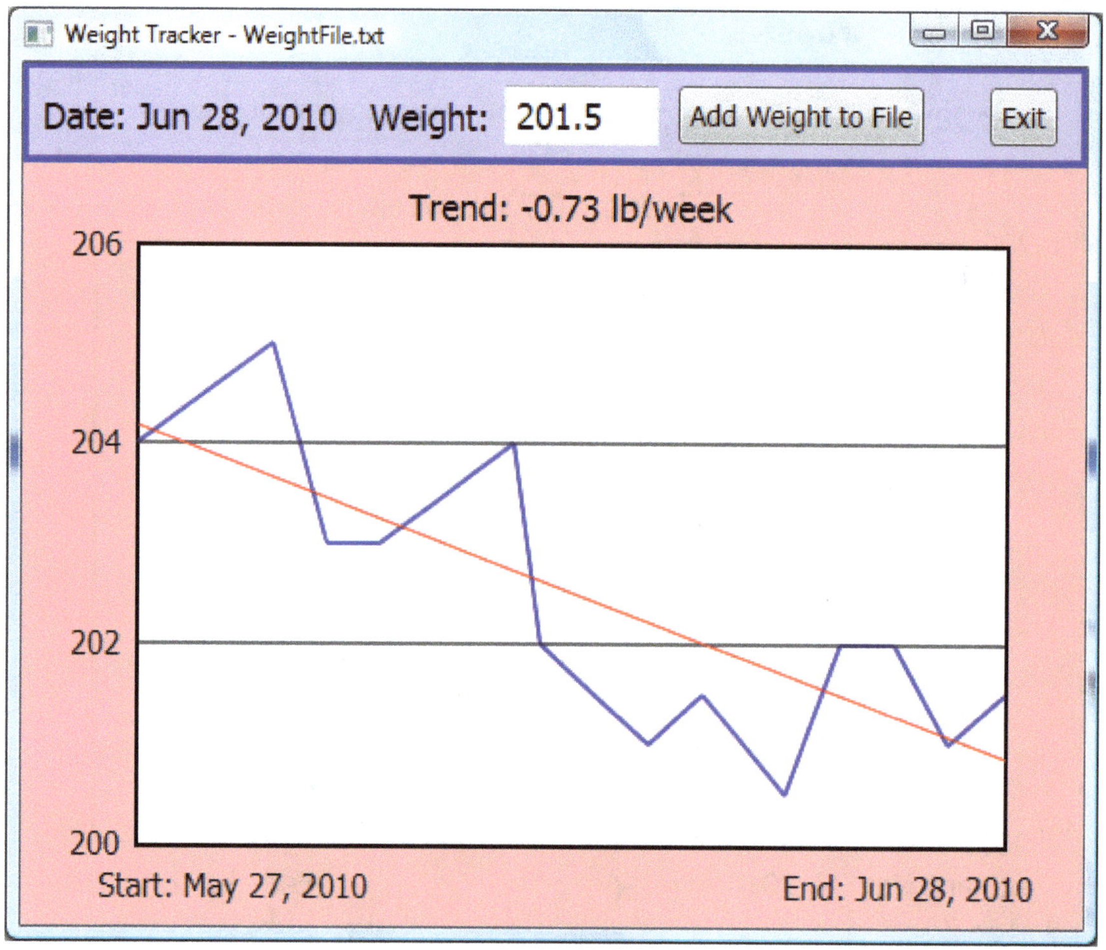

This case only occurs when you run the weight monitor program more than once in the same day.

The **Weight Monitor Project** code is complete. But, it's time to stop using the sample weight file and use your own.

Code Design – Using a New Weight File

We've built and tested the weight monitor project using a sample weight file. Obviously, you'd like to get started with your own file. The process is simple. Just change this line of code in **InitializeProgram**:

```
WeightFile = "WeightFile.txt"
```

Replace **WeightFile.txt** with a name for your file (we suggest keeping the .txt extension).

Once you've changed the code, **Save** and **Run** the program. You will be asked to enter your weight for the current day. No plot will be drawn since you only have a single entry. Click **Exit** and your one line file will be saved in your program folder. Then, on subsequent days, **Run** the program and enter additional weights. Over time, you will build up your own weight profile.

We can test this process. First, change **WeightFile** to **WeightFile1.txt**:

```
WeightFile = "WeightFile1.txt"
```

You can pick another file name if you'd like.

Save and **Run** the program. You will see:

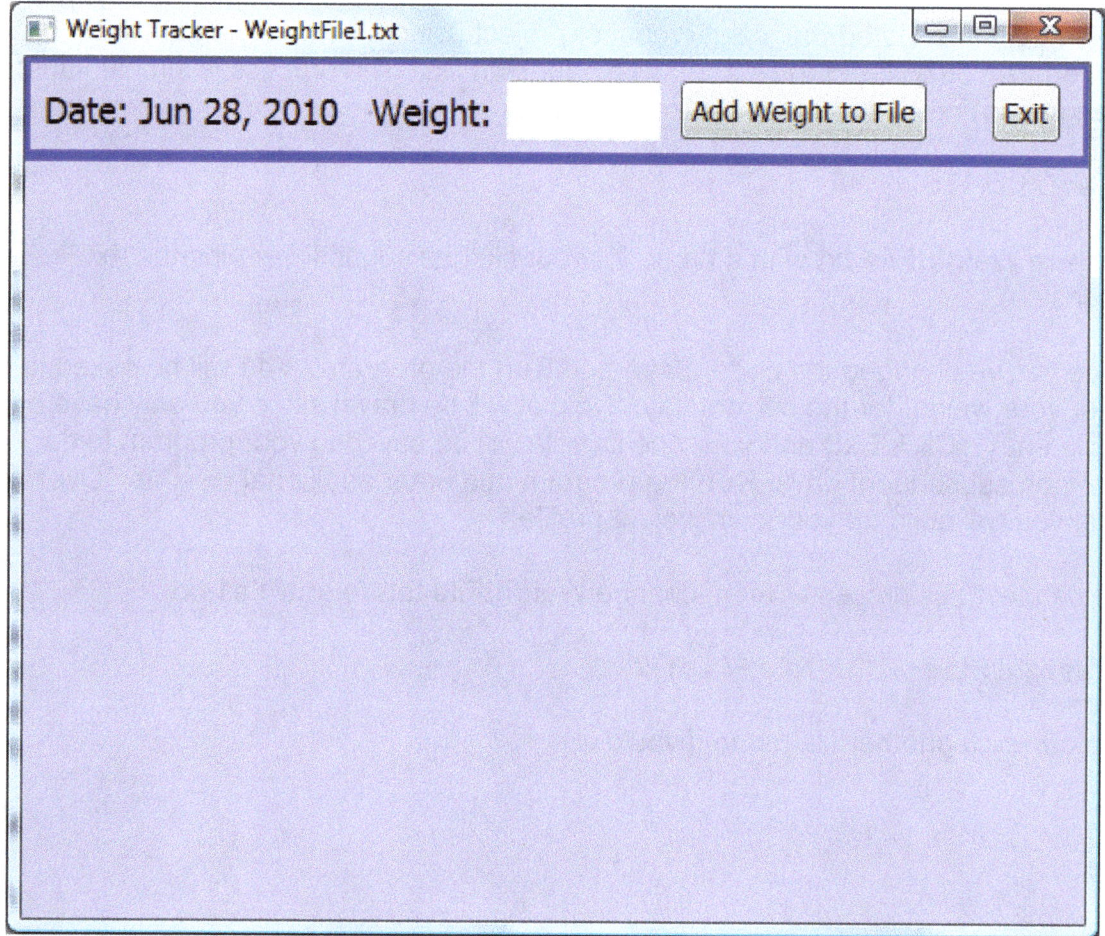

You will have another date displayed. Enter a weight value (I used 200). Click **Exit**.

Go to your program folder and open **WeightFile1.txt**. It should have one line:

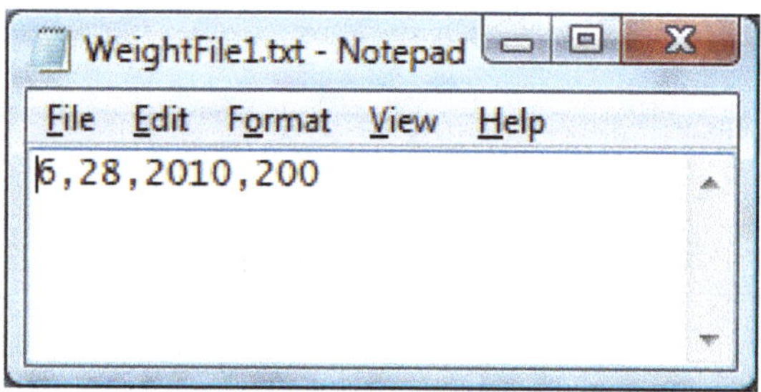

To see a plot, you need to wait until tomorrow or some later day to add another weight value. If you know how (and feel comfortable doing it), you can advanced your computer's calendar ahead one day and try it. If you do, make sure you change it back immediately or your computer's file structure will be kind of messed up.

Now you have the ability to use the **Weight Monitor Project** with your own weight file. I usually change file every few months or so, saving my older files. I have been using a version of this program for nearly 20 years to keep track of my weight. I hope you find it useful.

Weight Monitor Project Code Listing

Here is the complete listing of the **Weight Monitor** Small Basic program:

```
' Weight Tracker
InitializeProgram()

Sub InitializeProgram
  'graphics window
  GraphicsWindow.Width = 550
  GraphicsWindow.Height = 430
  GraphicsWindow.Title = "Weight Tracker"
  GraphicsWindow.BackgroundColor =
GraphicsWindow.GetColorFromRGB(192, 192, 255)
  GraphicsWindow.PenColor = "Blue"
  GraphicsWindow.PenWidth = 5
  GraphicsWindow.DrawRectangle(0, 0, GraphicsWindow.Width, 49)
  'month arrays
  MonthName[1] = "Jan"
  MonthName[2] = "Feb"
  MonthName[3] = "Mar"
  MonthName[4] = "Apr"
  MonthName[5] = "May"
  MonthName[6] = "Jun"
  MonthName[7] = "Jul"
  MonthName[8] = "Aug"
  MonthName[9] = "Sep"
  MonthName[10] = "Oct"
  MonthName[11] = "Nov"
  MonthName[12] = "Dec"
  'date
  GraphicsWindow.BrushColor = "Black"
  GraphicsWindow.FontBold = "false"
  GraphicsWindow.FontSize = 18
  GraphicsWindow.DrawText(10, 15, "Date: " +
MonthName[Clock.Month] + " " + Clock.Day + ", " + Clock.year)
  'weight
  GraphicsWindow.DrawText(180, 15, "Weight: ")
  WeightTextBox = Controls.AddTextBox(250, 10)
  Controls.SetSize(WeightTextBox, 80, 30)
  'buttons
  GraphicsWindow.BrushColor = "Black"
  GraphicsWindow.FontSize = 14
  GraphicsWindow.FontBold = "false"
  AddWeightButton = Controls.AddButton("Add Weight to File", 340,
10)
```

```
  ExitButton = Controls.AddButton("Exit", 500, 10)
  'specify weight file
  WeightFile = "WeightFile.txt"
  GraphicsWindow.Title = GraphicsWindow.Title + " - " + WeightFile
  OpenWeightFile()
  'get today's day number
  MM = Clock.Month
  DD = Clock.Day
  YY = Clock.Year
  ComputeElapsedDays()
  TodayDayNumber = ElapsedDays - FirstDayValue
  'if last value is today show it in text box
  If (DayNumber[NumberWeights] = TodayDayNumber) Then
    Controls.SetTextBoxText(WeightTextBox, Weight[NumberWeights])
  EndIf
  PlotWeightValues()
  Controls.ButtonClicked = ButtonClickedSub
  GraphicsWindow.KeyDown = KeyDownSub
EndSub

Sub OpenWeightFile
  NumberWeights = 0
  ReadWeight:
  FileLine = File.ReadLine(Program.Directory + "\" + WeightFile,
NumberWeights + 1)
  If (FileLine <> "") Then
    NumberWeights = NumberWeights + 1
    'find month/shorten FileLine
    CL = Text.GetIndexOf(FileLine, ",")
    WeightMonth[NumberWeights] = Text.GetSubText(FileLine, 1, CL -
1)
    FileLine = Text.GetSubTextToEnd(FileLine, CL + 1)
    'find day/shorten FileLine
    CL = Text.GetIndexOf(FileLine, ",")
    WeightDay[NumberWeights] = Text.GetSubText(FileLine, 1, CL -
1)
    FileLine = Text.GetSubTextToEnd(FileLine, CL + 1)
    'find year/shorten FileLine
    CL = Text.GetIndexOf(FileLine, ",")
    WeightYear[NumberWeights] = Text.GetSubText(FileLine, 1, CL -
1)
    'find weight (what's left)
    Weight[NumberWeights] = Text.GetSubTextToEnd(FileLine, CL + 1)
    'establish day number
    MM = WeightMonth[NumberWeights]
    DD = WeightDay[NumberWeights]
```

```
    YY = WeightYear[NumberWeights]
    ComputeElapsedDays()
    If (NumberWeights = 1) Then
      FirstDayValue = ElapsedDays
      DayNumber[1] = 0
    Else
      DayNumber[NumberWeights] = ElapsedDays - FirstDayValue
    EndIf
    Goto ReadWeight
  EndIf
EndSub

Sub PlotWeightValues
  If (NumberWeights < 2) Then
    Goto ExitPlotWeightValues
  EndIf
  'clear weight panel
  GraphicsWindow.BrushColor = GraphicsWindow.GetColorFromRGB(255,
192, 192)
  GraphicsWindow.FillRectangle(0, 50, 550, 380)
  GraphicsWindow.BrushColor = "White"
  PlotLeft = 60
  PlotTop = 90
  PlotWidth = 450
  PlotHeight = 300
  GraphicsWindow.FillRectangle(PlotLeft, PlotTop, PlotWidth,
PlotHeight)
  GraphicsWindow.PenColor = "Black"
  GraphicsWindow.PenWidth = 2
  GraphicsWindow.DrawRectangle(PlotLeft, PlotTop, PlotWidth,
PlotHeight)
  Wmin = 1000.0
  Wmax = 0.0
  SumD = 0.0
  SumD2 = 0.0
  SumW = 0.0
  SumDW = 0.0
  For I = 1 To NumberWeights
    Wmin = Math.Min(Weight[I], Wmin)
    Wmax = Math.Max(Weight[I], Wmax)
    'values for trend line
    SumD = SumD + DayNumber[I]
    SumD2 = SumD2 + DayNumber[I] * DayNumber[I]
    SumW = SumW + Weight[I]
    SumDW = SumDW + DayNumber[I] * Weight[I]
  EndFor
```

```
'adjust Wmin/Wmax for 'nice' intervals
If (Wmin = Wmax) Then
  Wmin = Wmax - 1
EndIf
Wmax = Math.Ceiling(Wmax + 0.5) 'round up
Wmin = Math.Floor(Wmin - 0.5) 'round down
If (Wmax - Wmin) <= 5.0 Then
  GridSpacing = 1.0
ElseIf (Wmax - Wmin <= 10.0) Then
  GridSpacing = 2.0
ElseIf (Wmax - Wmin <= 25.0) Then
  GridSpacing = 5.0
ElseIf (Wmax - Wmin <= 50.0) Then
  GridSpacing = 10.0
Else
  GridSpacing = 20.0
EndIf
If (Math.Remainder(Wmax, GridSpacing) <> 0) Then
  Wmax = GridSpacing * Math.Floor(Wmax / GridSpacing) +
GridSpacing
EndIf
If (Math.Remainder(Wmin, GridSpacing) <> 0) Then
  Wmin = GridSpacing * Math.Floor(Wmin / GridSpacing)
EndIf
Intervals = Math.Floor((Wmax - Wmin) / GridSpacing)
GraphicsWindow.PenColor = "Blue"
GraphicsWindow.PenWidth = 2
XPrevious = PlotLeft
YPrevious = PlotTop + (Wmax - Weight[1]) * (PlotHeight - 1) /
(Wmax - Wmin)
For I = 2 To NumberWeights
  'connect current point to previous point
  XCurrent = PlotLeft + DayNumber[I] * (PlotWidth - 1) /
DayNumber[NumberWeights]
  YCurrent = PlotTop + (Wmax - Weight[I]) * (PlotHeight - 1) /
(Wmax - Wmin)
  GraphicsWindow.DrawLine(XPrevious, YPrevious, XCurrent,
YCurrent)
  XPrevious = XCurrent
  YPrevious = YCurrent
EndFor
GraphicsWindow.PenColor = "Black"
GraphicsWindow.PenWidth = 1
WLegend = Wmin
GraphicsWindow.BrushColor = "Black"
GraphicsWindow.FontSize = 16
```

```
  GraphicsWindow.FontBold = "false"
  For I = 0 To Intervals
    YLegend = PlotTop + Math.Floor((Wmax - WLegend) * (PlotHeight
- 1) / (Wmax - Wmin))
    'add label
    GraphicsWindow.DrawText(PlotLeft - 35, YLegend - 10, WLegend)
    'draw grid line (except at top and bottom)
    If (I > 0 And I < Intervals) Then
      GraphicsWindow.DrawLine(PlotLeft, YLegend, PlotLeft +
PlotWidth, YLegend)
    EndIf
    WLegend = WLegend + GridSpacing
  EndFor
  'add x legends
  GraphicsWindow.DrawText(PlotLeft - 20, PlotTop + PlotHeight +10,
"Start: " + MonthName[WeightMonth[1]] + " " + WeightDay[1] + ", "+
WeightYear[1])
  GraphicsWindow.DrawText(PlotLeft + 335, PlotTop + PlotHeight +
10, "End: " + MonthName[WeightMonth[NumberWeights]] + " " +
WeightDay[NumberWeights] + ", "+ WeightYear[NumberWeights])
  'trend computations
  T = (NumberWeights * SumDW - SumD * SumW) / (NumberWeights *
SumD2 - SumD * SumD)
  W0 = (SumD2 * SumW - SumD * SumDW) / (NumberWeights * SumD2 -
SumD * SumD)
  'draw line
  Y1 = PlotTop + Math.Floor((Wmax - W0) * (PlotHeight - 1) / (Wmax
- Wmin))
  Y2 = PlotTop + Math.Floor((Wmax - (T * DayNumber[NumberWeights]
+ W0)) * (PlotHeight - 1) / (Wmax - Wmin))
  GraphicsWindow.PenColor = "Red"
  GraphicsWindow.PenWidth = 1
  GraphicsWindow.DrawLine(PlotLeft, Y1, PlotLeft + PlotWidth , Y2)
  'draw trend title
  GraphicsWindow.BrushColor = "Black"
  GraphicsWindow.FontSize = 18
  S = "Trend: "
  If (T > 0) Then
    S = S + "+"
  EndIf
  S = S + Math.Floor(7 * 100 * T) / 100 + " lb/week"
  GraphicsWindow.DrawText(200, 60, S)
ExitPlotWeightValues:
EndSub

Sub ComputeElapsedDays
```

```
'number of days in each month
MonthDays[1] = 31
MonthDays[2] = 28
MonthDays[3] = 31
MonthDays[4] = 30
MonthDays[5] = 31
MonthDays[6] = 30
MonthDays[7] = 31
MonthDays[8] = 31
MonthDays[9] = 30
MonthDays[10] = 31
MonthDays[11] = 30
MonthDays[12] = 31
'January 1, 2010 is Day 1
ElapsedDays = 0
BaseYear = 2010
'Difference in years
DeltaY = YY - BaseYear
If (DeltaY > 0) Then
  'move to January 1 of current year
  For J = BaseYear To YY - 1
    'leap year?      'Leap year?
    If (Math.Remainder(J, 4) = 0) Then
      ElapsedDays = ElapsedDays + 366
    Else
      ElapsedDays = ElapsedDays + 365
    EndIf
  EndFor
EndIf
'Difference in months
DeltaM = MM - 1
If (DeltaM > 0) Then
  'move to current month
  For J = 1 To MM - 1
    'if february, leap year?
    If (J = 2) Then
      If (Math.Remainder(YY, 4) = 0) Then
        ElapsedDays = ElapsedDays + 29
      Else
        ElapsedDays = ElapsedDays + 28
      EndIf
    Else
      ElapsedDays = ElapsedDays + MonthDays[J]
    EndIf
  EndFor
EndIf
```

```
  'difference in days
  ElapsedDays = ElapsedDays + DD - 1
EndSub

Sub ButtonClickedSub
  B = Controls.LastClickedButton
  If (B = AddWeightButton) Then
    AddWeightButtonClicked()
  ElseIf (B = ExitButton) Then
    'write out file and stop program
    For I = 1 To NumberWeights
      FileLine = WeightMonth[I] + "," + WeightDay[I] + "," +
WeightYear[I] + "," + Weight[I]
      File.WriteLine(Program.Directory + "\" + WeightFile, I,
FileLine)
    EndFor
    Program.End()
  EndIf
EndSub

Sub AddWeightButtonClicked
  'is weight valid?
  NumberToCheck = Controls.GetTextBoxText(WeightTextBox)
  ValidateNumber()
  If (NumberIsValid) Then
    'are adding or replacing today's weight?
    If (DayNumber[NumberWeights] <> TodayDayNumber) Then
      'adding value
      NumberWeights = NumberWeights + 1
      WeightMonth[NumberWeights] = Clock.Month
      WeightDay[NumberWeights] = Clock.Day
      WeightYear[NumberWeights] = Clock.Year
      DayNumber[NumberWeights] = TodayDayNumber
    EndIf
    Weight[NumberWeights] = Controls.GetTextBoxText(WeightTextBox)
    PlotWeightValues()
  Else
    GraphicsWindow.ShowMessage("Entered weight is invalid format
or blank.  Please correct.", "Invalid Entry")
  EndIf
EndSub

Sub ValidateNumber
  'sees if NumberToCheck has only digits and a single decimal and
is not blank
  NumberIsValid = "true"
```

```
  If (NumberToCheck = "") Then
    NumberIsValid = "false"
    Goto ExitValidateNumber
  EndIf
  DecimalCount = 0
  For I = 1 To Text.GetLength(NumberToCheck)
    CC = Text.GetCharacterCode(Text.GetSubText(NumberToCheck, I,
1))
    If (CC = Text.GetCharacterCode(".")) Then
      DecimalCount = DecimalCount + 1
      If (DecimalCount > 1) Then
        NumberIsValid = "false"
        Goto ExitValidateNumber
      EndIf
    ElseIf (CC < Text.GetCharacterCode("0") Or CC >
Text.GetCharacterCode("9")) Then
      NumberIsValid = "false"
      Goto ExitValidateNumber
    EndIf
  EndFor
ExitValidateNumber:
EndSub

Sub KeyDownSub
  If (GraphicsWindow.LastKey = "Return") Then
    AddWeightButtonClicked()
  EndIf
EndSub
```

Weight Monitor Project Review

The **Weight Monitor Project** is now complete. **Save** and **Run** the project and make sure it works as designed. Use the program to track your weight each day (or let your family try it). Hopefully the program can become an integral part of an overall health program.

If there are errors in your implementation, go back over the steps of window and code design. Use the debugger when needed. Go over the developed code – make sure you understand how different parts of the project were coded. As mentioned in the beginning of this chapter, the completed project is saved as **Weight** in the **HomeSB\HomeSB Projects\Weight** folder.

While completing this project, new concepts and skills you should have gained include:

- Input/output of variables with sequential files.
- Doing unit conversions need for plotting.
- Making "nice" intervals for plots.

Weight Monitor Project Enhancements

Possible enhancements to the weight monitor project include:

- Add the possibility of editing previously entered values or entering values for missed days.
- For large weight changes, the computed trend line may extend outside the borders of the plot rectangle. Can you write code that keeps this from happening?
- Many times, you are trying to achieve a certain weight goal. Modify the program to allow a user to enter a desired goal and a desired goal date. Provide computations that show how well the user to doing in trying the reach this goal. Draw a "goal" line on the weight plot.
- As implemented, weights need to be in pounds. Most of the world uses kilograms for weight. Add the capability to choose either unit for weight. You'll have to decide if you want to change any current values to the new units or just keep file in one particular set of units.
- Add the ability to pick a weight file to edit (rather than having the file name "hard-coded"). This would allow several users to use the same program. We had such ability in the multiple choice exam project earlier in these notes. Look over that code for help.

This page intentionally not left blank.

10. Home Inventory Manager Project

Review and Preview

The **Home Inventory Manager Project** helps you keep track of your valuable belongings. For every item in your inventory, the program stores a description, location, serial number, purchase information, and even a photo!

Home Inventory Manager Project Preview

In this chapter, we will build a **home inventory manager** program. This program lets you keep a record of your belongings.

The finished project is saved as **Inventory** in the **HomeSB\HomeSB Projects\Inventory** folder. Start Small Basic and open the finished project. Run the project (click **Run** in the toolbar or press <**F5**>). The program has a built-in sample inventory file – the first item in that file will display (items are listed alphabetically by **Description**):

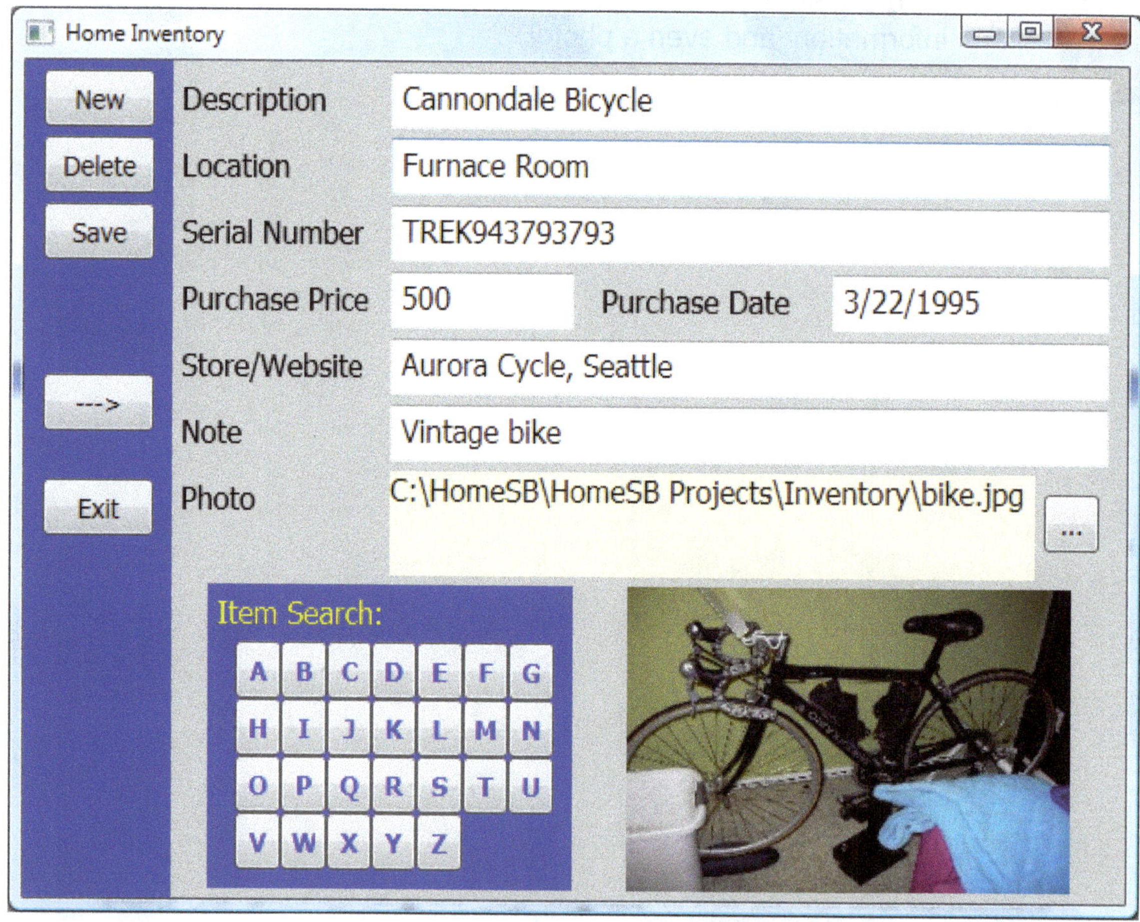

You will, of course, be able to replace the built-in file with your own belongings, but for now, let's see how the program works.

The idea of the program is to enter and/or view descriptive information about each item in your inventory. You can enter:

Description	A description of the item (required)
Location	Description of where item is located
Serial Number	Item serial number
Purchase Price	How much you paid for the item.
Purchase Date	When you purchased the item.
Store/Website	Where you purchased the item.
Note	Any additional information about the item.
Photo	View a stored JPEG photo of the item.

On the left are two buttons marked **<---** (**Previous Item**) and **--->** (**Next Item**). Use these to move from one item to the next. The sample file has 10 items to view. In the **Item Search** group box are 26 buttons, each with a letter of the alphabet. These are used to search through the inventory for items beginning with the clicked letter. Try searching the sample inventory, if you'd like.

A primary task of the home inventory manager is to add, edit, save and delete inventory items. To add an item, you click the **Add** button. You then enter the necessary information and click the **Save** button. To edit an existing item, you first display the item to edit. Make the desired changes and click **Save**. To delete an item, you display the item, then click the **Delete** button. Let's try the editing features.

Navigate to one of the existing items in the sample file (use the **Previous** or **Next** arrow buttons or try a search). I moved to Toby, my ever faithful dog:

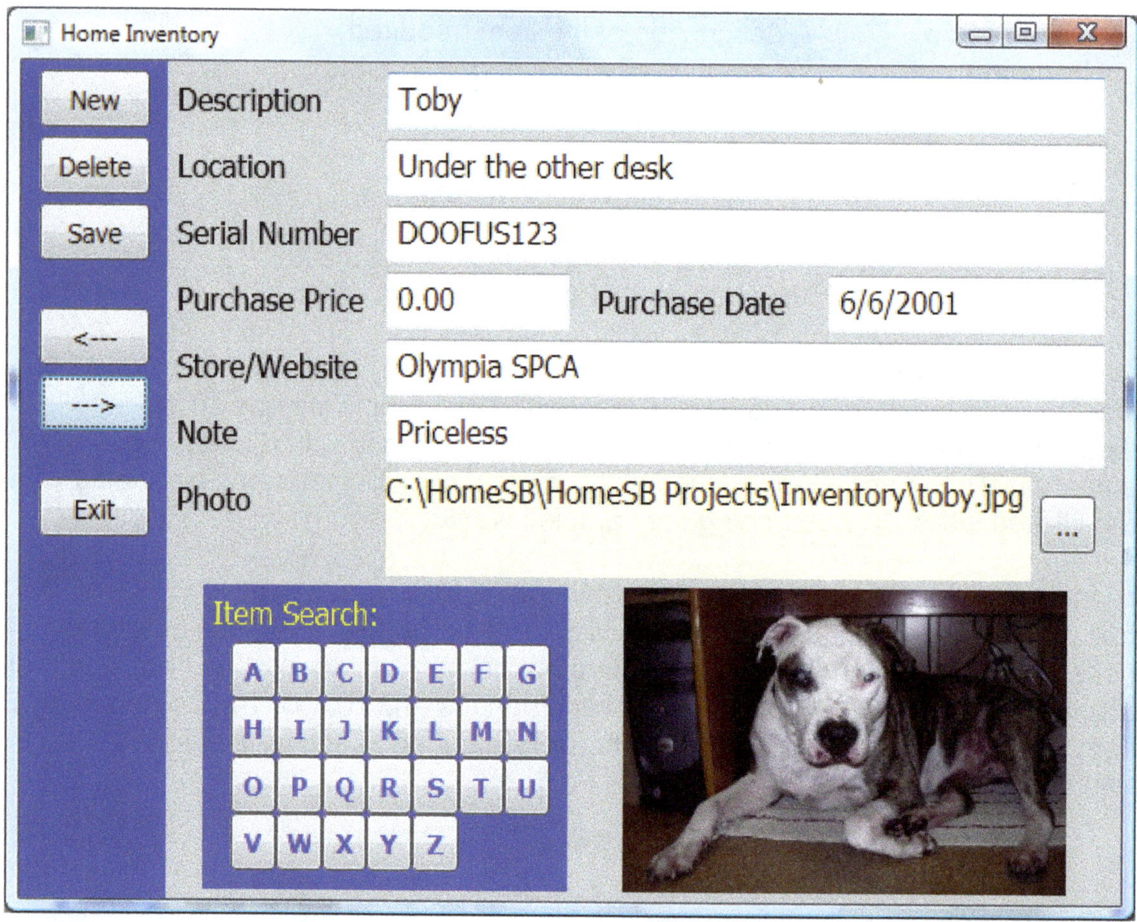

We'll delete this item, then rebuild it to demonstrate how to enter information. Click the **Delete** button. The display will show the next item in the inventory. Click the **New** button to start a new item.

The blank inventory screen appears as:

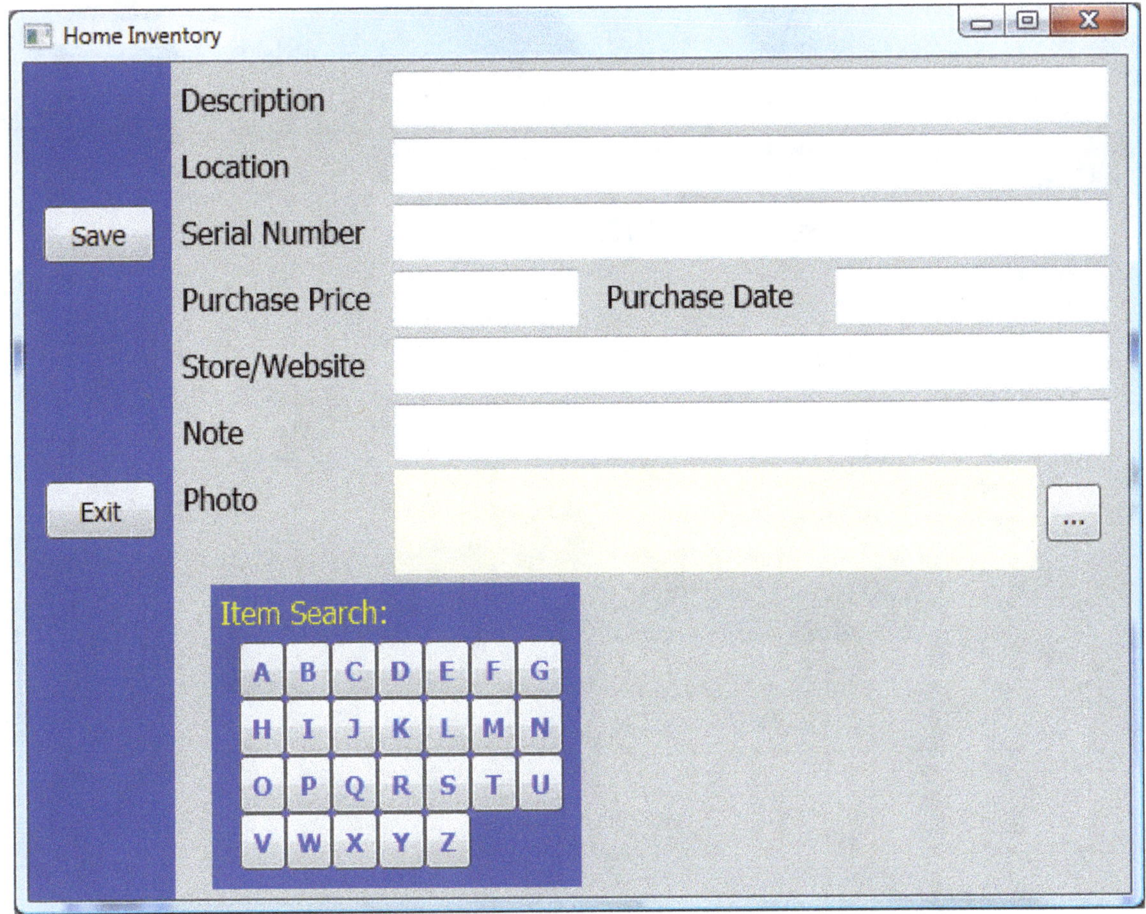

At this point, you simply work your way down the form entering the desired information at the desired locations. When done, you click **Save** and the item is added to your inventory. We'll add Toby back to the file.

Under **Description**, type **Toby**. This is the only required piece of information – all other entries are optional. For **Location**, type **Under the other desk** for Toby (he's always there). Make up a **Serial Number** for Toby – I used **DOOFUS123**. We got Toby for free, so his **Purchase Price** is **0.00**. We got Toby on **June 6, 2001**. Under **Purchase Date**, enter **6/6/2001**. Under **Store/Website**, type **Olympia SPCA** (he's a pound puppy) and under **Note**, type **Priceless**.

At this point, the form should look like this:

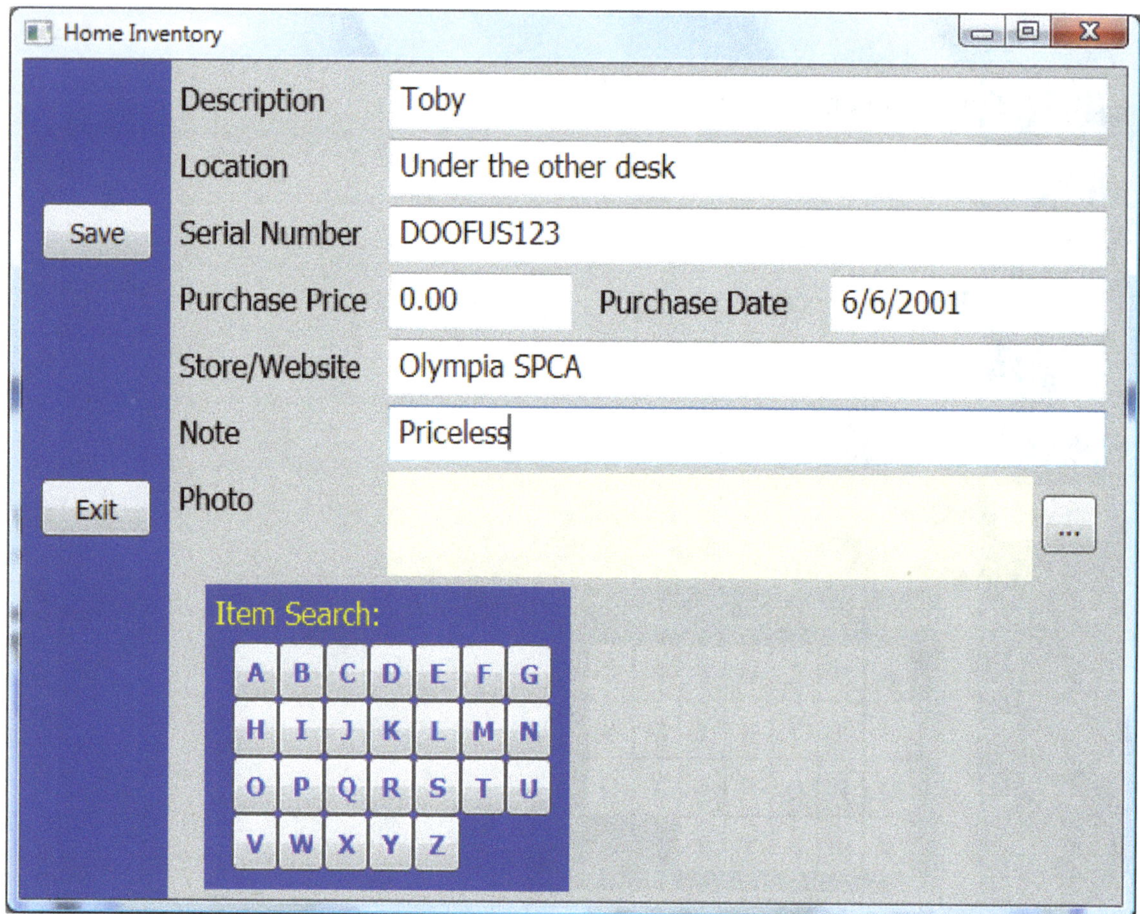

The last step is adding a photo.

Click the button with the ellipsis (**...**) next to the **Photo** label area. A text window will appear:

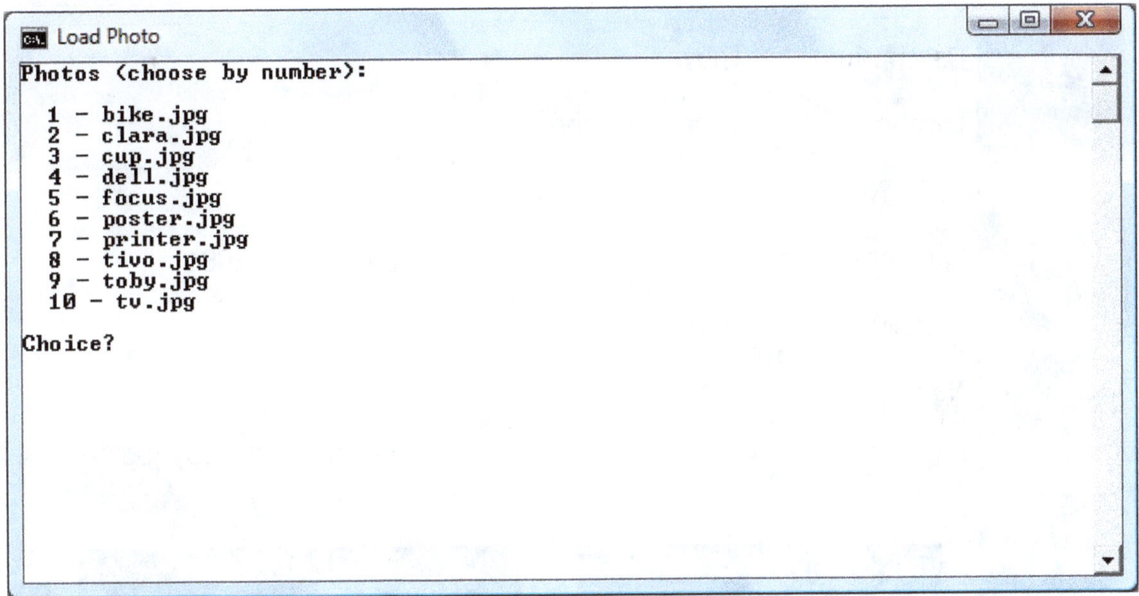
Load Photo
Photos (choose by number):
1 - bike.jpg
2 - clara.jpg
3 - cup.jpg
4 - dell.jpg
5 - focus.jpg
6 - poster.jpg
7 - printer.jpg
8 - tivo.jpg
9 - toby.jpg
10 - tv.jpg
Choice?

The photo can be any JPEG file (what a digital camera uses). The photos are stored in your program folder. This window shows the photo files it found in the program folder. Make your selection – in this case type 9 (**toby.jpg**) and press <**Enter**>. The photo will appear.

The final **Toby** inventory item page looks like this:

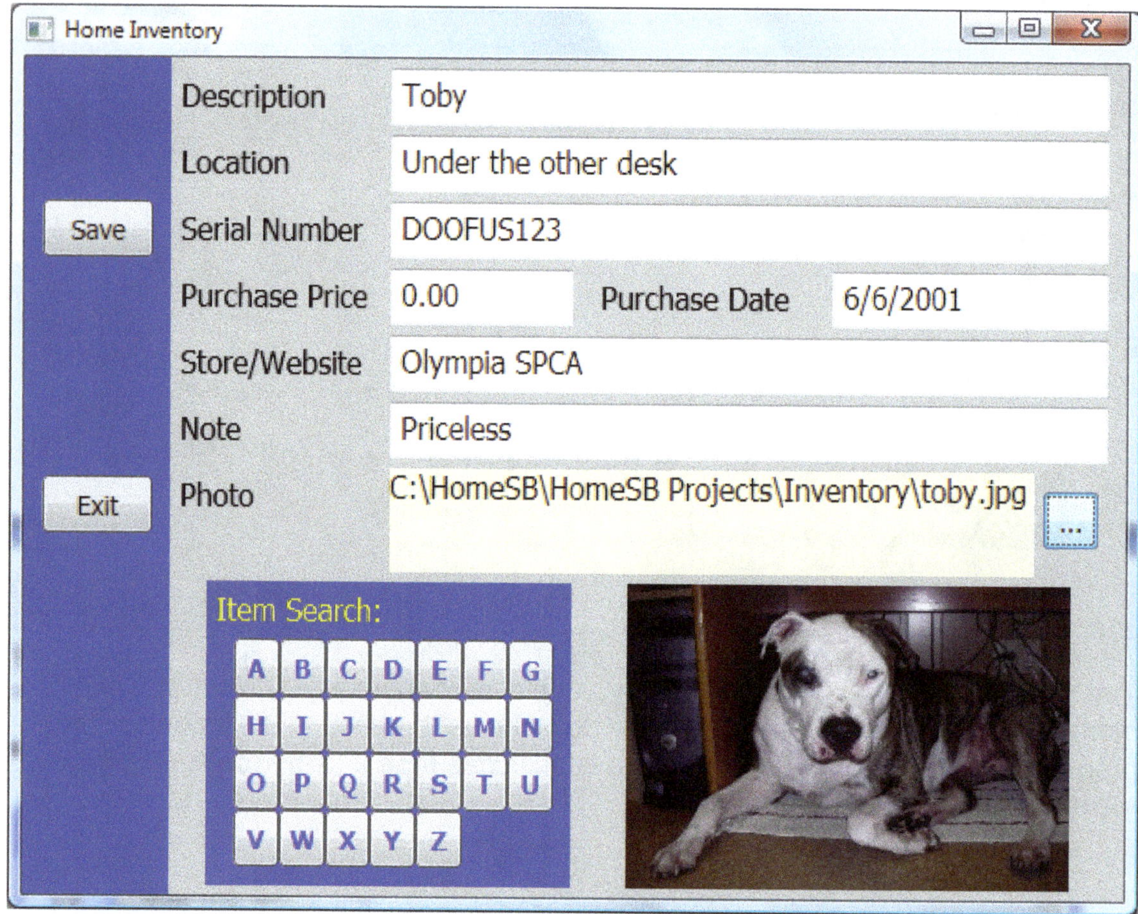

Notice the photo and the file name listed under **Photo**. At this point, click **Save** and Toby is back in the list (properly sorted alphabetically).

That's the idea of the program. Fill in an entry page for each item in your inventory and click **Save**. Click **Exit** when done. Upon exiting the program, all your inventory items are saved to a file (the built-in file currently holding the sample entries). This same file is automatically opened when you rerun the program, so your items are always available for additions, changes and deletions.

We will now build this program in several stages. We discuss **window design**. We discuss the controls used to build the window and establish initial properties. And, we address **code design** in detail. We discuss how to read and write the inventory file, how to perform the various editing features, how to load a photo file, and how to perform the search function.

Home Inventory Manager Window Design

Here is the sketch for the window layout of the **Home Inventory Manager** program:

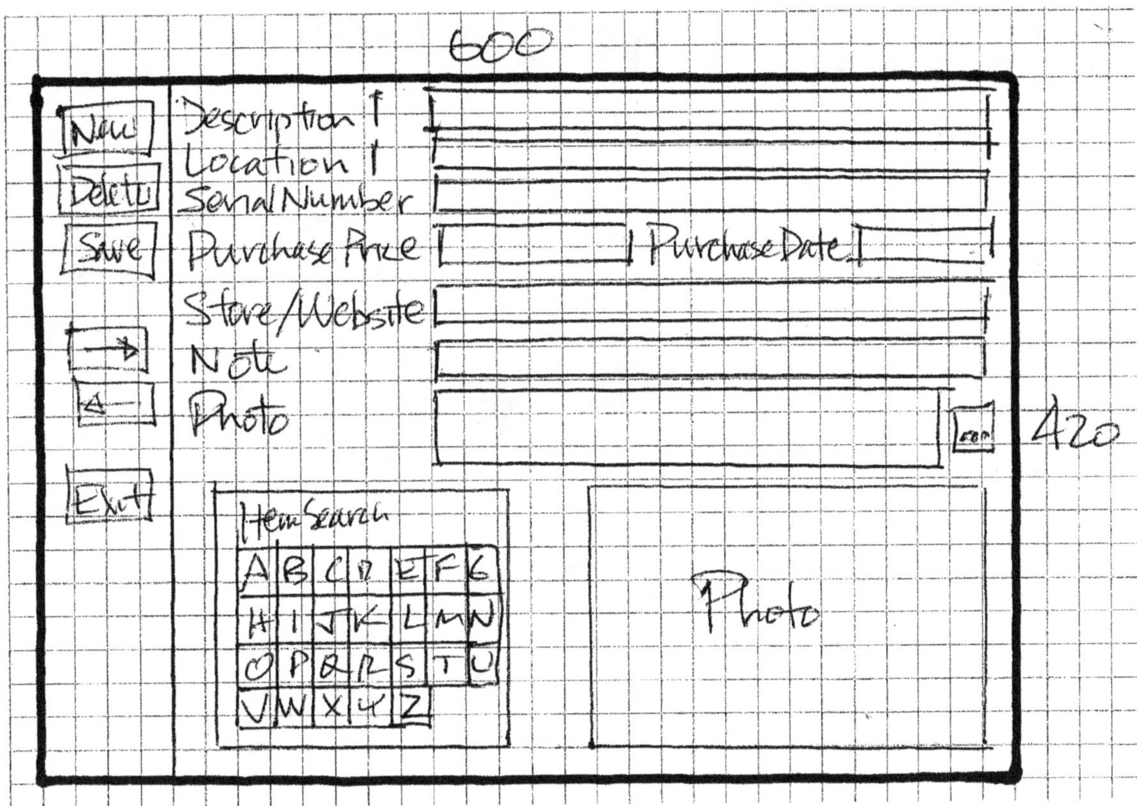

Buttons on the left are used to add, delete and save items from the inventory. There are also buttons to navigate from one item to the next. Information about an inventory item is entered with several text box controls. A button control (with an ellipsis) selects a photo to display. A rectangle holds buttons for searching.

We will begin writing code. As always, the code will be written in steps. We'll begin by writing code draws the user interface with the information display and button controls.

Start a new program in Small Basic. Once started, we suggest you immediately save the program with a name you choose. This sets up the folder and file structure needed for your program.

Window Design – Inventory Items

We begin by drawing the graphics window with the labeling and text boxes used to input and display the information about each inventory item (except the photo). Add this code to your program to initialize the window and display the **Description**, **Location, Serial Number**, **Purchase Price**, **Purchase Date, Store/Website**, and **Note**:

```
' Home Inventory
InitializeProgram()

Sub InitializeProgram
  'graphics window
  GraphicsWindow.Width = 600
  GraphicsWindow.Height = 440
  GraphicsWindow.Title = "Home Inventory"
  GraphicsWindow.BackgroundColor = "LightGray"
  'labels/textboxes
  GraphicsWindow.BrushColor = "Black"
  GraphicsWindow.FontSize = 16
  GraphicsWindow.FontBold = "false"
  GraphicsWindow.DrawText(85, 10, "Description")
  GraphicsWindow.DrawText(85, 45, "Location")
  GraphicsWindow.DrawText(85, 80, "Serial Number")
  GraphicsWindow.DrawText(85, 115, "Purchase Price")
  GraphicsWindow.DrawText(315, 115, "Purchase Date")
  GraphicsWindow.DrawText(85, 150, "Store/Website")
  GraphicsWindow.DrawText(85, 185, "Note")
  InventoryTextBox[1] = Controls.AddTextBox(200, 5)
  InventoryTextBox[2] = Controls.AddTextBox(200, 40)
  InventoryTextBox[3] = Controls.AddTextBox(200, 75)
  InventoryTextBox[4] = Controls.AddTextBox(200, 110)
  InventoryTextBox[5] = Controls.AddTextBox(440, 110)
  InventoryTextBox[6] = Controls.AddTextBox(200, 145)
  InventoryTextBox[7] = Controls.AddTextBox(200, 180)
  Controls.SetSize(InventoryTextBox[1], 390, 30)
  Controls.SetSize(InventoryTextBox[2], 390, 30)
  Controls.SetSize(InventoryTextBox[3], 390, 30)
  Controls.SetSize(InventoryTextBox[4], 100, 30)
  Controls.SetSize(InventoryTextBox[5], 150, 30)
  Controls.SetSize(InventoryTextBox[6], 390, 30)
  Controls.SetSize(InventoryTextBox[7], 390, 30)
EndSub
```

The first line of code calls a subroutine **InitializeProgram** where we will put all code needed to set up the program for use. All remaining code here goes in that subroutine.The array **InventoryTextBox** is used for the seven pieces of information.

Save and **Run** the program. You will see the nicely arranged text boxes and associated labeling:

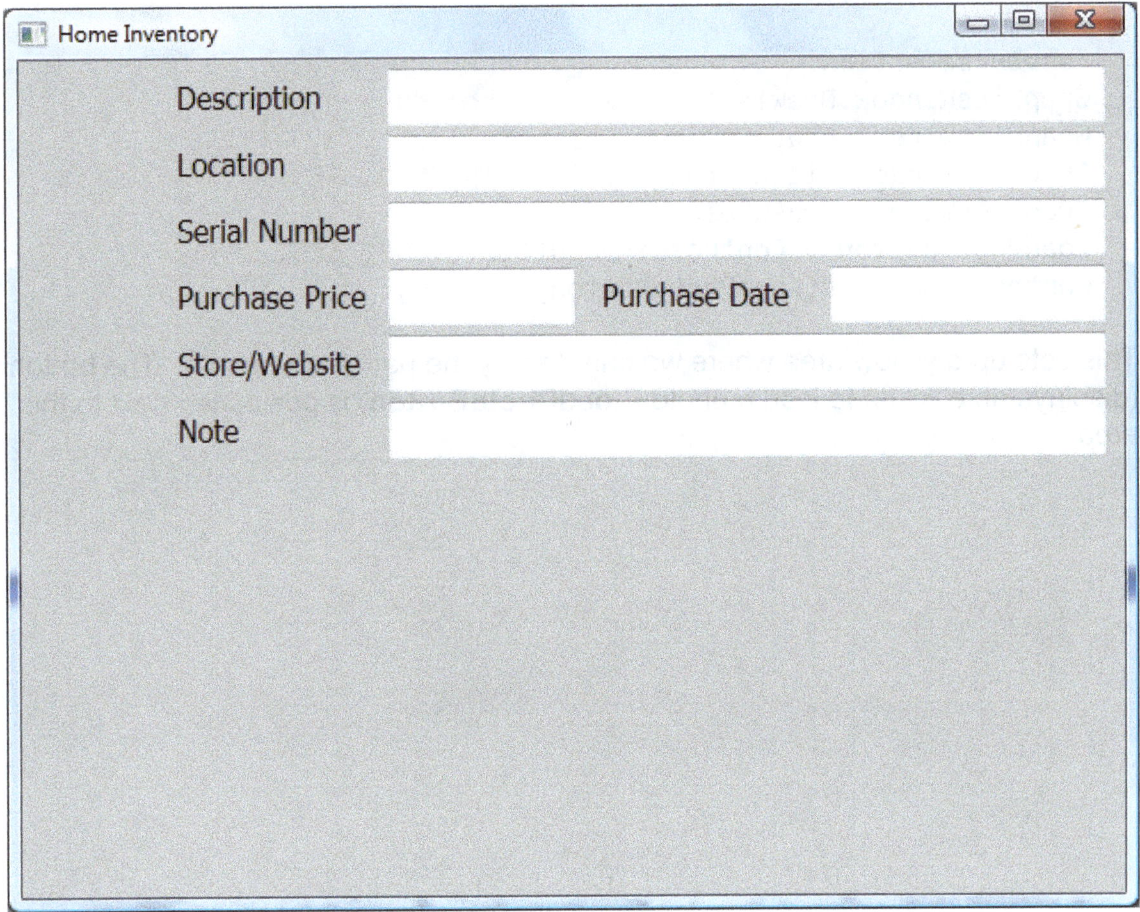

Window Design – Photo Selection

The photo selection process does not involve typing in information. When the **LoadPhoto** button is clicked, the available photos will be listed. The user makes a selection. The path of the photo is displayed along with the photo in the lower part of the graphics window. Let's build that interface.

Add this code to **InitializeProgram**:

```
'photo selection
GraphicsWindow.DrawText(85, 220, "Photo")
GraphicsWindow.BrushColor = "LightYellow"
GraphicsWindow.FillRectangle(200, 215, 350, 55)
GraphicsWindow.BrushColor = "Black"
LoadPhotoButton = Controls.AddButton("...", 555, 225)
Controls.SetSize(LoadPhotoButton, 30, 30)
```

This sets up a yellow area where we can display the path to the photo. The button (displays an ellipsis) to load a photo (**LoadPhotoButton**) is positioned next to this area.

Save and **Run** the program to see the additions:

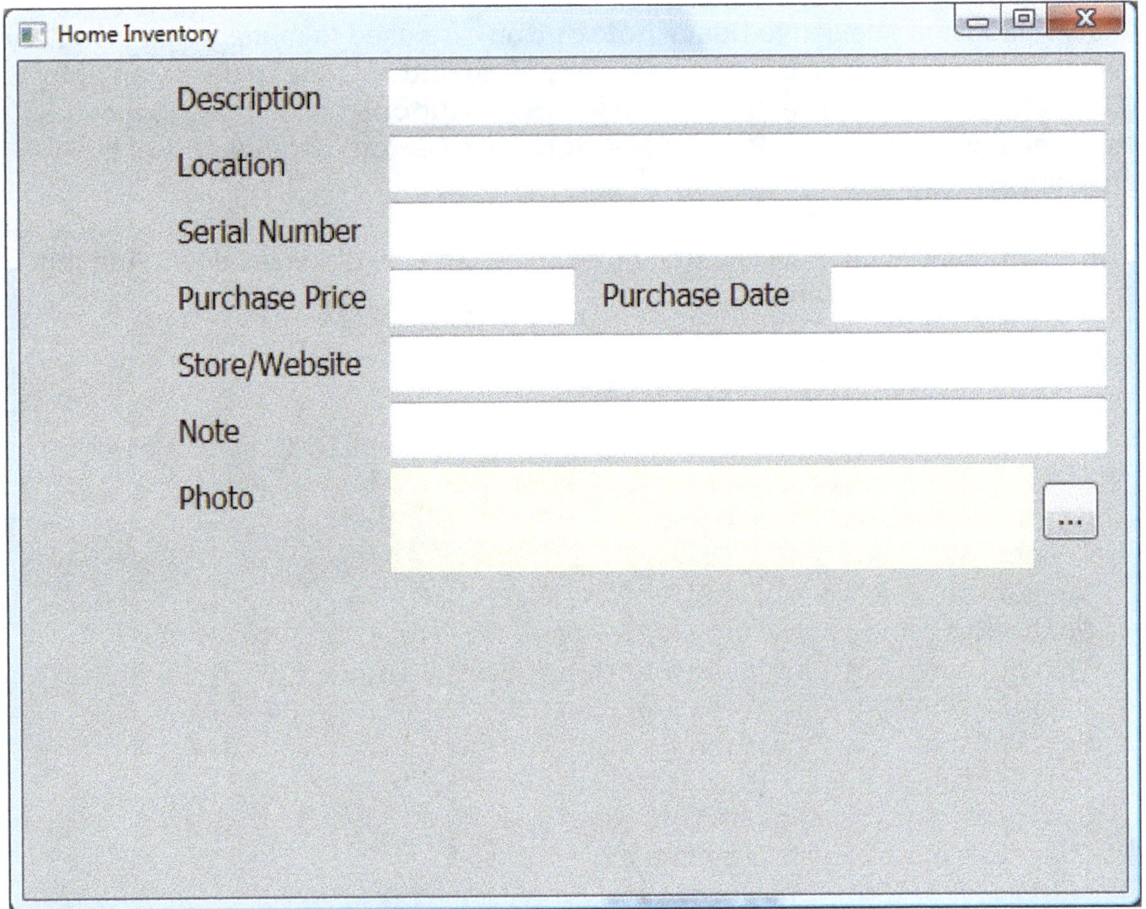

The photo will be displayed in the lower right corner of this window. We will write code to do that soon.

Window Design – Adding Buttons

Many buttons (in addition to **LoadPhotoButton**) are used to manage the inventory items. There is a button to add a new entry (**AddButton**), one to delete an entry (**DeleteButton**), one to save any changes (**SaveButton**), two buttons to move from one entry to the next (**PreviousButton**, **NextButton**) and one to exit the program (**ExitButton**).

Each button is placed in a blue rectangle on the left side of the window. Add this code to **InitializeProgram**:

```
'Buttons
GraphicsWindow.BrushColor = "Blue"
GraphicsWindow.FillRectangle(0, 0, 80, GraphicsWindow.Height)
GraphicsWindow.BrushColor = "Black"
GraphicsWindow.FontSize = 14
GraphicsWindow.FontBold = "false"
NewButton = Controls.AddButton("New", 10, 5)
DeleteButton = Controls.AddButton("Delete", 10, 40)
SaveButton = Controls.AddButton("Save", 10, 75)
PreviousButton = Controls.AddButton("<---", 10, 130)
NextButton = Controls.AddButton("--->", 10, 165)
ExitButton = Controls.AddButton("Exit", 10, 220)
Controls.SetSize(NewButton, 60, 30)
Controls.SetSize(DeleteButton, 60, 30)
Controls.SetSize(SaveButton, 60, 30)
Controls.SetSize(PreviousButton, 60, 30)
Controls.SetSize(NextButton, 60, 30)
Controls.SetSize(ExitButton, 60, 30)
```

Each button is made the same size to make things look nice.

Save and **Run** the program. The buttons will appear:

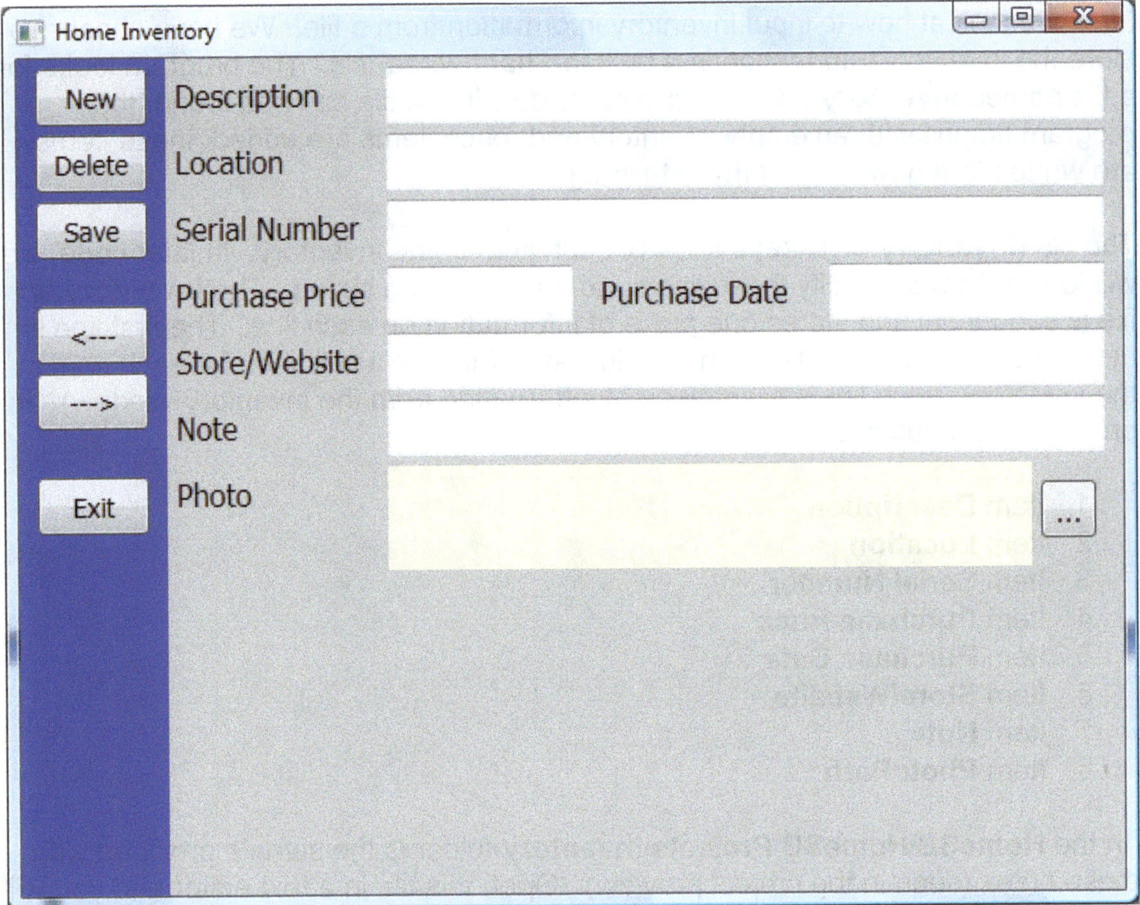

The only thing remaining in the interface are the search buttons. These will be added later when we discuss the code behind searching the inventory. We now start to write code to manage the inventory items.

Code Design – Inventory File Input

First, we look at how to input inventory information from a file. We have chosen to store the inventory information in a built-in, "hard-wired" file. The program looks for a file named **inventory.txt** in the project folder. If the file can't be found, the program begins with an empty inventory and, once items are added, these items are written to a new copy of **inventory.txt**.

The file (**inventory.txt**) keeps track of each item in the inventory. In later code, we will look at how to modify these items, so new ones are saved. The **inventory.txt** file is sequential and stores one piece of information on each line. The first line is the number of inventory items in the file. After this line are 8 lines for each item in the inventory (each line saving piece of information from the inventory window). In order, those items are:

1. Item **Description**
2. Item **Location**
3. Item **Serial Number**
4. Item **Purchase Price**
5. Item **Purchase Date**
6. Item **Store/Website**
7. Item **Note**
8. Item **PhotoPath**

In the **HomeSB\HomeSB Projects\Inventory** folder is the sample provided with these notes (seen in the project preview). Open this file in a text editor and you will see:

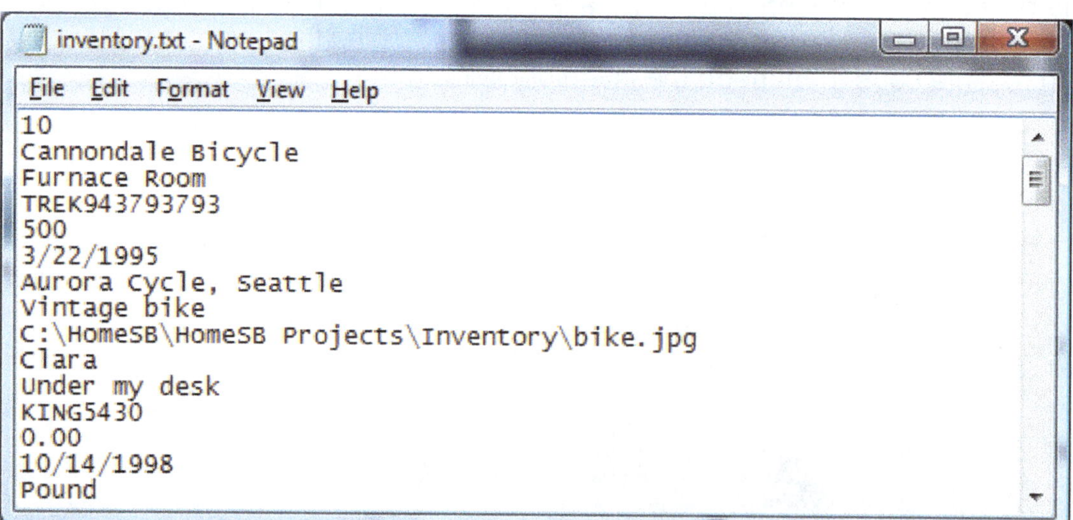

You see this file has 10 entries and there will be 8 lines per entry. You can see the first entry (**Cannondale Bicycle**) and the beginning of the second (**Clara**).

When the home inventory manager project begins, the program reads in the **inventory.txt** file to obtain inventory item information. The information will be stored in a two-dimensional array **InventoryItem**. For item **I,** the elements of the array are:

InventoryItem[I][1] - Item **Description**
InventoryItem[I][2] - Item **Location**
InventoryItem[I][3] - Item **Serial Number**
InventoryItem[I][4] - Item **Purchase Price**
InventoryItem[I][5] - Item **Purchase Date**
InventoryItem[I][6] - Item **Store/Website**
InventoryItem[I][7] - Item **Note**
InventoryItem[I][8] - Item **PhotoPath**

The array just fills the file elements in order. To fill this array, we first read the number of entries (**NumberEntries**) from **inventory.txt**. Then, for each entry in the file, read in the next eight lines (**NumberItems = 8**) and store the values in the corresponding array elements..

The code to read in the inventory file is placed in a subroutine **OpenInventoryFile**:

```
Sub OpenInventoryFile
  'read in inventory file
  NumberItems = 8
  NumberEntries = File.ReadLine(Program.Directory +
"\inventory.txt", 1)
  If (NumberEntries > 0) Then
    For I = 1 To NumberEntries
      For J = 1 to NumberItems
        InventoryItem[I][J] = File.ReadLine(Program.Directory +
"\inventory.txt", NumberItems * (I - 1) + J + 1)
      EndFor
    EndFor
  Else
    Controls.HideControl(NewButton)
    Controls.HideControl(DeleteButton)
    Controls.HideControl(PreviousButton)
    Controls.HideControl(NextButton)
  EndIf
EndSub
```

Let's take a look at this code. If the file is successfully opened, we read **NumberEntries**, then read each subsequent entry, creating a new **InventoryItem** array element for each entry. If **NumberEntries** is zero, (meaning the file couldn't be opened or truly had zero elements), we set the button controls so only a new item can be entered. To open the file, add this single line at the end of **InitializeProgram**:

```
OpenInventoryFile()
```

Let's try this code. Copy the sample **inventory.txt** file into your project's folder. **Save** and **Run** the project. If the file opens and reads successfully, you should see a blank window with all control buttons enabled:

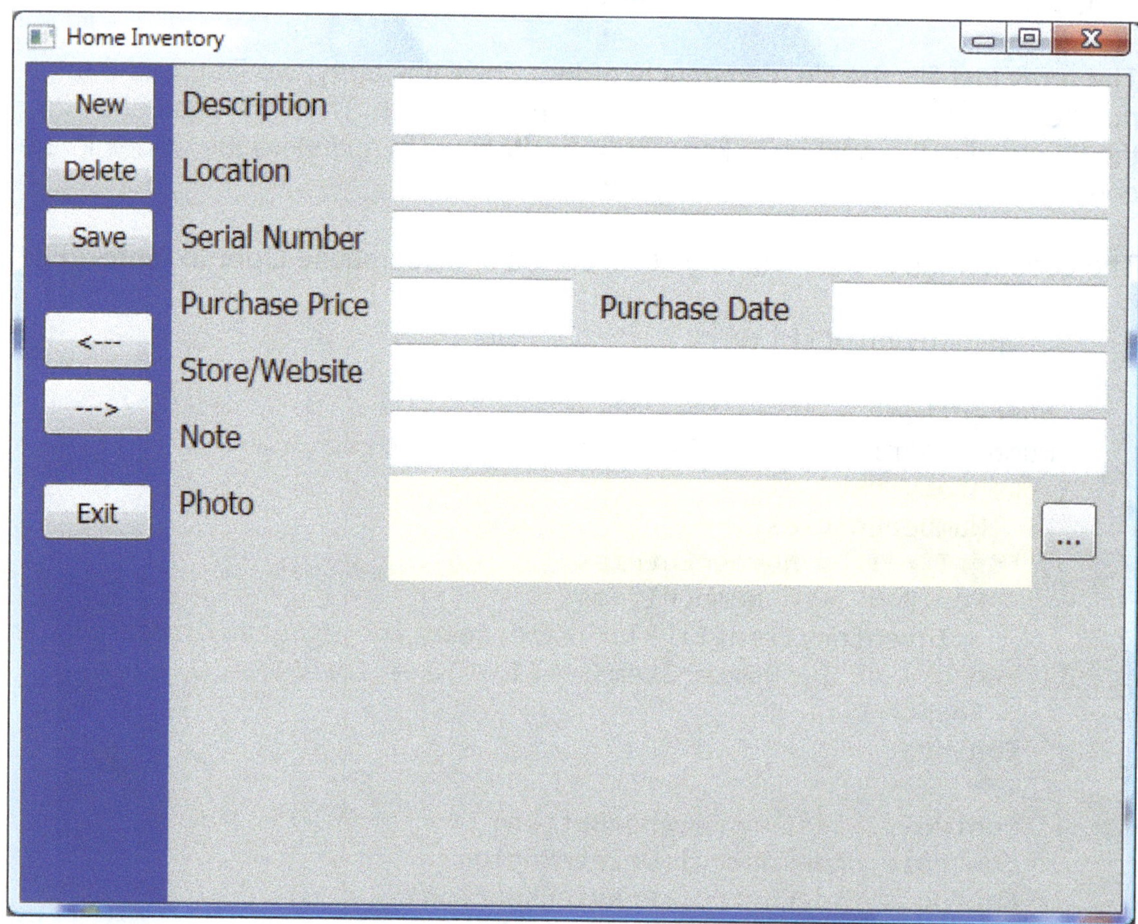

If only the **Save** button is enabled, there was an error in reading the file. If this occurs, make sure the file is in the correct folder and double-check the code.

Code Design – Viewing Inventory Item

We can now read in the input file, but it's not very satisfying not being able to see the results. We remedy that now by writing code to display an inventory item (including the photo). The code simply loads the appropriate elements of the **InventoryItem** array into corresponding text box controls (for all but the photo). For the photo, we display the path (**PhotoPath**) and the photo.

We will use a subroutine **ShowCurrentEntry** to display a single inventory item. **CurrentEntry** is the variable specifying the entry number to display:

```
Sub ShowCurrentEntry
  'display CurrentEntry
  For I =1 to NumberItems - 1
    Controls.SetTextBoxText(InventoryTextBox[I],
InventoryItem[CurrentEntry][I])
  EndFor
  PhotoPath = InventoryItem[CurrentEntry][NumberItems]
  ShowPhoto()
EndSub
```

This code simply transfers the elements of the **InventoryItem** array into the appropriate controls. To show a photo, we use **ShowPhoto**:

```
Sub ShowPhoto
  'clear previous path
  GraphicsWindow.BrushColor = "LightYellow"
  GraphicsWindow.FillRectangle(200, 215, 350, 55)
  'write path
  GraphicsWindow.BrushColor = "Black"
  GraphicsWindow.FontSize = 16
  GraphicsWindow.FontBold = "false"
  GraphicsWindow.DrawBoundText(200, 215, 350, PhotoPath)
  'clear any previous photo
  GraphicsWindow.BrushColor = GraphicsWindow.BackgroundColor
  GraphicsWindow.FillRectangle(330, 275, 240, 160)
  If (PhotoPath <> "") Then

GraphicsWindow.DrawResizedImage(ImageList.LoadImage(PhotoPath),
330, 275, 240, 160)
  EndIf
EndSub
```

Here, the **PhotoPath** is displayed in the yellow labeled area while the photo is loaded and displayed at the bottom of the window using the **DrawResizedImage** method. If **PhotoPath** is blank, no photo is displayed. The code assumes all photos are in your program folder. The photos used by the sample **inventory.txt** file are included in **HomeSB\HomeSB Projects\Inventory Photos**. Copy the photos from this folder to your program folder.

We need to modify the code we wrote to load the inventory file to establish a value for **CurrentEntry** and call the display routine. The changes to **OpenInventoryFile** are shaded:

```
Sub OpenInventoryFile
  'read in inventory file
  NumberItems = 8
  NumberEntries = File.ReadLine(Program.Directory +
"\inventory.txt", 1)
  If (NumberEntries > 0) Then
    For I = 1 To NumberEntries
      For J = 1 to NumberItems
        InventoryItem[I][J] = File.ReadLine(Program.Directory +
"\inventory.txt", NumberItems * (I - 1) + J + 1)
      EndFor
    EndFor
    CurrentEntry = 1
    ShowCurrentEntry()
  Else
    Controls.HideControl(NewButton)
    Controls.HideControl(DeleteButton)
    Controls.HideControl(PreviousButton)
    Controls.HideControl(NextButton)
    CurrentEntry = 0
  EndIf
EndSub
```

Make the noted changes.

Save and **Run** the project. You should now see the first item in the inventory displayed (including photo, assuming you properly copied the photos to your program folder):

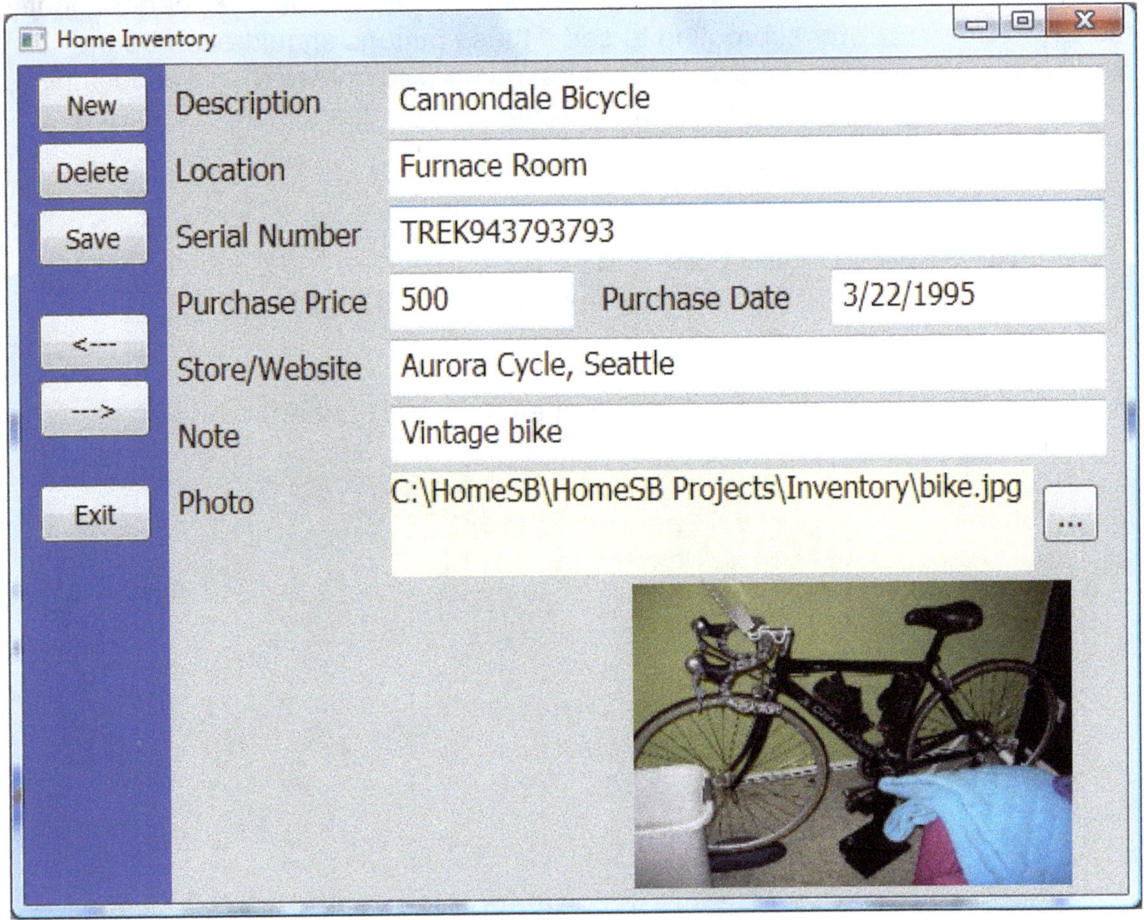

At this point, we would like to be able to move to the next item, or move backward. Let's write the code to do that.

Code Design – Navigation

Two button controls (**PreviousButton** and **NextButton**) are used to navigate from one item to the next. Before writing code behind these buttons, we need to modify the **ShowCurrentEntry** subroutine to see if these buttons should even been displayed. We hide/show these controls based on whether we're at the beginning, at the end or in the middle of the item list (changes are shaded):

```
Sub ShowCurrentEntry
  'display CurrentEntry
  For I =1 to NumberItems - 1
    Controls.SetTextBoxText(InventoryTextBox[I],
InventoryItem[CurrentEntry][I])
  EndFor
  PhotoPath = InventoryItem[CurrentEntry][NumberItems]
  ShowPhoto()
    'set status of previous/next buttons
  Controls.ShowControl(PreviousButton)
  Controls.ShowControl(NextButton)
  If (CurrentEntry = 1) Then
    Controls.HideControl(PreviousButton)
  EndIf
  If (CurrentEntry = NumberEntries) Then
    Controls.HideControl(NextButton)
  EndIf
EndSub
```

Make these changes. Only **NextButton** is shown if **CurrentEntry = 1**. Only **PreviousButton** is shown if **CurrentEntry = NumberEntries**. Otherwise, both buttons are shown.

Now, we need code for clicking either navigation button. Add this line at the end of **InitializeProgram** to enable detection of button clicks:

```
Controls.ButtonClicked = ButtonClickedSub
```

And add the corresponding **ButtonClickedSub** with code for both **PreviousButton** and **NextButton** clicks. In each case, we adjust **CurrentEntry** in the proper direction and display the item:

```
Sub ButtonClickedSub
  B = Controls.LastClickedButton
  If (B = PreviousButton) Then
    CurrentEntry = CurrentEntry - 1
    ShowCurrentEntry()
  ElseIf (B = NextButton) Then
    CurrentEntry = CurrentEntry + 1
    ShowCurrentEntry()
  EndIf
EndSub
```

Again, **Save** and **Run** the project. You should now be able to view all 10 items in the sample file by using the **Previous** and **Next** buttons in the toolbar. Give it a try. I moved to a display of my dog Toby:

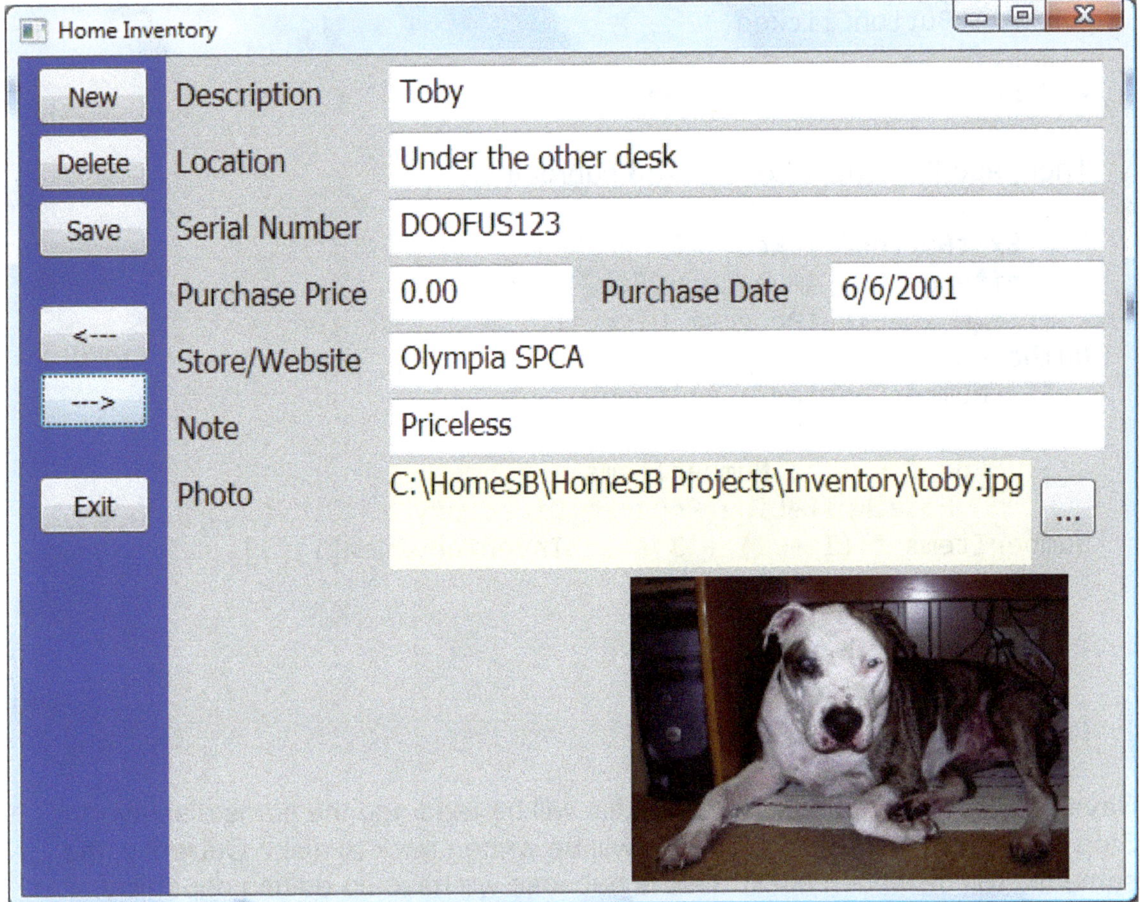

Notice both the previous and next buttons are seen.

Code Design – Inventory File Output

If inventory entries are edited or new items added (we'll see how to do this next), we want to save all entries back to the **inventory.txt** file. We do this output when the Exit button is clicked. The code to write the file is essentially the same as the code in the **OpenInventoryFile** procedure with the **ReadLine** lines replaced by **WriteLine** statements.

Make the shaded changed to **ButtonClickedSub** to recognize clicking **ExitButton**:

```
Sub ButtonClickedSub
  B = Controls.LastClickedButton
  If (B = PreviousButton) Then
    CurrentEntry = CurrentEntry - 1
    ShowCurrentEntry()
  ElseIf (B = NextButton) Then
    CurrentEntry = CurrentEntry + 1
    ShowCurrentEntry()
  ElseIf (B = ExitButton) Then
    ExitButtonClicked()
  EndIf
EndSub
```

Then, add the **ExitButtonClicked** subroutine:

```
Sub ExitButtonClicked
  'write out in inventory file
  File.WriteLine(Program.Directory + "\inventory.txt", 1,
NumberEntries)
  If (NumberEntries > 0) Then
    For I = 1 To NumberEntries
      For J = 1 to NumberItems
        File.WriteLine(Program.Directory + "\inventory.txt",
NumberItems * (I - 1) + J + 1, InventoryItem[I][J])
      EndFor
    EndFor
  EndIf
  Program.End()
EndSub
```

Save and **Run** the project. The input file will be read and the items displayed. Stop the project (click **Exit**). The file will be written back to disk. Currently, the same file will be written back. This is because we have no editing capability.

Code Design – Loading Photo

In anticipation of adding editing capability, let's write code to load a photo into the inventory. The code here is very similar to that written in the multiple choice exam project where we loaded exam files. In fact most of the code was taken directly from that project.

When a user clicks **LoadPhotoButton**, the program will display all the photo files in the program folder and ask the user to select one. Upon that selection, the **PhotoPath** is established and the photo displayed. Add the shaded code to **ButtonClickedSub** to detect clicks on this button:

```
Sub ButtonClickedSub
  B = Controls.LastClickedButton
  If (B = PreviousButton) Then
    CurrentEntry = CurrentEntry - 1
    ShowCurrentEntry()
  ElseIf (B = NextButton) Then
    CurrentEntry = CurrentEntry + 1
    ShowCurrentEntry()
  ElseIf (B = ExitButton) Then
    ExitButtonClicked()
  ElseIf (B = LoadPhotoButton) Then
    LoadPhotoButtonClicked()
  EndIf
EndSub
```

Add the **LoadPhotoButtonClicked** subroutine with the code needed to find photo files (files with **jpg** extensions):

```
Sub LoadPhotoButtonClicked
  GraphicsWindow.Hide()
  TextWindow.Show()
  TextWindow.BackgroundColor = "White"
  TextWindow.ForegroundColor = "Black"
  TextWindow.Clear()
  TextWindow.Title = "Load Photo"
  'find jpg files in program directory
  AllFiles = File.GetFiles(Program.Directory)
  NumberFiles = Array.GetItemCount(AllFiles)
  NumberJPGFiles = 0
  For I = 1 To NumberFiles
    'check for jpg extension
    If (Text.IsSubText(AllFiles[I], ".jpg")) Then
      NumberJPGFiles = NumberJPGFiles + 1
      JPGFiles[NumberJPGFiles] = AllFiles[I]
```

```
      EndIf
    EndFor
    If (NumberJPGFiles = 0) Then
      TextWindow.WriteLine("No photos found.")
      TextWindow.Pause()
    Else
      TextWindow.WriteLine("Photos (choose by number):")
      TextWindow.WriteLine("")
      For I = 1 To NumberJPGFiles
        TextWindow.CursorLeft = 2
        TextWindow.Write(I + " - ")
        'strip off directory for display of name
        TextWindow.WriteLine(text.GetSubTextToEnd(JPGFiles[I],
  Text.GetLength(Program.Directory) + 2))
      EndFor
      TextWindow.WriteLine("")
      GetFileNumber:
      TextWindow.Write("Choice? ")
      J = TextWindow.ReadNumber()
      If (J < 1 Or J > NumberJPGFiles) Then
        Goto GetFileNumber
      EndIf
      'read info from file
      PhotoPath = JPGFiles[J]
      ShowPhoto()
    EndIf
    TextWindow.Hide()
    GraphicsWindow.Show()
  EndSub
```

A text window is used to display the photo files. **AllFiles** contains all files in the **Program.Directory** folder. There are **NumberFiles** such files. We loop through these files looking for a **jpg** extension. All these files (there are **NumberJPGFiles** such files) are stored in the array **JPGFiles**. These files are listed (without the **Program.Directory**) for the user to choose from. Once the user makes a selection, **PhotoPath** is established and the corresponding photo shown using **ShowPhoto**.

Save and **Run** the program. Click the load photo button next to the path display. You should see this text window displaying the photo files it found:

Try opening a photo – I chose 9 (my dog Toby):

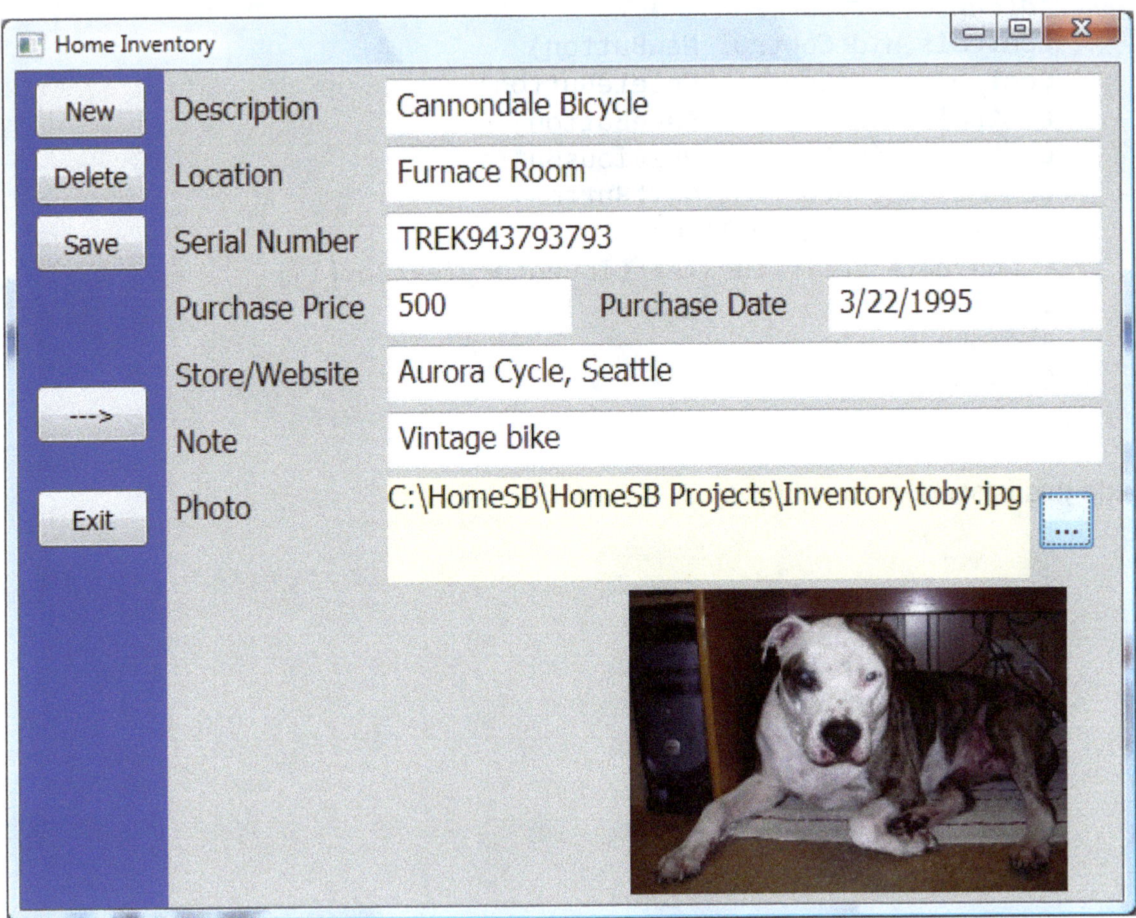

Notice the new **PhotoPath** value and displayed photo. You can change the photo back to a bicycle if you like (Choice 1). But, any changes to an item won't be saved. We now add editing capability to allow saving changes to existing and new inventory items.

Code Design – New Inventory Item

When the project first begins with an empty input file or when the user clicks the **New** button, we want the window to be in a state to accept a new set of inventory information. The steps are:

- Disable all buttons, except **SaveButton**.
- Blank out all text box controls.
- Blank out displayed photo and **PhotoPath** value.

The code for these steps is placed in a subroutine **BlankValues**. We use a subroutine because it is needed here, to start a new item, and later in the delete procedure (in case we delete the last item in the inventory). The procedure to implement the above steps is:

```
Sub BlankValues
  'blank input screen
  Controls.HideControl(NewButton)
  Controls.HideControl(DeleteButton)
  Controls.ShowControl(SaveButton)
  Controls.HideControl(PreviousButton)
  Controls.HideControl(NextButton)
  For I = 1 To NumberItems - 1
    Controls.SetTextBoxText(InventoryTextBox[I], "")
  EndFor
  PhotoPath = ""
  ShowPhoto()
EndSub
```

Add this procedure to your project.

Add the shaded code to **ButtonClickedSub** to call this subroutine when **NewButton** is clicked:

```
Sub ButtonClickedSub
  B = Controls.LastClickedButton
  If (B = PreviousButton) Then
    CurrentEntry = CurrentEntry - 1
    ShowCurrentEntry()
  ElseIf (B = NextButton) Then
    CurrentEntry = CurrentEntry + 1
    ShowCurrentEntry()
  ElseIf (B = ExitButton) Then
    ExitButtonClicked()
  ElseIf (B = LoadPhotoButton) Then
    LoadPhotoButtonClicked()
  ElseIf (B = NewButton) Then
    BlankValues()
  EndIf
EndSub
```

Now we need code to save entries for a new inventory item. When the user clicks the **Save** button, the following steps occur:

- Make sure there is an entry in **InventoryTextBox[1]** (**Description**, the only required input). Capitalize the first character (to insure proper ordering).
- Increment **NumberEntries**.
- Determine entry location in **InventoryItem** array (alphabetically, using **Description**)
- Once location is determined, move all items "below" location down one position in **InventoryItem** array.
- Establish values for new array entry.
- Display new entry.
- Show **NewButton**.
- Show **ButtonDelete**

Add the shaded code to **ButtonClickSub** to handle clicks on **SaveButton**:

```
Sub ButtonClickedSub
  B = Controls.LastClickedButton
  If (B = PreviousButton) Then
    CurrentEntry = CurrentEntry - 1
    ShowCurrentEntry()
  ElseIf (B = NextButton) Then
    CurrentEntry = CurrentEntry + 1
    ShowCurrentEntry()
  ElseIf (B = ExitButton) Then
    ExitButtonClicked()
  ElseIf (B = LoadPhotoButton) Then
    LoadPhotoButtonClicked()
  ElseIf (B = NewButton) Then
    BlankValues()
  ElseIf (B = SaveButton) Then
    SaveButtonClicked()
  EndIf
EndSub
```

The code for saving an entry is placed in the **SaveButtonClicked** subroutine:

```
Sub SaveButtonClicked
  'check for description
  Description = Controls.GetTextBoxText(InventoryTextBox[1])
  If (Description = "") Then
    GraphicsWindow.ShowMessage("Must Have Item Description.", 
"Error")
  Else
    'capitalize first letter
    FirstLetter = 
Text.ConvertToUpperCase(Text.GetSubText(Description, 1, 1))
    Description = FirstLetter + 
Text.GetSubTextToEnd(Description, 2)
    Controls.SetTextBoxText(InventoryTextBox[1], Description)
    NumberEntries = NumberEntries + 1
    'determine new current entry location based on first letter 
of description
    CurrentEntry = 1
    If NumberEntries <> 1 Then
      While (Text.GetCharacterCode(FirstLetter) >= 
Text.GetCharacterCode(Text.GetSubText(InventoryItem[CurrentEntr
y][1], 1, 1)))
        CurrentEntry = CurrentEntry + 1
        If (CurrentEntry = NumberEntries) Then
```

```
          Goto DoneLooping
        EndIf
      EndWhile
    EndIf
    'move all entries below new value down one position unless
at end
    DoneLooping:
    If CurrentEntry <> NumberEntries Then
      For I = NumberEntries To CurrentEntry + 1 Step -1
        For J = 1 To NumberItems
          InventoryItem[I][J] = InventoryItem[I - 1][J]
        EndFor
      EndFor
    EndIf
    For J = 1 To NumberItems - 1
      InventoryItem[CurrentEntry][J] =
Controls.GetTextBoxText(InventoryTextBox[J])
    EndFor
    InventoryItem[CurrentEntry][NumberItems] = PhotoPath
    ShowCurrentEntry()
    Controls.ShowControl(NewButton)
    Controls.ShowControl(DeleteButton)
  EndIf
EndSub
```

Study this code. If there is no entry in **InventoryTextBox[1]**, a message box is displayed. If there is an entry, capitalize the first character, to obtain proper ordering. We then determine the location of the new entry in the list of current entries. Once that position (**CurrentEntry**) is found, all other array elements are moved down one position. A new **InventoryItem** is created at **CurrentEntry** and the values placed in the appropriate array elements. Button status is modified.

A little confession – the inventory items are not really in alphabetic order. The current version of Small Basic does not allow comparison of strings. That is, we cannot test to see if "Jones" is greater than "Smith". In our code, we group items that start with the same first letter. We do this by comparing the ASCII code (**Text.GetCharacterCode**) of the first letters of each item **Description**. So, a "Cat" and a "Comb" would be near each other in the list, but not necessarily in alphabetical order.

Save and **Run** the project. You should now have the capability to add and save a new item to the inventory. Let's try it. Click the **New** button to see a blank form ready for input (only the **Save** button and **Exit** buttons are enabled):

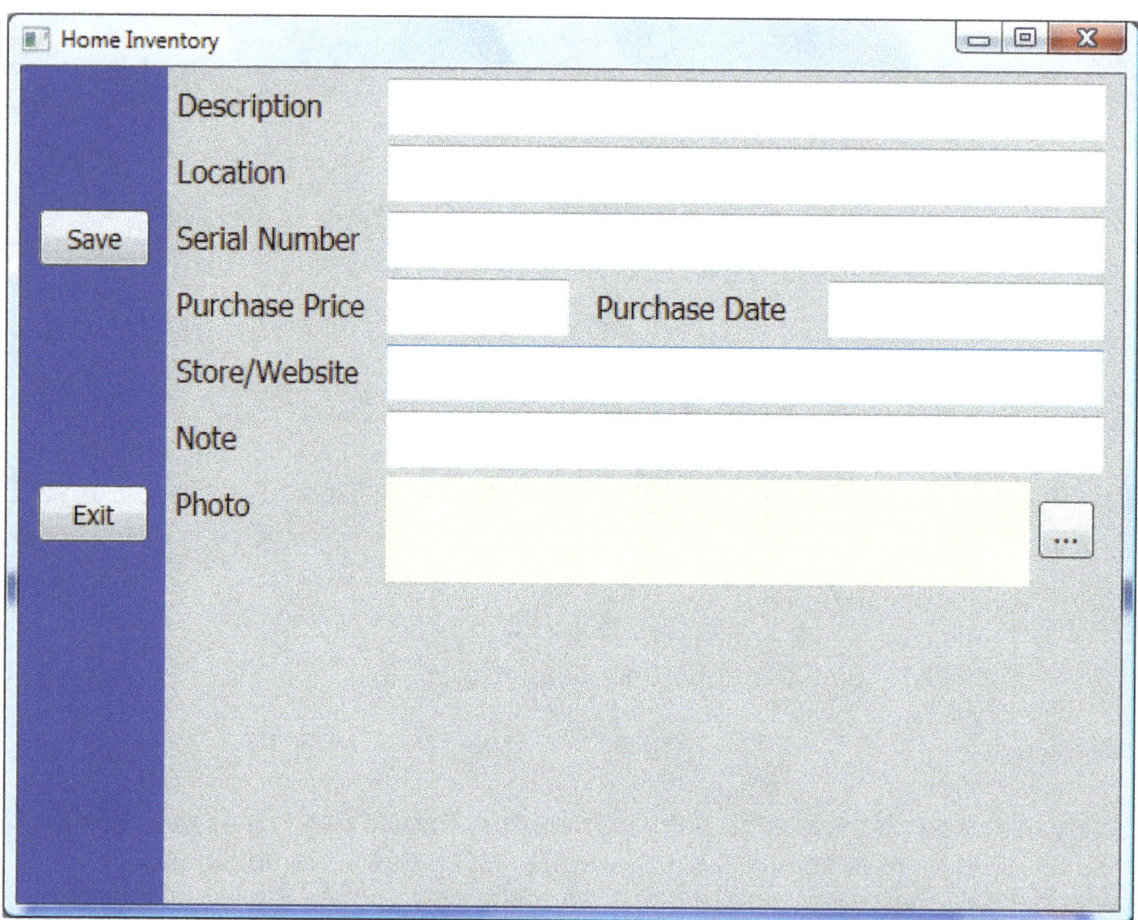

Type in some entries. Notice as you hit the <**Tab**> key, the cursor moves from text box to text box in an orderly fashion, making input easier. Add a photo if you have one. When done, click **Save** to make sure the item is properly sorted.

I added a **Garden Hose** to my inventory (no photo). After clicking **Save**, I see:

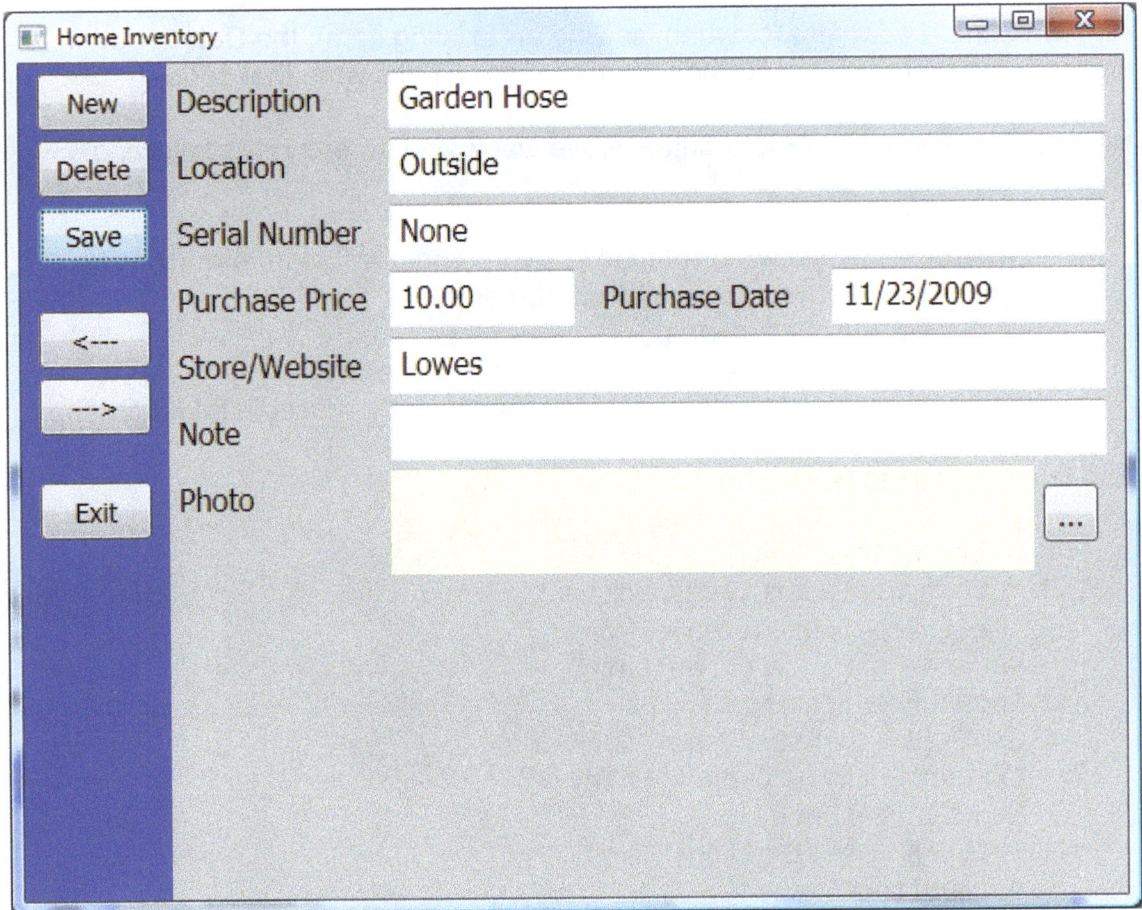

Notice all buttons are now active. I can add another item or move to another item. By clicking the **Previous** arrow button and **Next** arrow button, I can see that the item is properly located in the list (right after my **Ford**). Stop the project when you want.

Code Design – Deleting Inventory Items

After entering a new item (or when viewing an existing item), the **Delete** button is enabled, but there is no code "behind" the button. Let's write that code.

When a user clicks the **Delete** button while displaying an entry, the following should happen:

- Move all items "below" displayed entry up one position in **InventoryItem** array. This removes the entry from the array.
- Decrement **NumberEntries**.
- If entry deleted is last item, set form up for new entry.
- If more entries remain after deletion, display entry preceding deleted entry.

Add shaded code to **ButtonClickSub**:

```
Sub ButtonClickedSub
  B = Controls.LastClickedButton
  If (B = PreviousButton) Then
    CurrentEntry = CurrentEntry - 1
    ShowCurrentEntry()
  ElseIf (B = NextButton) Then
    CurrentEntry = CurrentEntry + 1
    ShowCurrentEntry()
  ElseIf (B = ExitButton) Then
    ExitButtonClicked()
  ElseIf (B = LoadPhotoButton) Then
    LoadPhotoButtonClicked()
  ElseIf (B = NewButton) Then
    BlankValues()
  ElseIf (B = SaveButton) Then
    SaveButtonClicked()
  ElseIf (B = DeleteButton) Then
    DeleteButtonClicked()
  EndIf
EndSub
```

Now, add the **DeleteButtonClicked** subroutine that covers the above steps:

```
Sub DeleteButtonClicked
  DeleteCurrentEntry()
  If (NumberEntries = 0) Then
    CurrentEntry = 0
    BlankValues()
  Else
    CurrentEntry = CurrentEntry - 1
    If (CurrentEntry = 0) Then
      CurrentEntry = 1
    EndIf
    ShowCurrentEntry()
  EndIf
EndSub
```

Notice if we delete the last item in the inventory, the form is 'blanked.' Otherwise, the entry preceding the deleted entry (if there is one) is displayed.

The above code uses a subroutine **DeleteCurrentEntry** to remove the **CurrentEntry** from the **InventoryItem** array. The code for this procedure is:

```
Sub DeleteCurrentEntry
  'delete entry CurrentEntry
  If (CurrentEntry <> NumberEntries) Then
    'move all entries under j up one level
    For I = CurrentEntry To NumberEntries - 1
      For J = 1 To NumberItems
        InventoryItem[I][J] = InventoryItem[I + 1][J]
      EndFor
    EndFor
  EndIf
  NumberEntries = NumberEntries - 1
EndSub
```

Save and **Run** the project with these changes. Make sure you can delete any entries you added earlier. I was able to successfully delete my **Garden Hose** from the inventory.

Code Design – Editing Inventory Items

There is one problem you may notice. If you edit a current entry in the inventory and click **Save**, a new item is added to the inventory, rather than a simple update of the existing item. We need to modify the save procedure to be able to handle editing an existing item.

The approach we take is that if we are editing an existing item and click **Save**, we first delete it, then treat the modified item as if it is a new item. This allows us to use the existing save code and also properly sorts the edited item (if the **Description** changed). We define a variable **NewItem** which is "**true**" if we are working with a new item, "**false**" if editing an existing item.

We need to set values for **NewItem** in a few places. Add the shaded code to **OpenInventoryFile** subroutine to establish values when the inventory file is first opened:

```
Sub OpenInventoryFile
  'read in inventory file
  NumberItems = 8
  NumberEntries = File.ReadLine(Program.Directory +
"\inventory.txt", 1)
  If (NumberEntries > 0) Then
    For I = 1 To NumberEntries
      For J = 1 to NumberItems
        InventoryItem[I][J] = File.ReadLine(Program.Directory +
"\inventory.txt", NumberItems * (I - 1) + J + 1)
      EndFor
    EndFor
    CurrentEntry = 1
    ShowCurrentEntry()
    NewItem = "false"
  Else
    Controls.HideControl(NewButton)
    Controls.HideControl(DeleteButton)
    Controls.HideControl(PreviousButton)
    Controls.HideControl(NextButton)
    CurrentEntry = 0
    NewItem = "true"
  EndIf
EndSub
```

We also need to set **NewItem** to "true" when we blank the form. Add the shaded line to **BlankValues**:

```
Sub BlankValues
  'blank input screen
  Controls.HideControl(NewButton)
  Controls.HideControl(DeleteButton)
  Controls.ShowControl(SaveButton)
  Controls.HideControl(PreviousButton)
  Controls.HideControl(NextButton)
  For I = 1 To NumberItems - 1
    Controls.SetTextBoxText(InventoryTextBox[I], "")
  EndFor
  PhotoPath = ""
  ShowPhoto()
  NewItem = "true"
EndSub
```

Now, the modified **SaveButtonClicked** subroutine is (changes are shaded, much unmodified code not shown):

```
Sub SaveButtonClicked
  'check for description
  Description = Controls.GetTextBoxText(InventoryTextBox[1])
  If (Description = "") Then
    GraphicsWindow.ShowMessage("Must Have Item Description.",
"Error")
  Else
    If (NewItem = "false") Then
      'if editing existing entry, delete entry then resave
      DeleteCurrentEntry()
    Else
      NewItem = "false"
    EndIf
    'capitalize first letter
   .
   .
  EndIf
EndSub
```

In this code, if **NewItem** is "**false**", we delete the existing item before resaving it.

Save and **Run** the project. You now have full editing capability in the home inventory manager project. You can view inventory items, add new items to your inventory, delete items, or modify existing items. All information can now be properly saved.

We still need to add search capabilities to our project. But, first we need to address one "small" annoyance. If you edit an existing item and then click **New**, the **Previous** or **Next** arrow, or **Exit** without clicking **Save**, your changes are lost. It would be nice if the program would "save us from ourselves" and save any changes we made. This is a straightforward modification. We essentially need to know if anything was changed for a particular item. If changes were made and we attempt to move away from that item (click **New**, **Previous** arrow or **Next** arrow) or **Exit** the program without clicking **Save**, the program will 'click' it for us (call the **SaveButtonClicked** subroutine).

We will use a variable **Edited** to help with this task. This variable will be **"true"** when a current inventory item has been edited. Modify the **ButtonClickedSub** subroutine the see if we want to do a save when **NewButton**, **PreviousButton**, **NextButton** or **ExitButton** is clicked. The changes are shaded (same code for each button click event):

```
Sub ButtonClickedSub
  B = Controls.LastClickedButton
  If (B = PreviousButton) Then
    If (Edited) Then
      SaveButtonClicked()
    EndIf
    CurrentEntry = CurrentEntry - 1
    ShowCurrentEntry()
  ElseIf (B = NextButton) Then
    If (Edited) Then
      SaveButtonClicked()
    EndIf
    CurrentEntry = CurrentEntry + 1
    ShowCurrentEntry()
  ElseIf (B = ExitButton) Then
    If (Edited) Then
      SaveButtonClicked()
    EndIf
    ExitButtonClicked()
  ElseIf (B = LoadPhotoButton) Then
    LoadPhotoButtonClicked()
  ElseIf (B = NewButton) Then
    If (Edited) Then
      SaveButtonClicked()
    EndIf
```

```
    BlankValues()
  ElseIf (B = SaveButton) Then
    SaveButtonClicked()
  ElseIf (B = DeleteButton) Then
    DeleteButtonClicked()
  EndIf
EndSub
```

We now need to modify the code to set **Edited** to the proper value at the proper locations. **Edited** should be **"false"** whenever a new inventory item is displayed. Add this single line:

```
Edited = "false"
```

as the last line in the **ShowEntry** subroutine.

How do we know if a user has edited a value associated with an inventory item? To know for sure if an edit occurred would take a bit of code. We could save the values when the item is first displayed. Then, when the **New**, **Previous**, **Next** or **Exit** button is clicked, we could recheck to see if any of the values were changed. Such code would have to involve questions of just what constitutes a "different" value. We take a simpler approach. If the user accesses any of the controls used to set an inventory item property, we set **Edited** to **"true"**. This is a safe approach. Even though nothing may have changed, we are assuming something did.

To see if something was edited, we need to see if a user accessed any of the text boxes used for input or loaded a photo. Whenever a user types in a text box, a **TextTyped** event is generated. Add this line of code at the end of **InitializeProgram** to recognize the event:

```
Controls.TextTyped = TextTypedSub
```

Then the **TextTypedSub** simply sets **Edited** to "**true**" when it is called:

```
Sub TextTypedSub
  Edited = "true"
EndSub
```

Lastly, add this line at the end of the **LoadPhotoButtonClicked** subroutine:

```
Edited = "true"
```

Save and **Run** the project. Add a new inventory item, make some entries describing the item and click **Save**. Now modify something about your new item and click **Previous** or **Next**. Navigate back to the previously modified item. Your changes were automatically saved for you.

Window Design – Inventory Item Search

As an inventory list grows, you would like to have some capability to search for particular items. In this project, we will use 26 button controls in a rectangle labeled **Item Search**. Each of these buttons will have a letter of the alphabet. When a letter is clicked, the first item in the inventory beginning with that letter (if there is such an item) is displayed on the form.

Here's what the search rectangle will look like:

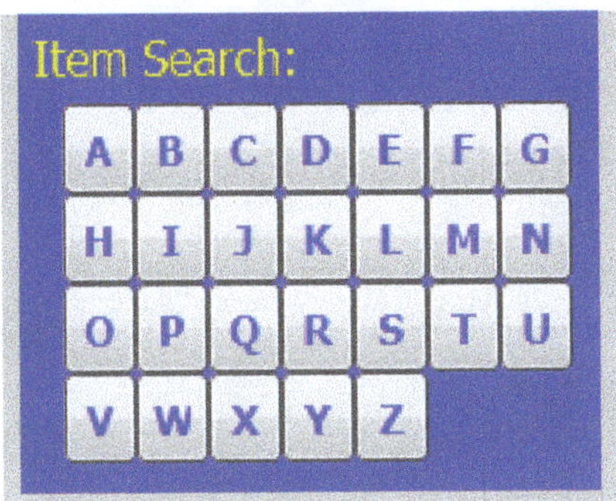

We draw four rows of buttons with seven buttons in each row. The buttons will be in an array **SearchButton**. The trickiest part is determining the height and width of each button and positioning within the rectangle. A lot of trial and error was used.

Add this code to the **InitializeProgram** subroutine (before the line calling the **OpenInventoryFile** subroutine):

```
'search buttons
GraphicsWindow.BrushColor = "Blue"
GraphicsWindow.FillRectangle(100, 275, 200, 160)
GraphicsWindow.BrushColor = "Yellow"
GraphicsWindow.FontBold = "false"
GraphicsWindow.DrawText(105, 280, "Item Search:")
GraphicsWindow.BrushColor = "Blue"
GraphicsWindow.FontSize = 14
GraphicsWindow.FontBold = "true"
W = 25
H = 30
L = 115
T = 305
For I = 1 To 26
  SearchButton[I] = Controls.AddButton(Text.GetCharacter(I +
64), L, T)
  Controls.SetSize(SearchButton[I], W, H)
```

```
    L = L + W
    'seven buttons per row
    If (Math.Remainder(I, 7) = 0) Then
      L = 115
      T = T + H
    EndIf
  EndFor
```

I did a lot of playing around with values used here before settling on this final set. Note how we place 7 buttons in each row.

You also need to add code to handle clicking on any of these buttons. Add the shaded lines to **ButtonClickedSub**:

```
Sub ButtonClickedSub
  B = Controls.LastClickedButton
  If (B = PreviousButton) Then
   .
  ElseIf (B = NextButton) Then
   .
  ElseIf (B = ExitButton) Then
   .
  ElseIf (B = LoadPhotoButton) Then
   .
  ElseIf (B = NewButton) Then
   .
  ElseIf (B = SaveButton) Then
   .
  ElseIf (B = DeleteButton) Then
   .
  Else
    SearchButtonClicked()
  EndIf
EndSub
```

This addition just says if we don't click **NewButton**, **DeleteButton**, **SaveButton**, **PreviousButton**, **NextButton**, **ExitButton** or **LoadPhotoButton**, we must have clicked one of the elements of the **SearchButton** array (the variable **B** holds the exact button clicked).

Add an empty **SearchButtonClicked** subroutine:

```
Sub SearchButtonClicked
EndSub
```

Save and **Run** the project. The search buttons should now appear on the form:

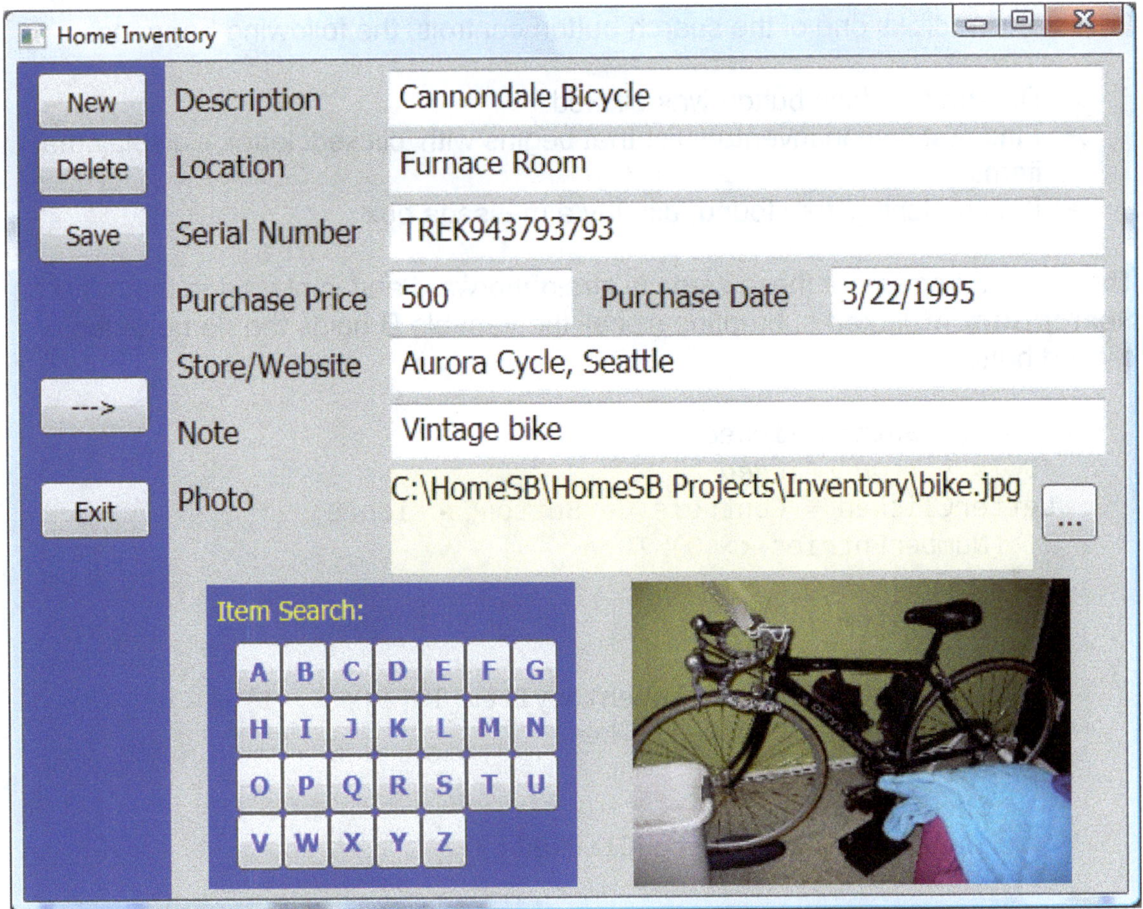

Now, we need code to implement the search.

Code Design – Inventory Item Search

When a user clicks one of the search button controls, the following happens:

- Determine which button was clicked.
- Find first item in inventory list that begins with 'clicked' letter – display that item.
- If no matching item found, display a message box.

The code to implement these steps is straightforward and is placed in the **SearchButtonClicked** subroutine (recall the variable **B** holds the name of the clicked button):

```
Sub SearchButtonClicked
  'B is button clicked
  LetterClicked = Controls.GetButtonCaption(B)
  If (NumberEntries <> 0) Then
    I = 0
  CheckNextItem:
    I = I + 1
    S = Text.GetSubText(InventoryItem[I][1], 1, 1)
    If (S = LetterClicked) Then
      CurrentEntry = I
      ShowCurrentEntry()
      Goto ExitSearchButtonClicked
    EndIf
    If (I = NumberEntries Or
Text.GetCharacterCode(Text.GetSubText(InventoryItem[I][1], 1,
1)) > Text.GetCharacterCode(LetterClicked)) Then
      GraphicsWindow.ShowMessage("No " + LetterClicked + "
inventory items.", "None Found")
    Else
      Goto CheckNextItem
    EndIf
  EndIf
  ExitSearchButtonClicked:
EndSub
```

We use the **Text.GetCharacterCode** to get the ASCII representation of the first letter of an item **Description** (**InventoryItem[I][1]**). Add this subroutine to your project.

Save and **Run** the project. Notice how the search buttons are properly created and positioned. When I click the '**T**' search button using the sample inventory, I see:

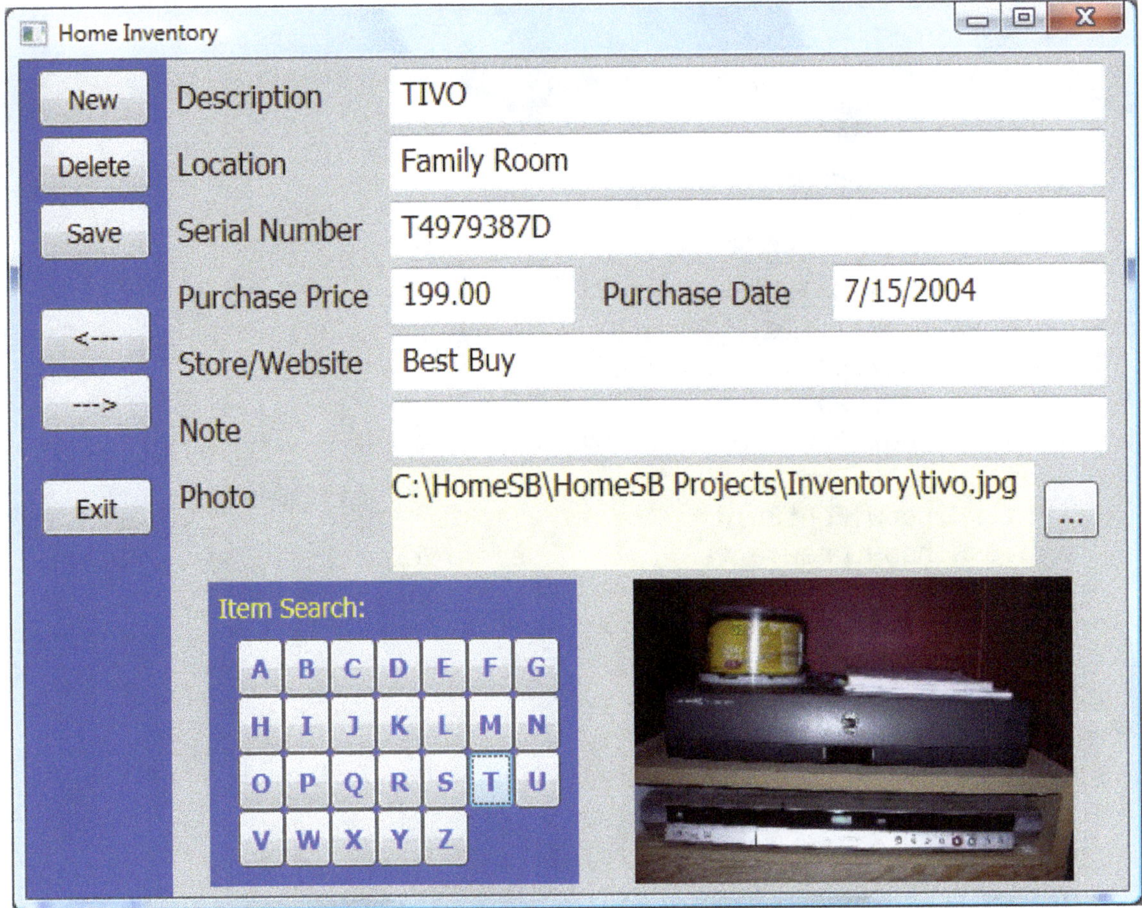

Notice we see the first T entry (**TIVO**). To see entries 'around' this choice, use the **Previous** and **Next** buttons. Click on '**R**' and you'll see:

Home Inventory Manager Project Code Listing

Here is the complete listing of the **Home Inventory Manager** Small Basic program:

```
' Home Inventory
InitializeProgram()

Sub InitializeProgram
  'graphics window
  GraphicsWindow.Width = 600
  GraphicsWindow.Height = 440
  GraphicsWindow.Title = "Home Inventory"
  GraphicsWindow.BackgroundColor = "LightGray"
  'labels/textboxes
  GraphicsWindow.BrushColor = "Black"
  GraphicsWindow.FontSize = 16
  GraphicsWindow.FontBold = "false"
  GraphicsWindow.DrawText(85, 10, "Description")
  GraphicsWindow.DrawText(85, 45, "Location")
  GraphicsWindow.DrawText(85, 80, "Serial Number")
  GraphicsWindow.DrawText(85, 115, "Purchase Price")
  GraphicsWindow.DrawText(315, 115, "Purchase Date")
  GraphicsWindow.DrawText(85, 150, "Store/Website")
  GraphicsWindow.DrawText(85, 185, "Note")
  InventoryTextBox[1] = Controls.AddTextBox(200, 5)
  InventoryTextBox[2] = Controls.AddTextBox(200, 40)
  InventoryTextBox[3] = Controls.AddTextBox(200, 75)
  InventoryTextBox[4] = Controls.AddTextBox(200, 110)
  InventoryTextBox[5] = Controls.AddTextBox(440, 110)
  InventoryTextBox[6] = Controls.AddTextBox(200, 145)
  InventoryTextBox[7] = Controls.AddTextBox(200, 180)
  Controls.SetSize(InventoryTextBox[1], 390, 30)
  Controls.SetSize(InventoryTextBox[2], 390, 30)
  Controls.SetSize(InventoryTextBox[3], 390, 30)
  Controls.SetSize(InventoryTextBox[4], 100, 30)
  Controls.SetSize(InventoryTextBox[5], 150, 30)
  Controls.SetSize(InventoryTextBox[6], 390, 30)
  Controls.SetSize(InventoryTextBox[7], 390, 30)
  'photo selection
  GraphicsWindow.DrawText(85, 220, "Photo")
  GraphicsWindow.BrushColor = "LightYellow"
  GraphicsWindow.FillRectangle(200, 215, 350, 55)
  GraphicsWindow.BrushColor = "Black"
  LoadPhotoButton = Controls.AddButton("...", 555, 225)
  Controls.SetSize(LoadPhotoButton, 30, 30)
```

```
  'Buttons
  GraphicsWindow.BrushColor = "Blue"
  GraphicsWindow.FillRectangle(0, 0, 80, GraphicsWindow.Height)
  GraphicsWindow.BrushColor = "Black"
  GraphicsWindow.FontSize = 14
  GraphicsWindow.FontBold = "false"
  NewButton = Controls.AddButton("New", 10, 5)
  DeleteButton = Controls.AddButton("Delete", 10, 40)
  SaveButton = Controls.AddButton("Save", 10, 75)
  PreviousButton = Controls.AddButton("<---", 10, 130)
  NextButton = Controls.AddButton("--->", 10, 165)
  ExitButton = Controls.AddButton("Exit", 10, 220)
  Controls.SetSize(NewButton, 60, 30)
  Controls.SetSize(DeleteButton, 60, 30)
  Controls.SetSize(SaveButton, 60, 30)
  Controls.SetSize(PreviousButton, 60, 30)
  Controls.SetSize(NextButton, 60, 30)
  Controls.SetSize(ExitButton, 60, 30)
  'search buttons
  GraphicsWindow.BrushColor = "Blue"
  GraphicsWindow.FillRectangle(100, 275, 200, 160)
  GraphicsWindow.BrushColor = "Yellow"
  GraphicsWindow.FontBold = "false"
  GraphicsWindow.DrawText(105, 280, "Item Search:")
  GraphicsWindow.BrushColor = "Blue"
  GraphicsWindow.FontSize = 14
  GraphicsWindow.FontBold = "true"
  W = 25
  H = 30
  L = 115
  T = 305
  For I = 1 To 26
    SearchButton[I] = Controls.AddButton(Text.GetCharacter(I +
64), L, T)
    Controls.SetSize(SearchButton[I], W, H)
    L = L + W
    'seven buttons per row
    If (Math.Remainder(I, 7) = 0) Then
      L = 115
      T = T + H
    EndIf
  EndFor
  OpenInventoryFile()
  Controls.ButtonClicked = ButtonClickedSub
  Controls.TextTyped = TextTypedSub
EndSub
```

```
Sub OpenInventoryFile
  'read in inventory file
  NumberItems = 8
  NumberEntries = File.ReadLine(Program.Directory +
"\inventory.txt", 1)
  If (NumberEntries > 0) Then
    For I = 1 To NumberEntries
      For J = 1 to NumberItems
        InventoryItem[I][J] = File.ReadLine(Program.Directory +
"\inventory.txt", NumberItems * (I - 1) + J + 1)
      EndFor
    EndFor
    CurrentEntry = 1
    ShowCurrentEntry()
    NewItem = "false"
  Else
    Controls.HideControl(NewButton)
    Controls.HideControl(DeleteButton)
    Controls.HideControl(PreviousButton)
    Controls.HideControl(NextButton)
    CurrentEntry = 0
    NewItem = "true"
  EndIf
EndSub

Sub ShowCurrentEntry
  'display CurrentEntry
  For I =1 to NumberItems - 1
    Controls.SetTextBoxText(InventoryTextBox[I],
InventoryItem[CurrentEntry][I])
  EndFor
  PhotoPath = InventoryItem[CurrentEntry][NumberItems]
  ShowPhoto()
    'set status of previous/next buttons
  Controls.ShowControl(PreviousButton)
  Controls.ShowControl(NextButton)
  If (CurrentEntry = 1) Then
    Controls.HideControl(PreviousButton)
  EndIf
  If (CurrentEntry = NumberEntries) Then
    Controls.HideControl(NextButton)
  EndIf
  Edited = "false"
EndSub
```

```
Sub ShowPhoto
  'clear previous path
  GraphicsWindow.BrushColor = "LightYellow"
  GraphicsWindow.FillRectangle(200, 215, 350, 55)
  'write path
  GraphicsWindow.BrushColor = "Black"
  GraphicsWindow.FontSize = 16
  GraphicsWindow.FontBold = "false"
  GraphicsWindow.DrawBoundText(200, 215, 350, PhotoPath)
  'clear any previous photo
  GraphicsWindow.BrushColor = GraphicsWindow.BackgroundColor
  GraphicsWindow.FillRectangle(330, 275, 240, 160)
  If (PhotoPath <> "") Then

GraphicsWindow.DrawResizedImage(ImageList.LoadImage(PhotoPath),
330, 275, 240, 160)
  EndIf
EndSub

Sub ButtonClickedSub
  B = Controls.LastClickedButton
  If (B = PreviousButton) Then
    If (Edited) Then
      SaveButtonClicked()
    EndIf
    CurrentEntry = CurrentEntry - 1
    ShowCurrentEntry()
  ElseIf (B = NextButton) Then
    If (Edited) Then
      SaveButtonClicked()
    EndIf
    CurrentEntry = CurrentEntry + 1
    ShowCurrentEntry()
  ElseIf (B = ExitButton) Then
    If (Edited) Then
      SaveButtonClicked()
    EndIf
    ExitButtonClicked()
  ElseIf (B = LoadPhotoButton) Then
    LoadPhotoButtonClicked()
  ElseIf (B = NewButton) Then
    If (Edited) Then
      SaveButtonClicked()
    EndIf
    BlankValues()
  ElseIf (B = SaveButton) Then
```

```
    SaveButtonClicked()
  ElseIf (B = DeleteButton) Then
    DeleteButtonClicked()
  Else
    SearchButtonClicked()
  EndIf
EndSub

Sub ExitButtonClicked
  'write out in inventory file
  File.WriteLine(Program.Directory + "\inventory.txt", 1,
NumberEntries)
  If (NumberEntries > 0) Then
    For I = 1 To NumberEntries
      For J = 1 to NumberItems
        File.WriteLine(Program.Directory + "\inventory.txt",
NumberItems * (I - 1) + J + 1, InventoryItem[I][J])
      EndFor
    EndFor
  EndIf
  Program.End()
EndSub

Sub LoadPhotoButtonClicked
  GraphicsWindow.Hide()
  TextWindow.Show()
  TextWindow.BackgroundColor = "White"
  TextWindow.ForegroundColor = "Black"
  TextWindow.Clear()
  TextWindow.Title = "Load Photo"
  'find jpg files in program directory
  AllFiles = File.GetFiles(Program.Directory)
  NumberFiles = Array.GetItemCount(AllFiles)
  NumberJPGFiles = 0
  For I = 1 To NumberFiles
    'check for jpg extension
    If (Text.IsSubText(AllFiles[I], ".jpg")) Then
      NumberJPGFiles = NumberJPGFiles + 1
      JPGFiles[NumberJPGFiles] = AllFiles[I]
    EndIf
  EndFor
  If (NumberJPGFiles = 0) Then
    TextWindow.WriteLine("No photos found.")
    TextWindow.Pause()
  Else
    TextWindow.WriteLine("Photos (choose by number):")
```

```
    TextWindow.WriteLine("")
    For I = 1 To NumberJPGFiles
      TextWindow.CursorLeft = 2
      TextWindow.Write(I + " - ")
      'strip off directory for display of name
      TextWindow.WriteLine(text.GetSubTextToEnd(JPGFiles[I],
Text.GetLength(Program.Directory) + 2))
    EndFor
    TextWindow.WriteLine("")
    GetFileNumber:
    TextWindow.Write("Choice? ")
    J = TextWindow.ReadNumber()
    If (J < 1 Or J > NumberJPGFiles) Then
      Goto GetFileNumber
    EndIf
    'read info from file
    PhotoPath = JPGFiles[J]
    ShowPhoto()
  EndIf
  TextWindow.Hide()
  GraphicsWindow.Show()
  Edited = "true"
EndSub

Sub BlankValues
  'blank input screen
  Controls.HideControl(NewButton)
  Controls.HideControl(DeleteButton)
  Controls.ShowControl(SaveButton)
  Controls.HideControl(PreviousButton)
  Controls.HideControl(NextButton)
  For I = 1 To NumberItems - 1
    Controls.SetTextBoxText(InventoryTextBox[I], "")
  EndFor
  PhotoPath = ""
  ShowPhoto()
  NewItem = "true"
EndSub

Sub SaveButtonClicked
  'check for description
  Description = Controls.GetTextBoxText(InventoryTextBox[1])
  If (Description = "") Then
    GraphicsWindow.ShowMessage("Must Have Item Description.",
"Error")
  Else
```

```
    If (NewItem = "false") Then
      'if editing existing entry, delete entry then resave
      DeleteCurrentEntry()
    Else
      NewItem = "false"
    EndIf
    'capitalize first letter
    FirstLetter =
Text.ConvertToUpperCase(Text.GetSubText(Description, 1, 1))
    Description = FirstLetter + Text.GetSubTextToEnd(Description,
2)
    Controls.SetTextBoxText(InventoryTextBox[1], Description)
    NumberEntries = NumberEntries + 1
    'determine new current entry location based on first letter of
description
    CurrentEntry = 1
    If NumberEntries <> 1 Then
      While (Text.GetCharacterCode(FirstLetter) >=
Text.GetCharacterCode(Text.GetSubText(InventoryItem[CurrentEntry][
1], 1, 1)))
        CurrentEntry = CurrentEntry + 1
        If (CurrentEntry = NumberEntries) Then
          Goto DoneLooping
        EndIf
      EndWhile
    EndIf
    'move all entries below new value down one position unless at
end
    DoneLooping:
    If CurrentEntry <> NumberEntries Then
      For I = NumberEntries To CurrentEntry + 1 Step -1
        For J = 1 To NumberItems
          InventoryItem[I][J] = InventoryItem[I - 1][J]
        EndFor
      EndFor
    EndIf
    For J = 1 To NumberItems - 1
      InventoryItem[CurrentEntry][J] =
Controls.GetTextBoxText(InventoryTextBox[J])
    EndFor
    InventoryItem[CurrentEntry][NumberItems] = PhotoPath
    ShowCurrentEntry()
    Controls.ShowControl(NewButton)
    Controls.ShowControl(DeleteButton)
  EndIf
EndSub
```

```
Sub DeleteButtonClicked
  DeleteCurrentEntry()
  If (NumberEntries = 0) Then
    CurrentEntry = 0
    BlankValues()
  Else
    CurrentEntry = CurrentEntry - 1
    If (CurrentEntry = 0) Then
      CurrentEntry = 1
    EndIf
    ShowCurrentEntry()
  EndIf
EndSub

Sub DeleteCurrentEntry
  'delete entry CurrentEntry
  If (CurrentEntry <> NumberEntries) Then
    'move all entries under j up one level
    For I = CurrentEntry To NumberEntries - 1
      For J = 1 To NumberItems
        InventoryItem[I][J] = InventoryItem[I + 1][J]
      EndFor
    EndFor
  EndIf
  NumberEntries = NumberEntries - 1
EndSub

Sub TextTypedSub
  Edited = "true"
EndSub

Sub SearchButtonClicked
  'B is button clicked
  LetterClicked = Controls.GetButtonCaption(B)
  If (NumberEntries <> 0) Then
    I = 0
  CheckNextItem:
    I = I + 1
    S = Text.GetSubText(InventoryItem[I][1], 1, 1)
    If (S = LetterClicked) Then
      CurrentEntry = I
      ShowCurrentEntry()
      Goto ExitSearchButtonClicked
    EndIf
```

```
    If (I = NumberEntries Or
Text.GetCharacterCode(Text.GetSubText(InventoryItem[I][1], 1, 1))
> Text.GetCharacterCode(LetterClicked)) Then
      GraphicsWindow.ShowMessage("No " + LetterClicked + "
inventory items.", "None Found")
    Else
      Goto CheckNextItem
    EndIf
  EndIf
  ExitSearchButtonClicked:
EndSub
```

Home Inventory Manager Project Review

The **Home Inventory Manager Project** is now complete. **Save** and **Run** the project and make sure it works as designed. Use the program to keep track of your belongings. You'll want to delete the **inventory.txt** file currently in the project folder and start over adding your own items.

If there are errors in your implementation, go back over the steps of window and code design. Use the debugger when needed. Go over the developed code – make sure you understand how different parts of the project were coded. As mentioned in the beginning of this chapter, the completed project is saved as **Inventory** in the **HomeSB\HomeSB Projects\Inventory** folder.

While completing this project, new concepts and skills you should have gained include:

- Selecting and displaying images.
- Writing sequential files to disk.
- Sorting things "alphabetically."

Home Inventory Manager Project Enhancements

Possible enhancements to the home inventory manager project include:

- After clicking the **New** button, you must add an item to the inventory and click **Save**. There is no **Cancel** option – add such an option.
- The implemented search is rather basic. Add a search capability that looks through all the information in the inventory for certain terms or parts of terms. Use the **Soundex** function from the **Multiple Choice Exam Project** to do "sound-alike" searches.
- Like the suggestion for the weight monitor project, modify the project to allow opening and saving of separate inventory files. That is, replace the built-in file (**inventory.txt**) with one you can select using code.
- When an item is deleted, there is no **Undo** possibility. Can you add such an option?

11. Snowball Toss Game Project

Review and Preview

In the final project, we'll have some fun. In the **Snowball Toss Game Project**, two players toss snowballs at each other or a single player plays against the computer - the most hits wins!

We introduce concepts needed for game programming – animation, collision detection, keyboard control, and sounds. And, we'll look at how to give our computer a semblance of intelligence.

Snowball Toss Game Project Preview

In this chapter, we will build a **Snowball Toss Game** program. This program lets two players compete in throwing snowballs at each other. Or, optionally, a single player can play against a computer with adjustable 'smarts'.

The finished project is saved as **Snowball** in the **HomeSB\HomeSB Projects\Snowball** folder. Start Small Basic and open the finished project. Run the project (click **Run** in the toolbar or press <**F5**>). When the game appears, click **Options**. You should see:

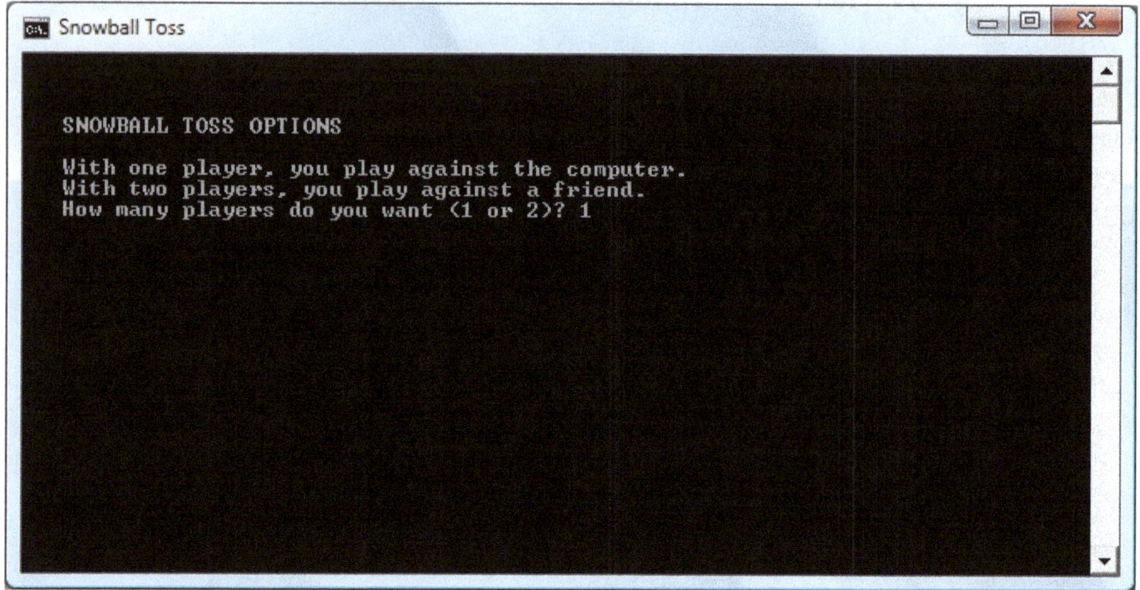
Snowball Toss
SNOWBALL TOSS OPTIONS
With one player, you play against the computer.
With two players, you play against a friend.
How many players do you want (1 or 2)? 1

In the snowball toss game, you can have two players competing against each other or one player against the computer. For now, enter **1** for **One Player**.

With a single player, you can also choose **Difficulty** (setting the intelligence level of the computer):

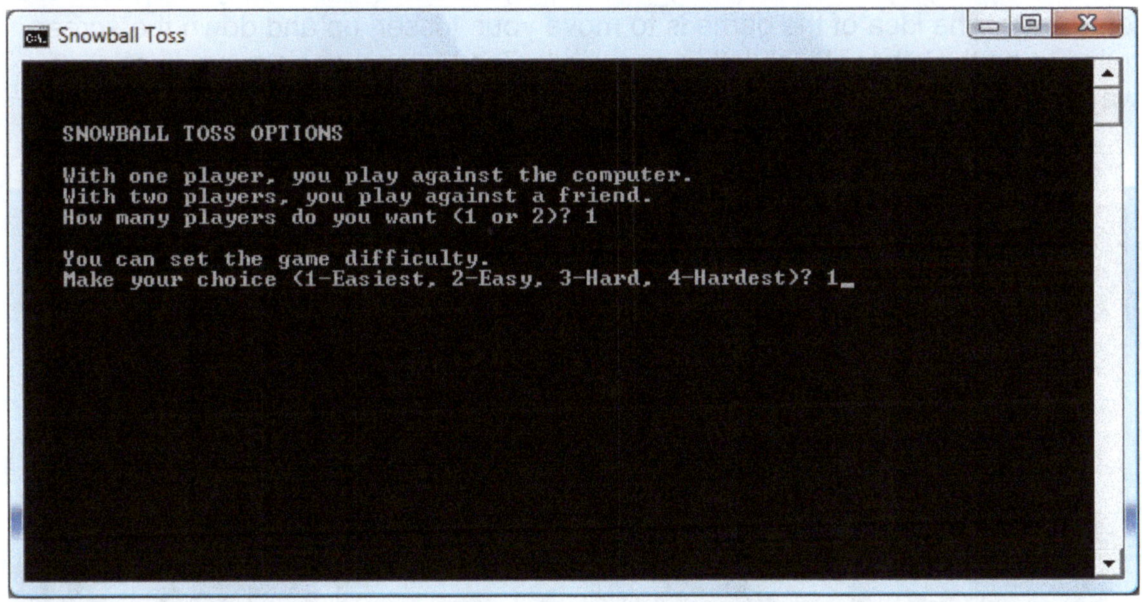
Snowball Toss
SNOWBALL TOSS OPTIONS
With one player, you play against the computer.
With two players, you play against a friend.
How many players do you want (1 or 2)? 1
You can set the game difficulty.
Make your choice (1-Easiest, 2-Easy, 3-Hard, 4-Hardest)? 1_

Select **1** (**Easiest)** and press **<Enter>** make the **Options** window disappear. Then, click **New Game**.

The game screen shows the two snowball tossing characters, one on each side of the screen (the players are identified by the labels at the top of the window). Also shown are the player scores (**Hits**) and displays showing how many snowballs are left (**Left**). The idea of the game is to move your 'tosser' up and down the screen, trying to hit the other player with a snowball. Zombie snowmen move in strange ways through the middle of the screen to act as cover and deflect some tosses:

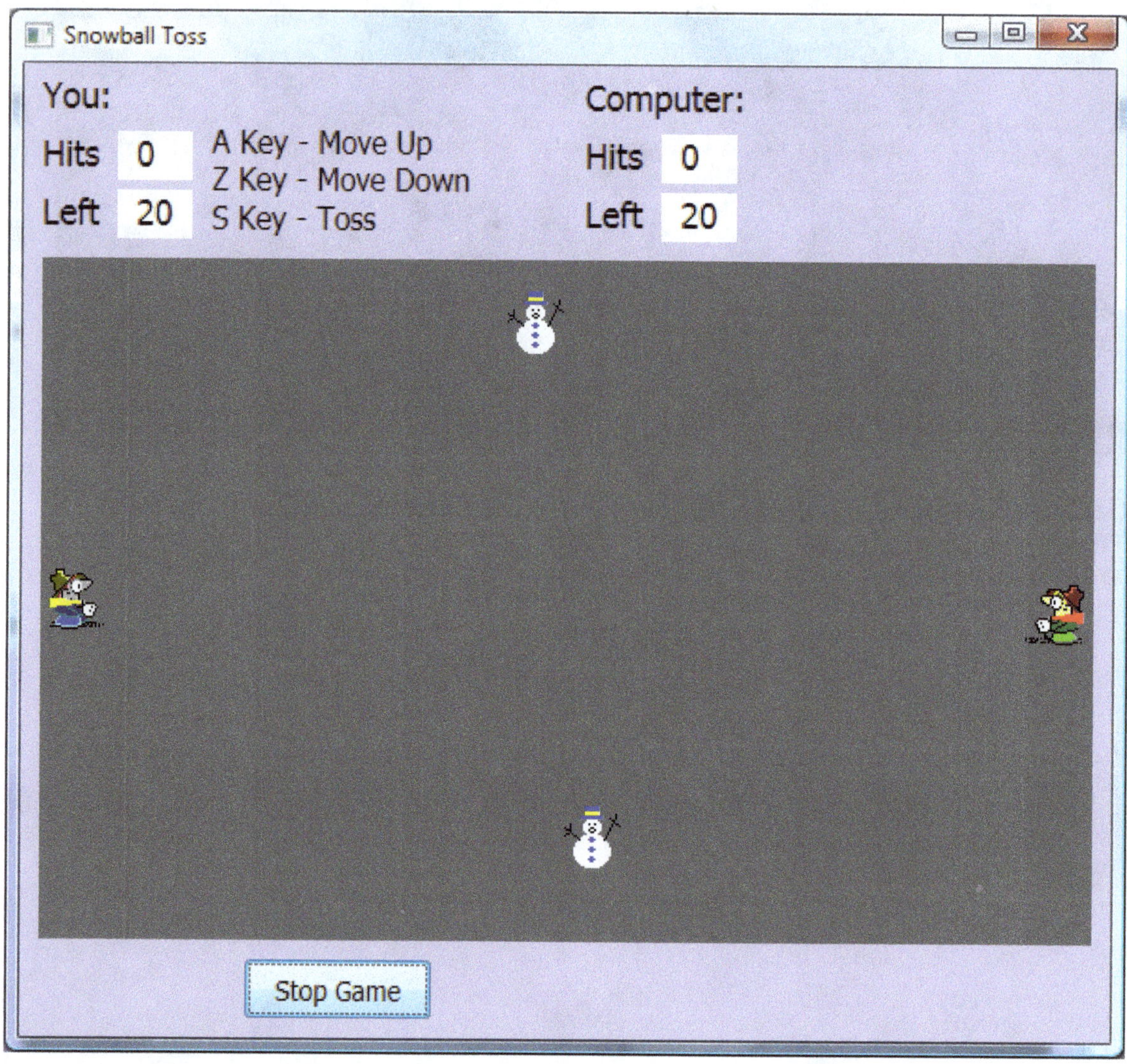

Watch out – the computer may make a toss at you.

Control of the players is via the keyboard. Player 1 (and the player when playing against the computer) uses the **A** key to move up, the **Z** key to move down, and the **S** key to toss a snowball. Player 2 uses the **K** key to move up, the **M** key to move down, and the **J** key to toss. These instructions are shown on the window. The game ends when all the snowballs have been thrown or when the **Stop Game** button is clicked.

Try moving your player up and down using the **A** and **Z** keys. When you want, take a toss at the other player by pressing the **S** key. You should hear a 'throwing' sound. Here's a throw I made:

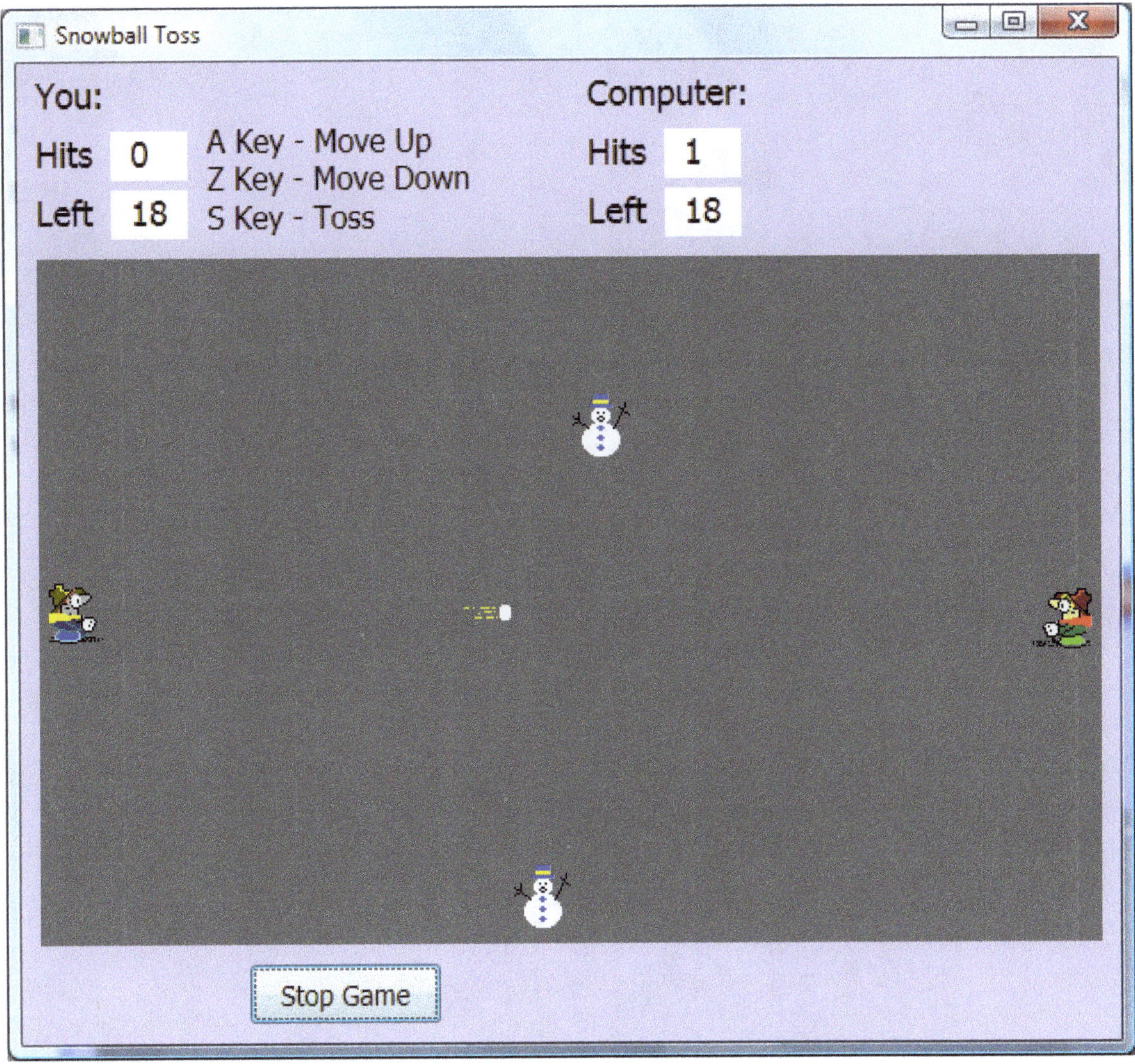

The snowball will move across the screen until it hits something or flies off the side of the window. If you hit the other player (resulting in an ouch sound), you earn one point. The player with the most points when the game stops is the winner.

That's all there is to this game. Conceptually, it is very simple. Just throw snowballs at each other until you're out of snowballs. Though simple, there are many topics we need to discuss to build the project.

The project will be built in several stages. We discuss **window design**. We discuss the controls used to build the window and establish initial properties. We show how to configure the window based on selected options. And, we address **code design**. We discuss several areas of game programming: animation, keyboard events, collision detection and sounds. Lastly, we look at how to give the computer intelligence in making decisions needed to play the game.

Snowball Toss Game Window Design

Here is the sketch for the window layout of the **Snowball Toss Game** program:

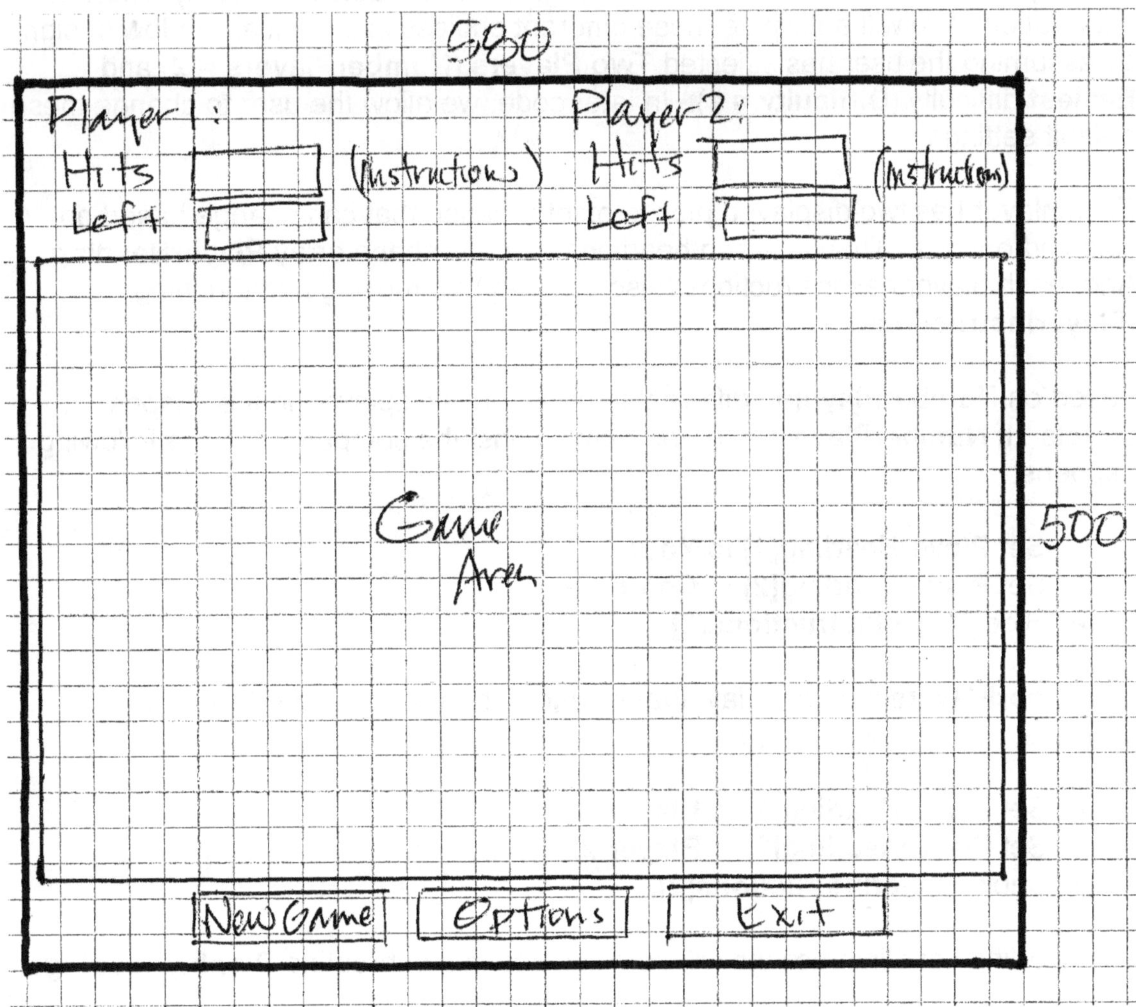

The labels and controls (**Shapes** objects with text) at the top of the window provide game status (score, snowballs left to toss and keys to use to move players). The rectangle in the middle is the game field. Three button controls are used to start/stop the game, set options (the number of players and the game difficulty (if playing against the computer) and stop the program.

We now begin writing project code. We first write code that establishes window status based on selected game options.

Start a new program in Small Basic. Once started, we suggest you immediately save the program with a name you choose. This sets up the folder and file structure needed for your program.

Window Design – Headings

When the game begins, a user usually chooses options (number of players and difficulty level). Based on these choices, the game window will display different information. We will anticipate these different choices in our initial window design by assuming the user has selected **Two Players** (**NumberPlayers = 2**) and **Easiest** difficulty (**Difficulty = 1**). In later code, we allow the user to change these default settings.

Each player has two displayed pieces of information that can change based on selected options. There are two headings in a text shape array **PlayerHeading**. And, each player has instructions (also an array) for moving and throwing (**PlayerInstructions**).

Based on **NumberPlayers,** different information is displayed in the shapes objects. If **NumberPlayers = 1**, you play against the computer and the following happens:

- Set **PlayerHeading[1]** to **You:**
- Set **PlayerHeading[2]** to **Computer:**
- Hide **PlayerInstructions[2]**.

If **NumberPlayers = 2**, you play against another person and the following happens:

- Set **PlayerHeading[1]** to **Player 1:**
- Set **PlayerHeading[2]** to **Player 2:**
- Show **PlayerInstructions[2].**

The headings and instructions will be displayed in a subroutine **DisplayHeadings**:

```
Sub DisplayHeadings
  If (NumberPlayers = 1) Then
    Shapes.SetText(PlayerHeading[1], "You:")
    Shapes.SetText(PlayerHeading[2], "Computer:")
    Shapes.HideShape(PlayerInstructions[2])
  Else
    Shapes.SetText(PlayerHeading[1], "Player 1:")
    Shapes.SetText(PlayerHeading[2], "Player 2:")
    Shapes.ShowShape(PlayerInstructions[2])
  EndIf
EndSub
```

Let's use this subroutine to start drawing our window.

Add this code to your program (above the **DisplayHeadings** subroutine):

```
' Snowball Toss
InitializeProgram()

Sub InitializeProgram
  'graphics window
  GraphicsWindow.Width = 580
  GraphicsWindow.Height = 500
  GraphicsWindow.Title = "Snowball Toss"
  GraphicsWindow.BackgroundColor =
GraphicsWindow.GetColorFromRGB(192, 192, 255)
  ' options
  NumberPlayers = 2
  Difficulty = 1
  'build instructions and show headings
  CRLF = Text.GetCharacter(13)
  GraphicsWindow.BrushColor = "Black"
  GraphicsWindow.FontSize = 18
  GraphicsWindow.FontBold = "false"
  PlayerHeading[1] = Shapes.AddText("")
  Shapes.Move(PlayerHeading[1], 10, 5)
  PlayerHeading[2] = Shapes.AddText("")
  Shapes.Move(PlayerHeading[2], 300, 5)
  GraphicsWindow.FontSize = 16
  PlayerInstructions[1] = Shapes.AddText("A Key - Move Up" +
CRLF + "Z Key - Move Down" + CRLF + "S Key - Toss")
  Shapes.Move(PlayerInstructions[1], 100, 30)
  PlayerInstructions[2] = Shapes.AddText("K Key - Move Up" +
CRLF + "M Key - Move Down" + CRLF + "J Key - Toss")
  Shapes.Move(PlayerInstructions[2], 390, 30)
  DisplayHeadings()
EndSub
```

The first line of code calls a subroutine **InitializeProgram** where we will put all code needed to set up the program for use. All remaining code here goes in that subroutine.Here we set the window size, establish values for **NumberPlayers** and **Difficulty** and position the needed **Shapes** objects array elements (**PlayerHeading** and **PlayerInstructions**). Notice how the player instructions shapes contain three lines of information (separated by a 'carriage return' character, **CRLF**). When done, we call the **DisplayHeadings** subroutine to set proper values based on the default options.

Save and **Run** the program to see the proper headings for two players:

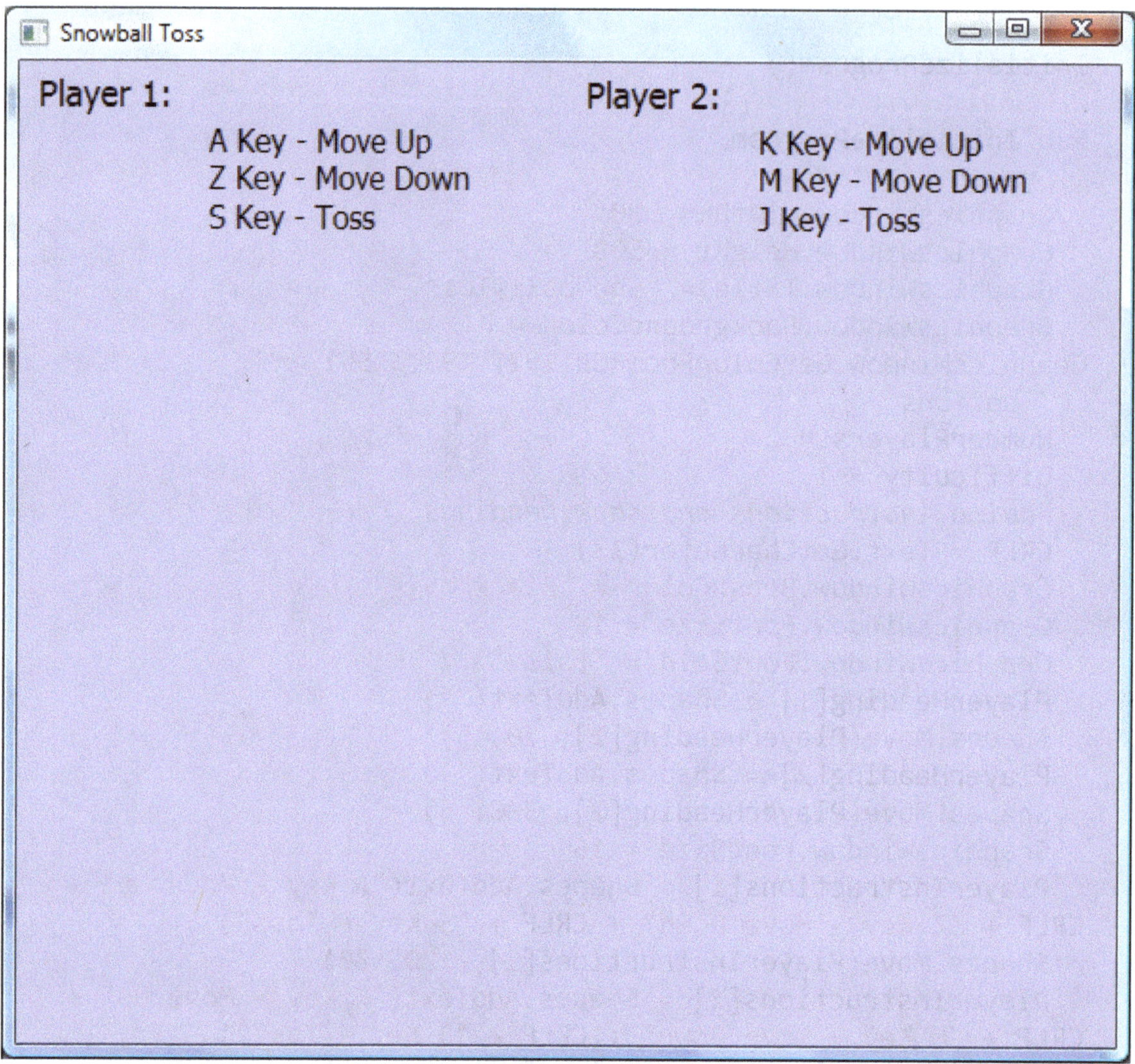

If you want, change **NumberPlayers** to **1** to see the alternate headings.

Window Design – Scoring and Game Area

Each player has two pieces of scoring information – the number of snowballs that have hit the other player (**PlayerHits**) and the number of snowballs left to throw (**NumberLeft**). These are two element arrays. The values are displayed in corresponding shape arrays, **PlayerHitsDisplay** and **NumberLeftDisplay**, positioned on white rectangle backgrounds. Each player starts with 20 snowballs (**MaximumBalls**).

The game area is a gray rectangle located at (**GameLeft**, **GameTop**) and is **GameWidth** by **GameHeight** pixels in size.

Add these elements to the game with this code in **InitializeProgram**:

```
'game variables
MaximumBalls = 20
'scoring
GraphicsWindow.BrushColor = "Black"
GraphicsWindow.FontSize = 18
GraphicsWindow.FontBold = "false"
GraphicsWindow.DrawText(10, 35, "Hits")
GraphicsWindow.DrawText(10, 65, "Left")
GraphicsWindow.DrawText(300, 35, "Hits")
GraphicsWindow.DrawText(300, 65, "Left")
GraphicsWindow.BrushColor = "White"
GraphicsWindow.FillRectangle(50, 35, 40, 25)
GraphicsWindow.FillRectangle(50, 65, 40, 25)
GraphicsWindow.FillRectangle(340, 35, 40, 25)
GraphicsWindow.FillRectangle(340, 65, 40, 25)
GraphicsWindow.BrushColor = "Black"
PlayerHitsDisplay[1] = Shapes.AddText("0")
Shapes.Move(PlayerHitsDisplay[1], 60, 35)
PlayerLeftDisplay[1] = Shapes.AddText(MaximumBalls)
Shapes.Move(PlayerLeftDisplay[1], 60, 65)
PlayerHitsDisplay[2] = Shapes.AddText("0")
Shapes.Move(PlayerHitsDisplay[2], 350, 35)
PlayerLeftDisplay[2] = Shapes.AddText(MaximumBalls)
Shapes.Move(PlayerLeftDisplay[2], 350, 65)
'game region
GameLeft = 10
GameTop = 100
GameWidth = 560
GameHeight = 350
GraphicsWindow.BrushColor = "Gray"
GraphicsWindow.FillRectangle(GameLeft, GameTop, GameWidth,
GameHeight)
```

We will add other variables under the '**game variables** comment as we build the game.

Save and **Run** the program. The initial scoring and game area will appear:

As desired, each player has 20 snowballs (**MaximumBalls**).

Window Design – Adding Buttons

We need a button to start and stop the game (**GameButton**), one to set options (**OptionsButton**) and one to exit the program (**ExitButton**). Add this code (in **InitializeProgram**) to put the buttons at the bottom of the window:

```
'buttons
GraphicsWindow.BrushColor = "Black"
GraphicsWindow.FontSize = 14
GraphicsWindow.FontBold = "false"
GameButton = Controls.AddButton("New Game", 120, 460)
Controls.SetSize(GameButton, 100, 30)
OptionsButton = Controls.AddButton("Options", 240, 460)
Controls.SetSize(OptionsButton, 100, 30)
ExitButton = Controls.AddButton("Exit", 360, 460)
Controls.SetSize(ExitButton, 100, 30)
```

Save and **Run** the program to see the buttons:

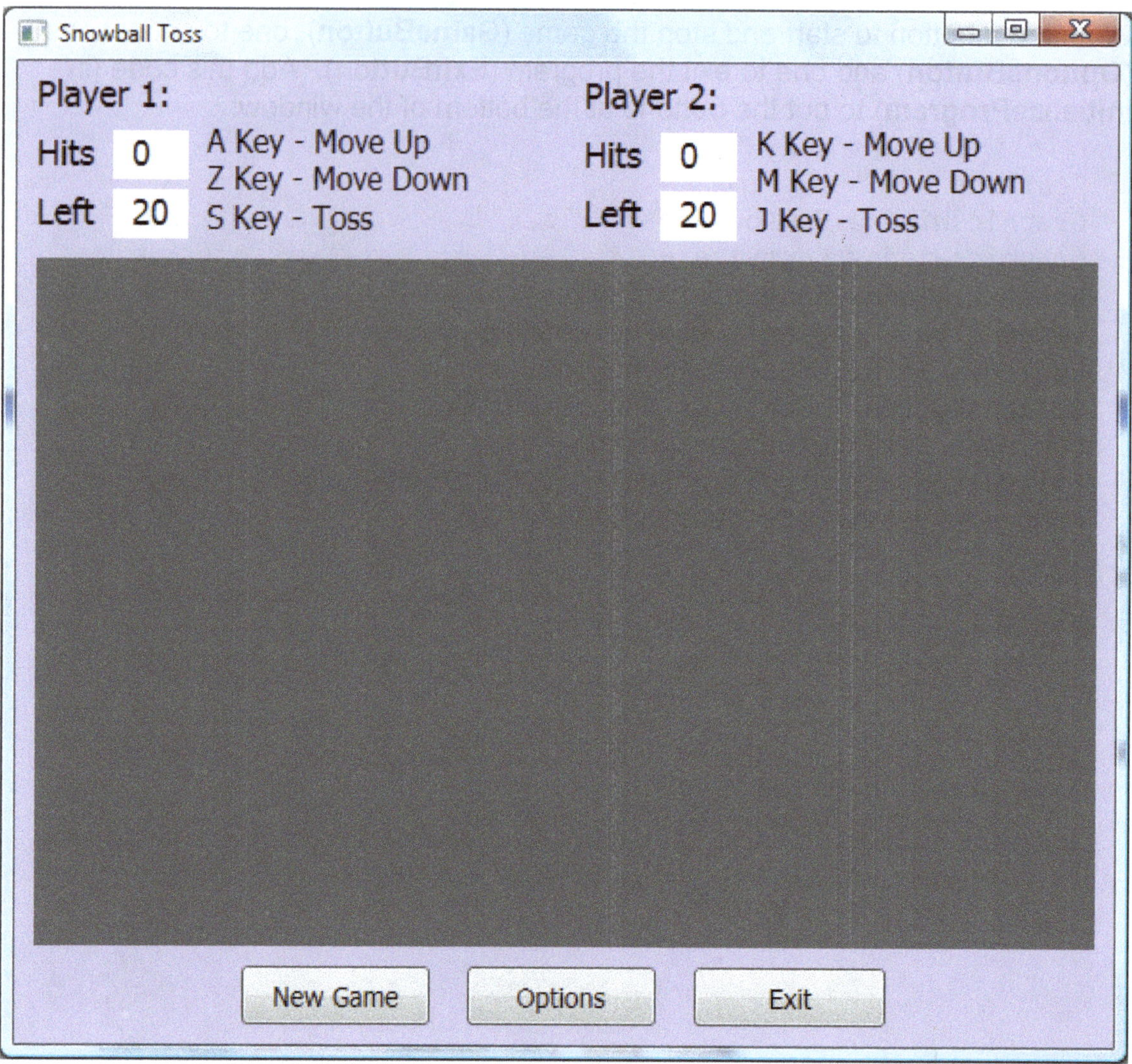

The window design is complete. We now write code for the game play, starting with setting the options.

Code Design – Choosing Options

As mentioned, the first thing a player usually does is set the game options by clicking the **Options** button. We will use the Small Basic text window to establish game options. We need to be able to detect button clicks so add this line at the end of **InitializeProgram**:

```
Controls.ButtonClicked = ButtonClickedSub
```

Then, add the **ButtonClickedSub** subroutine:

```
Sub ButtonClickedSub
  B = Controls.LastClickedButton
  If (B = OptionsButton) Then
    SetOptions()
  EndIf
EndSub
```

The options are set in the **SetOptions** subroutine – add this routine:

```
Sub SetOptions
  GraphicsWindow.Hide()
  TextWindow.Show()
  TextWindow.Title = "Snowball Toss"
  TextWindow.CursorLeft = 3
  TextWindow.CursorTop = 3
  TextWindow.WriteLine("SNOWBALL TOSS OPTIONS")
  TextWindow.WriteLine("")
  GetPlayers:
  TextWindow.CursorLeft = 3
  TextWindow.WriteLine("With one player, you play against the
computer.")
  TextWindow.CursorLeft = 3
  TextWindow.WriteLine("With two players, you play against a
friend.")
  TextWindow.CursorLeft = 3
  TextWindow.Write("How many players do you want (1 or 2)? ")
  NumberPlayers = TextWindow.ReadNumber()
  If (NumberPlayers < 1 Or NumberPlayers > 2) Then
    Goto GetPlayers
  EndIf
  If (NumberPlayers = 1) Then
    GetDifficulty:
    TextWindow.WriteLine("")
    TextWindow.CursorLeft = 3
    TextWindow.WriteLine("You can set the game difficulty.")
```

```
    TextWindow.CursorLeft = 3
    TextWindow.Write("Make your choice (1-Easiest, 2-Easy, 3-
Hard, 4-Hardest)? ")
    Difficulty = TextWindow.ReadNumber()
    If (Difficulty < 1 Or Difficulty > 4) Then
      Goto GetDifficulty
    EndIf
  EndIf
  DisplayHeadings()
  TextWindow.Hide()
  GraphicsWindow.Show()
EndSub
```

This routine hides the graphics window, displays a text window and asks the user questions necessary to establish the two options (**NumberPlayers**, **Difficulty**). Note, if two players are selected, there is no need to ask how difficult you want the game to be. Once the questions are answered, headings are established in **DisplayHeadings** and the program returns to the game in ‘stopped’ state.

Save and **Run** the program. Click the **Options** button to change options:

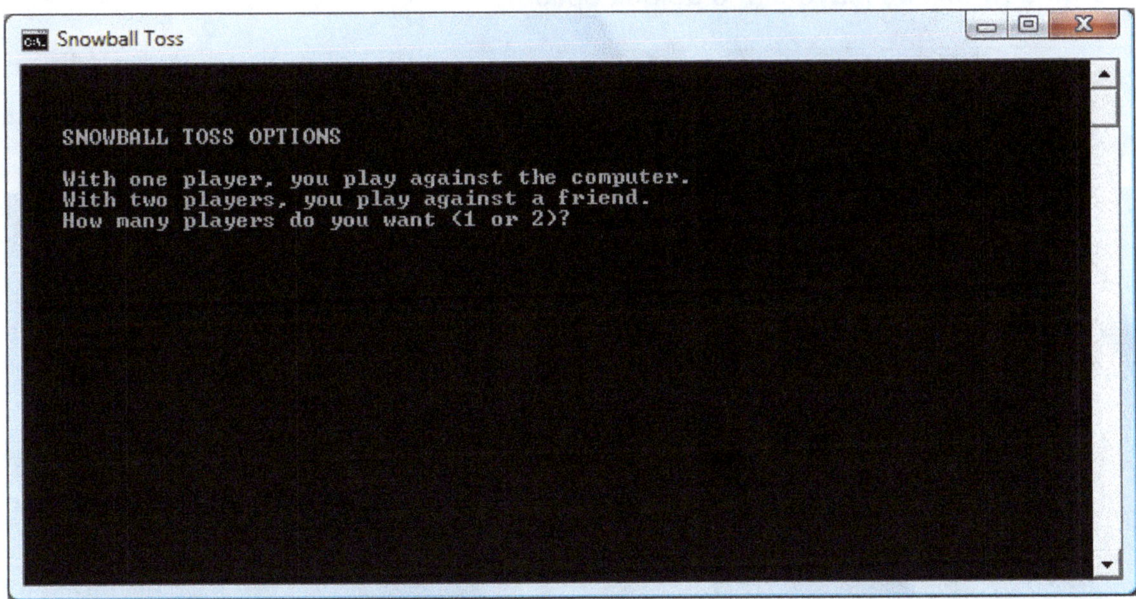
Snowball Toss
SNOWBALL TOSS OPTIONS
With one player, you play against the computer.
With two players, you play against a friend.
How many players do you want (1 or 2)?

Make your choices and press **Enter** after each. The **Snowball Toss** window will again appear.

Make sure the proper heading information appears based on your choices. Here's the window for two players (the default option):

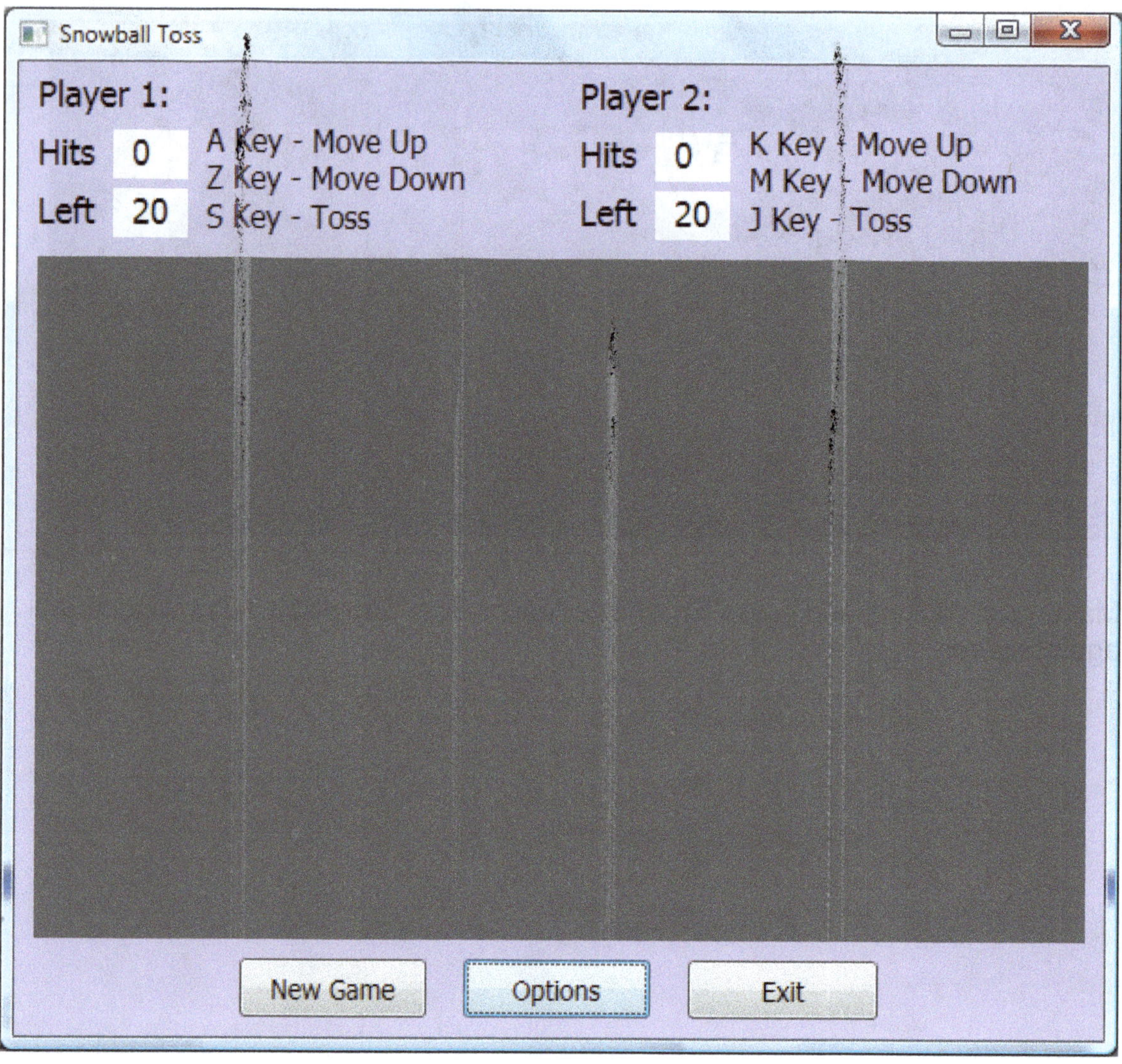

And, here's the window for one player, playing the computer:

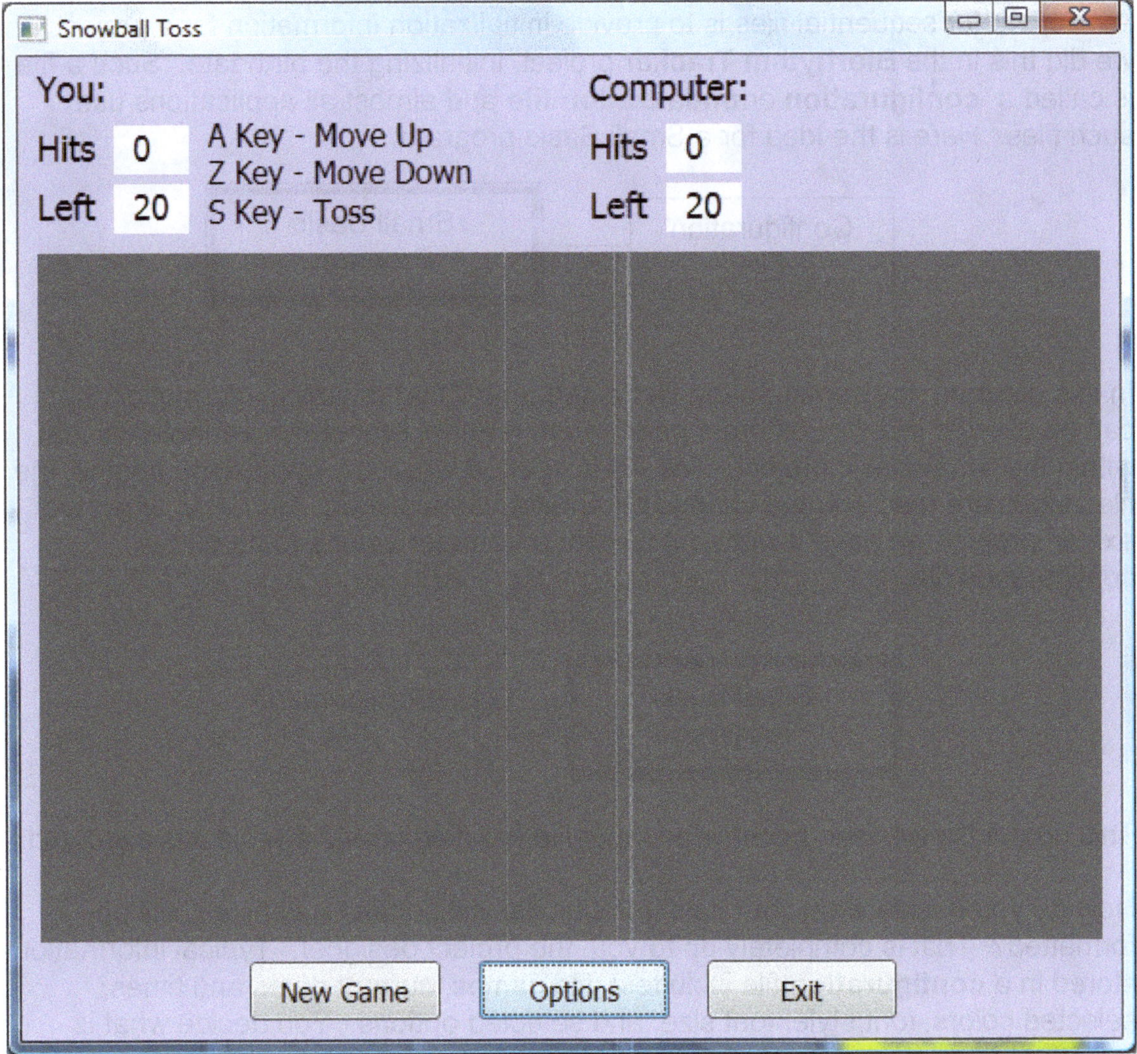

Each time you play the game, you would like the options you used the last time you played the game to be "pre-selected." A **configuration file** can handle this task.

Configuration Files

A nice use for sequential files is to provide initialization information for a project – we did this in the **Biorhythm Tracker** project, initializing the birthdate. Such a file is called a **configuration** or **initialization file** and almost all applications use such files. Here is the idea for a Small Basic program:

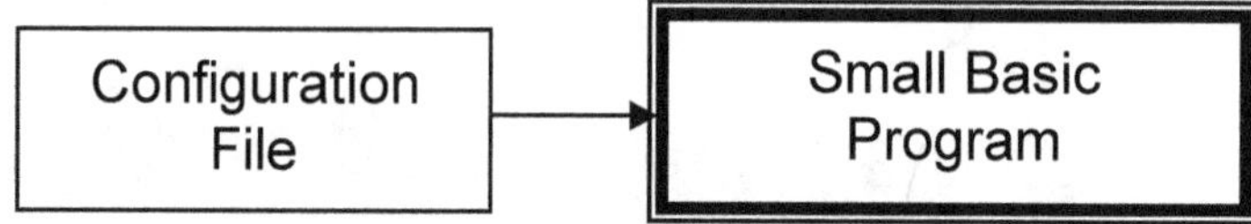

In this diagram, the configuration file (a sequential file) contains information that can be used to initialize different parameters (control properties, variable values) within the Small Basic project. The file is opened when the application begins, the file values are read and the various parameters established. Similarly, when we exit an project, we have it write out current parameter values to an output configuration file:

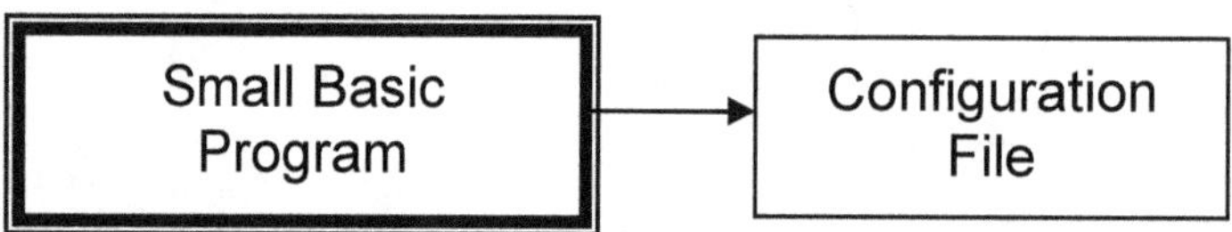

This output file will then become an input file the next time the project is executed.

How do you decide what your configuration file will contain and how it will be formatted? That is completely up to you, the project designer. Typical information stored in a **configuration** file includes: file names, current dates and times, selected colors, font style, font size, and selected options. You decide what is important in your project. You develop variables to save information and read and write these variables from and to the sequential configuration file. There is usually one variable (numeric, string) for each option being saved. In our game, the configuration file will have values for the two selected options (**NumberPlayers** and **Difficulty**).

Once you've decided on values to save and the format of your file, how do you proceed? A first step is to create an initial file using a text editor. If the number of variables being saved is relatively short, I suggest putting one variable on each line of the file. Save your configuration file in your program's folder. Configuration files will always be kept in the program path. And, the usual three letter file extension for a configuration file is **ini** (for initialization).

Once you have developed the configuration file, you need to write code to fit this framework:

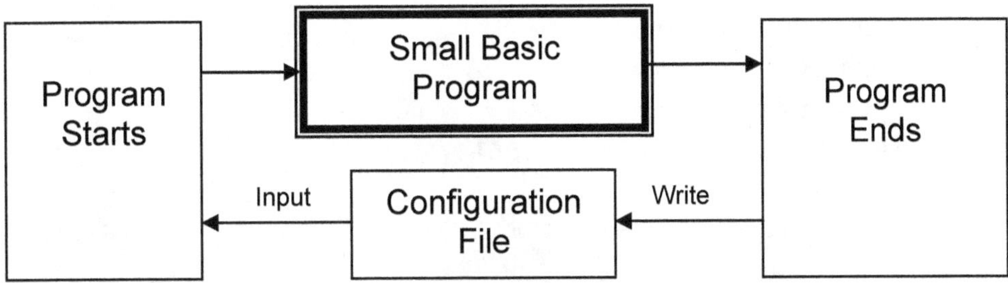

When your program starts, open and read the file and use the variables to establish t he respective options. When your program ends (usually by clicking an exit button), open and write variables back to the file.

Code Design – Configuration File

The configuration file (**snowball.ini**) here will hold two pieces of information: the number of players (**NumberPlayers**) and the difficulty (**Difficulty**). First, let's develop the code to write the configuration file to disk when the program ends (the **ExitButton** is clicked). This code goes in the **ButtonClickedSub** subroutine (changes are shaded):

```
Sub ButtonClickedSub
  B = Controls.LastClickedButton
  If (B = OptionsButton) Then
    SetOptions()
  ElseIf (B = ExitButton) Then
    File.WriteLine(Program.Directory + "\snowball.ini", 1,
NumberPlayers)
    File.WriteLine(Program.Directory + "\snowball.ini", 2,
Difficulty)
    Program.End()
  EndIf
EndSub
```

Note, the configuration file is in the program folder.

Save and **Run** the program. It will start using the default options (**NumberPlayers = 2**, **Difficulty = 1**). Click the **Exit** button. Go to your program folder and make sure the configuration file (**snowball.ini**) is there. Open it and you will see the two values (each on a separate line):

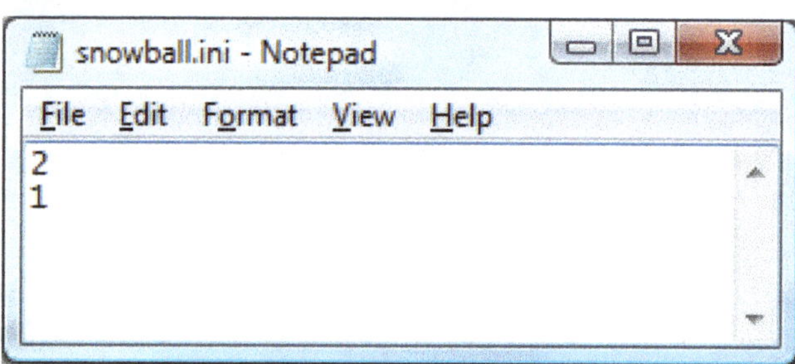

The configuration file is opened and read in when the program starts. Replace the two lines of code (in **InitializeProgram**) setting the default options:

```
' options
NumberPlayers = 2
Difficulty = 1
```

with these lines that read the options values (**NumberPlayers**, **Difficulty**) from the configuration file:

```
' options
NumberPlayers = File.ReadLine(Program.Directory +
"\snowball.ini", 1)
Difficulty = File.ReadLine(Program.Directory + "\snowball.ini",
2)
```

Save and **Run** the program. Choose some options. Make sure the window is properly configured after choosing the options. Stop the project – click **Exit**. **Run** the program again to make sure your last set of selected options is still selected and the window looks correct. Before stopping the program for the last time, make sure the **Two Player** option is selected. We will use this for most of our design work.

We're now ready to start programming the graphics features of the snowball game – moving the tossers up and down the screen, throwing snowballs, and moving the zombie snowmen up and down the screen.

Animation with Small Basic

Programming animated games in Small Basic requires a specific set of skills. We need to know how to develop a graphic image, how to move (animate) that image and how to see if one image collides with another image. We also want to add sounds to our games. As we build the snowball toss game, we will discuss these new skills. We start with **animation**.

Animation is fairly simple with Small Basic. We create a **Shapes** object holding an image. Then, using the **Shapes Move** method, we give the image an appearance of motion.

The first step to create a **Shapes** object is to load an image from a graphics file. This is done with:

```
MyImage = ImageList.LoadImage(FileName)
```

where **FileName** is a complete path to the graphics file. With this, the **Shapes** object displaying the image (**MyShape**) is created using:

```
MyShape = Shapes.AddImage(MyImage)
```

Once created, we position the **Shapes** object at (**X, Y**) using the **Move** method:

```
Shapes.Move(MyShape, X, Y)
```

This statement will remove **MyShape** at its previous location in the graphics window (if any) and move it to (**X, Y**). By periodically changing the value of (**X, Y**) and moving the shape to that new location we obtain a nice smooth animated motion. It really is that easy.

Two other **Shapes** methods useful in animation are the **HideShape** and **ShowShape** methods. To remove a shape (**MyShape**) from the graphics window, use:

```
Shapes.HideShape(MyShape)
```

Then, to make a hidden shape reappear, use:

```
Shapes.ShowShape(MyShape)
```

We're ready to start writing code to animate our snowball toss game, but first we need to answer one question that might be lingering. In discussing animation, we said the images we use are loaded from files. Your question might be – where do these files come from? The answer is you either need to find them from some source (the Internet is a good place to look) or create them yourself.

To create animation images, you could use a tool like the **Paint** program that ships with Windows. Draw your picture and save it as a bitmap file. Or you could use one of many available commercial paintbrush programs. In the snowball toss game, we use another tool to develop our images – a program called **IconEdit**.

Drawing Images with IconEdit

Several years ago, ***PC Magazine*** offered a free utility called **IconEdit** that allows you to design and save icons (a file with an **ico** extension). Icons are simply special cases of bitmap files that are 32 bits by 32 bits in size. Their size makes them very useful in games such as this. We will use **IconEdit** to create the images needed for our snowball toss program.

Included with these notes is the **IconEdit** program and other files (directory **HomeSB\HomeSB Projects\IconEdit**). To run **IconEdit**, click **Start** on the Windows task bar, and then click **Run**. Find the **IconEdit.exe** program (use **Browse** mode) and run it. You can also establish a shortcut to start **IconEdit** from your desktop, if desired. The following Editor window will appear when you choose the **New** option under the **File** menu:

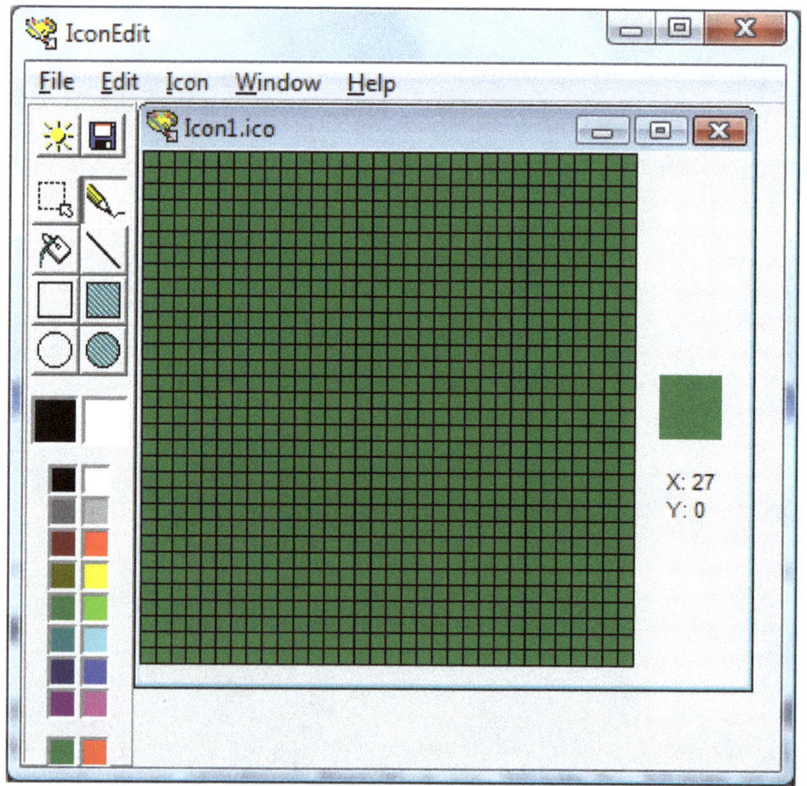

The basic idea of **IconEdit** is to draw an icon in the large 32 x 32 grid displayed. You can draw single points, lines, open rectangles and ovals, and filled rectangles and ovals. Various colors are available with simple mouse clicks. The displayed green color is a transparent color. As you draw in the large grid, the small grid to the right displays your finished icon. Once completed, the icon file can be saved for use within an application.

We won't go into a lot of detail on using the **IconEdit** program here - I just want you to know it exists and can be used to create and save icon files. Its use is fairly intuitive. Consult the help (click **Help** in the menu) that comes with the program for details.

All graphics used in the snowball toss game were created using **IconEdit**. These files are included in the **HomeSB\HomeSB Projects\Snowball** folder. Let's look at the files used to represent one of the two players. Start **IconEdit**. Choose **Open** under the **File** menu. An **Open Icon** dialog will appear. Navigate to the above folder. There are two files used to represent the players – **player1.ico** and **player2.ico**. Open **player1.ico** as shown:

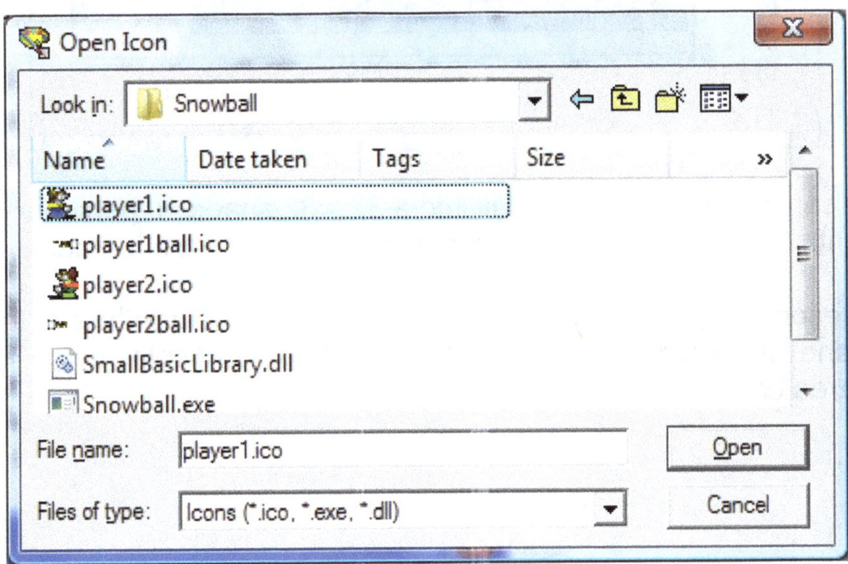

This cute little guy will appear:

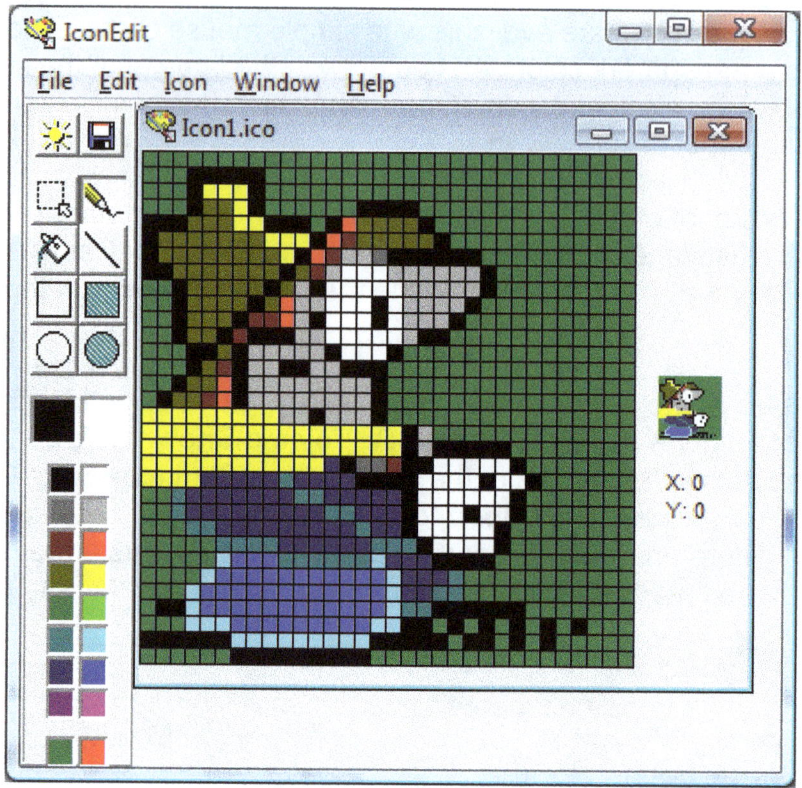

Notice you can get quite a lot of detail into a 32 x 32 space. I, personally, have no artistic talent. Someone drew all the graphics in this program for me.

Open the second player file if you like or look ahead at the graphics to represent snowmen and snowballs. Right now, let's look at how to display these little guys in the game area on our window.

Code Design – Start/Stop Game

We'll now write the code to display the players and to start and stop the game. Copy the **player1.ico** and **player2.ico** graphics files into your program's folder. Then, add this code (in **InitializeProgram** subroutine after code creating buttons) to create the player **Shapes** objects (**Player** array):

```
'Load images and put in shapes - all images 32 x 32
ImageW = 32
ImageH = 32
Player[1] =
Shapes.AddImage(ImageList.LoadImage(Program.Directory +
"\player1.ico"))
Shapes.HideShape(Player[1])
Player[2] =
Shapes.AddImage(ImageList.LoadImage(Program.Directory +
"\player2.ico"))
Shapes.HideShape(Player[2])
```

Since we are using icon files for all our graphics, they will all be the same size (32 x 32 pixels). These dimensions are stored in **ImageW** and **ImageH**. We hide the players initially.

When the user clicks **New Game** (**GameButton**) to start a game, the following preliminary steps should happen (more steps will be added later):

- Clear game rectangle.
- Change caption of **GameButton** to **Stop Game**.
- Hide **OptionsButton**.
- Hide **ExitButton**.
- Reset **PlayerHits[1]** and **PlayerHits[2]** to **0**.
- Reset **PlayerLeft[1]** and **PlayerLeft[2]** to **MaximumBalls**.
- Place **Player[1]** and **Player[2]** shapes in initial positions (use the **Move** method, followed by **ShowShape** method).

The code behind these steps is straightforward. The **Player[1]** shape will be centered vertically in the game rectangle near the left edge. The **Player[2]** shape will be centered vertically near the right edge.

This same button (**GameButton**) is used to stop a game. When a user clicks the button (when **Stop Game** is displayed), the following should happen:

- Hide **Player[1]** and **Player[2]** shapes (use **HideShape** method).
- Change caption of **GameButton** to **Start Game**.
- Show **OptionsButton**.
- Show **ExitButton**.
- Write **Game Over** message.

Make the shaded change to **ButtonClickedSub** to recognize clicking on **GameButton**:

```
Sub ButtonClickedSub
  B = Controls.LastClickedButton
  If (B = OptionsButton) Then
    SetOptions()
  ElseIf (B = ExitButton) Then
    File.WriteLine(Program.Directory + "\snowball.ini", 1,
NumberPlayers)
    File.WriteLine(Program.Directory + "\snowball.ini", 2,
Difficulty)
    Program.End()
  ElseIf (B = GameButton) Then
    GameButtonClicked()
  EndIf
EndSub
```

Then, the code for all the listed steps is placed in the **GameButtonClicked** subroutine. That code is:

```
Sub GameButtonClicked
  If (Controls.GetButtonCaption(GameButton) = "New Game") Then
    'clear game rectangle
    GraphicsWindow.BrushColor = "Gray"
    GraphicsWindow.FillRectangle(GameLeft, GameTop, GameWidth,
GameHeight)
    Controls.SetButtonCaption(GameButton, "Stop Game")
    Controls.HideControl(OptionsButton)
    Controls.HideControl(ExitButton)
    PlayerX[1] = GameLeft + 5
    PlayerY[1] = GameTop + 0.5 * GameHeight - 0.5 * ImageH
    PlayerX[2] = GameLeft + GameWidth - ImageW - 5
    PlayerY[2] = PlayerY[1]
    For I = 1 To 2
      PlayerHits[I] = 0
      Shapes.SetText(PlayerHitsDisplay[I], PlayerHits[I])
```

```
      PlayerLeft[I] = MaximumBalls
      Shapes.SetText(PlayerLeftDisplay[I], PlayerLeft[I])
      Shapes.Move(Player[I], PlayerX[I], PlayerY[I])
      Shapes.ShowShape(Player[I])
    EndFor
  Else
    For I = 1 To 2
      Shapes.HideShape(Player[I])
    EndFor
    Controls.SetButtonCaption(GameButton, "New Game")
    Controls.ShowControl(OptionsButton)
    Controls.ShowControl(ExitButton)
    GraphicsWindow.BrushColor = "Yellow"
    GraphicsWindow.FontSize = 36
    GraphicsWindow.DrawText(200, 250, "Game Over")
  EndIf
EndSub
```

Add this procedure to your project. The positioning of the **Game Over** message was obtained with trial and error.

Save and **Run** the project. Click **New Game** and the two guys should appear:

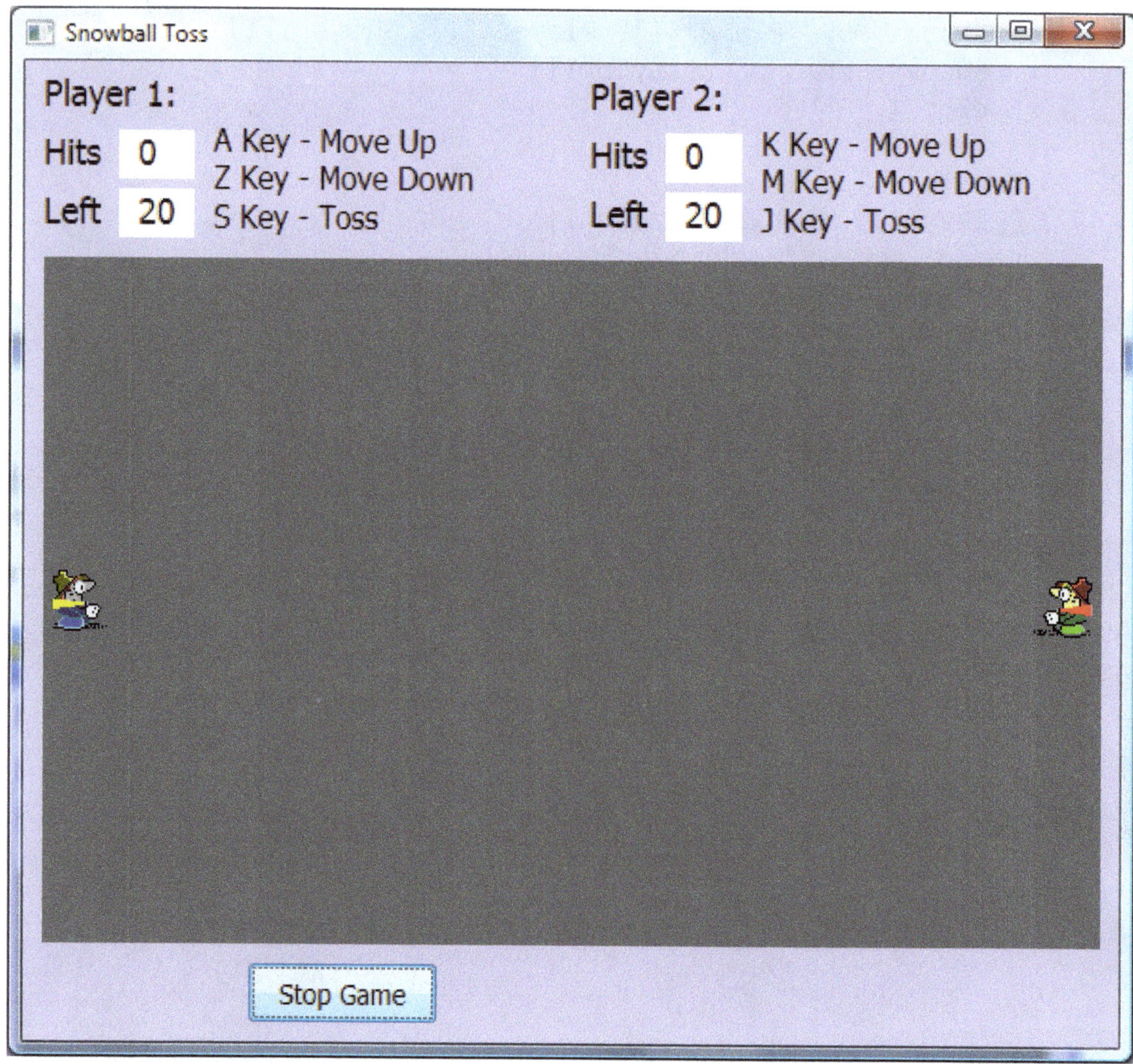

The game is ready to play – once we add the capability of moving the guys and throwing snowballs

Before leaving, click **Stop Game** to make sure the stop procedure works and **Game Over** appears:

At this point, you have the option to start a new game, change options or exit.

Code Design – Moving the Tossers

We need the capability to move our snowball tossers up and down in the game area. We choose to use the keyboard for control, using the **KeyDown** event. Add this line at the end of **InitializeProgram** to recognize key presses:

```
GraphicsWindow.KeyDown = KeyDownSub
```

In the snowball toss game, we choose the following keys to control player motion and tossing of snowballs (selected based on location on the keyboard):

Player 1	**A** – Move Up, **Z** – Move Down, **S** – Toss
Player 2	**K** – Move Up, **M** – Move Down, **J** – Toss

You can change these if you'd like.

Each time a movement key is pressed, we will move (using the **Move** method) the player an amount **PlayerIncrement** (a value you can adjust if needed) if going down and an amount **–PlayerIncrement** if going up. Add this variable under the **'game variables** comment in **InitializeProgram**:

```
PlayerIncrement = 5
```

You might wonder how I came up with this value. I tried several values finding one that resulted in smooth motion that wasn't too small or too large. Any time you program a game, you will have several adjustable parameters. There is no real science to setting values – just some guessing, trying and refining. Feel free to change any of the "built-in" values in the snowball toss game.

The code to move the tossers (we'll add throwing logic later) is placed in the **KeyDownSub** subroutine. That code is:

```
Sub KeyDownSub
  If (Controls.GetButtonCaption(GameButton) <> "New Game") Then
    PressedKey =
Text.ConvertToUpperCase(GraphicsWindow.LastKey)
    If (PressedKey = "A" Or PressedKey = "Z" Or PressedKey =
"S") Then
      PlayerID = 1
    Else
      PlayerID = 2
    EndIf
    If (PressedKey = "A" Or PressedKey = "K") Then
      MovePlayerUp()
    ElseIf (PressedKey = "Z" Or PressedKey = "M") Then
      MovePlayerDown()
    EndIf
  EndIf
EndSub
```

Notice we don't allow any key down events if we haven't started a game (that is, if **Game** is displaying **New Game**). We determine which player (**PlayerID**) has pressed a key, then based on the pressed key either call **MovePlayerUp** or **MovePlayerDown**.

The movement subroutines for **PlayerID** are:

```
Sub MovePlayerUp
  PlayerY[PlayerID] = PlayerY[PlayerID] - PlayerIncrement
  If (PlayerY[PlayerID] < GameTop) Then
    PlayerY[PlayerID] = GameTop
  EndIf
  Shapes.Move(Player[PlayerID], PlayerX[PlayerID],
PlayerY[PlayerID])
EndSub

Sub MovePlayerDown
  PlayerY[PlayerID] = PlayerY[PlayerID] + PlayerIncrement
  If (PlayerY[PlayerID] > GameTop + GameHeight - ImageH) Then
    PlayerY[PlayerID] = GameTop + GameHeight - ImageH
  EndIf
  Shapes.Move(Player[PlayerID], PlayerX[PlayerID],
PlayerY[PlayerID])
EndSub
```

Note we insure a player never leaves the playing field. Add these procedures to your project.

Save and **Run** the project. Select the **Two Players** option so you can see if both players can move. Click **New Game**. Press the **A** and **Z** keys to move **Player 1** (the guy on the left) and press the **K** and **M** keys to move **Player 2** (the guy on the right). Make sure they can't move off the top or bottom of the game area. Here's Player 1 at the top of the screen and Player 2 at the bottom:

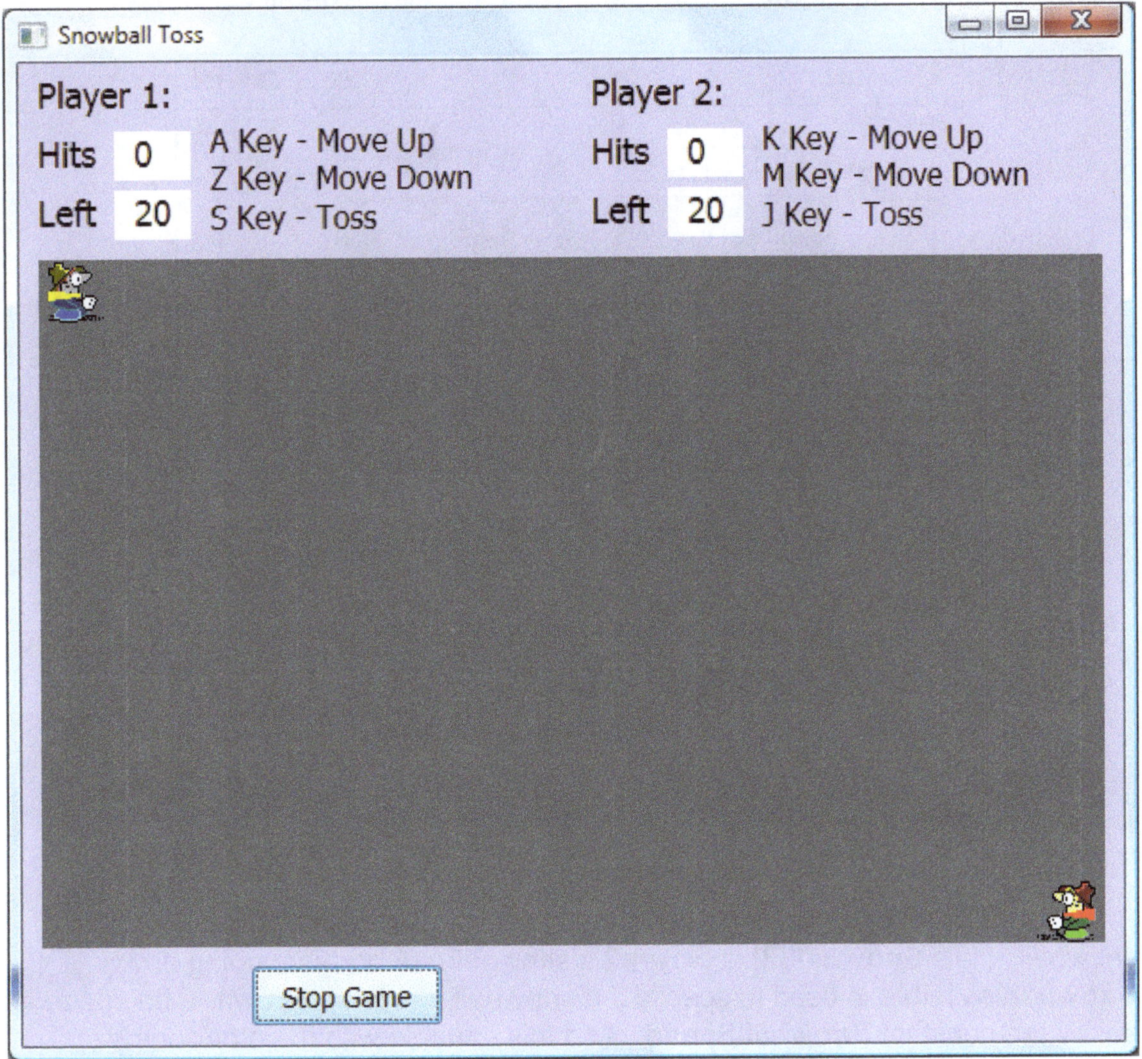

Now, let's start throwing some snowballs.

Code Design – Throwing Snowballs

We include two icon files to represent the snowballs (included in the **HomeSB\HomeSB Projects\Snowball** folder) named **player1ball.ico** and **player2ball.ico**. Move these files to your program folder. If you open **player1ball.ico** in the **IconEdit** program, you can see the detail:

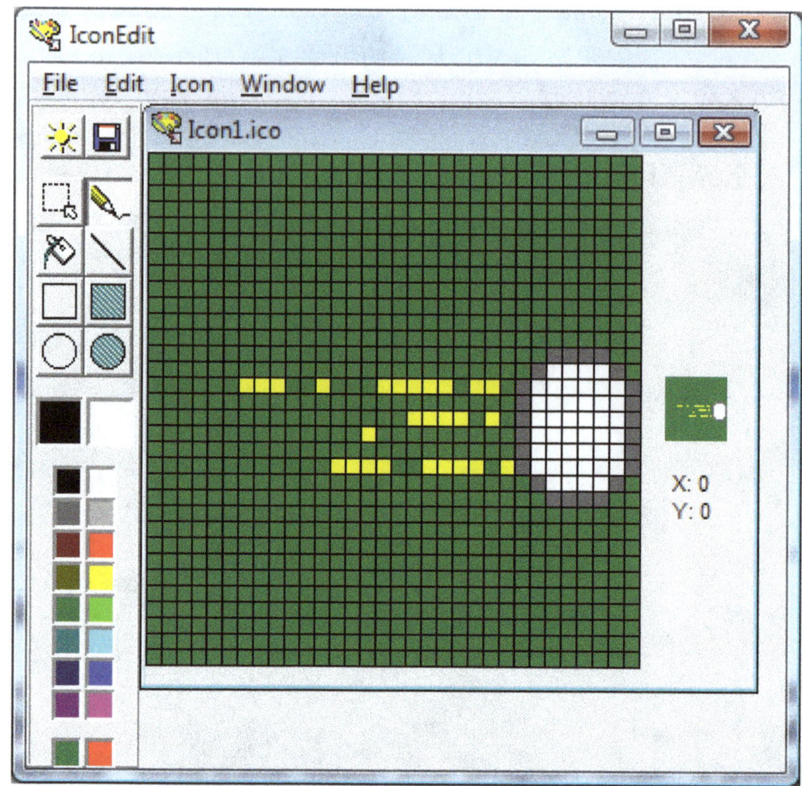

Snowballs are represented by two **Shapes** objects (**Snowball[1]** is player 1's snowball, while **Snowball[2]** is player 2's snowball). A corresponding array **SnowballIsVisible** is used to specify if a snowball has been thrown. The speed is set by the constant **SnowballSpeed**. Add this variable with the other game variables in **InitializeProgram**:

```
SnowballSpeed = 20
```

The speed is another parameter set by playing around with the program (again, a value you might like to change).

Snowballs are constructed in **InitializeProgram**. Add these lines (after the lines establishing the player **Shapes** objects):

```
Snowball[1] =
Shapes.AddImage(ImageList.LoadImage(Program.Directory +
"\player1ball.ico"))
Shapes.HideShape(Snowball[1])
SnowballIsVisible[1] = "false"
Snowball[2] =
Shapes.AddImage(ImageList.LoadImage(Program.Directory +
"\player2ball.ico"))
SnowballIsVisible[2] = "false"
Shapes.HideShape(Snowball[2])
```

Player 1 throws a snowball by pressing the **S** key. Player 2 throws a snowball by pressing the **J** key. We establish a couple of rules for throwing a snowball. First, we will only allow one snowball from each player to be on the screen at any one time (no multiple firings!). Second, the player can't throw a snowball if he is out of snowballs (obviously). Assuming these conditions are met, when a player makes a throw, the following steps occur:

- Decrement the number of snowballs left.
- Update display of snowballs left.
- Position snowball next to throwing player (just to right of Player 1, just to left of Player 2).
- Place snowball on game area using **Move** method (preceded by **ShowShape**).
- Set **SnowballIsVisible** to "**true**"

This 'throwing' code that implements these steps is placed in a subroutine **TossSnowball**. That code for **PlayerID** (either 1 or 2) is:

```
Sub TossSnowball
  If (SnowballIsVisible[PlayerID] = "false" And
PlayerLeft[PlayerID] > 0) Then
    PlayerLeft[PlayerID] = PlayerLeft[PlayerID] - 1
    Shapes.SetText(PlayerLeftDisplay[PlayerID],
PlayerLeft[PlayerID])
    If (PlayerID = 1) Then
      SnowballX[PlayerID] = PlayerX[PlayerID] + ImageW
    Else
      SnowballX[PlayerID] = PlayerX[PlayerID] - ImageW
    EndIf
    SnowballY[PlayerID] = PlayerY[PlayerID]
    Shapes.Move(Snowball[PlayerID], SnowballX[PlayerID],
SnowballY[PlayerID])
    Shapes.ShowShape(Snowball[PlayerID])
    SnowballIsVisible[PlayerID] = "true"
  EndIf
EndSub
```

The **TossSnowball** subroutine is called in the existing **KeyDownSub** subroutine (changes are shaded):

```
Sub KeyDownSub
  If (Controls.GetButtonCaption(GameButton) <> "New Game") Then
    PressedKey =
Text.ConvertToUpperCase(GraphicsWindow.LastKey)
    If (PressedKey = "A" Or PressedKey = "Z" Or PressedKey =
"S") Then
      PlayerID = 1
    Else
      PlayerID = 2
    EndIf
    If (PressedKey = "A" Or PressedKey = "K") Then
      MovePlayerUp()
    ElseIf (PressedKey = "Z" Or PressedKey = "M") Then
      MovePlayerDown()
    ElseIf (PressedKey = "S" Or PressedKey = "J") Then
      TossSnowball()
    EndIf
  EndIf
EndSub
```

Save and **Run** the program. Click **New Game**. Press the **S** and **J** keys to get snowballs started:

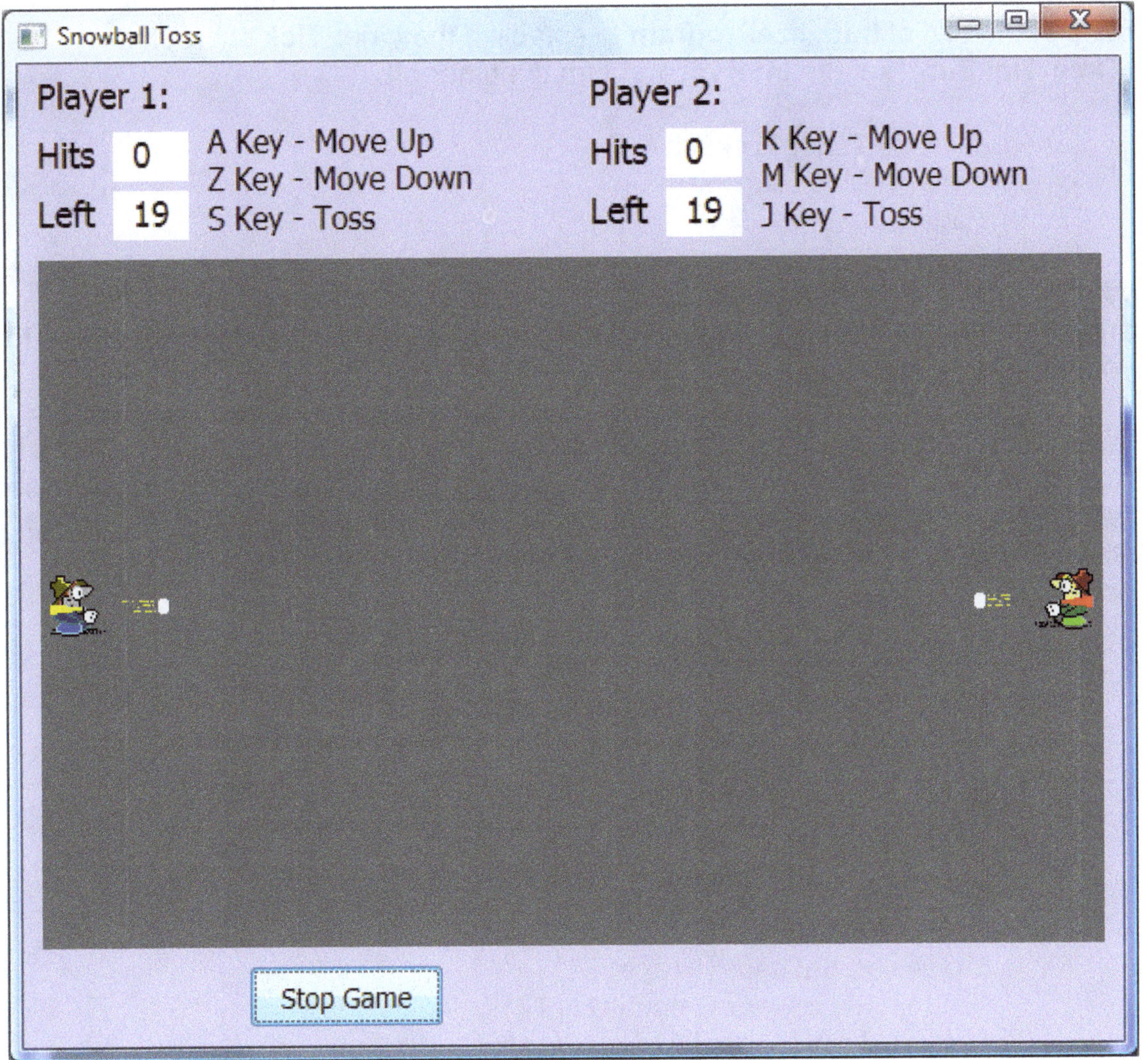

As seen, this code just gets a snowball started. Notice each player now has 19 snowballs left. Notice neither player can throw another snowball (since **SnowballIsVisible[1]** and **SnowballIsVisible[2]** are both "**true**"). Let's look at the code to get a snowball moving.

Code Design – Moving Snowballs

Once thrown, motion of the snowball(s) is updated by a **Timer** object. Add this code at the end of **InitializeProgram** to establish the timer **Tick** subroutine (**TimerTickSub**), set the **Interval** and turn the timer off:

```
Timer.Tick = TimerTickSub
Timer.Interval = 50
Timer.Pause()
```

We have selected an **Interval** property of **50** milliseconds for the timer. This is another parameter you may want to change to speed up or slow down the game to your liking.

We need code in the **GameButtonClicked** subroutine to start that timer (when **New Game** is clicked) and to stop the timer (when **Stop Game** is clicked. We also remove the snowballs when **Stop Game** is clicked. The modified **GameButtonClicked** procedure (changes are shaded, most unmodified code is not shown) is:

```
Sub GameButtonClicked
  If (Controls.GetButtonCaption(GameButton) = "New Game") Then
    .
    .
    Timer.Resume()
  Else
    Timer.Pause()
    For I = 1 To 2
      Shapes.HideShape(Player[I])
      Shapes.HideShape(Snowball[I])
      SnowballIsVisible[I] = "false"
    EndFor
    .
    .
  EndIf
EndSub
```

Add the new lines.

In the **TimerTickSub** subroutine, we update the position of thrown snowballs using the speed value and the **Move** method. We also check to see if a snowball goes off the edge of the game rectangle. If it does, we remove it from the rectangle to allow another throw. We also check for the end of the game (both players are out of snowballs and none are visible). If the game has ended, we 'click' **GameButton**. The code that does all this is:

```
Sub TimerTickSub
  'status of snowball 1
  If (SnowballIsVisible[1]) Then
    SnowballX[1] = SnowballX[1] + SnowballSpeed
    Shapes.Move(Snowball[1], SnowballX[1], SnowballY[1])
    If (SnowballX[1] > GameLeft + GameWidth) Then
      'off screen
      Shapes.HideShape(Snowball[1])
      SnowballIsVisible[1] = "false"
      Goto Snowball1Gone
    EndIf
  EndIf
  Snowball1Gone:
  'status of player 2 snowball
  If (SnowballIsVisible[2]) Then
    SnowballX[2] = SnowballX[2] - SnowballSpeed
    Shapes.Move(Snowball[2], SnowballX[2], SnowballY[2])
    If (SnowballX[2] < GameLeft - ImageW) Then
      'off screen
      Shapes.HideShape(Snowball[2])
      SnowballIsVisible[2] = "false"
      Goto Snowball2Gone
    EndIf
  EndIf
  Snowball2Gone:
  'check status of game
  If (SnowballIsVisible[1] = "false" And PlayerLeft[1] = 0 And
SnowballIsVisible[2] = "false" And PlayerLeft[2] = 0) Then
    GameButtonClicked()
  EndIf
EndSub
```

Add this subroutine to your project.

Save and **Run** the project. Make sure you are still using the two player option. Click **New Game**. Click **S** and **J** to throw snowballs. Make sure the displays reflect the proper number of remaining snowballs. Here is a run I made with a couple of snowballs flying:

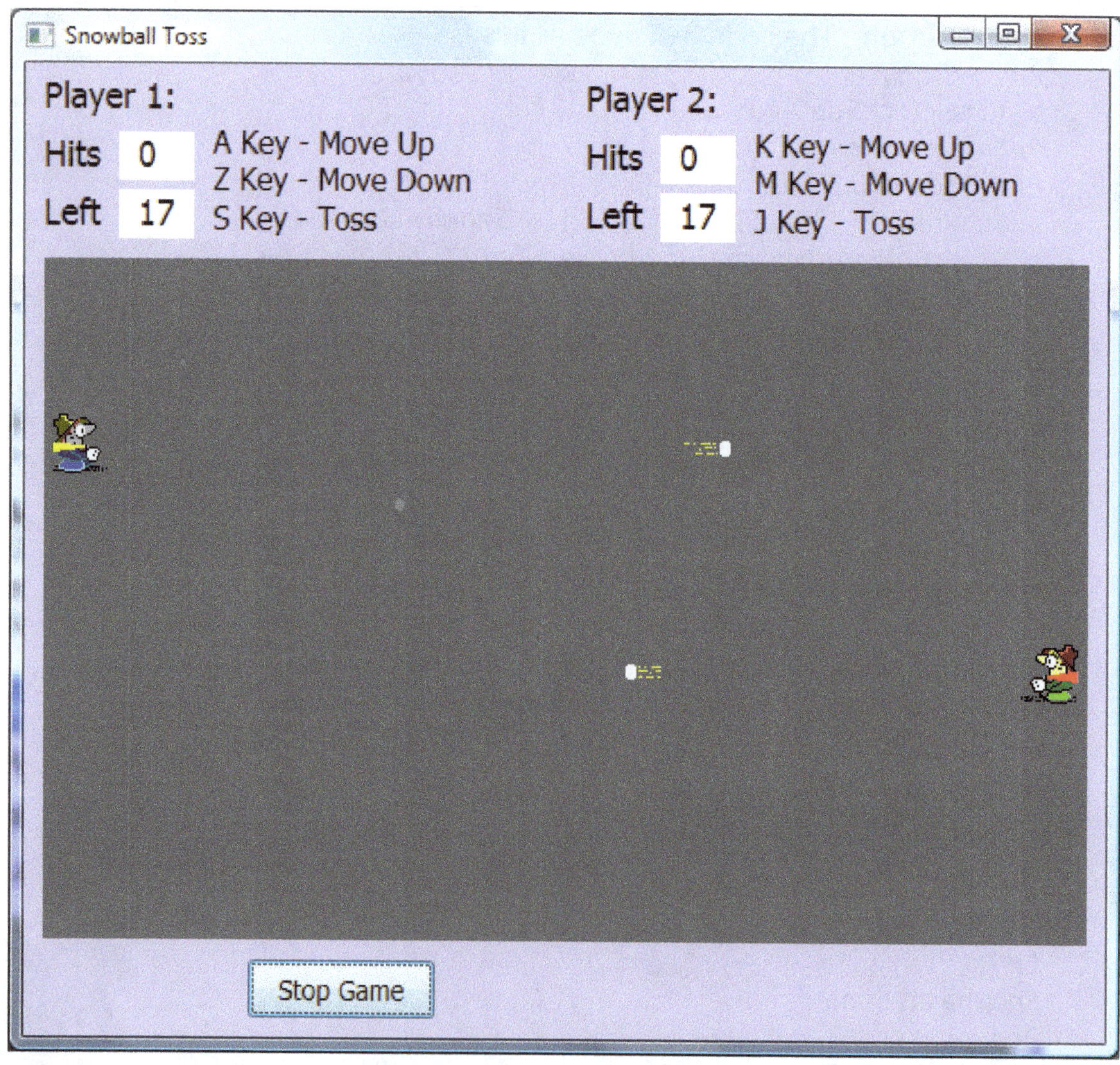

Stop the game when you want or throw snowballs until neither player has any remaining – the game will end. Notice we don't have any scoring (counting hits). To do this, we need collision logic, which is discussed next.

Code Design - Collision Detection

If a thrown snowball hits a player, the other player gets a point (a **Hit**). We need some way to check for such a 'collision'. Each shape is described by a rectangular area, so the **collision detection** problem is to see if two rectangles collide, or overlap. This check is done using each shape's position and dimensions.

Here are two shapes (**Shape[1]** and **Shape[2]**) in a window (to simplify things we assume each shape is the same size – **ShapeW** by **ShapeH** pixels):

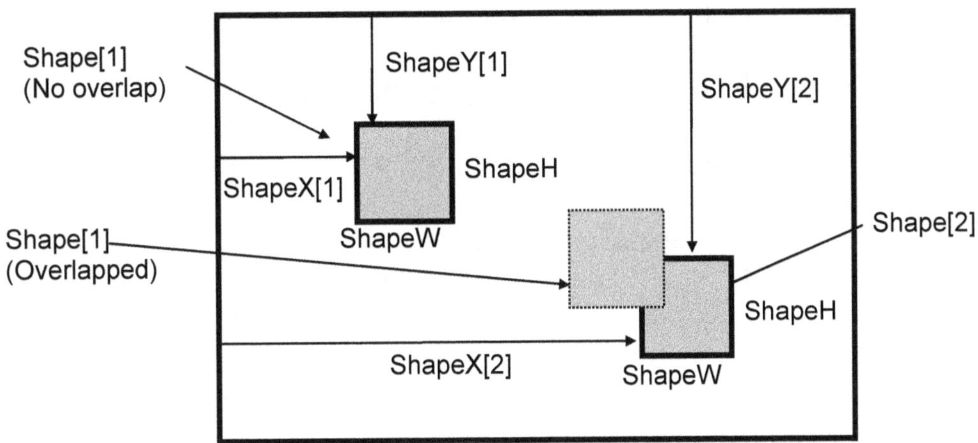

Shape[1] is positioned at (**ShapeX[1]**, **ShapeY[1]**), is **ShapeW** wide and **ShapeH** high. Similarly, **Shape[2]** is positioned at (**ShapeX[2]**, **ShapeY[2]**), is also **ShapeW** wide and **ShapeH** high.

Looking at this diagram, you should see there are four requirements for the two shapes to overlap:

1. The right side of Shape[1] (**ShapeX[1] + ShapeW**) must be "farther right" than the left side of Shape2 (**ShapeX[2]**)
2. The left side of Shape1 (**ShapeX[1]**) must be "farther left" than the right side of Shape2 (**ShapeX[2] + ShapeW**)
3. The bottom of Shape1 (**ShapeY[1] + ShapeH**) must be "farther down" than the top of Shape2 (**ShapeY[2]**)
4. The top of Shape1 (**ShapeY[1]**) must be "farther up" than the bottom of Shape2 (**ShapeY[2] + ShapeH**)

All four of these requirements must be met for a collision.

The Small Basic code to check if these shapes overlap is:

```
If ((ShapeX[1] + ShapeW) > ShapeX[2]) Then
  If (ShapeX[1] < (ShapeX[2] + ShapeW)) Then
    If ((ShapeY[1] + ShapeH) > ShapeY[2]) Then
      If (ShapeY[1] < (ShapeY[2] + ShapeH)) Then
        ' Small Basic code for overlap, or collision
      EndIf
    EndIf
  EndIf
EndIf
```

This code checks the four conditions for overlap using four "nested" If structures. The Small Basic code for a collision is executed only if all four conditions are found to be "**true**".

Add this subroutine (**CheckCollision**) to your program:

```
Sub CheckCollision
  Collision = "false"
  If ((ShapeX[1] + ImageW) > ShapeX[2]) Then
    If (ShapeX[1] < (ShapeX[2] + ImageW)) Then
      If ((ShapeY[1] + ImageH) > ShapeY[2]) Then
        If (ShapeY[1] < (ShapeY[2] + ImageH)) Then
          Collision = "true"
        EndIf
      EndIf
    EndIf
  EndIf
EndSub
```

To use this, you provide locations for two shapes in the **ShapeX** and **ShapeY** arrays. It determines a value for **Collision** ("**true**" if the shapes collided, "**false**" if not). Note the shapes are **ImageW** by **ImageH** in size.

As an example of using this subroutine, say we want to check if **Snowball[2]** has hit **Player[1]**. You would use this snippet of code:

```
ShapeX[1] = SnowballX[2]
ShapeY[1] = SnowballY[2]
ShapeX[2] = PlayerX[1]
ShapeY[2] = PlayerY[1]
CheckCollision()
```

If, after the call to **CheckCollision**, the variable **Collision** is "**true**", a collision has occurred. If a collision occurs, we remove the snowball and update the successful tosser's score.

We check for collisions between snowballs and players in the **TimerTickSub** subroutine. The modified code (shaded) checks for collisions and updates the score accordingly:

```
Sub TimerTickSub
  'status of snowball 1
  If (SnowballIsVisible[1]) Then
    SnowballX[1] = SnowballX[1] + SnowballSpeed
    Shapes.Move(Snowball[1], SnowballX[1], SnowballY[1])
    If (SnowballX[1] > GameLeft + GameWidth) Then
      'off screen
      Shapes.HideShape(Snowball[1])
      SnowballIsVisible[1] = "false"
      Goto Snowball1Gone
    Else
      'check for collision with player2
      ShapeX[1] = SnowballX[1]
      ShapeY[1] = SnowballY[1]
      ShapeX[2] = PlayerX[2]
      ShapeY[2] = PlayerY[2]
      CheckCollision()
      If (Collision) Then
        PlayerHits[1] = PlayerHits[1] + 1
        Shapes.SetText(PlayerHitsDisplay[1], PlayerHits[1])
        Shapes.HideShape(Snowball[1])
        SnowballIsVisible[1] = "false"
        Goto Snowball1Gone
      EndIf
    EndIf
  EndIf
  Snowball1Gone:
  'status of player 2 snowball
  If (SnowballIsVisible[2]) Then
    SnowballX[2] = SnowballX[2] - SnowballSpeed
    Shapes.Move(Snowball[2], SnowballX[2], SnowballY[2])
    If (SnowballX[2] < GameLeft - ImageW) Then
      'off screen
      Shapes.HideShape(Snowball[2])
      SnowballIsVisible[2] = "false"
      Goto Snowball2Gone
    Else
      'check for collision with player1
      ShapeX[1] = SnowballX[2]
      ShapeY[1] = SnowballY[2]
      ShapeX[2] = PlayerX[1]
      ShapeY[2] = PlayerY[1]
```

```
      CheckCollision()
      If (Collision) Then
        PlayerHits[2] = PlayerHits[2] + 1
        Shapes.SetText(PlayerHitsDisplay[2], PlayerHits[2])
        Shapes.HideShape(Snowball[2])
        SnowballIsVisible[2] = "false"
        Goto Snowball2Gone
      EndIf
    EndIf
  EndIf
  Snowball2Gone:
  'check status of game
  If (SnowballIsVisible[1] = "false" And PlayerLeft[1] = 0 And
SnowballIsVisible[2] = "false" And PlayerLeft[2] = 0) Then
    GameButtonClicked()
  EndIf
EndSub
```

Make the noted modifications.

Save and **Run** the project. Now if you throw a snowball and hit the other player, the snowball should disappear. Give it a try. Here's the middle of a game I played:

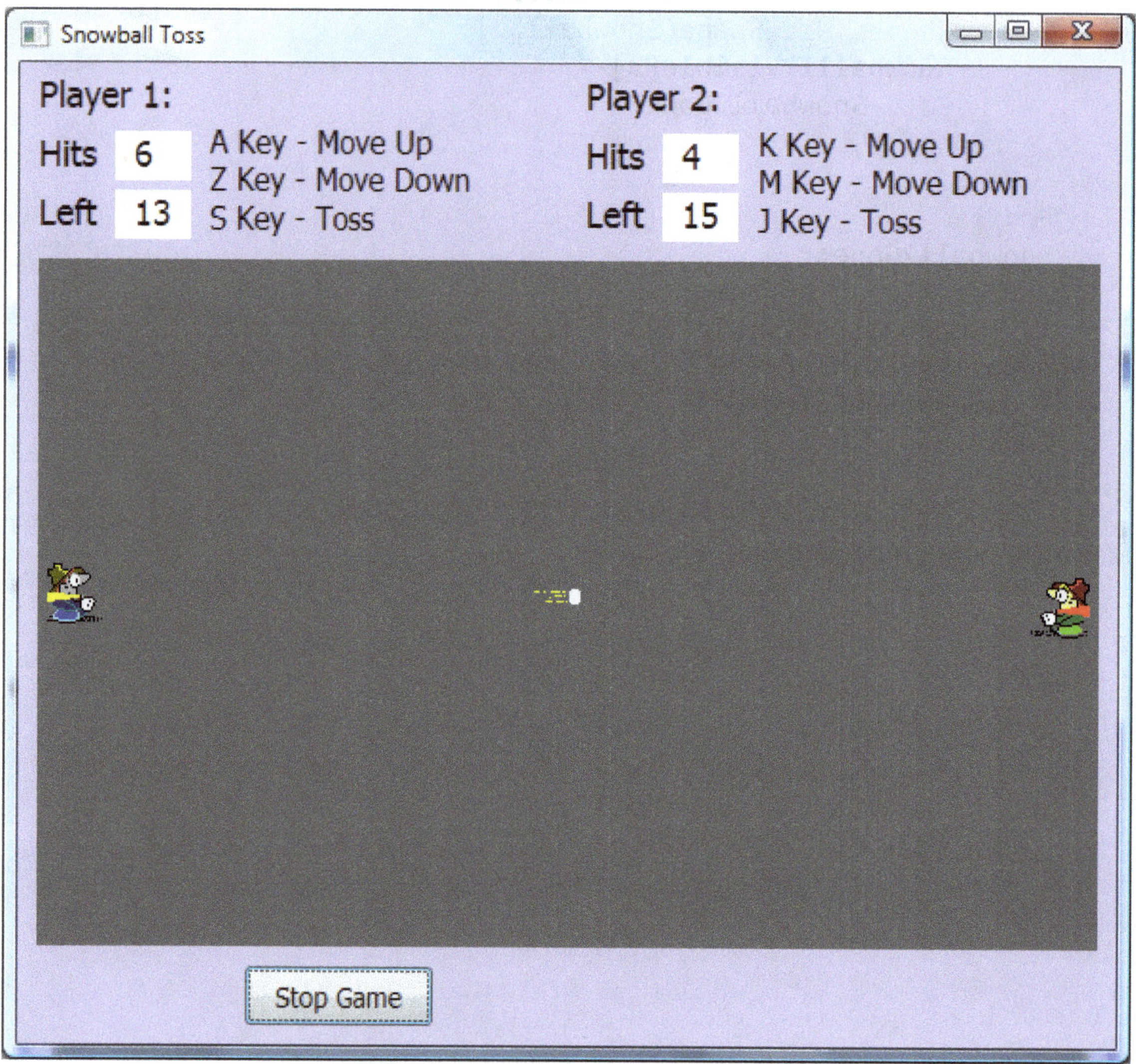

Make sure the score updates properly after each successful toss.

Code Design – Zombie Snowmen

As designed, the players have no protection from thrown snowballs other than their ability to move up and down. We'll change that now. We'll invent a tribe of "zombie" snowmen that roam up and down the middle of the playing field. These snowmen will deflect (stop) any snowball that has been thrown.

The icon file **snowman.ico** (included in the **HomeSB\HomeSB Projects\Snowball** folder) depicts a snowman. Move this file to your program folder. If you open **snowman.ico** in the **IconEdit** program, you can see the detail:

I know – he looks pretty happy for a zombie! We will have two snowmen (you can choose more if you want). Snowmen are represented by **Shapes** objects (in a **Snowman** array). Their motion will be random, with some restrictions.

Our snowmen will move according to some predetermined rules. **Snowman[1]** will move vertically just to the left of the center of game area, while **Snowman[2]** will move vertically just to the right of center. The speed (**SnowmanSpeed** array) will be a random value between 1 and 4 (a value you might want to change). The snowmen can move either up or down. If moving up, they start at the bottom of the field. If moving down, they start at the top. How did I come up with all these rules for my zombies? I made them up. That's the nice thing about being a game programmer. You can make your characters do whatever you want them to. Come up with rules for your own set of zombie snowmen if you want.

The snowmen are constructed in **InitializeProgram**. Add these lines (after the lines establishing the snowball shapes):

```
Snowman[1] =
Shapes.AddImage(ImageList.LoadImage(Program.Directory +
"\snowman.ico"))
Shapes.HideShape(Snowman[1])
Snowman[2] =
Shapes.AddImage(ImageList.LoadImage(Program.Directory +
"\snowman.ico"))
Shapes.HideShape(Snowman[2])
```

The snowmen are initially placed in the field when **New Game** is clicked. When this occurs, they are randomly placed within the vertical constraints of the game area. And, they are assigned a random speed. The snowmen are removed when **Stop Game** is clicked. The modified **GameButtonClicked** procedure that accomplishes these tasks (changes are shaded, with much unmodified code not shown) is:

```
Sub GameButtonClicked
  If (Controls.GetButtonCaption(GameButton) = "New Game") Then
   .
   .
    SnowmanX[1] = GameLeft + 0.5 * GameWidth - ImageW
    SnowmanY[1] = GameTop + Math.GetRandomNumber(GameHeight -
ImageH)
    SnowmanX[2] = GameLeft + 0.5 * GameWidth
    SnowmanY[2] = GameTop + Math.GetRandomNumber(GameHeight -
ImageH)
    For I = 1 To 2
   .
   .
      GetSnowmanSpeed()
      SnowmanSpeed[I] = Speed
      Shapes.Move(Snowman[I], SnowmanX[I], SnowmanY[I])
      Shapes.ShowShape(Snowman[I])
    EndFor
    Timer.Resume()
  Else
    Timer.Pause()
    For I = 1 To 2
      Shapes.HideShape(Player[I])
      Shapes.HideShape(Snowball[I])
      SnowballIsVisible[I] = "false"
      Shapes.HideShape(Snowman[I])
    EndFor
   .
   .
  EndIf
EndSub
```

Snowman[1] is just to the left of the middle of the game rectangle, while **Snowman[2]** is just to the right. Notice how the snowmen are randomly positioned vertically.

The snowman speed is determined using a subroutine **SnowmanSpeed**. As mentioned, we choose this value to be random, between 1 and 4. The speed can be positive (for downward motion) or negative (for upward motion). This choice of sign is also random. The code that incorporates this speed assignment is:

```
Sub GetSnowmanSpeed
  SpeedMin = 1
  SpeedMax = 4
  Speed = Math.GetRandomNumber(SpeedMax - SpeedMin + 1) +
SpeedMin - 1
  If (Math.GetRandomNumber(2) = 1) Then
    Speed = -Speed
  EndIf
EndSub
```

Computing the speed value (**Speed**) is straightforward. To choose the sign, we do a computerized "coin flip". This flip is done by looking at the value of:

```
Math.GetRandomNumber(2)
```

This can return one of two values, 1 ("heads") or 2 ("tails").

Snowman motion is updated in the **TimerTickSub** subroutine. At each update, for each snowman, we need to perform the following steps:

- Move the snowman using the current **SnowmanSpeed** value.
- Check to see if the snowman has moved to edge of the game area.
- If at the edge, do this:
  - Compute a new speed.
  - If speed is positive, position snowman at top of playing field so it can start moving down.
  - If speed is negative, position snowman at bottom of playing field so it can start moving up.
- After moving or repositioning snowman, check to see if a thrown snowball has collided with it. If there is a collision, remove the snowball from the field.

The modified **TimerTickSub** subroutine that implements these steps is (changes are shaded):

```
Sub TimerTickSub
  'move snowmen
  For I =1 to 2
    SnowmanY[I] = SnowmanY[I] + SnowmanSpeed[I]
    Shapes.Move(Snowman[I], SnowmanX[I], SnowmanY[I])
    If (SnowmanY[I] < GameTop Or SnowmanY[I] > GameTop +
GameHeight - ImageH) Then
      'recompute speed
      GetSnowmanSpeed()
      SnowmanSpeed[I] = Speed
      If (SnowmanSpeed[I] > 0) Then
        SnowmanY[I] = GameTop
      Else
        SnowmanY[I] = GameTop + GameHeight - ImageH
      EndIf
    EndIf
  EndFor
  'status of snowball 1
  If (SnowballIsVisible[1]) Then
    SnowballX[1] = SnowballX[1] + SnowballSpeed
    Shapes.Move(Snowball[1], SnowballX[1], SnowballY[1])
    If (SnowballX[1] > GameLeft + GameWidth) Then
      'off screen
      Shapes.HideShape(Snowball[1])
      SnowballIsVisible[1] = "false"
      Goto Snowball1Gone
    Else
      'check for collision with player2
      ShapeX[1] = SnowballX[1]
      ShapeY[1] = SnowballY[1]
      ShapeX[2] = PlayerX[2]
      ShapeY[2] = PlayerY[2]
      CheckCollision()
      If (Collision) Then
        PlayerHits[1] = PlayerHits[1] + 1
        Shapes.SetText(PlayerHitsDisplay[1], PlayerHits[1])
        Shapes.HideShape(Snowball[1])
        SnowballIsVisible[1] = "false"
        Goto Snowball1Gone
      EndIf
      'check for collision with either snowman
      For I = 1 To 2
        ShapeX[1] = SnowballX[1]
```

```
        ShapeY[1] = SnowballY[1]
        ShapeX[2] = SnowmanX[I]
        ShapeY[2] = SnowmanY[I]
        CheckCollision()
        If (Collision) Then
          Shapes.HideShape(Snowball[1])
          SnowballIsVisible[1] = "false"
          Goto Snowball1Gone
        EndIf
      EndFor
    EndIf
  EndIf
  Snowball1Gone:
  'status of player 2 snowball
  If (SnowballIsVisible[2]) Then
    SnowballX[2] = SnowballX[2] - SnowballSpeed
    Shapes.Move(Snowball[2], SnowballX[2], SnowballY[2])
    If (SnowballX[2] < GameLeft - ImageW) Then
      'off screen
      Shapes.HideShape(Snowball[2])
      SnowballIsVisible[2] = "false"
      Goto Snowball2Gone
    Else
      'check for collision with player1
      ShapeX[1] = SnowballX[2]
      ShapeY[1] = SnowballY[2]
      ShapeX[2] = PlayerX[1]
      ShapeY[2] = PlayerY[1]
      CheckCollision()
      If (Collision) Then
        PlayerHits[2] = PlayerHits[2] + 1
        Shapes.SetText(PlayerHitsDisplay[2], PlayerHits[2])
        Shapes.HideShape(Snowball[2])
        SnowballIsVisible[2] = "false"
        Goto Snowball2Gone
      EndIf
      'check for collision with either snowman
      For I = 1 To 2
        ShapeX[1] = SnowballX[2]
        ShapeY[1] = SnowballY[2]
        ShapeX[2] = SnowmanX[I]
        ShapeY[2] = SnowmanY[I]
        CheckCollision()
        If (Collision) Then
          Shapes.HideShape(Snowball[2])
          SnowballIsVisible[2] = "false"
```

```
          Goto Snowball2Gone
        EndIf
      EndFor
    EndIf
  EndIf
  Snowball2Gone:
  'check status of game
  If (SnowballIsVisible[1] = "false" And PlayerLeft[1] = 0 And
SnowballIsVisible[2] = "false" And PlayerLeft[2] = 0) Then
    GameButtonClicked()
  EndIf
EndSub
```

Make the noted changes. You should understand how all the zombie rules have been applied.

Save and **Run** the project. The snowmen should be moving through the middle of the field deflecting any snowballs they might block. They should move both up and down at varying speeds. Watch them for a while. Here's a run I made:

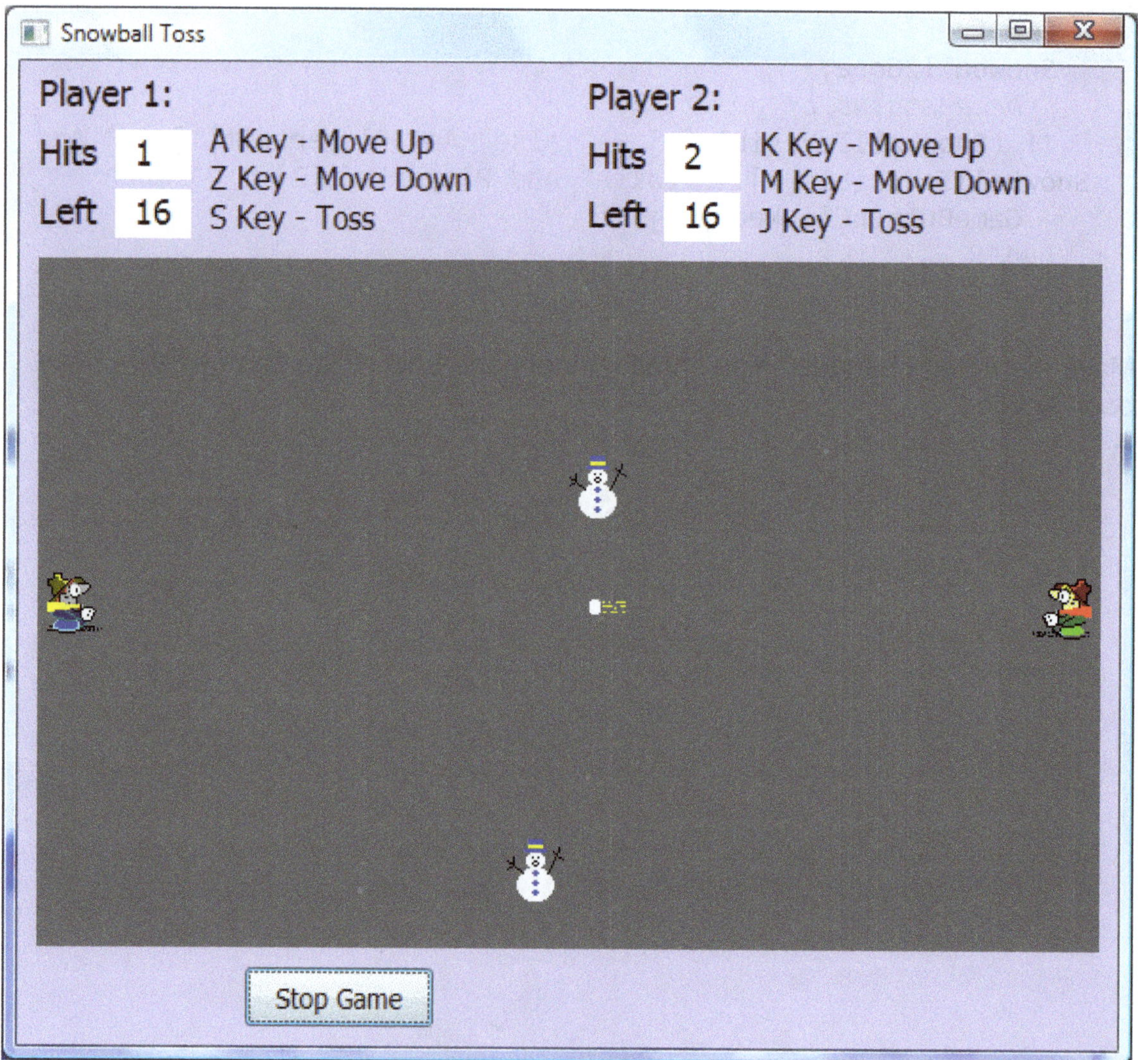

The two player version of the snowball toss game is essentially complete. All the animation steps are implemented – we can move the players, we can throw snowballs, the zombie snowmen can block snowballs and the score is properly kept. Next, we'll program the one player version, making the computer control Player 2.

Before doing the one player version, however, let's address one sorely lacking feature – sounds! Any good game has sound and we should have some in this game. Let's add a throwing sound, a splat sound when a snowman is hit and an "Ouch" sound when a player is hit. And, let's add a little tune when the game is over.

Code Design – Playing Sounds

There are a few built in sounds with Small Basic, but they are kind of boring. Games feature elaborate sounds that take advantage of stereo sound cards. By using the Small Basic **Sound** object, we can add such sounds to our snowball toss game.

The **Sound** object is used to play one particular type of sound, those represented by **wav** files (files with wav extensions). Most sounds you hear played in Windows applications are saved as **wav** files. These are the files formed when you record using one of the many sound recorder programs available. In the **HomeSB\HomeSB Projects\Snowball** folder are four **wav** files for use in this program:

throw.wav	sound to play when a snowball is thrown
splat.wav	sound to play when a snowball hits a snowman
ouch.wav	sound to play when a snowball hits a player
gameover.wav	sound to play when game is over (both players are out of snowballs)

You can play each of these sounds in your computer's media player if you want.

There are two ways to play a sound file. To play the sound (represented by **SoundFile**) to completion before executing any more code (delaying the program), use the single line:

```
Sound.PlayAndWait(SoundFile)
```

To start playing a sound and immediately continue executing code:

```
Sound.Stop(SoundFile)
Sound.Play(SoundFile)
```

We execute a **Stop** before playing a sound, just in case it's still playing from a previous call.

It is normal practice to include any sound files an application uses in the same folder as the program. This makes them easily accessible (use the **Program.Directory** parameter). Copy the four included sound files into your program's folder.

Let's modify the snowball toss game code to include the sounds. A throwing sound (**throw.wav**) will play when a snowball is thrown. This action occurs in the **TossSnowball** subroutine. The modified code (changes are shaded) is:

```
Sub TossSnowball
  If (SnowballIsVisible[PlayerID] = "false" And
PlayerLeft[PlayerID] > 0) Then
    Sound.Stop(Program.Directory + "\throw.wav")
    Sound.Play(Program.Directory + "\throw.wav")
    PlayerLeft[PlayerID] = PlayerLeft[PlayerID] - 1
    Shapes.SetText(PlayerLeftDisplay[PlayerID],
PlayerLeft[PlayerID])
    If (PlayerID = 1) Then
      SnowballX[PlayerID] = PlayerX[PlayerID] + ImageW
    Else
      SnowballX[PlayerID] = PlayerX[PlayerID] - ImageW
    EndIf
    SnowballY[PlayerID] = PlayerY[PlayerID]
    Shapes.Move(Snowball[PlayerID], SnowballX[PlayerID],
SnowballY[PlayerID])
    Shapes.ShowShape(Snowball[PlayerID])
    SnowballIsVisible[PlayerID] = "true"
  EndIf
EndSub
```

A splat sound (**splat.wav**) will play when a snowman is hit by a snowball, an ouch sound (**ouch.wav**) will play when a player is hit by a snowball and a game over sound (**gameover.wav**) will play when the players run out of snowballs. All of these actions occur in the **TimerTickSub** subroutine. The modified code (changes are shaded) is:

```
Sub TimerTickSub
  'move snowmen
  For I =1 to 2
    SnowmanY[I] = SnowmanY[I] + SnowmanSpeed[I]
    Shapes.Move(Snowman[I], SnowmanX[I], SnowmanY[I])
    If (SnowmanY[I] < GameTop Or SnowmanY[I] > GameTop +
GameHeight - ImageH) Then
      'recompute speed
      GetSnowmanSpeed()
      SnowmanSpeed[I] = Speed
      If (SnowmanSpeed[I] > 0) Then
        SnowmanY[I] = GameTop
      Else
        SnowmanY[I] = GameTop + GameHeight - ImageH
      EndIf
```

```
  EndIf
EndFor
'status of snowball 1
If (SnowballIsVisible[1]) Then
  SnowballX[1] = SnowballX[1] + SnowballSpeed
  Shapes.Move(Snowball[1], SnowballX[1], SnowballY[1])
  If (SnowballX[1] > GameLeft + GameWidth) Then
    'off screen
    Shapes.HideShape(Snowball[1])
    SnowballIsVisible[1] = "false"
    Goto Snowball1Gone
  Else
    'check for collision with player2
    ShapeX[1] = SnowballX[1]
    ShapeY[1] = SnowballY[1]
    ShapeX[2] = PlayerX[2]
    ShapeY[2] = PlayerY[2]
    CheckCollision()
    If (Collision) Then
      Sound.Stop(Program.Directory + "\ouch.wav")
      Sound.Play(Program.Directory + "\ouch.wav")
      PlayerHits[1] = PlayerHits[1] + 1
      Shapes.SetText(PlayerHitsDisplay[1], PlayerHits[1])
      Shapes.HideShape(Snowball[1])
      SnowballIsVisible[1] = "false"
      Goto Snowball1Gone
    EndIf
    'check for collision with either snowman
    For I = 1 To 2
      ShapeX[1] = SnowballX[1]
      ShapeY[1] = SnowballY[1]
      ShapeX[2] = SnowmanX[I]
      ShapeY[2] = SnowmanY[I]
      CheckCollision()
      If (Collision) Then
        Sound.Stop(Program.Directory + "\splat.wav")
        Sound.Play(Program.Directory + "\splat.wav")
        Shapes.HideShape(Snowball[1])
        SnowballIsVisible[1] = "false"
        Goto Snowball1Gone
      EndIf
    EndFor
  EndIf
EndIf
Snowball1Gone:
'status of player 2 snowball
```

```
If (SnowballIsVisible[2]) Then
  SnowballX[2] = SnowballX[2] - SnowballSpeed
  Shapes.Move(Snowball[2], SnowballX[2], SnowballY[2])
  If (SnowballX[2] < GameLeft - ImageW) Then
    'off screen
    Shapes.HideShape(Snowball[2])
    SnowballIsVisible[2] = "false"
    Goto Snowball2Gone
  Else
    'check for collision with player1
    ShapeX[1] = SnowballX[2]
    ShapeY[1] = SnowballY[2]
    ShapeX[2] = PlayerX[1]
    ShapeY[2] = PlayerY[1]
    CheckCollision()
    If (Collision) Then
      Sound.Stop(Program.Directory + "\ouch.wav")
      Sound.Play(Program.Directory + "\ouch.wav")
      PlayerHits[2] = PlayerHits[2] + 1
      Shapes.SetText(PlayerHitsDisplay[2], PlayerHits[2])
      Shapes.HideShape(Snowball[2])
      SnowballIsVisible[2] = "false"
      Goto Snowball2Gone
    EndIf
    'check for collision with either snowman
    For I = 1 To 2
      ShapeX[1] = SnowballX[2]
      ShapeY[1] = SnowballY[2]
      ShapeX[2] = SnowmanX[I]
      ShapeY[2] = SnowmanY[I]
      CheckCollision()
      If (Collision) Then
        Sound.Stop(Program.Directory + "\splat.wav")
        Sound.Play(Program.Directory + "\splat.wav")
        Shapes.HideShape(Snowball[2])
        SnowballIsVisible[2] = "false"
        Goto Snowball2Gone
      EndIf
    EndFor
  EndIf
EndIf
Snowball2Gone:
'check status of game
If (SnowballIsVisible[1] = "false" And PlayerLeft[1] = 0 And
SnowballIsVisible[2] = "false" And PlayerLeft[2] = 0) Then
  Sound.PlayAndWait(Program.Directory + "\gameover.wav")
```

```
    GameButtonClicked()
  EndIf
EndSub
```

Make these changes. The collision sounds are played immediately (**Play** method) so game play can continue. The **GameOverSound** is played using **PlayAndWait** – it must finish playing before user events can occur.

Save and **Run** the project. Play the two player game. Listen for the throw, splat and ouch sounds. And, play until all the snowballs are thrown to hear the cute little "game over" tune. Make these changes. I think you'll agree that the sounds make the game far more fun to play.

A Possible Problem

As implemented, sometimes when the program is run, you may see an error message like this:

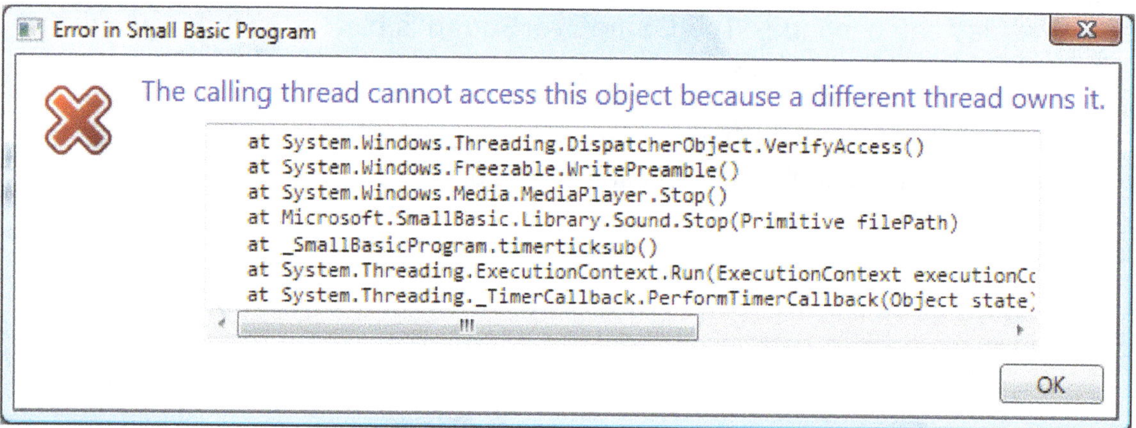

Error in Small Basic Program
The calling thread cannot access this object because a different thread owns it.
at System.Windows.Threading.DispatcherObject.VerifyAccess()
at System.Windows.Freezable.WritePreamble()
at System.Windows.Media.MediaPlayer.Stop()
at Microsoft.SmallBasic.Library.Sound.Stop(Primitive filePath)
at _SmallBasicProgram.timerticksub()
at System.Threading.ExecutionContext.Run(ExecutionContext executionCc
at System.Threading._TimerCallback.PerformTimerCallback(Object state)
OK

This message is related to the playing of sounds within the **TimerTickSub** subroutine.

A simple explanation is that there is a lot of computation going on in the **TimerTickSub** subroutine and it has just 50 milliseconds (0.05 seconds) to complete the tasks. Occasionally, especially when sounds are involved, it cannot perform all tasks in the allotted 0.05 seconds. In such a case, the current execution of the subroutine is halted and a new execution from the beginning is started - a new "**thread**" (the word that appears in the error message) begins. At that point, it has sounds playing and tries to start other sounds, confusing the Small Basic language. All it can do is stop.

So, what can we do? I am assuming this is a problem that will be fixed in later versions of Small Basic. We are currently working with Beta versions and errors do exist. For now, the only solution I have is to comment out the lines of code that stop/play sounds. I have found you can leave the throw sounds in, but all others should not be played for now. You decide which sounds you want.

Code Design – One Player Game

You can't always find someone to play a game with. So why not let the computer be your opponent? In a one player snowball toss game, we will let the computer control Player 2.

For such computer control, we need to develop some rules for the computer to use. In the **Blackjack** card game built earlier in these notes, we played against the computer. The rules used there by the computer were predetermined by those used in most casinos. Here, in the snowball toss game, we have no such rules. We need to develop them ourselves. This is a fun part of programming – giving the computer some semblance of intelligence. The logic presented here are ideas that I just made up as I went along. They seem to work. Feel free to make changes you think are needed.

There are two approaches we could take in writing code for a computer competitor. We could use very simple logic, perhaps making it easy for a human to win. Or, we could write more detailed logic, emulating steps you, as a human, might take in playing the game. With more detailed logic, it would be harder for a human to win. In the snowball toss game, we take both approaches. We first develop a simple, random game playing logic, then a more detailed logic. Then, we use the level of difficulty selected with the **Options** button to determine how often we use the random logic versus how often we use the detailed logic. The values I chose to use are:

Difficulty Level	Simple Logic (%)	Detailed Logic (%)
Easiest	100	0
Easy	75	25
Hard	50	50
Hardest	25	75

So, when the **Easiest** level is selected, we use the simple logic 100 percent of the time. When the **Hardest** level is selected, we use the simple logic 25 percent of the time (we don't want our computer to be too smart) and the detailed logic 75 percent of the time

Another value selected by the level of difficulty will be how often the computer makes a move. The computer moves will be controlled by the same **Timer** object that controls game play. We will have the computer make a move every **ComputerTicksMax** calls to the **TimerTickSub** subroutine. For easier games, we want a larger value for the **ComputerTicksMax**. This slows down the computer's thought process. The values I chose are:

Difficulty Level	ComputerTicksMax
Easiest	20
Easy	15
Hard	10
Hardest	5

So with the **Hardest** difficulty, the computer makes moves 4 times as often as when the **Easiest** difficulty is selected. A variable **ComputerTicks** will keep track of how many times the **TimerTickSub** subroutine has been called. Once **ComputerTicks** equals **ComputerTicksMax**, a computer move will be allowed.

We will use a variable **ComputerRandom** to represent the percentage of time simple logic is used. Values for **ComputerRandom** and **ComputerTicksMax** will be set (based on difficulty) in the subroutine **ComputerParameters**:

```
Sub GetComputerParameters
  If (Difficulty = 1) Then
    ComputerRandom = 100
    ComputerTicksMax = 20
  ElseIf (Difficulty = 2) Then
    ComputerRandom = 75
    ComputerTicksMax = 15
  ElseIf (Difficulty = 3) Then
    ComputerRandom = 50
    ComputerTicksMax = 10
  Else
    ComputerRandom = 25
    ComputerTicksMax = 5
  EndIf
EndSub
```

Add this subroutine to your project.

We call this subroutine (**GetComputerParameters**) in two places. First, after we read in the configuration file in **InitializeProgram** (establishing **NumberPlayers** and **Difficulty**) when the program begins. Place this line after the code reading in these values from the file:

```
GetComputerParameters()
```

Also, add this line at the shaded location in **SetOptions** (code setting **NumberPlayers** not shown):

```
Sub SetOptions
  GraphicsWindow.Hide()
  TextWindow.Show()
  TextWindow.Title = "Snowball Toss"
   .
   .
  If (NumberPlayers = 1) Then
    GetDifficulty:
    TextWindow.WriteLine("")
    TextWindow.CursorLeft = 3
    TextWindow.WriteLine("You can set the game difficulty.")
    TextWindow.CursorLeft = 3
    TextWindow.Write("Make your choice (1-Easiest, 2-Easy, 3-
Hard, 4-Hardest)? ")
    Difficulty = TextWindow.ReadNumber()
    If (Difficulty < 1 Or Difficulty > 4) Then
      Goto GetDifficulty
    EndIf
    GetComputerParameters()
  EndIf
  DisplayHeadings()
  TextWindow.Hide()
  GraphicsWindow.Show()
EndSub
```

We need to initialize **ComputerTicks** to zero when a game is started. This is done in the **GameButtonClicked** (new line is shaded):

```
Sub GameButtonClicked
  If (Controls.GetButtonCaption(GameButton) = "New Game") Then
    'clear game rectangle
    GraphicsWindow.BrushColor = "Gray"
    GraphicsWindow.FillRectangle(GameLeft, GameTop, GameWidth,
GameHeight)
    Controls.SetButtonCaption(GameButton, "Stop Game")
    Controls.HideControl(OptionsButton)
    Controls.HideControl(ExitButton)
    PlayerX[1] = GameLeft + 5
    PlayerY[1] = GameTop + 0.5 * GameHeight - 0.5 * ImageH
    PlayerX[2] = GameLeft + GameWidth - ImageW - 5
    PlayerY[2] = PlayerY[1]
    SnowmanX[1] = GameLeft + 0.5 * GameWidth - ImageW
    SnowmanY[1] = GameTop + Math.GetRandomNumber(GameHeight -
ImageH)
    SnowmanX[2] = GameLeft + 0.5 * GameWidth
    SnowmanY[2] = GameTop + Math.GetRandomNumber(GameHeight -
ImageH)
    For I = 1 To 2
      PlayerHits[I] = 0
      Shapes.SetText(PlayerHitsDisplay[I], PlayerHits[I])
      PlayerLeft[I] = MaximumBalls
      Shapes.SetText(PlayerLeftDisplay[I], PlayerLeft[I])
      Shapes.Move(Player[I], PlayerX[I], PlayerY[I])
      Shapes.ShowShape(Player[I])
      GetSnowmanSpeed()
      SnowmanSpeed[I] = Speed
      Shapes.Move(Snowman[I], SnowmanX[I], SnowmanY[I])
      Shapes.ShowShape(Snowman[I])
    EndFor
    ComputerTicks = 0
    Timer.Resume()
  Else
    Timer.Pause()
    For I = 1 To 2
      Shapes.HideShape(Player[I])
      Shapes.HideShape(Snowball[I])
      SnowballIsVisible[I] = "false"
      Shapes.HideShape(Snowman[I])
    EndFor
    Controls.SetButtonCaption(GameButton, "New Game")
    Controls.ShowControl(OptionsButton)
```

```
      Controls.ShowControl(ExitButton)
      GraphicsWindow.BrushColor = "Yellow"
      GraphicsWindow.FontSize = 36
      GraphicsWindow.DrawText(200, 250, "Game Over")
    EndIf
  EndSub
```

We have listed the entire **GameButtonClicked** procedure – it is now complete.

Now, let's write the computer playing rules. We'll start with the simple, random rules. In these rules, the computer will just make random moves up and down the field, occasionally tossing a snowball. The only non-random element we add is that we only allow the computer to throw a snowball if it has at least as many snowballs left as the human player. This prevents the computer from tossing all its snowballs and becoming an easy target for the human. The rules I use are:

- Generate a random number from 1 to 5.
- If number is 1, toss snowball, if computer has at least as many snowballs as player.
- If number is 2 or 3, move up.
- If number is 4 or 5, move down.

With these rules, a snowball is thrown 1 out of 5 times the computer makes a move, the computer's player moves up 2 of 5 times and moves down 2 of 5 times. There's no real intelligence involved – just random moves. Let's write some more intelligent rules.

In writing more detailed (smarter) playing rules, just think about how you would play the game. Smarter rules would be if the other player is "in range", take a toss. Otherwise, move away from the other player if he's tossed a snowball (defensive move) or move toward the other player to keep him range (offensive move). In our rules, we define "in range" to mean the difference between the two players' vertical position no more than 80 percent of a player's height. The rules I used are:

- If "in range" and computer has at least as many snowballs as player, take toss.
- If human player has tossed snowball or computer has no snowballs remaining, make defensive move:
    - If human player is above computer player, move down.
    - If human player is below computer player, move up.
- Else, make offensive move:
    - If human player is above computer player, move up.
    - If human player is below computer player, move down.

Notice we still only toss a snowball when the computer has at least as many snowballs remaining as the player. We don't want the computer to run out of snowballs before the human player.

The code for both the simple and detailed computer logic is placed in the **TimerTickSub** subroutine. Recall a computer move will be made every time **ComputerTicks** (incremented with each call to **TimerTickSub**) equals **ComputerTicksMax**. Once a move is made, **ComputerTicks** is reset to zero to start counting up for the next move.

The code that implements the computer player logic is shaded in the final version of the **TimerTickSub** subroutine:

```
Sub TimerTickSub
  'move snowmen
  For I =1 to 2
    SnowmanY[I] = SnowmanY[I] + SnowmanSpeed[I]
    Shapes.Move(Snowman[I], SnowmanX[I], SnowmanY[I])
    If (SnowmanY[I] < GameTop Or SnowmanY[I] > GameTop +
GameHeight - ImageH) Then
      'recompute speed
      GetSnowmanSpeed()
      SnowmanSpeed[I] = Speed
      If (SnowmanSpeed[I] > 0) Then
        SnowmanY[I] = GameTop
      Else
        SnowmanY[I] = GameTop + GameHeight - ImageH
      EndIf
    EndIf
  EndFor
  'status of snowball 1
  If (SnowballIsVisible[1]) Then
    SnowballX[1] = SnowballX[1] + SnowballSpeed
    Shapes.Move(Snowball[1], SnowballX[1], SnowballY[1])
    If (SnowballX[1] > GameLeft + GameWidth) Then
      'off screen
      Shapes.HideShape(Snowball[1])
      SnowballIsVisible[1] = "false"
      Goto Snowball1Gone
    Else
      'check for collision with player2
      ShapeX[1] = SnowballX[1]
      ShapeY[1] = SnowballY[1]
      ShapeX[2] = PlayerX[2]
      ShapeY[2] = PlayerY[2]
      CheckCollision()
      If (Collision) Then
        Sound.Stop(Program.Directory + "\ouch.wav")
        Sound.Play(Program.Directory + "\ouch.wav")
        PlayerHits[1] = PlayerHits[1] + 1
        Shapes.SetText(PlayerHitsDisplay[1], PlayerHits[1])
        Shapes.HideShape(Snowball[1])
        SnowballIsVisible[1] = "false"
        Goto Snowball1Gone
      EndIf
      'check for collision with either snowman
```

```
      For I = 1 To 2
        ShapeX[1] = SnowballX[1]
        ShapeY[1] = SnowballY[1]
        ShapeX[2] = SnowmanX[I]
        ShapeY[2] = SnowmanY[I]
        CheckCollision()
        If (Collision) Then
          Sound.Stop(Program.Directory + "\splat.wav")
          Sound.Play(Program.Directory + "\splat.wav")
          Shapes.HideShape(Snowball[1])
          SnowballIsVisible[1] = "false"
          Goto Snowball1Gone
        EndIf
      EndFor
    EndIf
  EndIf
  Snowball1Gone:
  'status of player 2 snowball
  If (SnowballIsVisible[2]) Then
    SnowballX[2] = SnowballX[2] - SnowballSpeed
    Shapes.Move(Snowball[2], SnowballX[2], SnowballY[2])
    If (SnowballX[2] < GameLeft - ImageW) Then
      'off screen
      Shapes.HideShape(Snowball[2])
      SnowballIsVisible[2] = "false"
      Goto Snowball2Gone
    Else
      'check for collision with player1
      ShapeX[1] = SnowballX[2]
      ShapeY[1] = SnowballY[2]
      ShapeX[2] = PlayerX[1]
      ShapeY[2] = PlayerY[1]
      CheckCollision()
      If (Collision) Then
        Sound.Stop(Program.Directory + "\ouch.wav")
        Sound.Play(Program.Directory + "\ouch.wav")
        PlayerHits[2] = PlayerHits[2] + 1
        Shapes.SetText(PlayerHitsDisplay[2], PlayerHits[2])
        Shapes.HideShape(Snowball[2])
        SnowballIsVisible[2] = "false"
        Goto Snowball2Gone
      EndIf
      'check for collision with either snowman
      For I = 1 To 2
        ShapeX[1] = SnowballX[2]
        ShapeY[1] = SnowballY[2]
```

```
        ShapeX[2] = SnowmanX[I]
        ShapeY[2] = SnowmanY[I]
        CheckCollision()
        If (Collision) Then
          Sound.Stop(Program.Directory + "\splat.wav")
          Sound.Play(Program.Directory + "\splat.wav")
          Shapes.HideShape(Snowball[2])
          SnowballIsVisible[2] = "false"
          Goto Snowball2Gone
        EndIf
      EndFor
    EndIf
  EndIf
  Snowball2Gone:
  'check for computer move if one player
  If (NumberPlayers = 1) Then
    ComputerTicks = ComputerTicks + 1
    If (ComputerTicks >= ComputerTicksMax) Then
      ComputerTicks = 0
      PlayerID = 2
      If (Math.GetRandomNumber(100) <= ComputerRandom) Then
        'random action
        Action = Math.GetRandomNumber(5)
        If (Action = 1) Then
          If (PlayerLeft[2] >= PlayerLeft[1]) Then
            TossSnowball()
          EndIf
        ElseIf (Action =2 Or Action = 3) Then
          MovePlayerUp()
        Else
          MovePlayerDown()
        EndIf
      Else
        'if in range take a toss
        If (Math.Abs(PlayerY[1] - PlayerY[2]) < 0.8 * ImageH
And PlayerLeft[2] >= PlayerLeft[1]) Then
          TossSnowball()
        EndIf
        If (SnowballIsVisible[1] Or PlayerLeft[2] = 0) Then
          'defense - move away from Player 1
          If (PlayerY[1] - PlayerY[2] < 0) Then
            MovePlayerDown() ' move down
          Else
            MovePlayerUp() ' move up
          EndIf
        Else
```

```
          'offense - move toward Player 1
          If (PlayerY[1] - PlayerY[2] < 0) Then
            MovePlayerUp() ' move up
          Else
            MovePlayerDown() ' move down
          EndIf
        EndIf
      EndIf
    EndIf
  EndIf
  'check status of game
  If (SnowballIsVisible[1] = "false" And PlayerLeft[1] = 0 And
SnowballIsVisible[2] = "false" And PlayerLeft[2] = 0) Then
    Sound.PlayAndWait(Program.Directory + "\gameover.wav")
    GameButtonClicked()
  EndIf
EndSub
```

You should be able to identify each step in the different computer player logics. Make sure you understand how **ComputerTicks** works and how the **ComputerRandom** value is used to determine whether simple or detailed logic is used. Notice when the computer player is moving or throwing, the **PlayerID** value is set to **2**.

Save and **Run** the project. Click **Options**, select a **One Player** game. Select a difficulty level. Once done, click **New Game**. Then, watch out, the computer opponent will start tossing snowballs at you!

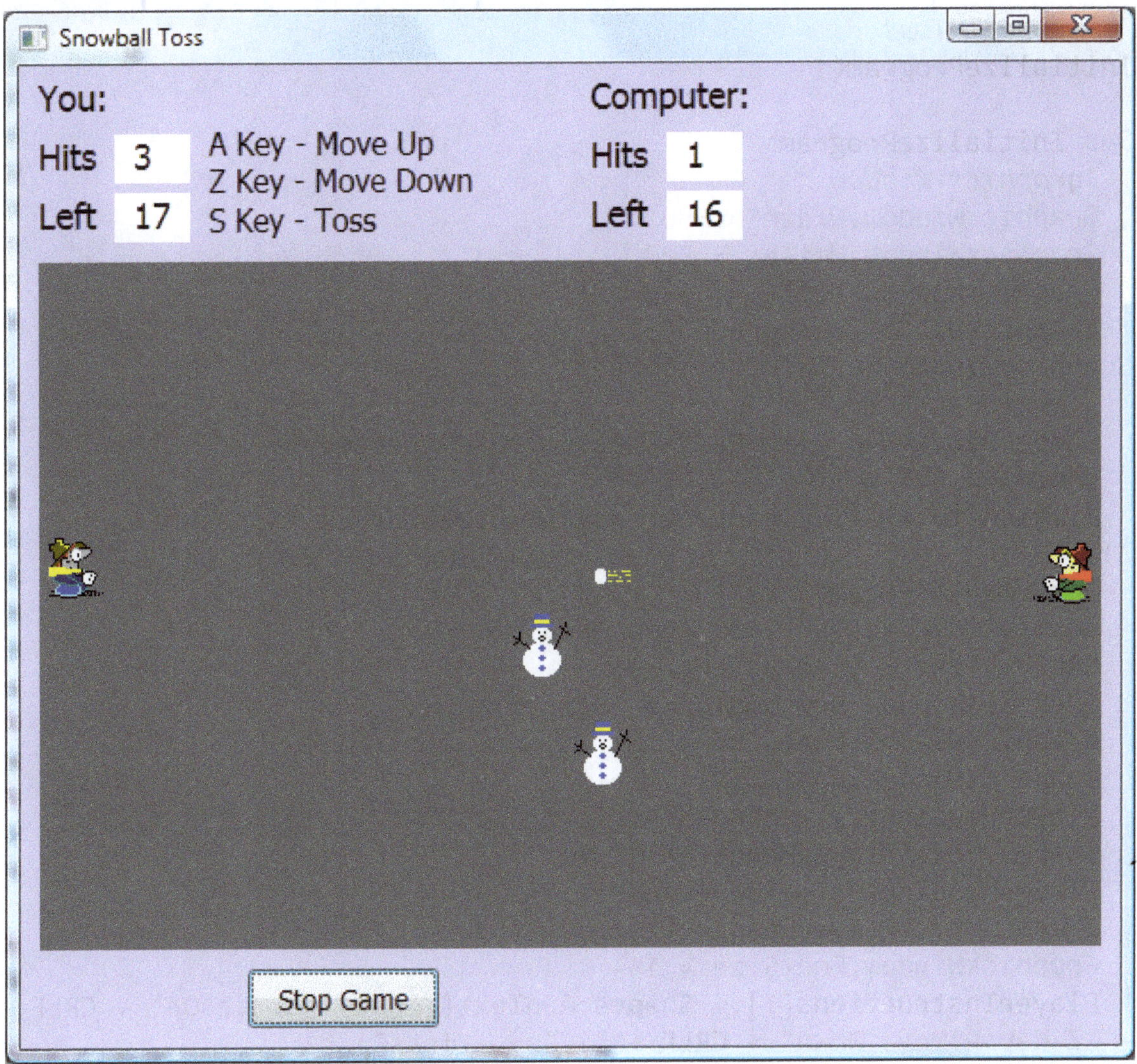

This completes the snowball toss game. As you play the game, against another player or against the computer, you'll find modifications you want to make. This is a fun part of game programming – tailoring the game play to your desires and needs.

Snowball Toss Game Project Code Listing

Here is the complete listing of the **Snowball Toss Game** Small Basic program:

```
' Snowball Toss
InitializeProgram()

Sub InitializeProgram
  'graphics window
  GraphicsWindow.Width = 580
  GraphicsWindow.Height = 500
  GraphicsWindow.Title = "Snowball Toss"
  GraphicsWindow.BackgroundColor =
GraphicsWindow.GetColorFromRGB(192, 192, 255)
  ' options
  NumberPlayers = File.ReadLine(Program.Directory +
"\snowball.ini", 1)
  Difficulty = File.ReadLine(Program.Directory + "\snowball.ini",
2)
  GetComputerParameters()
  'build instructions and show headings
  CRLF = Text.GetCharacter(13)
  GraphicsWindow.BrushColor = "Black"
  GraphicsWindow.FontSize = 18
  GraphicsWindow.FontBold = "false"
  PlayerHeading[1] = Shapes.AddText("")
  Shapes.Move(PlayerHeading[1], 10, 5)
  PlayerHeading[2] = Shapes.AddText("")
  Shapes.Move(PlayerHeading[2], 300, 5)
  GraphicsWindow.FontSize = 16
  PlayerInstructions[1] = Shapes.AddText("A Key - Move Up" + CRLF
+ "Z Key - Move Down" + CRLF + "S Key - Toss")
  Shapes.Move(PlayerInstructions[1], 100, 30)
  PlayerInstructions[2] = Shapes.AddText("K Key - Move Up" + CRLF
+ "M Key - Move Down" + CRLF + "J Key - Toss")
  Shapes.Move(PlayerInstructions[2], 390, 30)
  DisplayHeadings()
  'game variables
  MaximumBalls = 20
  PlayerIncrement = 5
  SnowballSpeed = 20
  'scoring
  GraphicsWindow.BrushColor = "Black"
  GraphicsWindow.FontSize = 18
  GraphicsWindow.FontBold = "false"
  GraphicsWindow.DrawText(10, 35, "Hits")
```

```
  GraphicsWindow.DrawText(10, 65, "Left")
  GraphicsWindow.DrawText(300, 35, "Hits")
  GraphicsWindow.DrawText(300, 65, "Left")
  GraphicsWindow.BrushColor = "White"
  GraphicsWindow.FillRectangle(50, 35, 40, 25)
  GraphicsWindow.FillRectangle(50, 65, 40, 25)
  GraphicsWindow.FillRectangle(340, 35, 40, 25)
  GraphicsWindow.FillRectangle(340, 65, 40, 25)
  GraphicsWindow.BrushColor = "Black"
  PlayerHitsDisplay[1] = Shapes.AddText("0")
  Shapes.Move(PlayerHitsDisplay[1], 60, 35)
  PlayerLeftDisplay[1] = Shapes.AddText(MaximumBalls)
  Shapes.Move(PlayerLeftDisplay[1], 60, 65)
  PlayerHitsDisplay[2] = Shapes.AddText("0")
  Shapes.Move(PlayerHitsDisplay[2], 350, 35)
  PlayerLeftDisplay[2] = Shapes.AddText(MaximumBalls)
  Shapes.Move(PlayerLeftDisplay[2], 350, 65)
  'game region
  GameLeft = 10
  GameTop = 100
  GameWidth = 560
  GameHeight = 350
  GraphicsWindow.BrushColor = "Gray"
  GraphicsWindow.FillRectangle(GameLeft, GameTop, GameWidth,
GameHeight)
  'buttons
  GraphicsWindow.BrushColor = "Black"
  GraphicsWindow.FontSize = 14
  GraphicsWindow.FontBold = "false"
  GameButton = Controls.AddButton("New Game", 120, 460)
  Controls.SetSize(GameButton, 100, 30)
  OptionsButton = Controls.AddButton("Options", 240, 460)
  Controls.SetSize(OptionsButton, 100, 30)
  ExitButton = Controls.AddButton("Exit", 360, 460)
  Controls.SetSize(ExitButton, 100, 30)
  'Load images and put in shapes - all images 32 x 32
  ImageW = 32
  ImageH = 32
  Player[1] =
Shapes.AddImage(ImageList.LoadImage(Program.Directory +
"\player1.ico"))
  Shapes.HideShape(Player[1])
  Player[2] =
Shapes.AddImage(ImageList.LoadImage(Program.Directory +
"\player2.ico"))
  Shapes.HideShape(Player[2])
```

```
  Snowball[1] =
Shapes.AddImage(ImageList.LoadImage(Program.Directory +
"\player1ball.ico"))
  Shapes.HideShape(Snowball[1])
  SnowballIsVisible[1] = "false"
  Snowball[2] =
Shapes.AddImage(ImageList.LoadImage(Program.Directory +
"\player2ball.ico"))
  SnowballIsVisible[2] = "false"
  Shapes.HideShape(Snowball[2])
  Snowman[1] =
Shapes.AddImage(ImageList.LoadImage(Program.Directory +
"\snowman.ico"))
  Shapes.HideShape(Snowman[1])
  Snowman[2] =
Shapes.AddImage(ImageList.LoadImage(Program.Directory +
"\snowman.ico"))
  Shapes.HideShape(Snowman[2])
  Controls.ButtonClicked = ButtonClickedSub
  GraphicsWindow.KeyDown = KeyDownSub
  Timer.Tick = TimerTickSub
  Timer.Interval = 50
  Timer.Pause()
EndSub

Sub DisplayHeadings
  If (NumberPlayers = 1) Then
    Shapes.SetText(PlayerHeading[1], "You:")
    Shapes.SetText(PlayerHeading[2], "Computer:")
    Shapes.HideShape(PlayerInstructions[2])
  Else
    Shapes.SetText(PlayerHeading[1], "Player 1:")
    Shapes.SetText(PlayerHeading[2], "Player 2:")
    Shapes.ShowShape(PlayerInstructions[2])
  EndIf
EndSub

Sub ButtonClickedSub
  B = Controls.LastClickedButton
  If (B = OptionsButton) Then
    SetOptions()
  ElseIf (B = ExitButton) Then
    File.WriteLine(Program.Directory + "\snowball.ini", 1,
NumberPlayers)
    File.WriteLine(Program.Directory + "\snowball.ini", 2,
Difficulty)
```

```
    Program.End()
  ElseIf (B = GameButton) Then
    GameButtonClicked()
  EndIf
EndSub

Sub SetOptions
  GraphicsWindow.Hide()
  TextWindow.Show()
  TextWindow.Title = "Snowball Toss"
  TextWindow.CursorLeft = 3
  TextWindow.CursorTop = 3
  TextWindow.WriteLine("SNOWBALL TOSS OPTIONS")
  TextWindow.WriteLine("")
  GetPlayers:
  TextWindow.CursorLeft = 3
  TextWindow.WriteLine("With one player, you play against the
computer.")
  TextWindow.CursorLeft = 3
  TextWindow.WriteLine("With two players, you play against a
friend.")
  TextWindow.CursorLeft = 3
  TextWindow.Write("How many players do you want (1 or 2)? ")
  NumberPlayers = TextWindow.ReadNumber()
  If (NumberPlayers < 1 Or NumberPlayers > 2) Then
    Goto GetPlayers
  EndIf
  If (NumberPlayers = 1) Then
    GetDifficulty:
    TextWindow.WriteLine("")
    TextWindow.CursorLeft = 3
    TextWindow.WriteLine("You can set the game difficulty.")
    TextWindow.CursorLeft = 3
    TextWindow.Write("Make your choice (1-Easiest, 2-Easy, 3-Hard,
4-Hardest)? ")
    Difficulty = TextWindow.ReadNumber()
    If (Difficulty < 1 Or Difficulty > 4) Then
      Goto GetDifficulty
    EndIf
    GetComputerParameters()
  EndIf
  DisplayHeadings()
  TextWindow.Hide()
  GraphicsWindow.Show()
EndSub
```

```
Sub GameButtonClicked
  If (Controls.GetButtonCaption(GameButton) = "New Game") Then
    'clear game rectangle
    GraphicsWindow.BrushColor = "Gray"
    GraphicsWindow.FillRectangle(GameLeft, GameTop, GameWidth,
GameHeight)
    Controls.SetButtonCaption(GameButton, "Stop Game")
    Controls.HideControl(OptionsButton)
    Controls.HideControl(ExitButton)
    PlayerX[1] = GameLeft + 5
    PlayerY[1] = GameTop + 0.5 * GameHeight - 0.5 * ImageH
    PlayerX[2] = GameLeft + GameWidth - ImageW - 5
    PlayerY[2] = PlayerY[1]
    SnowmanX[1] = GameLeft + 0.5 * GameWidth - ImageW
    SnowmanY[1] = GameTop + Math.GetRandomNumber(GameHeight -
ImageH)
    SnowmanX[2] = GameLeft + 0.5 * GameWidth
    SnowmanY[2] = GameTop + Math.GetRandomNumber(GameHeight -
ImageH)
    For I = 1 To 2
      PlayerHits[I] = 0
      Shapes.SetText(PlayerHitsDisplay[I], PlayerHits[I])
      PlayerLeft[I] = MaximumBalls
      Shapes.SetText(PlayerLeftDisplay[I], PlayerLeft[I])
      Shapes.Move(Player[I], PlayerX[I], PlayerY[I])
      Shapes.ShowShape(Player[I])
      GetSnowmanSpeed()
      SnowmanSpeed[I] = Speed
      Shapes.Move(Snowman[I], SnowmanX[I], SnowmanY[I])
      Shapes.ShowShape(Snowman[I])
    EndFor
    ComputerTicks = 0
    Timer.Resume()
  Else
    Timer.Pause()
    For I = 1 To 2
      Shapes.HideShape(Player[I])
      Shapes.HideShape(Snowball[I])
      SnowballIsVisible[I] = "false"
      Shapes.HideShape(Snowman[I])
    EndFor
    Controls.SetButtonCaption(GameButton, "New Game")
    Controls.ShowControl(OptionsButton)
    Controls.ShowControl(ExitButton)
    GraphicsWindow.BrushColor = "Yellow"
    GraphicsWindow.FontSize = 36
```

```
    GraphicsWindow.DrawText(200, 250, "Game Over")
  EndIf
EndSub

Sub KeyDownSub
  If (Controls.GetButtonCaption(GameButton) <> "New Game") Then
    PressedKey = Text.ConvertToUpperCase(GraphicsWindow.LastKey)
    If (PressedKey = "A" Or PressedKey = "Z" Or PressedKey = "S")
Then
      PlayerID = 1
    Else
      PlayerID = 2
    EndIf
    If (PressedKey = "A" Or PressedKey = "K") Then
      MovePlayerUp()
    ElseIf (PressedKey = "Z" Or PressedKey = "M") Then
      MovePlayerDown()
    ElseIf (PressedKey = "S" Or PressedKey = "J") Then
      TossSnowball()
    EndIf
  EndIf
EndSub

Sub MovePlayerUp
  PlayerY[PlayerID] = PlayerY[PlayerID] - PlayerIncrement
  If (PlayerY[PlayerID] < GameTop) Then
    PlayerY[PlayerID] = GameTop
  EndIf
  Shapes.Move(Player[PlayerID], PlayerX[PlayerID],
PlayerY[PlayerID])
EndSub

Sub MovePlayerDown
  PlayerY[PlayerID] = PlayerY[PlayerID] + PlayerIncrement
  If (PlayerY[PlayerID] > GameTop + GameHeight - ImageH) Then
    PlayerY[PlayerID] = GameTop + GameHeight - ImageH
  EndIf
  Shapes.Move(Player[PlayerID], PlayerX[PlayerID],
PlayerY[PlayerID])
EndSub

Sub TossSnowball
  If (SnowballIsVisible[PlayerID] = "false" And
PlayerLeft[PlayerID] > 0) Then
    Sound.Stop(Program.Directory + "\throw.wav")
    Sound.Play(Program.Directory + "\throw.wav")
```

```
    PlayerLeft[PlayerID] = PlayerLeft[PlayerID] - 1
    Shapes.SetText(PlayerLeftDisplay[PlayerID],
PlayerLeft[PlayerID])
    If (PlayerID = 1) Then
      SnowballX[PlayerID] = PlayerX[PlayerID] + ImageW
    Else
      SnowballX[PlayerID] = PlayerX[PlayerID] - ImageW
    EndIf
    SnowballY[PlayerID] = PlayerY[PlayerID]
    Shapes.Move(Snowball[PlayerID], SnowballX[PlayerID],
SnowballY[PlayerID])
    Shapes.ShowShape(Snowball[PlayerID])
    SnowballIsVisible[PlayerID] = "true"
  EndIf
EndSub

Sub TimerTickSub
  'move snowmen
  For I =1 to 2
    SnowmanY[I] = SnowmanY[I] + SnowmanSpeed[I]
    Shapes.Move(Snowman[I], SnowmanX[I], SnowmanY[I])
    If (SnowmanY[I] < GameTop Or SnowmanY[I] > GameTop +
GameHeight - ImageH) Then
      'recompute speed
      GetSnowmanSpeed()
      SnowmanSpeed[I] = Speed
      If (SnowmanSpeed[I] > 0) Then
        SnowmanY[I] = GameTop
      Else
        SnowmanY[I] = GameTop + GameHeight - ImageH
      EndIf
    EndIf
  EndFor
  'status of snowball 1
  If (SnowballIsVisible[1]) Then
    SnowballX[1] = SnowballX[1] + SnowballSpeed
    Shapes.Move(Snowball[1], SnowballX[1], SnowballY[1])
    If (SnowballX[1] > GameLeft + GameWidth) Then
      'off screen
      Shapes.HideShape(Snowball[1])
      SnowballIsVisible[1] = "false"
      Goto Snowball1Gone
    Else
      'check for collision with player2
      ShapeX[1] = SnowballX[1]
      ShapeY[1] = SnowballY[1]
```

```
    ShapeX[2] = PlayerX[2]
    ShapeY[2] = PlayerY[2]
    CheckCollision()
    If (Collision) Then
      Sound.Stop(Program.Directory + "\ouch.wav")
      Sound.Play(Program.Directory + "\ouch.wav")
      PlayerHits[1] = PlayerHits[1] + 1
      Shapes.SetText(PlayerHitsDisplay[1], PlayerHits[1])
      Shapes.HideShape(Snowball[1])
      SnowballIsVisible[1] = "false"
      Goto Snowball1Gone
    EndIf
    'check for collision with either snowman
    For I = 1 To 2
      ShapeX[1] = SnowballX[1]
      ShapeY[1] = SnowballY[1]
      ShapeX[2] = SnowmanX[I]
      ShapeY[2] = SnowmanY[I]
      CheckCollision()
      If (Collision) Then
        Sound.Stop(Program.Directory + "\splat.wav")
        Sound.Play(Program.Directory + "\splat.wav")
        Shapes.HideShape(Snowball[1])
        SnowballIsVisible[1] = "false"
        Goto Snowball1Gone
      EndIf
    EndFor
  EndIf
EndIf
Snowball1Gone:
'status of player 2 snowball
If (SnowballIsVisible[2]) Then
  SnowballX[2] = SnowballX[2] - SnowballSpeed
  Shapes.Move(Snowball[2], SnowballX[2], SnowballY[2])
  If (SnowballX[2] < GameLeft - ImageW) Then
    'off screen
    Shapes.HideShape(Snowball[2])
    SnowballIsVisible[2] = "false"
    Goto Snowball2Gone
  Else
    'check for collision with player1
    ShapeX[1] = SnowballX[2]
    ShapeY[1] = SnowballY[2]
    ShapeX[2] = PlayerX[1]
    ShapeY[2] = PlayerY[1]
    CheckCollision()
```

```
      If (Collision) Then
        Sound.Stop(Program.Directory + "\ouch.wav")
        Sound.Play(Program.Directory + "\ouch.wav")
        PlayerHits[2] = PlayerHits[2] + 1
        Shapes.SetText(PlayerHitsDisplay[2], PlayerHits[2])
        Shapes.HideShape(Snowball[2])
        SnowballIsVisible[2] = "false"
        Goto Snowball2Gone
      EndIf
      'check for collision with either snowman
      For I = 1 To 2
        ShapeX[1] = SnowballX[2]
        ShapeY[1] = SnowballY[2]
        ShapeX[2] = SnowmanX[I]
        ShapeY[2] = SnowmanY[I]
        CheckCollision()
        If (Collision) Then
          Sound.Stop(Program.Directory + "\splat.wav")
          Sound.Play(Program.Directory + "\splat.wav")
          Shapes.HideShape(Snowball[2])
          SnowballIsVisible[2] = "false"
          Goto Snowball2Gone
        EndIf
      EndFor
    EndIf
  EndIf
  Snowball2Gone:
  'check for computer move if one player
  If (NumberPlayers = 1) Then
    ComputerTicks = ComputerTicks + 1
    If (ComputerTicks >= ComputerTicksMax) Then
      ComputerTicks = 0
      PlayerID = 2
      If (Math.GetRandomNumber(100) <= ComputerRandom) Then
        'random action
        Action = Math.GetRandomNumber(5)
        If (Action = 1) Then
          If (PlayerLeft[2] >= PlayerLeft[1]) Then
            TossSnowball()
          EndIf
        ElseIf (Action =2 Or Action = 3) Then
          MovePlayerUp()
        Else
          MovePlayerDown()
        EndIf
      Else
```

```
        'if in range take a toss
        If (Math.Abs(PlayerY[1] - PlayerY[2]) < 0.8 * ImageH And
PlayerLeft[2] >= PlayerLeft[1]) Then
          TossSnowball()
        EndIf
        If (SnowballIsVisible[1] Or PlayerLeft[2] = 0) Then
          'defense - move away from Player 1
          If (PlayerY[1] - PlayerY[2] < 0) Then
            MovePlayerDown() ' move down
          Else
            MovePlayerUp() ' move up
          EndIf
        Else
          'offense - move toward Player 1
          If (PlayerY[1] - PlayerY[2] < 0) Then
            MovePlayerUp() ' move up
          Else
            MovePlayerDown() ' move down
          EndIf
        EndIf
      EndIf
    EndIf
  EndIf
  'check status of game
  If (SnowballIsVisible[1] = "false" And PlayerLeft[1] = 0 And
SnowballIsVisible[2] = "false" And PlayerLeft[2] = 0) Then
    Sound.PlayAndWait(Program.Directory + "\gameover.wav")
    GameButtonClicked()
  EndIf
EndSub

Sub CheckCollision
  Collision = "false"
  If ((ShapeX[1] + ImageW) > ShapeX[2]) Then
    If (ShapeX[1] < (ShapeX[2] + ImageW)) Then
      If ((ShapeY[1] + ImageH) > ShapeY[2]) Then
        If (ShapeY[1] < (ShapeY[2] + ImageH)) Then
          Collision = "true"
        EndIf
      EndIf
    EndIf
  EndIf
EndSub

Sub GetSnowmanSpeed
  SpeedMin = 1
```

```
  SpeedMax = 4
  Speed = Math.GetRandomNumber(SpeedMax - SpeedMin + 1) + SpeedMin
- 1
  If (Math.GetRandomNumber(2) = 1) Then
    Speed = -Speed
  EndIf
EndSub

Sub GetComputerParameters
  If (Difficulty = 1) Then
    ComputerRandom = 100
    ComputerTicksMax = 20
  ElseIf (Difficulty = 2) Then
    ComputerRandom = 75
    ComputerTicksMax = 15
  ElseIf (Difficulty = 3) Then
    ComputerRandom = 50
    ComputerTicksMax = 10
  Else
    ComputerRandom = 25
    ComputerTicksMax = 5
  EndIf
EndSub
```

Snowball Toss Game Project Review

The **Snowball Toss Game Project** is now complete. **Save** and **Run** the project and make sure it works as designed. Have fun playing the game against friends and family or against the computer. In Appendix II, we'll show you how you can share this game (or any other project) with other users.

If there are errors in your implementation, go back over the steps of window and code design. Use the debugger when needed. Go over the developed code – make sure you understand how different parts of the project were coded. As mentioned in the beginning of this chapter, the completed project is saved as **Snowball** in the **HomeSB\HomeSB Projects\Snowball** folder.

While completing this project, new concepts and skills you should have gained include:

- Use of the **Shapes** object in graphics.
- How the **Move** method is used.
- Using a tool like **IconEdit** to develop graphics files.
- Using the keyboard for control of animated characters.
- Detecting collisions between shapes.
- How to play sounds.
- How to develop game playing rules for the computer.

This is the last project in these notes. By now, you should be a fairly competent Small Basic programmer. There's always more to learn though. Consult the Internet and bookstores for more books about skills you might want to gain.

Snowball Toss Game Project Enhancements

Possible enhancements to the snowball toss game project include:

- Add another option to allow the user to select the number of snowballs to use. Just add another question to the **SetOptions** routine. Modify the configuration file so this value is saved.
- Players like to see their name “in lights.” Add an option to have player’s name placed on the window instead of the generic titling information used now. You might want to save the names in the configuration file.
- Add some horizontal motion to the zombie snowmen.
- In the computer playing logic, no consideration is given to position of the zombie snowmen. Modify the logic so a toss is taken only when a snowman is not blocking the toss.
- If you play the game against a ‘smart’ computer, you will find it is possible to trap the computer player at the top or bottom of the playing field and fire away. Modify the code to have the computer player move away from such trapped situations.
- In the one player game, it is still possible to control the computer player manually using the J, K and M keys. Can you write code so this is not possible?

Appendix I. Small Basic Colors

Color	Name	RGB Value
	AliceBlue	#F0F8FF
	AntiqueWhite	#FAEBD7
	Aqua	#00FFFF
	Aquamarine	#7FFFD4
	Azure	#F0FFFF
	Beige	#F5F5DC
	Bisque	#FFE4C4
	Black	#000000
	BlanchedAlmond	#FFEBCD
	Blue	#0000FF
	BlueViolet	#8A2BE2
	Brown	#A52A2A
	BurlyWood	#DEB887
	CadetBlue	#5F9EA0
	Chartreuse	#7FFF00
	Chocolate	#D2691E
	Coral	#FF7F50
	CornflowerBlue	#6495ED

	Cornsilk	#FFF8DC
	Crimson	#DC143C
	Cyan	#00FFFF
	DarkBlue	#00008B
	DarkCyan	#008B8B
	DarkGoldenrod	#B8860B
	DarkGray / DarkGrey†	#A9A9A9
	DarkGreen	#006400
	DarkKhaki	#BDB76B
	DarkMagenta	#8B008B
	DarkOliveGreen	#556B2F
	DarkOrange	#FF8C00
	DarkOrchid	#9932CC
	DarkRed	#8B0000
	DarkSalmon	#E9967A
	DarkSeaGreen	#8FBC8F
	DarkSlateBlue	#483D8B
	DarkSlateGray / DarkSlateGrey†	#2F4F4F
	DarkTurquoise	#00CED1
	DarkViolet	#9400D3
	DeepPink	#FF1493

	DeepSkyBlue	#00BFFF
	DimGray / DimGrey[†]	#696969
	DodgerBlue	#1E90FF
	FireBrick	#B22222
	FloralWhite	#FFFAF0
	ForestGreen	#228B22
	Fuchsia	#FF00FF
	Gainsboro	#DCDCDC
	GhostWhite	#F8F8FF
	Gold	#FFD700
	Goldenrod	#DAA520
	Gray / Grey[†]	#808080
	Green	#008000
	GreenYellow	#ADFF2F
	Honeydew	#F0FFF0
	HotPink	#FF69B4
	IndianRed	#CD5C5C
	Indigo	#4B0082
	Ivory	#FFFFF0
	Khaki	#F0E68C
	Lavender	#E6E6FA

	LavenderBlush	#FFF0F5
	LawnGreen	#7CFC00
	LemonChiffon	#FFFACD
	LightBlue	#ADD8E6
	LightCoral	#F08080
	LightCyan	#E0FFFF
	LightGoldenrodYellow	#FAFAD2
	LightGreen	#90EE90
	LightGray† / LightGrey	#D3D3D3
	LightPink	#FFB6C1
	LightSalmon	#FFA07A
	LightSeaGreen	#20B2AA
	LightSkyBlue	#87CEFA
	LightSlateGray / LightSlateGrey†	#778899
	LightSteelBlue	#B0C4DE
	LightYellow	#FFFFE0
	Lime	#00FF00
	LimeGreen	#32CD32
	Linen	#FAF0E6
	Magenta	#FF00FF
	Maroon	#800000

Appendix II. Sharing a Small Basic Program

I bet you're ready to show your friends and colleagues some of the programs you have built using Small Basic. Just give them a copy of your code, ask them to install Small Basic and learn how to open and run a program. Then, have them open your program and run it. I think you'll agree this might be asking a lot of your friends, colleagues, and, ultimately, your user base. We need to know how to run a program **without** Small Basic.

To run a program without Small Basic, you need to create an **executable** version of the program. So, how is an executable created? A little secret is that Small Basic builds an executable version of a program every time we run the program! This executable file is in the same folder you save your program in. Open the folder for any program you have built and you'll see a file with your program name of type **Application**.

For example, if I open the program folder for the **Snowball** program we just built:

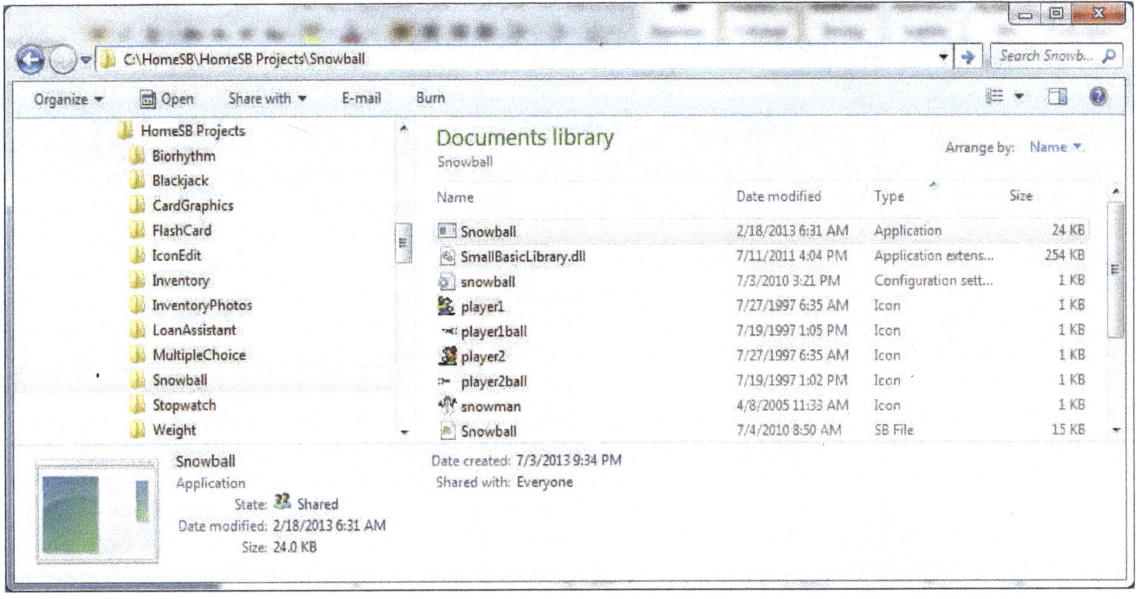

The file named **Snowball.exe** of type **Application** (size 24 KB) is the executable version of the program. If I make sure Small Basic is not running and double-click this file, the following appears:

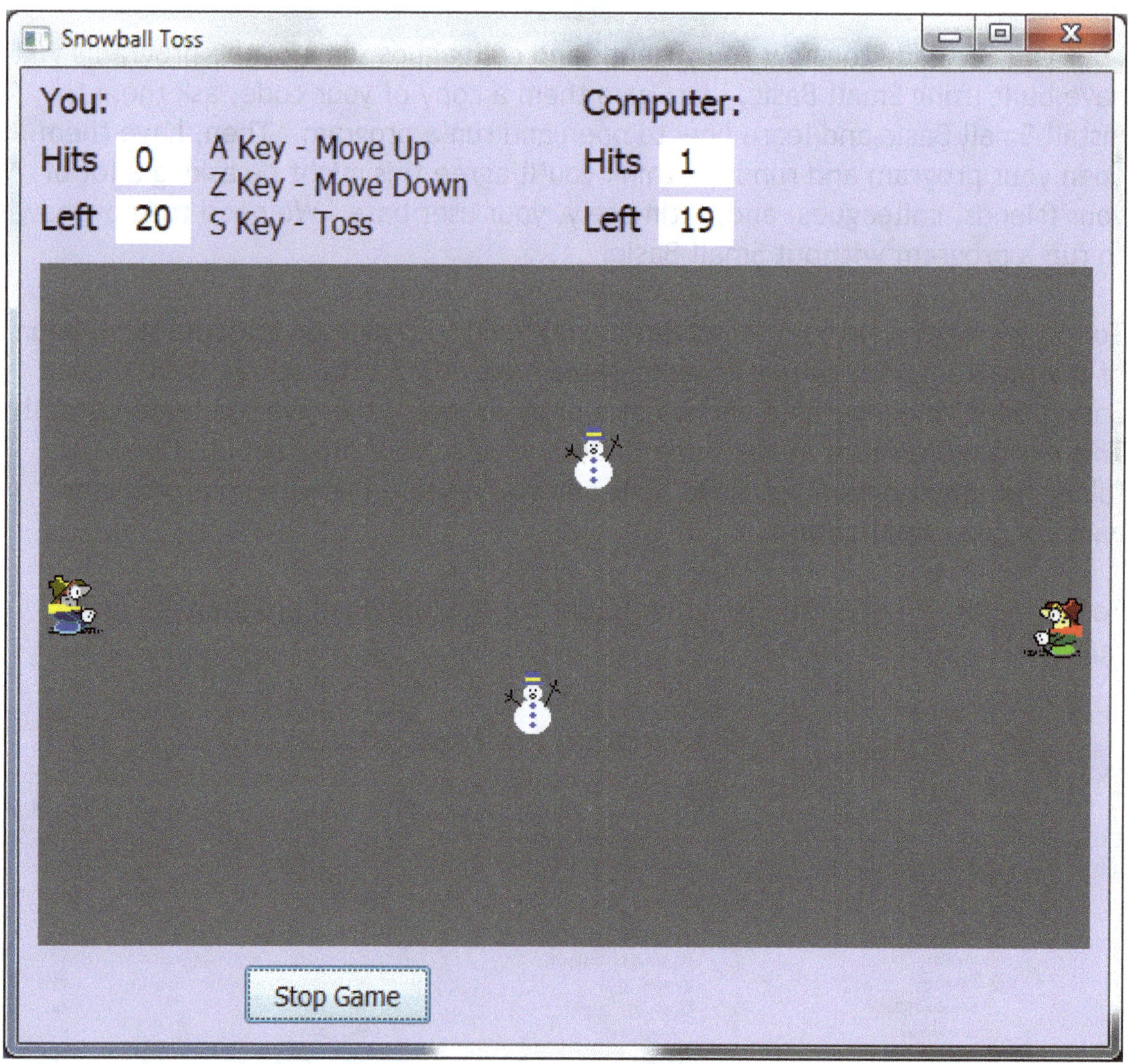

Voila! The **Snowball** program is running outside of the Small Basic development environment! Go ahead and play the game if you like.

So distributing a Small Basic program is as simple as giving your user a copy of the executable file (and the **SmallBasicLibrary.dll** file in your program folder - this has some support code), having them place the files in a folder on their computer and double-clicking the executable file to run it? Maybe. This worked on my computer (and will work on yours) because I have a very important set of files known as the **.NET Framework** installed (they are installed when Small Basic is installed). Every Small Basic program needs the .NET Framework to be installed on the hosting computer.

The next question is: how do you know if your user has the .NET Framework installed on his or her computer? And, if they don't, how can you get it installed? These are difficult questions. So, in addition to our program's executable file, we also need to give a potential user the Microsoft .NET Framework files and inform them how to install and register these files on their computer. Things are getting complicated. Let's look at an easier and very flashy solution - letting users access and run your programs over the Internet!

Start Small Basic and take a look at the toolbar. There are two buttons there we haven't talked about yet. Between the buttons to open and save files and the ones for editing are buttons marked **Import** and **Publish**:

These are remarkable buttons. Clicking **Import** will take you to a Microsoft website where you can import and open a program stored on the Internet by you or other users. **Publish** allows you to store your programs on the Internet for others to use.

Make sure your computer is connected to the Internet. Go ahead and click **Import**. You should see:

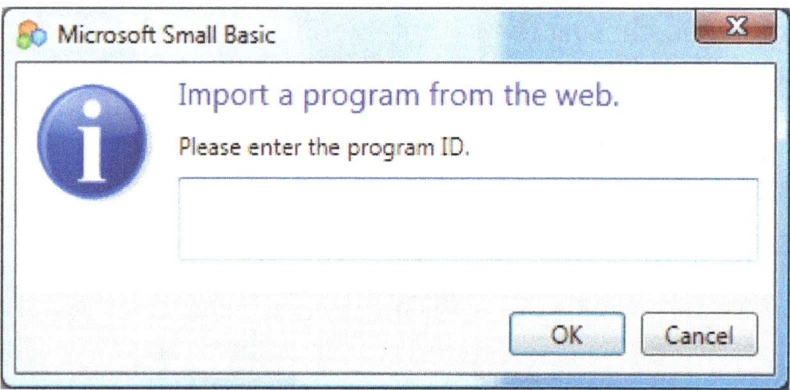

To import a program, you require a **Program ID**. How do you get such an ID? It is assigned when you **Publish** a program, so let's try that. Click the **Cancel** button for now.

When you publish a program, it will be available for all to see and use. And, for now, there is no way to "unpublish" a program. So, be careful what you publish. You may be leary about just giving your hard work away. For the example here, I will use a very simple two line program just to show how things work. You can decide what you want to publish.

Here is the program I will use:

```
GraphicsWindow.Show()
GraphicsWindow.DrawText(10, 10 , "I can publish!!")
```

Type in this code (or use some other program), then click **Publish**. You will see a message something like this:

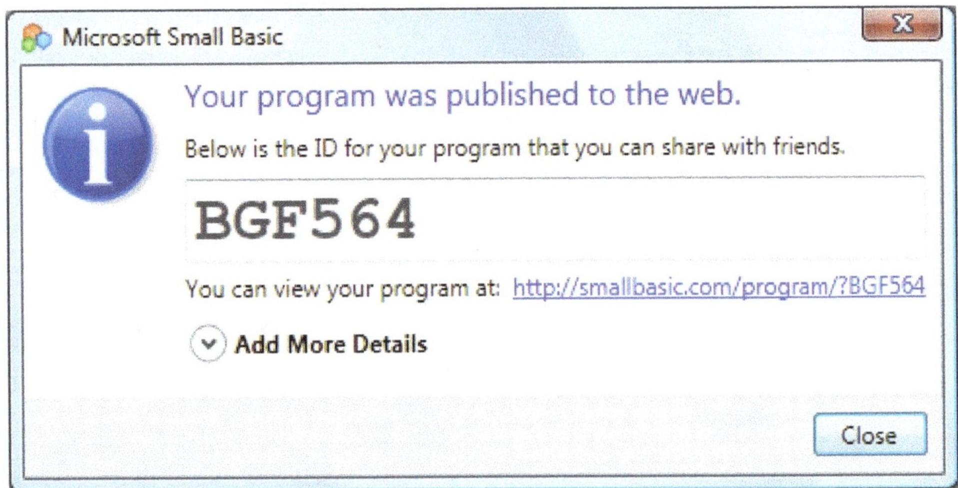

Your program is assigned a Program **ID** (remember we need this to import a program).

Click **Add More Details:**

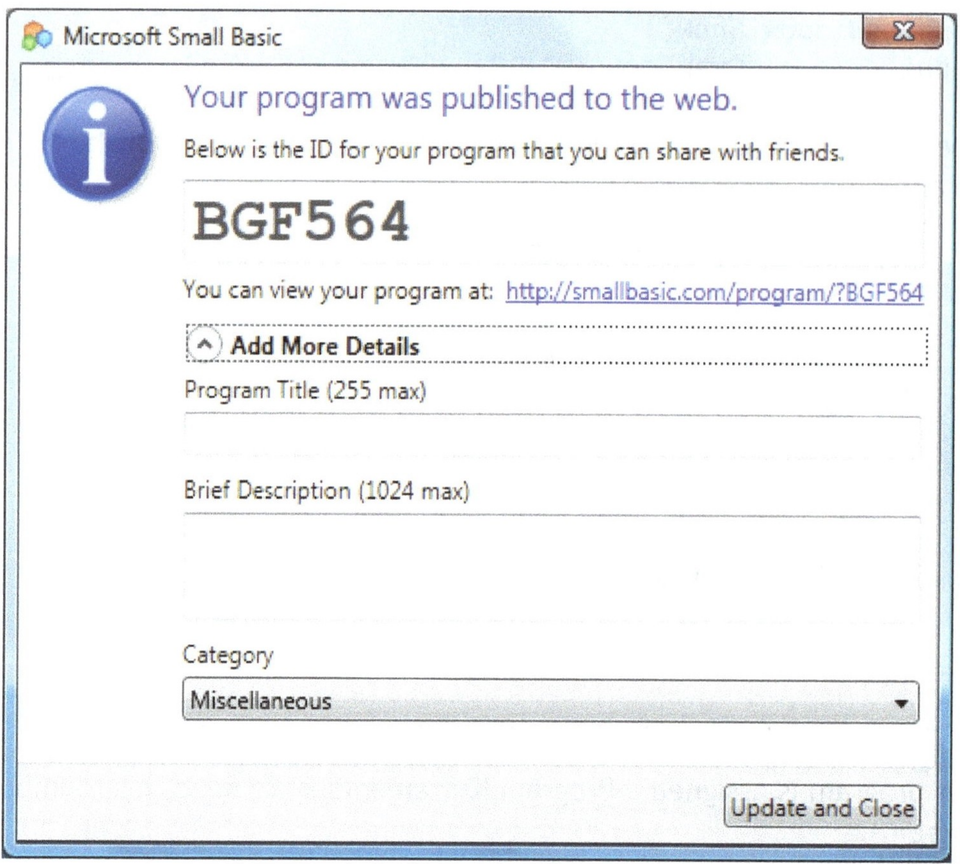

Here, you can describe what your program is and what it does. You can provide a category. This will help users find your program

Also listed in this window is this very interesting piece of information:

You can view your program at:
http://smallbasic.com/program/?BGF564

If you click this link (or give the link to others and let them click it), "magic" occurs.

When I click the link, I am taken to this website hosted by Microsoft:

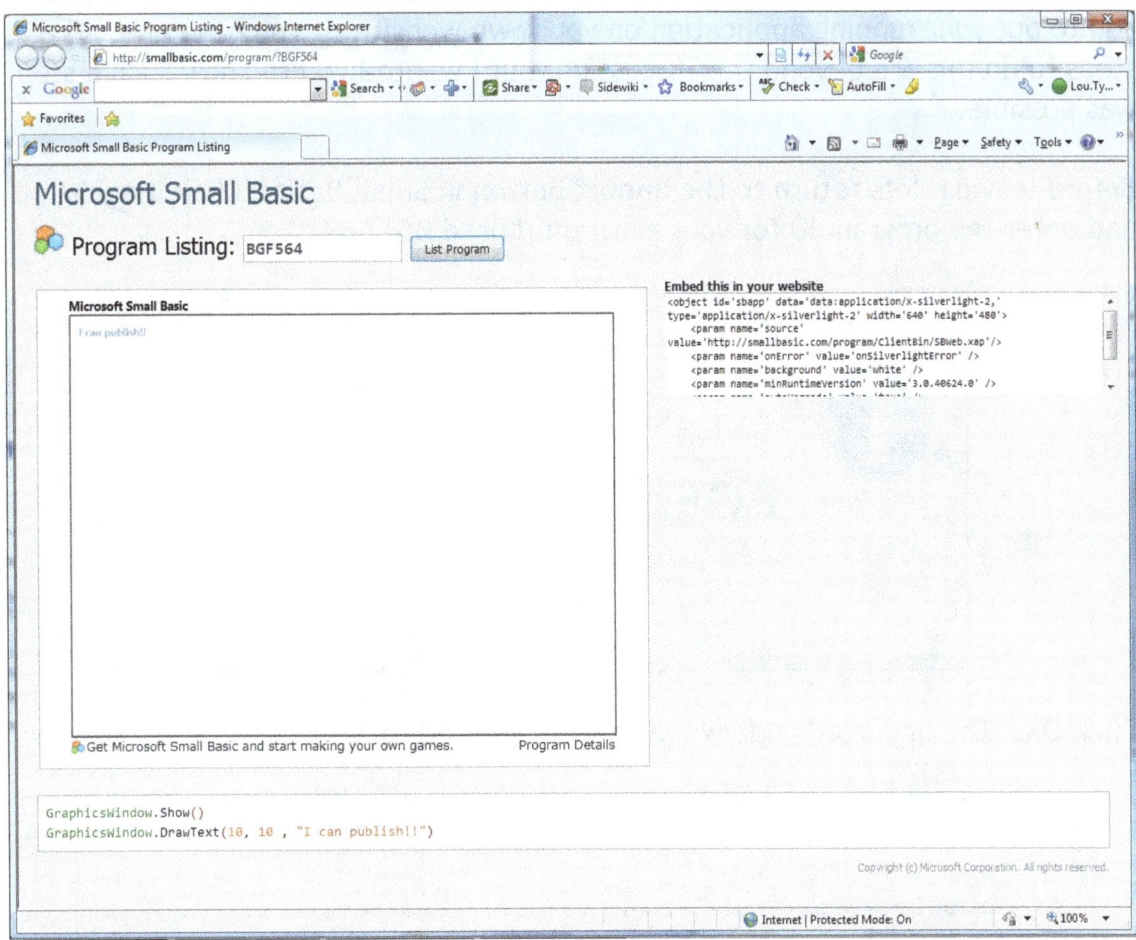

The running program is shown, along with a code listing.

I think you'll agree this pretty neat. To share your programs with other users, **Publish** them, then give them the program link given to you. If they click the link, they can run the program. Well, almost. To use this feature, a user's computer must have a Microsoft product called **Silverlight** installed on their computer. It can be downloaded from this website:

http://www.silverlight.net/

If a user attempts to access your Small Basic program via a provided link and they do not have the required Silverlight product, they will be taken through the installation steps.

Return to the website with your running program. In the upper right corner is a box marked **Embed this in your website.** In this box is some code that allows you to put your running application on your own website, if you have one. The steps to do this are beyond this discussion, but I wanted you to know such a step was possible.

Before leaving, lets return to the **Import** button in Small Basic. Click it again and enter the program ID for your program (I used **BGF564**):

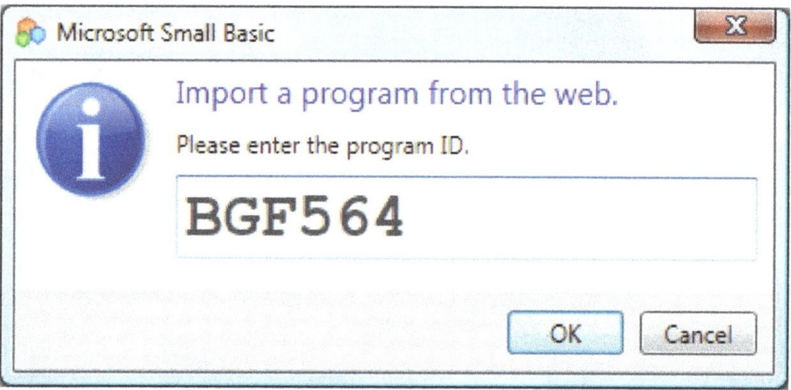

Click **OK.** The imported code will appear in your editor:

BGF564 - Imported *

```
GraphicsWindow.Show()
GraphicsWindow.DrawText(10, 10 , "I can publish!!")
```

So, you have access to any code published to the Microsoft Small Basic library. I'm guessing this library will be growing very quickly.

We publish several Self-Study or Instructor-Led Computer Programming Tutorials for Microsoft® Small Basic:

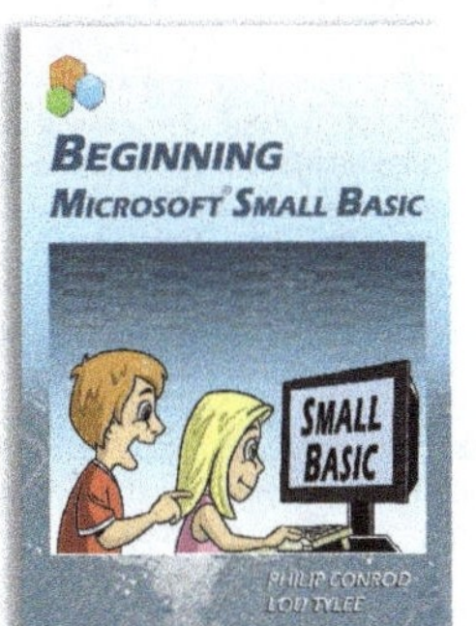

The Beginning Microsoft Small Basic Programming Tutorial is a self-study first semester "beginner" programming tutorial consisting of 11 chapters explaining (in simple, easy-to-follow terms) how to write Microsoft Small Basic programs. The last chapter of this tutorial shows you how four different Small Basic games could port to Visual Basic, Visual C# and Java. This beginning level self-paced tutorial can be used at home or at school.

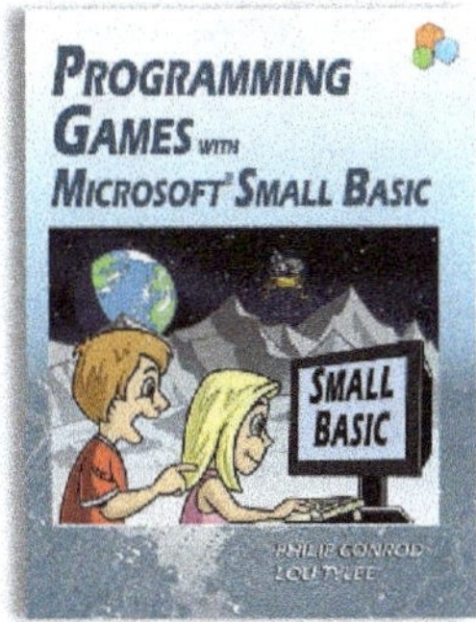

Programming Games with Microsoft Small Basic is a self-paced second semester "intermediate" level programming tutorial consisting of 10 chapters explaining (in simple, easy-to-follow terms) how to write video games in Microsoft Small Basic. The games built are non-violent, family-friendly, and teach logical thinking skills. Students will learn how to program the following Small Basic video games: Safecracker, Tic Tac Toe, Match Game, Pizza Delivery, Moon Landing, and Leap Frog. This intermediate level self-paced tutorial can be used at home or school. The tutorial is simple enough for kids yet engaging enough for beginning adults.

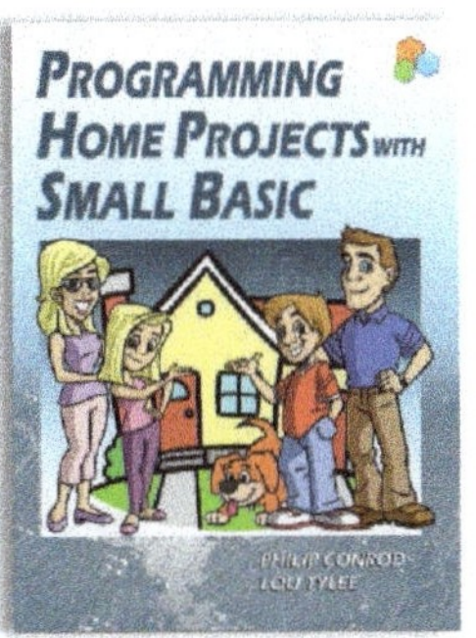

Programming Home Projects with Microsoft Small Basic is a self-paced programming tutorial explains (in simple, easy-to-follow terms) how to build Small Basic Windows applications. Students learn about program design, Small Basic objects, many elements of the Small Basic language, and how to debug and distribute finished programs. Sequential file input and output is also introduced.. The projects built include a Dual-Mode Stopwatch, Flash Card Math Quiz, Multiple Choice Exam, Blackjack Card Game, Weight Monitor, Home Inventory Manager and a Snowball Toss Game.

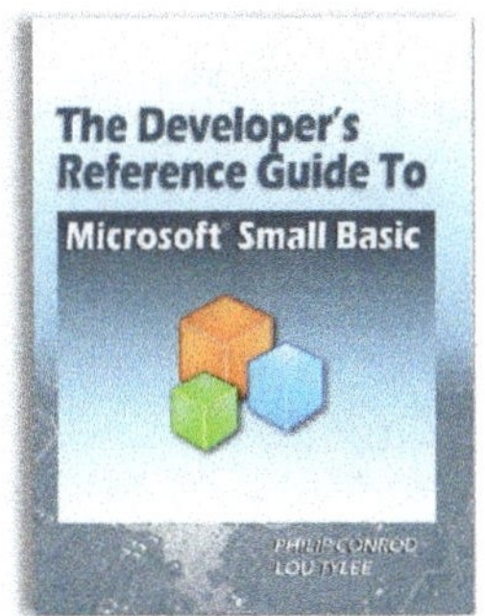

The Developer's Reference Guide to Microsoft Small Basic
While developing all the different Microsoft Small Basic tutorials we found it necessary to write The Developer's Reference Guide to Microsoft Small Basic . The Developer's Reference Guide to Microsoft Small Basic is over 500 pages long and includes over 100 Small Basic programming examples for you to learn from and include in your own Microsoft Small Basic programs. It is a detailed reference guide for new developers.

David Ahl's Small Basic Computer Adventures is a Microsoft Small Basic re-make of the classic *Basic Computer Games* programming *book* originally written by David H. Ahl. This new book includes the following classic adventure simulations; Marco Polo, Westward Ho!, The Longest Automobile Race, The Orient Express, Amelia Earhart: Around the World Flight, Tour de France, Subway Scavenger, Hong Kong Hustle, and Voyage to Neptune. Learn how to program these classic computer simulations in Microsoft Small Basic. This "intermediate" level self-paced tutorial can be used at home or school.

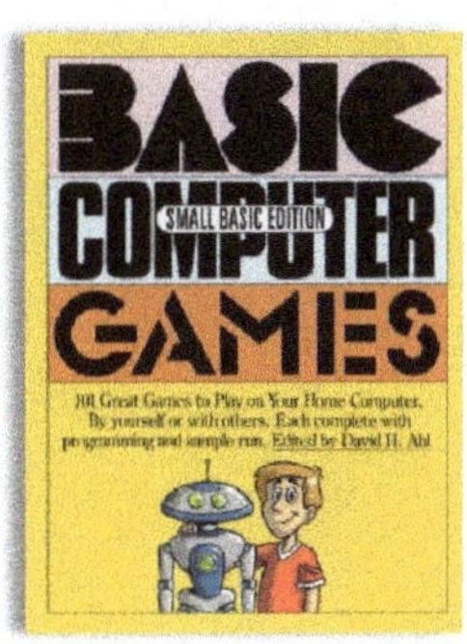

Basic Computer Games - Small Basic Edition is a re-make of the classic BASIC COMPUTER GAMES book originally edited by David H. Ahl. It contains 100 of the original text based BASIC games that inspired a whole generation of programmers. Now these classic BASIC games have been re-written in Microsoft Small Basic for a new generation to enjoy! The new Small Basic games look and act like the original text based games. The book includes all the original spaghetti code GOTO commands and it will make you appreciate the structured programming techniques found in our other tutorials.

We also publish several Self-Study or Instructor-Led Computer Programming Tutorials for Microsoft® Visual Basic® Express and Visual C#® Express:

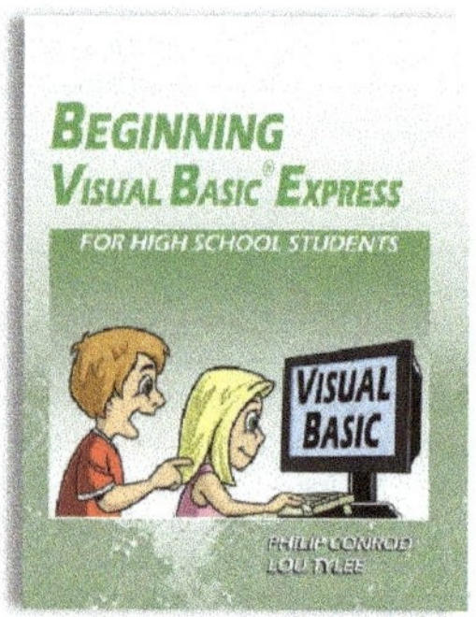

Beginning Visual Basic® Express is a semester long self-paced "beginner" programming tutorial consisting of 10 chapters explaining (in simple, easy-to-follow terms) how to build a Visual Basic Express Windows application. The tutorial includes several detailed computer projects for students to build and try. These projects include a number guessing game, card game, allowance calculator, drawing program, state capitals game, and a couple of video games like Pong. We also include several college prep bonus projects including a loan calculator, portfolio manager, and checkbook balancer.

Programming Games with Visual Basic® Express is a semester long "intermediate" programming tutorial consisting of 10 chapters explaining (in simple, easy-to-follow terms) how to build Visual Basic Video Games. The games built are non-violent, family-friendly, and teach logical thinking skills. Students will learn how to program the following Visual Basic video games: Safecracker, Tic Tac Toe, Match Game, Pizza Delivery, Moon Landing, and Leap Frog. This intermediate level self-paced tutorial can be used at home or school. The tutorial is simple enough for kids yet engaging enough for beginning adults.

Programming Home Projects with Visual Basic® Express is a semester long self-paced programming tutorial explains (in simple, easy-to-follow terms) how to build a Visual Basic Express Windows project. Students learn about project design, the Visual Basic Express toolbox, many elements of the Visual Basic language, and how to debug and distribute finished projects. The projects built include a Dual-Mode Stopwatch, Flash Card Math Quiz, Multiple Choice Exam, Blackjack Card Game, Weight Monitor, Home Inventory Manager and a Snowball Toss Game.

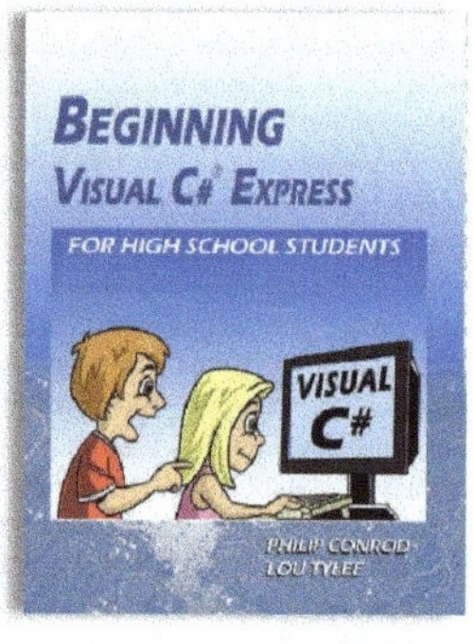

Beginning Visual C#® Express is a semester long "beginning" programming tutorial consisting of 10 chapters explaining (in simple, easy-to-follow terms) how to build a C# Express Windows application. The tutorial includes several detailed computer projects for students to build and try. These projects include a number guessing game, card game, allowance calculator, drawing program, state capitals game, and a couple of video games like Pong. We also include several college prep bonus projects including a loan calculator, portfolio manager, and checkbook balancer.

Programming Games with Visual C#® Express is a semester long "intermediate" programming tutorial consisting of 10 chapters explaining (in simple, easy-to-follow terms) how to build a Visual C# Video Games. The games built are non-violent, family-friendly and teach logical thinking skills. Students will learn how to program the following Visual C# video games: Safecracker, Tic Tac Toe, Match Game, Pizza Delivery, Moon Landing, and Leap Frog. This intermediate level self-paced tutorial can be used at home or school. The tutorial is simple enough for kids yet engaging enough for beginning adults.

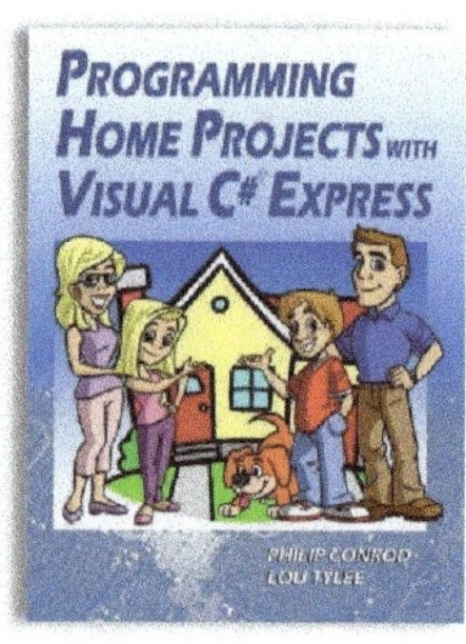

Programming Home Projects with Visual C#® Express is a semester long self-paced programming tutorial explains (in simple, easy-to-follow terms) how to build a Visual C# Express Windows project. Students learn about project design, the Visual C# Express toolbox, many elements of the Visual C# language, and how to debug and distribute finished projects. The projects built include a Dual-Mode Stopwatch, Flash Card Math Quiz, Multiple Choice Exam, Blackjack Card Game, Weight Monitor, Home Inventory Manager and a Snowball Toss Game.

We also publish several Self-Study or Instructor-Led Computer Programming Tutorials for Oracle® Java® :

Beginning Java™ is a semester long "beginning" programming tutorial consisting of 10 chapters explaining (in simple, easy-to-follow terms) how to build a Java application. The games built are non-violent and teach logical thinking skills. The tutorial includes several detailed computer projects for students to build and try. These projects include a number guessing game, card game, allowance calculator, drawing program, state capitals game, and a couple of video games like Pong. We also include several college prep bonus projects including a loan calculator, portfolio manager, and checkbook balancer.

Learn Java™ GUI Applications is a 9 lesson Tutorial covering object-oriented programming concepts, using a integrated development environment to create and test Java projects, building and distributing GUI applications, understanding and using the Swing control library, exception handling, sequential file access, graphics, multimedia, advanced topics such as printing, and help system authoring. **Our Beginning Java tutorial is a pre-requisite for this tutorial.**

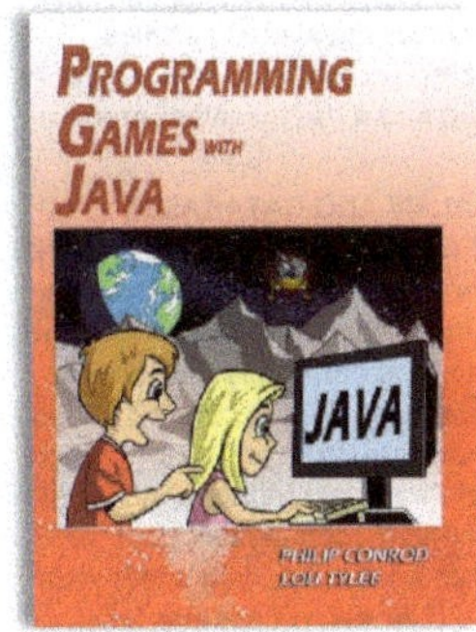

Programming Games with Java™ is a semester long "intermediate" programming tutorial consisting of 10 chapters explaining (in simple, easy-to-follow terms) how to build a Visual C# Video Games. The games built are non-violent, family-friendly and teach logical thinking skills. Students will learn how to program the following Visual C# video games: Safecracker, Tic Tac Toe, Match Game, Pizza Delivery, Moon Landing, and Leap Frog. This intermediate level self-paced tutorial can be used at home or school. The tutorial is simple enough for kids yet engaging enough for beginning adults. **Our Beginning Java and Learn Java GUI Applications tutorials are required pre-requisites for this tutorial.**

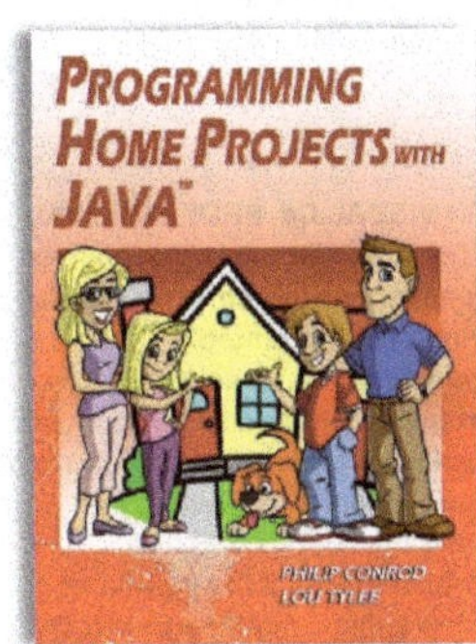

Programming Home Projects with Java™ is a Java GUI Swing tutorial covering object-oriented programming concepts. It explains (in simple, easy-to-follow terms) how to build Java GUI project to use around the home. Students learn about project design, the Java Swing controls, many elements of the Java language, and how to distribute finished projects. The projects built include a Dual-Mode Stopwatch, Flash Card Math Quiz, Multiple Choice Exam, Blackjack Card Game, Weight Monitor, Home Inventory Manager and a Snowball Toss Game. **Our Beginning Java and Learn Java GUI Applications tutorials are pre-requisites for this tutorial.**

We also publish several advanced Self-Study or Instructor-Led "College Prep" Self-Study Computer Programming Tutorials for Microsoft® Visual Basic® Professional Edition and Visual C#® Professional Edition:

LEARN VISUAL BASIC PROFESSIONAL EDITION is a comprehensive college prep programming tutorial covering object-oriented programming, the Visual Basic integrated development environment, building and distributing Windows applications using the Windows Installer, exception handling, sequential file access, graphics, multimedia, advanced topics such as web access, printing, and HTML help system authoring. The tutorial also introduces database applications (using ADO .NET) and web applications (using ASP.NET).

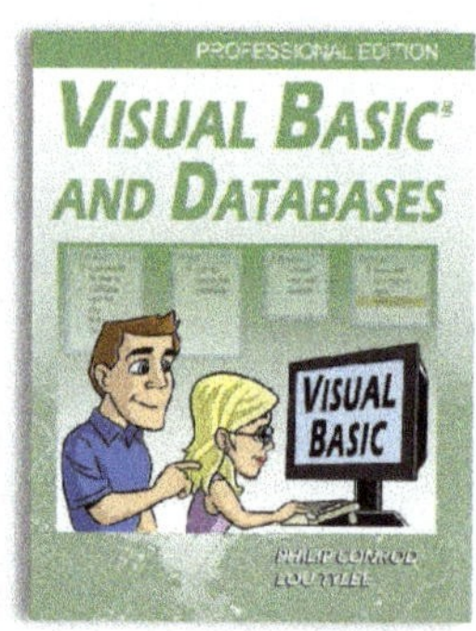

VISUAL BASIC AND DATABASES PROFESSIONAL EDITION is a tutorial that provides a detailed introduction to using Visual Basic for accessing and maintaining databases for desktop applications. Topics covered include: database structure, database design, Visual Basic project building, ADO .NET data objects (connection, data adapter, command, data table), data bound controls, proper interface design, structured query language (SQL), creating databases using Access, SQL Server and ADOX, and database reports. Actual projects developed include a books tracking system, a sales invoicing program, a home inventory system and a daily weather monitor.

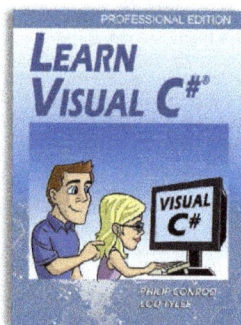

LEARN VISUAL C# PROFESSIONAL EDITION is a comprehensive college prep computer programming tutorial covering object-oriented programming, the Visual C# integrated development environment and toolbox, building and distributing Windows applications (using the Windows Installer), exception handling, sequential file input and output, graphics, multimedia effects (animation and sounds), advanced topics such as web access, printing, and HTML help system authoring. The tutorial also introduces database applications (using ADO .NET) and web applications (using ASP.NET).

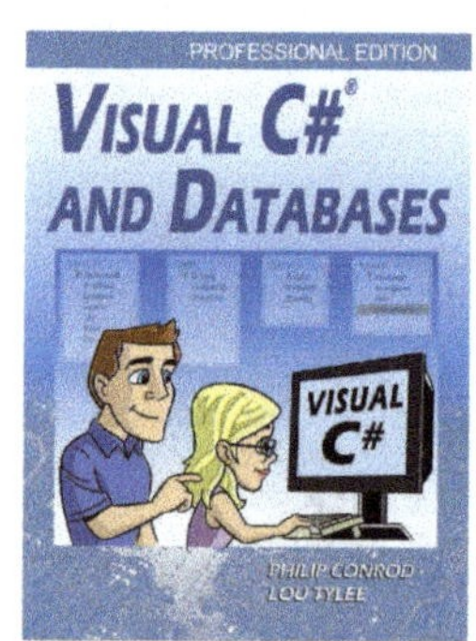

VISUAL C# AND DATABASES PROFESSIONAL EDITION is a tutorial that provides a detailed introduction to using Visual C# for accessing and maintaining databases for desktop applications. Topics covered include: database structure, database design, Visual C# project building, ADO .NET data objects (connection, data adapter, command, data table), data bound controls, proper interface design, structured query language (SQL), creating databases using Access, SQL Server and ADOX, and database reports. Actual projects developed include a books tracking system, a sales invoicing program, a home inventory system and a daily weather monitor.

	MediumAquamarine	#66CDAA
	MediumBlue	#0000CD
	MediumOrchid	#BA55D3
	MediumPurple	#9370DB
	MediumSeaGreen	#3CB371
	MediumSlateBlue	#7B68EE
	MediumSpringGreen	#00FA9A
	MediumTurquoise	#48D1CC
	MediumVioletRed	#C71585
	MidnightBlue	#191970
	MintCream	#F5FFFA
	MistyRose	#FFE4E1
	Moccasin	#FFE4B5
	NavajoWhite	#FFDEAD
	Navy	#000080
	OldLace	#FDF5E6
	Olive	#808000
	OliveDrab	#6B8E23
	Orange	#FFA500
	OrangeRed	#FF4500
	Orchid	#DA70D6

	PaleGoldenrod	#EEE8AA
	PaleGreen	#98FB98
	PaleTurquoise	#AFEEEE
	PaleVioletRed	#DB7093
	PapayaWhip	#FFEFD5
	PeachPuff	#FFDAB9
	Peru	#CD853F
	Pink	#FFC0CB
	Plum	#DDA0DD
	PowderBlue	#B0E0E6
	Purple	#800080
	Red	#FF0000
	RosyBrown	#BC8F8F
	RoyalBlue	#4169E1
	SaddleBrown	#8B4513
	Salmon	#FA8072
	SandyBrown	#F4A460
	SeaGreen	#2E8B57
	Seashell	#FFF5EE
	Sienna	#A0522D
	Silver	#C0C0C0

	SkyBlue	#87CEEB
	SlateBlue	#6A5ACD
	SlateGray / SlateGrey[†]	#708090
	Snow	#FFFAFA
	SpringGreen	#00FF7F
	SteelBlue	#4682B4
	Tan	#D2B48C
	Teal	#008080
	Thistle	#D8BFD8
	Tomato	#FF6347
	Turquoise	#40E0D0
	Violet	#EE82EE
	Wheat	#F5DEB3
	White	#FFFFFF
	WhiteSmoke	#F5F5F5
	Yellow	#FFFF00
	YellowGreen	#9ACD32

This page intentionally not left blank.